CIVIL PROCEDURE IN CALIFORNIA:

STATE AND FEDERAL

Supplemental Materials for use with all Civil Procedure Casebooks

1994 Edition

By

Mary Kay Kane

Dean, University of California
Hastings College of the Law

Facts
Issue(s)
Lower courts
decision &
rationale

and

David I. Levine

Professor of Law, University of California
Hastings College of the Law

AMERICAN CASEBOOK SERIES®

WEST PUBLISHING CO.
ST. PAUL, MINN., 1994

COPYRIGHT © 1989, 1991, 1992 WEST PUBLISHING CO.

COPYRIGHT © 1994 By WEST PUBLISHING CO.
  610 Opperman Drive
  P.O. Box 64526
  St. Paul, MN 55164–0526
  1–800–328–9352

ISBN 0–314–04170–2
ISSN 1063–0805

 TEXT IS PRINTED ON 10% POST
CONSUMER RECYCLED PAPER

Preface to the 1994 Edition

In learning Civil Procedure, it is often quite useful to compare how different judicial systems handle certain problems. Indeed, in many places, a lawyer cannot practice without familiarity with at least two systems of procedure, one for the state courts and one for federal court; some states, notably California, have not adopted the Federal Rules of Civil Procedure for use in their own courts. For these reasons, we thought that it would be useful to compile a compact rule book and case supplement that would enable professors of Civil Procedure, particularly those teaching in California law schools, to use a comparative perspective. The book is designed to be used in conjunction with any of the existing casebooks in Civil Procedure.

This edition includes: a complete version of the Federal Rules of Civil Procedure with selected Advisory Committee Notes, as well as selected Federal Rules of Appellate Procedure (with amendments announced April 29, 1994 appended); a substantial selection of contrasting provisions from the California Code of Civil Procedure; selected federal and California constitutional provisions; California Rules of Court; a comparative table; and edited cases from California appellate courts. The cases were selected as being illustrative of areas in which California procedure differs from its federal counterpart. In editing the judicial opinions and the notes of the Advisory Committee on the Federal Rules of Civil Procedure, case and statute citations, as well as footnotes, have been omitted without so specifying; numbered footnotes retain the original numbering.

MKK
DIL

San Francisco, California
May, 1994

*

Table of Contents

*

Comparative Table

Fed.R.Civ.P.	Cal.Civ.Proc.Code
2	§ 307 *
3	§§ 350 *, 411.10
4	§§ 412.20, 412.30–417.30, 485.010, 485.210–.240, 492.010
4(m)	§§ 583.210, 583.250
5	§§ 465 *, 1011–13a
6(b)	§§ 12–13(b) *
7	§§ 422.10, 1010
8	§§ 425.10–.12, 431.10–.30
8(c)	§ 360.5
9	§§ 456–57 *
10	§§ 422.30–.40 *
11	§§ 128.5, 177.5, 178, 446
12	§§ 418.10, 430.10–.80, 472a–472c, 1014
12(c)	§ 597
12(f)	§§ 435–37
13	§§ 426.10–.60, 428.20, 428.50, 428.80
14	§§ 428.10, 428.70
15	§§ 469–70, 471.5–472, 473
15(b)	§ 309
15(d)	§ 464
17(a)	§§ 367 *, 369 *, 374 *
18	§§ 427.10 *, 428.30
19	§ 389 *
20(a)	§§ 378–79 *, 382
22	§§ 386–386.6
24	§ 387
26	§§ 2017–19, 2024, 2034
27	§§ 2035–36
30	§§ 2020–21, 2025
31	§ 2028
33	§ 2030
34	§ 2031
35	§ 2032
36	§ 2033
37	§§ 1991, 1991.1, 1992, 2023
38	§§ 592, 631
40	§§ 629–30
41	§§ 581, 583.310, 583.330, 583.360, 583.410, 583.420

* not included due to similarity to Fed.R.Civ.P.

Fed.R.Civ.P.	Cal.Civ.Proc.Code
41(b)	§ 583.130
42	§ 1048
45	§§ 1985–87, 1989
48	§§ 193, 194, 197, 198, 203, 204, 205, 613, 618
49	§§ 624–25
50	§ 581c
51	§ 607a
52	§§ 632, 909
54	§§ 1032, 1033.5
54(d)	§§ 1021, 1021.5–.7
55	§§ 473.5, 474, 585, 587
56	§§ 437c, 2015.5
57	§ 106c *
59	§§ 657, 659, 659a, 662, 662.5, 663
60(b)	§ 473
65	§§ 527, 529
66	§ 564
68	§ 998

Fed.R.Civ.P.	Cal.Civ.Proc.Code
38	§§ 907, 916, 917.1

* not included due to similarity to Fed.R.Civ.P.

CIVIL PROCEDURE IN CALIFORNIA:

STATE AND FEDERAL

*

FEDERAL RULES OF CIVIL PROCEDURE FOR THE UNITED STATES DISTRICT COURTS

As Amended to December 1, 1993

Table of Rules

I. Scope of Rules—One Form of Action

II. Commencement of Action; Service of Process, Pleadings, Motions and Orders

III. Pleadings and Motions

IV. Parties

V. Depositions and Discovery

VI. Trials

VII. Judgment

VIII. Provisional and Final Remedies

IX. Special Proceedings

APPENDIX OF FORMS

I. SCOPE OF RULES—ONE FORM OF ACTION

Rule 1. Scope and Purpose of Rules

These rules govern the procedure in the United States district courts in all suits of a civil nature whether cognizable as cases at law or in equity or in admiralty, with the exceptions stated in Rule 81. They shall be construed and administered to secure the just, speedy, and inexpensive determination of every action.

(As amended Dec. 29, 1948, eff. Oct. 20, 1949; Feb. 28, 1966, eff. July 1, 1966; Apr. 22, 1993, eff. Dec. 1, 1993.)

Rule 2. One Form of Action

There shall be one form of action to be known as "civil action".

II. COMMENCEMENT OF ACTION; SERVICE OF PROCESS, PLEADINGS, MOTIONS AND ORDERS

Rule 3. Commencement of Action

A civil action is commenced by filing a complaint with the court.

NOTES OF ADVISORY COMMITTEE ON RULES

* * *

4. This rule provides that the first step in an action is the filing of the complaint. Under Rule 4(a) this is to be followed forthwith by issuance of a summons and its delivery to an officer for service. Other rules providing for dismissal for failure to prosecute suggest a method available to attack unreasonable delay in prosecuting an action after it has been commenced. When a federal or state statute of limitations is pleaded as a defense, a question may arise under this rule whether the mere filing of the complaint stops the running of the statute, or whether any further step is required, such as, service of the summons and complaint or their delivery to the marshal for service. The answer to this question may depend on whether it is competent for the Supreme Court, exercising the power to make rules of procedure without affecting substantive rights, to vary the operation of statutes of limitations. The requirement of Rule 4(a) that the clerk shall forthwith issue the summons and deliver it to the marshal for service will reduce the chances of such a question arising.

Rule 4. Summons

(a) **Form.** The summons shall be signed by the clerk, bear the seal of the court, identify the court and the parties, be directed to the defendant, and state the name and address of the plaintiff's attorney or, if unrepresented, of the plaintiff. It shall also state the time within which the defendant must appear and defend, and notify the defendant that failure to do so will result in a judgment by default against the defendant for the relief demanded in the complaint. The court may allow a summons to be amended.

(b) Issuance. Upon or after filing the complaint, the plaintiff may present a summons to the clerk for signature and seal. If the summons is in proper form, the clerk shall sign, seal, and issue it to the plaintiff for service on the defendant. A summons, or a copy of the summons if addressed to multiple defendants, shall be issued for each defendant to be served.

(c) Service With Complaint; by Whom Made.

(1) A summons shall be served together with a copy of the complaint. The plaintiff is responsible for service of a summons and complaint within the time allowed under subdivision (m) and shall furnish the person effecting service with the necessary copies of the summons and complaint.

(2) Service may be effected by any person who is not a party and who is at least 18 years of age. At the request of the plaintiff, however, the court may direct that service be effected by a United States marshal, deputy United States marshal, or other person or officer specially appointed by the court for that purpose. Such an appointment must be made when the plaintiff is authorized to proceed in forma pauperis pursuant to 28 U.S.C. § 1915 or is authorized to proceed as a seaman under 28 U.S.C. § 1916.

(d) Waiver of Service; Duty to Save Costs of Service; Request to Waive.

(1) A defendant who waives service of a summons does not thereby waive any objection to the venue or to the jurisdiction of the court over the person of the defendant.

(2) An individual, corporation, or association that is subject to service under subdivision (e), (f), or (h) and that receives notice of an action in the manner provided in this paragraph has a duty to avoid unnecessary costs of serving the summons. To avoid costs, the plaintiff may notify such a defendant of the commencement of the action and request that the defendant waive service of a summons. The notice and request

(A) shall be in writing and shall be addressed directly to the defendant, if an individual, or else to an officer or managing or general agent (or other agent authorized by appointment or law to receive service of process) of a defendant subject to service under subdivision (h);

(B) shall be dispatched through first-class mail or other reliable means;

(C) shall be accompanied by a copy of the complaint and shall identify the court in which it has been filed;

(D) shall inform the defendant, by means of a text prescribed in an official form promulgated pursuant to Rule 84, of the consequences of compliance and of a failure to comply with the request;

(E) shall set forth the date on which the request is sent;

(F) shall allow the defendant a reasonable time to return the waiver, which shall be at least 30 days from the date on which the request is sent, or 60 days from that date if the defendant is addressed outside any judicial district of the United States; and

(G) shall provide the defendant with an extra copy of the notice and request, as well as a prepaid means of compliance in writing.

If a defendant located within the United States fails to comply with a request for waiver made by a plaintiff located within the United States, the court shall impose the costs subsequently incurred in effecting service on the defendant unless good cause for the failure be shown.

(3) A defendant that, before being served with process, timely returns a waiver so requested is not required to serve an answer to the complaint until 60 days after the date on which the request for waiver of service was sent, or 90 days after that date if the defendant was addressed outside any judicial district of the United States.

(4) When the plaintiff files a waiver of service with the court, the action shall proceed, except as provided in paragraph (3), as if a summons and complaint had been served at the time of filing the waiver, and no proof of service shall be required.

(5) The costs to be imposed on a defendant under paragraph (2) for failure to comply with a request to waive service of a summons shall include the costs subsequently incurred in effecting service under subdivision (e), (f), or (h), together with the costs, including a reasonable attorney's fee, of any motion required to collect the costs of service.

(e) Service Upon Individuals Within a Judicial District of the United States. Unless otherwise provided by federal law, service upon an individual from whom a waiver has not been obtained and filed, other than an infant or an incompetent person, may be effected in any judicial district of the United States:

(1) pursuant to the law of the state in which the district court is located, or in which service is effected, for the service of a summons upon the defendant in an action brought in the courts of general jurisdiction of the State; or

(2) by delivering a copy of the summons and of the complaint to the individual personally or by leaving copies thereof at the individual's dwelling house or usual place of abode with some person of suitable age and discretion then residing therein or by delivering a copy of the summons and of the complaint to an agent authorized by appointment or by law to receive service of process.

(f) Service Upon Individuals in a Foreign Country. Unless otherwise provided by federal law, service upon an individual from whom a waiver has not been obtained and filed, other than an infant or an incompetent person, may be effected in a place not within any judicial district of the United States:

(1) by any internationally agreed means reasonably calculated to give notice, such as those means authorized by the Hague Convention on the Service Abroad of Judicial and Extrajudicial Documents; or

(2) if there is no internationally agreed means of service or the applicable international agreement allows other means of service, provided that service is reasonably calculated to give notice:

> **(A)** in the manner prescribed by the law of the foreign country for service in that country in an action in any of its courts of general jurisdiction; or

> **(B)** as directed by the foreign authority in response to a letter rogatory or letter of request; or

> **(C)** unless prohibited by the law of the foreign country, by

>> **(i)** delivery to the individual personally of a copy of the summons and the complaint; or

>> **(ii)** any form of mail requiring a signed receipt, to be addressed and dispatched by the clerk of the court to the party to be served; or

(3) by other means not prohibited by international agreement as may be directed by the court.

(g) Service Upon Infants and Incompetent Persons. Service upon an infant or an incompetent person in a judicial district of the United States shall be effected in the manner prescribed by the law of the state in which the service is made for the service of summons or other like process upon any such defendant in an action brought in the courts of general jurisdiction of that state. Service upon an infant or an incompetent person in a place not within any judicial district of the United States shall be effected in the manner prescribed by paragraph (2)(A) or (2)(B) of subdivision (f) or by such means as the court may direct.

(h) Service Upon Corporations and Associations. Unless otherwise provided by federal law, service upon a domestic or foreign corporation or upon a partnership or other unincorporated association that is subject to suit under a common name, and from which a waiver of service has not been obtained and filed, shall be effected:

(1) in a judicial district of the United States in the manner prescribed for individuals by subdivision (e)(1), or by delivering a copy of the summons and of the complaint to an officer, a managing or general agent, or to any other agent authorized by appointment or by law to receive service of process and, if the agent is one authorized by statute to receive service and the statute so requires, by also mailing a copy to the defendant, or

(2) in a place not within any judicial district of the United States in any manner prescribed for individuals by subdivision (f) except personal delivery as provided in paragraph (2)(C)(i) thereof.

(i) Service Upon the United States, and Its Agencies, Corporations, or Officers.

(1) Service upon the United States shall be effected

(A) by delivering a copy of the summons and of the complaint to the United States attorney for the district in which the action is brought or to an assistant United States attorney or clerical employee designated by the United States attorney in a writing filed with the clerk of the court or by sending a copy of the summons and of the complaint by registered or certified mail addressed to the civil process clerk at the office of the United States attorney and

(B) by also sending a copy of the summons and of the complaint by registered or certified mail to the Attorney General of the United States at Washington, District of Columbia, and

(C) in any action attacking the validity of an order of an officer or agency of the United States not made a party, by also sending a copy of the summons and of the complaint by registered or certified mail to the officer or agency.

(2) Service upon an officer, agency, or corporation of the United States shall be effected by serving the United States in the manner prescribed by paragraph (1) of this subdivision and by also sending a copy of the summons and of the complaint by registered or certified mail to the officer, agency, or corporation.

(3) The court shall allow a reasonable time for service of process under this subdivision for the purpose of curing the failure to serve multiple officers, agencies, or corporations of the United States if the plaintiff has effected service on either the United States attorney or the Attorney General of the United States.

(j) Service Upon Foreign, State, or Local Governments.

(1) Service upon a foreign state or a political subdivision, agency, or instrumentality thereof shall be effected pursuant to 28 U.S.C. § 1608.

(2) Service upon a state, municipal corporation, or other governmental organization subject to suit shall be effected by delivering a copy of the summons and of the complaint to its chief executive officer or by serving the summons and complaint in the manner prescribed by the law of that state for the service of summons or other like process upon any such defendant.

(k) Territorial Limits of Effective Service.

(1) Service of a summons or filing a waiver of service is effective to establish jurisdiction over the person of a defendant

(A) who could be subjected to the jurisdiction of a court of general jurisdiction in the state in which the district court is located, or

(B) who is a party joined under Rule 14 or Rule 19 and is served at a place within a judicial district of the United States and not more than 100 miles from the place from which the summons issues, or

(C) who is subject to the federal interpleader jurisdiction under 28 U.S.C. § 1335, or

(D) when authorized by a statute of the United States.

(2) If the exercise of jurisdiction is consistent with the Constitution and laws of the United States, serving a summons or filing a waiver of service is also effective, with respect to claims arising under federal law, to establish personal jurisdiction over the person of any defendant who is not subject to the jurisdiction of the courts of general jurisdiction of any state.

(*l*) Proof of Service. If service is not waived, the person effecting service shall make proof thereof to the court. If service is made by a person other than a United States marshal or deputy United States marshal, the person shall make affidavit thereof. Proof of service in a place not within any judicial district of the United States shall, if effected under paragraph (1) of subdivision (f), be made pursuant to the applicable treaty or convention, and shall, if effected under paragraph (2) or (3) thereof, include a receipt signed by the addressee or other evidence of delivery to the addressee satisfactory to the court. Failure to make proof of service does not affect the validity of the service. The court may allow proof of service to be amended.

(m) Time Limit for Service. If service of the summons and complaint is not made upon a defendant within 120 days after the filing of the complaint, the court, upon motion or on its own initiative after notice to the plaintiff, shall dismiss the action without prejudice as to that defendant or direct that service be effected within a specified time; provided that if the plaintiff shows good cause for the failure, the court shall extend the time for service for an appropriate period. This subdivision does not apply to service in a foreign country pursuant to subdivision (f) or (j)(1).

(n) Seizure of Property; Service of Summons Not Feasible.

(1) If a statute of the United States so provides, the court may assert jurisdiction over property. Notice to claimants of the property shall then be sent in the manner provided by the statute or by service of a summons under this rule.

(2) Upon a showing that personal jurisdiction over a defendant cannot, in the district where the action is brought, be obtained with reasonable efforts by service of summons in any manner authorized by this rule, the court may assert jurisdiction over any of the defendant's assets found within the district by seizing the assets under the circumstances and in the manner provided by the law of the state in which the district court is located.

(As amended Jan. 21, 1963, eff. July 1, 1963; Feb. 28, 1966, eff. July 1, 1966; Apr. 29, 1980, eff. Aug. 1, 1980; Pub.L. 97–462, § 2, Jan. 12, 1983, 96 Stat. 2527; Mar. 2, 1987, eff. Aug. 1, 1987; Apr. 22, 1993, eff. Dec. 1, 1993.)

NOTES OF ADVISORY COMMITTEE ON RULES
1993 AMENDMENT

* * *

Purposes of Revision. The general purpose of this revision is to facilitate the service of the summons and complaint. The revised rule explicitly authorizes a means for service of the summons and complaint on any defendant. While the methods of service so authorized always provide appropriate notice to persons against whom claims are made, effective service under this rule does not assure that personal jurisdiction has been established over the defendant served.

First, the revised rule authorizes the use of any means of service provided by the law not only of the forum state, but also of the state in which a defendant is served, unless the defendant is a minor or incompetent.

Second, the revised rule clarifies and enhances the cost-saving practice of securing the assent of the defendant to dispense with actual service of the summons and complaint. This practice was introduced to the rule in 1983 by an act of Congress authorizing "service-by-mail," a procedure that effects economic service with cooperation of the defendant. Defendants that magnify costs of service by requiring expensive service not necessary to achieve full notice of an action brought against them are required to bear the wasteful costs. This provision is made available in actions against defendants who cannot be served in the districts in which the actions are brought.

Third, the revision reduces the hazard of commencing an action against the United States or its officers, agencies, and corporations. A party failing to effect service on all the offices of the United States as required by the rule is assured adequate time to cure defects in service.

Fourth, the revision calls attention to the important effect of the Hague Convention and other treaties bearing on service of documents in foreign countries and favors the use of internationally agreed means of service. In some respects, these treaties have facilitated service in foreign countries but are not fully known to the bar.

Finally, the revised rule extends the reach of federal courts to impose jurisdiction over the person of all defendants against whom federal law claims are made and who can be constitutionally subjected to the jurisdiction of the courts of the United States. The present territorial limits on the effectiveness of service to subject a defendant to the jurisdiction of the court over the defendant's person are retained for all actions in which there is a state in which personal jurisdiction can be asserted consistently with state law and the Fourteenth Amendment. A new provision enables district courts to exercise jurisdiction, if permissible under the Constitution and not precluded by statute, when a federal claim is made against a defendant not subject to the jurisdiction of any single state.

* * *

Rule 4.1. Service of Other Process

(a) **Generally.** Process other than a summons as provided in Rule 4 or subpoena as provided in Rule 45 shall be served by a United States marshal, a deputy United States marshal, or a person specially appointed for that purpose, who shall make proof of service as provided in Rule 4(1). The process may be served anywhere within the territorial limits of the state in which the district court is located, and, when authorized by a statute of the United States, beyond the territorial limits of that state.

(b) **Enforcement of Orders: Commitment for Civil Contempt.** An order of civil commitment of a person held to be in contempt of a decree or injunction issued to enforce the laws of the United States may be served and enforced in any district. Other orders in civil contempt proceedings shall be served in the state in which the court issuing the order to be enforced is located or elsewhere within the United States if not more than 100 miles from the place at which the order to be enforced was issued.

(Added Apr. 22, 1993, eff. Dec. 1, 1993.)

NOTES OF ADVISORY COMMITTEE ON RULES
1993 ADOPTION

This is a new rule. Its purpose is to separate those few provisions of the former Rule 4 bearing on matters other than service of a summons to allow greater textual clarity in Rule 4. Subdivision (a) contains no new language.

Subdivision (b) replaces the final clause of the penultimate sentence of the former subdivision 4(f), a clause added to the rule in 1963. The new rule provides for nationwide service of orders of civil commitment enforcing decrees of injunctions issued to compel compliance with federal law. The rule makes no change in the practice with respect to the enforcement of injunctions or decrees not involving the enforcement of federally-created rights.

* * *

Rule 5. Service and Filing of Pleadings and Other Papers

(a) **Service: When Required.** Except as otherwise provided in these rules, every order required by its terms to be served, every pleading subsequent to the original complaint unless the court otherwise orders because of numerous defendants, every paper relating to discovery required to be served upon a party unless the court otherwise orders, every written motion other than one which may be heard ex parte, and every written notice, appearance, demand, offer of judgment, designation of record on appeal, and similar paper shall be served upon each of the parties. No service need be made on parties in default for failure to appear except that pleadings asserting new or additional claims for relief against them shall be served upon them in the manner provided for service of summons in Rule 4.

In an action begun by seizure of property, in which no person need be or is named as defendant, any service required to be made prior to the filing of an answer, claim, or appearance shall be made upon the person having custody or possession of the property at the time of its seizure.

(b) Same: How Made. Whenever under these rules service is required or permitted to be made upon a party represented by an attorney the service shall be made upon the attorney unless service upon the party is ordered by the court. Service upon the attorney or upon a party shall be made by delivering a copy to the attorney or party or by mailing it to the attorney or party at the attorney's or party's last known address or, if no address is known, by leaving it with the clerk of the court. Delivery of a copy within this rule means: handing it to the attorney or to the party; or leaving it at the attorney's or party's office with a clerk or other person in charge thereof; or, if there is no one in charge, leaving it in a conspicuous place therein; or, if the office is closed or the person to be served has no office, leaving it at the person's dwelling house or usual place of abode with some person of suitable age and discretion then residing therein. Service by mail is complete upon mailing.

(c) Same: Numerous Defendants. In any action in which there are unusually large numbers of defendants, the court, upon motion or of its own initiative, may order that service of the pleadings of the defendants and replies thereto need not be made as between the defendants and that any cross-claim, counterclaim, or matter constituting an avoidance or affirmative defense contained therein shall be deemed to be denied or avoided by all other parties and that the filing of any such pleading and service thereof upon the plaintiff constitutes due notice of it to the parties. A copy of every such order shall be served upon the parties in such manner and form as the court directs.

(d) Filing; Certificate of Service. All papers after the complaint required to be served upon a party, together with a certificate of service, shall be filed with the court within a reasonable time after service, but the court may on motion of a party or on its own initiative order that depositions upon oral examination and interrogatories, requests for documents, requests for admission, and answers and responses thereto not be filed unless on order of the court or for use in the proceeding.

(e) Filing With the Court Defined. The filing of papers with the court as required by these rules shall be made by filing them with the clerk of the court, except that the judge may permit the papers to be filed with the judge, in which event the judge shall note thereon the filing date and forthwith transmit them to the office of the clerk. A court may, by local rule, permit papers to be filed by facsimile or other electronic means if such means are authorized by and consistent with standards established by the Judicial Conference of the United States. The clerk shall not refuse to accept for filing any paper presented for that purpose solely because it is not presented in proper form as required by these rules or any local rules or practices.

(As amended Jan. 21, 1963, eff. July 1, 1963; Mar. 30, 1970, eff. July 1, 1970; Apr. 29, 1980, eff. Aug. 1, 1980; Mar. 2, 1987, eff. Aug. 1, 1987; Apr. 30, 1991, eff. Dec. 1, 1991; Apr. 22, 1993, eff. Dec. 1, 1993.)

Rule 6. Time

(a) **Computation.** In computing any period of time prescribed or allowed by these rules, by the local rules of any district court, by order of court, or by any applicable statute, the day of the act, event, or default from which the designated period of time begins to run shall not be included. The last day of the period so computed shall be included, unless it is a Saturday, a Sunday, or a legal holiday, or, when the act to be done is the filing of a paper in court, a day on which weather or other conditions have made the office of the clerk of the district court inaccessible, in which event the period runs until the end of the next day which is not one of the aforementioned days. When the period of time prescribed or allowed is less than 11 days, intermediate Saturdays, Sundays, and legal holidays shall be excluded in the computation. As used in this rule and in Rule 77(c), "legal holiday" includes New Year's Day, Birthday of Martin Luther King, Jr., Washington's Birthday, Memorial Day, Independence Day, Labor Day, Columbus Day, Veterans Day, Thanksgiving Day, Christmas Day, and any other day appointed as a holiday by the President or the Congress of the United States, or by the state in which the district court is held.

(b) **Enlargement.** When by these rules or by a notice given thereunder or by order of court an act is required or allowed to be done at or within a specified time, the court for cause shown may at any time in its discretion (1) with or without motion or notice order the period enlarged if request therefor is made before the expiration of the period originally prescribed or as extended by a previous order, or (2) upon motion made after the expiration of the specified period permit the act to be done where the failure to act was the result of excusable neglect; but it may not extend the time for taking any action under Rules 50(b) and (c)(2), 52(b), 59(b), (d) and (e), 60(b), and 74(a), except to the extent and under the conditions stated in them.

(c) [**Rescinded. Feb. 28, 1966, eff. July 1, 1966.**]

(d) **For Motions—Affidavits.** A written motion, other than one which may be heard ex parte, and notice of the hearing thereof shall be served not later than 5 days before the time specified for the hearing, unless a different period is fixed by these rules or by order of the court. Such an order may for cause shown be made on ex parte application. When a motion is supported by affidavit, the affidavit shall be served with the motion; and, except as otherwise provided in Rule 59(c), opposing affidavits may be served not later than 1 day before the hearing, unless the court permits them to be served at some other time.

(e) Additional Time After Service by Mail. Whenever a party has the right or is required to do some act or take some proceedings within a prescribed period after the service of a notice or other paper upon the party and the notice or paper is served upon the party by mail, 3 days shall be added to the prescribed period.

(As amended Dec. 27, 1946, eff. Mar. 19, 1948; Jan. 21, 1963, eff. July 1, 1963; Feb. 28, 1966, eff. July 1, 1966; Dec. 4, 1967, eff. July 1, 1968; Mar. 1, 1971, eff. July 1, 1971; Apr. 28, 1983, eff. Aug. 1, 1983; Apr. 29, 1985, eff. Aug. 1, 1985; Mar. 2, 1987, eff. Aug. 1, 1987.)

III.   PLEADINGS AND MOTIONS

Rule 7.   Pleadings Allowed; Form of Motions

(a) Pleadings. There shall be a complaint and an answer; a reply to a counterclaim denominated as such; an answer to a cross-claim, if the answer contains a cross-claim; a third-party complaint, if a person who was not an original party is summoned under the provisions of Rule 14; and a third-party answer, if a third-party complaint is served. No other pleading shall be allowed, except that the court may order a reply to an answer or a third-party answer.

(b) Motions and Other Papers.

(1) An application to the court for an order shall be by motion which, unless made during a hearing or trial, shall be made in writing, shall state with particularity the grounds therefor, and shall set forth the relief or order sought. The requirement of writing is fulfilled if the motion is stated in a written notice of the hearing of the motion.

(2) The rules applicable to captions and other matters of form of pleadings apply to all motions and other papers provided for by these rules.

(3) All motions shall be signed in accordance with Rule 11.

(c) Demurrers, Pleas, etc., Abolished. Demurrers, pleas, and exceptions for insufficiency of a pleading shall not be used.

(As amended Dec. 27, 1946, eff. Mar. 19, 1948; Jan. 21, 1963, eff. July 1, 1963; Apr. 28, 1983, eff. Aug. 1, 1983.)

Rule 8.   General Rules of Pleading

(a) Claims for Relief. A pleading which sets forth a claim for relief, whether an original claim, counterclaim, cross-claim, or third-party claim, shall contain (1) a short and plain statement of the grounds upon which the court's jurisdiction depends, unless the court already has jurisdiction and the claim needs no new grounds of jurisdiction to support it, (2) a short and plain statement of the claim showing that the pleader is entitled to relief, and (3) a demand for judgment for the relief the pleader seeks. Relief in the alternative or of several different types may be demanded.

(b) Defenses; Form of Denials. A party shall state in short and plain terms the party's defenses to each claim asserted and shall admit or deny the averments upon which the adverse party relies. If a party is without knowledge or information sufficient to form a belief as to the truth of an averment, the party shall so state and this has the effect of a denial. Denials shall fairly meet the substance of the averments denied. When a pleader intends in good faith to deny only a part or a qualification of an averment, the pleader shall specify so much of it as is true and material and shall deny only the remainder. Unless the pleader intends in good faith to controvert all the averments of the preceding pleading, the pleader may make denials as specific denials of designated averments or paragraphs or may generally deny all the averments except such designated averments or paragraphs as the pleader expressly admits; but, when the pleader does so intend to controvert all its averments, including averments of the grounds upon which the court's jurisdiction depends, the pleader may do so by general denial subject to the obligations set forth in Rule 11.

(c) Affirmative Defenses. In pleading to a preceding pleading, a party shall set forth affirmatively accord and satisfaction, arbitration and award, assumption of risk, contributory negligence, discharge in bankruptcy, duress, estoppel, failure of consideration, fraud, illegality, injury by fellow servant, laches, license, payment, release, res judicata, statute of frauds, statute of limitations, waiver, and any other matter constituting an avoidance or affirmative defense. When a party has mistakenly designated a defense as a counterclaim or a counterclaim as a defense, the court on terms, if justice so requires, shall treat the pleading as if there had been a proper designation.

(d) Effect of Failure to Deny. Averments in a pleading to which a responsive pleading is required, other than those as to the amount of damage, are admitted when not denied in the responsive pleading. Averments in a pleading to which no responsive pleading is required or permitted shall be taken as denied or avoided.

(e) Pleading to Be Concise and Direct; Consistency.

(1) Each averment of a pleading shall be simple, concise, and direct. No technical forms of pleading or motions are required.

(2) A party may set forth two or more statements of a claim or defense alternately or hypothetically, either in one count or defense or in separate counts or defenses. When two or more statements are made in the alternative and one of them if made independently would be sufficient, the pleading is not made insufficient by the insufficiency of one or more of the alternative statements. A party may also state as many separate claims or defenses as the party has regardless of consistency and whether based on legal, equitable, or maritime grounds. All statements shall be made subject to the obligations set forth in Rule 11.

(f) Construction of Pleadings. All pleadings shall be so construed as to do substantial justice.

(As amended Feb. 28, 1966, eff. July 1, 1966; Mar. 2, 1987, eff. Aug. 1, 1987.)

Rule 9. Pleading Special Matters

(a) Capacity. It is not necessary to aver the capacity of a party to sue or be sued or the authority of a party to sue or be sued in a representative capacity or the legal existence of an organized association of persons that is made a party, except to the extent required to show the jurisdiction of the court. When a party desires to raise an issue as to the legal existence of any party or the capacity of any party to sue or be sued or the authority of a party to sue or be sued in a representative capacity, the party desiring to raise the issue shall do so by specific negative averment, which shall include such supporting particulars as are peculiarly within the pleader's knowledge.

(b) Fraud, Mistake, Condition of the Mind. In all averments of fraud or mistake, the circumstances constituting fraud or mistake shall be stated with particularity. Malice, intent, knowledge, and other condition of mind of a person may be averred generally.

(c) Conditions Precedent. In pleading the performance or occurrence of conditions precedent, it is sufficient to aver generally that all conditions precedent have been performed or have occurred. A denial of performance or occurrence shall be made specifically and with particularity.

(d) Official Document or Act. In pleading an official document or official act it is sufficient to aver that the document was issued or the act done in compliance with law.

(e) Judgment. In pleading a judgment or decision of a domestic or foreign court, judicial or quasijudicial tribunal, or of a board or officer, it is sufficient to aver the judgment or decision without setting forth matter showing jurisdiction to render it.

(f) Time and Place. For the purpose of testing the sufficiency of a pleading, averments of time and place are material and shall be considered like all other averments of material matter.

(g) Special Damage. When items of special damage are claimed, they shall be specifically stated.

(h) Admiralty and Maritime Claims. A pleading or count setting forth a claim for relief within the admiralty and maritime jurisdiction that is also within the jurisdiction of the district court on some other ground may contain a statement identifying the claim as an admiralty or maritime claim for the purposes of Rules 14(c), 38(e), 82, and the Supplemental Rules for Certain Admiralty and Maritime Claims. If the claim is cognizable only in admiralty, it is an admiralty or maritime claim for those purposes whether so identified or not. The amendment of a pleading to add or withdraw an identifying statement is governed by the principles of Rule 15. The reference in Title 28, U.S.C. § 1292(a)(3), to admiralty cases shall be construed to mean admiralty and maritime claims within the meaning of this subdivision (h).

(As amended Feb. 28, 1966, eff. July 1, 1966; Dec. 4, 1967, eff. July 1, 1968; Mar. 30, 1970, eff. July 1, 1970; Mar. 2, 1987, eff. Aug. 1, 1987.)

Rule 10. Form of Pleadings

(a) **Caption; Names of Parties.** Every pleading shall contain a caption setting forth the name of the court, the title of the action, the file number, and a designation as in Rule 7(a). In the complaint the title of the action shall include the names of all the parties, but in other pleadings it is sufficient to state the name of the first party on each side with an appropriate indication of other parties.

(b) **Paragraphs; Separate Statements.** All averments of claim or defense shall be made in numbered paragraphs, the contents of each of which shall be limited as far as practicable to a statement of a single set of circumstances; and a paragraph may be referred to by number in all succeeding pleadings. Each claim founded upon a separate transaction or occurrence and each defense other than denials shall be stated in a separate count or defense whenever a separation facilitates the clear presentation of the matters set forth.

(c) **Adoption by Reference; Exhibits.** Statements in a pleading may be adopted by reference in a different part of the same pleading or in another pleading or in any motion. A copy of any written instrument which is an exhibit to a pleading is a part thereof for all purposes.

Rule 11. Signing of Pleadings, Motions, and Other Papers; Representations to Court; Sanctions

(a) **Signature.** Every pleading, written motion, and other paper shall be signed by at least one attorney of record in the attorney's individual name, or, if the party is not represented by an attorney, shall be signed by the party. Each paper shall state the signer's address and telephone number, if any. Except when otherwise specifically provided by rule or statute, pleadings need not be verified or accompanied by affidavit. An unsigned paper shall be stricken unless omission of the signature is corrected promptly after being called to the attention of the attorney or party.

(b) **Representations to Court.** By presenting to the court (whether by signing, filing, submitting, or later advocating) a pleading, written motion, or other paper, an attorney or unrepresented party is certifying that to the best of the person's knowledge, information, and belief, formed after an inquiry reasonable under the circumstances

(1) it is not being presented for any improper purpose, such as to harass or to cause unnecessary delay or needless increase in the cost of litigation;

(2) the claims, defenses, and other legal contentions therein are warranted by existing law or by a nonfrivolous argument for the extension, modification, or reversal of existing law or the establishment of new law;

(3) the allegations and other factual contentions have evidentiary support or, if specifically so identified, are likely to have evidentiary support after a reasonable opportunity for further investigation or discovery; and

(4) the denials of factual contentions are warranted on the evidence or, if specifically so identified, are reasonably based on a lack of information or belief.

(c) Sanctions. If, after notice and a reasonable opportunity to respond, the court determines that subdivision (b) has been violated, the court may, subject to the conditions stated below, impose an appropriate sanction upon the attorneys, law firms, or parties that have violated subdivision (b) or are responsible for the violation.

(1) *How Initiated.*

(A) *By Motion.* A motion for sanctions under this rule shall be made separately from other motions or requests and shall describe the specific conduct alleged to violate subdivision (b). It shall be served as provided in Rule 5, but shall not be filed with or presented to the court unless, within 21 days after service of the motion (or such other period as the court may prescribe), the challenged paper, claim, defense, contention, allegation, or denial is not withdrawn or appropriately corrected. If warranted, the court may award to the party prevailing on the motion the reasonable expenses and attorney's fees incurred in presenting or opposing the motion. Absent exceptional circumstances, a law firm shall be held jointly responsible for violations committed by its partners, associates, and employees.

(B) *On Court's Initiative.* On its own initiative, the court may enter an order describing the specific conduct that appears to violate subdivision (b) and directing an attorney, law firm, or party to show cause why it has not violated subdivision (b) with respect thereto.

(2) *Nature of Sanction; Limitations.* A sanction imposed for violation of this rule shall be limited to what is sufficient to deter repetition of such conduct or comparable conduct by others similarly situated. Subject to the limitations in subparagraphs (A) and (B), the sanction may consist of, or include, directives of a nonmonetary nature, an order to pay a penalty into court, or, if imposed on motion and warranted for effective deterrence, an order directing payment to the movant of some or all of the reasonable attorneys' fees and other expenses incurred as a direct result of the violation.

(A) Monetary sanctions may not be awarded against a represented party for a violation of subdivision (b)(2).

(B) Monetary sanctions may not be awarded on the court's initiative unless the court issues its order to show cause before a voluntary dismissal or settlement of the claims made by or against the party which is, or whose attorneys are, to be sanctioned.

(3) *Order.* When imposing sanctions, the court shall describe the conduct determined to constitute a violation of this rule and explain the basis for the sanction imposed.

(d) Inapplicability to Discovery. Subdivisions (a) through (c) of this rule do not apply to disclosures and discovery requests, responses, objections, and motions that are subject to the provisions of Rules 26 through 37.

(As amended Apr. 28, 1983, eff. Aug. 1, 1983; Mar. 2, 1987, eff. Aug. 1, 1987; Apr. 22, 1993, eff. Dec. 1, 1993.)

NOTES OF ADVISORY COMMITTEE ON RULES
1993 AMENDMENT

Purpose of revision. This revision is intended to remedy problems that have arisen in the interpretation and application of the 1983 revision of the rule. * * *

The rule retains the principle that attorneys and pro se litigants have an obligation to the court to refrain from conduct that frustrates the aims of Rule 1. The revision broadens the scope of this obligation, but places greater constraints on the imposition of sanctions and should reduce the number of motions for sanctions presented to the court. New subdivision (d) removes from the ambit of this rule all discovery requests, responses, objections, and motions subject to the provisions of Rule 26 through 37.

Subdivision (a). Retained in this subdivision are the provisions requiring signatures on pleadings, written motions, and other papers. Unsigned papers are to be received by the Clerk, but then are to be stricken if the omission of the signature is not corrected promptly after being called to the attention of the attorney or pro se litigant. * * *

Subdivisions (b) and (c). These subdivisions restate the provisions requiring attorneys and pro se litigants to conduct a reasonable inquiry into the law and facts before signing pleadings, written motions, and other documents, and prescribing sanctions for violation of these obligations. The revision in part expands the responsibilities of litigants to the court, while providing greater constraints and flexibility in dealing with infractions of the rule. The rule continues to require litigants to "stop-and-think" before initially making legal or factual contentions. It also, however, emphasizes the duty of candor by subjecting litigants to potential sanctions for insisting upon a position after it is no longer tenable and by generally providing protection against sanctions if they withdraw or correct contentions after a potential violation is called to their attention.

The rule applies only to assertions contained in papers filed with or submitted to the court. It does not cover matters arising for the first time during oral presentations to the court, when counsel may make statements that would not have been made if there had been more time for study and reflection. However, a litigant's obligations with respect to the contents of these papers are not measured solely as of the time they are filed with or submitted to the court, but include reaffirming to the court and advocating positions contained in those pleadings and motions after learning that they cease to have any merit. For example, an attorney who during a pretrial conference insists on a claim or defense should be viewed as "presenting to the court" that contention and would be subject to the obligations of subdivision (b) measured as of that time. Similarly, if after a notice of removal is filed, a party urges in federal court the allegations of a pleading filed in state court (whether as claims, defenses, or in disputes regarding removal or remand), it would be viewed as "presenting"—and hence certifying to the district court under Rule 11—those allegations.

The certification with respect to allegations and other factual contentions is revised in recognition that sometimes a litigant may have good reason to believe that a fact is true or false but may need discovery, formal or informal, from opposing parties or third persons to gather and confirm the evidentiary basis for the allegation. Tolerance of factual contentions in initial pleadings by plaintiffs or defendants when specifically identified as made on information and belief does not relieve litigants from the obligation to conduct an appropriate investigation into the facts that is reasonable under the circumstances; it is not a license to join parties, make claims, or present defenses without any factual basis or justification. Moreover, if evidentiary support is not obtained after a reasonable opportunity for further investigation or discovery, the party has a duty under the rule not to persist with that contention. Subdivision (b) does not require a formal amendment to pleadings for which evidentiary support is not obtained, but rather calls upon a litigant not thereafter to advocate such claims or defenses.

The certification is that there is (or likely will be) "evidentiary support" for the allegation, not that the party will prevail with respect to its contention regarding the fact. That summary judgment is rendered against a party does not necessarily mean, for purposes of this certification, that it had no evidentiary support for its position. On the other hand, if a party has evidence with respect to a contention that would suffice to defeat a motion for summary judgment based thereon, it would have sufficient "evidentiary support" for purposes of Rule 11.

Denials of factual contentions involve somewhat different considerations. Often, of course, a denial is premised upon the existence of evidence contradicting the alleged fact. At other times a denial is permissible because, after an appropriate investigation, a party has no information concerning the matter or, indeed, has a reasonable basis for doubting the credibility of the only evidence relevant to the matter. A party should not deny an allegation it knows to be true; but it is not required, simply because it lacks contradictory evidence, to admit an allegation that it believes is not true.

The changes in subdivisions (b)(3) and (b)(4) will serve to equalize the burden of the rule upon plaintiffs and defendants, who under Rule 8(b) are in effect allowed to deny allegations by stating that from their initial investigation they lack sufficient information to form a belief as to the truth of the allegation. If, after further investigation or discovery, a denial is no longer warranted, the defendant should not continue to insist on that denial. While sometimes helpful, formal amendment of the pleadings to withdraw an allegation or denial is not required by subdivision (b).

Arguments for extensions, modifications, or reversals of existing law or for creation of new law do not violate subdivision (b)(2) provided they are "nonfrivolous." This establishes an objective standard, intended to eliminate any "empty-head pure-heart" justification for patently frivolous arguments. However, the extent to which a litigant has researched the issues and found some support for its theories even in minority opinions, in law review articles, or through consultation with other attorneys should certainly be taken into account in determining whether paragraph (2) has been violated. Although arguments for a change of law are not required to be specifically so identified, a contention that is so identified should be viewed with greater tolerance under the rule.

The court has available a variety of possible sanctions to impose for violations, such as striking the offending paper; issuing an admonition, reprimand, or censure; requiring participation in seminars or other educational programs; ordering a fine payable to the court; referring the matter to disciplinary authorities (or, in the case of government attorneys, to the Attorney General, Inspector General, or agency head), etc. *See Manual for Complex Litigation, Second,* § 42.3. The rule does not attempt to enumerate the factors a court should consider in deciding whether to impose a sanction or what sanctions would be appropriate in the circumstances; but, for emphasis, it does specifically note that a sanction may be nonmonetary as well as monetary. Whether the improper conduct was willful, or negligent; whether it was part of a pattern of activity, or an isolated event; whether it infected the entire pleading, or only one particular count or defense; whether the person has engaged in similar conduct in other litigation; whether it was intended to injure; what effect it had on the litigation process in time or expense; whether the responsible person is trained in the law; what amount, given the financial resources of the responsible person, is needed to deter that person from repetition in the same case; what amount is needed to deter similar activity by other litigants: all of these may in a particular case be proper considerations. The court has significant discretion in determining what sanctions, if any, should be imposed for a violation, subject to the principle that the sanctions should not be more severe than reasonably necessary to deter repetition of the conduct by the offending person or comparable conduct by similarly situated persons.

Since the purpose of Rule 11 sanctions is to deter rather than to compensate, the rule provides that, if a monetary sanction is imposed, it should ordinarily be paid into court as a penalty. However, under unusual circumstances, particularly for (b)(1) violations, deterrence may be ineffective unless the sanction not only requires the person violating the rule to make a monetary payment, but also directs that some or all of this payment be made to those injured by the violation. Accordingly, the rule authorizes the court, if requested in a motion and if so warranted, to award attorney's fees to another party. Any such award to another party, however, should not exceed the expenses and attorneys' fees for the services directly and unavoidably caused by the violation of the certification requirement. * * *

The sanction should be imposed on the persons—whether attorneys, law firms, or parties—who have violated the rule or who may be determined to be responsible for the violation. The person signing, filing, submitting, or advocating a document has a nondelegable responsibility to the court, and in most situations is the person to be sanctioned for a violation. Absent exceptional circumstances, a law firm is to be held also responsible when, as a result of a motion under subdivision (c)(1)(A), one of its partners, associates, or employees is determined to have violated the rule. Since such a motion may be filed only if the offending paper is not withdrawn or corrected within 21 days after service of the motion, it is appropriate that the law firm ordinarily be viewed as jointly responsible under established principles of agency. This provision is designed to remove the restrictions of the former rule. *Cf. Pavelic & LeFlore v. Marvel Entertainment Group,* 493 U.S. 120 (1989) (1983 version of Rule 11 does not permit sanctions against law firm of attorney signing groundless complaint).

The revision permits the court to consider whether other attorneys in the firm, co-counsel, other law firms, or the party itself should be held accountable for their part in causing a violation. * * *

Sanctions that involve monetary awards (such as a fine or an award of attorney's fees) may not be imposed on a represented party for causing a violation of subdivision (b)(2), involving frivolous contentions of law. Monetary responsibility for such violations is more properly placed solely on the party's attorneys. With this limitation, the rule should not be subject to attack under the Rules Enabling Act. *See Willy v. Coastal Corp.,* —— U.S. —— (1992); *Business Guides, Inc. v. Chromatic Communications Enter. Inc.,* —— U.S. —— (1991). This restriction does not limit the court's power to impose sanctions or remedial orders that may have collateral financial consequences upon a party, such as dismissal of a claim, preclusion of a defense, or preparation of amended pleadings.

* * *

Rule 11 motions should not be made or threatened for minor, inconsequential violations of the standards prescribed by subdivision (b). They should not be employed as a discovery device or to test the legal sufficiency or efficacy of allegations in the pleadings; other motions are available for those purposes. Nor should Rule 11 motions be prepared to emphasize the merits of a party's position, to exact an unjust settlement, to intimidate an adversary into withdrawing contentions that are fairly debatable, to increase the costs of litigation, to create a conflict of interest between attorney and client, or to seek disclosure of matters otherwise protected by the attorney-client privilege or the work-product doctrine.

* * *

The rule provides that requests for sanctions must be made as a separate motion, *i.e.,* not simply included as an additional prayer for relief contained in another motion. The motion for sanctions is not, however, to be filed until at least 21 days (or such other period as the court may set) after being served. If, during this period, the alleged violation is corrected, as by withdrawing (whether formally or informally) some allegation or contention, the motion should not be filed with the court. These provisions are intended to provide a type of "safe harbor" against motions under Rule 11 in that a party will not be subject to sanctions on the basis of another party's motion unless, after receiving the motion, it refuses to withdraw that position or to acknowledge candidly that it does not currently have evidence to support a specified allegation. Under the former rule, parties were sometimes reluctant to abandon a questionable contention lest that be viewed as evidence of a violation of Rule 11; under the revision, the timely withdrawal of a contention will protect a party against a motion for sanctions.

To stress the seriousness of a motion for sanctions and to define precisely the conduct claimed to violate the rule, the revision provides that the "safe harbor" period begins to run only upon service of the motion. In most cases, however, counsel should be expected to give informal notice to the other party, whether in person or by a telephone call or letter, of a potential violation before proceeding to prepare and serve a Rule 11 motion.

As under former Rule 11, the filing of a motion for sanctions is itself subject to the requirements of the rule and can lead to sanctions. However, service of a cross motion under Rule 11 should rarely be needed since under the revision the court may award to the person who prevails on a motion under Rule 11—whether the movant or the target of the motion—reasonable expenses, including attorney's fees, incurred in presenting or opposing the motion.

The power of the court to act on its own initiative is retained, but with the condition that this be done through a show cause order. This procedure provides the person with notice and an opportunity to respond. The revision provides that a monetary sanction imposed after a court-initiated show cause order be limited to a penalty payable to the court and that it be imposed only if the show cause order is issued before any voluntary dismissal or an agreement of the parties to settle the claims made by or against the litigant. Parties settling a case should not be subsequently faced with an unexpected order from the court leading to monetary sanctions that might have affected their willingness to settle or voluntarily dismiss a case. Since show cause orders will ordinarily be issued only in situations that are akin to a contempt of court, the rule does not provide a "safe harbor" to a litigant for withdrawing a claim, defense, etc., after a show cause order has been issued on the court's own initiative. Such corrective action, however, should be taken into account in deciding what—if any—sanction to impose if, after consideration of the litigant's response, the court concludes that a violation has occurred.

Subdivision (d). Rules 26(g) and 37 establish certification standards and sanctions that apply to discovery disclosures, requests, responses, objections, and motions. It is appropriate that Rules 26 through 37, which are specially designed for the discovery process, govern such documents and conduct rather than the more general provisions of Rule 11. Subdivision (d) has been added to accomplish this result.

Rule 11 is not the exclusive source for control of improper presentations of claims, defenses, or contentions. It does not supplant statutes permitting awards of attorney's fees to prevailing parties or alter the principles governing such awards. It does not inhibit the court in punishing for contempt, in exercising its inherent powers, or in imposing sanctions, awarding expenses, or directing remedial action authorized under other rules or under 28 U.S.C. § 1927. *See Chambers v. NASCO,* __ U.S. __ (1991). *Chambers* cautions, however, against reliance upon inherent powers if appropriate sanctions can be imposed under provisions such as Rule 11, and the procedures specified in

Rule 11—notice, opportunity to respond, and findings—should ordinarily be employed when imposing a sanction under the court's inherent powers. Finally, it should be noted that Rule 11 does not preclude a party from initiating an independent action for malicious prosecution or abuse of process.

Rule 12. Defenses and Objections—When and How Presented—By Pleading or Motion—Motion for Judgment on the Pleadings

(a) **When Presented.**

(1) Unless a different time is prescribed in a statute of the United States, a defendant shall serve an answer

(A) within 20 days after being served with the summons and complaint, or

(B) if service of the summons has been timely waived on request under Rule 4(d), within 60 days after the date when the request for waiver was sent, or within 90 days after that date if the defendant was addressed outside any judicial district of the United States.

(2) A party served with a pleading stating a cross-claim against that party shall serve an answer thereto within 20 days after being served. The plaintiff shall serve a reply to a counterclaim in the answer within 20 days after service of the answer, or, if a reply is ordered by the court, within 20 days after service of the order, unless the order otherwise directs.

(3) The United States or an officer or agency thereof shall serve an answer to the complaint or to a cross-claim, or a reply to a counterclaim, within 60 days after the service upon the United States attorney of the pleading in which the claim is asserted.

(4) Unless a different time is fixed by court order, the service of a motion permitted under this rule alters these periods of time as follows:

(A) if the court denies the motion or postpones its disposition until the trial on the merits, the responsive pleading shall be served within 10 days after notice of the court's action; or

(B) if the court grants a motion for a more definite statement, the responsive pleading shall be served within 10 days after the service of the more definite statement.

(b) **How Presented.** Every defense, in law or fact, to a claim for relief in any pleading, whether a claim, counterclaim, cross-claim, or third-party claim, shall be asserted in the responsive pleading thereto if one is required, except that the following defenses may at the option of the pleader be made by motion: (1) lack of jurisdiction over the subject matter, (2) lack of jurisdiction over the person, (3) improper venue, (4) insufficiency of process, (5) insufficiency of service of process, (6) failure to state a claim upon which relief can be granted, (7) failure to join a party under Rule 19. A motion making any of these defenses shall be made before pleading if a further pleading is permitted. No defense or objection is waived by being joined with one or more other defenses or objections in a responsive pleading or motion. If a pleading sets forth a claim for relief to which the adverse party is not required to serve a responsive pleading, the adverse party may assert at the trial any defense in law or fact to that claim for relief. If, on a motion asserting the defense numbered (6) to dismiss for failure of the pleading to state a claim upon which relief can be granted, matters outside the pleading are presented to and not excluded by the court, the motion shall be treated as one for summary judgment and disposed of as provided in Rule 56, and all parties shall be given reasonable opportunity to present all material made pertinent to such a motion by Rule 56.

(c) Motion for Judgment on the Pleadings. After the pleadings are closed but within such time as not to delay the trial, any party may move for judgment on the pleadings. If, on a motion for judgment on the pleadings, matters outside the pleadings are presented to and not excluded by the court, the motion shall be treated as one for summary judgment and disposed of as provided in Rule 56, and all parties shall be given reasonable opportunity to present all material made pertinent to such a motion by Rule 56.

(d) Preliminary Hearings. The defenses specifically enumerated (1)–(7) in subdivision (b) of this rule, whether made in a pleading or by motion, and the motion for judgment mentioned in subdivision (c) of this rule shall be heard and determined before trial on application of any party, unless the court orders that the hearing and determination thereof be deferred until the trial.

(e) Motion for More Definite Statement. If a pleading to which a responsive pleading is permitted is so vague or ambiguous that a party cannot reasonably be required to frame a responsive pleading, the party may move for a more definite statement before interposing a responsive pleading. The motion shall point out the defects complained of and the details desired. If the motion is granted and the order of the court is not obeyed within 10 days after notice of the order or within such other time as the court may fix, the court may strike the pleading to which the motion was directed or make such order as it deems just.

(f) Motion to Strike. Upon motion made by a party before responding to a pleading or, if no responsive pleading is permitted by these rules, upon motion made by a party within 20 days after the service of the pleading upon the party or upon the court's own initiative at any time, the court may order stricken from any pleading any insufficient defense or any redundant, immaterial, impertinent, or scandalous matter.

(g) Consolidation of Defenses in Motion. A party who makes a motion under this rule may join with it any other motions herein provided for and then available to the party. If a party makes a motion under this rule but omits therefrom any defense or objection then available to the party which this rule permits to be raised by motion, the party shall not thereafter make a motion based on the defense or objection so omitted, except a motion as provided in subdivision (h)(2) hereof on any of the grounds there stated.

(h) Waiver or Preservation of Certain Defenses.

(**1**) A defense of lack of jurisdiction over the person, improper venue, insufficiency of process, or insufficiency of service of process is waived (A) if omitted from a motion in the circumstances described in subdivision (g), or (B) if it is neither made by motion under this rule nor included in a responsive pleading or an amendment thereof permitted by Rule 15(a) to be made as a matter of course.

(**2**) A defense of failure to state a claim upon which relief can be granted, a defense of failure to join a party indispensable under Rule 19, and an objection of failure to state a legal defense to a claim may be made in any pleading permitted or ordered under Rule 7(a), or by motion for judgment on the pleadings, or at the trial on the merits.

(**3**) Whenever it appears by suggestion of the parties or otherwise that the court lacks jurisdiction of the subject matter, the court shall dismiss the action.

(As amended Dec. 27, 1946, eff. Mar. 19, 1948; Jan. 21, 1963, eff. July 1, 1963; Feb. 28, 1966, eff. July 1, 1966; Mar. 2, 1987, eff. Aug. 1, 1987; Apr. 22, 1993, eff. Dec. 1, 1993.)

NOTES OF ADVISORY COMMITTEE ON RULES

* * *

Subdivision (b). * * *

Rule 12(b)(6), permitting a motion to dismiss for failure of the complaint to state a claim on which relief can be granted, is substantially the same as the old demurrer for failure of a pleading to state a cause of action. Some courts have held that as the rule by its terms refers to statements in the complaint, extraneous matter on affidavits, depositions or otherwise, may not be introduced in support of the motion, or to resist it. On the other hand, in many cases the district courts have permitted the introduction of such material. * * * In dealing with such situations the Second Circuit has made the sound suggestion that whatever its label or original basis, the motion may be treated as a motion for summary judgment and disposed of as such. *Samara v. United States,* C.C.A.2, 1942, 129 F.2d 594, certiorari denied 63 S.Ct. 258, 317 U.S. 686, 87 L.Ed. 549; *Boro Hall Corp. v. General Motors Corp.,* C.C.A.2, 1942, 124 F.2d 822, certiorari denied 63 S.Ct. 436, 317 U.S. 695, 87 L.Ed. 556. See, also, *Kithcart v. Metropolitan Life Ins. Co.,* C.C.A. 8, 1945, 150 F.2d 997.

It has also been suggested that this practice could be justified on the ground that the federal rules permit "speaking" motions. The Committee entertains the view that on motion under Rule 12(b)(6) to dismiss for failure of the complaint to state a good claim, the trial court should have authority to permit the introduction of extraneous matter, such as may be offered on a motion for summary judgment, and if it does not exclude such matter the motion should then be treated as a motion for summary judgment and disposed of in the manner and on the conditions stated in Rule 56 relating to summary judgments, and, of course, in such a situation, when the case reaches the circuit court of appeals, that court should treat the motion in the same way. The Committee believes that such practice, however, should be tied to the summary judgment rule. The term "speaking motion" is not mentioned in the rules, and if there is such a thing its limitations are undefined. Where extraneous matter is received, by tying further proceedings to the summary judgment rule the courts have a definite basis in the rules for disposing of the motion.

The Committee emphasizes particularly the fact that the summary judgment rule does not permit a case to be disposed of by judgment on the merits on affidavits, which disclose a conflict on a material issue of fact, and unless this practice is tied to the summary judgment rule, the extent to which a court, on the introduction of such extraneous matter, may resolve questions of fact on conflicting proof would be left uncertain.

* * *

Subdivision (e). References in this subdivision to a bill of particulars have been deleted, and the motion provided for is confined to one for more definite statement to be obtained only in cases where the movant cannot reasonably be required to frame an answer or other responsive pleading to the pleading in question. With respect to preparations for trial, the party is properly relegated to the various methods of examination and discovery provided in the rules for that purpose. * * *

Rule 12(e) as originally drawn has been the subject of more judicial rulings than any other part of the rules, and has been much criticized by commentators, judges and members of the bar. * * * The tendency of some courts freely to grant extended bills of particulars has served to neutralize any helpful benefits derived from Rule 8, and has overlooked the intended use of the rules on depositions and discovery. The words "or to prepare for trial"—eliminated by the proposed amendment—have sometimes been seized upon as grounds for compulsory statement in the opposing pleading of all the details which the movant would have to meet at the trial. On the other hand, many courts have in effect read these words out of the rule. * * *

Rule 13. Counterclaim and Cross–Claim

(a) Compulsory Counterclaims. A pleading shall state as a counterclaim any claim which at the time of serving the pleading the pleader has against any opposing party, if it arises out of the transaction or occurrence that is the subject matter of the opposing party's claim and does not require for its adjudication the presence of third parties of whom the court cannot acquire jurisdiction. But the pleader need not state the claim if (1) at the time the action was commenced the claim was the subject of another pending action, or (2) the opposing party brought suit upon the claim by attachment or other process by which the court did not acquire jurisdiction to render a personal judgment on that claim, and the pleader is not stating any counterclaim under this Rule 13.

(b) Permissive Counterclaims. A pleading may state as a counterclaim any claim against an opposing party not arising out of the transaction or occurrence that is the subject matter of the opposing party's claim.

(c) Counterclaim Exceeding Opposing Claim. A counterclaim may or may not diminish or defeat the recovery sought by the opposing party. It may claim relief exceeding in amount or different in kind from that sought in the pleading of the opposing party.

(d) Counterclaim Against the United States. These rules shall not be construed to enlarge beyond the limits now fixed by law the right to assert counterclaims or to claim credits against the United States or an officer or agency thereof.

(e) Counterclaim Maturing or Acquired After Pleading. A claim which either matured or was acquired by the pleader after serving a pleading may, with the permission of the court, be presented as a counterclaim by supplemental pleading.

(f) Omitted Counterclaim. When a pleader fails to set up a counterclaim through oversight, inadvertence, or excusable neglect, or when justice requires, the pleader may by leave of court set up the counterclaim by amendment.

(g) Cross–Claim Against Co–party. A pleading may state as a cross-claim any claim by one party against a co-party arising out of the transaction or occurrence that is the subject matter either of the original action or of a counterclaim therein or relating to any property that is the subject matter of the original action. Such cross-claim may include a claim that the party against whom it is asserted is or may be liable to the cross-claimant for all or part of a claim asserted in the action against the cross-claimant.

(h) Joinder of Additional Parties. Persons other than those made parties to the original action may be made parties to a counterclaim or cross-claim in accordance with the provisions of Rules 19 and 20.

(i) Separate Trials; Separate Judgments. If the court orders separate trials as provided in Rule 42(b), judgment on a counterclaim or cross-claim may be rendered in accordance with the terms of Rule 54(b) when the court has jurisdiction so to do, even if the claims of the opposing party have been dismissed or otherwise disposed of.

(As amended Dec. 27, 1946, eff. Mar. 19, 1948; Jan. 21, 1963, eff. July 1, 1963; Feb. 28, 1966, eff. July 1, 1966; Mar. 2, 1987, eff. Aug. 1, 1987.)

Rule 14. Third Party Practice

(a) When Defendant May Bring in Third Party. At any time after commencement of the action a defending party, as a third-party plaintiff, may cause a summons and complaint to be served upon a person not a party to the action who is or may be liable to the third-party plaintiff for all or part of the plaintiff's claim against the third-party plaintiff. The third-party plaintiff need not obtain leave to make the service if the third-party plaintiff files the third-party complaint not later than 10 days after serving the original answer. Otherwise the third-party plaintiff must obtain leave on motion upon notice to all parties to the action. The person served with the summons and third-party complaint, hereinafter called the third-party defendant, shall make any defenses to the third-party plaintiff's claim as provided in Rule 12 and any counterclaims against the third-party plaintiff and cross-claims against other third-party defendants as provided in Rule 13. The third-party defendant may assert against the plaintiff any defenses which the third-party plaintiff has to the plaintiff's claim. The third-party defendant may also assert any claim against the plaintiff arising out of the transaction or occurrence that is the subject matter of the plaintiff's claim against the third-party plaintiff. The plaintiff may assert any claim against the third-party defendant arising out of the transaction or occurrence that is the subject matter of the plaintiff's claim against the third-party plaintiff, and the third-party defendant thereupon shall assert any defenses as provided in Rule 12 and any counterclaims and cross-claims as provided in Rule 13. Any party may move to strike the third-party claim, or for its severance or separate trial. A third-party defendant may proceed under this rule against any person not a party to the action who is or may be liable to the third-party defendant for all or part of the claim made in the action against the third-party defendant. The third-party complaint, if within the admiralty and maritime jurisdiction, may be in rem against a vessel, cargo, or other property subject to admiralty or maritime process in rem, in which case references in this rule to the summons include the warrant of arrest, and references to the third-party plaintiff or defendant include, where appropriate, the claimant of the property arrested.

(b) When Plaintiff May Bring in Third Party. When a counterclaim is asserted against a plaintiff, the plaintiff may cause a third party to be brought in under circumstances which under this rule would entitle a defendant to do so.

(c) Admiralty and Maritime Claims. When a plaintiff asserts an admiralty or maritime claim within the meaning of Rule 9(h), the defendant or claimant, as a third-party plaintiff, may bring in a third-party defendant who may be wholly or partly liable, either to the plaintiff or to the third-party plaintiff, by way of remedy over, contribution, or otherwise on account of the same transaction, occurrence, or series of transactions or occurrences. In such a case the third-party plaintiff may also demand judgment against the third-party defendant in favor of the plaintiff, in which event the third-party defendant shall make any defenses to the claim of the plaintiff as well as to that of the third-party plaintiff in the manner provided in Rule 12 and the action shall proceed as if the plaintiff had commenced it against the third-party defendant as well as the third-party plaintiff.

(As amended Dec. 27, 1946, eff. Mar. 19, 1948; Jan. 21, 1963, eff. July 1, 1963; Feb. 28, 1966, eff. July 1, 1966; Mar. 2, 1987, eff. Aug. 1, 1987.)

Rule 15.   Amended and Supplemental Pleadings

(a) Amendments.   A party may amend the party's pleading once as a matter of course at any time before a responsive pleading is served or, if the pleading is one to which no responsive pleading is permitted and the action has not been placed upon the trial calendar, the party may so amend it at any time within 20 days after it is served.   Otherwise a party may amend the party's pleading only by leave of court or by written consent of the adverse party; and leave shall be freely given when justice so requires.   A party shall plead in response to an amended pleading within the time remaining for response to the original pleading or within 10 days after service of the amended pleading, whichever period may be the longer, unless the court otherwise orders.

(b) Amendments to Conform to the Evidence.   When issues not raised by the pleadings are tried by express or implied consent of the parties, they shall be treated in all respects as if they had been raised in the pleadings.   Such amendment of the pleadings as may be necessary to cause them to conform to the evidence and to raise these issues may be made upon motion of any party at any time, even after judgment; but failure so to amend does not affect the result of the trial of these issues. If evidence is objected to at the trial on the ground that it is not within the issues made by the pleadings, the court may allow the pleadings to be amended and shall do so freely when the presentation of the merits of the action will be subserved thereby and the objecting party fails to satisfy the court that the admission of such evidence would prejudice the party in maintaining the party's action or defense upon the merits.   The court may grant a continuance to enable the objecting party to meet such evidence.

(c) Relation Back of Amendments.   An amendment of a pleading relates back to the date of the original pleading when

(1) relation back is permitted by the law that provides the statute of limitations applicable to the action, or

(2) the claim or defense asserted in the amended pleading arose out of the conduct, transaction, or occurrence set forth or attempted to be set forth in the original pleading, or

(3) the amendment changes the party or the naming of the party against whom a claim is asserted if the foregoing provision (2) is satisfied and, within the period provided by Rule 4(m) for service of the summons and complaint, the party to be brought in by amendment (A) has received such notice of the institution of the action that the party will not be prejudiced in maintaining a defense on the merits, and (B) knew or should have known that, but for a mistake concerning the identity of the proper party, the action would have been brought against the party.

The delivery or mailing of process to the United States Attorney, or United States Attorney's designee, or the Attorney General of the United States, or an agency or officer who would have been a proper defendant if named, satisfies the requirement of subparagraphs (A) and (B) of this paragraph (3) with respect to the United States or any agency or officer thereof to be brought into the action as a defendant.

(d) Supplemental Pleadings. Upon motion of a party the court may, upon reasonable notice and upon such terms as are just, permit the party to serve a supplemental pleading setting forth transactions or occurrences or events which have happened since the date of the pleading sought to be supplemented. Permission may be granted even though the original pleading is defective in its statement of a claim for relief or defense. If the court deems it advisable that the adverse party plead to the supplemental pleading, it shall so order, specifying the time therefor.

(As amended Jan. 21, 1963, eff. July 1, 1963; Feb. 28, 1966, eff. July 1, 1966; Mar. 2, 1987, eff. Aug. 1, 1987; Apr. 30, 1991, eff. Dec. 1, 1991; Act of Dec. 9, 1991, Pub.L. 102–198, 105 Stat. 1623; Apr. 22, 1993, eff. Dec. 1, 1993.)

NOTES OF ADVISORY COMMITTEE ON RULES
1991 AMENDMENT

The rule has been revised to prevent parties against whom claims are made from taking unjust advantage of otherwise inconsequential pleading errors to sustain a limitations defense.

Paragraph (c)(1). This provision is new. It is intended to make it clear that the rule does not apply to preclude any relation back that may be permitted under the applicable limitations law. * * * Whatever may be the controlling body of limitations law, if that law affords a more forgiving principle of relation back than the one provided in this rule, it should be available to save the claim. If *Schiavone v. Fortune,* 106 S.Ct. 2379 (1986) implies the contrary, this paragraph is intended to make a material change in the rule.

Paragraph (c)(3). This paragraph has been revised to change the result in *Schiavone v. Fortune, supra,* with respect to the problem of a misnamed defendant. An intended defendant who is notified of an action within the period allowed by Rule 4[(j)] for service of a summons and complaint may not under the revised rule defeat the action on account of a defect in the pleading with respect to the defendant's name, provided that the requirements of clauses (A) and (B) have been met. If the notice requirement is met within the Rule 4[(j)] period, a complaint may be amended at any time to correct a formal defect such as a misnomer or misidentification. On the basis of the text of the former rule, the Court reached a result in *Schiavone v. Fortune* that was inconsistent with the liberal pleading practices secured by Rule 8. * * *

In allowing a name-correcting amendment within the time allowed by Rule 4[(j)], this rule allows not only the 120 days specified in that rule, but also any additional time resulting from any extension ordered by the court pursuant to that rule, as may be granted, for example, if the defendant is a fugitive from service of the summons.

* * *

Rule 16. Pretrial Conferences; Scheduling; Management

(a) Pretrial Conferences; Objectives. In any action, the court may in its discretion direct the attorneys for the parties and any unrepresented parties to appear before it for a conference or conferences before trial for such purposes as

(1) expediting the disposition of the action;

(2) establishing early and continuing control so that the case will not be protracted because of lack of management;

(3) discouraging wasteful pretrial activities;

(4) improving the quality of the trial through more thorough preparation, and;

(5) facilitating the settlement of the case.

(b) Scheduling and Planning. Except in categories of actions exempted by district court rule as inappropriate, the district judge, or a magistrate judge when authorized by district court rule, shall, after receiving the report from the parties under Rule 26(f) or after consulting with the attorneys for the parties and any unrepresented parties by a scheduling conference, telephone, mail, or other suitable means, enter a scheduling order that limits the time

(1) to join other parties and to amend the pleadings;

(2) to file motions; and

(3) to complete discovery.

The scheduling order also may include

(4) modifications of the times for disclosures under Rules 26(a) and 26(e)(1) and of the extent of discovery to be permitted;

(5) the date or dates for conferences before trial, a final pretrial conference, and trial; and

(6) any other matters appropriate in the circumstances of the case.

The order shall issue as soon as practicable but in any event within 90 days after the appearance of a defendant and within 120 days after the complaint has been served on a defendant. A schedule shall not be modified except upon a showing of good cause and by leave of the district judge or, when authorized by local rule, by a magistrate judge.

(c) Subjects for Consideration at Pretrial Conferences. At any conference under this rule consideration may be given, and the court may take appropriate action, with respect to

(1) the formulation and simplification of the issues, including the elimination of frivolous claims or defenses;

(2) the necessity or desirability of amendments to the pleadings;

(3) the possibility of obtaining admissions of fact and of documents which will avoid unnecessary proof, stipulations regarding the authenticity of documents, and advance rulings from the court on the admissibility of evidence;

(4) the avoidance of unnecessary proof and of cumulative evidence, and limitations or restrictions on the use of testimony under Rule 702 of the Federal Rules of Evidence;

(5) the appropriateness and timing of summary adjudication under Rule 56;

(6) the control and scheduling of discovery, including orders affecting disclosures and discovery pursuant to Rule 26 and Rules 29 through 37;

(7) the identification of witnesses and documents, the need and schedule for filing and exchanging pretrial briefs, and the date or dates for further conferences and for trial;

(8) the advisability of referring matters to a magistrate judge or master;

(9) settlement and the use of special procedures to assist in resolving the dispute when authorized by statute or local rule;

(10) the form and substance of the pretrial order;

(11) the disposition of pending motions;

(12) the need for adopting special procedures for managing potentially difficult or protracted actions that may involve complex issues, multiple parties, difficult legal questions, or unusual proof problems;

(13) an order for a separate trial pursuant to Rule 42(b) with respect to a claim, counterclaim, cross-claim, or third-party claim, or with respect to any particular issue in the case;

(14) an order directing a party or parties to present evidence early in the trial with respect to a manageable issue that could, on the evidence, be the basis for a judgment as a matter of law under Rule 50(a) or a judgment on partial findings under Rule 52(c);

(15) an order establishing a reasonable limit on the time allowed for presenting evidence; and

(16) such other matters as may facilitate the just, speedy, and inexpensive disposition of the action.

At least one of the attorneys for each party participating in any conference before trial shall have authority to enter into stipulations and to make admissions regarding all matters that the participants may reasonably anticipate may be discussed. If appropriate, the court may require that a party or its representative be present or reasonably available by telephone in order to consider possible settlement of the dispute.

(d) Final Pretrial Conference. Any final pretrial conference shall be held as close to the time of trial as reasonable under the circumstances. The participants at any such conference shall formulate a plan for trial, including a program for facilitating the admission of evidence. The conference shall be attended by at least one of the attorneys who will conduct the trial for each of the parties and by any unrepresented parties.

(e) Pretrial Orders. After any conference held pursuant to this rule, an order shall be entered reciting the action taken. This order shall control the subsequent course of the action unless modified by a subsequent order. The order following a final pretrial conference shall be modified only to prevent manifest injustice.

(f) Sanctions. If a party or party's attorney fails to obey a scheduling or pretrial order, or if no appearance is made on behalf of a party at a scheduling or pretrial conference, or if a party or party's attorney is substantially unprepared to participate in the conference, or if a party or party's attorney fails to participate in good faith, the judge, upon motion or the judge's own initiative, may make such orders with regard thereto as are just, and among others any of the orders provided in Rule 37(b)(2)(B), (C), (D). In lieu of or in addition to any other sanction, the judge shall require the party or the attorney representing the party or both to pay the reasonable expenses incurred because of any noncompliance with this rule, including attorney's fees, unless the judge finds that the noncompliance was substantially justified or that other circumstances make an award of expenses unjust.

(As amended Apr. 28, 1983, eff. Aug. 1, 1983; Mar. 2, 1987, eff. Aug. 1, 1987; Apr. 22, 1993, eff. Dec. 1, 1993.)

NOTES OF ADVISORY COMMITTEE ON RULES
1983 AMENDMENT

Introduction

* * *

Given the significant changes in federal civil litigation since 1938 that are not reflected in Rule 16, it has been extensively rewritten and expanded to meet the challenges of modern litigation. Empirical studies reveal that when a trial judge intervenes personally at an early stage to assume judicial control over a case and to schedule dates for completion by the parties of the principal pretrial steps, the case is disposed of by settlement or trial more efficiently and with less cost and delay than when the parties are left to their own devices. Flanders, *Case Management and Court Management in United States District Courts* 17, Federal Judicial Center (1977). Thus, the rule mandates a pretrial scheduling order. However, although scheduling and pretrial conferences are encouraged in appropriate cases, they are not mandated.

Discussion

Subdivision (a); Pretrial Conferences; Objectives. The amended rule makes scheduling and case management an express goal of pretrial procedure. This is done in Rule 16(a) by shifting the emphasis away from a conference focused solely on the trial and toward a process of judicial management that embraces the entire pretrial phase, especially motions and discovery. In addition, the amendment explicitly recognizes some of the objectives of pretrial conferences and the powers that many courts already have assumed. Rule 16 thus will be a more accurate reflection of actual practice.

Subdivision (b); Scheduling and Planning. The most significant change in Rule 16 is the mandatory scheduling order described in Rule 16(b), which is based in part on Wisconsin Civil Procedure Rule 802.10. The idea of scheduling orders is not new. It has been used by many federal courts.

Although a mandatory scheduling order encourages the court to become involved in case management early in the litigation, it represents a degree of judicial involvement that is not warranted in many cases. Thus, subdivision (b) permits each district court to promulgate a local rule under Rule 83 exempting certain categories of cases in which the burdens of scheduling orders exceed the administrative efficiencies that would be gained. Logical candidates for this treatment include social security disability matters, habeas corpus petitions, forfeitures, and reviews of certain administrative actions.

* * *

Rule 16(b) assures that the judge will take some early control over the litigation, even when its character does not warrant holding a scheduling conference. * * *

Subdivision (c); Subjects to Be Discussed at Pretrial Conferences. This subdivision expands upon the list of things that may be discussed at a pretrial conference that appeared in original Rule 16. The intention is to encourage better planning and management of litigation. Increased judicial control during the pretrial process accelerates the processing and termination of cases.

The reference in Rule 16(c)(1) to "formulation" is intended to clarify and confirm the court's power to identify the litigable issues. It has been added in the hope of promoting efficiency and conserving judicial resources by identifying the real issues prior to trial, thereby saving time and expense for everyone. See generally *Meadow Gold Prods. Co. v. Wright*, 278 F.2d 867 (D.C.Cir.1960). The notion is emphasized by expressly authorizing the elimination of frivolous claims or defenses at a pretrial conference. There is no reason to require that this await a formal motion for summary judgment. Nor is there any reason for the court to wait for the parties to initiate the process called for in Rule 16(c)(1).

The timing of any attempt at issue formulation is a matter of judicial discretion. In relatively simple cases it may not be necessary or may take the form of a stipulation between counsel or a request by the court that counsel work together to draft a proposed order.

Counsel bear a substantial responsibility for assisting the court in identifying the factual issues worthy of trial. If counsel fail to identify an issue for the court, the right to have the issue tried is waived. Although an order specifying the issues is intended to be binding, it may be amended at trial to avoid manifest injustice. See Rule 16(e). However, the rule's effectiveness depends on the court employing its discretion sparingly.

Clause [(8)] acknowledges the widespread availability and use of magistrates. The corresponding provision in the original rule referred only to masters and limited the function of the reference to the making of "findings to be used as evidence" in a case to be tried to a jury. The new text is not limited and broadens the potential use of a magistrate to that permitted by the Magistrate's Act.

Clause [(9)] explicitly recognizes that it has become commonplace to discuss settlement at pretrial conferences. Since it obviously eases crowded court dockets and results in savings to the litigants and the judicial system, settlement should be facilitated at as early a stage of the litigation as possible. * * *

A settlement conference is appropriate at any time. It may be held in conjunction with a pretrial or discovery conference, although various objectives of pretrial management, such as moving the case toward trial, may not always be compatible with settlement negotiations, and thus a separate settlement conference may be desirable.

In addition to settlement, Rule 16(c)[(9)] refers to exploring the use of procedures other than litigation to resolve the dispute. This includes urging the litigants to employ adjudicatory techniques outside the courthouse.

Rule 16(c)[(12)] authorizes the use of special pretrial procedures to expedite the adjudication of potentially difficult or protracted cases. Some district courts obviously have done so for many years. See Rubin, *The Managed Calendar: Some Pragmatic Suggestions About Achieving the Just, Speedy and Inexpensive Determination of Civil Cases in Federal Courts*, 4 Just.Sys.J. 135 (1976). Clause ([12]) provides an explicit authorization for such procedures and encourages their use. No particular techniques have been described; the Committee felt that flexibility and experience are the keys to efficient management of complex cases. Extensive guidance is offered in such documents as the *Manual for Complex Litigation.*

The rule simply identifies characteristics that make a case a strong candidate for special treatment. The four mentioned are illustrative, not exhaustive, and overlap to some degree. But experience has shown that one or more of them will be present in every protracted or difficult case and it seems desirable to set them out.

* * *

Subdivision (d); Final Pretrial Conference. This provision has been added to make it clear that the time between any final pretrial conference (which in a simple case may be the only pretrial conference) and trial should be as short as possible to be certain that the litigants make substantial progress with the case and avoid the inefficiency of having that preparation repeated when there is a delay between the last pretrial conference and trial. * * * the timing has been left to the court's discretion.

At least one of the attorneys who will conduct the trial for each party must be present at the final pretrial conference. At this late date there should be no doubt as to which attorney or attorneys this will be. Since the agreements and stipulations made at this final conference will control the trial, the presence of lawyers who will be involved in it is especially useful to assist the judge in structuring the case, and to lead to a more effective trial.

Subdivision (e); Pretrial Orders. Rule 16(e) does not substantially change the portion of the original rule dealing with pretrial orders. The purpose of an order is to guide the course of the litigation and the language of the original rule making that clear has been retained.

* * *

Once formulated, pretrial orders should not be changed lightly; but total inflexibility is undesirable. See, *e.g., Clark v. Pennsylvania R.R. Co.,* 328 F.2d 591 (2d Cir.1964). The exact words used to describe the standard for amending the pretrial order probably are less important than the meaning given them in practice. By not imposing any limitation on the ability to modify a pretrial order, the rule reflects the reality that in any process of continuous management what is done at one conference may have to be altered at the next. In the case of the final pretrial order, however, a more stringent standard is called for and the words "to prevent manifest injustice," which appeared in the original rule, have been retained. They have the virtue of familiarity and adequately describe the restraint the trial judge should exercise.

Many local rules make the plaintiff's attorney responsible for drafting a proposed pretrial order, either before or after the conference. Others allow the court to appoint any of the attorneys to perform the task, and others leave it to the court. See Note, *Pretrial Conference: A Critical Examination of Local Rules Adopted by Federal District Courts,* 64 Va.L.Rev. 467 (1978). Rule 16 has never addressed this matter. Since there is no consensus about which method of drafting the order works best and there is no reason to believe that nationwide uniformity is needed, the rule has been left silent on the point. See *Handbook for Effective Pretrial Procedure,* 37 F.R.D. 225 (1964).

Subdivision (f); Sanctions. Original Rule 16 did not mention the sanctions that might be imposed for failing to comply with the rule. However, courts have not hesitated to enforce it by appropriate measures. * * *

To reflect that existing practice, and to obviate dependence upon Rule 41(b) or the court's inherent power to regulate litigation, *cf. Societe Internationale Pour Participations Industrielles et Commerciales, S.A. v. Rogers,* 357 U.S. 197 (1958), Rule 16(f) expressly provides for imposing sanctions on disobedient or recalcitrant parties, their attorneys, or both in four types of situations. Rodes, Ripple & Mooney, *Sanctions Imposable for Violations of the Federal Rules of Civil Procedure* 65–67, 80–84, Federal Judicial Center (1981). Furthermore, explicit reference to sanctions reenforces the rule's intention to encourage forceful judicial management.

Rule 16(f) incorporates portions of Rule 37(b)(2), which prescribes sanctions for failing to make discovery. This should facilitate application of Rule 16(f), since courts and lawyers already are familiar with the Rule 37 standards. Among the sanctions authorized by the new subdivision are: preclusion order, striking a pleading, staying the proceeding, default judgment, contempt, and charging a party, his attorney, or both with the expenses, including attorney's fees, caused by noncompliance. The contempt sanction, however, is only available for a violation of a court order. The references in Rule 16(f) are not exhaustive.

As is true under Rule 37(b)(2), the imposition of sanctions may be sought by either the court or a party. In addition, the court has discretion to impose whichever sanction it feels is appropriate under the circumstances. Its action is reviewable under the abuse-of-discretion standard. See *National Hockey League v. Metropolitan Hockey Club, Inc.*, 427 U.S. 639 (1976).

1993 AMENDMENT

Subdivision (b). One purpose of this amendment is to provide a more appropriate deadline for the initial scheduling order required by the rule. * * * The longer time provided by the revision is not intended to encourage unnecessary delays in entering the scheduling order. Indeed, in most cases the order can and should be entered at a much earlier date. Rather, the additional time is intended to alleviate problems in multi-defendant cases and should ordinarily be adequate to enable participation by all defendants initially named in the action.

* * *

New paragraph (4) has been added to highlight that it will frequently be desirable for the scheduling order to include provisions relating to the timing of disclosures under Rule 26(a). * * *

Subdivision (c). The primary purposes of the changes in subdivision (c) are to call attention to the opportunities for structuring of trial under Rules 42, 50, and 52 and to eliminate questions that have occasionally been raised regarding the authority of the court to make appropriate orders designed either to facilitate settlement or to provide for an efficient and economical trial. The prefatory language of this subdivision is revised to clarify the court's power to enter appropriate orders at a conference notwithstanding the objection of a party. Of course settlement is dependent upon agreement by the parties and, indeed, a conference is most effective and productive when the parties participate in a spirit of cooperation and mindful of their responsibilities under Rule 1.

* * *

IV. PARTIES

Rule 17. Parties Plaintiff and Defendant; Capacity

(a) Real Party in Interest. Every action shall be prosecuted in the name of the real party in interest. An executor, administrator, guardian, bailee, trustee of an express trust, a party with whom or in whose name a contract has been made for the benefit of another, or a party authorized by statute may sue in that person's own name without joining the party for whose benefit the action is brought; and when a statute of the United States so provides, an action for the use or benefit of another shall be brought in the name of the United States. No action shall be dismissed on the ground that it is not prosecuted in the name of the real party in interest until a reasonable time has been allowed after objection for ratification of commencement of the action by, or joinder or substitution of, the real party in interest; and such ratification, joinder, or substitution shall have the same effect as if the action had been commenced in the name of the real party in interest.

(b) Capacity to Sue or Be Sued. The capacity of an individual, other than one acting in a representative capacity, to sue or be sued shall be determined by the law of the individual's domicile. The capacity of a corporation to sue or be sued shall be determined by the law under which it was organized. In all other cases capacity to sue or be sued shall be determined by the law of the state in which the district court is held, except (1) that a partnership or other unincorporated association, which has no such capacity by the law of such state, may sue or be sued in its common name for the purpose of enforcing for or against it a substantive right existing under the Constitution or laws of the United States, and (2) that the capacity of a receiver appointed by a court of the United States to sue or be sued in a court of the United States is governed by Title 28, U.S.C. §§ 754 and 959(a).

(c) Infants or Incompetent Persons. Whenever an infant or incompetent person has a representative, such as a general guardian, committee, conservator, or other like fiduciary, the representative may sue or defend on behalf of the infant or incompetent person. An infant or incompetent person who does not have a duly appointed representative may sue by next friend or by a guardian ad litem. The court shall appoint a guardian ad litem for an infant or incompetent person not otherwise represented in an action or shall make such other order as it deems proper for the protection of the infant or incompetent person.

(As amended Dec. 27, 1946, eff. Mar. 19, 1948; Dec. 29, 1948, eff. Oct. 20, 1949; Feb. 28, 1966, eff. July 1, 1966; Mar. 2, 1987, eff. Aug. 1, 1987; Apr. 25, 1988, eff. Aug. 1, 1988; Nov. 18, 1988, Pub.L. 100–690, § 7049, 102 Stat. 4401.)

Rule 18.   Joinder of Claims and Remedies

(a) Joinder of Claims. A party asserting a claim to relief as an original claim, counterclaim, cross-claim, or third-party claim, may join, either as independent or as alternate claims, as many claims, legal, equitable, or maritime, as the party has against an opposing party.

(b) Joinder of Remedies; Fraudulent Conveyances. Whenever a claim is one heretofore cognizable only after another claim has been prosecuted to a conclusion, the two claims may be joined in a single action; but the court shall grant relief in that action only in accordance with the relative substantive rights of the parties. In particular, a plaintiff may state a claim for money and a claim to have set aside a conveyance fraudulent as to that plaintiff, without first having obtained a judgment establishing the claim for money.

(As amended Feb. 28, 1966, eff. July 1, 1966; Mar. 2, 1987, eff. Aug. 1, 1987.)

Rule 19.   Joinder of Persons Needed for Just Adjudication

(a) Persons to Be Joined if Feasible. A person who is subject to service of process and whose joinder will not deprive the court of jurisdiction over the subject matter of the action shall be joined as a party in the action if (1) in the person's absence complete relief cannot be accorded among those already parties, or (2) the person claims an interest relating to the subject of the action and is so situated that the disposition of the action in the person's absence may (i) as a practical matter impair or impede the person's ability to protect that interest or (ii) leave any of the persons already parties subject to a substantial risk of incurring double, multiple, or otherwise inconsistent obligations by reason of the claimed interest. If the person has not been so joined, the court shall order that the person be made a party. If the person should join as a plaintiff but refuses to do so, the person may be made a defendant, or, in a proper case, an involuntary plaintiff. If the joined party objects to venue and joinder of that party would render the venue of the action improper, that party shall be dismissed from the action.

(b) Determination by Court Whenever Joinder not Feasible. If a person as described in subdivision (a)(1)–(2) hereof cannot be made a party, the court shall determine whether in equity and good conscience the action should proceed among the parties before it, or should be dismissed, the absent person being thus regarded as indispensable. The factors to be considered by the court include: first, to what extent a judgment rendered in the person's absence might be prejudicial to the person or those already parties; second, the extent to which, by protective provisions in the judgment, by the shaping of relief, or other measures, the prejudice can be lessened or avoided; third, whether a judgment rendered in the person's absence will be adequate; fourth, whether the plaintiff will have an adequate remedy if the action is dismissed for nonjoinder.

(c) Pleading Reasons for Nonjoinder. A pleading asserting a claim for relief shall state the names, if known to the pleader, of any persons as described in subdivision (a)(1)–(2) hereof who are not joined, and the reasons why they are not joined.

(d) Exception of Class Actions. This rule is subject to the provisions of Rule 23.

(As amended Feb. 28, 1966, eff. July 1, 1966; Mar. 2, 1987, eff. Aug. 1, 1987.)

NOTES OF ADVISORY COMMITTEE ON RULES
1966 AMENDMENT

* * *

THE AMENDED RULE

* * *

The subdivision (a) definition of persons to be joined is not couched in terms of the abstract nature of their interests—"joint," "united," "separable," or the like. * * * It should be noted particularly, however, that the description is not at variance with the settled authorities holding that a tortfeasor with the usual "joint-and-several" liability is merely a permissive party to an action against another with like liability. * * * Joinder of these tortfeasors continues to be regulated by Rule 20; compare Rule 14 on third-party practice.

* * *

Subdivision (b).—When a person as described in subdivision (a)(1)–(2) cannot be made a party, the court is to determine whether in equity and good conscience the action should proceed among the parties already before it, or should be dismissed. That this decision is to be made in the light of pragmatic considerations has often been acknowledged by the courts. See *Roos v. Texas Co.,* 23 F.2d 171 (2d Cir.1927), cert. denied, 277 U.S. 587 (1928); *Niles–Bement–Pond Co. v. Iron Moulders' Union,* 254 U.S. 77, 80 (1920). The subdivision sets out four relevant considerations drawn from the experience revealed in the decided cases. The factors are to a certain extent overlapping, and they are not intended to exclude other considerations which may be applicable in particular situations.

The first factor brings in a consideration of what a judgment in the action would mean to the absentee. Would the absentee be adversely affected in a practical sense, and if so, would the prejudice be immediate and serious, or remote and minor? The possible collateral consequences of the judgment upon the parties already joined are also to be appraised. Would any party be exposed to a fresh action by the absentee, and if so, how serious is the threat?   * * *

The second factor calls attention to the measures by which prejudice may be averted or lessened. The "shaping of relief" is a familiar expedient to this end. See, e.g., the award of money damages in lieu of specific relief where the latter might affect an absentee adversely.   * * *

Sometimes the party is himself able to take measures to avoid prejudice. Thus a defendant faced with a prospect of a second suit by an absentee may be in a position to bring the latter into the action by defensive interpleader.   * * * So also the absentee may sometimes be able to avert prejudice to himself by voluntarily appearing in the action or intervening on an ancillary basis.   * * * The court should consider whether this, in turn, would impose undue hardship on the absentee.   * * *

The third factor—whether an "adequate" judgment can be rendered in the absence of a given person—calls attention to the extent of the relief that can be accorded among the parties joined. It meshes with the other factors, especially the "shaping of relief" mentioned under the second factor. Cf. *Kroese v. General Steel Castings Corp.,* 179 F.2d 760 (3d Cir.1949), cert. denied, 339 U.S. 983 (1950).

The fourth factor, looking to the practical effects of a dismissal, indicates that the court should consider whether there is any assurance that the plaintiff, if dismissed, could sue effectively in another forum where better joinder would be possible.   * * *

The subdivision uses the word "indispensable" only in a conclusory sense, that is, a person is "regarded as indispensable" when he cannot be made a party and, upon consideration of the factors above mentioned, it is determined that in his absence it would be preferable to dismiss the action, rather than to retain it.

* * *

Rule 20. Permissive Joinder of Parties

(a) Permissive Joinder. All persons may join in one action as plaintiffs if they assert any right to relief jointly, severally, or in the alternative in respect of or arising out of the same transaction, occurrence, or series of transactions or occurrences and if any question of law or fact common to all these persons will arise in the action. All persons (and any vessel, cargo or other property subject to admiralty process in rem) may be joined in one action as defendants if there is asserted against them jointly, severally, or in the alternative, any right to relief in respect of or arising out of the same transaction, occurrence, or series of transactions or occurrences and if any question of law or fact common to all defendants will arise in the action. A plaintiff or defendant need not be interested in obtaining or defending against all the relief demanded. Judgment may be given for one or more of the plaintiffs according to their respective rights to relief, and against one or more defendants according to their respective liabilities.

(b) Separate Trials. The court may make such orders as will prevent a party from being embarrassed, delayed, or put to expense by the inclusion of a party against whom the party asserts no claim and who asserts no claim against the party, and may order separate trials or make other orders to prevent delay or prejudice.

(As amended Feb. 28, 1966, eff. July 1, 1966; Mar. 2, 1987, eff. Aug. 1, 1987.)

Rule 21. Misjoinder and Non–joinder of Parties

Misjoinder of parties is not ground for dismissal of an action. Parties may be dropped or added by order of the court on motion of any party or of its own initiative at any stage of the action and on such terms as are just. Any claim against a party may be severed and proceeded with separately.

Rule 22. Interpleader

(1) Persons having claims against the plaintiff may be joined as defendants and required to interplead when their claims are such that the plaintiff is or may be exposed to double or multiple liability. It is not ground for objection to the joinder that the claims of the several claimants or the titles on which their claims depend do not have a common origin or are not identical but are adverse to and independent of one another, or that the plaintiff avers that the plaintiff is not liable in whole or in part to any or all of the claimants. A defendant exposed to similar liability may obtain such interpleader by way of cross-claim or counterclaim. The provisions of this rule supplement and do not in any way limit the joinder of parties permitted in Rule 20.

(2) The remedy herein provided is in addition to and in no way supersedes or limits the remedy provided by Title 28, U.S.C. §§ 1335, 1397, and 2361. Actions under those provisions shall be conducted in accordance with these rules.

(As amended Dec. 29, 1948, eff. Oct. 20, 1949; Mar. 2, 1987, eff. Aug. 1, 1987.)

Rule 23. Class Actions

(a) **Prerequisites to a Class Action.** One or more members of a class may sue or be sued as representative parties on behalf of all only if (1) the class is so numerous that joinder of all members is impracticable, (2) there are questions of law or fact common to the class, (3) the claims or defenses of the representative parties are typical of the claims or defenses of the class, and (4) the representative parties will fairly and adequately protect the interests of the class.

(b) **Class Actions Maintainable.** An action may be maintained as a class action if the prerequisites of subdivision (a) are satisfied, and in addition:

(1) the prosecution of separate actions by or against individual members of the class would create a risk of

(A) inconsistent or varying adjudications with respect to individual members of the class which would establish incompatible standards of conduct for the party opposing the class; or

(B) adjudications with respect to individual members of the class which would as a practical matter be dispositive of the interests of the other members not parties to the adjudications or substantially impair or impede their ability to protect their interests; or

(2) the party opposing the class has acted or refused to act on grounds generally applicable to the class, thereby making appropriate final injunctive relief or corresponding declaratory relief with respect to the class as a whole; or

(3) the court finds that the questions of law or fact common to the members of the class predominate over any questions affecting only individual members, and that a class action is superior to other available methods for the fair and efficient adjudication of the controversy. The matters pertinent to the findings include: (A) the interest of members of the class in individually controlling the prosecution or defense of separate actions; (B) the extent and nature of any litigation concerning the controversy already commenced by or against members of the class; (C) the desirability or undesirability of concentrating the litigation of the claims in the particular forum; (D) the difficulties likely to be encountered in the management of a class action.

(c) **Determination by Order Whether Class Action to Be Maintained; Notice; Judgment; Actions Conducted Partially as Class Actions.**

(1) As soon as practicable after the commencement of an action brought as a class action, the court shall determine by order whether it

is to be so maintained. An order under this subdivision may be conditional, and may be altered or amended before the decision on the merits.

(2) In any class action maintained under subdivision (b)(3), the court shall direct to the members of the class the best notice practicable under the circumstances, including individual notice to all members who can be identified through reasonable effort. The notice shall advise each member that (A) the court will exclude the member from the class if the member so requests by a specified date; (B) the judgment, whether favorable or not, will include all members who do not request exclusion; and (C) any member who does not request exclusion may, if the member desires, enter an appearance through counsel.

(3) The judgment in an action maintained as a class action under subdivision (b)(1) or (b)(2), whether or not favorable to the class, shall include and describe those whom the court finds to be members of the class. The judgment in an action maintained as a class action under subdivision (b)(3), whether or not favorable to the class, shall include and specify or describe those to whom the notice provided in subdivision (c)(2) was directed, and who have not requested exclusion, and whom the court finds to be members of the class.

(4) When appropriate (A) an action may be brought or maintained as a class action with respect to particular issues, or (B) a class may be divided into subclasses and each subclass treated as a class, and the provisions of this rule shall then be construed and applied accordingly.

(d) Orders in Conduct of Actions. In the conduct of actions to which this rule applies, the court may make appropriate orders: (1) determining the course of proceedings or prescribing measures to prevent undue repetition or complication in the presentation of evidence or argument; (2) requiring, for the protection of the members of the class or otherwise for the fair conduct of the action, that notice be given in such manner as the court may direct to some or all of the members of any step in the action, or of the proposed extent of the judgment, or of the opportunity of members to signify whether they consider the representation fair and adequate, to intervene and present claims or defenses, or otherwise to come into the action; (3) imposing conditions on the representative parties or on intervenors; (4) requiring that the pleadings be amended to eliminate therefrom allegations as to representation of absent persons, and that the action proceed accordingly; (5) dealing with similar procedural matters. The orders may be combined with an order under Rule 16, and may be altered or amended as may be desirable from time to time.

(e) Dismissal or Compromise. A class action shall not be dismissed or compromised without the approval of the court, and notice of the proposed dismissal or compromise shall be given to all members of the class in such manner as the court directs.

(As amended Feb. 28, 1966, eff. July 1, 1966; Mar. 2, 1987, eff. Aug. 1, 1987.)

NOTES OF ADVISORY COMMITTEE ON RULES
1966 AMENDMENT

Difficulties with the original rule. The categories of class actions in the original rule were defined in terms of the abstract nature of the rights involved: the so-called "true" category was defined as involving "joint, common, or secondary rights"; the "hybrid" category, as involving "several" rights related to "specific property"; the "spurious" category, as involving "several" rights affected by a common question and related to common relief. It was thought that the definitions accurately described the situations amenable to the class-suit device, and also would indicate the proper extent of the judgment in each category, which would in turn help to determine the res judicata effect of the judgment if questioned in a later action. Thus the judgments in "true" and "hybrid" class actions would extend to the class (although in somewhat different ways); the judgment in a "spurious" class action would extend only to the parties including intervenors. See Moore, Federal Rules of Civil Procedure: Some Problems Raised by the Preliminary Draft, 25 Geo.L.J. 551, 570–76 (1937).

In practice the terms "joint," "common," etc., which were used as the basis of the Rule 23 classification proved obscure and uncertain. * * *

Nor did the rule provide an adequate guide to the proper extent of the judgments in class actions. First, we find instances of the courts classifying actions as "true" or intimating that the judgments would be decisive for the class where these results seemed appropriate but were reached by dint of depriving the word "several" of coherent meaning. * * * Second, we find cases classified by the courts as "spurious" in which, on a realistic view, it would seem fitting for the judgments to extend to the class. * * *

The "spurious" action envisaged by original Rule 23 was in any event an anomaly because, although denominated a "class" action and pleaded as such, it was supposed not to adjudicate the rights or liabilities of any person not a party. It was believed to be an advantage of the "spurious" category that it would invite decisions that a member of the "class" could, like a member of the class in a "true" or "hybrid" action, intervene on an ancillary basis without being required to show an independent basis of Federal jurisdiction, and have the benefit of the date of the commencement of the action for purposes of the statute of limitations. See 3 Moore's Federal Practice, pars. 23.10[1], 23.12 (2d ed. 1963). These results were attained in some instances but not in others. * * *

Finally, the original rule did not squarely address itself to the question of the measures that might be taken during the course of the action to assure procedural fairness, particularly giving notice to members of the class, which may in turn be related in some instances to the extension of the judgment to the class. * * *

The amended rule describes in more practical terms the occasions for maintaining class actions; provides that all class actions maintained to the end as such will result in judgments including those whom the court finds to be members of the class, whether or not the judgment is favorable to the class; and refers to the measures which can be taken to assure the fair conduct of these actions.

Subdivision (a) states the prerequisites for maintaining any class action in terms of the numerousness of the class making joinder of the members impracticable, the existence of questions common to the class, and the desired qualifications of the representative parties. * * * These are necessary but not sufficient conditions for a class action. * * * Subdivision (b) describes the additional elements which in varying situations justify the use of a class action.

Subdivision (b)(1). The difficulties which would be likely to arise if resort were had to separate actions by or against the individual members of the class here furnish the reasons for, and the principal key to, the propriety and value of utilizing the class-action device. The considerations stated under clauses (A) and (B) are comparable to certain of the elements which define the persons whose joinder in an action is desirable as stated in Rule 19(a), as amended. * * *

Clause (A): One person may have rights against, or be under duties toward, numerous persons constituting a class, and be so positioned that conflicting or varying adjudications in lawsuits with individual members of the class might establish incompatible standards to govern his conduct. The class action device can be used effectively to obviate the actual or virtual dilemma which would thus confront the party opposing the class. * * * To illustrate: Separate actions by individuals against a municipality to declare a bond issue invalid or condition or limit it, to prevent or limit the making of a particular appropriation or to compel or invalidate an assessment, might create a risk of inconsistent or varying determinations. In the same way, individual litigations of the rights and duties of riparian owners, or of landowners' rights and duties respecting a claimed nuisance, could create a possibility of incompatible adjudications. Actions by or against a class provide a ready and fair means of achieving unitary adjudication. * * *

Clause (B): This clause takes in situations where the judgment in a nonclass action by or against an individual member of the class, while not technically concluding the other members, might do so as a practical matter. The vice of an individual action would lie in the fact that the other members of the class, thus practically concluded, would have had no representation in the lawsuit. In an action by policy holders against a fraternal benefit association attacking a financial reorganization of the society, it would hardly have been practical, if indeed it would have been possible, to confine the effects of a validation of the reorganization to the individual plaintiffs. * * * For much the same reason actions by shareholders to compel the declaration of a dividend, the proper recognition and handling of redemption or pre-emption rights, or the like (or actions by the corporation for corresponding declarations of rights), should ordinarily be conducted as class actions, although the matter has been much obscured by the insistence that each shareholder has an individual claim. * * * These shareholders' actions are to be distinguished from derivative actions by shareholders dealt with in new Rule 23.1. The same reasoning applies to an action which charges a breach of trust by an indenture trustee or other fiduciary similarly affecting the members of a larger class of security holders or other beneficiaries, and which requires an accounting or like measures to restore the subject of the trust. * * *.

In various situations an adjudication as to one or more members of the class will necessarily or probably have an adverse practical effect on the interests of other members who should therefore be represented in the lawsuit. This is plainly the case when claims are made by numerous persons against a fund insufficient to satisfy all claims. A class action by or against representative members to settle the validity of the claims as a whole, or in groups, followed by separate proof of the amount of each valid claim and proportionate distribution of the fund, meets the problem. * * *. The same reasoning applies to an action by a creditor to set aside a fraudulent conveyance by the debtor and to appropriate the property to his claim, when the debtor's assets are insufficient to pay all creditors' claims. * * *. Similar problems, however, can arise in the absence of a fund either present or potential. A negative or mandatory injunction secured by one of a numerous class may disable the opposing party from performing claimed duties toward the other members of the class or materially affect his ability to do so. An adjudication as to movie "clearances and runs" nominally affecting only one exhibitor would often have practical effects on all the exhibitors in the same territorial area. Cf. *United States v. Paramount Pictures, Inc.,* 66 F.Supp. 323, 341–46 (S.D.N.Y.1946); 334 U.S. 131, 144–48 (1948). Assuming a sufficiently numerous class of exhibitors, a class action would be advisable. (Here representation of subclasses of exhibitors could become necessary; see subdivision (c)(3)(B).)

Subdivision (b)(2). This subdivision is intended to reach situations where a party has taken action or refused to take action with respect to a class, and final relief of an injunctive nature or of a corresponding declaratory nature, settling the legality of the behavior with respect to the class as a whole, is appropriate. Declaratory relief "corresponds" to injunctive relief when as a practical matter it affords injunctive relief or serves as a basis for later injunctive relief. The subdivision does not extend to cases in which the appropriate final relief relates exclusively or predominantly to money damages. Action or inaction is directed to a class within the meaning of this subdivision even if it has taken effect or is threatened only as to one or a few members of the class, provided it is based on grounds which have general application to the class.

* * *

Subdivision (b)(3). In the situations to which this subdivision relates, class-action treatment is not as clearly called for as in those described above, but it may nevertheless be convenient and desirable depending upon the particular facts. Subdivision (b)(3) encompasses those cases in which a class action would achieve economies of time, effort, and expense, and promote uniformity of decision as to persons similarly situated, without sacrificing procedural fairness or bringing about other undesirable results. * * *.

The court is required to find, as a condition of holding that a class action may be maintained under this subdivision, that the questions common to the class predominate over the questions affecting individual members. It is only where this predominance exists that economies can be achieved by means of the class-action device. In this view, a fraud perpetrated on numerous persons by the use of similar misrepresentations may be an appealing situation for a class action, and it may remain so despite the need, if liability is found, for separate determination of the damages suffered by individuals within the class. On the other hand, although having some common core, a fraud case may be unsuited for treatment as a class action if there was material variation in the representations made or in the kinds or degrees of reliance by the persons to whom they were addressed. * * * A "mass accident" resulting in injuries to numerous persons is ordinarily not appropriate for a class action because of the likelihood that significant questions, not only of damages but of liability and defenses of liability, would be present, affecting the individuals in different ways. In these circumstances an action conducted nominally as a class action would degenerate in practice into multiple lawsuits separately tried. * * * Private damage claims by numerous individuals arising out of concerted antitrust violations may or may not involve predominating common questions. * * *

That common questions predominate is not itself sufficient to justify a class action under subdivision (b)(3), for another method of handling the litigious situation may be available which has greater practical advantages. Thus one or more actions agreed to by the parties as test or model actions may be preferable to a class action; or it may prove feasible and preferable to consolidate actions. * * * Even when a number of separate actions are proceeding simultaneously, experience shows that the burdens on the parties and the courts can sometimes be reduced by arrangements for avoiding repetitious discovery or the like. * * *

Factors (A)–(D) are listed, non-exhaustively, as pertinent to the findings. The court is to consider the interests of individual members of the class in controlling their own litigations and carrying them on as they see fit. * * *

In this connection the court should inform itself of any litigation actually pending by or against the individuals. The interests of individuals in conducting separate lawsuits may be so strong as to call for denial of a class action. On the other hand, these interests may be theoretic rather than practical; the class may have a high degree of cohesion and prosecution of the action through representatives would be quite unobjectionable, or the amounts at stake for individuals may be so small that separate suits would be impracticable. The burden that separate suits would impose on the party opposing the class, or upon the court calendars, may also fairly be considered. (See the discussion, under subdivision (c)(2) below, of the right of members to be excluded from the class upon their request.)

Also pertinent is the question of the desirability of concentrating the trial of the claims in the particular forum by means of a class action, in contrast to allowing the claims to be litigated separately in forums to which they would ordinarily be brought. Finally, the court should consider the problems of management which are likely to arise in the conduct of a class action.

Subdivision (c)(1). In order to give clear definition to the action, this provision requires the court to determine, as early in the proceedings as may be practicable, whether an action brought as a class action is to be so maintained. The determination depends in each case on satisfaction of the terms of subdivision (a) and the relevant provisions of subdivision (b).

An order embodying a determination can be conditional; the court may rule, for example, that a class action may be maintained only if the representation is improved through intervention of additional parties of a stated type. A determination once made can be altered or amended before the decision on the merits if, upon fuller development of the facts, the original determination appears unsound. A negative determination means that the action should be stripped of its character as a class action. See subdivision (d)(4). Although an action thus becomes a nonclass action, the court may still be receptive to interventions before the decision on the merits so that the litigation may cover as many interests as can be conveniently handled; the questions whether the intervenors in the nonclass action shall be permitted to claim "ancillary" jurisdiction or the benefit of the date of the commencement of the action for purposes of the statute of limitations are to be decided by reference to the laws governing jurisdiction and limitations as they apply in particular contexts.

Whether the court should require notice to be given to members of the class of its intention to make a determination, or of the order embodying it, is left to the court's discretion under subdivision (d)(2).

Subdivision (c)(2) makes special provision for class actions maintained under subdivision (b)(3). As noted in the discussion of the latter subdivision, the interests of the individuals in pursuing their own litigations may be so strong here as to warrant denial of a class action altogether. Even when a class action is maintained under subdivision (b)(3), this individual interest is respected. Thus the court is required to direct notice to the members of the class of the right of each member to be excluded from the class upon his request. A member who does not request exclusion may, if he wishes, enter an appearance in the action through his counsel; whether or not he does so, the judgment in the action will embrace him.

The notice, setting forth the alternatives open to the members of the class, is to be the best practicable under the circumstances, and shall include individual notice to the members who can be identified through reasonable effort. (For further discussion of this notice, see the statement under subdivision (d)(2) below.)

Subdivision (c)(3). The judgment in a class action maintained as such to the end will embrace the class, that is, in a class action under subdivision (b)(1) or (b)(2), those found by the court to be class members; in a class action under subdivision (b)(3), those to whom the notice prescribed by subdivision (c)(2) was directed, excepting those who requested exclusion or who are ultimately found by the court not to be members of the class. The judgment has this scope whether it is favorable or unfavorable to the class. In a (b)(1) or (b)(2) action the judgment "describes" the members of the class, but need not specify the individual members; in a (b)(3) action the judgment "specifies" the individual members who have been identified and describes the others.

* * *

Hitherto, in a few actions conducted as "spurious" class actions and thus nominally designed to extend only to parties and others intervening before the determination of liability, courts have held or intimated that class members might be permitted to intervene after a decision on the merits favorable to their interests, in order to secure the benefits of the decision for themselves, although they would presumably be unaffected by an unfavorable decision. * * * Under proposed subdivision (c)(3), one-way intervention is excluded; the action will have been early determined to be a class or nonclass action, and in the former case the judgment, whether or not favorable, will include the class, as above stated.

Although thus declaring that the judgment in a class action includes the class, as defined, subdivision (c)(3) does not disturb the recognized principle that the court conducting the action cannot predetermine the res judicata effect of the judgment; this can be tested only in a subsequent action. See Restatement, Judgments § 86, comment (h), § 116 (1942). The court, however, in framing the judgment in any suit brought as a class action, must decide what its extent or coverage shall be, and if the matter is carefully considered, questions of res judicata are less likely to be raised at a later time and if raised will be more satisfactorily answered. * * *

Subdivision (c)(4). This provision recognizes that an action may be maintained as a class action as to particular issues only. For example, in a fraud or similar case the action may retain its "class" character only through the adjudication of liability to the class; the members of the class may thereafter be required to come in individually and prove the amounts of their respective claims.

Two or more classes may be represented in a single action. Where a class is found to include subclasses divergent in interest, the class may be divided correspondingly, and each subclass treated as a class.

* * *

Subdivision (d)(2) does not require notice at any stage, but rather calls attention to its availability and invokes the court's discretion. In the degree that there is cohesiveness or unity in the class and the representation is effective, the need for notice to the class will tend toward a minimum. These indicators suggest that notice under subdivision (d)(2) may be particularly useful and advisable in certain class actions maintained under subdivision (b)(3), for example, to permit members of the class to object to the representation. Indeed, under subdivision (c)(2), notice must be ordered, and is not merely discretionary, to give the members in a subdivision (b)(3) class action an opportunity to secure exclusion from the class. This mandatory notice pursuant to subdivision (c)(2), together with any discretionary notice which the court may find it advisable to give under subdivision (d)(2), is designed to fulfill requirements of due process to which the class action procedure is of course subject. See *Hansberry v. Lee,* 311 U.S. 32 (1940); *Mullane v. Central Hanover Bank & Trust Co.,* 339 U.S. 306 (1950) * * *.

Notice to members of the class, whenever employed under amended Rule 23, should be accommodated to the particular purpose but need not comply with the formalities for service of process. * * * The fact that notice is given at one stage of the action does not mean that it must be given at subsequent stages. Notice is available fundamentally "for the protection of the members of the class or otherwise for the fair conduct of the action" and should not be used merely as a device for the undesirable solicitation of claims. * * *

* * *

Rule 23.1   Derivative Actions by Shareholders

In a derivative action brought by one or more shareholders or members to enforce a right of a corporation or of an unincorporated association, the corporation or association having failed to enforce a right which may properly be asserted by it, the complaint shall be verified and shall allege (1) that the plaintiff was a shareholder or member at the time of the transaction of which the plaintiff complains or that the plaintiff's share or membership thereafter devolved on the plaintiff by operation of law, and (2) that the action is not a collusive one to confer jurisdiction on a court of the United States which it would not otherwise have.   The complaint shall also allege with particularity the efforts, if any, made by the plaintiff to obtain the action the plaintiff desires from the directors or comparable authority and, if necessary, from the shareholders or members, and the reasons for the plaintiff's failure to obtain the action or for not making the effort.   The derivative action may not be maintained if it appears that the plaintiff does not fairly and adequately represent the interests of the shareholders or members similarly situated in enforcing the right of the corporation or association.   The action shall not be dismissed or compromised without the approval of the court, and notice of the proposed dismissal or compromise shall be given to shareholders or members in such manner as the court directs.

(Added Feb. 28, 1966, eff. July 1, 1966, and amended Mar. 2, 1987, eff. Aug. 1, 1987.)

Rule 23.2   Actions Relating to Unincorporated Associations

An action brought by or against the members of an unincorporated association as a class by naming certain members as representative parties may be maintained only if it appears that the representative parties will fairly and adequately protect the interests of the association and its members.   In the conduct of the action the court may make appropriate orders corresponding with those described in Rule 23(d), and the procedure for dismissal or compromise of the action shall correspond with that provided in Rule 23(e).

(Added Feb. 28, 1966, eff. July 1, 1966.)

Rule 24.   Intervention

(a) Intervention of Right.   Upon timely application anyone shall be permitted to intervene in an action: (1) when a statute of the United States confers an unconditional right to intervene; or (2) when the applicant claims an interest relating to the property or transaction which is the subject of the action and the applicant is so situated that the disposition of the action may as a practical matter impair or impede the applicant's ability to protect that interest, unless the applicant's interest is adequately represented by existing parties.

(b) Permissive Intervention.   Upon timely application anyone may be permitted to intervene in an action: (1) when a statute of the

United States confers a conditional right to intervene; or (2) when an applicant's claim or defense and the main action have a question of law or fact in common. When a party to an action relies for ground of claim or defense upon any statute or executive order administered by a federal or state governmental officer or agency or upon any regulation, order, requirement or agreement issued or made pursuant to the statute or executive order, the officer or agency upon timely application may be permitted to intervene in the action. In exercising its discretion the court shall consider whether the intervention will unduly delay or prejudice the adjudication of the rights of the original parties.

(c) Procedure. A person desiring to intervene shall serve a motion to intervene upon the parties as provided in Rule 5. The motion shall state the grounds therefor and shall be accompanied by a pleading setting forth the claim or defense for which intervention is sought. The same procedure shall be followed when a statute of the United States gives a right to intervene. When the constitutionality of an act of Congress affecting the public interest is drawn in question in any action to which the United States or an officer, agency, or employee thereof is not a party, the court shall notify the Attorney General of the United States as provided in Title 28, U.S.C. § 2403. When the constitutionality of any statute of a State affecting the public interest is drawn in question in any action in which that State or any agency, officer, or employee thereof is not a party, the court shall notify the attorney general of the State as provided in Title 28, U.S.C. § 2403. A party challenging the constitutionality of legislation should call the attention of the court to its consequential duty, but failure to do so is not a waiver of any constitutional right otherwise timely asserted.

(As amended Dec. 27, 1946, eff. Mar. 19, 1948; Dec. 29, 1948, eff. Oct. 20, 1949; Jan. 21, 1963, eff. July 1, 1963; Feb. 28, 1966, eff. July 1, 1966; Mar. 2, 1987, eff. Aug. 1, 1987; Apr. 30, 1991, eff. Dec. 1, 1991.)

NOTES OF ADVISORY COMMITTEE ON RULES
1966 AMENDMENT

In attempting to overcome certain difficulties which have arisen in the application of present Rule 24(a)(2) and (3), this amendment draws upon the revision of the related Rules 19 (joinder of persons needed for just adjudication) and 23 (class actions), and the reasoning underlying that revision.

Rule 24(a)(3) as amended in 1948 provided for intervention of right where the applicant established that he would be adversely affected by the distribution or disposition of property involved in an action to which he had not been made a party. Significantly, some decided cases virtually disregarded the language of this provision. * * * This development was quite natural, for Rule 24(a)(3) was unduly restricted. If an absentee would be substantially affected in a practical sense by the determination made in an action, he should, as a general rule, be entitled to intervene, and his right to do so should not depend on whether there is a fund to be distributed or otherwise disposed of. Intervention of right is here seen to be a kind of counterpart to Rule 19(a)(2)(i) on joinder of persons needed for a just adjudication: where, upon motion of a party in an action, an absentee should be joined so that he may protect his interest which as a practical matter may be substantially impaired by the disposition of the action, he ought to have a right to intervene in the action on his own motion.   * * *

The general purpose of original Rule 24(a)(2) was to entitle an absentee, purportedly represented by a party, to intervene in the action if he could establish with fair probability that the representation was inadequate. Thus, where an action is being prosecuted or defended by a trustee, a beneficiary of the trust should have a right to intervene if he can show that the trustee's representation of his interest probably is inadequate; similarly a member of a class should have the right to intervene in a class action if he can show the inadequacy of the representation of his interest by the representative parties before the court.

Original Rule 24(a)(2), however, made it a condition of intervention that "the applicant is or may be bound by a judgment in the action," and this created difficulties with intervention in class actions. If the "bound" language was read literally in the sense of res judicata, it could defeat intervention in some meritorious cases. A member of a class to whom a judgment in a class action extended by its terms (see Rule 23(c)(3), as amended) might be entitled to show in a later action, when the judgment in the class action was claimed to operate as res judicata against him, that the "representative" in the class action had not in fact adequately represented him. If he could make this showing, the class-action judgment might be held not to bind him. See *Hansberry v. Lee,* 311 U.S. 32 (1940). If a class member sought to intervene in the class action proper, while it was still pending, on grounds of inadequacy of representation, he could be met with the argument: if the representation was in fact inadequate, he would not be "bound" by the judgment when it was subsequently asserted against him as res judicata, hence he was not entitled to intervene; if the representation was in fact adequate, there was no occasion or ground for intervention. See *Sam Fox Publishing Co., v. United States,* 366 U.S. 683 (1961); cf. *Sutphen Estates, Inc. v. United States,* 342 U.S. 19 (1951). This reasoning might be linguistically justified by original Rule 24(a)(2); but it could lead to poor results.   * * * A class member who claims that his "representative" does not adequately represent him, and is able to establish that proposition with sufficient probability, should not be put to the risk of having a judgment entered in the action which by its terms extends to him, and be obliged to test the validity of the judgment as applied to his interest by a later collateral attack. Rather he should, as a general rule, be entitled to intervene in the action.

The amendment provides that an applicant is entitled to intervene in an action when his position is comparable to that of a person under Rule 19(a)(2)(i), as amended, unless his interest is already adequately represented in the action by existing parties. The Rule 19(a)(2)(i) criterion imports practical considerations, and the deletion of the "bound" language similarly frees the rule from undue preoccupation with strict considerations of res judicata.

The representation whose adequacy comes into question under the amended rule is not confined to formal representation like that provided by a trustee for his beneficiary or a representative party in a class action for a member of the class. A party to an action may provide practical representation to the absentee seeking intervention although no such formal relationship exists between them, and the adequacy of this practical representation will then have to be weighed. * * *

An intervention of right under the amended rule may be subject to appropriate conditions or restrictions responsive among other things to the requirements of efficient conduct of the proceedings.

Rule 25. Substitution of Parties

(a) Death.

(1) If a party dies and the claim is not thereby extinguished, the court may order substitution of the proper parties. The motion for substitution may be made by any party or by the successors or representatives of the deceased party and, together with the notice of hearing, shall be served on the parties as provided in Rule 5 and upon persons not parties in the manner provided in Rule 4 for the service of a summons, and may be served in any judicial district. Unless the motion for substitution is made not later than 90 days after the death is suggested upon the record by service of a statement of the fact of the death as provided herein for the service of the motion, the action shall be dismissed as to the deceased party.

(2) In the event of the death of one or more of the plaintiffs or of one or more of the defendants in an action in which the right sought to be enforced survives only to the surviving plaintiffs or only against the surviving defendants, the action does not abate. The death shall be suggested upon the record and the action shall proceed in favor of or against the surviving parties.

(b) Incompetency. If a party becomes incompetent, the court upon motion served as provided in subdivision (a) of this rule may allow the action to be continued by or against the party's representative.

(c) Transfer of Interest. In case of any transfer of interest, the action may be continued by or against the original party, unless the court upon motion directs the person to whom the interest is transferred to be substituted in the action or joined with the original party. Service of the motion shall be made as provided in subdivision (a) of this rule.

(d) Public Officers; Death or Separation From Office.

(1) When a public officer is a party to an action in an official capacity and during its pendency dies, resigns, or otherwise ceases to hold office, the action does not abate and the officer's successor is automatically substituted as a party. Proceedings following the substitution shall be in the name of the substituted party, but any misnomer not affecting the substantial rights of the parties shall be disregarded. An order of substitution may be entered at any time, but the omission to enter such an order shall not affect the substitution.

(2) A public officer who sues or is sued in an official capacity may be described as a party by the officer's official title rather than by name; but the court may require the officer's name to be added.

(As amended Dec. 29, 1948, eff. Oct. 20, 1949; Apr. 17, 1961, eff. July 19, 1961; Jan. 21, 1963, eff. July 1, 1963; Mar. 2, 1987, eff. Aug. 1, 1987.)

V. DEPOSITIONS AND DISCOVERY

ADVISORY COMMITTEE'S EXPLANATORY STATEMENT CONCERNING 1970 AMENDMENTS OF THE DISCOVERY RULES

This statement is intended to serve as a general introduction to the amendments of Rules 26–37, concerning discovery, as well as related amendments of other rules. A separate note of customary scope is appended to amendments proposed for each rule. This statement provides a framework for the consideration of individual rule changes.

CHANGES IN THE DISCOVERY RULES

The discovery rules, as adopted in 1938, were a striking and imaginative departure from tradition. It was expected from the outset that they would be important, but experience has shown them to play an even larger role than was initially foreseen. Although the discovery rules have been amended since 1938, the changes were relatively few and narrowly focused, made in order to remedy specific defects. The amendments now proposed reflect the first comprehensive review of the discovery rules undertaken since 1938. These amendments make substantial changes in the discovery rules. Those summarized here are among the more important changes.

Scope of Discovery. New provisions are made and existing provisions changed affecting the scope of discovery: (1) The contents of insurance policies are made discoverable (Rule 26(b)(2)). (2) A showing of good cause is no longer required for discovery of documents and things and entry upon land (Rule 34). However, a showing of need is required for discovery of "trial preparation" materials other than a party's discovery of his own statement and a witness' discovery of his own statement; and protection is afforded against disclosure in such documents of mental impressions, conclusions, opinions, or legal theories concerning the litigation. (Rule 26(b)(3)). (3) Provision is made for discovery with respect to experts retained for trial preparation, and particularly those experts who will be called to testify at trial (Rule 26(b)(4)). (4) It is provided that interrogatories and requests for admission are not objectionable simply because they relate to matters of opinion or contention, subject of course to the supervisory power of the court (Rules 33(b), 36(a)). (5) Medical examination is made available as to certain nonparties. (Rule 35(a)).

Mechanics of Discovery. A variety of changes are made in the mechanics of the discovery process, affecting the sequence and timing of discovery, the respective obligations of the parties with respect to requests, responses, and motions for court orders, and the related powers of the court to enforce discovery requests and to protect against their abusive use. A new provision eliminates the automatic grant of priority in discovery to one side (Rule 26(d)). Another provides that a party is not under a duty to supplement his responses to requests for discovery, except as specified (Rule 26(e)).

Other changes in the mechanics of discovery are designed to encourage extrajudicial discovery with a minimum of court intervention. Among these are the following: (1) The requirement that a plaintiff seek leave of court for early discovery requests is eliminated or reduced, and motions for a court order under Rule 34 are made unnecessary. Motions under Rule 35 are continued. (2) Answers and objections are to be served together and an enlargement of the time for response is provided. (3) The party seeking discovery, rather than the objecting party, is made responsible for invoking judicial determination of discovery disputes not resolved by the parties. (4) Judicial sanctions are tightened with respect to unjustified insistence upon or objection to discovery. These changes bring Rules 33, 34, and 36 substantially into line with the procedure now provided for depositions.

Failure to amend Rule 35 in the same way is based upon two considerations. First, the Columbia Survey finds that only about 5 percent of medical examinations require court motions, of which about half result in court orders. Second and of greater importance, the interest of the person to be examined in the privacy of his person was recently stressed by the Supreme Court in *Schlagenhauf v. Holder,* 379 U.S. 104 (1964). The court emphasized the trial judge's responsibility to assure that the medical examination was justified, particularly as to its scope.

* * *

Optional Procedures. In two instances, new optional procedures have been made available. A new procedure is provided to a party seeking to take the deposition of a corporation or other organization (Rule 30(b)(6)). A party on whom interrogatories have been served requesting information derivable from his business records may under specified circumstances produce the records rather than give answers (Rule 33(c)).

* * *

Rule 26. General Provisions Governing Discovery; Duty of Disclosure

(a) Required Disclosures; Methods to Discover Additional Matter.

(1) *Initial Disclosures.* Except to the extent otherwise stipulated or directed by order or local rule, a party shall, without waiting a discovery request, provide to other parties:

(A) the name and, if known, the address and telephone number of each individual likely to have discoverable information relevant to disputed facts alleged with particularity in the pleadings, identifying the subjects of the information;

(B) a copy of, or a description by category and location of, all documents, data compilations, and tangible things in the possession, custody, or control of the party that are relevant to disputed facts alleged with particularity in the pleadings;

(C) a computation of any category of damages claimed by the disclosing party, making available for inspection and copying as under Rule 34 the documents or other evidentiary material, not privileged or protected from disclosure, on which such computation is based, including materials bearing on the nature and extent of injuries suffered; and

(D) for inspection and copying as under Rule 34 any insurance agreement under which any person carrying on an insurance business may be liable to satisfy part or all of a judgment which may be entered in the action or to indemnify or reimburse for payments made to satisfy the judgment.

Unless otherwise stipulated or directed by the court, these disclosures shall be made at or within 10 days after the meeting of the parties under subdivision (f). A party shall make its initial disclosures based on the information then reasonably available to it and is not excused from making its disclosures because it has not fully completed its investigation of the case or because it challenges the sufficiency of another party's disclosures or because another party has not made its disclosures.

(2) *Disclosure of Expert Testimony.*

(A) In addition to the disclosures required by paragraph (1), a party shall disclose to other parties the identity of any person who may be used at trial to present evidence under Rules 702, 703, or 705 of the Federal Rules of Evidence.

(B) Except as otherwise stipulated or directed by the court, this disclosure shall, with respect to a witness who is retained or specially employed to provide expert testimony in the case or whose duties as an employee of the party regularly involve giving expert testimony, be accompanied by a written report prepared and signed by the witness. The report shall contain a complete statement of all opinions to be expressed and the basis and reasons therefor; the data or other information considered by the witness in forming the opinions; any exhibits to be used as a summary of or support for the opinions; the qualifications of the witness, including a list of all publications authored by the witness within the preceding ten years; the compensation to be paid for the study and testimony; and a listing of any other cases in which the witness has testified as an expert at trial or by deposition within the preceding four years.

(C) These disclosures shall be made at the times and in the sequence directed by the court. In the absence of other directions from the court or stipulation by the parties, the disclosures shall be made at least 90 days before the trial date or the date the case is to be ready for trial or, if the evidence is intended solely to contradict or rebut evidence on the same subject matter identified by another party under paragraph (2)(B), within 30 days after the disclosure made by the other party. The parties shall supplement these disclosures when required under subdivision (e)(1).

(3) *Pretrial Disclosures.* In addition to the disclosures required in the preceding paragraphs, a party shall provide to other parties the following information regarding the evidence that it may present at trial other than solely for impeachment purposes:

(A) the name and, if not previously provided, the address and telephone number of each witness, separately identifying those whom the party expects to present and those whom the party may call if the need arises;

(B) the designation of those witnesses whose testimony is expected to be presented by means of a deposition and, if not taken stenographically, a transcript of the pertinent portions of the deposition testimony; and

(C) an appropriate identification of each document or other exhibit, including summaries of other evidence, separately identifying those which the party expects to offer and those which the party may offer if the need arises.

Unless otherwise directed by the court, these disclosures shall be made at least 30 days before trial. Within 14 days thereafter, unless a different time is specified by the court, a party may serve and file a list disclosing (i) any objections to the use under Rule 32(a) of a deposition designated by another party under subparagraph (B) and (ii) any objection, together with the grounds therefor, that may be made to the admissibility of materials identified under subparagraph (C). Objections not so disclosed, other than objections under Rules 402 and 403 of the Federal Rules of Evidence, shall be deemed waived unless excused by the court for good cause shown.

(4) *Form of Disclosures; Filing.* Unless otherwise directed by order or local rule, all disclosures under paragraphs (1) through (3) shall be made in writing, signed, served, and promptly filed with the court.

(5) *Methods to Discover Additional Matter.* Parties may obtain discovery by one or more of the following methods: depositions upon oral examination or written questions; written interrogatories; production of documents or things or permission to enter upon land or other property under Rule 34 or 45(a)(1)(C), for inspection and other purposes; physical and mental examinations; and requests for admission.

(b) **Discovery Scope and Limits.** Unless otherwise limited by order of the court in accordance with these rules, the scope of discovery is as follows:

(1) *In General.* Parties may obtain discovery regarding any matter, not privileged, which is relevant to the subject matter involved in the pending action, whether it relates to the claim or defense of the party seeking discovery or to the claim or defense of any other party, including the existence, description, nature, custody, condition, and

location of any books, documents, or other tangible things and the identity and location of persons having knowledge of any discoverable matter. The information sought need not be admissible at the trial if the information sought appears reasonably calculated to lead to the discovery of admissible evidence.

(2) *Limitations.* By order or by local rule, the court may alter the limits in these rules on the number of depositions and interrogatories and may also limit the length of depositions under Rule 30 and the number of requests under Rule 36. The frequency or extent of use of the discovery methods otherwise permitted under these rules and by any local rule shall be limited by the court if it determines that: (i) the discovery sought is unreasonably cumulative or duplicative, or is obtainable from some other source that is more convenient, less burdensome, or less expensive; (ii) the party seeking discovery has had ample opportunity by discovery in the action to obtain the information sought; or (iii) the burden or expense of the proposed discovery outweighs its likely benefit, taking into account the needs of the case, the amount in controversy, the parties' resources, the importance of the issues at stake in the litigation, and the importance of the proposed discovery in resolving the issues. The court may act upon its own initiative after reasonable notice or pursuant to a motion under subdivision (c).

(3) *Trial Preparation: Materials.* Subject to the provisions of subdivision (b)(4) of this rule, a party may obtain discovery of documents and tangible things otherwise discoverable under subdivision (b)(1) of this rule and prepared in anticipation of litigation or for trial by or for another party or by or for that other party's representative (including the other party's attorney, consultant, surety, indemnitor, insurer, or agent) only upon a showing that the party seeking discovery has substantial need of the materials in the preparation of the party's case and that the party is unable without undue hardship to obtain the substantial equivalent of the materials by other means. In ordering discovery of such materials when the required showing has been made, the court shall protect against disclosure of the mental impressions, conclusions, opinions, or legal theories of an attorney or other representative of a party concerning the litigation.

A party may obtain without the required showing a statement concerning the action or its subject matter previously made by that party. Upon request, a person not a party may obtain without the required showing a statement concerning the action or its subject matter previously made by that person. If the request is refused, the person may move for a court order. The provisions of Rule 37(a)(4) apply to the award of expenses incurred in relation to the motion. For purposes of this paragraph, a statement previously made is (A) a written statement signed or otherwise adopted or approved by the person making it, or (B) a stenographic, mechanical, electrical, or other recording, or a transcription thereof, which is a substantially verbatim recital of an oral statement by the person making it and contemporaneously recorded.

(4) *Trial Preparation: Experts.*

(A) A party may depose any person who has been identified as an expert whose opinions may be presented at trial. If a report from the expert is required under subdivision (a)(2)(B), the deposition shall not be conducted until after the report is provided.

(B) A party may, through interrogatories or by deposition, discover facts known or opinions held by an expert who has been retained or specially employed by another party in anticipation of litigation or preparation for trial and who is not expected to be called as a witness at trial only as provided in Rule 35(b) or upon a showing of exceptional circumstances under which it is impracticable for the party seeking discovery to obtain facts or opinions on the same subject by other means.

(C) Unless manifest injustice would result, (i) the court shall require that the party seeking discovery pay the expert a reasonable fee for time spent in responding to discovery under this subdivision; and (ii) with respect to discovery obtained under subdivision (b)(4)(B) of this rule the court shall require the party seeking discovery to pay the other party a fair portion of the fees and expenses reasonably incurred by the latter party in obtaining facts and opinions from the expert.

(5) *Claims of Privilege or Protection of Trial Preparation Materials.* When a party withholds information otherwise discoverable under these rules by claiming that it is privileged or subject to protection as trial preparation material, the party shall make the claim expressly and shall describe the nature of the documents, communications, or things not produced or disclosed in a manner that, without revealing information itself privileged or protected, will enable other parties to assess the applicability of the privilege or protection.

(c) Protective Orders. Upon motion by a party or by the person from whom discovery is sought, accompanied by a certification that the movant has in good faith conferred or attempted to confer with other affected parties in an effort to resolve the dispute without court action, and for good cause shown, the court in which the action is pending or alternatively, on matters relating to a deposition, the court in the district where the deposition is to be taken may make any order which justice requires to protect a party or person from annoyance, embarrassment, oppression, or undue burden or expense, including one or more of the following:

(1) that the disclosure or discovery not be had;

(2) that the disclosure or discovery may be had only on specified terms and conditions, including a designation of the time or place;

(3) that the discovery may be had only by a method of discovery other than that selected by the party seeking discovery;

(4) that certain matters not be inquired into, or that the scope of the disclosure or discovery be limited to certain matters;

(5) that discovery be conducted with no one present except persons designated by the court;

(6) that a deposition, after being sealed, be opened only by order of the court;

(7) that a trade secret or other confidential research, development, or commercial information not be revealed or be revealed only in a designated way; and

(8) that the parties simultaneously file specified documents or information enclosed in sealed envelopes to be opened as directed by the court.

If the motion for a protective order is denied in whole or in part, the court may, on such terms and conditions as are just, order that any party or other person provide or permit discovery. The provisions of Rule 37(a)(4) apply to the award of expenses incurred in relation to the motion.

(d) Timing and Sequence of Discovery. Except when authorized under these rules or by local rule, order, or agreement of the parties, a party may not seek discovery from any source before the parties have met and conferred as required by subdivision (f). Unless the court upon motion, for the convenience of parties and witnesses and in the interests of justice, orders otherwise, methods of discovery may be used in any sequence, and the fact that a party is conducting discovery, whether by deposition or otherwise, shall not operate to delay any other party's discovery.

(e) Supplementation of Disclosures and Responses. A party who has made a disclosure under subdivision (a) or responded to a request for discovery with a disclosure or response is under a duty to supplement or correct the disclosure or response to include information thereafter acquired if ordered by the court or in the following circumstances:

(1) A party is under a duty to supplement at appropriate intervals its disclosures under subdivision (a) if the party learns that in some material respect the information disclosed is incomplete or incorrect and if the additional or corrective information has not otherwise been made known to the other parties during the discovery process or in writing. With respect to testimony of an expert from whom a report is required under subdivision (a)(2)(B) the duty extends both to information contained in the report and to information provided through a deposition of the expert, and any additions or other changes to this information shall be disclosed by the time the party's disclosures under Rule 26(a)(3) are due.

(2) A party is under a duty seasonably to amend a prior response to an interrogatory, request for production, or request for admission if the party learns that the response is in some material respect incomplete or incorrect and if the additional or corrective information has not otherwise been made known to the other parties during the discovery process or in writing.

(f) Meeting of Parties: Planning for Discovery. Except in actions exempted by local rule or when otherwise ordered, the parties shall, as soon as practicable and in any event at least 14 days before a scheduling conference is held or a scheduling order is due under Rule 16(b), meet to discuss the nature and basis of their claims and defenses and the possibilities for a prompt settlement or resolution of the case, to make or arrange for the disclosures required by subdivision (a)(1), and to develop a proposed discovery plan. The plan shall indicate the parties' views and proposals concerning:

(1) what changes should be made in the timing, form, or requirement for disclosures under subdivision (a) or local rule, including a statement as to when disclosures under subdivision (a)(1) were made or will be made;

(2) the subjects on which discovery may be needed, when discovery should be completed, and whether discovery should be conducted in phases or be limited to or focused upon particular issues;

(3) what changes should be made in the limitations on discovery imposed under these rules or by local rule, and what other limitations should be imposed; and

(4) any other orders that should be entered by the court under subdivision (c) or under Rule 16(b) and (c).

The attorneys of record and all unrepresented parties that have appeared in the case are jointly responsible for arranging and being present or represented at the meeting, for attempting in good faith to agree on the proposed discovery plan, and for submitting to the court within 10 days after the meeting a written report outlining the plan.

(g) Signing of Disclosures, Discovery Requests, Responses, and Objections.

(1) Every disclosure made pursuant to subdivision (a)(1) or subdivision (a)(3) shall be signed by at least one attorney of record in the attorney's individual name, whose address shall be stated. An unrepresented party shall sign the disclosure and state the party's address. The signature of the attorney or party constitutes a certification that to the best of the signer's knowledge, information, and belief, formed after a reasonable inquiry, the disclosure is complete and correct as of the time it is made.

(2) Every discovery request, response, or objection made by a party represented by an attorney shall be signed by at least one attorney of record in the attorney's individual name, whose address shall be stated. An unrepresented party shall sign the request, response, or objection and state the party's address. The signature of the attorney or party constitutes a certification that to the best of the signer's knowledge, information, and belief, formed after a reasonable inquiry, the request, response, or objection is:

(A) consistent with these rules and warranted by existing law or a good faith argument for the extension, modification, or reversal of existing law;

(B) not interposed for any improper purpose, such as to harass or to cause unnecessary delay or needless increase in the cost of litigation; and

(C) not unreasonable or unduly burdensome or expensive, given the needs of the case, the discovery already had in the case, the amount in controversy, and the importance of the issues at stake in the litigation.

If a request, response, or objection is not signed, it shall be stricken unless it is signed promptly after the omission is called to the attention of the party making the request, response, or objection, and a party shall not be obligated to take any action with respect to it until it is signed.

(3) If without substantial justification a certification is made in violation of the rule, the court, upon motion or upon its own initiative, shall impose upon the person who made the certification, the party on whose behalf the disclosure, request, response, or objection is made, or both, an appropriate sanction, which may include an order to pay the amount of the reasonable expenses incurred because of the violation, including a reasonable attorney's fee.

(As amended Dec. 27, 1946, eff. Mar. 19, 1948; Jan. 21, 1963, eff. July 1, 1963; Feb. 28, 1966, eff. July 1, 1966; Mar. 30, 1970, eff. July 1, 1970; Apr. 29, 1980, eff. Aug. 1, 1980; Apr. 28, 1983, eff. Aug. 1, 1983; Mar. 2, 1987, eff. Aug. 1, 1987; Apr. 22, 1993, Dec. 1, 1993.)

NOTES OF ADVISORY COMMITTEE ON RULES
1970 AMENDMENT

* * *

Subdivision (b)(3)—Trial Preparation: Materials. Some of the most controversial and vexing problems to emerge from the discovery rules have arisen out of requests for the production of documents or things prepared in anticipation of litigation or for trial. The existing rules make no explicit provision for such materials. Yet, two verbally distinct doctrines have developed, each conferring a qualified immunity on these materials— the "good cause" requirement in Rule 34 (now generally held applicable to discovery of documents via deposition under Rule 45 and interrogatories under Rule 33) and the work-product doctrine of *Hickman v. Taylor*, 329 U.S. 495 (1947). Both demand a showing of justification before production can be had, the one of "good cause" and the other variously described in the *Hickman* case: "necessity or justification," "denial * * * would unduly prejudice the preparation of petitioner's case," or "cause hardship or injustice". 329 U.S. at 509–510.

In deciding the *Hickman* case, the Supreme Court appears to have expressed a preference in 1947 for an approach to the problem of trial preparation materials by judicial decision rather than by rule. Sufficient experience has accumulated, however, with lower court applications of the *Hickman* decision to warrant a reappraisal.

The major difficulties visible in the existing case law are (1) confusion and disagreement as to whether "good cause" is made out by a showing of relevance and lack of privilege, or requires an additional showing of necessity, (2) confusion and disagreement as to the scope of the *Hickman* work-product doctrine, particularly whether it extends beyond work actually performed by lawyers, and (3) the resulting difficulty of relating the "good cause" required by Rule 34 and the "necessity or justification" of the work-product doctrine, so that their respective roles and the distinctions between them are understood.

Basic Standard.—* * *

The rules are amended by eliminating the general requirement of "good cause" from Rule 34 but retaining a requirement of a special showing for trial preparation materials in this subdivision. The required showing is expressed, not in terms of "good cause" whose generality has tended to encourage confusion and controversy, but in terms of the elements of the special showing to be made: substantial need of the materials in the preparation of the case and inability without undue hardship to obtain the substantial equivalent of the materials by other means.

These changes conform to the holdings of the cases, when viewed in light of their facts. Apart from trial preparation, the fact that the materials sought are documentary does not in and of itself require a special showing beyond relevance and absence of privilege. The protective provisions are of course available, and if the party from whom production is sought raises a special issue of privacy (as with respect to income tax returns or grand jury minutes) or points to evidence primarily impeaching, or can show serious burden or expense, the court will exercise its traditional power to decide whether to issue a protective order. On the other hand, the requirement of a special showing for discovery of trial preparation materials reflects the view that each side's informal evaluation of its case should be protected, that each side should be encouraged to prepare independently, and that one side should not automatically have the benefit of the detailed preparatory work of the other side. * * *

Elimination of a "good cause" requirement from Rule 34 and the establishment of a requirement of a special showing in this subdivision will eliminate the confusion caused by having two verbally distinct requirements of justification that the courts have been unable to distinguish clearly. Moreover, the language of the subdivision suggests the factors which the courts should consider in determining whether the requisite showing has been made. The importance of the materials sought to the party seeking them in preparation of his case and the difficulty he will have obtaining them by other means are factors noted in the *Hickman* case. The courts should also consider the likelihood that the party, even if he obtains the information by independent means, will not have the substantial equivalent of the documents the production of which he seeks.

Consideration of these factors may well lead the court to distinguish between witness statements taken by an investigator, on the one hand, and other parts of the investigative file, on the other. * * * The witness may have given a fresh and contemporaneous account in a written statement while he is available to the party seeking discovery only a substantial time thereafter. * * * Or he may be reluctant or hostile. * * * Or he may have a lapse of memory. * * * Or he may probably be deviating from his prior statement. * * * On the other hand, a much stronger showing is needed to obtain evaluative materials in an investigator's reports. * * *

Materials assembled in the ordinary course of business, or pursuant to public requirements unrelated to litigation, or for other nonlitigation purposes are not under the qualified immunity provided by this subdivision. * * * No change is made in the existing doctrine, noted in the *Hickman* case, that one party may discover relevant facts known or available to the other party, even though such facts are contained in a document which is not itself discoverable.

Treatment of Lawyers; Special Protection of Mental Impressions, Conclusions, Opinions, and Legal Theories Concerning the Litigation.—

* * *

Subdivision (b)(3) reflects the trend of the cases by requiring a special showing, not merely as to materials prepared by an attorney, but also as to materials prepared in anticipation of litigation or preparation for trial by or for a party or any representative acting on his behalf. The subdivision then goes on to protect against disclosure the mental impressions, conclusions, opinions, or legal theories concerning the litigation of an attorney or other representative of a party. The *Hickman* opinion drew special attention to the need for protecting an attorney against discovery of memoranda prepared from recollection of oral interviews. The courts have steadfastly safeguarded against disclosure of lawyers' mental impressions and legal theories, as well as mental impressions and subjective evaluations of investigators and claim-agents. In enforcing this provision of the subdivision, the courts will sometimes find it necessary to order disclosure of a document but with portions deleted.

Rules 33 and 36 have been revised in order to permit discovery calling for opinions, contentions, and admissions relating not only to fact but also to the application of law to fact. Under those rules, a party and his attorney or other representative may be required to disclose, to some extent, mental impressions, opinions, or conclusions. But documents or parts of documents containing these matters are protected against discovery by this subdivision. Even though a party may ultimately have to disclose in response to interrogatories or requests to admit, he is entitled to keep confidential documents containing such matters prepared for internal use.

Party's Right to Own Statement.—An exception to the requirement of this subdivision enables a party to secure production of his own statement without any special showing. The cases are divided. * * *

Courts which treat a party's statement as though it were that of any witness overlook the fact that the party's statement is, without more, admissible in evidence. Ordinarily, a party gives a statement without insisting on a copy because he does not yet have a lawyer and does not understand the legal consequences of his actions. Thus, the statement is given at a time when he functions at a disadvantage. Discrepancies between his trial testimony and earlier statement may result from lapse of memory or ordinary inaccuracy; a written statement produced for the first time at trial may give such discrepancies a prominence which they do not deserve. In appropriate cases the court may order a party to be deposed before his statement is produced.

* * *

Witness' Right to Own Statement.—A second exception to the requirement of this subdivision permits a non-party witness to obtain a copy of his own statement without any special showing. Many, though not all, of the considerations supporting a party's right to obtain his statement apply also to the non-party witness. Insurance companies are increasingly recognizing that a witness is entitled to a copy of his statement and are modifying their regular practice accordingly.

* * *

1993 AMENDMENT

Subdivision (a). Through the addition of paragraphs (1)–(4), this subdivision imposes on parties a duty to disclose, without awaiting formal discovery requests, certain basic information that is needed in most cases to prepare for trial or make an informed decision about settlement. The rule requires all parties (1) early in the case to exchange information regarding potential witnesses, documentary evidence, damages, and insurance, (2) at an appropriate time during the discovery period to identify expert witnesses and provide a detailed written statement of the testimony that may be offered at trial through specially retained experts, and (3) as the trial date approaches to identify the particular evidence that may be offered at trial. The enumeration in Rule 26(a) of items to be disclosed does not prevent a court from requiring by order or local rule that the parties disclose additional information without a discovery request. Nor are parties precluded from using traditional discovery methods to obtain further information regarding these matters, as for example asking an expert during a deposition about testimony given in other litigation beyond the four-year period specified in Rule 26(a)(2)(B).

A major purpose of the revision is to accelerate the exchange of basic information about the case and to eliminate the paper work involved in requesting such information, and the rule should be applied in a manner to achieve those objectives. The concepts of imposing a duty of disclosure were set forth in Brazil, *The Adversary Character of Civil Discovery: A Critique and Proposals for Change*, 31 *Vand.L.Rev.* 1348 (1978), and Schwarzer, *The Federal Rules, the Adversary Process, and Discovery Reform*, 50 *U.Pitt.L.Rev.* 703, 721–23 (1989).

The rule is based upon the experience of district courts that have required disclosure of some of this information through local rules, court-approved standard interrogatories, and standing orders. Most have required pretrial disclosure of the kind of information described in Rule 26(a)(3). Many have required written reports from experts containing information like that specified in Rule 26(a)(2)(B). While far more limited, the experience of the few state and federal courts that have required pre-discovery exchange of core information such as is contemplated in Rule 26(a)(1) indicates that savings in time and expense can be achieved, particularly if the litigants meet and discuss the issues in the case as a predicate for this exchange and if a judge supports the process, as by using the results to guide further proceedings in the case. Courts in Canada and the United Kingdom have for many years required disclosure of certain information without awaiting a request from an adversary.

Paragraph (1). As the functional equivalent of court-ordered interrogatories, this paragraph requires early disclosure, without need for any request, of four types of information that have been customarily secured early in litigation through formal discovery. The introductory clause permits the court, by local rule, to exempt all or particular types of cases from these disclosure requirement [sic] or to modify the nature of the information to be disclosed. It is expected that courts would, for example, exempt cases like Social Security reviews and government collection cases in which discovery would not be appropriate or would be unlikely. By order the court may eliminate or modify the disclosure requirements in a particular case, and similarly the parties, unless precluded by order or local rule, can stipulate to elimination or modification of the requirements for that case. The disclosure obligations specified in paragraph (1) will not be appropriate for all cases, and it is expected that changes in these obligations will be made by the court or parties when the circumstances warrant.

Authorization of these local variations is, in large measure, included in order to accommodate the Civil Justice Reform Act of 1990, which implicitly directs districts to experiment during the study period with differing procedures to reduce the time and expense of civil litigation. * * * While these studies may indicate the desirability of further changes in Rule 26(a)(1), these changes probably could not become effective before December 1998 at the earliest. In the meantime, the present revision puts in place a series of disclosure obligations that, unless a court acts affirmatively to impose other requirements or indeed to reject all such requirements for the present, are designed to eliminate certain discovery, help focus the discovery that is needed, and facilitate preparation for trial or settlement.

Subparagraph (A) requires identification of all persons who, based on the investigation conducted thus far, are likely to have discoverable information relevant to the factual disputes between the parties. All persons with such information should be disclosed, whether or not their testimony will be supportive of the position of the disclosing party. As officers of the court, counsel are expected to disclose the identity of those persons who may be used by them as witnesses or who, if their potential testimony were known, might reasonably be expected to be deposed or called as a witness by any of the other parties. Indicating briefly the general topics on which such persons have information should not be burdensome, and will assist other parties in deciding which depositions will actually be needed.

Subparagraph (B) is included as a substitute for the inquiries routinely made about the existence and location of documents and other tangible things in the possession, custody, or control of the disclosing party. Although, unlike subdivision (a)(3)(C), an itemized listing of each exhibit is not required, the disclosure should describe and categorize, to the extent identified during the initial investigation, the nature and location of potentially relevant documents and records, including computerized data and other electronically-recorded information, sufficiently to enable opposing parties (1) to make an informed decision concerning which documents might need to be examined, at least initially, and (2) to frame their document requests in a manner likely to avoid squabbles resulting from the wording of the requests. As with potential witnesses, the requirement for disclosure of documents applies to all potentially relevant items then known to the party, whether or not supportive of its contentions in the case.

Unlike subparagraphs (C) and (D), subparagraph (B) does not require production of any documents. Of course, in cases involving few documents a disclosing party may prefer to provide copies of the documents rather than describe them, and the rule is written to afford this option to the disclosing party. If, as will be more typical, only the description is provided, the other parties are expected to obtain the documents desired by proceeding under Rule 34 or through informal requests. The disclosing party does not, by describing documents under subparagraph (B), waive its right to object to production on the basis of privilege or work product protection, or to assert that the documents are not sufficiently relevant to justify the burden or expense of production.

The initial disclosure requirements of subparagraphs (A) and (B) are limited to identification of potential evidence "relevant to disputed facts alleged with particularity in the pleadings." There is no need for a party to identify potential evidence with respect to allegations that are admitted. Broad, vague, and conclusory allegations sometimes tolerated in notice pleading—for example, the assertion that a product with many component parts is defective in some unspecified manner—should not impose upon responding parties the obligation at that point to search for and identify all persons possibly involved in, or all documents affecting, the design, manufacture, and assembly of the product. The greater the specificity and clarity of the allegations in the pleadings, the more complete should be the listing of potential witnesses and types of documentary evidence. Although paragraphs (1)(A) and (1)(B) by their terms refer to the factual disputes defined in the pleadings, the rule contemplates that these issues would be informally refined and clarified during the meeting of the parties under subdivision (f) and that the disclosure obligations would be adjusted in the light of these discussions. The disclosure requirements should, in short, be applied with common sense in light of the principles of Rule 1, keeping in mind the salutary purposes that the rule is intended to accomplish. The litigants should not indulge in gamemanship with respect to the disclosure obligations.

Subparagraph (C) imposes a burden of disclosure that includes the functional equivalent of a standing Request for Production under Rule 34. A party claiming damages or other monetary relief must, in addition to disclosing the calculation of such damages, make available the supporting documents for inspection and copying as if a request for such materials had been made under Rule 34. This obligation applies only with respect to documents then reasonably available to it and not privileged or protected as work product. Likewise, a party would not be expected to provide a calculation of damages which, as in many patent infringement actions, depends on information in the possession of another party or person.

Subparagraph (D) replaces subdivision (b)(2) of Rule 26, and provides that liability insurance policies be made available for inspection and copying. The last two sentences of that subdivision have been omitted as unnecessary, not to signify any change of law. The disclosure of insurance information does not thereby render such information admissible in evidence. See Rule 411, Federal Rules of Evidence. Nor does subparagraph (D) require disclosure of applications for insurance, though in particular cases such information may be discoverable in accordance with revised subdivision (a)(5).

Unless the court directs a different time, the disclosures required by subdivision (a)(1) are to be made at or within 10 days after the meeting of the parties under subdivision (f). One of the purposes of this meeting is to refine the factual disputes with respect to which disclosures should be made under paragraphs (1)(A) and (1)(B), particularly if an answer has not been filed by a defendant, or, indeed, to afford the parties an opportunity to modify by stipulation the timing or scope of these obligations. The time of this meeting is generally left to the parties provided it is held at least 14 days before a scheduling conference is held or before a scheduling order is due under Rule 16(b). In cases in which no scheduling conference is held, this will mean that the meeting must ordinarily be held within 75 days after a defendant has first appeared in the case and hence that the initial disclosures would be due no later than 85 days after the first appearance of a defendant.

Before making its disclosures, a party has the obligation under subdivision (g)(1) to make a reasonable inquiry into the facts of the case. The rule does not demand an exhaustive investigation at this stage of the case, but one that is reasonable under the circumstances, focusing on the facts that are alleged with particularity in the pleadings. The type of investigation that can be expected at this point will vary based upon such factors as the number and complexity of the issues; the location, nature, number, and availability of potentially relevant witnesses and documents; the extent of past working relationships between the attorney and the client, particularly in handling related or similar litigation; and of course how long the party has to conduct an investigation, either before or after filing of the case. As provided in the last sentence of subdivision (a)(1), a party is not excused from the duty of disclosure merely because its investigation is incomplete. The party should make its initial disclosures based on the pleadings and the information then reasonably available to it. As its investigation continues and as the issues in the pleadings are clarified, it should supplement its disclosures as required by subdivision (e)(1). A party is not relieved from its obligation of disclosure merely because another party has not made its disclosures or has made an inadequate disclosure.

It will often be desirable, particularly if the claims made in the complaint are broadly stated, for the parties to have their Rule 26(f) meeting early in the case, perhaps before a defendant has answered the complaint or had time to conduct other than a cursory investigation. In such circumstances, in order to facilitate more meaningful and useful initial disclosures, they can and should stipulate to a period of more than 10 days after the meeting in which to make these disclosures, at least for defendants who had no advance notice of the potential litigation. A stipulation at an early meeting affording such a defendant at least 60 days after receiving the complaint in which to make its disclosures under subdivision (a)(1)—a period that is two weeks longer than the time formerly specified for responding to interrogatories served with a complaint—should be adequate and appropriate in most cases.

Paragraph (2). This paragraph imposes an additional duty to disclose information regarding expert testimony sufficiently in advance of trial that opposing parties have a reasonable opportunity to prepare for effective cross examination and perhaps arrange for expert testimony from other witnesses. Normally the court should prescribe a time for these disclosures in a scheduling order under Rule 16(b), and in most cases the party with the burden of proof on an issue should disclose its expert testimony on that issue before other parties are required to make their disclosures with respect to that issue. In the absence of such a direction, the disclosures are to be made by all parties at least 90 days before the trial date or the date by which the case is to be ready for trial, except that an additional 30 days is allowed (unless the court specifies another time) for disclosure of expert testimony to be used solely to contradict or rebut the testimony that may be presented by another party's expert. For a discussion of procedures that have been used to enhance the reliability of expert testimony, see M. Graham, *Expert Witness Testimony and the Federal Rules of Evidence: Insuring Adequate Assurance of Trustworthiness,* 1986 *U.Ill.L.Rev.* 90.

Paragraph (2)(B) requires that persons retained or specially employed to provide expert testimony, or whose duties as an employee of the party regularly involve the giving of expert testimony, must prepare a detailed and complete written report, stating the testimony the witness is expected to present during direct examination, together with the reasons therefor. The information disclosed under the former rule in answering interrogatories about the "substance" of expert testimony was frequently so sketchy and vague that it rarely dispensed with the need to depose the expert and often was even of little help in preparing for a deposition of the witness. Revised Rule 37(c)(1) provides an incentive for full disclosure; namely, that a party will not ordinarily be permitted to use on direct examination any expert testimony not so disclosed. Rule 26(a)(2)(B) does not preclude counsel from providing assistance to experts in preparing the reports, and indeed, with experts such as automobile mechanics, this assistance may be needed. Nevertheless, the report, which is intended to set forth the substance of the direct examination, should be written in a manner that reflects the testimony to be given by the witness and it must be signed by the witness.

The report is to disclose the data and other information considered by the expert and any exhibits or charts that summarize or support the expert's opinions. Given this obligation of disclosure, litigants should no longer be able to argue that materials furnished to their experts to be used in forming their opinions—whether or not ultimately relied upon by the expert—are privileged or otherwise protected from disclosure when such persons are testifying or being deposed.

Revised subdivision (b)(4)(A) authorizes the deposition of expert witnesses. Since depositions of experts required to prepare a written report may be taken only after the report has been served, the length of the deposition of such experts should be reduced, and in many cases the report may eliminate the need for a deposition. Revised subdivision (e)(1) requires disclosure of any material changes made in the opinions of an expert from whom a report is required, whether the changes are in the written report or in testimony given at a deposition.

For convenience, this rule and revised Rule 30 continue to use the term "expert" to refer to those persons who will testify under Rule 702 of the Federal Rules of Evidence with respect to scientific, technical, and other specialized matters. The requirement of a written report in paragraph (2)(B), however, applies only to those experts who are retained or specially employed to provide such testimony in the case or whose duties as an employee of a party regularly involve the giving of such testimony. A treating physician, for example, can be deposed or called to testify at trial without any requirement for a written report. By local rule, order, or written stipulation, the requirement of a written report may be waived for particular experts or imposed upon additional persons who will provide opinions under Rule 702.

Paragraph (3). This paragraph imposes an additional duty to disclose, without any request, information customarily needed in final preparation for trial. These disclosures are to be made in accordance with schedules adopted by the court under Rule 16(b) or by special order. If no such schedule is directed by the court, the disclosures are to be made at least 30 days before commencement of the trial. By its terms, rule 26(a)(3) does not require disclosure of evidence to be used solely for impeachment purposes; however, disclosure of such evidence—as well as other items relating to conduct of trial—may be required by local rule or a pretrial order.

Subparagraph (A) requires the parties to designate the persons whose testimony they may present as substantive evidence at trial, whether in person or by deposition. Those who will probably be called as witnesses should be listed separately from those who are not likely to be called but who are being listed in order to preserve the right to do so if needed because of developments during trial. Revised Rule 37(c)(1) provides that only persons so listed may be used at trial to present substantive evidence. This restriction does not apply unless the omission was "without substantial justification" and hence would not bar an unlisted witness if the need for such testimony is based upon developments during trial that could not reasonably have been anticipated—*e.g.,* a change of testimony.

Listing a witness does not obligate the party to secure the attendance of the person at trial, but should preclude the party from objecting if the person is called to testify by another party who did not list the person as a witness.

Subparagraph (B) requires the party to indicate which of these potential witnesses will be presented by deposition at trial. A party expecting to use at trial a deposition not recorded by stenographic means is required by revised Rule 32 to provide the court with a transcript of the pertinent portions of such depositions. This rule requires that copies of the transcript of a nonstenographic deposition be provided to other parties in advance of trial for verification, an obvious concern since counsel often utilize their own personnel to prepare transcripts from audio or video tapes. By order or local rule, the court may require that parties designate the particular portions of stenographic depositions to be used at trial.

Subparagraph (C) requires disclosure of exhibits, including summaries (whether to be offered in lieu of other documentary evidence or to be used as an aid in understanding such evidence), that may be offered as substantive evidence. The rule requires a separate listing of each such exhibit, though it should permit voluminous items of a similar or standardized character to be described by meaningful categories. For example, unless the court has otherwise directed, a series of vouchers might be shown collectively as a single exhibit with their starting and ending dates. As with witnesses, the exhibits that will probably be offered are to be listed separately from those which are unlikely to be offered but which are listed in order to preserve the right to do so if needed because of developments during trial. Under revised Rule 37(c)(1) the court can permit use of unlisted documents the need for which could not reasonably have been anticipated in advance of trial.

Upon receipt of these final pretrial disclosures, other parties have 14 days (unless a different time is specified by the court) to disclose any objections they wish to preserve to the usability of the deposition testimony or to the admissibility of the documentary evidence (other than under Rules 402 and 403 of the Federal Rules of Evidence). Similar provisions have become commonplace either in pretrial orders or by local rules, and significantly expedite the presentation of evidence at trial, as well as eliminate the need to have available witnesses to provide "foundation" testimony for most items of documentary evidence. The listing of a potential objection does not constitute the making of that objection or require the court to rule on the objection; rather, it preserves the right of the party to make the objection when and as appropriate during trial. The court may, however, elect to treat the listing as a motion "in limine" and rule upon the objections in advance of trial to the extent appropriate.

The time specified in the rule for the final pretrial disclosures is relatively close to the trial date. The objective is to eliminate the time and expense in making these disclosures of evidence and objections in those cases that settle shortly before trial, while affording a reasonable time for final preparation for trial in those cases that do not settle. In many cases, it will be desirable for the court in a scheduling or pretrial order to set an earlier time for disclosures of evidence and provide more time for disclosing potential objections.

Paragraph (4). This paragraph prescribes the form of disclosures. A signed written statement is required, reminding the parties and counsel of the solemnity of the obligations imposed; and the signature on the initial or pretrial disclosure is a certification under subdivision (g)(1) that it is complete and correct as of the time when made. Consistent with Rule 5(d), these disclosures are to be filed with the court unless otherwise directed. It is anticipated that many courts will direct that expert reports required under paragraph (2)(B) not be filed until needed in connection with a motion or for trial.

Paragraph (5). This paragraph is revised to take note of the availability of revised Rule 45 for inspection from non-parties of documents and premises without the need for a deposition.

Subdivision (b). This subdivision is revised in several respects. First, former paragraph (1) is subdivided into two paragraphs for ease of reference and to avoid renumbering of paragraphs (3) and (4). Textual changes are then made in new paragraph (2) to enable the court to keep tighter rein on the extent of discovery. The information explosion of recent decades has greatly increased both the potential cost of wide-ranging discovery and the potential for discovery to be used as an instrument for delay or oppression. Amendments to Rules 30, 31, and 33 place presumptive limits on the number of depositions and interrogatories, subject to leave of court to pursue additional discovery. The revisions in Rule 26(b)(2) are intended to provide the court with broader discretion to impose additional restrictions on the scope and extent of discovery and to authorize courts that develop case tracking systems based on the complexity of cases to increase or decrease by local rule the presumptive number of depositions and interrogatories allowed in particular types or classifications of cases. The revision also dispels any doubt as to the power of the court to impose limitations on the length of depositions under Rule 30 or on the number of requests for admission under Rule 36.

Second, former paragraph (2), relating to insurance, has been relocated as part of the required initial disclosures under subdivision (a)(1)(D), and revised to provide for disclosure of the policy itself.

Third, paragraph (4)(A) is revised to provide that experts who are expected to be witnesses will be subject to deposition prior to trial, conforming the norm stated in the rule to the actual practice followed in most courts, in which depositions of experts have become standard. Concerns regarding the expense of such depositions should be mitigated by the fact that the expert's fees for the deposition will ordinarily be borne by the party taking the deposition. The requirement under subdivision (a)(2)(B) of a complete and detailed report of the expected testimony of certain forensic experts may, moreover, eliminate the need for some such depositions or at least reduce the length of the depositions. Accordingly, the deposition of an expert required by subdivision (a)(2)(B) to provide a written report may be taken only after the report has been served.

Paragraph (4)(C), bearing on compensation of experts, is revised to take account of the changes in paragraph (4)(A).

Paragraph (5) is a new provision. A party must notify other parties if it is withholding materials otherwise subject to disclosure under the rule or pursuant to a discovery request because it is asserting a claim of privilege or work product protection. To withhold materials without such notice is contrary to the rule, subjects the party to sanctions under Rule 37(b)(2), and may be viewed as a waiver of the privilege or protection.

The party must also provide sufficient information to enable other parties to evaluate the applicability of the claimed privilege or protection. Although the person from whom the discovery is sought decides whether to claim a privilege or protection, the court ultimately decides whether, if this claim is challenged, the privilege or protection applies. Providing information pertinent to the applicability of the privilege or protection should reduce the need for in camera examination of the documents.

The rule does not attempt to define for each case what information must be provided when a party asserts a claim of privilege or work product protection. Details concerning time, persons, general subject matter, etc., may be appropriate if only a few items are withheld, but may be unduly burdensome when voluminous documents are claimed to be privileged or protected, particularly if the items can be described by categories. A party can seek relief through a protective order under subdivision (c) if compliance with the requirement for providing this information would be an unreasonable burden. In rare circumstances some of the pertinent information affecting applicability of the claim, such as the identity of the client, may itself be privileged; the rule provides that such information need not be disclosed.

The obligation to provide pertinent information concerning withheld privileged materials applies only to items "otherwise discoverable." If a broad discovery request is made—for example, for all documents of a particular type during a twenty year period—and the responding party believes in good faith that production of documents for more than the past three years would be unduly burdensome, it should make its objection to the breadth of the request and, with respect to the documents generated in that three year period, produce the unprivileged documents and describe those withheld under the claim of privilege. If the court later rules that documents for a seven year period are properly discoverable, the documents for the additional four years should then be either produced (if not privileged) or described (if claimed to be privileged).

Subdivision (c). The revision requires that before filing a motion for a protective order the movant must confer—either in person or by telephone—with the other affected parties in a good faith effort to resolve the discovery dispute without the need for court intervention. If the movant is unable to get opposing parties even to discuss the matter, the efforts in attempting to arrange such a conference should be indicated in the certificate.

Subdivision (d). This subdivision is revised to provide that formal discovery—as distinguished from interviews of potential witnesses and other informal discovery—not commence until the parties have met and conferred as required by subdivision (f). Discovery can begin earlier if authorized under Rule 30(a)(2)(C) (deposition of person about to leave the country) or by local rule, order, or stipulation. This will be appropriate in some cases, such as those involving requests for a preliminary injunction or motions challenging personal jurisdiction. If a local rule exempts any types of cases in which discovery may be needed from the requirement of a meeting under Rule 26(f), it should specify when discovery may commence in those cases.

The meeting of counsel is to take place as soon as practicable and in any event at least 14 days before the date of the scheduling conference under Rule 16(b) or the date a scheduling order is due under Rule 16(b). The court can assure that discovery is not unduly delayed either by entering a special order or by setting the case for a scheduling conference.

Subdivision (e). This subdivision is revised to provide that the requirement for supplementation applies to all disclosures required by subdivisions (a)(1)–(3). Like the former rule, the duty, while imposed on a "party," applies whether the corrective information is learned by the client or by the attorney. Supplementations need not be made as each new item of information is learned but should be made at appropriate intervals during the discovery period, and with special promptness as the trial date approaches. It may be useful for the scheduling order to specify the time or times when supplementations should be made.

The revision also clarifies that the obligation to supplement responses to formal discovery requests applies to interrogatories, requests for production, and requests for admissions, but not ordinarily to deposition testimony. However, with respect to experts from whom a written report is required under subdivision (a)(2)(B), changes in the opinions expressed by the expert whether in the report or at a subsequent deposition are subject to a duty of supplemental disclosure under subdivision (e)(1).

The obligation to supplement disclosures and discovery responses applies whenever a party learns that its prior disclosures or responses are in some material respect incomplete or incorrect. There is, however, no obligation to provide supplemental or corrective information that has been otherwise made known to the parties in writing or during the discovery process, as when a witness not previously disclosed is identified during the taking of a deposition or when an expert during a deposition corrects information contained in an earlier report.

Subdivision (f). This subdivision was added in 1980 to provide a party threatened with abusive discovery with a special means for obtaining judicial intervention other than through discrete motions under Rules 26(c) and 37(a). The amendment envisioned a two-step process: first, the parties would attempt to frame a mutually agreeable plan; second, the court would hold a "discovery conference" and then enter an order establishing a schedule and limitations for the conduct of discovery. It was contemplated that the procedure, an elective one triggered on request of a party, would be used in special cases rather than as a routine matter. As expected, the device has been used only sparingly in most courts, and judicial controls over the discovery process have ordinarily been imposed through scheduling orders under Rule 16(b) or through rulings on discovery motions.

The provisions relating to a conference with the court are removed from subdivision (f). This change does not signal any lessening of the importance of judicial supervision. Indeed, there is a greater need for early judicial involvement to consider the scope and timing of the disclosure requirements of Rule 26(a) and the presumptive limits on discovery imposed under these rules or by local rules. Rather, the change is made because the provisions addressing the use of conferences with the court to control discovery are more properly included in Rule 16, which is being revised to highlight the court's powers regarding the discovery process.

* * *

As noted above, former subdivision (f) envisioned the development of proposed discovery plans as an optional procedure to be used in relatively few cases. The revised rule directs that in all cases not exempted by local rule or special order the litigants must meet in person and plan for discovery. Following this meeting, the parties submit to the court their proposals for a discovery plan and can begin formal discovery. Their report will assist the court in seeing that the timing and scope of disclosures under revised Rule 26(a) and the limitations on the extent of discovery under these rules and local rules are tailored to the circumstances of the particular case.

To assure that the court has the litigants' proposals before deciding on a scheduling order and that the commencement of discovery is not delayed unduly, the rule provides that the meeting of the parties take place as soon as practicable and in any event at least 14 days before a scheduling conference is held or before a scheduling order is due under Rule 16(b). (Rule 16(b) requires that a scheduling order be entered within 90 days after the first appearance of a defendant or, if earlier, within 120 days after the complaint has been served on any defendant.) The obligation to participate in the planning process is imposed on all parties that have appeared in the case, including defendants who, because of a pending Rule 12 motion, may not have yet filed an answer in the case. Each such party should attend the meeting, either through one of its attorneys or in person if unrepresented. If more parties are joined or appear after the initial meeting, an additional meeting may be desirable.

Subdivision (f) describes certain matters that should be accomplished at the meeting and included in the proposed discovery plan. This listing does not exclude consideration of other subjects, such as the time when any dispositive motions should be filed and when the case should be ready for trial.

The parties are directed under subdivision (a)(1) to make the disclosures required by that subdivision at or within 10 days after this meeting. In many cases the parties should use the meeting to exchange, discuss, and clarify their respective disclosures. In other cases, it may be more useful if the disclosures are delayed until after the parties have discussed at the meeting the claims and defenses in order to define the issues with respect to which the initial disclosures should be made. As discussed in the Notes to subdivision (a)(1), the parties may also need to consider whether a stipulation extending this 10–day period would be appropriate, as when a defendant would otherwise have less than 60 days after being served in which to make its initial disclosure. The parties should also discuss at the meeting what additional information, although not subject to the disclosure requirements, can be made available informally without the necessity for formal discovery requests.

The report is to be submitted to the court within 10 days after the meeting and should not be difficult to prepare. In most cases counsel should be able to agree that one of them will be responsible for its preparation and submission to the court. Form 35 has been added in the Appendix to the Rules, both to illustrate the type of report that is contemplated and to serve as a checklist for the meeting.

The litigants are expected to attempt in good faith to agree on the contents of the proposed discovery plan. If they cannot agree on all aspects of the plan, their report to the court should indicate the competing proposals of the parties on those items, as well as the matters on which they agree. Unfortunately, there may be cases in which, because of disagreements about time or place or for other reasons, the meeting is not attended by all parties or, indeed, no meeting takes place. In such situations, the report—or reports—should describe the circumstances and the court may need to consider sanctions under Rule 37(g).

By local rule or special order, the court can exempt particular cases or types of cases from the meet-and-confer requirement of subdivision (f). In general this should include any types of cases which are exempted by local rule from the requirement for a scheduling order under Rule 16(b), such as cases in which there will be no discovery (*e.g.,* bankruptcy appeals and reviews of social security determinations). In addition, the court may want to exempt cases in which discovery is rarely needed (*e.g.,* government collection cases and proceedings to enforce administrative summonses) or in which a meeting of the parties might be impracticable (*e.g.,* actions by unrepresented prisoners). Note that if a court exempts from the requirements for a meeting any types of cases in which discovery may be needed, it should indicate when discovery may commence in those cases.

Subdivision (g). Paragraph (1) is added to require signatures on disclosures, a requirement that parallels the provisions of paragraph (2) with respect to discovery requests, responses, and objections. The provisions of paragraph (3) have been modified to be consistent with Rules 37(a)(4) and 37(c)(1); in combination, these rules establish sanctions for violation of the rules regarding disclosures and discovery matters. Amended Rule 11 no longer applies to such violations.

Rule 27. Depositions Before Action or Pending Appeal

(a) Before Action.

(1) *Petition.* A person who desires to perpetuate testimony regarding any matter that may be cognizable in any court of the United States may file a verified petition in the United States district court in the district of the residence of any expected adverse party. The petition shall be entitled in the name of the petitioner and shall show: 1, that the petitioner expects to be a party to an action cognizable in a court of the United States but is presently unable to bring it or cause it to be brought, 2, the subject matter of the expected action and the petitioner's interest therein, 3, the facts which the petitioner desires to establish by the proposed testimony and the reasons for desiring to perpetuate it, 4, the names or a description of the persons the petitioner expects will be adverse parties and their addresses so far as known, and 5, the names and addresses of the persons to be examined and the substance of the testimony which the petitioner expects to elicit from each, and shall ask for an order authorizing the petitioner to take the depositions of the persons to be examined named in the petition, for the purpose of perpetuating their testimony.

(2) *Notice and Service.* The petitioner shall thereafter serve a notice upon each person named in the petition as an expected adverse party, together with a copy of the petition, stating that the petitioner will apply to the court, at a time and place named therein, for the order described in the petition. At least 20 days before the date of hearing the notice shall be served either within or without the district or state in the manner provided in Rule 4(d) for service of summons; but if such service cannot with due diligence be made upon any expected adverse party named in the petition, the court may make such order as is just for service by publication or otherwise, and shall appoint, for persons not served in the manner provided in Rule 4(d), an attorney who shall represent them, and, in case they are not otherwise represented, shall cross-examine the deponent. If any expected adverse party is a minor or incompetent the provisions of Rule 17(c) apply.

(3) *Order and Examination.* If the court is satisfied that the perpetuation of the testimony may prevent a failure or delay of justice, it shall make an order designating or describing the persons whose depositions may be taken and specifying the subject matter of the examination and whether the depositions shall be taken upon oral examination or written interrogatories. The depositions may then be taken in accordance with these rules; and the court may make orders of the character provided for by Rules 34 and 35. For the purpose of applying these rules to depositions for perpetuating testimony, each reference therein to the court in which the action is pending shall be deemed to refer to the court in which the petition for such deposition was filed.

(4) *Use of Deposition.* If a deposition to perpetuate testimony is taken under these rules or if, although not so taken, it would be admissible in evidence in the courts of the state in which it is taken, it may be used in any action involving the same subject matter subsequently brought in a United States district court, in accordance with the provisions of Rule 32(a).

(b) Pending Appeal. If an appeal has been taken from a judgment of a district court or before the taking of an appeal if the time therefor has not expired, the district court in which the judgment was rendered may allow the taking of the depositions of witnesses to perpetuate their testimony for use in the event of further proceedings in the district court. In such case the party who desires to perpetuate the testimony may make a motion in the district court for leave to take the depositions, upon the same notice and service thereof as if the action was pending in the district court. The motion shall show (1) the names and addresses of persons to be examined and the substance of the testimony which the party expects to elicit from each; (2) the reasons for perpetuating their testimony. If the court finds that the perpetuation of the testimony is proper to avoid a failure or delay of justice, it may make an order allowing the depositions to be taken and may make orders of the character provided for by Rules 34 and 35, and thereupon the depositions may be taken and used in the same manner and under the same conditions as are prescribed in these rules for depositions taken in actions pending in the district court.

(c) Perpetuation by Action. This rule does not limit the power of a court to entertain an action to perpetuate testimony.

(As amended Dec. 27, 1946, eff. Mar. 19, 1948; Dec. 29, 1948, eff. Oct. 20, 1949; Mar. 1, 1971, eff. July 1, 1971; Mar. 2, 1987, eff. Aug. 1, 1987.)

Rule 28.   Persons Before Whom Depositions May Be Taken

(a) **Within the United States.** Within the United States or within a territory or insular possession subject to the jurisdiction of the United States, depositions shall be taken before an officer authorized to administer oaths by the laws of the United States or of the place where the examination is held, or before a person appointed by the court in which the action is pending.   A person so appointed has power to administer oaths and take testimony.   The term officer as used in Rules 30, 31, and 32 includes a person appointed by the court or designated by the parties under Rule 29.

(b) **In Foreign Countries.** Depositions may be taken in a foreign country (1) pursuant to any applicable treaty or convention, or (2) pursuant to a letter of request (whether or not captioned a letter rogatory), or (3) on notice before a person authorized to administer oaths in the place where the examination is held, either by the law thereof or by the law of the United States, or (4) before a person commissioned by the court, and a person so commissioned shall have the power by virtue of the commission to administer any necessary oath and take testimony. A commission or a letter of request shall be issued on application and notice and on terms that are just and appropriate.   It is not requisite to the issuance of a commission or a letter of request that the taking of the deposition in any other manner is impracticable or inconvenient; and both a commission and a letter of request may be issued in proper cases. A notice or commission may designate the person before whom the deposition is to be taken either by name or descriptive title.   A letter of request may be addressed "To the Appropriate Authority in [here name the country]."   When a letter of request or any other device is used pursuant to any applicable treaty or convention, it shall be captioned in the form prescribed by that treaty or convention.   Evidence obtained in response to a letter of request need not be excluded merely because it is not a verbatim transcript, because the testimony was not taken under oath, or because of any similar departure from the requirements for depositions taken within the United States under these rules.

(c) **Disqualification for Interest.** No deposition shall be taken before a person who is a relative or employee or attorney or counsel of any of the parties, or is a relative or employee of such attorney or counsel, or is financially interested in the action.

(As amended Dec. 27, 1946, eff. Mar. 19, 1948; Jan. 21, 1963, eff. July 1, 1963; Apr. 29, 1980, eff. Aug. 1, 1980; Mar. 2, 1987, eff. Aug. 1, 1987; Apr. 22, 1993, eff. Dec. 1, 1993.)

Rule 29.   Stipulations Regarding Discovery Procedure

Unless otherwise directed by the court, the parties may by written stipulation (1) provide that depositions may be taken before any person, at any time or place, upon any notice, and in any manner and when so taken may be used like other depositions, and (2) modify other procedures governing or limitations placed upon discovery, except that stipulations extending the time provided in Rules 33, 34, and 36 for responses to discovery may, if they would interfere with any time set for completion of discovery, for hearing of a motion, or for trial, be made only with the approval of the court.

(As amended Mar. 30, 1970, eff. July 1, 1970; Apr. 22, 1993, eff. Dec. 1, 1993.)

Rule 30. Depositions Upon Oral Examination

(a) When Depositions May Be Taken; When Leave Required.

(1) A party may take the testimony of any person, including a party, by deposition upon oral examination without leave of court except as provided in paragraph (2). The attendance of witnesses may be compelled by subpoena as provided in Rule 45.

(2) A party must obtain leave of court, which shall be granted to the extent consistent with the principles stated in Rule 26(b)(2), if the person to be examined is confined in prison or if, without the written stipulation of the parties.

(A) a proposed deposition would result in more than ten depositions being taken under this rule or Rule 31 by the plaintiffs, or by the defendants, or by third-party defendants;

(B) the person to be examined already has been deposed in the case; or

(C) a party seeks to take a deposition before the time specified in Rule 26(d) unless the notice contains a certification, with supporting facts, that the person to be examined is expected to leave the United States and be unavailable for examination in this country unless deposed before that time.

(b) Notice of Examination: General Requirements; Method of Recording; Production of Documents and Things; Deposition of Organization; Deposition by Telephone.

(1) A party desiring to take the deposition of any person upon oral examination shall give reasonable notice in writing to every other party to the action. The notice shall state the time and place for taking the deposition and the name and address of each person to be examined, if known, and, if the name is not known, a general description sufficient to identify the person or the particular class or group to which the person belongs. If a subpoena duces tecum is to be served on the person to be examined, the designation of the materials to be produced as set forth in the subpoena shall be attached to, or included in, the notice.

(2) The party taking the deposition shall state in the notice the method by which the testimony shall be recorded. Unless the court orders otherwise, it may be recorded by sound, sound-and-visual, or stenographic means, and the party taking the deposition shall bear the cost of the recording. Any party may arrange for a transcription to be made from the recording of a deposition taken by nonstenographic means.

(3) With prior notice to the deponent and other parties, any party may designate another method to record the deponent's testimony in addition to the method specified by the person taking the deposition. The additional record or transcript shall be made at that party's expense unless the court otherwise orders.

(4) Unless otherwise agreed by the parties, a deposition shall be conducted before an officer appointed or designated under Rule 28 and shall begin with a statement on the record by the officer that includes (A) the officer's name and business address; (B) the date, time, and place of the deposition; (C) the name of the deponent; (D) the administration of the oath or affirmation to the deponent; and (E) an identification of all persons present. If the deposition is recorded other than stenographically, the officer shall repeat items (A) through (C) at the beginning of each unit of recorded tape or other recording medium. The appearance or demeanor of deponents or attorneys shall not be distorted through camera or sound-recording techniques. At the end of the deposition, the officer shall state on the record that the deposition is complete and shall set forth any stipulations made by counsel concerning the custody of the transcript or recording and the exhibits, or concerning other pertinent matters.

(5) The notice to a party deponent may be accompanied by a request made in compliance with Rule 34 for the production of documents and tangible things at the taking of the deposition. The procedure of Rule 34 shall apply to the request.

(6) A party may in the party's notice and in a subpoena name as the deponent a public or private corporation or a partnership or association or governmental agency and describe with reasonable particularity the matters on which examination is requested. In that event, the organization so named shall designate one or more officers, directors, or managing agents, or other persons who consent to testify on its behalf, and may set forth, for each person designated, the matters on which the person will testify. A subpoena shall advise a non-party organization of its duty to make such a designation. The persons so designated shall testify as to matters known or reasonably available to the organization. This subdivision (b)(6) does not preclude taking a deposition by any other procedure authorized in these rules.

(7) The parties may stipulate in writing or the court may upon motion order that a deposition be taken by telephone or other remote electronic means. For the purposes of this rule and Rules 28(a), 37(a)(1), and 37(b)(1) a deposition taken by such means is taken in the district and at the place where the deponent is to answer questions.

(c) **Examination and Cross–Examination; Record of Examination; Oath; Objections.** Examination and cross-examination of witnesses may proceed as permitted at the trial under the provisions of the Federal Rules of Evidence except Rules 103 and 615. The officer before whom the deposition is to be taken shall put the witness on oath or affirmation and shall personally, or by someone acting under the officer's direction and in the officer's presence, record the testimony of the witness. The testimony shall be taken stenographically or recorded by any other method authorized by subdivision (b)(2) of this rule. All objections made at the time of the examination to the qualifications of the officer taking the deposition, to the manner of taking it, to the evidence presented, to the conduct of any party, or to any other aspect of the proceedings shall be noted by the officer upon the record of the deposition; but the examination shall proceed, with the testimony being taken subject to the objections. In lieu of participating in the oral examination, parties may serve written questions in a sealed envelope on the party taking the deposition and the party taking the deposition shall transmit them to the officer, who shall propound them to the witness and record the answers verbatim.

(d) Schedule and Duration; Motion to Terminate or Limit Examination.

(1) Any objection to evidence during a deposition shall be stated concisely and in a non-argumentative and non-suggestive manner. A party may instruct a deponent not to answer only when necessary to preserve a privilege, to enforce a limitation on evidence directed by the court, or to present a motion under paragraph (3).

(2) By order or local rule, the court may limit the time permitted for the conduct of a deposition, but shall allow additional time consistent with Rule 26(b)(2) if needed for a fair examination of the deponent or if the deponent or another party impedes or delays the examination. If the court finds such an impediment, delay, or other conduct that has frustrated the fair examination of the deponent, it may impose upon the persons responsible an appropriate sanction, including the reasonable costs and attorney's fees incurred by any parties as a result thereof.

(3) At any time during a deposition, on motion of a party or of the deponent and upon a showing that the examination is being conducted in bad faith or in such manner as unreasonably to annoy, embarrass, or oppress the deponent or party, the court in which the action is pending or the court in the district where the deposition is being taken may order the officer conducting the examination to cease forthwith from taking the deposition, or may limit the scope and manner of the taking of the deposition as provided in Rule 26(c). If the order made terminates the examination, it shall be resumed thereafter only upon the order of the court in which the action is pending. Upon demand of the objecting party or deponent, the taking of the deposition shall be suspended for the time necessary to make a motion for an order. The provisions of Rule 37(a)(4) apply to the award of expenses incurred in relation to the motion.

(e) Review by Witness; Changes; Signing. If requested by the deponent or a party before completion of the deposition, the deponent shall have 30 days after being notified by the officer that the transcript or recording is available in which to review the transcript or recording and, if there are changes in form or substance, to sign a statement reciting such changes and the reasons given by the deponent for making them. The officer shall indicate in the certificate prescribed by subdivision (f)(1) whether any review was requested and, if so, shall append any changes made by the deponent during the period allowed.

(f) Certification and Filing by Officer; Exhibits; Copies; Notice of Filing.

(1) The officer shall certify that the witness was duly sworn by the officer and that the deposition is a true record of the testimony given by the witness. This certificate shall be in writing and accompany the record of the deposition. Unless otherwise ordered by the court, the officer shall securely seal the deposition in an envelope or package indorsed with the title of the action and marked "Deposition of [here insert name of witness]" and shall promptly file it with the court in which the action is pending or send it to the attorney who arranged for the transcript or recording, who shall store it under conditions that will protect it against loss, destruction, tampering, or deterioration. Documents and things produced for inspection during the examination of the witness, shall, upon the request of a party, be marked for identification and annexed to the deposition and may be inspected and copied by any party, except that if the person producing the materials desires to retain them the person may (A) offer copies to be marked for identification and annexed to the deposition and to serve thereafter as originals if the person affords to all parties fair opportunity to verify the copies by comparison with the originals, or (B) offer the originals to be marked for identification, after giving to each party an opportunity to inspect and copy them, in which event the materials may then be used in the same manner as if annexed to the deposition. Any party may move for an order that the original be annexed to and returned with the deposition to the court, pending final disposition of the case.

(2) Unless otherwise ordered by the court or agreed by the parties, the officer shall retain stenographic notes of any deposition taken stenographically or a copy of the recording of any deposition taken by another method. Upon payment of reasonable charges therefor, the officer shall furnish a copy of the transcript or other recording of the deposition to any party or to the deponent.

(3) The party taking the deposition shall give prompt notice of its filing to all other parties.

(g) Failure to Attend or to Serve Subpoena; Expenses.

(1) If the party giving the notice of the taking of a deposition fails to attend and proceed therewith and another party attends in person or by attorney pursuant to the notice, the court may order the party giving the notice to pay to such other party the reasonable expenses incurred by that party and that party's attorney in attending, including reasonable attorney's fees.

(2) If the party giving the notice of the taking of a deposition of a witness fails to serve a subpoena upon the witness and the witness because of such failure does not attend, and if another party attends in person or by attorney because that party expects the deposition of that witness to be taken, the court may order the party giving the notice to pay to such other party the reasonable expenses incurred by that party and that party's attorney in attending, including reasonable attorney's fees.

(As amended Jan. 21, 1963, eff. July 1, 1963; Mar. 30, 1970, eff. July 1, 1970; Mar. 1, 1971, eff. July 1, 1971; Nov. 20, 1972, eff. July 1, 1975; Apr. 29, 1980, eff. Aug. 1, 1980; Mar. 2, 1987, eff. Aug. 1, 1987; Apr. 22, 1993, eff. Dec. 1, 1993.)

NOTES OF ADVISORY COMMITTEE ON RULES
1993 AMENDMENT

Subdivision (a). Paragraph (1) retains the first and third sentences from the former subdivision (a) without significant modification. The second and fourth sentences are relocated.

Paragraph (2) collects all provisions bearing on requirements of leave of court to take a deposition.

Paragraph (2)(A) is new. It provides a limit on the number of depositions the parties may take, absent leave of court or stipulation with the other parties. One aim of this revision is to assure judicial review under the standards stated in Rule 26(b)(2) before any side will be allowed to take more than ten depositions in a case without agreement of the other parties. A second objective is to emphasize that counsel have a professional obligation to develop a mutual cost-effective plan for discovery in the case. Leave to take additional depositions should be granted when consistent with the principles of Rule 26(b)(2), and in some cases the ten-per-side limit should be reduced in accordance with those same principles. Consideration should ordinarily be given at the planning meeting of the parties under Rule 26(f) and at the time of a scheduling conference under Rule 16(b) as to enlargements or reductions in the number of depositions, eliminating the need for special motions.

A deposition under Rule 30(b)(6) should, for purposes of this limit, be treated as a single deposition even though more than one person may be designated to testify.

In multi-party cases, the parties on any side are expected to confer and agree as to which depositions are most needed, given the presumptive limit on the number of depositions they can take without leave of court. If these disputes cannot be amicably resolved, the court can be requested to resolve the dispute or permit additional depositions.

Paragraph (2)(B) is new. It requires leave of court if any witness is to be deposed in the action more than once. This requirement does not apply when a deposition is temporarily recessed for convenience of counsel or the deponent or to enable additional materials to be gathered before resuming the deposition. If significant travel costs would be incurred to resume the deposition, the parties should consider the feasibility of conducting the balance of the examination by telephonic means.

Paragraph (2)(C) revises the second sentence of the former subdivision (a) as to when depositions may be taken. Consistent with the changes made in Rule 26(d), providing that formal discovery ordinarily not commence until after the litigants have met and conferred as directed in revised Rule 26(f), the rule requires leave of court or agreement of the parties if a deposition is to be taken before that time (except when a witness is about to leave the country).

Subdivision (b). The primary change in subdivision (b) is that parties will be authorized to record deposition testimony by nonstenographic means without first having to obtain permission of the court or agreement from other counsel.

* * *

New paragraph (2) confers on the party taking the deposition the choice of the method of recording, without the need to obtain prior court approval for one taken other than stenographically. A party choosing to record a deposition only by videotape or audiotape should understand that a transcript will be required by Rule 26(a)(3)(B) and Rule 32(c) if the deposition is later to be offered as evidence at trial or on a dispositive motion under Rule 56. Objections to the nonstenographic recording of a deposition, when warranted by the circumstances, can be presented to the court under Rule 26(c).

Paragraph (3) provides that other parties may arrange, at their own expense, for the recording of a deposition by a means (stenographic, visual, or sound) in addition to the method designated by the person noticing the deposition. The former provisions of this paragraph, relating to the court's power to change the date of a deposition, have been eliminated as redundant in view of Rule 26(c)(2).

Revised paragraph (4) requires that all depositions be recorded by an officer designated or appointed under Rule 28 and contains special provisions designed to provide basic safeguards to assure the utility and integrity of recordings taken other than stenographically.

Paragraph (7) is revised to authorize the taking of a deposition not only by telephone but also by other remote electronic means, such as satellite television, when agreed to by the parties or authorized by the court.

Subdivision (c). Minor changes are made in this subdivision to reflect those made in subdivision (b) and to complement the new provisions of subdivision (d)(1), aimed at reducing the number of interruptions during depositions.

In addition, the revision addresses a recurring problem as to whether other potential deponents can attend a deposition. Courts have disagreed, some holding that witnesses should be excluded through invocation of Rule 615 of the evidence rules, and others holding that witnesses may attend unless excluded by an order under Rule 26(c)(5). The revision provides that other witnesses are not automatically excluded from a deposition simply by the request of a party. Exclusion, however, can be ordered under Rule 26(c)(5) when appropriate; and, if exclusion is ordered, consideration should be given as to whether the excluded witnesses likewise should be precluded from reading, or being otherwise informed about, the testimony given in the earlier depositions. The revision addresses only the matter of attendance by potential deponents, and does not attempt to resolve issues concerning attendance by others, such as members of the public or press.

Subdivision (d). The first sentence of new paragraph (1) provides that any objections during a deposition must be made concisely and in a non-argumentative and non-suggestive manner. Depositions frequently have been unduly prolonged, if not unfairly frustrated, by lengthy objections and colloquy, often suggesting how the deponent should respond. While objections may, under the revised rule, be made during a deposition, they ordinarily should be limited to those that under Rule 32(d)(3) might be waived if not made at that time, i.e., objections on grounds that might be immediately obviated, removed, or cured, such as to the form of a question or the responsiveness of an answer. Under Rule 32(b), other objections can, even without the so-called "usual stipulation" preserving objections, be raised for the first time at trial and therefore should be kept to a minimum during a deposition.

Directions to a deponent not to answer a question can be even more disruptive than objections. The second sentence of new paragraph (1) prohibits such directions except in the three circumstances indicated: to claim a privilege or protection against disclosure (e.g., as work product), to enforce a court directive limiting the scope or length of permissible discovery, or to suspend a deposition to enable presentation of a motion under paragraph (3).

Paragraph (2) is added to this subdivision to dispel any doubts regarding the power of the court by order or local rule to establish limits on the length of depositions. The rule also explicitly authorizes the court to impose the cost resulting from obstructive tactics that unreasonably prolong a deposition on the person engaged in such obstruction. This sanction may be imposed on a non-party witness as well as a party or attorney, but is otherwise congruent with Rule 26(g).

It is anticipated that limits on the length of depositions prescribed by local rules would be presumptive only, subject to modification by the court or by agreement of the parties. Such modifications typically should be discussed by the parties in their meeting under Rule 26(f) and included in the scheduling order required by Rule 16(b). Additional time, moreover, should be allowed under the revised rule when justified under the principles stated in Rule 26(b)(2). To reduce the number of special motions, local rules should ordinarily permit—and indeed encourage—the parties to agree to additional time, as when, during the taking of a deposition, it becomes clear that some additional examination is needed.

Paragraph (3) authorizes appropriate sanctions not only when a deposition is unreasonably prolonged, but also when an attorney engages in other practices that improperly frustrate the fair examination of the deponent, such as making improper objections or giving directions not to answer prohibited by paragraph (1). In general, counsel should not engage in any conduct during a deposition that would not be allowed in the presence of a judicial officer. The making of an excessive number of unnecessary objections may itself constitute sanctionable conduct, as may the refusal of an attorney to agree with other counsel on a fair apportionment of the time allowed for examination of a deponent or a refusal to agree to a reasonable request for some additional time to complete a deposition, when that is permitted by the local rule or order.

Subdivision (e). Various changes are made in this subdivision to reduce problems sometimes encountered when depositions are taken stenographically. Reporters frequently have difficulties obtaining signatures— and the return of depositions—from deponents. Under the revision prefiling review by the deponent is required only if requested before the deposition is completed. If review is requested, the deponent will be allowed 30 days to review the transcript or recording and to indicate any changes in form or substance. Signature of the deponent will be required only if review is requested and changes are made.

Subdivision (f). Minor changes are made in this subdivision to reflect those made in subdivision (b). In courts which direct that depositions not be automatically filed, the reporter can transmit the transcript or recording to the attorney taking the deposition (or ordering the transcript or record), who then becomes custodian for the court of the original record of the deposition. Pursuant to subdivision (f)(2), as under the prior rule, any other party is entitled to secure a copy of the deposition from the officer designated to take the deposition; accordingly, unless ordered or agreed, the officer must retain a copy of the recording or the stenographic notes.

Rule 31. Depositions Upon Written Questions

(a) Serving Questions; Notice.

(1) A party may take the testimony of any person, including a party, by deposition upon written questions without leave of court except as provided in paragraph (2). The attendance of witnesses may be compelled by the use of subpoena as provided in Rule 45.

(2) A party must obtain leave of court, which shall be granted to the extent consistent with the principles stated in Rule 26(b)(2), if the person to be examined is confined in prison or if, without the written stipulation of the parties:

(A) a proposed deposition would result in more than ten depositions being taken under this rule or Rule 30 by the plaintiffs, or by the defendants, or by third-party defendants;

(B) the person to be examined has already been deposed in the case; or

(C) a party seeks to take a deposition before the time specified in Rule 26(d).

(3) A party desiring to take a deposition upon written questions shall serve them upon every other party with a notice stating (1) the name and address of the person who is to answer them, if known, and if the name is not known, a general description sufficient to identify the person or the particular class or group to which the person belongs, and (2) the name or descriptive title and address of the officer before whom the deposition is to be taken. A deposition upon written questions may be taken of a public or private corporation or a partnership or association or governmental agency in accordance with the provisions of Rule 30(b)(6).

(4) Within 14 days after the notice and written questions are served, a party may serve cross questions upon all other parties. Within 7 days after being served with cross questions, a party may serve redirect questions upon all other parties. Within 7 days after being served with redirect questions, a party may serve recross questions upon all other parties. The court may for cause shown enlarge or shorten the time.

(b) Officer to Take Responses and Prepare Record. A copy of the notice and copies of all questions served shall be delivered by the party taking the deposition to the officer designated in the notice, who shall proceed promptly, in the manner provided by Rule 30(c), (e), and (f), to take the testimony of the witness in response to the questions and to prepare, certify, and file or mail the deposition, attaching thereto the copy of the notice and the questions received by the officer.

(c) Notice of Filing. When the deposition is filed the party taking it shall promptly give notice thereof to all other parties.

(As amended Mar. 30, 1970, eff. July 1, 1970; Mar. 2, 1987, eff. Aug. 1, 1987; Apr. 22, 1993, eff. Dec. 1, 1993.)

Rule 32. Use of Depositions in Court Proceedings

(a) Use of Depositions. At the trial or upon the hearing of a motion or an interlocutory proceeding, any part or all of a deposition, so far as admissible under the rules of evidence applied as though the witness were then present and testifying, may be used against any party who was present or represented at the taking of the deposition or who had reasonable notice thereof, in accordance with any of the following provisions:

(1) Any deposition may be used by any party for the purpose of contradicting or impeaching the testimony of deponent as a witness, or for any other purpose permitted by the Federal Rules of Evidence.

(2) The deposition of a party or of anyone who at the time of taking the deposition was an officer, director, or managing agent, or a person designated under Rule 30(b)(6) or 31(a) to testify on behalf of a public or private corporation, partnership or association or governmental agency which is a party may be used by an adverse party for any purpose.

(3) The deposition of a witness, whether or not a party, may be used by any party for any purpose if the court finds:

(A) that the witness is dead; or

(B) that the witness is at a greater distance than 100 miles from the place of trial or hearing, or is out of the United States, unless it appears that the absence of the witness was procured by the party offering the deposition; or

(C) that the witness is unable to attend or testify because of age, illness, infirmity, or imprisonment; or

(D) that the party offering the deposition has been unable to procure the attendance of the witness by subpoena; or

(E) upon application and notice, that such exceptional circumstances exist as to make it desirable, in the interest of justice and with due regard to the importance of presenting the testimony of witnesses orally in open court, to allow the deposition to be used.

A deposition taken without leave of court pursuant to a notice under Rule 30(a)(2)(C) shall not be used against a party who demonstrates that, when served with the notice, it was unable through the exercise of diligence to obtain counsel to represent it at the taking of the deposition; nor shall a deposition be used against a party who, having received less than 11 days notice of a deposition, has promptly upon receiving such notice filed a motion for a protective order under Rule 26(c)(2) requesting that the deposition not be held or be held at a different time or place and such motion is pending at the time the deposition is held.

(4) If only part of a deposition is offered in evidence by a party, an adverse party may require the offeror to introduce any other part which ought in fairness to be considered with the part introduced, and any party may introduce any other parts.

Substitution of parties pursuant to Rule 25 does not affect the right to use depositions previously taken; and, when an action has been brought in any court of the United States or of any State and another action involving the same subject matter is afterward brought between the same parties or their representatives or successors in interest, all depositions lawfully taken and duly filed in the former action may be used in the latter as if originally taken therefor. A deposition previously taken may also be used as permitted by the Federal Rules of Evidence.

(b) Objections to Admissibility. Subject to the provisions of Rule 28(b) and subdivision (d)(3) of this rule, objection may be made at the trial or hearing to receiving in evidence any deposition or part thereof for any reason which would require the exclusion of the evidence if the witness were then present and testifying.

(c) Form of Presentation. Except as otherwise directed by the court, a party offering deposition testimony pursuant to this rule may offer it in stenographic or nonstenographic form, but, if in nonstenographic form, the party shall also provide the court with a transcript of the portions so offered. On request of any party in a case tried before a jury, deposition testimony offered other than for impeachment purposes shall be presented in nonstenographic form, if available, unless the court for good cause orders otherwise.

(d) Effect of Errors and Irregularities in Depositions.

(1) *As to Notice.* All errors and irregularities in the notice for taking a deposition are waived unless written objection is promptly served upon the party giving the notice.

(2) *As to Disqualification of Officer.* Objection to taking a deposition because of disqualification of the officer before whom it is to be taken is waived unless made before the taking of the deposition begins or as soon thereafter as the disqualification becomes known or could be discovered with reasonable diligence.

(3) *As to Taking of Deposition.*

(A) Objections to the competency of a witness or to the competency, relevancy, or materiality of testimony are not waived by failure to make them before or during the taking of the deposition, unless the ground of the objection is one which might have been obviated or removed if presented at that time.

(B) Errors and irregularities occurring at the oral examination in the manner of taking the deposition, in the form of the questions or answers, in the oath or affirmation, or in the conduct of parties, and errors of any kind which might be obviated, removed, or cured if promptly presented, are waived unless seasonable objection thereto is made at the taking of the deposition.

(C) Objections to the form of written questions submitted under Rule 31 are waived unless served in writing upon the party propounding them within the time allowed for serving the succeeding cross or other questions and within 5 days after service of the last questions authorized.

(4) *As to Completion and Return of Deposition.* Errors and irregularities in the manner in which the testimony is transcribed or the deposition is prepared, signed, certified, sealed, indorsed, transmitted, filed, or otherwise dealt with by the officer under Rules 30 and 31 are waived unless a motion to suppress the deposition or some part thereof is made with reasonable promptness after such defect is, or with due diligence might have been, ascertained.

(As amended Mar. 30, 1970, eff. July 1, 1970; Nov. 20, 1972, eff. July 1, 1975; Apr. 29, 1980, eff. Aug. 1, 1980; Mar. 2, 1987, eff. Aug. 1, 1987; Apr. 22, 1993, eff. Dec. 1, 1993.)

Rule 33. Interrogatories to Parties

(a) Availability. Without leave of court or written stipulation, any party may serve upon any other party written interrogatories, not exceeding 25 in number including all discrete subparts, to be answered by the party served or, if the party served is a public or private corporation or a partnership or association or governmental agency, by any officer or agent, who shall furnish such information as is available to the party. Leave to serve additional interrogatories shall be granted to the extent consistent with the principles of Rule 26(b)(2). Without leave of court or written stipulation, interrogatories may not be served before the time specified in Rule 26(d).

(b) Answers and Objections.

(1) Each interrogatory shall be answered separately and fully in writing under oath, unless it is objected to, in which event the objecting party shall state the reasons for objection and shall answer to the extent the interrogatory is not objectionable.

(2) The answers are to be signed by the person making them, and the objections signed by the attorney making them.

(3) The party upon whom the interrogatories have been served shall serve a copy of the answers, and objections if any, within 30 days after the service of the interrogatories. A shorter or longer time may be directed by the court or, in the absence of such an order, agreed to in writing by the parties subject to Rule 29.

(4) All grounds for an objection to an interrogatory shall be stated with specificity. Any ground not stated in a timely objection is waived unless the party's failure to object is excused by the court for good cause shown.

(5) The party submitting the interrogatories may move for an order under Rule 37(a) with respect to any objection to or other failure to answer an interrogatory.

(c) Scope; Use at Trial. Interrogatories may relate to any matters which can be inquired into under Rule 26(b)(1), and the answers may be used to the extent permitted by the rules of evidence.

An interrogatory otherwise proper is not necessarily objectionable merely because an answer to the interrogatory involves an opinion or contention that relates to fact or the application of law to fact, but the court may order that such an interrogatory need not be answered until after designated discovery has been completed or until a pre-trial conference or other later time.

(d) Option to Produce Business Records. Where the answer to an interrogatory may be derived or ascertained from the business records of the party upon whom the interrogatory has been served or from an examination, audit or inspection of such business records, including a compilation, abstract or summary thereof and the burden of deriving or ascertaining the answer is substantially the same for the party serving the interrogatory as for the party served, it is a sufficient answer to such interrogatory to specify the records from which the answer may be derived or ascertained and to afford to the party serving the interrogatory reasonable opportunity to examine, audit or inspect such records and to make copies, compilations, abstracts or summaries. A specification shall be in sufficient detail to permit the interrogating party to locate and to identify, as readily as can the party served, the records from which the answer may be ascertained.

(As amended Dec. 27, 1946, eff. Mar. 19, 1948; Mar. 30, 1970, eff. July 1, 1970; Apr. 29, 1980, eff. Aug. 1, 1980; Apr. 22, 1993, eff. Dec. 1, 1993.)

NOTES OF ADVISORY COMMITTEE ON RULES
1970 AMENDMENT
* * *

Subdivision [(c)]. * * *

Rule 33 is amended to provide that an interrogatory is not objectionable merely because it calls for an opinion or contention that relates to fact or the application of law to fact. Efforts to draw sharp lines between facts and opinions have invariably been unsuccessful, and the clear trend of the cases is to permit "factual" opinions. As to requests for opinions or contentions that call for the application of law to fact, they can be most useful in narrowing and sharpening the issues, which is a major purpose of discovery. * * * On the other hand, under the new language interrogatories may not extend to issues of "pure law," *i.e.,* legal issues unrelated to the facts of the case.

Since interrogatories involving mixed questions of law and fact may create disputes between the parties which are best resolved after much or all of the other discovery has been completed, the court is expressly authorized to defer an answer. Likewise, the court may delay determination until pretrial conference, if it believes that the dispute is best resolved in the presence of the judge.

The principal question raised with respect to the cases permitting such interrogatories is whether they reintroduce undesirable aspects of the prior pleading practice, whereby parties were chained to misconceived contentions or theories, and ultimate determination on the merits was frustrated. * * * But there are few if any instances in the recorded cases demonstrating that such frustration has occurred. The general rule governing the use of answers to interrogatories is that under ordinary circumstances they do not limit proof. * * * Although in exceptional circumstances reliance on an answer may cause such prejudice that the court will hold the answering party bound to his answer, *e.g., Zielinski v. Philadelphia Piers, Inc.,* 139 F.Supp. 408 (E.D.Pa.1956), the interrogating party will ordinarily not be entitled to rely on the unchanging character of the answers he receives and cannot base prejudice on such reliance. The rule does not affect the power of a court to permit withdrawal or amendment of answers to interrogatories.

The use of answers to interrogatories at trial is made subject to the rules of evidence. The provisions governing use of depositions, to which Rule 33 presently refers, are not entirely apposite to answers to interrogatories, since deposition practice contemplates that all parties will ordinarily participate through cross-examination.

* * *

1980 AMENDMENT

Subdivision [(d)]. The Committee is advised that parties upon whom interrogatories are served have occasionally responded by directing the interrogating party to a mass of business records or by offering to make all of their records available, justifying the response by the option provided by this subdivision. Such practices are an abuse of the option. A party who is permitted by the terms of this subdivision to offer records for inspection in lieu of answering an interrogatory should offer them in a manner that permits the same direct and economical access that is available to the party. If the information sought exists in the form of compilations, abstracts or summaries then available to the responding party, those should be made available to the interrogating party. The final sentence is added to make it clear that a responding party has the duty to specify, by category and location, the records from which answers to interrogatories can be derived.

1993 AMENDMENT

* * *

Subdivision (a). Revision of this subdivision limits interrogatory practice. Because Rule 26(a)(1)(3) requires disclosure of much of the information previously obtained by this form of discovery, there should be less occasion to use it. Experience in over half of the district courts has confirmed that limitations on the number of interrogatories are useful and manageable. Moreover, because the device can be costly and may be used as a means of harassment, it is desirable to subject its use to the control of the court consistent with the principles stated in Rule 26(b)(2), particularly in multi-party cases where it has not been unusual for the same interrogatory to be propounded to a party by more than one of its adversaries.

* * *

Subdivision (b). * * * Language is added to paragraph (1) of this subdivision to emphasize the duty of the responding party to provide full answers to the extent not objectionable. If, for example, an interrogatory seeking information about numerous facilities or products is deemed objectionable, but an interrogatory seeking information about a lesser number of facilities or products would not have been objectionable, the interrogatory should be answered with respect to the latter even though an objection is raised as to the balance of the facilities or products. Similarly, the fact that additional time may be needed to respond to some questions (or to some aspects of questions) should not justify a delay in responding to those questions (or other aspects of questions) that can be answered within the prescribed time.

Paragraph (4) is added to make clear that objections must be specifically justified, and that unstated or untimely grounds for objection ordinarily are waived. Note also the provisions of revised Rule 26(b)(5), which require a responding party to indicate when it is withholding information under a claim of privilege or as trial preparation materials.

These provisions should be read in light of Rule 26(g), authorizing the court to impose sanctions on a party and attorney making an unfounded objection to an interrogatory.

* * *

Rule 34. Production of Documents and Things and Entry Upon Land for Inspection and Other Purposes

(a) Scope. Any party may serve on any other party a request (1) to produce and permit the party making the request, or someone acting on the requestor's behalf, to inspect and copy, any designated documents (including writings, drawings, graphs, charts, photographs, phono records, and other data compilations from which information can be obtained, translated, if necessary, by the respondent through detection devices into reasonably usable form), or to inspect and copy, test, or sample any tangible things which constitute or contain matters within the scope of Rule 26(b) and which are in the possession, custody or control of the party upon whom the request is served; or (2) to permit entry upon designated land or other property in the possession or control of the party upon whom the request is served for the purpose of inspection and measuring, surveying, photographing, testing, or sampling the property or any designated object or operation thereon, within the scope of Rule 26(b).

(b) Procedure. The request shall set forth, either by individual item or by category, the items to be inspected, and describe each with reasonable particularity. The request shall specify a reasonable time, place, and manner of making the inspection and performing the related acts. Without leave of court or written stipulation, a request may not be served before the time specified in Rule 26(d).

The party upon whom the request is served shall serve a written response within 30 days after the service of the request. A shorter or longer time may be directed by the court or, in the absence of such an order, agreed to in writing by the parties, subject to Rule 29. The response shall state, with respect to each item or category, that inspection and related activities will be permitted as requested, unless the request is objected to, in which event the reasons for the objection shall be stated. If objection is made to part of an item or category, the part shall be specified and inspection permitted of the remaining parts. The party submitting the request may move for an order under Rule 37(a) with respect to any objection to or other failure to respond to the request or any part thereof, or any failure to permit inspection as requested.

A party who produces documents for inspection shall produce them as they are kept in the usual course of business or shall organize and label them to correspond with the categories in the request.

(c) Persons Not Parties. A person not a party to the action may be compelled to produce documents and things or to submit to an inspection as provided in Rule 45.

(As amended Dec. 27, 1946, eff. Mar. 19, 1948; Mar. 30, 1970, eff. July 1, 1970; Apr. 29, 1980, eff. Aug. 1, 1980; Mar. 2, 1987, eff. Aug. 1, 1987; Apr. 30, 1991, eff. Dec. 1, 1991; Apr. 22, 1993, eff. Dec. 1, 1993.)

Rule 35. Physical and Mental Examination of Persons

(a) Order for Examination. When the mental or physical condition (including the blood group) of a party, or of a person in the custody or under the legal control of a party, is in controversy, the court in which the action is pending may order the party to submit to a physical or mental examination by a suitably licensed or certified examiner or to produce for examination the person in the party's custody or legal control. The order may be made only on motion for good cause shown and upon notice to the person to be examined and to all parties and shall specify the time, place, manner, conditions, and scope of the examination and the person or persons by whom it is to be made.

(b) Report of Examiner.

(1) If requested by the party against whom an order is made under Rule 35(a) or the person examined, the party causing the examination to be made shall deliver to the requesting party a copy of a detailed written report of the examiner setting out the examiner's findings, including results of all tests made, diagnoses and conclusions, together with like reports of all earlier examinations of the same condition. After delivery the party causing the examination shall be entitled upon request to receive from the party against whom the order is made a like report of any examination, previously or thereafter made, of the same condition, unless, in the case of a report of examination of a person not a party, the party shows that the party is unable to obtain it. The court on motion may make an order against a party requiring delivery of a report on such terms as are just, and if an examiner fails or refuses to make a report the court may exclude the examiner's testimony if offered at the trial.

(2) By requesting and obtaining a report of the examination so ordered or by taking the deposition of the examiner, the party examined waives any privilege the party may have in that action or any other involving the same controversy, regarding the testimony of every other person who has examined or may thereafter examine the party in respect of the same mental or physical condition.

(3) This subdivision applies to examinations made by agreement of the parties, unless the agreement expressly provides otherwise. This subdivision does not preclude discovery of a report of an examiner or the taking of a deposition of the examiner in accordance with the provisions of any other rule.

(c) Definitions. For the purpose of this rule, a psychologist is a psychologist licensed or certified by a State or the District of Columbia.

(As amended Mar. 30, 1970, eff. July 1, 1970; Mar. 2, 1987, eff. Aug. 1, 1987; Act of Nov. 18, 1988, § 7047(b), Pub.L. 100–690, 102 Stat. 4181; Apr. 30, 1991, eff. Dec. 1, 1991.)

NOTES OF ADVISORY COMMITTEE ON RULES
1970 AMENDMENT

Subdivision (a). Rule 35(a) has hitherto provided only for an order requiring a party to submit to an examination. It is desirable to extend the rule to provide for an order against the party for examination of a person in his custody or under his legal control. As appears from the provisions of amended Rule 37(b)(2) and the comment under that rule, an order to "produce" the third person imposes only an obligation to use good faith efforts to produce the person.

The amendment will settle beyond doubt that a parent or guardian suing to recover for injuries to a minor may be ordered to produce the minor for examination. Further, the amendment expressly includes blood examination within the kinds of examinations that can be ordered under the rule. See *Beach v. Beach,* 114 F.2d 479 (D.C.Cir.1940). Provisions similar to the amendment have been adopted in at least 10 States; Calif.Code Civ.Proc. § 2032; Ida.R.Civ.P. 35; Ill. S–H Ann. c. 110A, § 215; Md.R.P. 420; Mich.Gen.Ct.R. 311; Minn.R.Civ.P. 35; Mo.Vern.Ann.R.Civ.P. 60.01; N.Dak.R.Civ.P. 35; N.Y.C.P.L. § 3121; Wyo.R.Civ.P. 35.

The amendment makes no change in the requirements of Rule 35 that, before a court order may issue the relevant physical or mental condition must be shown to be "in controversy" and "good cause" must be shown for the examination. Thus, the amendment has no effect on the recent decision of the Supreme Court in *Schlagenhauf v. Holder,* 379 U.S. 104 (1964), stressing the importance of these requirements and applying them to the facts of the case. The amendment makes no reference to employees of a party. Provisions relating to employees in the State statutes and rules cited above appear to have been virtually unused.

* * *

Subdivision (b)(3). This new subdivision removes any possible doubt that reports of examination may be obtained although no order for examination has been made under Rule 35(a). Examinations are very frequently made by agreement, and sometimes before the party examined has an attorney. * * *

The subdivision also makes clear that reports of examining physicians are discoverable not only under Rule 35(b), but under other rules as well. To be sure, if the report is privileged, then discovery is not permissible under any rule other than Rule 35(b) and it is permissible under Rule 35(b) only if the party requests a copy of the report of examination made by the other party's doctor. *Sher v. De Haven,* 199 F.2d 777 (D.C.Cir.1952), *cert. denied* 345 U.S. 936 (1953). But if the report is unprivileged and is subject to discovery under the provisions of rules other than Rule 35(b)—such as Rules 34 or 26(b)(3) or (4)—discovery should not depend upon whether the person examined demands a copy of the report. * * *

1991 AMENDMENT

The revision authorizes the court to require physical or mental examinations conducted by any person who is suitably licensed or certified.

* * *

The requirement that the examiner be *suitably* licensed or certified is a new requirement. The court is thus expressly authorized to assess the credentials of the examiner to assure that no person is subjected to a court-ordered examination by an examiner whose testimony would be of such limited value that it would be unjust to require the person to undergo the invasion of privacy associated with the examination. This authority is not wholly new, for under the former rule, the court retained discretion to refuse to order an examination, or to restrict an examination. The revision is intended to encourage the exercise of this discretion, especially with respect to examinations by persons having narrow qualifications.

The court's responsibility to determine the suitability of the examiner's qualifications applies even to a proposed examination by a physician. If the proposed examination and testimony calls for an expertise that the proposed examiner does not have, it should not be ordered, even if the proposed examiner is a physician. The rule does not, however, require that the license or certificate be conferred by the jurisdiction in which the examination is conducted.

Rule 36.   Requests for Admission

(a) Request for Admission. A party may serve upon any other party a written request for the admission, for purposes of the pending action only, of the truth of any matters within the scope of Rule 26(b)(1) set forth in the request that relate to statements or opinions of fact or of the application of law to fact including the genuineness of any documents described in the request. Copies of documents shall be served with the request unless they have been or are otherwise furnished or made available for inspection and copying. Without leave of court or written stipulation, requests for admission may not be served before the time specified in Rule 26(d).

Each matter of which an admission is requested shall be separately set forth. The matter is admitted unless, within 30 days after service of the request, or within such shorter or longer time as the court may allow or as the parties may agree to in writing, subject to Rule 29, the party to whom the request is directed serves upon the party requesting the admission a written answer or objection addressed to the matter, signed by the party or by the party's attorney. If objection is made, the reasons therefor shall be stated. The answer shall specifically deny the matter or set forth in detail the reasons why the answering party cannot truthfully admit or deny the matter. A denial shall fairly meet the substance of the requested admission, and when good faith requires that a party qualify an answer or deny only a part of the matter of which an admission is requested, the party shall specify so much of it as is true and qualify or deny the remainder. An answering party may not give lack of information or knowledge as a reason for failure to admit or deny unless the party states that the party has made reasonable inquiry and that the information known or readily obtainable by the party is insufficient to enable the party to admit or deny. A party who considers that a matter of which an admission has been requested presents a genuine issue for trial may not, on that ground alone, object to the request; the party may, subject to the provisions of Rule 37(c), deny the matter or set forth reasons why the party cannot admit or deny it.

The party who has requested the admissions may move to determine the sufficiency of the answers or objections. Unless the court determines that an objection is justified, it shall order that an answer be served. If the court determines that an answer does not comply with the requirements of this rule, it may order either that the matter is admitted or that an amended answer be served. The court may, in lieu of these orders, determine that final disposition of the request be made at a pre-trial conference or at a designated time prior to trial. The provisions of Rule 37(a)(4) apply to the award of expenses incurred in relation to the motion.

(b) Effect of Admission. Any matter admitted under this rule is conclusively established unless the court on motion permits withdrawal or amendment of the admission. Subject to the provision of Rule 16 governing amendment of a pre-trial order, the court may permit withdrawal or amendment when the presentation of the merits of the action will be subserved thereby and the party who obtained the admission fails to satisfy the court that withdrawal or amendment will prejudice that party in maintaining the action or defense on the merits. Any admission made by a party under this rule is for the purpose of the pending action only and is not an admission for any other purpose nor may it be used against the party in any other proceeding.

(As amended Dec. 27, 1946, eff. Mar. 19, 1948; Mar. 30, 1970, eff. July 1, 1970; Mar. 2, 1987, eff. Aug. 1, 1987.)

NOTES OF ADVISORY COMMITTEE ON RULES
1970 AMENDMENT

Rule 36 serves two vital purposes, both of which are designed to reduce trial time. Admissions are sought, first to facilitate proof with respect to issues that cannot be eliminated from the case, and secondly, to narrow the issues by eliminating those that can be. The changes made in the rule are designed to serve these purposes more effectively. * * *

Subdivision (a). As revised, the subdivision provides that a request may be made to admit any matters within the scope of Rule 26(b) that relate to statements or opinions of fact or of the application of law to fact. It thereby eliminates the requirement that the matters be "of fact." * * *

Not only is it difficult as a practical matter to separate "fact" from "opinion," * * * but an admission on a matter of opinion may facilitate proof or narrow the issues or both. An admission of a matter involving the application of law to fact may, in a given case, even more clearly narrow the issues. For example, an admission that an employee acted in the scope of his employment may remove a major issue from the trial. * * * The amended provision does not authorize requests for admissions of law unrelated to the facts of the case.

Requests for admission involving the application of law to fact may create disputes between the parties which are best resolved in the presence of the judge after much or all of the other discovery has been completed. Power is therefore expressly conferred upon the court to defer decision until a pretrial conference is held or until a designated time prior to trial. On the other hand, the court should not automatically defer decision; in many instances, the importance of the admission lies in enabling the requesting party to avoid the burdensome accumulation of proof prior to the pretrial conference.

Courts have also divided on whether an answering party may properly object to requests for admission as to matters which that party regards as "in dispute". * * * The proper response in such cases is an answer. The very purpose of the request is to ascertain whether the answering party is prepared to admit or regards the matter as presenting a genuine issue for trial. In his answer, the party may deny, or he may give as his reason for inability to admit or deny the existence of a genuine issue. The party runs no risk of sanctions if the matter is genuinely in issue since Rule 37(c) provides a sanction of costs only when there are no good reasons for a failure to admit.

On the other hand, requests to admit may be so voluminous and so framed that the answering party finds the task of identifying what is in dispute and what is not unduly burdensome. If so, the responding party may obtain a protective order under Rule 26(c). * * *

Another sharp split of authority exists on the question whether a party may base his answer on lack of information or knowledge without seeking out additional information. * * *

The revised rule requires only that the answering party make reasonable inquiry and secure such knowledge and information as are readily obtainable by him. In most instances, the investigation will be necessary either to his own case or to preparation for rebuttal. Even when it is not, the information may be close enough at hand to be "readily obtainable." Rule 36 requires only that the party state that he has taken these steps. The sanction for failure of a party to inform himself before he answers lies in the award of costs after trial, as provided in Rule 37(c).

* * *

A problem peculiar to Rule 36 arises if the responding party serves answers that are not in conformity with the requirements of the rule—for example, a denial is not "specific," or the explanation of inability to admit or deny is not "in detail." Rule 36 now makes no provision for court scrutiny of such answers before trial, and it seems to contemplate that defective answers bring about admissions just as effectively as if no answer had been served. Some cases have so held. * * *

Giving a defective answer the automatic effect of an admission may cause unfair surprise. A responding party who purported to deny or to be unable to admit or deny will for the first time at trial confront the contention that he has made a binding admission. Since it is not always easy to know whether a denial is "specific" or an explanation is "in detail," neither party can know how the court will rule at trial and whether proof must be prepared. Some courts, therefore, have entertained motions to rule on defective answers. They have at times ordered that amended answers be served, when the defects were technical, and at other times have declared that the matter was admitted. * * * The rule as revised conforms to the latter practice.

Subdivision (b). * * *

The new provisions give an admission a conclusively binding effect, for purposes only of the pending action, unless the admission is withdrawn or amended. In form and substance a Rule 36 admission is comparable to an admission in pleadings or a stipulation drafted by counsel for use at trial, rather than to an evidentiary admission of a party. Louisell, *Modern California Discovery* § 8.07 (1963); 2A Barron & Holtzoff, *Federal Practice and Procedure* § 838 (Wright ed. 1961). Unless the party securing an admission can depend on its binding effect, he cannot safely avoid the expense of preparing to prove the very matters on which he has secured the admission, and the purpose of the rule is defeated.

Provision is made for withdrawal or amendment of an admission. This provision emphasizes the importance of having the action resolved on the merits, while at the same time assuring each party that justified reliance on an admission in preparation for trial will not operate to his prejudice.

Rule 37. Failure to Make Disclosure or Cooperate in Discovery: Sanctions

(a) Motion for Order Compelling Disclosure or Discovery. A party, upon reasonable notice to other parties and all persons affected thereby, may apply for an order compelling discovery as follows:

(1) *Appropriate Court.* An application for an order to a party shall be made to the court in which the action is pending. An application for an order to a person who is not a party shall be made to the court in the district where the discovery is being, or is to be, taken.

(2) *Motion.*

(A) If a party fails to make a disclosure required by Rule 26(a), any other party may move to compel disclosure and for appropriate sanctions. The motion must include a certification that the movant has in good faith conferred or attempted to confer with the party not making the disclosure in an effort to secure the disclosure without court action.

(B) If a deponent fails to answer a question propounded or submitted under Rules 30 or 31, or a corporation or other entity fails to make a designation under Rule 30(b)(6) or 31(a), or a party fails to answer an interrogatory submitted under Rule 33, or if a party, in response to a request for inspection submitted under Rule 34, fails to respond that inspection will be permitted as requested or fails to permit inspection as requested, the discovering party may move for an order compelling an answer, or a designation, or an order compelling inspection in accordance with the request. The motion must include a certification that the movant has in good faith conferred or attempted to confer with the person or party failing to make the discovery in an effort to secure the information or material without court action. When taking a deposition on oral examination, the proponent of the question may complete or adjourn the examination before applying for an order.

(3) *Evasive or Incomplete Disclosure, Answer, or Response.* For purposes of this subdivision an evasive or incomplete disclosure, answer, or response is to be treated as a failure to disclose, answer, or respond.

(4) *Expenses and Sanctions.*

(A) If the motion is granted or if the disclosure or requested discovery is provided after the motion was filed, the court shall, after affording an opportunity to be heard, require the party or deponent whose conduct necessitated the motion or the party or attorney advising such conduct or both of them to pay to the moving party the reasonable expenses incurred in making the motion, including attorney's fees, unless the court finds that the motion was filed without the movant's first making a good faith effort to obtain the disclosure or discovery without court action, or that the opposing party's nondisclosure, response, or objection was substantially justified, or that other circumstances make an award of expenses unjust.

(B) If the motion is denied, the court may enter any protective order authorized under Rule 26(c) and shall, after affording an opportunity to be heard, require the moving party or the attorney filing the motion or both of them to pay to the party or deponent who opposed the motion the reasonable expenses incurred in opposing the motion, including attorney's fees, unless the court finds that the making of the motion was substantially justified or that other circumstances make an award of expenses unjust.

(C) If the motion is granted in part and denied in part, the court may enter any protective order authorized under Rule 26(c) and may, after affording an opportunity to be heard, apportion the reasonable expenses incurred in relation to the motion among the parties and persons in a just manner.

(b) Failure to Comply With Order.

(1) *Sanctions by Court in District Where Deposition Is Taken.* If a deponent fails to be sworn or to answer a question after being directed to do so by the court in the district in which the deposition is being taken, the failure may be considered a contempt of that court.

(2) *Sanctions by Court in Which Action Is Pending.* If a party or an officer, director, or managing agent of a party or a person designated under Rule 30(b)(6) or 31(a) to testify on behalf of a party fails to obey an order to provide or permit discovery, including an order made under subdivision (a) of this rule or Rule 35, or if a party fails to obey an order entered under Rule 26(f), the court in which the action is pending may make such orders in regard to the failure as are just, and among others the following:

(A) An order that the matters regarding which the order was made or any other designated facts shall be taken to be established for the purposes of the action in accordance with the claim of the party obtaining the order;

(B) An order refusing to allow the disobedient party to support or oppose designated claims or defenses, or prohibiting that party from introducing designated matters in evidence;

(C) An order striking out pleadings or parts thereof, or staying further proceedings until the order is obeyed, or dismissing the action or proceeding or any part thereof, or rendering a judgment by default against the disobedient party;

(D) In lieu of any of the foregoing orders or in addition thereto, an order treating as a contempt of court the failure to obey any orders except an order to submit to a physical or mental examination;

(E) Where a party has failed to comply with an order under Rule 35(a) requiring that party to produce another for examination, such orders as are listed in paragraphs (A), (B), and (C) of this subdivision, unless the party failing to comply shows that that party is unable to produce such person for examination.

In lieu of any of the foregoing orders or in addition thereto, the court shall require the party failing to obey the order or the attorney advising that party or both to pay the reasonable expenses, including attorney's fees, caused by the failure, unless the court finds that the failure was substantially justified or that other circumstances make an award of expenses unjust.

(c) Failure to Disclose; False or Misleading Disclosure; Refusal to Admit.

(1) A party that without substantial justification fails to disclose information required by Rule 26(a) or 26(e)(1) shall not, unless such failure is harmless, be permitted to use as evidence at a trial, at a hearing, or on a motion any witness or information not so disclosed. In addition to or in lieu of this sanction, the court, on motion and after affording an opportunity to be heard, may impose other appropriate sanctions. In addition to requiring payment of reasonable expenses, including attorney's fees, caused by the failure, these sanctions may include any of the actions authorized under subparagraphs (A), (B), and (C) of subdivision (b)(2) of this rule and may include informing the jury of the failure to make the disclosure.

(2) If a party fails to admit the genuineness of any document or the truth of any matter as requested under Rule 36, and if the party requesting the admissions thereafter proves the genuineness of the document or the truth of the matter, the requesting party may apply to the court for an order requiring the other party to pay the reasonable expenses incurred in making that proof, including reasonable attorney's fees. The court shall make the order unless it finds that (A) the request was held objectionable pursuant to Rule 36(a), or (B) the admission sought was of no substantial importance, or (C) the party failing to admit had reasonable ground to believe that the party might prevail on the matter, or (D) there was other good reason for the failure to admit.

(d) Failure of Party to Attend at Own Deposition or Serve Answers to Interrogatories or Respond to Request for Inspection. If a party or an officer, director, or managing agent of a party or a person designated under Rule 30(b)(6) or 31(a) to testify on behalf of a party fails (1) to appear before the officer who is to take the deposition, after being served with a proper notice, or (2) to serve answers or objections to interrogatories submitted under Rule 33, after proper service of the interrogatories, or (3) to serve a written response to a request for inspection submitted under Rule 34, after proper service of the request, the court in which the action is pending on motion may make such orders in regard to the failure as are just, and among others it may take any action authorized under subparagraphs (A), (B), and (C) of subdivision (b)(2) of this rule. Any motion specifying a failure under clause (2) or (3) of this subdivision shall include a certification that the movant has in good faith conferred or attempted to confer with the party failing to answer or respond in an effort to obtain such answer or response without court action. In lieu of any order or in addition thereto, the court shall require the party failing to act or the attorney advising that party or both to pay the reasonable expenses, including attorney's fees, caused by the failure unless the court finds that the failure was substantially justified or that other circumstances make an award of expenses unjust.

The failure to act described in this subdivision may not be excused on the ground that the discovery sought is objectionable unless the party failing to act has a pending motion for a protective order as provided by Rule 26(c).

(e) [Abrogated]

(f) [Repealed. Pub.L. 96–481, Title II, § 205(a), Oct. 21, 1980, 94 Stat. 2330.]

(g) Failure to Participate in the Framing of a Discovery Plan. If a party or a party's attorney fails to participate in good faith in the development and submission of a proposed discovery plan by agreement as is required by Rule 26(f), the court may, after opportunity for hearing, require such party or attorney to pay to any other party the reasonable expenses, including attorney's fees, caused by the failure.

(As amended Dec. 29, 1948, eff. Oct. 20, 1949; Mar. 30, 1970, eff. July 1, 1970; Apr. 29, 1980, eff. Aug. 1, 1980; Pub.L. 96–481, Title II, § 205(a), Oct. 21, 1980, 94 Stat. 2330; Mar. 2, 1987, eff. Aug. 1, 1987; Apr. 22, 1993, eff. Dec. 1, 1993.)

NOTES OF ADVISORY COMMITTEE ON RULES
1993 AMENDMENT

Subdivision (a). This subdivision is revised to reflect the revision of Rule 26(a), requiring disclosure of matters without a discovery request.

Pursuant to new subdivision (a)(2)(A), a party dissatisfied with the disclosure made by an opposing party may under this rule move for an order to compel disclosure. In providing for such a motion, the revised rule parallels the provisions of the former rule dealing with failures to answer particular interrogatories. Such a motion may be needed when the information to be disclosed might be helpful to the party seeking the disclosure but not to the party required to make the disclosure. If the party required to make the disclosure would need the material to support its own contentions, the more effective enforcement of the disclosure requirement will be to exclude the evidence not disclosed, as provided in subdivision (c)(1) of this revised rule.

Language is included in the new paragraph and added to the subparagraph (B) that requires litigants to seek to resolve discovery disputes by informal means before filing a motion with the court. This requirement is based on successful experience with similar local rules of court promulgated pursuant to Rule 83.

* * *

Under revised paragraph (3), evasive or incomplete disclosures and responses to interrogatories and production requests are treated as failures

to disclose or respond.   Interrogatories and requests for production should
not be read or interpreted in an artificially restrictive or hypertechnical
manner to avoid disclosure of information fairly covered by the discovery
request, and to do so is subject to appropriate sanctions under subdivision
(a).

* * *

Subdivision (c).   The revision provides a self-executing sanction for
failure to make a disclosure required by Rule 26(a), without need for a
motion under subdivision (a)(2)(A).

Paragraph (1) prevents a party from using as evidence any witnesses or
information that, without substantial justification, has not been disclosed as
required by Rules 26(a) and 26(e)(1).   This automatic sanction provides a
strong inducement for disclosure of material that the disclosing party would
expect to use as evidence, whether at a trial, at a hearing, or on a motion,
such as one under Rule 56.   As disclosure of evidence offered solely for
impeachment purposes is not required under those rules, this preclusion
sanction likewise does not apply to that evidence.

Limiting the automatic sanction to violations "without substantial justification," coupled with the exception for violations that are "harmless," is
needed to avoid unduly harsh penalties in a variety of situations: e.g., the
inadvertent omission from a Rule 26(a)(1)(A) disclosure of the name of a
potential witness known to all parties; the failure to list as a trial witness a
person so listed by another party; or the lack of knowledge of a pro se
litigant of the requirement to make disclosures.   In the latter situation,
however, exclusion would be proper if the requirement for disclosure had
been called to the litigant's attention by either the court or another party.

Preclusion of evidence is not an effective incentive to compel disclosure
of information that, being supportive of the position of the opposing party,
might advantageously be concealed by the disclosing party.   However, the
rule provides the court with a wide range of other sanctions—such as
declaring specified facts to be established, preventing contradictory evidence,
or, like spoliation of evidence, allowing the jury to be informed of the fact of
nondisclosure—that, though not self-executing, can be imposed when found
to be warranted after a hearing.   The failure to identify a witness or
document in a disclosure statement would be admissible under the Federal
Rules of Evidence under the same principles that allow a party's interrogatory answers to be offered against it.

Subdivision (d).   This subdivision is revised to require that, where a
party fails to file any response to interrogatories or a Rule 34 request, the
discovering party should informally seek to obtain such responses before
filing a motion for sanctions.

The last sentence of this subdivision is revised to clarify that it is the
pendency of a motion for protective order that may be urged as an excuse for
a violation of subdivision (d).   If a party's motion has been denied, the party
cannot argue that its subsequent failure to comply would be justified.   In
this connection, it should be noted that the filing of a motion under Rule

26(c) is not self-executing—the relief authorized under that rule depends on obtaining the court's order to that effect.

* * *

VI. TRIALS

Rule 38. Jury Trial of Right

(a) **Right Preserved.** The right of trial by jury as declared by the Seventh Amendment to the Constitution or as given by a statute of the United States shall be preserved to the parties inviolate.

(b) **Demand.** Any party may demand a trial by jury of any issue triable of right by a jury by (1) serving upon the other parties a demand therefor in writing at any time after the commencement of the action and not later than 10 days after the service of the last pleading directed to such issue, and (2) filing the demand as required by Rule 5(d). Such demand may be indorsed upon a pleading of the party.

(c) **Same: Specification of Issues.** In the demand a party may specify the issues which the party wishes so tried; otherwise the party shall be deemed to have demanded trial by jury for all the issues so triable. If the party has demanded trial by jury for only some of the issues, any other party within 10 days after service of the demand or such lesser time as the court may order, may serve a demand for trial by jury of any other or all of the issues of fact in the action.

(d) **Waiver.** The failure of a party to serve and file a demand as required by this rule constitutes a waiver by the party of trial by jury. A demand for trial by jury made as herein provided may not be withdrawn without the consent of the parties.

(e) **Admiralty and Maritime Claims.** These rules shall not be construed to create a right to trial by jury of the issues in an admiralty or maritime claim within the meaning of Rule 9(h).

(As amended Feb. 28, 1966, eff. July 1, 1966; Mar. 2, 1987, eff. Aug. 1, 1987; Apr. 22, 1993, eff. Dec. 1, 1993.)

Rule 39. Trial by Jury or by the Court

(a) **By Jury.** When trial by jury has been demanded as provided in Rule 38, the action shall be designated upon the docket as a jury action. The trial of all issues so demanded shall be by jury, unless (1) the parties or their attorneys of record, by written stipulation filed with the court or by an oral stipulation made in open court and entered in the record, consent to trial by the court sitting without a jury or (2) the court upon motion or of its own initiative finds that a right of trial by jury of some or all of those issues does not exist under the Constitution or statutes of the United States.

(b) **By the Court.** Issues not demanded for trial by jury as provided in Rule 38 shall be tried by the court; but, notwithstanding the failure of a party to demand a jury in an action in which such a demand might have been made of right, the court in its discretion upon motion may order a trial by a jury of any or all issues.

(c) Advisory Jury and Trial by Consent. In all actions not triable of right by a jury the court upon motion or of its own initiative may try any issue with an advisory jury or, except in actions against the United States when a statute of the United States provides for trial without a jury, the court, with the consent of both parties, may order a trial with a jury whose verdict has the same effect as if trial by jury had been a matter of right.

Rule 40. Assignment of Cases for Trial

The district courts shall provide by rule for the placing of actions upon the trial calendar (1) without request of the parties or (2) upon request of a party and notice to the other parties or (3) in such other manner as the courts deem expedient. Precedence shall be given to actions entitled thereto by any statute of the United States.

Rule 41. Dismissal of Actions

(a) Voluntary Dismissal: Effect Thereof.

(1) *By Plaintiff; by Stipulation.* Subject to the provisions of Rule 23(e), of Rule 66, and of any statute of the United States, an action may be dismissed by the plaintiff without order of court (i) by filing a notice of dismissal at any time before service by the adverse party of an answer or of a motion for summary judgment, whichever first occurs, or (ii) by filing a stipulation of dismissal signed by all parties who have appeared in the action. Unless otherwise stated in the notice of dismissal or stipulation, the dismissal is without prejudice, except that a notice of dismissal operates as an adjudication upon the merits when filed by a plaintiff who has once dismissed in any court of the United States or of any state an action based on or including the same claim.

(2) *By Order of Court.* Except as provided in paragraph (1) of this subdivision of this rule, an action shall not be dismissed at the plaintiff's instance save upon order of the court and upon such terms and conditions as the court deems proper. If a counterclaim has been pleaded by a defendant prior to the service upon the defendant of the plaintiff's motion to dismiss, the action shall not be dismissed against the defendant's objection unless the counterclaim can remain pending for independent adjudication by the court. Unless otherwise specified in the order, a dismissal under this paragraph is without prejudice.

(b) Involuntary Dismissal: Effect Thereof. For failure of the plaintiff to prosecute or to comply with these rules or any order of court, a defendant may move for dismissal of an action or of any claim against the defendant. Unless the court in its order for dismissal otherwise specifies, a dismissal under this subdivision and any dismissal not provided for in this rule, other than a dismissal for lack of jurisdiction, for improper venue, or for failure to join a party under Rule 19, operates as an adjudication upon the merits.

(c) Dismissal of Counterclaim, Cross–Claim, or Third–Party Claim. The provisions of this rule apply to the dismissal of any counterclaim, cross-claim, or third-party claim. A voluntary dismissal by the claimant alone pursuant to paragraph (1) of subdivision (a) of this rule shall be made before a responsive pleading is served or, if there is none, before the introduction of evidence at the trial or hearing.

(d) Costs of Previously Dismissed Action. If a plaintiff who has once dismissed an action in any court commences an action based upon or including the same claim against the same defendant, the court may make such order for the payment of costs of the action previously dismissed as it may deem proper and may stay the proceedings in the action until the plaintiff has complied with the order.

(As amended Dec. 27, 1946, eff. Mar. 19, 1948; Jan. 21, 1963, eff. July 1, 1963; Feb. 28, 1966, eff. July 1, 1966; Dec. 4, 1967, eff. July 1, 1968; Mar. 2, 1987, eff. Aug. 1, 1987; Apr. 30, 1991, eff. Dec. 1, 1991.)

Rule 42. Consolidation; Separate Trials

(a) Consolidation. When actions involving a common question of law or fact are pending before the court, it may order a joint hearing or trial of any or all the matters in issue in the actions; it may order all the actions consolidated; and it may make such orders concerning proceedings therein as may tend to avoid unnecessary costs or delay.

(b) Separate Trials. The court, in furtherance of convenience or to avoid prejudice, or when separate trials will be conducive to expedition and economy, may order a separate trial of any claim, cross-claim, counterclaim, or third-party claim, or of any separate issue or of any number of claims, cross-claims, counterclaims, third-party claims, or issues, always preserving inviolate the right of trial by jury as declared by the Seventh Amendment to the Constitution or as given by a statute of the United States.

(As amended Feb. 28, 1966, eff. July 1, 1966.)

Rule 43. Taking of Testimony

(a) Form. In all trials the testimony of witnesses shall be taken orally in open court, unless otherwise provided by an Act of Congress or by these rules, the Federal Rules of Evidence, or other rules adopted by the Supreme Court.

(b), (c) [Abrogated]

(d) Affirmation in Lieu of Oath. Whenever under these rules an oath is required to be taken, a solemn affirmation may be accepted in lieu thereof.

(e) Evidence on Motions. When a motion is based on facts not appearing of record the court may hear the matter on affidavits presented by the respective parties, but the court may direct that the matter be heard wholly or partly on oral testimony or deposition.

(f) Interpreters. The court may appoint an interpreter of its own selection and may fix the interpreter's reasonable compensation. The compensation shall be paid out of funds provided by law or by one or more of the parties as the court may direct, and may be taxed ultimately as costs, in the discretion of the court.

(As amended Feb. 28, 1966, eff. July 1, 1966; Nov. 20, 1972, eff. July 1, 1975; Dec. 18, 1972, eff. July 1, 1975; Mar. 2, 1987, eff. Aug. 1, 1987).

Rule 44. Proof of Official Record

(a) Authentication.

(1) *Domestic.* An official record kept within the United States, or any state, district, or commonwealth, or within a territory subject to the administrative or judicial jurisdiction of the United States, or an entry therein, when admissible for any purpose, may be evidenced by an official publication thereof or by a copy attested by the officer having the legal custody of the record, or by the officer's deputy, and accompanied by a certificate that such officer has the custody. The certificate may be made by a judge of a court of record of the district or political subdivision in which the record is kept, authenticated by the seal of the court, or may be made by any public officer having a seal of office and having official duties in the district or political subdivision in which the record is kept, authenticated by the seal of the officer's office.

(2) *Foreign.* A foreign official record, or an entry therein, when admissible for any purpose, may be evidenced by an official publication thereof; or a copy thereof, attested by a person authorized to make the attestation, and accompanied by a final certification as to the genuineness of the signature and official position (i) of the attesting person, or (ii) of any foreign official whose certificate of genuineness of signature and official position relates to the attestation or is in a chain of certificates of genuineness of signature and official position relating to the attestation. A final certification may be made by a secretary of embassy or legation, consul general, vice consul, or consular agent of the United States, or a diplomatic or consular official of the foreign country assigned or accredited to the United States. If reasonable opportunity has been given to all parties to investigate the authenticity and accuracy of the documents, the court may, for good cause shown, (i) admit an attested copy without final certification or (ii) permit the foreign official record to be evidenced by an attested summary with or without a final certification. The final certification is unnecessary if the record and the attestation are certified as provided in a treaty or convention to which the United States and the foreign country in which the official record is located are parties.

(b) Lack of Record. A written statement that after diligent search no record or entry of a specified tenor is found to exist in the records designated by the statement, authenticated as provided in subdivision (a)(1) of this rule in the case of a domestic record, or complying with the requirements of subdivision (a)(2) of this rule for a summary in the case of a foreign record, is admissible as evidence that the records contain no such record or entry.

(c) Other Proof. This rule does not prevent the proof of official records or of entry or lack of entry therein by any other method authorized by law.

(As amended Feb. 28, 1966, eff. July 1, 1966; Mar. 2, 1987, eff. Aug. 1, 1987; Apr. 30, 1991, eff. Dec. 1, 1991.)

Rule 44.1   Determination of Foreign Law

A party who intends to raise an issue concerning the law of a foreign country shall give notice by pleadings or other reasonable written notice. The court, in determining foreign law, may consider any relevant material or source, including testimony, whether or not submitted by a party or admissible under the Federal Rules of Evidence. The court's determination shall be treated as a ruling on a question of law.

(Added Feb. 28, 1966, eff. July 1, 1966, and amended Nov. 20, 1972, eff. July 1, 1975; Mar. 2, 1987, eff. Aug. 1, 1987.)

Rule 45.   Subpoena

(a) Form; Issuance.

(1) Every subpoena shall

(A) state the name of the court from which it is issued; and

(B) state the title of the action, the name of the court in which it is pending, and its civil action number; and

(C) command each person to whom it is directed to attend and give testimony or to produce and permit inspection and copying of designated books, documents or tangible things in the possession, custody or control of that person, or to permit inspection of premises, at a time and place therein specified; and

(D) set forth the text of subdivisions (c) and (d) of this rule.

A command to produce evidence or to permit inspection may be joined with a command to appear at trial or hearing or at deposition, or may be issued separately.

(2) A subpoena commanding attendance at a trial or hearing shall issue from the court for the district in which the hearing or trial is to be held. A subpoena for attendance at a deposition shall issue from the court for the district designated by the notice of deposition as the district in which the deposition is to be taken. If separate from a subpoena commanding the attendance of a person, a subpoena for production or inspection shall issue from the court for the district in which the production or inspection is to be made.

(3) The clerk shall issue a subpoena, signed but otherwise in blank, to a party requesting it, who shall complete it before service. An attorney as officer of the court may also issue and sign a subpoena on behalf of

   (A) a court in which the attorney is authorized to practice; or

   (B) a court for a district in which a deposition or production is compelled by the subpoena, if the deposition or production pertains to an action pending in a court in which the attorney is authorized to practice.

(b) Service.

(1) A subpoena may be served by any person who is not a party and is not less than 18 years of age. Service of a subpoena upon a person named therein shall be made by delivering a copy thereof to such person and, if the person's attendance is commanded, by tendering to that person the fees for one day's attendance and the mileage allowed by law. When the subpoena is issued on behalf of the United States or an officer or agency thereof, fees and mileage need not be tendered. Prior notice of any commanded production of documents and things or inspection of premises before trial shall be served on each party in the manner prescribed by Rule 5(b).

(2) Subject to the provisions of clause (ii) of subparagraph (c)(3)(A) of this rule, a subpoena may be served at any place within the district of the court by which it is issued, or at any place without the district that is within 100 miles of the place of the deposition, hearing, trial, production, or inspection specified in the subpoena or at any place within the state where a state statute or rule of court permits service of a subpoena issued by a state court of general jurisdiction sitting in the place of the deposition, hearing, trial, production, or inspection specified in the subpoena. When a statute of the United States provides therefor, the court upon proper application and cause shown may authorize the service of a subpoena at any other place. A subpoena directed to a witness in a foreign country who is a national or resident of the United States shall issue under the circumstances and in the manner and be served as provided in Title 28, U.S.C. § 1783.

(3) Proof of service when necessary shall be made by filing with the clerk of the court by which the subpoena is issued a statement of the date and manner of service and of the names of the persons served, certified by the person who made the service.

(c) Protection of Persons Subject to Subpoenas.

(1) A party or an attorney responsible for the issuance and service of a subpoena shall take reasonable steps to avoid imposing undue burden or expense on a person subject to that subpoena. The court on behalf of which the subpoena was issued shall enforce this duty and impose upon the party or attorney in breach of this duty an appropriate sanction, which may include, but is not limited to, lost earnings and a reasonable attorney's fee.

(2)(A) A person commanded to produce and permit inspection and copying of designated books, papers, documents or tangible things, or inspection of premises need not appear in person at the place of production or inspection unless commanded to appear for deposition, hearing or trial.

(B) Subject to paragraph (d)(2) of this rule, a person commanded to produce and permit inspection and copying may, within 14 days after service of the subpoena or before the time specified for compliance if such time is less than 14 days after service, serve upon the party or attorney designated in the subpoena written objection to inspection or copying of any or all of the designated materials or of the premises. If objection is made, the party serving the subpoena shall not be entitled to inspect and copy the materials or inspect the premises except pursuant to an order of the court by which the subpoena was issued. If objection has been made, the party serving the subpoena may, upon notice to the person commanded to produce, move at any time for an order to compel the production. Such an order to compel production shall protect any person who is not a party or an officer of a party from significant expense resulting from the inspection and copying commanded.

(3)(A) On timely motion, the court by which a subpoena was issued shall quash or modify the subpoena if it

(i) fails to allow reasonable time for compliance;

(ii) requires a person who is not a party or an officer of a party to travel to a place more than 100 miles from the place where that person resides, is employed or regularly transacts business in person, except that, subject to the provisions of clause (c)(3)(B)(iii) of this rule, such a person may in order to attend trial be commanded to travel from any such place within the state in which the trial is held, or

(iii) requires disclosure of privileged or other protected matter and no exception or waiver applies, or

(iv) subjects a person to undue burden.

(B) If a subpoena

(i) requires disclosure of a trade secret or other confidential research, development, or commercial information, or

(ii) requires disclosure of an unretained expert's opinion or information not describing specific events or occurrences in dispute and resulting from the expert's study made not at the request of any party, or

(iii) requires a person who is not a party or an officer of a party to incur substantial expense to travel more than 100 miles to attend trial, the court may, to protect a person subject to or affected by the subpoena, quash or modify the subpoena or, if the party in whose behalf the subpoena is issued shows a substantial need for the testimony or material that cannot be otherwise met without undue hardship and assures that the person to whom the subpoena is addressed will be reasonably compensated, the court may order appearance or production only upon specified conditions.

(d) Duties in Responding to Subpoena.

(1) A person responding to a subpoena to produce documents shall produce them as they are kept in the usual course of business or shall organize and label them to correspond with the categories in the demand.

(2) When information subject to a subpoena is withheld on a claim that it is privileged or subject to protection as trial preparation materials, the claim shall be made expressly and shall be supported by a description of the nature of the documents, communications, or things not produced that is sufficient to enable the demanding party to contest the claim.

(e) Contempt. Failure by any person without adequate excuse to obey a subpoena served upon that person may be deemed a contempt of the court from which the subpoena issued. An adequate cause for failure to obey exists when a subpoena purports to require a non-party to attend or produce at a place not within the limits provided by clause (ii) of subparagraph (c)(3)(A).

(As amended Dec. 27, 1946, eff. Mar. 19, 1948; Dec. 29, 1948, eff. Oct. 20, 1949; Mar. 30, 1970, eff. July 1, 1970; Apr. 29, 1980, eff. Aug. 1, 1980; Apr. 29, 1985, eff. Aug. 1, 1985; Mar. 2, 1987, eff. Aug. 1, 1987; Apr. 30, 1991, eff. Dec. 1, 1991.)

NOTES OF ADVISORY COMMITTEE ON RULES
1991 AMENDMENT

* * *

Subdivision (a). This subdivision is amended in seven significant respects.

First, Paragraph (a)(3) modifies the requirement that a subpoena be issued by the clerk of court. Provision is made for the issuance of subpoenas by attorneys as officers of the court. This revision perhaps culminates an evolution. Subpoenas were long issued by specific order of the court. As this became a burden to the court, general orders were made authorizing clerks to issue subpoenas on request. Since 1948, they have been issued in blank by the clerk of any federal court to any lawyer, the clerk serving as stationer to the bar. In allowing counsel to issue the subpoena, the rule is merely a recognition of present reality.

Although the subpoena is in a sense the command of the attorney who completes the form, defiance of a subpoena is nevertheless an act in defiance of a court order and exposes the defiant witness to contempt sanctions.

* * *

Necessarily accompanying the evolution of this power of the lawyer as officer of the court is the development of increased responsibility and liability for the misuse of this power. The latter development is reflected in the provisions of subdivision (c) of this rule, and also in the requirement imposed by paragraph (3) of this subdivision that the attorney issuing a subpoena must sign it.

Second, Paragraph (a)(3) authorizes attorneys in distant districts to serve as officers authorized to issue commands in the name of the court. Any attorney permitted to represent a client in a federal court, even one admitted pro haec vice, has the same authority as a clerk to issue a subpoena from any federal court for the district in which the subpoena is served and enforced. In authorizing attorneys to issue subpoenas from distant courts, the amended rule effectively authorizes service of a subpoena anywhere in the United States by an attorney representing any party. * * *

Third, in order to relieve attorneys of the need to secure an appropriate seal to affix to a subpoena issued as an officer of a distant court, the requirement that a subpoena be under seal is abolished by the provisions of Paragraph (a)(1).

Fourth, Paragraph (a)(1) authorizes the issuance of a subpoena to compel a non-party to produce evidence independent of any deposition. This revision spares the necessity of a deposition of the custodian of evidentiary material required to be produced. A party seeking additional production from a person subject to such a subpoena may serve an additional subpoena requiring additional production at the same time and place.

Fifth, Paragraph (a)(2) makes clear that the person subject to the subpoena is required to produce materials in that person's control whether or not the materials are located within the district or within the territory within which the subpoena can be served. The non-party witness is subject to the same scope of discovery under this rule as that person would be as a party to whom a request is addressed pursuant to Rule 34.

Sixth, Paragraph (a)(1) requires that the subpoena include a statement of the rights and duties of witnesses by setting forth in full the text of the new subdivisions (c) and (d).

Seventh, the revised rule authorizes the issuance of a subpoena to compel the inspection of premises in the possession of a non-party. Rule 34 has authorized such inspections of premises in the possession of a party as discovery compelled under Rule 37, but prior practice required an independent proceeding to secure such relief ancillary to the federal proceeding when the premises were not in the possession of a party. Practice in some states has long authorized such use of a subpoena for this purpose without apparent adverse consequence.

* * *

Subdivision (c). This provision is new and states the rights of witnesses. It is not intended to diminish rights conferred by Rules 26–37 or any other authority.

Paragraph (c)(1) gives specific application to the principle stated in Rule 26(g) and specifies liability for earnings lost by a non-party witness as a result of a misuse of the subpoena. No change in existing law is thereby effected. Abuse of a subpoena is an actionable tort, and the duty of the attorney to the non-party is also embodied in Model Rule of Professional Conduct 4.4. The liability of the attorney is correlative to the expanded power of the attorney to issue subpoenas. The liability may include the cost of fees to collect attorneys' fees owed as a result of a breach of this duty.

* * *

A non-party required to produce documents or materials is protected against significant expense resulting from involuntary assistance to the court. This provision applies, for example, to a non-party required to provide a list of class members.

* * *

Clause (c)(3)(B)(ii) provides appropriate protection for the intellectual property of the non-party witness; it does not apply to the expert retained by a party, whose information is subject to the provisions of Rule 26(b)(4). A growing problem has been the use of subpoenas to compel the giving of evidence and information by unretained experts. Experts are not exempt from the duty to give evidence, even if they cannot be compelled to prepare themselves to give effective testimony, but compulsion to give evidence may threaten the intellectual property of experts denied the opportunity to bargain for the value of their services. Arguably the compulsion to testify can be regarded as a "taking" of intellectual property. The rule establishes the right of such persons to withhold their expertise, at least unless the party seeking it makes the kind of showing required for a conditional denial of a motion to quash as provided in the final sentence of subparagraph (c)(3)(B); that requirement is the same as that necessary to secure work product under Rule 26(b)(3) and gives assurance of reasonable compensation.

* * *

Rule 46. Exceptions Unnecessary

Formal exceptions to rulings or orders of the court are unnecessary; but for all purposes for which an exception has heretofore been necessary it is sufficient that a party, at the time the ruling or order of the court is made or sought, makes known to the court the action which the party desires the court to take or the party's objection to the action of the court and the grounds therefor; and, if a party has no opportunity to object to a ruling or order at the time it is made, the absence of an objection does not thereafter prejudice the party.

(As amended Mar. 2, 1987, eff. Aug. 1, 1987.)

Rule 47. Jurors

(a) **Examination of Jurors.** The court may permit the parties or their attorneys to conduct the examination of prospective jurors or may itself conduct the examination. In the latter event, the court shall permit the parties or their attorneys to supplement the examination by such further inquiry as it deems proper or shall itself submit to the prospective jurors such additional questions of the parties or their attorneys as it deems proper.

(b) **Peremptory Challenges.** The court shall allow the number of peremptory challenges provided by 28 U.S.C. § 1870.

(c) **Excuse.** The court may for good cause excuse a juror from service during trial or deliberation.

(As amended Feb. 28, 1966, eff. July 1, 1966; Apr. 30, 1991, eff. Dec. 1, 1991.)

Rule 48. Number of Jurors—Participation in Verdict

The court shall seat a jury of not fewer than six and not more than twelve members and all jurors shall participate in the verdict unless excused from service by the court pursuant to Rule 47(c). Unless the parties otherwise stipulate, (1) the verdict shall be unanimous and (2) no verdict shall be taken from a jury reduced in size to fewer than six members.

(As amended Apr. 30, 1991, eff. Dec. 1, 1991.)

Rule 49. Special Verdicts and Interrogatories

(a) **Special Verdicts.** The court may require a jury to return only a special verdict in the form of a special written finding upon each issue of fact. In that event the court may submit to the jury written questions susceptible of categorical or other brief answer or may submit written forms of the several special findings which might properly be made under the pleadings and evidence; or it may use such other method of submitting the issues and requiring the written findings thereon as it deems most appropriate. The court shall give to the jury such explanation and instruction concerning the matter thus submitted as may be necessary to enable the jury to make its findings upon each issue. If in so doing the court omits any issue of fact raised by the pleadings or by the evidence, each party waives the right to a trial by jury of the issue so omitted unless before the jury retires the party demands its submission to the jury. As to an issue omitted without such demand the court may make a finding; or, if it fails to do so, it shall be deemed to have made a finding in accord with the judgment on the special verdict.

(b) **General Verdict Accompanied by Answer to Interrogatories.** The court may submit to the jury, together with appropriate forms for a general verdict, written interrogatories upon one or more issues of fact the decision of which is necessary to a verdict. The court shall give such explanation or instruction as may be necessary to enable the jury both to make answers to the interrogatories and to render a general verdict, and the court shall direct the jury both to make written answers and to render a general verdict. When the general verdict and the answers are harmonious, the appropriate judgment upon the verdict and answers shall be entered pursuant to Rule 58. When the answers are consistent with each other but one or more is inconsistent with the general verdict, judgment may be entered pursuant to Rule 58 in accordance with the answers, notwithstanding the general verdict, or the court may return the jury for further consideration of its answers and verdict or may order a new trial. When the answers are inconsistent with each other and one or more is likewise inconsistent with the general verdict, judgment shall not be entered, but the court shall return the jury for further consideration of its answers and verdict or shall order a new trial.

(As amended Jan. 21, 1963, eff. July 1, 1963; Mar. 2, 1987, eff. Aug. 1, 1987.)

Rule 50. Judgment as a Matter of Law in Actions Tried by Jury; Alternative Motion for New Trial; Conditional Rulings

(a) Judgment as a Matter of Law.

(1) If during a trial by jury a party has been fully heard on an issue and there is no legally sufficient evidentiary basis for a reasonable jury to find for that party on that issue, the court may determine the issue against that party and may grant a motion for judgment as a matter of law against that party with respect to a claim or defense that cannot under the controlling law be maintained or defeated without a favorable finding on that issue.

(2) Motions for judgment as a matter of law may be made at any time before submission of the case to the jury. Such a motion shall specify the judgment sought and the law and the facts on which the moving party is entitled to the judgment.

(b) Renewal of Motion for Judgment After Trial; Alternative Motion for New Trial.

Whenever a motion for a judgment as a matter of law made at the close of all the evidence is denied or for any reason is not granted, the court is deemed to have submitted the action to the jury subject to a later determination of the legal questions raised by the motion. Such a motion may be renewed by service and filing not later than 10 days after entry of judgment. A motion for a new trial under Rule 59 may be joined with a renewal of the motion for judgment as a matter of law, or a new trial may be requested in the alternative. If a verdict was returned, the court may, in disposing of the renewed motion, allow the judgment to stand or may reopen the judgment and either order a new trial or direct the entry of judgment as a matter of law. If no verdict was returned, the court may, in disposing of the renewed motion, direct the entry of judgment as a matter of law or may order a new trial.

(c) Same: Conditional Rulings on Grant of Motion for Judgment as a Matter of Law.

(1) If the renewed motion for judgment as a matter of law is granted, the court shall also rule on the motion for a new trial, if any, by determining whether it should be granted if the judgment is thereafter vacated or reversed, and shall specify the grounds for granting or denying the motion for the new trial. If the motion for a new trial is thus conditionally granted, the order thereon does not affect the finality of the judgment. In case the motion for a new trial has been conditionally granted and the judgment is reversed on appeal, the new trial shall

proceed unless the appellate court has otherwise ordered. In case the motion for a new trial has been conditionally denied, the appellee on appeal may assert error in that denial; and if the judgment is reversed on appeal, subsequent proceedings shall be in accordance with the order of the appellate court.

(2) The party against whom judgment as a matter of law has been rendered may serve a motion for a new trial pursuant to Rule 59 not later than 10 days after entry of the judgment.

(d) Same: Denial of Motion for Judgment as a Matter of Law. If the motion for judgment as a matter of law is denied, the party who prevailed on that motion may, as appellee, assert grounds entitling the party to a new trial in the event the appellate court concludes that the trial court erred in denying the motion for judgment. If the appellate court reverses the judgment, nothing in this rule precludes it from determining that the appellee is entitled to a new trial, or from directing the trial court to determine whether a new trial shall be granted.

(As amended Jan. 21, 1963, eff. July 1, 1963; Mar. 2, 1987, eff. Aug. 1, 1987; Apr. 30, 1991, eff. Dec. 1, 1991; Apr. 22, 1993, eff. Dec. 1, 1993.)

NOTES OF ADVISORY COMMITTEE ON RULES
1991 AMENDMENT

* * *

The revision abandons the familiar terminology of *direction of verdict* for several reasons. The term is misleading as a description of the relationship between judge and jury. It is also freighted with anachronisms some of which are the subject of the text of former subdivision (a) of this rule that is deleted in this revision. Thus, it should not be necessary to state in the text of this rule that a motion made pursuant to it is not a waiver of the right to jury trial, and only the antiquities of directed verdict practice suggest that it might have been. The term "judgment as a matter of law" is an almost equally familiar term and appears in the text of Rule 56; its use in Rule 50 calls attention to the relationship between the two rules. Finally, the change enables the rule to refer to pre-verdict and post-verdict motions with a terminology that does not conceal the common identity of two motions made at different times in the proceeding.

* * *

Paragraph (a)(1) articulates the standard for the granting of a motion for judgment as a matter of law. It effects no change in the existing standard. That existing standard was not expressed in the former rule, but was articulated in long-standing case law. The expressed standard makes clear that action taken under the rule is a performance of the court's duty to assure enforcement of the controlling law and is not an intrusion on any responsibility for factual determinations conferred on the jury by the Seventh Amendment or any other provision of federal law. Because this standard is also used as a reference point for entry of summary judgment under 56(a), it serves to link the two related provisions.

The revision authorizes the court to perform its duty to enter judgment as a matter of law at any time during the trial, as soon as it is apparent that either party is unable to carry a burden of proof that is essential to that party's case. Thus, the second sentence of paragraph (a)(1) authorizes the court to consider a motion for judgment as a matter of law as soon as a party has completed a presentation on a fact essential to that party's case. Such early action is appropriate when economy and expedition will be served. In no event, however, should the court enter judgment against a party who has not been apprised of the materiality of the dispositive fact and been afforded an opportunity to present any available evidence bearing on that fact. * * *

Paragraph (a)(2) retains the requirement that a motion for judgment be made prior to the close of the trial, subject to renewal after a jury verdict has been rendered. The purpose of this requirement is to assure the responding party an opportunity to cure any deficiency in that party's proof that may have been overlooked until called to the party's attention by a late motion for judgment.

* * *

Subdivision (b). This provision retains the concept of the former rule that the post-verdict motion is a renewal of an earlier motion made at the close of the evidence. One purpose of this concept was to avoid any question arising under the Seventh Amendment. It remains useful as a means of defining the appropriate issue posed by the post-verdict motion. A post-trial motion for judgment can be granted only on grounds advanced in the pre-verdict motion.

Often it appears to the court or to the moving party that a motion for judgment as a matter of law made at the close of the evidence should be reserved for a post-verdict decision. This is so because a jury verdict for the moving party moots the issue and because a pre-verdict ruling gambles that a reversal may result in a new trial that might have been avoided. For these reasons, the court may often wisely decline to rule on a motion for judgment as a matter of law made at the close of the evidence, and it is not inappropriate for the moving party to suggest such a postponement of the ruling until after the verdict has been rendered.

* * *

Rule 51. Instructions to Jury; Objection

At the close of the evidence or at such earlier time during the trial as the court reasonably directs, any party may file written requests that the court instruct the jury on the law as set forth in the requests. The court shall inform counsel of its proposed action upon the requests prior to their arguments to the jury. The court, at its election, may instruct the jury before or after argument, or both. No party may assign as error the giving or the failure to give an instruction unless that party objects thereto before the jury retires to consider its verdict, stating distinctly the matter objected to and the grounds of the objection. Opportunity shall be given to make the objection out of the hearing of the jury.

(As amended Mar. 2, 1987, eff. Aug. 1, 1987.)

Rule 52. Findings by the Court; Judgment on Partial Findings

(a) **Effect.** In all actions tried upon the facts without a jury or with an advisory jury, the court shall find the facts specially and state separately its conclusions of law thereon, and judgment shall be entered pursuant to Rule 58; and in granting or refusing interlocutory injunctions the court shall similarly set forth the findings of fact and conclusions of law which constitute the grounds of its action. Requests for findings are not necessary for purposes of review. Findings of fact, whether based on oral or documentary evidence, shall not be set aside unless clearly erroneous, and due regard shall be given to the opportunity of the trial court to judge of the credibility of the witnesses. The findings of a master, to the extent that the court adopts them, shall be considered as the findings of the court. It will be sufficient if the findings of fact and conclusions of law are stated orally and recorded in open court following the close of the evidence or appear in an opinion or memorandum of decision filed by the court. Findings of fact and conclusions of law are unnecessary on decisions of motions under Rules 12 or 56 or any other motion except as provided in subdivision (c) of this rule.

(b) **Amendment.** Upon motion of a party made not later than 10 days after entry of judgment the court may amend its findings or make additional findings and may amend the judgment accordingly. The motion may be made with a motion for a new trial pursuant to Rule 59. When findings of fact are made in actions tried by the court without a jury, the question of the sufficiency of the evidence to support the findings may thereafter be raised whether or not the party raising the question has made in the district court an objection to such findings or has made a motion to amend them or a motion for judgment.

(c) **Judgment on Partial Findings.** If during a trial without a jury a party has been fully heard on an issue and the court finds against the party on that issue, the court may enter judgment as a matter of law against that party with respect to a claim or defense that cannot under the controlling law be maintained or defeated without a favorable finding on that issue, or the court may decline to render any judgment until the close of all the evidence. Such a judgment shall be supported by findings of fact and conclusions of law as required by subdivision (a) of this rule.

(As amended Dec. 27, 1946, eff. Mar. 19, 1948; Jan. 21, 1963, eff. July 1, 1963; Apr. 28, 1983, eff. Aug. 1, 1983; Apr. 29, 1985, eff. Aug. 1, 1985; Apr. 30, 1991, eff. Dec. 1, 1991; Apr. 22, 1993, eff. Dec. 1, 1993.)

NOTES OF ADVISORY COMMITTEE ON RULES

1985 AMENDMENT

Rule 52(a) has been amended (1) to avoid continued confusion and conflicts among the circuits as to the standard of appellate review of findings of fact by the court, (2) to eliminate the disparity between the standard of review as literally stated in Rule 52(a) and the practice of some courts of appeals, and (3) to promote nationwide uniformity.

Some courts of appeal have stated that when a trial court's findings do not rest on demeanor evidence and evaluation of a witness' credibility, there is no reason to defer to the trial court's findings and the appellate court more readily can find them to be clearly erroneous. * * * Others go further, holding that appellate review may be had without application of the "clearly erroneous" test since the appellate court is in as good a position as the trial court to review a purely documentary record. * * *

A third group has adopted the view that the "clearly erroneous" rule applies in all nonjury cases even when findings are based solely on documentary evidence or on inferences from undisputed facts.

* * *

The principal argument advanced in favor of a more searching appellate review of findings by the district court based solely on documentary evidence is that the rationale of Rule 52(a) does not apply when the findings do not rest on the trial court's assessment of credibility of the witnesses but on an evaluation of documentary proof and the drawing of inferences from it, thus eliminating the need for any special deference to the trial court's findings. These considerations are outweighed by the public interest in the stability and judicial economy that would be promoted by recognizing that the trial court, not the appellate tribunal, should be the finder of the facts. To permit courts of appeals to share more actively in the fact-finding function would tend to undermine the legitimacy of the district courts in the eyes of litigants, multiply appeals by encouraging appellate retrial of some factual issues, and needlessly reallocate judicial authority.

Rule 53. Masters

(a) Appointment and Compensation. The court in which any action is pending may appoint a special master therein. As used in these rules the word "master" includes a referee, an auditor, an examiner, and an assessor. The compensation to be allowed to a master shall be fixed by the court, and shall be charged upon such of the parties or paid out of any fund or subject matter of the action, which is in the custody and control of the court as the court may direct; provided that this provision for compensation shall not apply when a United States magistrate judge is designated to serve as a master. The master shall not retain the master's report as security for the master's compensation; but when the party ordered to pay the compensation allowed by the court does not pay it after notice and within the time prescribed by the court, the master is entitled to a writ of execution against the delinquent party.

(b) Reference. A reference to a master shall be the exception and not the rule. In actions to be tried by a jury, a reference shall be made only when the issues are complicated; in actions to be tried without a jury, save in matters of account and of difficult computation of damages, a reference shall be made only upon a showing that some exceptional condition requires it. Upon the consent of the parties, a magistrate judge may be designated to serve as a special master without regard to the provisions of this subdivision.

(c) Powers. The order of reference to the master may specify or limit the master's powers and may direct the master to report only upon particular issues or to do or perform particular acts or to receive and report evidence only and may fix the time and place for beginning and closing the hearings and for the filing of the master's report. Subject to the specifications and limitations stated in the order, the master has and shall exercise the power to regulate all proceedings in every hearing before the master and to do all acts and take all measures necessary or proper for the efficient performance of the master's duties under the order. The master may require the production before the master of evidence upon all matters embraced in the reference, including the production of all books, papers, vouchers, documents, and writings applicable thereto. The master may rule upon the admissibility of evidence unless otherwise directed by the order of reference and has the authority to put witnesses on oath and may examine them and may call the parties to the action and examine them upon oath. When a party so requests, the master shall make a record of the evidence offered and excluded in the same manner and subject to the same limitations as provided in the Federal Rules of Evidence for a court sitting without a jury.

(d) Proceedings.

(1) *Meetings.* When a reference is made, the clerk shall forthwith furnish the master with a copy of the order of reference. Upon receipt thereof unless the order of reference otherwise provides, the master shall forthwith set a time and place for the first meeting of the parties or their attorneys to be held within 20 days after the date of the order of reference and shall notify the parties or their attorneys. It is the duty of the master to proceed with all reasonable diligence. Either party, on notice to the parties and master, may apply to the court for an order requiring the master to speed the proceedings and to make the report. If a party fails to appear at the time and place appointed, the master may proceed ex parte or, in the master's discretion, adjourn the proceedings to a future day, giving notice to the absent party of the adjournment.

(2) *Witnesses.* The parties may procure the attendance of witnesses before the master by the issuance and service of subpoenas as provided in Rule 45. If without adequate excuse a witness fails to appear or give evidence, the witness may be punished as for a contempt and be subjected to the consequences, penalties, and remedies provided in Rules 37 and 45.

(3) *Statement of Accounts.* When matters of accounting are in issue before the master, the master may prescribe the form in which the accounts shall be submitted and in any proper case may require or receive in evidence a statement by a certified public accountant who is called as a witness. Upon objection of a party to any of the items thus submitted or upon a showing that the form of statement is insufficient, the master may require a different form of statement to be furnished, or the accounts or specific items thereof to be proved by oral examination of the accounting parties or upon written interrogatories or in such other manner as the master directs.

(e) Report.

(1) *Contents and Filing.* The master shall prepare a report upon the matters submitted to the master by the order of reference and, if required to make findings of fact and conclusions of law, the master shall set them forth in the report. The master shall file the report with the clerk of the court and serve on all parties notice of the filing. In an action to be tried without a jury, unless otherwise directed by the order of reference, the master shall file with the report a transcript of the proceedings and of the evidence and the original exhibits. Unless otherwise directed by the order of reference, the master shall serve a copy of the report on each party.

(2) *In Non–Jury Actions.* In an action to be tried without a jury the court shall accept the master's findings of fact unless clearly erroneous. Within 10 days after being served with notice of the filing of the report any party may serve written objections thereto upon the other parties. Application to the court for action upon the report and upon objections thereto shall be by motion and upon notice as prescribed in Rule 6(d). The court after hearing may adopt the report or may modify it or may reject it in whole or in part or may receive further evidence or may recommit it with instructions.

(3) *In Jury Actions.* In an action to be tried by a jury the master shall not be directed to report the evidence. The master's findings upon the issues submitted to the master are admissible as evidence of the matters found and may be read to the jury, subject to the ruling of the court upon any objections in point of law which may be made to the report.

(4) *Stipulation as to Findings.* The effect of a master's report is the same whether or not the parties have consented to the reference; but, when the parties stipulate that a master's findings of fact shall be final, only questions of law arising upon the report shall thereafter be considered.

(5) *Draft Report.* Before filing the master's report a master may submit a draft thereof to counsel for all parties for the purpose of receiving their suggestions.

(f) Application to Magistrate Judge. A magistrate judge is subject to this rule only when the order referring a matter to the magistrate judge expressly provides that the reference is made under this Rule.

(As amended Feb. 28, 1966, eff. July 1, 1966; Apr. 28, 1983, eff. Aug. 1, 1983; Mar. 2, 1987, eff. Aug. 1, 1987; Apr. 30, 1991, eff. Dec. 1, 1991; Apr. 22, 1993, eff. Dec. 1, 1993.)

VII. JUDGMENT

Rule 54. Judgments; Costs

(a) Definition; Form. "Judgment" as used in these rules includes a decree and any order from which an appeal lies. A judgment shall not contain a recital of pleadings, the report of a master, or the record of prior proceedings.

(b) Judgment Upon Multiple Claims or Involving Multiple Parties. When more than one claim for relief is presented in an action, whether as a claim, counterclaim, cross-claim, or third-party claim, or when multiple parties are involved, the court may direct the entry of a final judgment as to one or more but fewer than all of the claims or parties only upon an express determination that there is no just reason for delay and upon an express direction for the entry of judgment. In the absence of such determination and direction, any order or other form of decision, however designated, which adjudicates fewer than all the claims or the rights and liabilities of fewer than all the parties shall not terminate the action as to any of the claims or parties, and the order or other form of decision is subject to revision at any time before the entry of judgment adjudicating all the claims and the rights and liabilities of all the parties.

(c) Demand for Judgment. A judgment by default shall not be different in kind from or exceed in amount that prayed for in the demand for judgment. Except as to a party against whom a judgment is entered by default, every final judgment shall grant the relief to which the party in whose favor it is rendered is entitled, even if the party has not demanded such relief in the party's pleadings.

(d) Costs; Attorneys' Fees.

(1) *Costs Other than Attorneys' Fees.* Except when express provision therefor is made either in a statute of the United States or in these rules, costs other than attorneys' fees shall be allowed as of course to the prevailing party unless the court otherwise directs; but costs against the United States, its officers, and agencies shall be imposed only to the extent permitted by law. Such costs may be taxed by the clerk on one day's notice. On motion served within 5 days thereafter, the action of the clerk may be reviewed by the court.

(2) *Attorneys' Fees.*

(A) Claims for attorneys' fees and related nontaxable expenses shall be made by motion unless the substantive law governing the action provides for the recovery of such fees as an element of damages to be proved at trial.

(B) Unless otherwise provided by statute or order of the court, the motion must be filed and served no later than 14 days after entry of judgment; must specify the judgment and the statute, rule, or other grounds entitling the moving party to the award; and must state the amount or provide a fair estimate of the amount sought. If directed by the court, the motion shall also disclose the terms of any agreement with respect to fees to be paid for the services for which claim is made.

(C) On request of a party or class member, the court shall afford an opportunity for adversary submissions with respect to the motion in accordance with Rule 43(e) or Rule 78. The court may determine issues of liability for fees before receiving submissions bearing on issues of evaluation of services for which liability is imposed by the court. The court shall find the facts and state its conclusions of law as provided in Rule 52(a), and a judgment shall be set forth in a separate document as provided in Rule 58.

(D) By local rule the court may establish special procedures by which issues relating to such fees may be resolved without extensive evidentiary hearings. In addition, the court may refer issues relating to the value of services to a special master under Rule 53 without regard to the provisions of subdivision (b) thereof and may refer a motion for attorneys' fees to a magistrate judge under Rule 72(b) as if it were a dispositive pretrial matter.

(E) The provisions of subparagraphs (A) through (D) do not apply to claims for fees and expenses as sanctions for violations of these rules or under 28 U.S.C. § 1927.

(As amended Dec. 27, 1946, eff. Mar. 19, 1948; Apr. 17, 1961, eff. July 19, 1961; Mar. 2, 1987, eff. Aug. 1, 1987; Apr. 22, 1993, eff. Dec. 1, 1993.)

Rule 55. Default

(a) **Entry.** When a party against whom a judgment for affirmative relief is sought has failed to plead or otherwise defend as provided by these rules and that fact is made to appear by affidavit or otherwise, the clerk shall enter the party's default.

(b) **Judgment.** Judgment by default may be entered as follows:

(1) *By the Clerk.* When the plaintiff's claim against a defendant is for a sum certain or for a sum which can by computation be made certain, the clerk upon request of the plaintiff and upon affidavit of the amount due shall enter judgment for that amount and costs against the defendant, if the defendant has been defaulted for failure to appear and if he is not an infant or incompetent person.

(2) *By the Court.* In all other cases the party entitled to a judgment by default shall apply to the court therefor; but no judgment by default shall be entered against an infant or incompetent person unless represented in the action by a general guardian, committee, conservator, or other such representative who has appeared therein. If the party against whom judgment by default is sought has appeared in the action, the party (or, if appearing by representative, the party's representative) shall be served with written notice of the application for judgment at least 3 days prior to the hearing on such application. If, in

order to enable the court to enter judgment or to carry it into effect, it is necessary to take an account or to determine the amount of damages or to establish the truth of any averment by evidence or to make an investigation of any other matter, the court may conduct such hearings or order such references as it deems necessary and proper and shall accord a right of trial by jury to the parties when and as required by any statute of the United States.

(c) **Setting Aside Default.** For good cause shown the court may set aside an entry of default and, if a judgment by default has been entered, may likewise set it aside in accordance with Rule 60(b).

(d) **Plaintiffs, Counterclaimants, Cross–Claimants.** The provisions of this rule apply whether the party entitled to the judgment by default is a plaintiff, a third-party plaintiff, or a party who has pleaded a cross-claim or counterclaim. In all cases a judgment by default is subject to the limitations of Rule 54(c).

(e) **Judgment Against the United States.** No judgment by default shall be entered against the United States or an officer or agency thereof unless the claimant establishes a claim or right to relief by evidence satisfactory to the court.

(As amended Mar. 2, 1987, eff. Aug. 1, 1987.)

Rule 56. Summary Judgment

(a) **For Claimant.** A party seeking to recover upon a claim, counterclaim, or cross-claim or to obtain a declaratory judgment may, at any time after the expiration of 20 days from the commencement of the action or after service of a motion for summary judgment by the adverse party, move with or without supporting affidavits for a summary judgment in the party's favor upon all or any part thereof.

(b) **For Defending Party.** A party against whom a claim, counterclaim, or cross-claim is asserted or a declaratory judgment is sought may, at any time, move with or without supporting affidavits for a summary judgment in the party's favor as to all or any part thereof.

(c) **Motions and Proceedings Thereon.** The motion shall be served at least 10 days before the time fixed for the hearing. The adverse party prior to the day of hearing may serve opposing affidavits. The judgment sought shall be rendered forthwith if the pleadings, depositions, answers to interrogatories, and admissions on file, together with the affidavits, if any, show that there is no genuine issue as to any material fact and that the moving party is entitled to a judgment as a matter of law. A summary judgment, interlocutory in character, may be rendered on the issue of liability alone although there is a genuine issue as to the amount of damages.

(d) **Case Not Fully Adjudicated on Motion.** If on motion under this rule judgment is not rendered upon the whole case or for all the relief asked and a trial is necessary, the court at the hearing of the motion, by examining the pleadings and the evidence before it and by interrogating counsel, shall if practicable ascertain what material facts exist without substantial controversy and what material facts are actually and in good faith controverted. It shall thereupon make an order specifying the facts that appear without substantial controversy, including the extent to which the amount of damages or other relief is not in controversy, and directing such further proceedings in the action as are just. Upon the trial of the action the facts so specified shall be deemed established, and the trial shall be conducted accordingly.

(e) Form of Affidavits; Further Testimony; Defense Required. Supporting and opposing affidavits shall be made on personal knowledge, shall set forth such facts as would be admissible in evidence, and shall show affirmatively that the affiant is competent to testify to the matters stated therein. Sworn or certified copies of all papers or parts thereof referred to in an affidavit shall be attached thereto or served therewith. The court may permit affidavits to be supplemented or opposed by depositions, answers to interrogatories, or further affidavits. When a motion for summary judgment is made and supported as provided in this rule, an adverse party may not rest upon the mere allegations or denials of the adverse party's pleading, but the adverse party's response, by affidavits or as otherwise provided in this rule, must set forth specific facts showing that there is a genuine issue for trial. If the adverse party does not so respond, summary judgment, if appropriate, shall be entered against the adverse party.

(f) When Affidavits are Unavailable. Should it appear from the affidavits of a party opposing the motion that the party cannot for reasons stated present by affidavit facts essential to justify the party's opposition, the court may refuse the application for judgment or may order a continuance to permit affidavits to be obtained or depositions to be taken or discovery to be had or may make such other order as is just.

(g) Affidavits Made in Bad Faith. Should it appear to the satisfaction of the court at any time that any of the affidavits presented pursuant to this rule are presented in bad faith or solely for the purpose of delay, the court shall forthwith order the party employing them to pay to the other party the amount of the reasonable expenses which the filing of the affidavits caused the other party to incur, including reasonable attorney's fees, and any offending party or attorney may be adjudged guilty of contempt.

(As amended Dec. 27, 1946, eff. Mar. 19, 1948; Jan. 21, 1963, eff. July 1, 1963; Mar. 2, 1987, eff. Aug. 1, 1987.)

NOTES OF ADVISORY COMMITTEE ON RULES
1963 AMENDMENT

Subdivision (e). * * *

The last two sentences are added to overcome a line of cases, chiefly in the Third Circuit, which has impaired the utility of the summary judgment device. A typical case is as follows: A party supports his motion for summary judgment by affidavits or other evidentiary matter sufficient to show that there is no genuine issue as to a material fact. The adverse party, in opposing the motion, does not produce any evidentiary matter, or produces some but not enough to establish that there is a genuine issue for trial. Instead, the adverse party rests on averments of his pleadings which on their face present an issue. In this situation Third Circuit cases have taken the view that summary judgment must be denied, at least if the averments are "well-pleaded," and not suppositious, conclusory, or ultimate. * * *

The very mission of the summary judgment procedure is to pierce the pleadings and to assess the proof in order to see whether there is a genuine need for trial. The Third Circuit doctrine, which permits the pleadings themselves to stand in the way of granting an otherwise justified summary judgment, is incompatible with the basic purpose of the rule. * * *

The amendment is not intended to derogate from the solemnity of the pleadings. Rather it recognizes that, despite the best efforts of counsel to make his pleadings accurate, they may be overwhelmingly contradicted by the proof available to his adversary.

Nor is the amendment designed to affect the ordinary standards applicable to the summary judgment motion. So, for example: Where an issue as to a material fact cannot be resolved without observation of the demeanor of witnesses in order to evaluate their credibility, summary judgment is not appropriate. Where the evidentiary matter in support of the motion does not establish the absence of a genuine issue, summary judgment must be denied even if no opposing evidentiary matter is presented. And summary judgment may be inappropriate where the party opposing it shows under subdivision (f) that he cannot at the time present facts essential to justify his opposition.

Rule 57. Declaratory Judgments

The procedure for obtaining a declaratory judgment pursuant to Title 28 U.S.C. § 2201, shall be in accordance with these rules, and the right to trial by jury may be demanded under the circumstances and in the manner provided in Rules 38 and 39. The existence of another adequate remedy does not preclude a judgment for declaratory relief in cases where it is appropriate. The court may order a speedy hearing of an action for a declaratory judgment and may advance it on the calendar.

(As amended Dec. 29, 1948, eff. Oct. 20, 1949.)

Rule 58. Entry of Judgment

Subject to the provisions of Rule 54(b): (1) upon a general verdict of a jury, or upon a decision by the court that a party shall recover only a sum certain or costs or that all relief shall be denied, the clerk, unless the court otherwise orders, shall forthwith prepare, sign, and enter the judgment without awaiting any direction by the court; (2) upon a decision by the court granting other relief, or upon a special verdict or a general verdict accompanied by answers to interrogatories, the court shall promptly approve the form of the judgment, and the clerk shall thereupon enter it. Every judgment shall be set forth on a separate document. A judgment is effective only when so set forth and when entered as provided in Rule 79(a). Entry of the judgment shall not be delayed, nor the time for appeal extended, in order to tax costs or award fees, except that, when a timely motion for attorneys' fees is made under Rule 54(d)(2), the court, before a notice of appeal has been filed and has become effective, may order that the motion have the same effect under Rule 4(a)(4) of the Federal Rules of Appellate Procedure as a timely motion under Rule 59. Attorneys shall not submit forms of judgment except upon direction of the court, and these directions shall not be given as a matter of course.

(As amended Dec. 27, 1946, eff. Mar. 19, 1948; Jan. 21, 1963, eff. July 1, 1963; Apr. 22, 1993, eff. Dec. 1, 1993.)

Rule 59. New Trials; Amendment of Judgments

(a) **Grounds.** A new trial may be granted to all or any of the parties and on all or part of the issues (1) in an action in which there has been a trial by jury, for any of the reasons for which new trials have heretofore been granted in actions at law in the courts of the United States; and (2) in an action tried without a jury, for any of the reasons for which rehearings have heretofore been granted in suits in equity in the courts of the United States. On a motion for a new trial in an action tried without a jury, the court may open the judgment if one has been entered, take additional testimony, amend findings of fact and conclusions of law or make new findings and conclusions, and direct the entry of a new judgment.

(b) **Time for Motion.** A motion for a new trial shall be served not later than 10 days after the entry of the judgment.

(c) **Time for Serving Affidavits.** When a motion for new trial is based upon affidavits they shall be served with the motion. The opposing party has 10 days after such service within which to serve opposing affidavits, which period may be extended for an additional period not exceeding 20 days either by the court for good cause shown or by the parties by written stipulation. The court may permit reply affidavits.

(d) **On Initiative of Court.** Not later than 10 days after entry of judgment the court of its own initiative may order a new trial for any reason for which it might have granted a new trial on motion of a party. After giving the parties notice and an opportunity to be heard on the matter, the court may grant a motion for a new trial, timely served, for a reason not stated in the motion. In either case, the court shall specify in the order the grounds therefor.

(e) **Motion to Alter or Amend a Judgment.** A motion to alter or amend the judgment shall be served not later than 10 days after entry of the judgment.

(As amended Dec. 27, 1946, eff. Mar. 19, 1948; Feb. 28, 1966, eff. July 1, 1966.)

Rule 60. Relief From Judgment or Order

(a) **Clerical Mistakes.** Clerical mistakes in judgments, orders or other parts of the record and errors therein arising from oversight or omission may be corrected by the court at any time of its own initiative or on the motion of any party and after such notice, if any, as the court orders. During the pendency of an appeal, such mistakes may be so corrected before the appeal is docketed in the appellate court, and thereafter while the appeal is pending may be so corrected with leave of the appellate court.

(b) Mistakes; Inadvertence; Excusable Neglect; Newly Discovered Evidence; Fraud, etc. On motion and upon such terms as are just, the court may relieve a party or a party's legal representative from a final judgment, order, or proceeding for the following reasons: (1) mistake, inadvertence, surprise, or excusable neglect; (2) newly discovered evidence which by due diligence could not have been discovered in time to move for a new trial under Rule 59(b); (3) fraud (whether heretofore denominated intrinsic or extrinsic), misrepresentation, or other misconduct of an adverse party; (4) the judgment is void; (5) the judgment has been satisfied, released, or discharged, or a prior judgment upon which it is based has been reversed or otherwise vacated, or it is no longer equitable that the judgment should have prospective application; or (6) any other reason justifying relief from the operation of the judgment. The motion shall be made within a reasonable time, and for reasons (1), (2), and (3) not more than one year after the judgment, order, or proceeding was entered or taken. A motion under this subdivision (b) does not affect the finality of a judgment or suspend its operation. This rule does not limit the power of a court to entertain an independent action to relieve a party from a judgment, order, or proceeding, or to grant relief to a defendant not actually personally notified as provided in Title 28, U.S.C., § 1655, or to set aside a judgment for fraud upon the court. Writs of coram nobis, coram vobis, audita querela, and bills of review and bills in the nature of a bill of review, are abolished, and the procedure for obtaining any relief from a judgment shall be by motion as prescribed in these rules or by an independent action.

(As amended Dec. 27, 1946, eff. Mar. 19, 1948; Dec. 29, 1948, eff. Oct. 20, 1949; Mar. 2, 1987, eff. Aug. 1, 1987.)

Rule 61.   Harmless Error

No error in either the admission or the exclusion of evidence and no error or defect in any ruling or order or in anything done or omitted by the court or by any of the parties is ground for granting a new trial or for setting aside a verdict or for vacating, modifying or otherwise disturbing a judgment or order, unless refusal to take such action appears to the court inconsistent with substantial justice. The court at every stage of the proceeding must disregard any error or defect in the proceeding which does not affect the substantial rights of the parties.

Rule 62.   Stay of Proceedings to Enforce a Judgment

(a) Automatic Stay; Exceptions—Injunctions, Receiverships, and Patent Accountings. Except as stated herein, no execution shall issue upon a judgment nor shall proceedings be taken for its enforcement until the expiration of 10 days after its entry. Unless otherwise ordered by the court, an interlocutory or final judgment in an action for an injunction or in a receivership action, or a judgment or order directing an accounting in an action for infringement of letters patent, shall not be stayed during the period after its entry and until an appeal is taken or during the pendency of an appeal. The provisions of subdivision (c) of this rule govern the suspending, modifying, restoring, or granting of an injunction during the pendency of an appeal.

(b) Stay on Motion for New Trial or for Judgment. In its discretion and on such conditions for the security of the adverse party as are proper, the court may stay the execution of or any proceedings to enforce a judgment pending the disposition of a motion for a new trial or to alter or amend a judgment made pursuant to Rule 59, or of a motion for relief from a judgment or order made pursuant to Rule 60, or of a motion for judgment in accordance with a motion for a directed verdict made pursuant to Rule 50, or of a motion for amendment to the findings or for additional findings made pursuant to Rule 52(b).

(c) Injunction Pending Appeal. When an appeal is taken from an interlocutory or final judgment granting, dissolving, or denying an injunction, the court in its discretion may suspend, modify, restore, or grant an injunction during the pendency of the appeal upon such terms as to bond or otherwise as it considers proper for the security of the rights of the adverse party. If the judgment appealed from is rendered by a district court of three judges specially constituted pursuant to a statute of the United States, no such order shall be made except (1) by such court sitting in open court or (2) by the assent of all the judges of such court evidenced by their signatures to the order.

(d) Stay Upon Appeal. When an appeal is taken the appellant by giving a supersedeas bond may obtain a stay subject to the exceptions contained in subdivision (a) of this rule. The bond may be given at or after the time of filing the notice of appeal or of procuring the order allowing the appeal, as the case may be. The stay is effective when the supersedeas bond is approved by the court.

(e) Stay in Favor of the United States or Agency Thereof. When an appeal is taken by the United States or an officer or agency thereof or by direction of any department of the Government of the United States and the operation or enforcement of the judgment is stayed, no bond, obligation, or other security shall be required from the appellant.

(f) Stay According to State Law. In any state in which a judgment is a lien upon the property of the judgment debtor and in which the judgment debtor is entitled to a stay of execution, a judgment debtor is entitled, in the district court held therein, to such stay as would be accorded the judgment debtor had the action been maintained in the courts of that state.

(g) Power of Appellate Court Not Limited. The provisions in this rule do not limit any power of an appellate court or of a judge or justice thereof to stay proceedings during the pendency of an appeal or to suspend, modify, restore, or grant an injunction during the pendency of an appeal or to make any order appropriate to preserve the status quo or the effectiveness of the judgment subsequently to be entered.

(h) Stay of Judgment as to Multiple Claims or Multiple Parties. When a court has ordered a final judgment under the conditions stated in Rule 54(b), the court may stay enforcement of that judgment until the entering of a subsequent judgment or judgments and may prescribe such conditions as are necessary to secure the benefit thereof to the party in whose favor the judgment is entered.

(As amended Dec. 27, 1946, eff. Mar. 19, 1948; Dec. 29, 1948, eff. Oct. 20, 1949; Apr. 17, 1961, eff. July 19, 1961; Mar. 2, 1987, eff. Aug. 1, 1987.)

Rule 63. Inability of a Judge to Proceed

If a trial or hearing has been commenced and the judge is unable to proceed, any other judge may proceed with it upon certifying familiarity with the record and determining that the proceedings in the case may be completed without prejudice to the parties. In a hearing or trial without a jury, the successor judge shall at the request of a party recall any witness whose testimony is material and disputed and who is available to testify again without undue burden. The successor judge may also recall any other witness.

(As amended Mar. 2, 1987, eff. Aug. 1, 1987; Apr. 30, 1991, eff. Dec. 1, 1991.)

VIII. PROVISIONAL AND FINAL REMEDIES

Rule 64. Seizure of Person or Property

At the commencement of and during the course of an action, all remedies providing for seizure of person or property for the purpose of securing satisfaction of the judgment ultimately to be entered in the action are available under the circumstances and in the manner provided by the law of the state in which the district court is held, existing at the time the remedy is sought, subject to the following qualifications: (1) any existing statute of the United States governs to the extent to which it is applicable; (2) the action in which any of the foregoing remedies is used shall be commenced and prosecuted or, if removed from a state court, shall be prosecuted after removal, pursuant to these rules. The remedies thus available include arrest, attachment, garnishment, replevin, sequestration, and other corresponding or equivalent remedies, however designated and regardless of whether by state procedure the remedy is ancillary to an action or must be obtained by an independent action.

Rule 65. Injunctions

(a) Preliminary Injunction.

(1) *Notice.* No preliminary injunction shall be issued without notice to the adverse party.

(2) *Consolidation of Hearing With Trial on Merits.* Before or after the commencement of the hearing of an application for a preliminary injunction, the court may order the trial of the action on the merits to be advanced and consolidated with the hearing of the application. Even when this consolidation is not ordered, any evidence received upon an application for a preliminary injunction which would be admissible upon the trial on the merits becomes part of the record on the trial and need not be repeated upon the trial. This subdivision (a)(2) shall be so construed and applied as to save to the parties any rights they may have to trial by jury.

(b) Temporary Restraining Order; Notice; Hearing; Duration. A temporary restraining order may be granted without written or oral notice to the adverse party or that party's attorney only if (1) it clearly appears from specific facts shown by affidavit or by the verified complaint that immediate and irreparable injury, loss, or damage will result to the applicant before the adverse party or that party's attorney can be heard in opposition, and (2) the applicant's attorney certifies to the court in writing the efforts, if any, which have been made to give the notice and the reasons supporting the claim that notice should not be required. Every temporary restraining order granted without notice shall be indorsed with the date and hour of issuance; shall be filed forthwith in the clerk's office and entered of record; shall define the injury and state why it is irreparable and why the order was granted without notice; and shall expire by its terms within such time after entry, not to exceed 10 days, as the court fixes, unless within the time so fixed the order, for good cause shown, is extended for a like period or unless the party against whom the order is directed consents that it may be extended for a longer period. The reasons for the extension shall be entered of record. In case a temporary restraining order is granted without notice, the motion for a preliminary injunction shall be set down for hearing at the earliest possible time and takes precedence of all matters except older matters of the same character; and when the motion comes on for hearing the party who obtained the temporary restraining order shall proceed with the application for a preliminary injunction and, if the party does not do so, the court shall dissolve the temporary restraining order. On 2 days' notice to the party who obtained the temporary restraining order without notice or on such shorter notice to that party as the court may prescribe, the adverse party may appear and move its dissolution or modification and in that event the court shall proceed to hear and determine such motion as expeditiously as the ends of justice require.

(c) Security. No restraining order or preliminary injunction shall issue except upon the giving of security by the applicant, in such sum as the court deems proper, for the payment of such costs and damages as may be incurred or suffered by any party who is found to have been wrongfully enjoined or restrained. No such security shall be required of the United States or of an officer or agency thereof.

The provisions of Rule 65.1 apply to a surety upon a bond or undertaking under this rule.

(d) Form and Scope of Injunction or Restraining Order. Every order granting an injunction and every restraining order shall set forth the reasons for its issuance; shall be specific in terms; shall describe in reasonable detail, and not by reference to the complaint or other document, the act or acts sought to be restrained; and is binding only upon the parties to the action, their officers, agents, servants, employees, and attorneys, and upon those persons in active concert or participation with them who receive actual notice of the order by personal service or otherwise.

(e) Employer and Employee; Interpleader; Constitutional Cases. These rules do not modify any statute of the United States relating to temporary restraining orders and preliminary injunctions in actions affecting employer and employee; or the provisions of Title 28, U.S.C., § 2361, relating to preliminary injunctions in actions of interpleader or in the nature of interpleader; or Title 28, U.S.C., § 2284, relating to actions required by Act of Congress to be heard and determined by a district court of three judges.

(As amended Dec. 27, 1946, eff. Mar. 19, 1948; Dec. 29, 1948, eff. Oct. 20, 1949; Feb. 28, 1966, eff. July 1, 1966; Mar. 2, 1987, eff. Aug. 1, 1987.)

Rule 65.1   Security: Proceedings Against Sureties

Whenever these rules, including the Supplemental Rules for Certain Admiralty and Maritime Claims, require or permit the giving of security by a party, and security is given in the form of a bond or stipulation or other undertaking with one or more sureties, each surety submits to the jurisdiction of the court and irrevocably appoints the clerk of the court as the surety's agent upon whom any papers affecting the surety's liability on the bond or undertaking may be served. The surety's liability may be enforced on motion without the necessity of an independent action. The motion and such notice of the motion as the court prescribes may be served on the clerk of the court, who shall forthwith mail copies to the sureties if their addresses are known.

(Added Feb. 28, 1966, eff. July 1, 1966, and amended Mar. 2, 1987, eff. Aug. 1, 1987.)

Rule 66.   Receivers Appointed by Federal Courts

An action wherein a receiver has been appointed shall not be dismissed except by order of the court. The practice in the administration of estates by receivers or by other similar officers appointed by the court shall be in accordance with the practice heretofore followed in the courts of the United States or as provided in rules promulgated by the district courts. In all other respects the action in which the appointment of a receiver is sought or which is brought by or against a receiver is governed by these rules.

(As amended Dec. 27, 1946, eff. Mar. 19, 1948; Dec. 29, 1948, eff. Oct. 20, 1949.)

Rule 67. Deposit in Court

In an action in which any part of the relief sought is a judgment for a sum of money or the disposition of a sum of money or the disposition of any other thing capable of delivery, a party, upon notice to every other party, and by leave of court, may deposit with the court all or any part of such sum or thing, whether or not that party claims all or any part of the sum or thing. The party making the deposit shall serve the order permitting deposit on the clerk of the court. Money paid into court under this rule shall be deposited and withdrawn in accordance with the provisions of Title 28, U.S.C., §§ 2041, and 2042; the Act of June 26, 1934, c. 756, § 23, as amended (48 Stat. 1236, 58 Stat. 845), U.S.C., Title 31, § 725v; or any like statute. The fund shall be deposited in an interest-bearing account or invested in an interest-bearing instrument approved by the court.

(As amended Dec. 29, 1948, eff. Oct. 20, 1949; Apr. 28, 1983, eff. Aug. 1, 1983.)

Rule 68. Offer of Judgment

At any time more than 10 days before the trial begins, a party defending against a claim may serve upon the adverse party an offer to allow judgment to be taken against the defending party for the money or property or to the effect specified in the offer, with costs then accrued. If within 10 days after the service of the offer the adverse party serves written notice that the offer is accepted, either party may then file the offer and notice of acceptance together with proof of service thereof and thereupon the clerk shall enter judgment. An offer not accepted shall be deemed withdrawn and evidence thereof is not admissible except in a proceeding to determine costs. If the judgment finally obtained by the offeree is not more favorable than the offer, the offeree must pay the costs incurred after the making of the offer. The fact that an offer is made but not accepted does not preclude a subsequent offer. When the liability of one party to another has been determined by verdict or order or judgment, but the amount or extent of the liability remains to be determined by further proceedings, the party adjudged liable may make an offer of judgment, which shall have the same effect as an offer made before trial if it is served within a reasonable time not less than 10 days prior to the commencement of hearings to determine the amount or extent of liability.

(As amended Dec. 27, 1946, eff. Mar. 19, 1948; Feb. 28, 1966, eff. July 1, 1966; Mar. 2, 1987, eff. Aug. 1, 1987.)

Rule 69. Execution

(a) **In General.** Process to enforce a judgment for the payment of money shall be a writ of execution, unless the court directs otherwise. The procedure on execution, in proceedings supplementary to and in aid of a judgment, and in proceedings on and in aid of execution shall be in accordance with the practice and procedure of the state in which the district court is held, existing at the time the remedy is sought, except that any statute of the United States governs to the extent that it is applicable. In aid of the judgment or execution, the judgment creditor or a successor in interest when that interest appears of record, may obtain discovery from any person, including the judgment debtor, in the manner provided in these rules or in the manner provided by the practice of the state in which the district court is held.

(b) Against Certain Public Officers. When a judgment has been entered against a collector or other officer of revenue under the circumstances stated in Title 28, U.S.C., § 2006, or against an officer of Congress in an action mentioned in the Act of March 3, 1875, ch. 130, § 8 (18 Stat. 401), U.S.C., Title 2, § 118, and when the court has given the certificate of probable cause for the officer's act as provided in those statutes, execution shall not issue against the officer or the officer's property but the final judgment shall be satisfied as provided in such statutes.

(As amended Dec. 29, 1948, eff. Oct. 20, 1949; Mar. 30, 1970, eff. July 1, 1970; Mar. 2, 1987, eff. Aug. 1, 1987.)

Rule 70. Judgment for Specific Acts; Vesting Title

If a judgment directs a party to execute a conveyance of land or to deliver deeds or other documents or to perform any other specific act and the party fails to comply within the time specified, the court may direct the act to be done at the cost of the disobedient party by some other person appointed by the court and the act when so done has like effect as if done by the party. On application of the party entitled to performance, the clerk shall issue a writ of attachment or sequestration against the property of the disobedient party to compel obedience to the judgment. The court may also in proper cases adjudge the party in contempt. If real or personal property is within the district, the court in lieu of directing a conveyance thereof may enter a judgment divesting the title of any party and vesting it in others and such judgment has the effect of a conveyance executed in due form of law. When any order or judgment is for the delivery of possession, the party in whose favor it is entered is entitled to a writ of execution or assistance upon application to the clerk.

IX. SPECIAL PROCEEDINGS

Rule 71. Process in Behalf of and Against Persons Not Parties

When an order is made in favor of a person who is not a party to the action, that person may enforce obedience to the order by the same process as if a party; and, when obedience to an order may be lawfully enforced against a person who is not a party, that person is liable to the same process for enforcing obedience to the order as if a party.

(As amended Mar. 2, 1987, eff. Aug. 1, 1987.)

Rule 71A. Condemnation of Property

(a) Applicability of Other Rules. The Rules of Civil Procedure for the United States District Courts govern the procedure for the condemnation of real and personal property under the power of eminent domain, except as otherwise provided in this rule.

(b) Joinder of Properties. The plaintiff may join in the same action one or more separate pieces of property, whether in the same or different ownership and whether or not sought for the same use.

(c) Complaint.

(1) *Caption.* The complaint shall contain a caption as provided in Rule 10(a), except that the plaintiff shall name as defendants the property, designated generally by kind, quantity, and location, and at least one of the owners of some part of or interest in the property.

(2) *Contents.* The complaint shall contain a short and plain statement of the authority for the taking, the use for which the property is to be taken, a description of the property sufficient for its identification, the interests to be acquired, and as to each separate piece of property a designation of the defendants who have been joined as owners thereof or of some interest therein. Upon the commencement of the action, the plaintiff need join as defendants only the persons having or claiming an interest in the property whose names are then known, but prior to any hearing involving the compensation to be paid for a piece of property, the plaintiff shall add as defendants all persons having or claiming an interest in that property whose names can be ascertained by a reasonably diligent search of the records, considering the character and value of the property involved and the interests to be acquired, and also those whose names have otherwise been learned. All others may be made defendants under the designation "Unknown Owners." Process shall be served as provided in subdivision (d) of this rule upon all defendants, whether named as defendants at the time of the commencement of the action or subsequently added, and a defendant may answer as provided in subdivision (e) of this rule. The court meanwhile may order such distribution of a deposit as the facts warrant.

(3) *Filing.* In addition to filing the complaint with the court, the plaintiff shall furnish to the clerk at least one copy thereof for the use of the defendants and additional copies at the request of the clerk or of a defendant.

(d) Process.

(1) *Notice; Delivery.* Upon the filing of the complaint the plaintiff shall forthwith deliver to the clerk joint or several notices directed to the defendants named or designated in the complaint. Additional notices directed to defendants subsequently added shall be so delivered. The delivery of the notice and its service have the same effect as the delivery and service of the summons under Rule 4.

(2) *Same; Form.* Each notice shall state the court, the title of the action, the name of the defendant to whom it is directed, that the action is to condemn property, a description of the defendant's property sufficient for its identification, the interest to be taken, the authority for the taking, the uses for which the property is to be taken, that the defendant may serve upon the plaintiff's attorney an answer within 20 days after service of the notice, and that the failure so to serve an answer constitutes a consent to the taking and to the authority of the court to proceed to hear the action and to fix the compensation. The notice shall conclude with the name of the plaintiff's attorney and an address within the district in which action is brought where the attorney may be served. The notice need contain a description of no other property than that to be taken from the defendants to whom it is directed.

(3) *Service of Notice.*

(A) *Personal Service.*   Personal service of the notice (but without copies of the complaint) shall be made in accordance with Rule 4 upon a defendant whose residence is known and who resides within the United States or a territory subject to the administrative or judicial jurisdiction of the United States.

(B) *Service by Publication.*   Upon the filing of a certificate of the plaintiff's attorney stating that the attorney believes a defendant cannot be personally served, because after diligent inquiry within the state in which the complaint is filed the defendant's place of residence cannot be ascertained by the plaintiff or, if ascertained, that it is beyond the territorial limits of personal service as provided in this rule, service of the notice shall be made on this defendant by publication in a newspaper published in the county where the property is located, or if there is no such newspaper, then in a newspaper having a general circulation where the property is located, once a week for not less than three successive weeks. Prior to the last publication, a copy of the notice shall also be mailed to a defendant who cannot be personally served as provided in this rule but whose place of residence is then known. Unknown owners may be served by publication in like manner by a notice addressed to "Unknown Owners."

Service by publication is complete upon the date of the last publication. Proof of publication and mailing shall be made by certificate of the plaintiff's attorney, to which shall be attached a printed copy of the published notice with the name and dates of the newspaper marked thereon.

(4) *Return; Amendment.*   Proof of service of the notice shall be made and amendment of the notice or proof of its service allowed in the manner provided for the return and amendment of the summons under Rule 4.

(e) **Appearance or Answer.**   If a defendant has no objection or defense to the taking of the defendant's property, the defendant may serve a notice of appearance designating the property in which the defendant claims to be interested. Thereafter, the defendant shall receive notice of all proceedings affecting it. If a defendant has any objection or defense to the taking of the property, the defendant shall serve an answer within 20 days after the service of notice upon the defendant. The answer shall identify the property in which the defendant claims to have an interest, state the nature and extent of the interest claimed, and state all the defendant's objections and defenses to the taking of the property. A defendant waives all defenses and objections not so presented, but at the trial of the issue of just compensation, whether or not the defendant has previously appeared or answered, the defendant may present evidence as to the amount of the compensation to be paid for the property, and the defendant may share in the distribution of the award. No other pleading or motion asserting any additional defense or objection shall be allowed.

(f) **Amendment of Pleadings.** Without leave of court, the plaintiff may amend the complaint at any time before the trial of the issue of compensation and as many times as desired, but no amendment shall be made which will result in a dismissal forbidden by subdivision (i) of this rule. The plaintiff need not serve a copy of an amendment, but shall serve notice of the filing, as provided in Rule 5(b), upon any party affected thereby who has appeared and, in the manner provided in subdivision (d) of this rule, upon any party affected thereby who has not appeared. The plaintiff shall furnish to the clerk of the court for the use of the defendants at least one copy of each amendment and shall furnish additional copies on the request of the clerk or of a defendant. Within the time allowed by subdivision (e) of this rule a defendant may serve an answer to the amended pleading, in the form and manner and with the same effect as there provided.

(g) **Substitution of Parties.** If a defendant dies or becomes incompetent or transfers an interest after the defendant's joinder, the court may order substitution of the proper party upon motion and notice of hearing. If the motion and notice of hearing are to be served upon a person not already a party, service shall be made as provided in subdivision (d)(3) of this rule.

(h) **Trial.** If the action involves the exercise of the power of eminent domain under the law of the United States, any tribunal specially constituted by an Act of Congress governing the case for the trial of the issue of just compensation shall be the tribunal for the determination of that issue; but if there is no such specially constituted tribunal any party may have a trial by jury of the issue of just compensation by filing a demand therefor within the time allowed for answer or within such further time as the court may fix, unless the court in its discretion orders that, because of the character, location, or quantity of the property to be condemned, or for other reasons in the interest of justice, the issue of compensation shall be determined by a commission of three persons appointed by it.

In the event that a commission is appointed the court may direct that not more than two additional persons serve as alternate commissioners to hear the case and replace commissioners who, prior to the time when a decision is filed, are found by the court to be unable or disqualified to perform their duties. An alternate who does not replace a regular commissioner shall be discharged after the commission renders its final decision. Before appointing the members of the commission and alternates the court shall advise the parties of the identity and qualifications of each prospective commissioner and alternate and may permit the parties to examine each such designee. The parties shall not be permitted or required by the court to suggest nominees. Each party shall have the right to object for valid cause to the appointment of any person as a commissioner or alternate. If a commission is appointed it shall have the powers of a master provided in subdivision (c) of Rule 53 and proceedings before it shall be governed by the provisions of paragraphs (1) and (2) of subdivision (d) of Rule 53. Its action and report shall be determined by a majority and its findings and report shall have the effect, and be dealt with by the court in accordance with the practice, prescribed in paragraph (2) of subdivision (e) of Rule 53. Trial of all issues shall otherwise be by the court.

(i) Dismissal of Action.

(1) *As of Right.* If no hearing has begun to determine the compensation to be paid for a piece of property and the plaintiff has not acquired the title or a lesser interest in or taken possession, the plaintiff may dismiss the action as to that property, without an order of the court, by filing a notice of dismissal setting forth a brief description of the property as to which the action is dismissed.

(2) *By Stipulation.* Before the entry of any judgment vesting the plaintiff with title or a lesser interest in or possession of property, the action may be dismissed in whole or in part, without an order of the court, as to any property by filing a stipulation of dismissal by the plaintiff and the defendant affected thereby; and, if the parties so stipulate, the court may vacate any judgment that has been entered.

(3) *By Order of the Court.* At any time before compensation for a piece of property has been determined and paid and after motion and hearing, the court may dismiss the action as to that property, except that it shall not dismiss the action as to any part of the property of which the plaintiff has taken possession or in which the plaintiff has taken title or a lesser interest, but shall award just compensation for the possession, title or lesser interest so taken. The court at any time may drop a defendant unnecessarily or improperly joined.

(4) *Effect.* Except as otherwise provided in the notice, or stipulation of dismissal, or order of the court, any dismissal is without prejudice.

(j) Deposit and Its Distribution. The plaintiff shall deposit with the court any money required by law as a condition to the exercise of the power of eminent domain; and, although not so required, may make a deposit when permitted by statute. In such cases the court and attorneys shall expedite the proceedings for the distribution of the money so deposited and for the ascertainment and payment of just compensation. If the compensation finally awarded to any defendant exceeds the amount which has been paid to that defendant on distribution of the deposit, the court shall enter judgment against the plaintiff and in favor of that defendant for the deficiency. If the compensation finally awarded to any defendant is less than the amount which has been paid to that defendant, the court shall enter judgment against that defendant and in favor of the plaintiff for the overpayment.

(k) Condemnation Under a State's Power of Eminent Domain. The practice as herein prescribed governs in actions involving the exercise of the power of eminent domain under the law of a state, provided that if the state law makes provision for trial of any issue by jury, or for trial of the issue of compensation by jury or commission or both, that provision shall be followed.

(*l*) Costs. Costs are not subject to Rule 54(d).

(Added Apr. 30, 1951, eff. Aug. 1, 1951, and amended Jan. 21, 1963, eff. July 1, 1963; Apr. 29, 1985, eff. Aug. 1, 1985; Mar. 2, 1987, eff. Aug. 1, 1987; Apr. 25, 1988, eff. Aug. 1, 1988; Nov. 18, 1988, Pub.L. 100–690, § 7050, 102 Stat. 4401; Apr. 22, 1993, eff. Dec. 1, 1993.)

Rule 72. Magistrate Judges; Pretrial Orders

(a) Nondispositive Matters. A magistrate judge to whom a pretrial matter not dispositive of a claim or defense of a party is referred to hear and determine shall promptly conduct such proceedings as are required and when appropriate enter into the record a written order setting forth the disposition of the matter. Within 10 days after being served with a copy of the magistrate judge's order, a party may serve and file objections to the order; a party may not thereafter assign as error a defect in the magistrate judge's order to which objection was not timely made. The district judge to whom the case is assigned shall consider such objections and shall modify or set aside any portion of the magistrate judge's order found to be clearly erroneous or contrary to law.

(b) Dispositive Motions and Prisoner Petitions. A magistrate judge assigned without consent of the parties to hear a pretrial matter dispositive of a claim or defense of a party or a prisoner petition challenging the conditions of confinement shall promptly conduct such proceedings as are required. A record shall be made of all evidentiary proceedings before the magistrate judge, and a record may be made of such other proceedings as the magistrate judge deems necessary. The magistrate judge shall enter into the record a recommendation for disposition of the matter, including proposed findings of fact when appropriate. The clerk shall forthwith mail copies to all parties.

A party objecting to the recommended disposition of the matter shall promptly arrange for the transcription of the record, or portions of it as all parties may agree upon or the magistrate judge deems sufficient, unless the district judge otherwise directs. Within 10 days after being served with a copy of the recommended disposition, a party may serve and file specific, written objections to the proposed findings and recommendations. A party may respond to another party's objections within 10 days after being served with a copy thereof. The district judge to whom the case is assigned shall make a de novo determination upon the record, or after additional evidence, of any portion of the magistrate judge's disposition to which specific written objection has been made in accordance with this rule. The district judge may accept, reject, or modify the recommended decision, receive further evidence, or recommit the matter to the magistrate judge with instructions.

(Added Apr. 28, 1983, eff. Aug. 1, 1983, and amended Apr. 30, 1991, eff. Dec. 1, 1991; Apr. 22, 1993, eff. Dec. 1, 1993.)

Rule 73. Magistrate Judges; Trial by Consent and Appeal Options

(a) **Powers; Procedure.** When specially designated to exercise such jurisdiction by local rule or order of the district court and when all parties consent thereto, a magistrate judge may exercise the authority provided by Title 28, U.S.C. § 636(c) and may conduct any or all proceedings, including a jury or nonjury trial, in a civil case. A record of the proceedings shall be made in accordance with the requirements of Title 28, U.S.C. § 636(c)(7).

(b) **Consent.** When a magistrate judge has been designated to exercise civil trial jurisdiction, the clerk shall give written notice to the parties of their opportunity to consent to the exercise by a magistrate judge of civil jurisdiction over the case, as authorized by Title 28, U.S.C. § 636(c). If, within the period specified by local rule, the parties agree to a magistrate judge's exercise of such authority, they shall execute and file a joint form of consent or separate forms of consent setting forth such election.

A district judge, magistrate judge, or other court official may again advise the parties of the availability of the magistrate judge, but, in so doing, shall also advise the parties that they are free to withhold consent without adverse substantive consequences. A district judge or magistrate judge shall not be informed of a party's response to the clerk's notification, unless all parties have consented to the referral of the matter to a magistrate judge.

The district judge, for good cause shown on the judge's own initiative, or under extraordinary circumstances shown by a party, may vacate a reference of a civil matter to a magistrate judge under this subdivision.

(c) **Normal Appeal Route.** In accordance with Title 28, U.S.C. § 636(c)(3), unless the parties otherwise agree to the optional appeal route provided for in subdivision (d) of this rule, appeal from a judgment entered upon direction of a magistrate judge in proceedings under this rule will lie to the court of appeals as it would from a judgment of the district court.

(d) **Optional Appeal Route.** In accordance with Title 28, U.S.C. § 636(c)(4), at the time of reference to a magistrate judge, the parties may consent to appeal on the record to a district judge of the court and thereafter, by petition only, to the court of appeals.

(Added Apr. 28, 1983, eff. Aug. 1, 1983, and amended Mar. 2, 1987, eff. Aug. 1, 1987; Apr. 22, 1993, eff. Dec. 1, 1993.)

Rule 74. Method of Appeal From Magistrate Judge to District Judge Under Title 28, U.S.C. § 636(c)(4) and Rule 73(d)

(a) **When Taken.** When the parties have elected under Rule 73(d) to proceed by appeal to a district judge from an appealable decision made by a magistrate judge under the consent provisions of Title 28, U.S.C. § 636(c)(4), an appeal may be taken from the decision of a magistrate judge by filing with the clerk of the district court a notice of appeal within 30 days of the date of entry of the judgment appealed from; but if the United States or an officer or agency thereof is a party, the notice of appeal may be filed by any party within 60 days of such entry. If a timely notice of appeal is filed by a party, any other party may file a notice of appeal within 14 days thereafter, or within the time otherwise prescribed by this subdivision, whichever period last expires.

The running of the time for filing a notice of appeal is terminated as to all parties by the timely filing of any of the following motions with the magistrate judge by any party, and the full time for appeal from the judgment entered by the magistrate judge commences to run anew from entry of any of the following orders: (1) granting or denying a motion for judgment under Rule 50(b); (2) granting or denying a motion under Rule 52(b) to amend or make additional findings of fact, whether or not an alteration of the judgment would be required if the motion is granted; (3) granting or denying a motion under Rule 59 to alter or amend the judgment; (4) denying a motion for a new trial under Rule 59.

An interlocutory decision or order by a magistrate judge which, if made by a district judge, could be appealed under any provision of law, may be appealed to a district judge by filing a notice of appeal within 15 days after entry of the decision or order, provided the parties have elected to appeal to a district judge under Rule 73(d). An appeal of such interlocutory decision or order shall not stay the proceedings before the magistrate judge unless the magistrate judge or district judge shall so order.

Upon a showing of excusable neglect, the magistrate judge may extend the time for filing a notice of appeal upon motion filed not later than 20 days after the expiration of the time otherwise prescribed by this rule.

(b) **Notice of Appeal; Service.** The notice of appeal shall specify the party or parties taking the appeal, designate the judgment, order or part thereof appealed from, and state that the appeal is to a judge of the district court. The clerk shall mail copies of the notice to all other parties and note the date of mailing in the civil docket.

(c) **Stay Pending Appeal.** Upon a showing that the magistrate judge has refused or otherwise failed to stay the judgment pending appeal to the district judge under Rule 73(d), the appellant may make application for a stay to the district judge with reasonable notice to all parties. The stay may be conditioned upon the filing in the district court of a bond or other appropriate security.

(d) Dismissal. For failure to comply with these rules or any local rule or order, the district judge may take such action as is deemed appropriate, including dismissal of the appeal. The district judge also may dismiss the appeal upon the filing of a stipulation signed by all parties, or upon motion and notice by the appellant.

(Added Apr. 28, 1983, eff. Aug. 1, 1983, and amended Apr. 22, 1993, eff. Dec. 1, 1993.)

Rule 75. Proceedings on Appeal From Magistrate Judge to District Judge Under Rule 73(d)

(a) Applicability. In proceedings under Title 28, U.S.C. § 636(c), when the parties have previously elected under Rule 73(d) to appeal to a district judge rather than to the court of appeals, this rule shall govern the proceedings on appeal.

(b) Record on Appeal.

(1) *Composition.* The original papers and exhibits filed with the clerk of the district court, the transcript of the proceedings, if any, and the docket entries shall constitute the record on appeal. In lieu of this record the parties, within 10 days after the filing of the notice of appeal, may file a joint statement of the case showing how the issues presented by the appeal arose and were decided by the magistrate judge, and setting forth only so many of the facts averred and proved or sought to be proved as are essential to a decision of the issues presented.

(2) *Transcript.* Within 10 days after filing the notice of appeal the appellant shall make arrangements for the production of a transcript of such parts of the proceedings as the appellant deems necessary. Unless the entire transcript is to be included, the appellant, within the time provided above, shall serve on the appellee and file with the court a description of the parts of the transcript which the appellant intends to present on the appeal. If the appellee deems a transcript of other parts of the proceedings to be necessary, within 10 days after the service of the statement of the appellant, the appellee shall serve on the appellant and file with the court a designation of additional parts to be included. The appellant shall promptly make arrangements for the inclusion of all such parts unless the magistrate judge, upon motion, exempts the appellant from providing certain parts, in which case the appellee may provide for their transcription.

(3) *Statement in Lieu of Transcript.* If no record of the proceedings is available for transcription, the parties shall, within 10 days after the filing of the notice of appeal, file a statement of the evidence from the best available means to be submitted in lieu of the transcript. If the parties cannot agree they shall submit a statement of their differences to the magistrate judge for settlement.

(c) **Time for Filing Briefs.** Unless a local rule or court order otherwise provides, the following time limits for filing briefs shall apply.

(1) The appellant shall serve and file the appellant's brief within 20 days after the filing of the transcript, statement of the case, or statement of the evidence.

(2) The appellee shall serve and file the appellee's brief within 20 days after service of the brief of the appellant.

(3) The appellant may serve and file a reply brief within 10 days after service of the brief of the appellee.

(4) If the appellee has filed a cross-appeal, the appellee may file a reply brief limited to the issues on the cross-appeal within 10 days after service of the reply brief of the appellant.

(d) **Length and Form of Briefs.** Briefs may be typewritten. The length and form of briefs shall be governed by local rule.

(e) **Oral Argument.** The opportunity for the parties to be heard on oral argument shall be governed by local rule.

(Added Apr. 28, 1983, eff. Aug. 1, 1983, and amended Mar. 2, 1987, eff. Aug. 1, 1987, Apr. 22, 1993, eff. Dec. 1, 1993.)

Rule 76. Judgment of the District Judge on the Appeal Under Rule 73(d) and Costs

(a) **Entry of Judgment.** When the parties have elected under Rule 73(d) to appeal from a judgment of the magistrate judge to a district judge, the clerk shall prepare, sign, and enter judgment in accordance with the order or decision of the district judge following an appeal from a judgment of the magistrate judge, unless the district judge directs otherwise. The clerk shall mail to all parties a copy of the order or decision of the district judge.

(b) **Stay of Judgments.** The decision of the district judge shall be stayed for 10 days during which time a party may petition the district judge for rehearing, and a timely petition shall stay the decision of the district judge pending disposition of a petition for rehearing. Upon the motion of a party, the decision of the district judge may be stayed in order to allow a party to petition the court of appeals for leave to appeal.

(c) **Costs.** Except as otherwise provided by law or ordered by the district judge, costs shall be taxed against the losing party; if a judgment of the magistrate judge is affirmed in part or reversed in part, or is vacated, costs shall be allowed only as ordered by the district judge. The cost of the transcript, if necessary for the determination of the appeal, and the premiums paid for bonds to preserve rights pending appeal shall be taxed as costs by the clerk.

(Added Apr. 28, 1983, eff. Aug. 1, 1983, and amended Apr. 22, 1993, eff. Dec. 1, 1993.)

X. DISTRICT COURTS AND CLERKS

Rule 77. District Courts and Clerks

(a) District Courts Always Open. The district courts shall be deemed always open for the purpose of filing any pleading or other proper paper, of issuing and returning mesne and final process, and of making and directing all interlocutory motions, orders, and rules.

(b) Trials and Hearings; Orders in Chambers. All trials upon the merits shall be conducted in open court and so far as convenient in a regular court room. All other acts or proceedings may be done or conducted by a judge in chambers, without the attendance of the clerk or other court officials and at any place either within or without the district; but no hearing, other than one ex parte, shall be conducted outside the district without the consent of all parties affected thereby.

(c) Clerk's Office and Orders by Clerk. The clerk's office with the clerk or a deputy in attendance shall be open during business hours on all days except Saturdays, Sundays, and legal holidays, but a district court may provide by local rule or order that its clerk's office shall be open for specified hours on Saturdays or part:cular legal holidays other than New Year's Day, Birthday of Martin Luther King, Jr., Washington's Birthday, Memorial Day, Independence Day, Labor Day, Columbus Day, Veterans Day, Thanksgiving Day, and Christmas Day. All motions and applications in the clerk's office for issuing mesne process, for issuing final process to enforce and execute judgments, for entering defaults or judgments by default, and for other proceedings which do not require allowance or order of the court are grantable of course by the clerk; but the clerk's action may be suspended or altered or rescinded by the court upon cause shown.

(d) Notice of Orders or Judgments. Immediately upon the entry of an order or judgment the clerk shall serve a notice of the entry by mail in the manner provided for in Rule 5 upon each party who is not in default for failure to appear, and shall make a note in the docket of the mailing. Any party may in addition serve a notice of such entry in the manner provided in Rule 5 for the service of papers. Lack of notice of the entry by the clerk does not affect the time to appeal or relieve or authorize the court to relieve a party for failure to appeal within the time allowed, except as permitted in Rule 4(a) of the Federal Rules of Appellate Procedure.

(As amended Dec. 27, 1946, eff. Mar. 19, 1948; Jan. 21, 1963, eff. July 1, 1963; Dec. 4, 1967, eff. July 1, 1968; Mar. 1, 1971, eff. July 1, 1971; Mar. 2, 1987, eff. Aug. 1, 1987; Apr. 30, 1991, eff. Dec. 1, 1991.)

Rule 78. Motion Day

Unless local conditions make it impracticable, each district court shall establish regular times and places, at intervals sufficiently frequent for the prompt dispatch of business, at which motions requiring notice and hearing may be heard and disposed of; but the judge at any time or place and on such notice, if any, as the judge considers reasonable may make orders for the advancement, conduct, and hearing of actions.

To expedite its business, the court may make provision by rule or order for the submission and determination of motions without oral hearing upon brief written statements of reasons in support and opposition.

(As amended Mar. 2, 1987, eff. Aug. 1, 1987.)

Rule 79. Books and Records Kept by the Clerk and Entries Therein

(a) Civil Docket. The clerk shall keep a book known as "civil docket" of such form and style as may be prescribed by the Director of the Administrative Office of the United States Courts with the approval of the Judicial Conference of the United States, and shall enter therein each civil action to which these rules are made applicable. Actions shall be assigned consecutive file numbers. The file number of each action shall be noted on the folio of the docket whereon the first entry of the action is made. All papers filed with the clerk, all process issued and returns made thereon, all appearances, orders, verdicts, and judgments shall be entered chronologically in the civil docket on the folio assigned to the action and shall be marked with its file number. These entries shall be brief but shall show the nature of each paper filed or writ issued and the substance of each order or judgment of the court and of the returns showing execution of process. The entry of an order or judgment shall show the date the entry is made. When in an action trial by jury has been properly demanded or ordered the clerk shall enter the word "jury" on the folio assigned to that action.

(b) Civil Judgments and Orders. The clerk shall keep, in such form and manner as the Director of the Administrative Office of the United States Courts with the approval of the Judicial Conference of the United States may prescribe, a correct copy of every final judgment or appealable order, or order affecting title to or lien upon real or personal property, and any other order which the court may direct to be kept.

(c) Indices; Calendars. Suitable indices of the civil docket and of every civil judgment and order referred to in subdivision (b) of this rule shall be kept by the clerk under the direction of the court. There shall be prepared under the direction of the court calendars of all actions ready for trial, which shall distinguish "jury actions" from "court actions."

(d) Other Books and Records of the Clerk. The clerk shall also keep such other books and records as may be required from time to time by the Director of the Administrative Office of the United States Courts with the approval of the Judicial Conference of the United States.

(As amended Dec. 27, 1946, eff. Mar. 19, 1948; Dec. 29, 1948, eff. Oct. 20, 1949; Jan. 21, 1963, eff. July 1, 1963.)

Rule 80. Stenographer; Stenographic Report or Transcript as Evidence

(a), (b) [Abrogated]

(c) Stenographic Report or Transcript as Evidence. Whenever the testimony of a witness at a trial or hearing which was stenographically reported is admissible in evidence at a later trial, it may be proved by the transcript thereof duly certified by the person who reported the testimony.

(As amended Dec. 27, 1946, eff. Mar. 19, 1948.)

XI.   GENERAL PROVISIONS

Rule 81. Applicability in General

(a) To What Proceedings Applicable.

(1) These rules do not apply to prize proceedings in admiralty governed by Title 10, U.S.C. §§ 7651–7681. They do not apply to proceedings in bankruptcy or proceedings in copyright under Title 17, U.S.C., except in so far as they may be made applicable thereto by rules promulgated by Supreme Court of the United States. They do not apply to mental health proceedings in the United States District Court for the District of Columbia.

(2) These rules are applicable to proceedings for admission to citizenship, habeas corpus, and quo warranto, to the extent that the practice in such proceedings is not set forth in statutes of the United States and has heretofore conformed to the practice in civil actions. The writ of habeas corpus, or order to show cause, shall be directed to the person having custody of the person detained. It shall be returned within 3 days unless for good cause shown additional time is allowed which in cases brought under 28 U.S.C. § 2254 shall not exceed 40 days, and in all other cases shall not exceed 20 days.

(3) In proceedings under Title 9, U.S.C., relating to arbitration, or under the Act of May 20, 1926, ch. 347, § 9 (44 Stat. 585), U.S.C., Title 45, § 159, relating to boards of arbitration of railway labor disputes, these rules apply only to the extent that matters of procedure are not provided for in those statutes. These rules apply to proceedings to compel the giving of testimony or production of documents in accordance with a subpoena issued by an officer or agency of the United States under any statute of the United States except as otherwise provided by statute or by rules of the district court or by order of the court in the proceedings.

(4) These rules do not alter the method prescribed by the Act of February 18, 1922, c. 57, § 2 (42 Stat. 388), U.S.C., Title 7, § 292; or by the Act of June 10, 1930, c. 436, § 7 (46 Stat. 534), as amended, U.S.C., Title 7, § 499g(c), for instituting proceedings in the United States district courts to review orders of the Secretary of Agriculture; or prescribed by the Act of June 25, 1934, c. 742, § 2 (48 Stat. 1214),

U.S.C., Title 15, § 522, for instituting proceedings to review orders of the Secretary of the Interior; or prescribed by the Act of February 22, 1935, c. 18, § 5 (49 Stat. 31), U.S.C., Title 15, § 715d(c), as extended, for instituting proceedings to review orders of petroleum control boards; but the conduct of such proceedings in the district courts shall be made to conform to these rules so far as applicable.

(5) These rules do not alter the practice in the United States district courts prescribed in the Act of July 5, 1935, c. 372, §§ 9 and 10 (49 Stat. 453), as amended, U.S.C., Title 29, §§ 159 and 160, for beginning and conducting proceedings to enforce orders of the National Labor Relations Board; and in respects not covered by those statutes, the practice in the district courts shall conform to these rules so far as applicable.

(6) These rules apply to proceedings for enforcement or review of compensation orders under the Longshoremen's and Harbor Workers' Compensation Act, Act of March 4, 1927, c. 509, §§ 18, 21 (44 Stat. 1434, 1436), as amended, U.S.C., Title 33, §§ 918, 921, except to the extent that matters of procedure are provided for in that Act. The provisions for service by publication and for answer in proceedings to cancel certificates of citizenship under the Act of June 27, 1952, c. 477, Title III, c. 2, § 340 (66 Stat. 260), U.S.C., Title 8, § 1451, remain in effect.

(7) [Abrogated]

(b) Scire Facias and Mandamus. The writs of scire facias and mandamus are abolished. Relief heretofore available by mandamus or scire facias may be obtained by appropriate action or by appropriate motion under the practice prescribed in these rules.

(c) Removed Actions. These rules apply to civil actions removed to the United States district courts from the state courts and govern procedure after removal. Repleading is not necessary unless the court so orders. In a removed action in which the defendant has not answered, the defendant shall answer or present the other defenses or objections available under these rules within 20 days after the receipt through service or otherwise of a copy of the initial pleading setting forth the claim for relief upon which the action or proceeding is based, or within 20 days after the service of summons upon such initial pleading, then filed, or within 5 days after the filing of the petition for removal, whichever period is longest. If at the time of removal all necessary pleadings have been served, a party entitled to trial by jury under Rule 38 shall be accorded it, if the party's demand therefor is served within 10 days after the petition for removal is filed if the party is the petitioner, or if not the petitioner within 10 days after service on the party of the notice of filing the petition. A party who, prior to removal, has made an express demand for trial by jury in accordance with state law, need not make a demand after removal. If state law applicable in the court from which the case is removed does not require the parties to make express demands in order to claim trial by jury, they need not make demands after removal unless the court directs that they do so within a specified time if they desire to claim trial by jury. The court may make this direction on its own motion and shall do so as a matter of course at the request of any party. The failure of a party to make demand as directed constitutes a waiver by that party of trial by jury.

(d) [Abrogated]

(e) Law Applicable. Whenever in these rules the law of the state in which the district court is held is made applicable, the law applied in the District of Columbia governs proceedings in the United States District Court for the District of Columbia. When the word "state" is used, it includes, if appropriate, the District of Columbia. When the term "statute of the United States" is used, it includes, so far as concerns proceedings in the United States District Court for the District of Columbia, any Act of Congress locally applicable to and in force in the District of Columbia. When the law of a state is referred to, the word "law" includes the statutes of that state and the state judicial decisions construing them.

(f) References to Officer of the United States. Under any rule in which reference is made to an officer or agency of the United States, the term "officer" includes a district director of internal revenue, a former district director or collector of internal revenue, or the personal representative of a deceased district director or collector of internal revenue.

(As amended Dec. 27, 1946, eff. Mar. 19, 1948; Dec. 29, 1948, eff. Oct. 20, 1949; Apr. 30, 1951, eff. Aug. 1, 1951; Jan. 21, 1963, eff. July 1, 1963; Feb. 28, 1966, eff. July 1, 1966; Dec. 4, 1967, eff. July 1, 1968; Mar. 1, 1971, eff. July 1, 1971; Mar. 2, 1987, eff. Aug. 1, 1987.)

Rule 82.   Jurisdiction and Venue Unaffected

These rules shall not be construed to extend or limit the jurisdiction of the United States district courts or the venue of actions therein. An admiralty or maritime claim within the meaning of Rule 9(h) shall not be treated as a civil action for the purposes of Title 28, U.S.C. §§ 1391–93.

(As amended Dec. 29, 1948, eff. Oct. 20, 1949; Feb. 28, 1966, eff. July 1, 1966.)

Rule 83.   Rules by District Courts

Each district court by action of a majority of the judges thereof may from time to time, after giving appropriate public notice and an opportunity to comment, make and amend rules governing its practice not inconsistent with these rules. A local rule so adopted shall take effect upon the date specified by the district court and shall remain in effect unless amended by the district court or abrogated by the judicial council of the circuit in which the district is located. Copies of rules and amendments so made by any district court shall upon their promulgation be furnished to the judicial council and the Administrative Office of the United States Courts and be made available to the public. In all cases not provided for by rule, the district judges and magistrates may regulate their practice in any manner not inconsistent with these rules or those of the district in which they act.

(As amended Apr. 29, 1985, eff. Aug. 1, 1985.)

Rule 84.　Forms

The forms contained in the Appendix of Forms are sufficient under the rules and are intended to indicate the simplicity and brevity of statement which the rules contemplate.

(As amended Dec. 27, 1946, eff. Mar. 19, 1948.)

Rule 85.　Title

These rules may be known and cited as the Federal Rules of Civil Procedure.

Rule 86.　Effective Date

(a) [Effective Date of Original Rules]. These rules will take effect on the day which is 3 months subsequent to the adjournment of the second regular session of the 75th Congress, but if that day is prior to September 1, 1938, then these rules will take effect on September 1, 1938. They govern all proceedings in actions brought after they take effect and also all further proceedings in actions then pending, except to the extent that in the opinion of the court their application in a particular action pending when the rules take effect would not be feasible or would work injustice, in which event the former procedure applies.

(b) Effective Date of Amendments. The amendments adopted by the Supreme Court on December 27, 1946, and transmitted to the Attorney General on January 2, 1947, shall take effect on the day which is three months subsequent to the adjournment of the first regular session of the 80th Congress, but, if that day is prior to September 1, 1947, then these amendments shall take effect on September 1, 1947. They govern all proceedings in actions brought after they take effect and also all further proceedings in actions then pending, except to the extent that in the opinion of the court their application in a particular action pending when the amendments take effect would not be feasible or would work injustice, in which event the former procedure applies.

(c) Effective Date of Amendments. The amendments adopted by the Supreme Court on December 29, 1948, and transmitted to the Attorney General on December 31, 1948, shall take effect on the day following the adjournment of the first regular session of the 81st Congress.

(d) Effective Date of Amendments. The amendments adopted by the Supreme Court on April 17, 1961, and transmitted to the Congress on April 18, 1961, shall take effect on July 19, 1961. They govern all proceedings in actions brought after they take effect and also all further proceedings in actions then pending, except to the extent that in the opinion of the court their application in a particular action pending when the amendments take effect would not be feasible or would work injustice, in which event the former procedure applies.

(e) Effective Date of Amendments. The amendments adopted by the Supreme Court on January 21, 1963, and transmitted to the Congress on January 21, 1963, shall take effect on July 1, 1963. They govern all proceedings in actions brought after they take effect and also all further proceedings in actions then pending, except to the extent that in the opinion of the court their application in a particular action pending when the amendments take effect would not be feasible or would work injustice, in which event the former procedure applies.

(As amended Dec. 27, 1946, eff. Mar. 19, 1948; Dec. 29, 1948, eff. Oct. 20, 1949; Apr. 17, 1961, eff. July 19, 1961; Jan. 21, 1963, and Mar. 18, 1963, eff. July 1, 1963.)

APPENDIX OF FORMS

(See Rule 84)

Introductory Statement

1. The following forms are intended for illustration only. They are limited in number. No attempt is made to furnish a manual of forms. Each form assumes the action to be brought in the Southern District of New York. If the district in which an action is brought has divisions, the division should be indicated in the caption.

2. Except where otherwise indicated each pleading, motion, and other paper should have a caption similar to that of the summons, with the designation of the particular paper substituted for the word "Summons". In the caption of the summons and in the caption of the complaint all parties must be named but in other pleadings and papers, it is sufficient to state the name of the first party on either side, with an appropriate indication of other parties. See Rules 4(b), 7(b)(2), and 10(a).

3. In Form 3 and the forms following, the words, "Allegation of jurisdiction," are used to indicate the appropriate allegation in Form 2.

4. Each pleading, motion, and other paper is to be signed in his individual name by at least one attorney of record (Rule 11). The attorney's name is to be followed by his address as indicated in Form 3. In forms following Form 3 the signature and address are not indicated.

5. If a party is not represented by an attorney, the signature and address of the party are required in place of those of the attorney.

Form 1.
SUMMONS
UNITED STATES DISTRICT COURT FOR THE SOUTHERN DISTRICT OF NEW YORK
Civil Action, File Number _____

A. B., Plaintiff   )
)
           v.   ) *Summons*
)
C.D., Defendant   )

To the above-named Defendant:

You are hereby summoned and required to serve upon _____, plaintiff's attorney, whose address is _____, an answer to the complaint which is herewith served upon you, within 20[1] days after service of this summons upon you, exclusive of the day of service. If you fail to do so, judgment by default will be taken against you for the relief demanded in the complaint.

                               _____,
                                  Clerk of Court.

[Seal of the U.S. District Court]
Dated _____

(This summons is issued pursuant to Rule 4 of the Federal Rules of Civil Procedure).

(As amended Dec. 29, 1948, eff. Oct. 20, 1949.)

1. If the United States or an officer or agency thereof is a defendant, the time to be inserted as to it is 60 days.

Form 1A.
NOTICE OF LAWSUIT AND REQUEST FOR WAIVER OF SERVICE OF SUMMONS

TO: _____(A)_____ [as _____(B)_____ of _____(C)_____]

A lawsuit has been commenced against you (or the entity on whose behalf you are addressed). A copy of the complaint is attached to this notice. It has been filed in the United States District Court for the _(D)_____ and has been assigned docket number _____(E)_____.

This is not a formal summons or notification from the court, but rather my request that you sign and return the enclosed waiver of service in order to save the cost of serving you with a judicial summons and an additional copy of the complaint. The cost of service will be avoided if I receive a signed copy of the waiver within _____(F)_____ days after the date designated below as the date on which this Notice and Request is sent. I enclose a stamped and addressed envelope (or other means of cost-free return) for your use. An extra copy of the waiver is also attached for your records.

If you comply with this request and return the signed waiver, it will be filed with the court and no summons will be served on you. The action will then proceed as if you had been served on the date the waiver is filed, except that you will not be obligated to answer the complaint before 60 days from the date designated below as the date on which this notice is sent (or before 90 days from that date if your address is not in any judicial district of the United States).

If you do not return the signed waiver within the time indicated, I will take appropriate steps to effect formal service in a manner authorized by the Federal Rules of Civil Procedure and will then, to the extent authorized by those Rules, ask the court to require you (or the party on whose behalf you are addressed) to pay the full costs of such service. In that connection, please read the statement concerning the duty of parties to waive the service of the summons, which is set forth on the reverse side (or at the foot) of the waiver form.

I affirm that this request is being sent to you on behalf of the plaintiff, this _____ day of _____, ___.

_____

Signature of Plaintiff's Attorney or Unrepresented Plaintiff

Notes:

A—Name of individual defendant (or name of officer or agent of corporate defendant)

B—Title, or other relationship of individual to corporate defendant

C—Name of corporate defendant, if any

D—District

E—Docket number of action

F—Addressee must be given at least 30 days (60 days if located in foreign country) in which to return waiver

(Added Apr. 22, 1993, eff. Dec. 1, 1993.)

Form 1B.
WAIVER OF SERVICE OF SUMMONS

TO: (name of plaintiff's attorney or unrepresented plaintiff)

I acknowledge receipt of your request that I waive service of a summons in the action of   (caption of action) , which is case number (docket number)   in the United States District Court for the   (district) . I have also received a copy of the complaint in the action, two copies of this instrument, and a means by which I can return the signed waiver to you without cost to me.

I agree to save the cost of service of a summons and an additional copy of the complaint in this lawsuit by not requiring that I (or the entity on whose behalf I am acting) be served with judicial process in the manner provided by Rule 4.

I (or the entity on whose behalf I am acting) will retain all defenses or objections to the lawsuit or to the jurisdiction or venue of the court except for objections based on a defect in the summons or in the service of the summons.

I understand that a judgment may be entered against me (or the party on whose behalf I am acting) if an answer or motion under Rule 12 is not served upon you within 60 days after __(date request was sent)__ , or within 90 days after that date if the request was sent outside the United States.

_____   _____
Date   Signature
                                        Printed/typed name: _____
                                        [as _____]
                                        [of _____]

To be printed on reverse side of the waiver form or set forth at the foot of the form:

Duty to Avoid Unnecessary Costs of Service of Summons

Rule 4 of the Federal Rules of Civil Procedure requires certain parties to cooperate in saving unnecessary costs of service of the summons and complaint. A defendant located in the United States who, after being notified of an action and asked by a plaintiff located in the United States to waive service of a summons, fails to do so will be required to bear the cost of such service unless good cause be shown for its failure to sign and return the waiver.

It is not good cause for a failure to waive service that a party believes that the complaint is unfounded, or that the action has been brought in an improper place or in a court that lacks jurisdiction over the subject matter of the action or over its person or property. A party who waives service of the summons retains all defenses and objections (except any relating to the summons or to the service of the summons), and may later object to the jurisdiction of the court or to the place where the action has been brought.

A defendant who waives service must within the time specified on the waiver form serve on the plaintiff's attorney (or unrepresented plaintiff) a response to the complaint and must also file a signed copy of the response with the court. If the answer or motion is not served within this time, a default judgment may be taken against that defendant. By waiving service, a defendant is allowed more time to answer than if the summons had been actually served when the request for waiver of service was received.

(Added Apr. 22, 1993, eff. Dec. 1, 1993.)

Form 2.
ALLEGATION OF JURISDICTION

(a) Jurisdiction founded on diversity of citizenship and amount.

Plaintiff is a [citizen of the State of Connecticut] [1] [corporation incorporated under the laws of the State of Connecticut having its principal place of business in the State of Connecticut] and defendant is a corporation incorporated under the laws of the State of New York having its principal place of business in a State other than the State of Connecticut. The matter in controversy exceeds, exclusive of interest and costs, the sum of fifty thousand dollars.

(b) Jurisdiction founded on the existence of a Federal question.

The action arises under [the Constitution of the United States, Article __, Section __]; [the __ Amendment to the Constitution of the United States, Section __]; [the Act of __, __ Stat. __; U.S.C., Title __, § __]; [the Treaty of the United States (here describe the treaty)],[2] as hereinafter more fully appears.

(c) Jurisdiction founded on the existence of a question arising under particular statutes.

The action arises under the Act of __, __ Stat. __ U.S.C., Title __, § __, as hereinafter more fully appears.

(d) Jurisdiction founded on the admiralty or maritime character of the claim.

This is a case of admiralty and maritime jurisdiction, as hereinafter more fully appears. [If the pleader wishes to invoke the distinctively maritime procedures referred to in Rule 9(h), add the following or its substantial equivalent: This is an admiralty or maritime claim within the meaning of Rule 9(h).]

(As amended Apr. 17, 1961, eff. July 19, 1961; Feb. 28, 1966, eff. July 1, 1966; Apr. 22, 1993, eff. Dec. 1, 1993.)

1. Form for natural person.

2. Use the appropriate phrase or phrases. The general allegation of the existence of a Federal question is ineffective unless the matters constituting the claim for relief as set forth in the complaint raise a Federal question.

Form 3.
COMPLAINT ON A PROMISSORY NOTE

1. Allegation of jurisdiction.

2. Defendant on or about June 1, 1935, executed and delivered to plaintiff a promissory note [in the following words and figures: (here set out the note verbatim)]; [a copy of which is hereto annexed as Exhibit A]; [whereby defendant promised to pay to plaintiff or order on June 1, 1936 the sum of _____ dollars with interest thereon at the rate of six percent per annum].

3. Defendant owes to plaintiff the amount of said note and interest.

Wherefore plaintiff demands judgment against defendant for the sum of _____ dollars, interest, and costs.

Signed: _____

Attorney for Plaintiff

Address: _____

(As amended Jan. 21, 1963, eff. July 1, 1963.)

NOTES

1. The pleader may use the material in one of the three sets of brackets. His choice will depend upon whether he desires to plead the document verbatim, or by exhibit, or according to its legal effect.

2. Under the rules free joinder of claims is permitted. See rules 8(e) and 18. Consequently the claims set forth in each and all of the following forms may be joined with this complaint or with each other. Ordinarily each claim should be stated in a separate division of the complaint, and the divisions should be designated as counts successively numbered. In particular the rules permit alternative and inconsistent pleading. See Form 10.

Form 4.
COMPLAINT ON AN ACCOUNT

1. Allegation of jurisdiction.

2. Defendant owes plaintiff _____ dollars according to the account hereto annexed as Exhibit A.

Wherefore (etc. as in Form 3).

(As amended Jan. 21, 1963, eff. July 1, 1963.)

Form 5.
COMPLAINT FOR GOODS SOLD AND DELIVERED

1. Allegation of jurisdiction.

2. Defendant owes plaintiff _____ dollars for goods sold and delivered by plaintiff to defendant between June 1, 1936 and December 1, 1936.

Wherefore (etc. as in Form 3).

(As amended Jan. 21, 1963, eff. July 1, 1963.)

NOTE

This form may be used where the action is for an agreed price or for the reasonable value of the goods.

Form 6.
COMPLAINT FOR MONEY LENT

1. Allegation of jurisdiction.

2. Defendant owes plaintiff _____ dollars for money lent by plaintiff to defendant on June 1, 1936.

Wherefore (etc. as in Form 3).

(As amended Jan. 21, 1963, eff. July 1, 1963.)

Form 7.
COMPLAINT FOR MONEY PAID BY MISTAKE

1. Allegation of jurisdiction.

2. Defendant owes plaintiff _____ dollars for money paid by plaintiff to defendant by mistake on June 1, 1936, under the following circumstances: [here state the circumstances with particularity—see Rule 9(b)].

Wherefore (etc. as in Form 3).

(As amended Jan. 21, 1963, eff. July 1, 1963.)

Form 8.
COMPLAINT FOR MONEY HAD AND RECEIVED

1. Allegation of jurisdiction.

2. Defendant owes plaintiff _____ dollars for money had and received from one G.H. on June 1, 1936, to be paid by defendant to plaintiff.

Wherefore (etc. as in Form 3).

(As amended Jan. 21, 1963, eff. July 1, 1963.)

Form 9.
COMPLAINT FOR NEGLIGENCE

1. Allegation of jurisdiction.

2. On June 1, 1936, in a public highway called Boylston Street in Boston, Massachusetts, defendant negligently drove a motor vehicle against plaintiff who was then crossing said highway.

3. As a result plaintiff was thrown down and had his leg broken and was otherwise injured, was prevented from transacting his business, suffered great pain of body and mind, and incurred expenses for medical attention and hospitalization in the sum of one thousand dollars.

Wherefore plaintiff demands judgment against defendant in the sum of _____ dollars and costs.

(As amended Jan. 21, 1963, eff. July 1, 1963.)

NOTE

Since contributory negligence is an affirmative defense, the complaint need contain no allegation of due care of plaintiff.

Form 10.

COMPLAINT FOR NEGLIGENCE WHERE PLAINTIFF IS UNABLE TO DETERMINE DEFINITELY WHETHER THE PERSON RESPONSIBLE IS C.D. OR E.F. OR WHETHER BOTH ARE RESPONSIBLE AND WHERE HIS EVIDENCE MAY JUSTIFY A FINDING OF WILFULNESS OR OF RECKLESSNESS OR OF NEGLIGENCE

A.B., Plaintiff   )
)
     v.   ) *Complaint*
)
C.D. and E.F., Defendants   )

1. Allegation of jurisdiction.

2. On June 1, 1936, in a public highway called Boylston Street in Boston, Massachusetts, defendant C.D. or defendant E.F., or both defendants C.D. and E.F. wilfully or recklessly or negligently drove or caused to be driven a motor vehicle against plaintiff who was then crossing said highway.

3. As a result plaintiff was thrown down and had his leg broken and was otherwise injured, was prevented from transacting his business, suffered great pain of body and mind, and incurred expenses for medical attention and hospitalization in the sum of one thousand dollars.

Wherefore plaintiff demands judgment against C.D. or against E.F. or against both in the sum of _____ dollars and costs.

(As amended Jan. 21, 1963, eff. July 1, 1963.)

Form 11.

COMPLAINT FOR CONVERSION

1. Allegation of jurisdiction.

2. On or about December 1, 1936, defendant converted to his own use ten bonds of the _____ Company (here insert brief identification as by number and issue) of the value of _____ dollars, the property of plaintiff.

Wherefore plaintiff demands judgment against defendant in the sum of _____ dollars, interest, and costs.

(As amended Jan. 21, 1963, eff. July 1, 1963.)

Form 12.

COMPLAINT FOR SPECIFIC PERFORMANCE OF CONTRACT TO CONVEY LAND

1. Allegation of jurisdiction.

2. On or about December 1, 1936, plaintiff and defendant entered into an agreement in writing a copy of which is hereto annexed as Exhibit A.

3. In accord with the provisions of said agreement plaintiff tendered to defendant the purchase price and requested a conveyance of the land, but defendant refused to accept the tender and refused to make the conveyance.

4. Plaintiff now offers to pay the purchase price.

Wherefore plaintiff demands (1) that defendant be required specifically to perform said agreement, (2) damages in the sum of one thousand dollars, and (3) that if specific performance is not granted plaintiff have judgment against defendant in the sum of _____ dollars.

(As amended Jan. 21, 1963, eff. July 1, 1963.)

NOTE

Here, as in Form 3, plaintiff may set forth the contract verbatim in the complaint or plead it, as indicated, by exhibit, or plead it according to its legal effect. Furthermore, plaintiff may seek legal or equitable relief or both even though this was impossible under the system in operation before these rules.

Form 13.
COMPLAINT ON CLAIM FOR DEBT AND TO SET ASIDE FRAUDULENT CONVEYANCE UNDER RULE 18(b)

A.B., Plaintiff   )
)
       v.   ) *Complaint*
)
C.D. and E.F., Defendants   )

1. Allegation of jurisdiction.

2. Defendant C.D. on or about _____ executed and delivered to plaintiff a promissory note [in the following words and figures: (here set out the note verbatim)]; [a copy of which is hereto annexed as Exhibit A]; [whereby defendant C.D. promised to pay to plaintiff or order on _____ the sum of five thousand dollars with interest thereon at the rate of _____ percent, per annum].

3. Defendant C.D. owes to plaintiff the amount of said note and interest.

4. Defendant C.D. on or about _____ conveyed all his property, real and personal [or specify and describe] to defendant E.F. for the purpose of defrauding plaintiff and hindering and delaying the collection of the indebtedness evidenced by the note above referred to.

Wherefore plaintiff demands:

(1) That plaintiff have judgment against defendant C.D. for _____ dollars and interest; (2) that the aforesaid conveyance to defendant E.F. be declared void and the judgment herein be declared a lien on said property; (3) that plaintiff have judgment against the defendants for costs.

(As amended Jan. 21, 1963, eff. July 1, 1963.)

Form 14.
COMPLAINT FOR NEGLIGENCE UNDER FEDERAL EMPLOYERS' LIABILITY ACT

1. Allegation of jurisdiction.

2. During all the times herein mentioned defendant owned and operated in interstate commerce a railroad which passed through a tunnel located at _____ and known as Tunnel No. _____.

3. On or about June 1, 1936, defendant was repairing and enlarging the tunnel in order to protect interstate trains and passengers and freight from injury and in order to make the tunnel more conveniently usable for interstate commerce.

4. In the course of thus repairing and enlarging the tunnel on said day defendant employed plaintiff as one of its workmen, and negligently put plaintiff to work in a portion of the tunnel which defendant had left unprotected and unsupported.

5. By reason of defendant's negligence in thus putting plaintiff to work in that portion of the tunnel, plaintiff was, while so working pursuant to defendant's orders, struck and crushed by a rock, which fell from the unsupported portion of the tunnel, and was (here describe plaintiff's injuries).

6. Prior to these injuries, plaintiff was a strong, able-bodied man, capable of earning and actually earning _____ dollars per day. By these injuries he has been made incapable of any gainful activity, has suffered great physical and mental pain, and has incurred expense in the amount of _____ dollars for medicine, medical attendance, and hospitalization.

Wherefore plaintiff demands judgment against defendant in the sum of _____ dollars and costs.

Form 15.
COMPLAINT FOR DAMAGES UNDER MERCHANT MARINE ACT

1. Allegation of jurisdiction. [If the pleader wishes to invoke the distinctively maritime procedures referred to in Rule 9(h), add the following or its substantial equivalent: This is an admiralty or maritime claim within the meaning of Rule 9(h).]

2. During all the times herein mentioned defendant was the owner of the steamship _____ and used it in the transportation of freight for hire by water in interstate and foreign commerce.

3. During the first part of (month and year) at _____ plaintiff entered the employ of defendant as an able seaman on said steamship under seamen's articles of customary form for a voyage from _____ ports to the Orient and return at a wage of _____ dollars per month and found, which is equal to a wage of _____ dollars per month as a shore worker.

4. On June 1, 1936, said steamship was about _____ days out of the port of _____ and was being navigated by the master and crew on

the return voyage to ———— ports. (Here describe weather conditions and the condition of the ship and state as in an ordinary complaint for personal injuries the negligent conduct of defendant.)

5. By reason of defendant's negligence in thus (brief statement of defendant's negligent conduct) and the unseaworthiness of said steamship, plaintiff was (here describe plaintiff's injuries).

6. Prior to these injuries, plaintiff was a strong, able-bodied man, capable of earning and actually earning ———— dollars per day. By these injuries he has been made incapable of any gainful activity; has suffered great physical and mental pain, and has incurred expense in the amount of ———— dollars for medicine, medical attendance, and hospitalization.

Wherefore plaintiff demands judgment against defendant in the sum of ———— dollars and costs.

(As amended Feb. 28, 1966, eff. July 1, 1966.)

Form 16.
COMPLAINT FOR INFRINGEMENT OF PATENT

1. Allegation of jurisdiction.

2. On May 16, 1934, United States Letters Patent No. ———— were duly and legally issued to plaintiff for an invention in an electric motor; and since that date plaintiff has been and still is the owner of those Letters Patent.

3. Defendant has for a long time past been and still is infringing those Letters Patent by making, selling, and using electric motors embodying the patented invention, and will continue to do so unless enjoined by this court.

4. Plaintiff has placed the required statutory notice on all electric motors manufactured and sold by him under said Letters Patent, and has given written notice to defendant of his said infringement.

Wherefore plaintiff demands a preliminary and final injunction against continued infringement, an accounting for damages, and an assessment of interest and costs against defendant.

(As amended Jan. 21, 1963, eff. July 1, 1963.)

Form 17.
COMPLAINT FOR INFRINGEMENT OF COPYRIGHT
AND UNFAIR COMPETITION

1. Allegation of jurisdiction.

2. Prior to March, 1936, plaintiff, who then was and ever since has been a citizen of the United States, created and wrote an original book, entitled ————.

3. This book contains a large amount of material wholly original with plaintiff and is copyrightable subject matter under the laws of the United States.

4. Between March 2, 1936, and March 10, 1936, plaintiff complied in all respects with the Act of (give citation) and all other laws governing copyright, and secured the exclusive rights and privileges in and to the copyright of said book, and received from the Register of Copyrights a certificate of registration, dated and identified as follows: "March 10, 1936, Class _____, No. _____."

5. Since March 10, 1936, said book has been published by plaintiff and all copies of it made by plaintiff or under his authority or license have been printed, bound, and published in strict conformity with the provisions of the Act of _____ and all other laws governing copyright.

6. Since March 10, 1936, plaintiff has been and still is the sole proprietor of all rights, title, and interest in and to the copyright in said book.

7. After March 10, 1936, defendant infringed said copyright by publishing and placing upon the market a book entitled _____, which was copied largely from plaintiff's copyrighted book, entitled _____.

8. A copy of plaintiff's copyrighted book is hereto attached as "Exhibit 1"; and a copy of defendant's infringing book is hereto attached as "Exhibit 2."

9. Plaintiff has notified defendant that defendant has infringed the copyright of plaintiff, and defendant has continued to infringe the copyright.

10. After March 10, 1936, and continuously since about _____, defendant has been publishing, selling and otherwise marketing the book entitled _____, and has thereby been engaging in unfair trade practices and unfair competition against plaintiff to plaintiff's irreparable damage.

Wherefore plaintiff demands:

(1) That defendant, his agents, and servants be enjoined during the pendency of this action and permanently from infringing said copyright of said plaintiff in any manner, and from publishing, selling, marketing or otherwise disposing of any copies of the book entitled _____.

(2) That defendant be required to pay to plaintiff such damages as plaintiff has sustained in consequence of defendant's infringement of said copyright and said unfair trade practices and unfair competition and to account for

(a) all gains, profits and advantages derived by defendant by said trade practices and unfair competition and

(b) all gains, profits, and advantages derived by defendant by his infringement of plaintiff's copyright or such damages as to the court shall appear proper within the provisions of the copyright statutes, but not less than two hundred and fifty dollars.

(3) That defendant be required to deliver up to be impounded during the pendency of this action all copies of said book entitled _____ in his possession or under his control and to deliver up for destruction all

infringing copies and all plates, molds, and other matter for making such infringing copies.

(4) That defendant pay to plaintiff the costs of this action and reasonable attorney's fees to be allowed to the plaintiff by the court.

(5) That plaintiff have such other and further relief as is just.

(As amended Dec. 27, 1946, eff. Mar. 19, 1948.)

Form 18.
COMPLAINT FOR INTERPLEADER AND DECLARATORY RELIEF

1.   Allegation of jurisdiction.

2.   On or about June 1, 1935, plaintiff issued to G.H. a policy of life insurance whereby plaintiff promised to pay to K.L. as beneficiary the sum of _____ dollars upon the death of G.H. The policy required the payment by G.H. of a stipulated premium on June 1, 1936, and annually thereafter as a condition precedent to its continuance in force.

3.   No part of the premium due June 1, 1936, was ever paid and the policy ceased to have any force or effect on July 1, 1936.

4.   Thereafter, on September 1, 1936, G.H. and K.L. died as the result of a collision between a locomotive and the automobile in which G.H. and K.L. were riding.

5.   Defendant C.D. is the duly appointed and acting executor of the will of G.H.; defendant E.F. is the duly appointed and acting executor of the will of K.L.; defendant X.Y. claims to have been duly designated as beneficiary of said policy in place of K.L.

6.   Each of defendants, C.D., E.F., and X.Y. is claiming that the above-mentioned policy was in full force and effect at the time of the death of G.H.; each of them is claiming to be the only person entitled to receive payment of the amount of the policy and has made demand for payment thereof.

7.   By reason of these conflicting claims of the defendants, plaintiff is in great doubt as to which defendant is entitled to be paid the amount of the policy, if it was in force at the death of G.H.

Wherefore plaintiff demands that the court adjudge:

(1) That none of the defendants is entitled to recover from plaintiff the amount of said policy or any part thereof.

(2) That each of the defendants be restrained from instituting any action against plaintiff for the recovery of the amount of said policy or any part thereof.

(3) That, if the court shall determine that said policy was in force at the death of G.H., the defendants be required to interplead and settle between themselves their rights to the money due under said policy, and that plaintiff be discharged from all liability in the premises except to the person whom the court shall adjudge entitled to the amount of said policy.

(4) That plaintiff recover its costs.

(As amended Jan. 21, 1963, eff. July 1, 1963.)

Form 19.

MOTION TO DISMISS, PRESENTING DEFENSES OF FAILURE TO STATE A CLAIM, OF LACK OF SERVICE OF PROCESS, OF IMPROPER VENUE, AND OF LACK OF JURISDICTION UNDER RULE 12(b)

The defendant moves the court as follows:

1. To dismiss the action because the complaint fails to state a claim against defendant upon which relief can be granted.

2. To dismiss the action or in lieu thereof to quash the return of service of summons on the grounds (a) that the defendant is a corporation organized under the laws of Delaware and was not and is not subject to service of process within the Southern District of New York, and (b) that the defendant has not been properly served with process in this action, all of which more clearly appears in the affidavits of M.N. and X.Y. hereto annexed as Exhibit A and Exhibit B respectively.

3. To dismiss the action on the ground that it is in the wrong district because (a) the jurisdiction of this court is invoked solely on the ground that the action arises under the Constitution and laws of the United States and (b) the defendant is a corporation incorporated under the laws of the State of Delaware and is not licensed to do or doing business in the Southern District of New York, all of which more clearly appears in the affidavits of K.L. and V.W. hereto annexed as Exhibits C and D, respectively.

4. To dismiss the action on the ground that the court lacks jurisdiction because the amount actually in controversy is less than ten thousand dollars exclusive of interest and costs.

Signed: _____
Attorney for Defendant.
Address: _____

Notice of Motion

To: _____
Attorney for Plaintiff.

_____

Please take notice, that the undersigned will bring the above motion on for hearing before this Court at Room _____, United States Court House, Foley Square, City of New York, on the _____ day of _____, 19___, at 10 o'clock in the forenoon of that day or as soon thereafter as counsel can be heard.

Signed: _____
Attorney for Defendant.
Address: _____

(As amended Dec. 29, 1948, eff. Oct. 20, 1949; Apr. 17, 1961, eff. July 19, 1961.)

Form 20.
ANSWER PRESENTING DEFENSES UNDER RULE 12(b)

First Defense

The complaint fails to state a claim against defendant upon which relief can be granted.

Second Defense

If defendant is indebted to plaintiffs for the goods mentioned in the complaint, he is indebted to them jointly with G.H. G.H. is alive; is a citizen of the State of New York and a resident of this district, is subject to the jurisdiction of this court, as to both service of process and venue; can be made a party without depriving this court of jurisdiction of the present parties, and has not been made a party.

Third Defense

Defendant admits the allegation contained in paragraphs 1 and 4 of the complaint; alleges that he is without knowledge or information sufficient to form a belief as to the truth of the allegations contained in paragraph 2 of the complaint; and denies each and every other allegation contained in the complaint.

Fourth Defense

The right of action set forth in the complaint did not accrue within six years next before the commencement of this action.

Counterclaim

(Here set forth any claim as a counterclaim in the manner in which a claim is pleaded in a complaint. No statement of the grounds on which the court's jurisdiction depends need be made unless the counterclaim requires independent grounds of jurisdiction.)

Cross–Claim Against Defendant M.N.

(Here set forth the claim constituting a cross-claim against defendant M.N. in the manner in which a claim is pleaded in a complaint. The statement of grounds upon which the court's jurisdiction depends need not be made unless the cross-claim requires independent grounds of jurisdiction.)

Form 21.
ANSWER TO COMPLAINT SET FORTH IN FORM 8, WITH COUNTERCLAIM FOR INTERPLEADER

Defense

Defendant admits the allegations stated in paragraph 1 of the complaint; and denies the allegations stated in paragraph 2 to the extent set forth in the counterclaim herein.

Counterclaim for Interpleader

1.   Defendant received the sum of _____ dollars as a deposit from E.F.

2.   Plaintiff has demanded the payment of such deposit to him by virtue of an assignment of it which he claims to have received from E.F.

3.   E.F. has notified the defendant that he claims such deposit, that the purported assignment is not valid, and that he holds the defendant responsible for the deposit.

Wherefore defendant demands:

(1) That the court order E.F. to be made a party defendant to respond to the complaint and to this counterclaim.[1]

(2) That the court order the plaintiff and E.F. to interplead their respective claims.

(3) That the court adjudge whether the plaintiff or E.F. is entitled to the sum of money.

(4) That the court discharge defendant from all liability in the premises except to the person it shall adjudge entitled to the sum of money.

(5) That the court award to the defendant its costs and attorney's fees.

(As amended Jan. 21, 1963, eff. July 1, 1963.)

1.   Rule 13(h) provides for the court ordering parties to a counterclaim, but who are not parties to the original action, to be brought in as defendants.

Form 22.

MOTION TO BRING IN THIRD–PARTY DEFENDANT

[Form 22 for motion to bring in third-party defendant, setting out as an exhibit summons and third-party complaint, and for notice of motion, was superseded by Forms 22–A and 22–B, setting out summons and complaint against third-party defendant, and motion to bring in third-party defendant, effective July 1, 1963.   See Advisory Committee notes under Forms 22–A and 22–B.]

(Superseded Jan. 21, 1963, eff. July 1, 1963.)

Form 22–A.

SUMMONS AND COMPLAINT AGAINST THIRD–PARTY DEFENDANT

UNITED STATES DISTRICT COURT FOR THE
SOUTHERN DISTRICT OF NEW YORK

Civil Action, File Number _____

A.B., Plaintiff	)	
	)	
v.	)	
	)	
C.D., Defendant and	)	Summons
Third-Party Plaintiff	)	
	)	
v.	)	
	)	
E.F., Third-Party Defendant	)	

To the above-named Third–Party Defendant:

You are hereby summoned and required to serve upon _____, plaintiff's attorney whose address is _____, and upon _____, who is attorney for C.D., defendant and third-party plaintiff, and whose address is _____, an answer to the third-party complaint which is herewith served upon you within 20 days after the service of this summons upon you exclusive of the day of service. If you fail to do so, judgment by default will be taken against you for the relief demanded in the third-party complaint. There is also served upon you herewith a copy of the complaint of the plaintiff which you may but are not required to answer.

_____
Clerk of Court.

[Seal of District Court]
Dated _____

UNITED STATES DISTRICT COURT FOR THE
SOUTHERN DISTRICT OF NEW YORK

Civil Action, File Number _____

A.B. Plaintiff	)	
	)	
v.	)	
	)	
C.D., Defendant and	)	Summons
Third-Party Plaintiff	)	
	)	
v.	)	
	)	
E.F., Third-Party Defendant	)	

1. Plaintiff A.B. has filed against defendant C.D. a complaint, a copy of which is hereto attached as "Exhibit A."

2. (Here state the grounds upon which C.D. is entitled to recover from E.F., all or part of what A.B. may recover from C.D. The statement should be framed as in an original complaint.)

Wherefore C.D. demands judgment against third-party defendant E.F. for all sums [1] that may be adjudged against defendant C.D. in favor of plaintiff A.B.

Signed: _____

> Attorney for C.D.,
> Third-Party Plaintiff
> Address: _____

(Added Jan. 21, 1963, eff. July 1, 1963.)

1. Make appropriate change where C.D. is entitled to only partial recovery-over against E.F.

Form 22–B.
MOTION TO BRING IN THIRD–PARTY DEFENDANT

Defendant moves for leave, as third-party plaintiff, to cause to be served upon E.F. a summons and third-party complaint, copies of which are hereto attached as Exhibit X.

Signed: _____

> Attorney for Defendant
> C.D.
> Address: _____

Notice of Motion

(Contents the same as in Form 19. The notice should be addressed to all parties to the action.)

Exhibit X

(Contents the same as in Form 22–A.)

(Added Jan. 21, 1963, eff. July 1, 1963.)

Form 23.
MOTION TO INTERVENE AS A DEFENDANT UNDER RULE 24
(Based upon the complaint, Form 16)
United States District Court for the Southern District of New York
Civil Action, File Number _____

A.B., Plaintiff   )
)
      v.   ) *Motion to intervene as a defendant*
)
C. D., Defendant   )
E. F., Applicant for intervention)

E.F. moves for leave to intervene as a defendant in this action, in order to assert the defenses set forth in his proposed answer, of which a copy is hereto attached, on the ground that he is the manufacturer and vendor to the defendant, as well as to others, of the articles alleged in the complaint to be an infringement of plaintiff's patent, and as such has a defense to plaintiff's claim presenting both questions of law and of fact which are common to the main action.[1]

Signed: _____.

Attorney for E. F.,
Applicant for Intervention.
Address: _____.

Notice of Motion

(Contents the same as in Form 19)

United States District Court for the Southern District of New York

Civil Action, File Number _____

A. B., Plaintiff   )
)
         v.   )   *Intervener's Answer*
)
C. D., Defendant   )
E. F., Intervener   )

First Defense

Intervener admits the allegations stated in paragraphs 1 and 4 of the complaint; denies the allegations in paragraph 3, and denies the allegations in paragraph 2 in so far as they assert the legality of the issuance of the Letters Patent to plaintiff.

Second Defense

Plaintiff is not the first inventor of the articles covered by the Letters Patent specified in his complaint, since articles substantially identical in character were previously patented in Letters Patent granted to intervener on January 5, 1920.

Signed: _____.

Attorney for E. F.,
Intervener
Address: _____.

(As amended Dec. 29, 1948, eff. Oct. 20, 1949.)

1. For other grounds of intervention, either of right or in the discretion of the court, see Rule 24(a) and (b).

Form 24.
REQUEST FOR PRODUCTION OF DOCUMENTS, ETC., UNDER RULE 34

Plaintiff A.B. requests defendant C.D. to respond within _____ days to the following requests:

(1) That defendant produce and permit plaintiff to inspect and to copy each of the following documents:

(Here list the documents either individually or by category and describe each of them.)

(Here state the time, place, and manner of making the inspection and performance of any related acts.)

(2) That defendant produce and permit plaintiff to inspect and to copy, test, or sample each of the following objects:

(Here list the objects either individually or by category and describe each of them.)

(Here state the time, place, and manner of making the inspection and performance of any related acts.)

(3) That defendant permit plaintiff to enter (here describe property to be entered) and to inspect and to photograph, test or sample (here describe the portion of the real property and the objects to be inspected).

(Here state the time, place, and manner of making the inspection and performance of any related acts.)

Signed: _____

Attorney for Plaintiff.

Address: _____

(As amended Mar. 30, 1970, eff. July 1, 1970.)

Form 25.
REQUEST FOR ADMISSION UNDER RULE 36

Plaintiff A.B. requests defendant C.D. within _____ days after service of this request to make the following admissions for the purpose of this action only and subject to all pertinent objections to admissibility which may be interposed at the trial:

1. That each of the following documents, exhibited with this request, is genuine.

(Here list the documents and describe each document.)

2. That each of the following statements is true.

(Here list the statements.)

Signed:

Attorney for Plaintiff.

Address: _____

(As amended Dec. 27, 1946, eff. Mar. 19, 1948.)

Form 26.
ALLEGATION OF REASON FOR OMITTING PARTY

When it is necessary, under Rule 19(c), for the pleader to set forth in his pleading the names of persons who ought to be made parties, but who are not so made, there should be an allegation such as the one set out below:

John Doe named in this complaint is not made a party to this action [because he is not subject to the jurisdiction of this court]; [because he cannot be made a party to this action without depriving this court of jurisdiction].

Form 27.
NOTICE OF APPEAL TO COURT OF APPEALS UNDER RULE 73(b)
[Abrogated Dec. 4, 1967, eff. July 1, 1968]

Form 28.
NOTICE: CONDEMNATION

United States District Court for the Southern District of New York

Civil Action, File Number _____

UNITED STATES OF AMERICA, Plaintiff)
)
v.)
)
1,000 ACRES OF LAND IN [here in-) Notice.
sert a general location as "City)
of _____" or "County of)
_____"], JOHN DOE ET)
AL., AND UNKNOWN OWNERS,)
Defendants)

To (here insert the names of the defendants to whom the notice is directed):

You are hereby notified that a complaint in condemnation has heretofore been filed in the office of the clerk of the United States District Court for the Southern District of New York, in the United States Court House in New York City, New York, for the taking (here state the interest to be acquired, as "an estate in fee simple") for use (here state briefly the use, "as a site for a post-office building") of the following described property in which you have or claim an interest.

(Here insert brief description of the property in which the defendants, to whom the notice is directed, have or claim an interest.)

The authority for the taking is (here state briefly, as "the Act of _____, _____ Stat. _____, U.S.C., Title _____, § _____".) [1]

You are further notified that if you desire to present any objection or defense to the taking of your property you are required to serve your answer on the plaintiff's attorney at the address herein designated within twenty days after _____.[2]

Your answer shall identify the property in which you claim to have an interest, state the nature and extent of the interest you claim, and state all of your objections and defenses to the taking of your property. All defenses and objections not so presented are waived. And in case of your failure so to answer the complaint, judgment of condemnation of that part of the above-described property in which you have or claim an interest will be rendered.

But without answering, you may serve on the plaintiff's attorney a notice of appearance designating the property in which you claim to be interested. Thereafter you will receive notice of all proceedings affecting it. At the trial of the issue of just compensation, whether or not you have previously appeared or answered, you may present evidence as to the amount of the compensation to be paid for your property, and you may share in the distribution of the award.

Signed: _____

United States Attorney.

Address _____

(Here state an address within the district where the United States Attorney may be served, as "United States Court House, New York, N.Y.")

Dated _____

(Added May 1, 1951, eff. Aug. 1, 1951.)

1. And where appropriate add a citation to any applicable Executive Order.

2. Here insert the words "personal service of this notice upon you," if personal service is to be made pursuant to subdivision (d)(3)(i) of this rule [Rule 71A]; or, insert the date of the last publication of notice, if service by publication is to be made pursuant to subdivision (d)(3)(ii) of this rule.

Form 29.

COMPLAINT: CONDEMNATION

United States District Court for the Southern District of New York

Civil Action, File Number _____

UNITED STATES OF AMERICA, Plaintiff)
)
         v.   )
)
1,000 ACRES OF LAND IN [here insert a general location as "City of _____" or "County of _____"], JOHN DOE ET AL., AND UNKNOWN OWNERS, Defendants)   Complaint.
)
)
)
)
)

1.   This is an action of a civil nature brought by the United States of America for the taking of property under the power of eminent domain and for the ascertainment and award of just compensation to the owners and parties in interest.[1]

2.   The authority for the taking is (here state briefly, as "the Act of _____, _____ Stat. _____, U.S.C., Title _____, § _____").[2]

3.   The use for which the property is to be taken is (here state briefly the use, "as a site for a post-office building").

4.   The interest to be acquired in the property is (here state the interest as "an estate in fee simple").

5.   The property so to be taken is (here set forth a description of the property sufficient for its identification) or (described in Exhibit A hereto attached and made a part hereof).

6.   The persons known to the plaintiff to have or claim an interest in the property [3] are:

> (Here set forth the names of such persons and the interests claimed.) [4]

7.   In addition to the persons named, there are or may be others who have or may claim some interest in the property to be taken, whose names are unknown to the plaintiff and on diligent inquiry have not been ascertained.   They are made parties to the action under the designation "Unknown Owners."

Wherefore the plaintiff demands judgment that the property be condemned and that just compensation for the taking be ascertained and awarded and for such other relief as may be lawful and proper.

Signed: _____
United States Attorney.
Address _____

(Here state an address within the district where the United States Attorney may be served, as "United States Court House, New York, N.Y.").

(Added May 1, 1951, eff. Aug. 1, 1951.)

1. If the plaintiff is not the United States, but is, for example, a corporation invoking the power of eminent domain delegated to it by the state, then this paragraph 1 of the complaint should be appropriately modified and should be preceded by a paragraph appropriately alleging federal jurisdiction for the action, such as diversity. See Form 2.

2. And where appropriate add a citation to any applicable Executive Order.

3. At the commencement of the action the plaintiff need name as defendants only the persons having or claiming an interest in the property whose names are then known, but prior to any hearing involving the compensation to be paid for a particular piece of property the plaintiff must add as defendants all persons having or claiming an interest in that property whose names can be ascertained by an appropriate search of the records and also those whose names have otherwise been learned. See Rule 71A(c)(2).

4. The plaintiff should designate, as to each separate piece of property, the defendants who have been joined as owners thereof or of some interest therein. See Rule 71A(c)(2).

Form 30.
SUGGESTION OF DEATH UPON THE
RECORD UNDER RULE 25(a)(1)

A.B. [describe as a party, or as executor, administrator, or other representative or successor of C.D., the deceased party] suggests upon the record, pursuant to Rule 25(a)(1), the death of C.D. [describe as party] during the pendency of this action.

(Added Jan. 21, 1963, eff. July 1, 1963.)

Form 31.
JUDGMENT ON JURY VERDICT
UNITED STATES DISTRICT COURT FOR THE
SOUTHERN DISTRICT OF NEW YORK

Civil Action, File Number _____

A. B., Plaintiff   )
)
        v.   ) Judgment
)
C. D., Defendant   )

This action came on for trial before the Court and a jury, Honorable John Marshall, District Judge, presiding, and the issues having been duly tried and the jury having duly rendered its verdict,

It is Ordered and Adjudged

[that the plaintiff A.B. recover of the defendant C.D. the sum of _____, with interest thereon at the rate of _____ per cent as provided by law, and his costs of action.]

[that the plaintiff take nothing, that the action be dismissed on the merits, and that the defendant C.D. recover of the plaintiff A.B. his costs of action.]

Dated at New York, New York, this _____ day of _____, 19__.

_____
Clerk of Court

(Added Jan. 21, 1963, eff. July 1, 1963.)

Form 32.
JUDGMENT ON DECISION BY THE COURT
UNITED STATES DISTRICT COURT FOR THE
SOUTHERN DISTRICT OF NEW YORK
Civil Action, File Number _____

A. B., Plaintiff   )
)
        v.   ) Judgment
)
C. D., Defendant   )

This action came on for [trial] [hearing] before the Court, Honorable John Marshall, District Judge, presiding, and the issues having been duly [tried] [heard] and a decision having been duly rendered,

It is Ordered and Adjudged

[that the plaintiff A.B. recover of the defendant C.D. the sum of _____, with interest thereon at the rate of _____ per cent as provided by law, and his costs of action.]

[that the plaintiff take nothing, that the action be dismissed on the merits, and that the defendant C.D. recover of the plaintiff A.B. his costs of action.]

Dated at New York, New York, this _____ day of _____, 19__.

_____

Clerk of Court

(Added Jan. 21, 1963, eff. July 1, 1963.)

Form 33.

NOTICE OF AVAILABILITY OF A MAGISTRATE JUDGE TO EXERCISE JURISDICTION AND APPEAL OPTION

In accordance with the provisions of Title 28, U.S.C. § 636(c), you are hereby notified that a United States magistrate judge of this district court is available to exercise the court's jurisdiction and to conduct any or all proceedings in this case including a jury or nonjury trial, and entry of a final judgment. Exercise of this jurisdiction by a magistrate judge is, however, permitted only if all parties voluntarily consent.

You may, without adverse substantive consequences, withhold your consent, but this will prevent the court's jurisdiction from being exercised by a magistrate judge. If any party withholds consent, the identity of the parties consenting or withholding consent will not be communicated to any magistrate judge or to the district judge to whom the case has been assigned.

An appeal from a judgment entered by a magistrate judge may be taken directly to the United States court of appeals for this judicial circuit in the same manner as an appeal from any other judgment of a district court. Alternatively, upon consent of all parties, an appeal from a judgment entered by a magistrate judge may be taken directly to a district judge. Cases in which an appeal is taken to a district judge may be reviewed by the United States court of appeals for this judicial circuit only by way of petition for leave to appeal.

Copies of the Form for the "Consent to Jurisdiction by a United States Magistrate Judge" and "Election of Appeal to a District Judge" are available from the clerk of the court.

(As amended Apr. 22, 1993, eff. Dec. 1, 1993.)

Form 34.
CONSENT TO EXERCISE OF JURISDICTION BY A UNITED STATES MAGISTRATE JUDGE, ELECTION OF APPEAL TO DISTRICT JUDGE
UNITED STATES DISTRICT COURT
_____ DISTRICT OF _____

Plaintiff,)
)
vs.) Docket No. _____
)
Defendant.)

CONSENT TO JURISDICTION BY A UNITED STATES MAGISTRATE JUDGE

In accordance with the provisions of Title 28, U.S.C. § 636(c), the undersigned party or parties to the above-captioned civil matter hereby voluntarily consent to have a United States magistrate judge conduct any and all further proceedings in the case, including trial, and order the entry of a final judgment.

_____   _____
Date   Signature

ELECTION OF APPEAL TO DISTRICT JUDGE

[Do not execute this portion of the Consent Form if you desire that the appeal lie directly to the court of appeals.]

In accordance with the provisions of Title 28, U.S.C. § 636(c)(4), the undersigned party or parties elect to take any appeal in this case to a district judge of this court.

_____   _____
Date   Signature

Note: Return this form to the Clerk of the Court if you consent to jurisdiction by a magistrate judge. Do not send a copy of this form to any district judge or magistrate judge.

(As amended Apr. 22, 1993, eff. Dec. 1, 1993.)

Form 34A.
ORDER OF REFERENCE
UNITED STATES DISTRICT COURT
_____ DISTRICT OF _____

Plaintiff,)
)
vs.) Docket No. _____
)
Defendant.)

ORDER OF REFERENCE

IT IS HEREBY ORDERED that the above-captioned matter be referred to United States Magistrate Judge _____ for all further proceedings and entry of judgment in accordance with Title 28, U.S.C. § 636(c) and the consent of the parties.

_____
U.S. District Judge

(Added Apr. 22, 1993, eff. Dec. 1, 1993.)

Form 35.
REPORT OF PARTIES' PLANNING MEETING

[Caption and Names of Parties]

1. Pursuant to Fed.R.Civ.P. 26(f), a meeting was held on __(date)__ at ___(place)___ and was attended by:

     ___(name)___ for plaintiff(s)

     ___(name)___ for defendant(s) ___(party name)___

     ___(name)___ for defendant(s) ___(party name)___

2. Pre–Discovery Disclosures. The parties [have exchanged] [will exchange by (date)] the information required by [Fed.R.Civ.P. 26(a)(1)] [local rule _____].

3. Discovery Plan. The parties jointly propose to the court the following discovery plan: [Use separate paragraphs or subparagraphs as necessary if parties disagree.]

     Discovery will be needed on the following subjects: ___(brief description of subjects on which discovery will be needed)___

     All discovery commenced in time to be completed by ___(date)___. [Discovery on ___(issue for early discovery)___ to be completed by ___(date)___.]

     Maximum of _____ interrogatories by each party to any other party. [Responses due _____ days after service.]

     Maximum of _____ requests for admission by each party to any other party. [Responses due _____ days after service.]

     Maximum of _____ depositions by plaintiff(s) and _____ by defendant(s).

     Each deposition [other than of _____] limited to maximum of _____ hours unless extended by agreement of parties.

     Reports from retained experts under Rule 26(a)(2) due:

         from plaintiff(s) by ___(date)___

         from defendant(s) by ___(date)___

Supplementations under Rule 26(e) due ___(time(s) or interval(s))___ .

4. Other Items. [Use separate paragraphs or subparagraphs as necessary if parties disagree.]

The parties [request] [do not request] a conference with the court before entry of the scheduling order.

The parties request a pretrial conference in ___(month and year)___ .

Plaintiff(s) should be allowed until ___(date)___ to join additional parties and until ___(date)___ to amend the pleadings.

Defendant(s) should be allowed until ___(date)___ to join additional parties and until ___(date)___ to amend the pleadings.

All potentially dispositive motions should be filed by ___(date)___ .

Settlement [is likely] [is unlikely] [cannot be evaluated prior to ___(date)___] [may be enhanced by use of the following alternative dispute resolution procedure: [_____].

Final lists of witnesses and exhibits under Rule 26(a)(3) should be due

from plaintiff(s) by ___(date)___

from defendant(s) by ___(date)___

Parties should have _____ days after service of final lists of witnesses and exhibits to list objections under Rule 26(a)(3).

The case should be ready for trial by ___(date)___ [and at this time is expected to take approximately ___(length of time)___].

[Other matters.]

Date: _____

(Added Apr. 22, 1993, eff. Dec. 1, 1993.)

SELECTED FEDERAL RULES OF APPELLATE PROCEDURE

As amended to December 1, 1993

Table of Rules

Title I. Applicability of Rules

TITLE I. APPLICABILITY OF RULES

Rule 1. Scope of Rules

(a) **Scope of Rules.**—These rules govern procedure in appeals to United States courts of appeals from the United States district courts and the United States Tax Court; in appeals from bankruptcy appellate panels; in proceedings in the courts of appeals for review or enforcement of orders of administrative agencies, boards, commissions and officers of the United States; and in applications for writs or other relief which a court of appeals or a judge thereof is competent to give. When these rules provide for the making of a motion or application in the district court, the procedure for making such motion or application shall be in accordance with the practice of the district court.

(b) **Rules Not to Affect Jurisdiction.** These rules shall not be construed to extend or limit the jurisdiction of the courts of appeals as established by law.

(As amended Apr. 30, 1979, eff. Aug. 1, 1979; Apr. 25, 1989, eff. Dec. 1, 1989.)

TITLE II. APPEALS FROM JUDGMENTS AND ORDERS OF DISTRICT COURTS

Rule 3. Appeal as of Right—How Taken

(a) Filing the Notice of Appeal. An appeal permitted by law as of right from a district court to a court of appeals shall be taken by filing a notice of appeal with the clerk of the district court within the time allowed by Rule 4. Failure of an appellant to take any step other than the timely filing of a notice of appeal does not affect the validity of the appeal, but is ground only for such action as the court of appeals deems appropriate, which may include dismissal of the appeal. Appeals by permission under 28 U.S.C. § 1292(b) and appeals in bankruptcy shall be taken in the manner prescribed by Rule 5 and Rule 6, respectively.

(b) Joint or Consolidated Appeals. If 2 or more persons are entitled to appeal from a judgment or order of a district court and their interests are such as to make joinder practicable, they may file a joint notice of appeal, or may join in appeal after filing separate timely notices of appeal, and they may thereafter proceed on appeal as a single appellant. Appeals may be consolidated by order of the court of appeals upon its own motion or upon motion of a party, or by stipulation of the parties to the several appeals.

(c) Content of the Notice of Appeal. A notice of appeal must specify the party or parties taking the appeal by naming each appellant in either the caption or the body of the notice of appeal. An attorney representing more than one party may fulfill this requirement by describing those parties with such terms as "all plaintiffs," "the defendants," "the plaintiffs A, B, et al.," or "all defendants except X." A notice of appeal filed pro se is filed on behalf of the party signing the notice and the signer's spouse and minor children, if they are parties, unless the notice of appeal clearly indicates a contrary intent. In a class action, whether or not the class has been certified, it is sufficient for the notice to name one person qualified to bring the appeal as representative of the class. A notice of appeal also must designate the judgment, order, or part thereof appealed from, and must name the court to which the appeal is taken. An appeal will not be dismissed for informality of form or title of the notice of appeal, or for failure to name a party whose intent to appeal is otherwise clear from the notice. Form 1 in the Appendix of Forms is a suggested form for a notice of appeal.

(d) Serving the Notice of Appeal. The clerk of the district court shall serve notice of the filing of a notice of appeal by mailing a copy to each party's counsel of record (apart from the appellant's), or, if a party is not represented by counsel, to the party's last known address. The clerk of the district court shall forthwith send a copy of the notice and of the docket entries to the clerk of the court of appeals named in the notice. The clerk of the district court shall likewise send a copy of any later docket entry in the case to the clerk of the court of appeals. When a defendant appeals in a criminal case, the clerk of the district court shall also serve a copy of the notice of appeal upon the defendant, either by personal service or by mail addressed to the defendant. The clerk shall note on each copy served the date when the notice of appeal was filed and, if the notice of appeal was filed in the manner provided in Rule 4(c) by an inmate confined in an institution, the date when the clerk received the notice of appeal. The clerk's failure to serve notice does not affect the validity of the appeal. Service is sufficient notwithstanding the death of a party or the party's counsel. The clerk shall note in the docket the names of the parties to whom the clerk mails copies, with the date of mailing.

(e) Payment of Fees. Upon the filing of any separate or joint notice of appeal from the district court, the appellant shall pay to the clerk of the district court such fees as are established by statute, and also the docket fee prescribed by the Judicial Conference of the United States, the latter to be received by the clerk of the district court on behalf of the court of appeals.

(As amended Apr. 30, 1979, eff. Aug. 1, 1979; Mar. 10, 1986, eff. July 1, 1986; Apr. 25, 1989, eff. Dec. 1, 1989; Apr. 22, 1993, eff. Dec. 1, 1993.)

Rule 4. Appeal as of Right—When Taken

(a) Appeal in a Civil Case.

(1) Except as provided in paragraph (a)(4) of this Rule, in a civil case in which an appeal is permitted by law as of right from a district court to a court of appeals the notice of appeal required by Rule 3 must be filed with the clerk of the district court within 30 days after the date of entry of the judgment or order appealed from; but if the United States or an officer or agency thereof is a party, the notice of appeal may be filed by any party within 60 days after such entry. If a notice of appeal is mistakenly filed in the court of appeals, the clerk of the court of appeals shall note thereon the date when the clerk received the notice and send it to the clerk of the district court and the notice will be treated as filed in the district court on the date so noted.

(2) A notice of appeal filed after the court announces a decision or order but before the entry of the judgment or order is treated as filed on the date of and after the entry.

(3) If one party timely files a notice of appeal, any other party may file a notice of appeal within 14 days after the date when the first notice was filed, or within the time otherwise prescribed by this Rule 4(a), whichever period last expires.

(4) If any party makes a timely motion of a type specified immediately below, the time for appeal for all parties runs from the entry of the order disposing of the last such motion outstanding. This provision applies to a timely motion under the Federal Rules of Civil Procedure:

(A) for judgment under Rule 50(b);

(B) to amend or make additional findings of fact under Rule 52(b), whether or not granting the motion would alter the judgment;

(C) to alter or amend the judgment under Rule 59;

(D) for attorney's fees under Rule 54 if a district court under Rule 58 extends the time for appeal;

(E) for a new trial under Rule 59; or

(F) for relief under Rule 60 if the motion is served within 10 days after the entry of judgment.

A notice of appeal filed after announcement or entry of the judgment but before disposition of any of the above motions is ineffective to appeal from the judgment or order, or part thereof, specified in the notice of appeal, until the date of the entry of the order disposing of the last such motion outstanding. Appellate review of an order disposing of any of the above motions requires the party, in compliance with Appellate Rule 3(c), to amend a previously filed notice of appeal. A party intending to challenge an alteration or amendment of the judgment shall file an amended notice of appeal within the time prescribed by this Rule 4 measured from the entry of the order disposing of the last such motion outstanding. No additional fees will be required for filing an amended notice.

(5) The district court, upon a showing of excusable neglect or good cause, may extend the time for filing a notice of appeal upon motion filed not later than 30 days after the expiration of the time prescribed by this Rule 4(a). Any such motion which is filed before expiration of the prescribed time may be *ex parte* unless the court otherwise requires. Notice of any such motion which is filed after expiration of the prescribed time shall be given to the other parties in accordance with local rules. No such extension shall exceed 30 days past such prescribed time or 10 days from the date of entry of the order granting the motion, whichever occurs later.

(6) The district court, if it finds (a) that a party entitled to notice of the entry of a judgment or order did not receive such notice from the clerk or any party within 21 days of its entry and (b) that no party would be prejudiced, may, upon motion filed within 180 days of entry of the judgment or order or within 7 days of receipt of such notice, whichever is earlier, reopen the time for appeal for a period of 14 days from the date of entry of the order reopening the time for appeal.

(7) A judgment or order is entered within the meaning of this Rule 4(a) when it is entered in compliance with Rules 58 and 79(a) of the Federal Rules of Civil Procedure.

(b) Appeal in a Criminal Case. In a criminal case, a defendant shall file the notice of appeal in the district court within 10 days after the entry either of the judgment or order appealed from, or of a notice of appeal by the Government. A notice of appeal filed after the announcement of a decision, sentence, or order—but before entry of the judgment or order—is treated as filed on the date of and after the entry. If a defendant makes a timely motion specified immediately below, in accordance with the Federal Rules of Criminal Procedure, an appeal from a judgment of conviction must be taken within 10 days after the entry of the order disposing of the last such motion outstanding, or within 10 days after the entry of the judgment of conviction, whichever is later. This provision applies to a timely motion:

(1) for judgment of acquittal;

(2) for arrest of judgment;

(3) for a new trial on any ground other than newly discovered evidence; or

(4) for a new trial based on the ground of newly discovered evidence if the motion is made before or within 10 days after entry of the judgment.

A notice of appeal filed after the court announces a decision, sentence, or order but before it disposes of any of the above motions, is ineffective until the date of the entry of the order disposing of the last such motion outstanding, or until the date of the entry of the judgment of conviction, whichever is later. Notwithstanding the provisions of Rule 3(c), a valid notice of appeal is effective without amendment to appeal from an order disposing of any of the above motions. When an appeal by the government is authorized by statute, the notice of appeal must be filed in the district court within 30 days after (i) the entry of the judgment or order appealed from or (ii) the filing of a notice of appeal by any defendant.

A judgment or order is entered within the meaning of this subdivision when it is entered on the criminal docket. Upon a showing of excusable neglect, the district court may—before or after the time has expired, with or without motion and notice—extend the time for filing a notice of appeal for a period not to exceed 30 days from the expiration of the time otherwise prescribed by this subdivision.

The filing of a notice of appeal under this Rule 4(b) does not divest a district court of jurisdiction to correct a sentence under Fed.R.Crim.P. 35(c), nor does the filing of a motion under Fed.R.Crim.P. 35(c) affect the validity of a notice of appeal filed before entry of the order disposing of the motion.

(c) Appeal by an Inmate Confined in an Institution. If an inmate confined in an institution files a notice of appeal in either a civil case or a criminal case, the notice of appeal is timely filed if it is deposited in the institution's internal mail system on or before the last day for filing. Timely filing may be shown by a notarized statement or by a declaration (in compliance with 28 U.S.C. § 1746) setting forth the date of deposit and stating that first-class postage has been prepaid. In a civil case in which the first notice of appeal is filed in the manner provided in this subdivision (c), the 14-day period provided in paragraph (a)(3) of this Rule 4 for another party to file a notice of appeal runs from the date when the district court receives the first notice of appeal. In a criminal case in which a defendant files a notice of appeal in the manner provided in this subdivision (c), the 30–day period for the government to file its notice of appeal runs from the entry of the judgment or order appealed from or from the district court's receipt of the defendant's notice of appeal.

(As amended Apr. 30, 1979, eff. Aug. 1, 1979; amended eff. Nov. 18, 1988; Apr. 30, 1991, eff. Dec. 1, 1991; Apr. 22, 1993, eff. Dec. 1, 1993.)

Rule 5. Appeals by Permission Under 28 U.S.C. § 1292(b)

(a) Petition for Permission to Appeal. An appeal from an interlocutory order containing the statement prescribed by 28 U.S.C. § 1292(b) may be sought by filing a petition for permission to appeal with the clerk of the court of appeals within 10 days after the entry of such order in the district court with proof of service on all other parties to the action in the district court. An order may be amended to include the prescribed statement at any time, and permission to appeal may be sought within 10 days after entry of the order as amended.

(b) Content of Petition; Answer. The petition shall contain a statement of the facts necessary to an understanding of the controlling question of law determined by the order of the district court; a statement of the question itself; and a statement of the reasons why a substantial basis exists for a difference of opinion on the question and why an immediate appeal may materially advance the termination of the litigation. The petition shall include or have annexed thereto a copy of the order from which appeal is sought and of any findings of fact, conclusions of law and opinion relating thereto. Within 7 days after service of the petition an adverse party may file an answer in opposition. The application and answer shall be submitted without oral argument unless otherwise ordered.

(c) Form of Papers; Number of Copies. All papers may be typewritten. Three copies shall be filed with the original, but the court may require that additional copies be furnished.

(d) Grant of Permission; Cost Bond; Filing of Record. Within 10 days after the entry of an order granting permission to appeal the appellant shall (1) pay to the clerk of the district court the fees established by statute and the docket fee prescribed by the Judicial Conference of the United States and (2) file a bond for costs if required pursuant to Rule 7. The clerk of the district court shall notify the clerk of the court of appeals of the payment of the fees. Upon receipt of such notice the clerk of the court of appeals shall enter the appeal upon the docket. The record shall be transmitted and filed in accordance with Rules 11 and 12(b). A notice of appeal need not be filed.

(As amended Apr. 30, 1979, eff. Aug. 1, 1979.)

Rule 7. Bond for Costs on Appeal in Civil Cases

The district court may require an appellant to file a bond or provide other security in such form and amount as it finds necessary to ensure payment of costs on appeal in a civil case. The provisions of Rule 8(b) apply to a surety upon a bond given pursuant to this rule.

(As amended Apr. 30, 1979, eff. Aug. 1, 1979.)

Rule 8. Stay or Injunction Pending Appeal

(a) **Stay Must Ordinarily Be Sought in the First Instance in District Court; Motion for Stay in Court of Appeals.** Application for a stay of the judgment or order of a district court pending appeal, or for approval of a supersedeas bond, or for an order suspending, modifying, restoring or granting an injunction during the pendency of an appeal must ordinarily be made in the first instance in the district court. A motion for such relief may be made to the court of appeals or to a judge thereof, but the motion shall show that application to the district court for the relief sought is not practicable, or that the district court has denied an application, or has failed to afford the relief which the applicant requested, with the reasons given by the district court for its action. The motion shall also show the reasons for the relief requested and the facts relied upon, and if the facts are subject to dispute the motion shall be supported by affidavits or other sworn statements or copies thereof. With the motion shall be filed such parts of the record as are relevant. Reasonable notice of the motion shall be given to all parties. The motion shall be filed with the clerk and normally will be considered by a panel or division of the court, but in exceptional cases where such procedure would be impracticable due to the requirements of time, the application may be made to and considered by a single judge of the court.

(b) **Stay May Be Conditioned Upon Giving of Bond; Proceedings Against Sureties.** Relief available in the court of appeals under this rule may be conditioned upon the filing of a bond or other appropriate security in the district court. If security is given in the form of a bond or stipulation or other undertaking with one or more sureties, each surety submits to the jurisdiction of the district court and irrevocably appoints the clerk of the district court as the surety's agent upon whom any papers affecting the surety's liability on the bond or undertaking may be served. A surety's liability may be enforced on motion in the district court without the necessity of an independent action. The motion and such notice of the motion as the district court prescribes may be served on the clerk of the district court, who shall forthwith mail copies to the sureties if their addresses are known.

(c) **Stays in Criminal Cases.** Stays in criminal cases shall be had in accordance with the provisions of Rule 38(a) of the Federal Rules of Criminal Procedure.

(As amended Mar. 10, 1986, eff. July 1, 1986.)

TITLE V.　EXTRAORDINARY WRITS

Rule 21.　Writs of Mandamus and Prohibition Directed to a Judge or Judges and Other Extraordinary Writs

(a) Mandamus or Prohibition to a Judge or Judges; Petition for Writ; Service and Filing. Application for a writ of mandamus or of prohibition directed to a judge or judges shall be made by filing a petition therefor with the clerk of the court of appeals with proof of service on the respondent judge or judges and on all parties to the action in the trial court. The petition shall contain a statement of the facts necessary to an understanding of the issues presented by the application; a statement of the issues presented and of the relief sought; a statement of the reasons why the writ should issue; and copies of any order or opinion or parts of the record which may be essential to an understanding of the matters set forth in the petition. Upon receipt of the prescribed docket fee, the clerk shall docket the petition and submit it to the court.

(b) Denial; Order Directing Answer. If the court is of the opinion that the writ should not be granted, it shall deny the petition. Otherwise, it shall order that an answer to the petition be filed by the respondents within the time fixed by the order. The order shall be served by the clerk on the judge or judges named respondents and on all other parties to the action in the trial court. All parties below other than the petitioner shall also be deemed respondents for all purposes. Two or more respondents may answer jointly. If the judge or judges named respondents do not desire to appear in the proceeding, they may so advise the clerk and all parties by letter, but the petition shall not thereby be taken as admitted. The clerk shall advise the parties of the dates on which briefs are to be filed, if briefs are required, and of the date of oral argument. The proceeding shall be given preference over ordinary civil cases.

(c) Other Extraordinary Writs. Application for extraordinary writs other than those provided for in subdivisions (a) and (b) of this rule shall be made by petition filed with the clerk of the court of appeals with proof of service on the parties named as respondents. Proceedings on such application shall conform, so far as is practicable, to the procedure prescribed in subdivisions (a) and (b) of this rule.

(d) Form of Papers; Number of Copies. All papers may be typewritten. Three copies shall be filed with the original, but the court may direct that additional copies be furnished.

TITLE VII.　GENERAL PROVISIONS

Rule 25.　Filing and Service

(a) Filing. Papers required or permitted to be filed in a court of appeals must be filed with the clerk. Filing may be accomplished by mail addressed to the clerk, but filing is not timely unless the clerk receives the papers within the time fixed for filing, except that briefs and appendices are treated as filed on the day of mailing if the most expeditious form of delivery by mail, except special delivery, is used. Papers filed by an inmate confined in an institution are timely filed if deposited in the institution's internal mail system on or before the last day for filing. Timely filing of papers by an inmate confined in an institution may be shown by a notarized statement or declaration (in compliance with 28 U.S.C. § 1746) setting forth the date of deposit and stating that first-class postage has been prepaid. If a motion requests relief that may be granted by a single judge, the judge may permit the motion to be filed with the judge, in which event the judge shall note thereon the date of filing and thereafter give it to the clerk. A court of appeals may, by local rule, permit papers to be filed by facsimile or other electronic means, provided such means are authorized by and consistent with standards established by the Judicial Conference of the United States.

(b) Service of All Papers Required. Copies of all papers filed by any party and not required by these rules to be served by the clerk shall, at or before the time of filing, be served by a party or person acting for that party on all other parties to the appeal or review. Service on a party represented by counsel shall be made on counsel.

(c) Manner of Service. Service may be personal or by mail. Personal service includes delivery of the copy to a clerk or other responsible person at the office of counsel. Service by mail is complete on mailing.

(d) Proof of Service. Papers presented for filing shall contain an acknowledgment of service by the person served or proof of service in the form of a statement of the date and manner of service and of the names of the person served, certified by the person who made service. Proof of service may appear on or be affixed to the papers filed. The clerk may permit papers to be filed without acknowledgment or proof of service but shall require such to be filed promptly thereafter.

(As amended Mar. 10, 1986, eff. July 1, 1986; Apr. 30, 1991, eff. Dec. 1, 1991; Apr. 22, 1993, eff. Dec. 1, 1993.)

Rule 26.   Computation and Extension of Time

(a) Computation of Time. In computing any period of time prescribed or allowed by these rules, by an order of court, or by any applicable statute, the day of the act, event, or default from which the designated period of time begins to run shall not be included. The last day of the period so computed shall be included, unless it is a Saturday, a Sunday, or a legal holiday, or, when the act to be done is the filing of a paper in court, a day on which weather or other conditions have made the office of the clerk of the court inaccessible, in which event the period runs until the end of the next day which is not one of the aforementioned days. When the period of time prescribed or allowed is less than 7 days, intermediate Saturdays, Sundays, and legal holidays shall be excluded in the computation. As used in this rule "legal holiday" includes New Year's Day, Birthday of Martin Luther King, Jr., Washington's Birthday, Memorial Day, Independence Day, Labor Day, Columbus Day, Veterans Day, Thanksgiving Day, Christmas Day, and any other day appointed as a holiday by the President or the Congress of the United States. It shall also include a day appointed as a holiday by the state wherein the district court which rendered the judgment or order which is or may be appealed from is situated, or by the state wherein the principal office of the clerk of the court of appeals in which the appeal is pending is located.

(b) Enlargement of Time. The court for good cause shown may upon motion enlarge the time prescribed by these rules or by its order for doing any act, or may permit an act to be done after the expiration of such time; but the court may not enlarge the time for filing a notice of appeal, a petition for allowance, or a petition for permission to appeal. Nor may the court enlarge the time prescribed by law for filing a petition to enjoin, set aside, suspend, modify, enforce or otherwise review, or a notice of appeal from, an order of an administrative agency, board, commission or officer of the United States, except as specifically authorized by law.

(c) Additional Time After Service by Mail. Whenever a party is required or permitted to do an act within a prescribed period after service of a paper upon that party and the paper is served by mail, 3 days shall be added to the prescribed period.

(As amended Mar. 1, 1971, eff. July 1, 1971; Mar. 10, 1986, eff. July 1, 1986; Apr. 25, 1989, eff. Dec. 1, 1989; Apr. 30, 1991, eff. Dec. 1, 1991.)

Rule 35. Determination of Causes by the Court in Banc

(a) When Hearing or Rehearing in Banc Will Be Ordered. A majority of the circuit judges who are in regular active service may order that an appeal or other proceeding be heard or reheard by the court of appeals in banc. Such a hearing or rehearing is not favored and ordinarily will not be ordered except (1) when consideration by the full court is necessary to secure or maintain uniformity of its decisions, or (2) when the proceeding involves a question of exceptional importance.

(b) Suggestion of a Party for Hearing or Rehearing in Banc. A party may suggest the appropriateness of a hearing or rehearing in banc. No response shall be filed unless the court shall so order. The clerk shall transmit any such suggestion to the members of the panel and the judges of the court who are in regular active service but a vote need not be taken to determine whether the cause shall be heard or reheard in banc unless a judge in regular active service or a judge who was a member of the panel that rendered a decision sought to be reheard requests a vote on such a suggestion made by a party.

(c) Time for Suggestion of a Party for Hearing or Rehearing in Banc; Suggestion Does Not Stay Mandate. If a party desires to suggest that an appeal be heard initially in banc, the suggestion must be made by the date on which the appellee's brief is filed. A suggestion for a rehearing in banc must be made within the time prescribed by Rule 40 for filing a petition for rehearing, whether the suggestion is made in such petition or otherwise. The pendency of such a suggestion whether or not included in a petition for rehearing shall not affect the finality of the judgment of the court of appeals or stay the issuance of the mandate.

(As amended Apr. 30, 1979, eff. Aug. 1, 1979.)

Rule 38. Damages for Delay

If a court of appeals shall determine that an appeal is frivolous, it may award just damages and single or double costs to the appellee.

Rule 39. Costs

(a) **To Whom Allowed.** Except as otherwise provided by law, if an appeal is dismissed, costs shall be taxed against the appellant unless otherwise agreed by the parties or ordered by the court; if a judgment is affirmed, costs shall be taxed against the appellant unless otherwise ordered; if a judgment is reversed, costs shall be taxed against the appellee unless otherwise ordered; if a judgment is affirmed or reversed in part, or is vacated, costs shall be allowed only as ordered by the court.

(b) **Costs for and Against the United States.** In cases involving the United States or an agency or officer thereof, if an award of costs against the United States is authorized by law, costs shall be awarded in accordance with the provisions of subdivision (a); otherwise, costs shall not be awarded for or against the United States.

(c) **Costs of Briefs, Appendices, and Copies of Records.** By local rule the court of appeals shall fix the maximum rate at which the cost of printing or otherwise producing necessary copies of briefs, appendices, and copies of records authorized by Rule 30(f) shall be taxable. Such rate shall not be higher than that generally charged for such work in the area where the clerk's office is located and shall encourage the use of economical methods of printing and copying.

(d) **Bill of Costs; Objections; Costs to Be Inserted in Mandate or Added Later.** A party who desires such costs to be taxed shall state them in an itemized and verified bill of costs which the party shall file with the clerk, with proof of service, within 14 days after the entry of judgment. Objections to the bill of costs must be filed within 10 days of service on the party against whom costs are to be taxed unless the time is extended by the court. The clerk shall prepare and certify an itemized statement of costs taxed in the court of appeals for insertion in the mandate, but the issuance of the mandate shall not be delayed for taxation of costs and if the mandate has been issued before final determination of costs, the statement, or any amendment thereof, shall be added to the mandate upon request by the clerk of the court of appeals to the clerk of the district court.

(e) Costs on Appeal Taxable in the District Courts.　Costs incurred in the preparation and transmission of the record, the cost of the reporter's transcript, if necessary for the determination of the appeal, the premiums paid for cost of supersedeas bonds or other bonds to preserve rights pending appeal, and the fee for filing the notice of appeal shall be taxed in the district court as costs of the appeal in favor of the party entitled to costs under this rule.

(As amended Apr. 30, 1979, eff. Aug. 1, 1979; Mar. 10, 1986, eff. July 1, 1986.)

AMENDMENTS TO FEDERAL RULES OF APPELLATE PROCEDURE ANNOUNCED APRIL 29, 1994

Absent contrary action by the Congress, the foregoing amendments will take effect December 1, 1994.

Table of Rules

Rule 1. Scope of Rules and Title

(a) Scope of Rules. These rules govern procedure in appeals to United States courts of appeals from the United States district courts and the United States Tax Court; in appeals from bankruptcy appellate panels; in proceedings in the courts of appeals for review or enforcement of orders of administrative agencies, boards, commissions and officers of the United States; and in applications for writs or other relief which a court of appeals or a judge thereof is competent to give. When these rules provide for the making of a motion or application in the district court, the procedure for making such motion or application shall be in accordance with the practice of the district court.

(b) Rules Not to Affect Jurisdiction. These rules shall not be construed to extend or limit the jurisdiction of the courts of appeals as established by law.

(c) Title. These rules may be known and cited as the Federal Rules of Appellate Procedure.

Rule 3. Appeal as of Right—How Taken

(a) Filing the Notice of Appeal. An appeal permitted by law as of right from a district court to a court of appeals must be taken by filing a notice of appeal with the clerk of the district court within the time allowed by Rule 4. At the time of filing, the appellant must furnish the clerk with sufficient copies of the notice of appeal to enable the clerk to comply promptly with the requirements of subdivision (d) of this Rule 3.

Failure of an appellant to take any step other than the timely filing of a notice of appeal does not affect the validity of the appeal, but is ground only for such action as the court of appeals deems appropriate, which may include dismissal of the appeal. Appeals by permission under 28 U.S.C. § 1292(b) and appeals in bankruptcy must be taken in the manner prescribed by Rule 5 and Rule 6 respectively.

* * *

Rule 5. Appeal by Permission Under 28 U.S.C. § 1292(b)

* * *

(c) **Form of Papers; Number of Copies.** All papers may be typewritten. An original and three copies must be filed unless the court requires the filing of a different number by local rule or by order in a particular case.

* * *

Rule 21. Writs of Mandamus and Prohibition Directed to a Judge or Judges and Other Extraordinary Writs

* * *

(d) **Form of Papers; Number of Copies.** All papers may be typewritten. An original and three copies must be filed unless the court requires the filing of a different number by local rule or by order in a particular case.

Rule 25. Filing and Service

(a) **Filing.** A paper required or permitted to be filed in a court of appeals must be filed with the clerk. Filing may be accomplished by mail addressed to the clerk, but filing is not timely unless the clerk receives the papers within the time fixed for filing, except that briefs and appendices are treated as filed on the day of mailing if the most expeditious form of delivery by mail, except special delivery, is used. Papers filed by an inmate confined in an institution are timely filed if deposited in the institution's internal mail system on or before the last day for filing. Timely filing of papers by an inmate confined in an institution may be shown by a notarized statement or declaration (in compliance with 28 U.S.C. § 1746) setting forth the date of deposit and stating that first-class postage has been prepaid. If a motion requests relief that may be granted by a single judge, the judge may permit the motion to be filed with the judge, in which event the judge shall note thereon the filing date and thereafter give it to the clerk. A court of appeals may, by local rule, permit papers to be filed by facsimile or other electronic means, provided much means are authorized by and consistent with standards established by the Judicial Conference of the United States. The clerk must not refuse to accept for filing any paper presented for that purpose solely because it is not presented in proper form as required by these rules or by any local rules or practices.

* * *

(d) Proof of Service. Papers presented for filing must contain an acknowledgment of service by the person served or proof of service in the form of a statement of the date and manner of service, of the names of the persons served, and of the addresses to which the papers were mailed or at which they were delivered, certified by the person who made service. Proof of service may appear on or be affixed to the papers filed.

(e) Number of Copies. Whenever these rules require the filing or furnishing of a number of copies, a court may require a different number by local rule or by order in a particular case.

Rule 35. Determination of Causes by the Court in Banc

* * *

(d) Number of Copies. The number of copies that must be filed may be prescribed by local rule and may be altered by order in a particular case.

Rule 38. Damages and Costs for Frivolous Appeals

If a court of appeals determines that an appeal is frivolous, it may, after a separately filed motion or notice from the court and reasonable opportunity to respond, award just damages and single or double costs to the appellee.

Rule 48. Masters

A court of appeals may appoint a special master to hold hearings, if necessary, and to make recommendations as to factual findings and disposition in matters ancillary to proceedings in the court. Unless the order referring a matter to a master specifies or limits the master's powers, a master shall have power to regulate all proceedings in every hearing before the master and to do all acts and take all measures necessary or proper for the efficient performance of the master's duties under the order including, but not limited to, requiring the production of evidence upon all matters embraced in the reference and putting witnesses and parties on oath and examining them. If the master is not a judge or court employee, the court shall determine the master's compensation and whether the cost will be charged to any of the parties.

SELECTED PROVISIONS OF THE UNITED STATES CONSTITUTION

Table of Contents

Preamble

We the People of the United States, in Order to form a more perfect Union, establish Justice, insure domestic Tranquility, provide for the common defence, promote the general Welfare, and secure the Blessings of Liberty to ourselves and our Posterity, do ordain and establish this Constitution for the United States of America.

ARTICLE I.

* * *

Section 8.   The Congress shall have Power To lay and collect Taxes, Duties, Imposts and Excises, to pay the Debts and provide for the common Defence and general Welfare of the United States; but all Duties, Imposts and Excises shall be uniform throughout the United States;

To borrow Money on the credit of the United States;

To regulate Commerce with foreign Nations, and among the several States, and with the Indian Tribes;

To establish an uniform Rule of Naturalization, and uniform Laws on the subject of Bankruptcies throughout the United States;

To coin Money, regulate the Value thereof, and of foreign Coin, and fix the Standard of Weights and Measures;

To provide for the Punishment of counterfeiting the Securities and current Coin of the United States;

To establish Post Offices and post Roads;

To promote the Progress of Science and useful Arts, by securing for limited Times to Authors and Inventors the exclusive Right to their respective Writings and Discoveries;

To constitute Tribunals inferior to the supreme Court;

To define and punish Piracies and Felonies committed on the high Seas, and Offences against the Law of Nations;

To declare War, grant Letters of Marque and Reprisal, and make Rules concerning Captures on Land and Water;

To raise and support Armies, but no Appropriation of Money to that Use shall be for a longer Term than two Years;

To provide and maintain a Navy;

To make Rules for the Government and Regulation of the land and naval Forces;

To provide for calling forth the Militia to execute the Laws of the Union, suppress Insurrections and repel Invasions;

To provide for organizing, arming, and disciplining, the Militia, and for governing such Part of them as may be employed in the Service of the United States, reserving to the States respectively, the Appointment of the Officers, and the Authority of training the Militia according to the discipline prescribed by Congress;

To exercise exclusive Legislation in all Cases whatsoever, over such District (not exceeding ten Miles square) as may, by Cession of particular States, and the Acceptance of Congress, become the Seat of the Government of the United States, and to exercise like Authority over all Places purchased by the Consent of the Legislature of the State in which the same shall be, for the Erection of Forts, Magazines, Arsenals, dock-Yards, and other needful Buildings;—And

To make all Laws which shall be necessary and proper for carrying into Execution the foregoing Powers, and all other Powers vested by this Constitution in the Government of the United States, or in any Department or Officer thereof.

* * *

ARTICLE III.

Section 1. The judicial Power of the United States, shall be vested in one supreme Court, and in such inferior Courts as the Congress may from time to time ordain and establish. The Judges, both of the supreme and inferior Courts, shall hold their Offices during good Behaviour, and shall, at stated Times, receive for their Services, a Compensation, which shall not be diminished during their Continuance in Office.

Section 2.   The judicial Power shall extend to all Cases, in Law and Equity, arising under this Constitution, the Laws of the United States, and Treaties made, or which shall be made, under their Authority;—to all Cases affecting Ambassadors, other public Ministers and Consuls;—to all Cases of admiralty and maritime Jurisdiction;—to Controversies to which the United States shall be a Party;—to Controversies between two or more States;—between a State and Citizens of another State;—between Citizens of different States;—between Citizens of the same State claiming Lands under Grants of different States, and between a State, or the Citizens thereof, and foreign States, Citizens or Subjects.

In all Cases affecting Ambassadors, other public Ministers and Consuls, and those in which a State shall be Party, the supreme Court shall have original Jurisdiction.   In all the other Cases before mentioned, the supreme Court shall have appellate Jurisdiction, both as to Law and Fact, with such Exceptions, and under such Regulations as the Congress shall make.

The Trial of all Crimes, except in Cases of Impeachment, shall be by Jury; and such Trial shall be held in the State where the said Crimes shall have been committed; but when not committed within any State, the Trial shall be at such Place or Places as the Congress may by Law have directed.

* * *

ARTICLE IV.

Section 1.   Full Faith and Credit shall be given in each State to the public Acts, Records, and judicial Proceedings of every other State.   And the Congress may by general Laws prescribe the Manner in which such Acts, Records and Proceedings shall be proved, and the Effect thereof.

Section 2.   The Citizens of each State shall be entitled to all Privileges and Immunities of Citizens in the several States.

ARTICLE VI.

* * *

This Constitution, and the Laws of the United States which shall be made in Pursuance thereof; and all Treaties made, or which shall be made, under the Authority of the United States, shall be the supreme Law of the Land; and the Judges in every State shall be bound thereby, any Thing in the Constitution or Laws of any State to the Contrary notwithstanding.

* * *

AMENDMENT I.   [1791]

Congress shall make no law respecting an establishment of religion, or prohibiting the free exercise thereof; or abridging the freedom of speech, or of the press; or the right of the people peaceably to assemble, and to petition the Government for a redress of grievances.

AMENDMENT IV. [1791]

The right of the people to be secure in their persons, houses, papers, and effects, against unreasonable searches and seizures, shall not be violated, and no Warrants shall issue, but upon probable cause, supported by Oath or affirmation, and particularly describing the place to be searched, and the persons or things to be seized.

AMENDMENT V. [1791]

No person shall be held to answer for a capital, or otherwise infamous crime, unless on a presentment or indictment of a Grand Jury, except in cases arising in the land or naval forces, or in the Militia, when in actual service in time of War or public danger; nor shall any person be subject for the same offence to be twice put in jeopardy of life or limb; nor shall be compelled in any criminal case to be a witness against himself, nor be deprived of life, liberty, or property, without due process of law; nor shall private property be taken for public use, without just compensation.

AMENDMENT VI. [1791]

In all criminal prosecutions, the accused shall enjoy the right to a speedy and public trial, by an impartial jury of the State and district wherein the crime shall have been committed, which district shall have been previously ascertained by law, and to be informed of the nature and cause of the accusation; to be confronted with the witnesses against him; to have compulsory process for obtaining witnesses in his favor, and to have the Assistance of Counsel for his defence.

AMENDMENT VII. [1791]

In Suits at common law, where the value in controversy shall exceed twenty dollars, the right of trial by jury shall be preserved, and no fact tried by a jury, shall be otherwise re-examined in any Court of the United States, than according to the rules of the common law.

AMENDMENT VIII. [1791]

Excessive bail shall not be required, nor excessive fines imposed, nor cruel and unusual punishments inflicted.

AMENDMENT IX. [1791]

The enumeration in the Constitution, of certain rights, shall not be construed to deny or disparage others retained by the people.

AMENDMENT X. [1791]

The powers not delegated to the United States by the Constitution, nor prohibited by it to the States, are reserved to the States respectively, or to the people.

AMENDMENT XI.   [1798]

The Judicial power of the United States shall not be construed to extend to any suit in law or equity, commenced or prosecuted against one of the United States by Citizens of another State, or by Citizens or Subjects of any Foreign State.

AMENDMENT XIV.   [1868]

Section 1. All persons born or naturalized in the United States, and subject to the jurisdiction thereof, are citizens of the United States and of the State wherein they reside. No State shall make or enforce any law which shall abridge the privileges or immunities of citizens of the United States; nor shall any State deprive any person of life, liberty, or property, without due process of law; nor deny to any person within its jurisdiction the equal protection of the laws.

* * *

Section 5. The Congress shall have power to enforce, by appropriate legislation, the provisions of this article.

SELECTED PROVISIONS OF TITLE 28, UNITED STATES CODE—JUDICIARY AND JUDICIAL PROCEDURE

As amended to January 1, 1994

Table of Contents

§ 41. Number and Composition of Circuits

The thirteen judicial circuits of the United States are constituted as follows:

Circuits	Composition
District of Columbia	District of Columbia.
First	Maine, Massachusetts, New Hampshire, Puerto Rico, Rhode Island.
Second	Connecticut, New York, Vermont.
Third	Delaware, New Jersey, Pennsylvania, Virgin Islands.
Fourth	Maryland, North Carolina, South Carolina, Virginia, West Virginia.
Fifth	District of the Canal Zone, Louisiana, Mississippi, Texas.
Sixth	Kentucky, Michigan, Ohio, Tennessee.
Seventh	Illinois, Indiana, Wisconsin.
Eighth	Arkansas, Iowa, Minnesota, Missouri, Nebraska, North Dakota, South Dakota.
Ninth	Alaska, Arizona, California, Idaho, Montana, Nevada, Oregon, Washington, Guam, Hawaii.
Tenth	Colorado, Kansas, New Mexico, Oklahoma, Utah, Wyoming.
Eleventh	Alabama, Florida, Georgia.
Federal	All Federal judicial districts.

(As amended Oct. 31, 1951, c. 655, § 34, 65 Stat. 723; Oct. 14, 1980, Pub.L. 96–452, § 2, 94 Stat. 1994; Apr. 2, 1982, Pub.L. 97–164, Title I, § 101, 96 Stat. 25.)

§ 133. Appointment and Number of District Judges

The President shall appoint, by and with the advice and consent of the Senate, district judges for the several judicial districts, as follows:

Districts	Judges
Alabama:	
Northern	7
Middle	3
Southern	3
Alaska	3
Arizona	8
Arkansas:	
Eastern	5
Western	3
California:	
Northern	14
Eastern	6
Central	27
Southern	8
Colorado	7
Connecticut	8
Delaware	4
District of Columbia	15
Florida:	
Northern	4
Middle	11
Southern	16
Georgia:	
Northern	11
Middle	4
Southern	3
Hawaii	3
Idaho	2
Illinois:	
Northern	22
Central	3
Southern	3
Indiana:	
Northern	5
Southern	5
Iowa:	
Northern	2
Southern	3
Kansas	5
Kentucky:	
Eastern	4
Western	4
Eastern and Western	1

Districts	Judges
Louisiana:	
Eastern	13
Middle	2
Western	7
Maine	3
Maryland	10
Massachusetts	13
Michigan:	
Eastern	15
Western	4
Minnesota	7
Mississippi:	
Northern	3
Southern	6
Missouri:	
Eastern	6
Western	5
Eastern and Western	2
Montana	3
Nebraska	3
Nevada	4
New Hampshire	3
New Jersey	17
New Mexico	5
New York:	
Northern	4
Southern	28
Eastern	15
Western	4
North Carolina:	
Eastern	4
Middle	4
Western	3
North Dakota	2
Ohio:	
Northern	11
Southern	8
Oklahoma:	
Northern	3
Eastern	1
Western	6
Northern, Eastern, and Western	6
Oregon	6
Pennsylvania:	
Eastern	22
Middle	6
Western	10
Puerto Rico	7
Rhode Island	3
South Carolina	9
South Dakota	3
Tennessee:	
Eastern	5
Middle	4

Districts	Judges
Western	5
Texas:	
Northern	12
Southern	18
Eastern	7
Western	10
Utah	5
Vermont	2
Virginia:	
Eastern	9
Western	4
Washington:	
Eastern	4
Western	7
West Virginia:	
Northern	3
Southern	5
Wisconsin:	
Eastern	4
Western	2
Wyoming	3

(As amended Aug. 3, 1949, c. 387, § 2(a), 63 Stat. 493; Aug. 14, 1950, c. 708, 64 Stat. 443; Aug. 29, 1950, c. 819, § 1, 64 Stat. 562; Sept. 5, 1950, c. 848, § 1, 64 Stat. 578; Feb. 10, 1954, c. 6, § 2(a)(3), 68 Stat. 9; Sept. 7, 1957, Pub.L. 85–310, 71 Stat. 631; July 7, 1958, Pub.L. 85–508, § 12(c), 72 Stat. 348; Mar. 18, 1959, Pub.L. 86–3, § 9(b), 73 Stat. 8; May 19, 1961, Pub.L. 87–36, § 2(d), 75 Stat. 81; July 30, 1962, Pub.L. 87–562, § 3, 76 Stat. 248; Oct. 7, 1965, Pub.L. 89–242, § 1(c), 79 Stat. 951; Mar. 18, 1966, Pub.L. 89–372, § 4, 80 Stat. 77; June 2, 1970, Pub.L. 91–272, § 1(c), (d), 84 Stat. 294, 295; Dec. 18, 1971, Pub.L. 92–208, § 3(d), 85 Stat. 742; Oct. 2, 1978, Pub.L. 95–408, § 4(b)(2), 92 Stat. 885; Oct. 20, 1978, Pub.L. 95–486, § 1(c), 92 Stat. 1630; Jan. 14, 1983, Pub.L. 97–471, § 3, 96 Stat. 2601; July 10, 1984, Pub.L. 98–353, Title II, § 202(e), 98 Stat. 348; Dec. 1, 1990, Pub.L. 101–650, § 203(d), 104 Stat. 5089.)

§ 636. Jurisdiction, Powers, and Temporary Assignment

(a) Each United States magistrate serving under this chapter shall have within the territorial jurisdiction prescribed by his appointment—

(1) all powers and duties conferred or imposed upon United States commissioners by law or by the Rules of Criminal Procedure for the United States District Courts;

(2) the power to administer oaths and affirmations, issue orders pursuant to section 3142 of title 18 concerning release or detention of persons pending trial, and take acknowledgements, affidavits, and depositions;

(3) the power to conduct trials under section 3401, title 18, United States Code, in conformity with and subject to the limitations of that section; and

(4) the power to enter a sentence for a misdemeanor or infraction with the consent of the parties.

(b)(1) Notwithstanding any provision of law to the contrary—

(A) a judge may designate a magistrate to hear and determine any pretrial matter pending before the court, except a motion for injunctive relief, for judgment on the pleadings, for summary judgment, to dismiss or quash an indictment or information made by the defendant, to suppress evidence in a criminal case, to dismiss or to permit maintenance of a class action, to dismiss for failure to state a claim upon which relief can be granted, and to involuntarily dismiss an action. A judge of the court may reconsider any pretrial matter under this subparagraph (A) where it has been shown that the magistrate's order is clearly erroneous or contrary to law.

(B) a judge may also designate a magistrate to conduct hearings, including evidentiary hearings, and to submit to a judge of the court proposed findings of fact and recommendations for the disposition, by a judge of the court, of any motion excepted in subparagraph (A), of applications for posttrial relief made by individuals convicted of criminal offenses and of prisoner petitions challenging conditions of confinement.

(C) the magistrate shall file his proposed findings and recommendations under subparagraph (B) with the court and a copy shall forthwith be mailed to all parties.

Within ten days after being served with a copy, any party may serve and file written objections to such proposed findings and recommendations as provided by rules of court. A judge of the court shall make a de novo determination of those portions of the report or specified proposed findings or recommendations to which objection is made. A judge of the court may accept, reject, or modify, in whole or in part, the findings or recommendations made by the magistrate. The judge may also receive further evidence or recommit the matter to the magistrate with instructions.

(2) A judge may designate a magistrate to serve as a special master pursuant to the applicable provisions of this title and the Federal Rules of Civil Procedure for the United States district courts. A judge may designate a magistrate to serve as a special master in any civil case, upon consent of the parties, without regard to the provisions of rule 53(b) of the Federal Rules of Civil Procedure for the United States district courts.

(3) A magistrate may be assigned such additional duties as are not inconsistent with the Constitution and laws of the United States.

(4) Each district court shall establish rules pursuant to which the magistrates shall discharge their duties.

(c) Notwithstanding any provision of law to the contrary—

(1) Upon the consent of the parties, a full-time United States magistrate or a part-time United States magistrate who serves as a full-time judicial officer may conduct any or all proceedings in a jury

or nonjury civil matter and order the entry of judgment in the case, when specially designated to exercise such jurisdiction by the district court or courts he serves. Upon the consent of the parties, pursuant to their specific written request, any other part-time magistrate may exercise such jurisdiction, if such magistrate meets the bar membership requirements set forth in section 631(b)(1) and the chief judge of the district court certifies that a full-time magistrate is not reasonably available in accordance with guidelines established by the judicial council of the circuit. When there is more than one judge of a district court, designation under this paragraph shall be by the concurrence of a majority of all the judges of such district court, and when there is no such concurrence, then by the chief judge.

(2) If a magistrate is designated to exercise civil jurisdiction under paragraph (1) of this subsection, the clerk of court shall, at the time the action is filed, notify the parties of the availability of a magistrate to exercise such jurisdiction. The decision of the parties shall be communicated to the clerk of court. Thereafter, either the district court judge or the magistrate may again advise the parties of the availability of the magistrate, but in so doing, shall also advise the parties that they are free to withhold consent without adverse substantive consequences. Rules of court for the reference of civil matters to magistrates shall include procedures to protect the voluntariness of the parties' consent.

(3) Upon entry of judgment in any case referred under paragraph (1) of this subsection, an aggrieved party may appeal directly to the appropriate United States court of appeals from the judgment of the magistrate in the same manner as an appeal from any other judgment of a district court. In this circumstance, the consent of the parties allows a magistrate designated to exercise civil jurisdiction under paragraph (1) of this subsection to direct the entry of a judgment of the district court in accordance with the Federal Rules of Civil Procedure. Nothing in this paragraph shall be construed as a limitation of any party's right to seek review by the Supreme Court of the United States.

(4) Notwithstanding the provisions of paragraph (3) of this subsection, at the time of reference to a magistrate, the parties may further consent to appeal on the record to a judge of the district court in the same manner as on an appeal from a judgment of the district court to a court of appeals. Wherever possible the local rules of the district court and the rules promulgated by the conference shall endeavor to make such appeal inexpensive. The district court may affirm, reverse, modify, or remand the magistrate's judgment.

(5) Cases in the district courts under paragraph (4) of this subsection may be reviewed by the appropriate United States court of appeals upon petition for leave to appeal by a party stating

specific objections to the judgment. Nothing in this paragraph shall be construed to be a limitation on any party's right to seek review by the Supreme Court of the United States.

(6) The court may, for good cause shown on its own motion, or under extraordinary circumstances shown by any party, vacate a reference of a civil matter to a magistrate under this subsection.

(7) The magistrate shall, subject to guidelines of the Judicial Conference, determine whether the record taken pursuant to this section shall be taken by electronic sound recording, by a court reporter, or by other means.

(d) The practice and procedure for the trial of cases before officers serving under this chapter, and for the taking and hearing of appeals to the district courts, shall conform to rules promulgated by the Supreme Court pursuant to section 2072 of this title.

(e) In a proceeding before a magistrate, any of the following acts or conduct shall constitute a contempt of the district court for the district wherein the magistrate is sitting: (1) disobedience or resistance to any lawful order, process, or writ; (2) misbehavior at a hearing or other proceeding, or so near the place thereof as to obstruct the same; (3) failure to produce, after having been ordered to do so, any pertinent document; (4) refusal to appear after having been subpoenaed or, upon appearing, refusal to take the oath or affirmation as a witness, or, having taken the oath or affirmation, refusal to be examined according to law; or (5) any other act or conduct which if committed before a judge of the district court would constitute contempt of such court. Upon the commission of any such act or conduct, the magistrate shall forthwith certify the facts to a judge of the district court and may serve or cause to be served upon any person whose behavior is brought into question under this section an order requiring such person to appear before a judge of that court upon a day certain to show cause why he should not be adjudged in contempt by reason of the facts so certified. A judge of the district court shall thereupon, in a summary manner, hear the evidence as to the act or conduct complained of and, if it is such as to warrant punishment, punish such person in the same manner and to the same extent as for a contempt committed before a judge of the court, or commit such person upon the conditions applicable in the case of defiance of the process of the district court or misconduct in the presence of a judge of that court.

(f) In an emergency and upon the concurrence of the chief judges of the districts involved, a United States magistrate may be temporarily assigned to perform any of the duties specified in subsection (a) or (b) of this section in a judicial district other than the judicial district for which he has been appointed. No magistrate shall perform any of such duties in a district to which he has been temporarily assigned until an order has been issued by the chief judge of such district specifying (1) the emergency by reason of which he has been transferred, (2) the duration of his assignment, and (3) the duties which he is authorized to perform.

A magistrate so assigned shall not be entitled to additional compensation but shall be reimbursed for actual and necessary expenses incurred in the performance of his duties in accordance with section 635.

(g) A United States magistrate may perform the verification function required by section 4107 of title 18, United States Code. A magistrate may be assigned by a judge of any United States district court to perform the verification required by section 4108 and the appointment of counsel authorized by section 4109 of title 18, United States Code, and may perform such functions beyond the territorial limits of the United States. A magistrate assigned such functions shall have no authority to perform any other function within the territory of a foreign country.

(h) A United States magistrate who has retired may, upon the consent of the chief judge of the district involved, be recalled to serve as a magistrate in any judicial district by the judicial council of the circuit within which such district is located. Upon recall, a magistrate may receive a salary for such service in accordance with regulations promulgated by the Judicial Conference, subject to the restrictions on the payment of an annuity set forth in section 377 of this title or in subchapter III of chapter 83, and chapter 84, of title 5 which are applicable to such magistrate. The requirements set forth in subsections (a), (b)(3), and (d) of section 631, and paragraph (1) of subsection (b) of such section to the extent such paragraph requires membership of the bar of the location in which an individual is to serve as a magistrate, shall not apply to the recall of a retired magistrate under this subsection or section 375 of this title. Any other requirement set forth in section 631(b) shall apply to the recall of a retired magistrate under this subsection or section 375 of this title unless such retired magistrate met such requirement upon appointment or reappointment as a magistrate under section 361.

(As amended Oct. 17, 1968, Pub.L. 90–578, Title I, § 101, 82 Stat. 1113; Mar. 1, 1972, Pub.L. 92–239, §§ 1, 2, 86 Stat. 47; Oct. 21, 1976, Pub.L. 94–577, § 1, 90 Stat. 2729; Oct. 28, 1977, Pub.L. 95–144, § 2, 91 Stat. 1220; Oct. 10, 1979, Pub.L. 96–82, § 2, 93 Stat. 643; Oct. 12, 1984, Pub.L. 98–473, Title II, § 208, 98 Stat. 1986; Nov. 8, 1984, Pub.L. 98–620, Title IV, § 402(29)(B), 98 Stat. 3359; Nov. 14, 1986, Pub.L. 99–651, Title II, § 201(a)(2), 100 Stat. 3647; Nov. 15, 1988, Pub.L. 100–659, § 4(c), 102 Stat. 3918; Nov. 18, 1988, Pub.L. 100–690, Title VII, § 7322, 102 Stat. 4467; Nov. 19, 1988, Pub.L. 100–702, Title IV, § 404(b)(1), Title X, § 1014, 102 Stat. 4651, 4669; Dec. 1, 1990, Pub.L. 101–650, Title III, § 308, 104 Stat. 5089.)

§ 1251. Original Jurisdiction

(a) The Supreme Court shall have original and exclusive jurisdiction of all controversies between two or more States.

(b) The Supreme Court shall have original but not exclusive jurisdiction of:

(1) All actions or proceedings to which ambassadors, other public ministers, consuls, or vice consuls of foreign states are parties;

(2) All controversies between the United States and a State;

(3) All actions or proceedings by a State against the citizens of another State or against aliens.

(As amended Sept. 30, 1978, Pub.L. 95–393, § 8(b), 92 Stat. 810.)

§ 1253. Direct Appeals From Decisions of Three-Judge Courts

Except as otherwise provided by law, any party may appeal to the Supreme Court from an order granting or denying, after notice and hearing, an interlocutory or permanent injunction in any civil action, suit or proceeding required by any Act of Congress to be heard and determined by a district court of three judges.

§ 1254. Courts of Appeals; Certiorari; Certified Questions

Cases in the courts of appeals may be reviewed by the Supreme Court by the following methods:

(1) By writ of certiorari granted upon the petition of any party to any civil or criminal case, before or after rendition of judgment or decree;

(2) By certification at any time by a court of appeals of any question of law in any civil or criminal case as to which instructions are desired, and upon such certification the Supreme Court may give binding instructions or require the entire record to be sent up for decision of the entire matter in controversy.

(As amended June 27, 1988, Pub.L. 100–352, §§ 2(a), (b), 7, 102 Stat. 662, 664.)

§ 1257. State Courts; Certiorari

(a) Final judgments or decrees rendered by the highest court of a State in which a decision could be had, may be reviewed by the Supreme Court by writ of certiorari where the validity of a treaty or statute of the United States is drawn in question or where the validity of a statute of any State is drawn in question on the ground of its being repugnant to the Constitution, treaties or laws of the United States, or where any title, right, privilege or immunity is specially set up or claimed under the Constitution or the treaties or statutes of, or commission held or authority exercised under, the United States.

(b) For the purposes of this section, the term "highest court of a State" includes the District of Columbia Court of Appeals.

(As amended July 29, 1970, Pub.L. 91–358, Title I, § 172(a)(1), 84 Stat. 590; June 27, 1988, Pub.L. 100–352, §§ 3, 7, 102 Stat. 662, 664.)

§ 1291. Final Decisions of District Courts

The courts of appeals (other than the United States Court of Appeals for the Federal Circuit) shall have jurisdiction of appeals from all final decisions of the district courts of the United States, the United States District Court for the District of the Canal Zone, the District Court of Guam, and the District Court of the Virgin Islands, except where a direct review may be had in the Supreme Court. The jurisdiction of the United States Court of Appeals for the Federal Circuit shall be limited to the jurisdiction described in sections 1292(c) and (d) and 1295 of this title.

(As amended Oct. 31, 1951, c. 655, § 48, 65 Stat. 726; July 7, 1958, Pub.L. 85–508, § 12(e), 72 Stat. 348; Apr. 2, 1982, Pub.L. 97–164, Title I, § 124, 96 Stat. 36.)

§ 1292. Interlocutory Decisions

(a) Except as provided in subsections (c) and (d) of this section, the courts of appeals shall have jurisdiction of appeals from:

(1) Interlocutory orders of the district courts of the United States, the United States District Court for the District of the Canal Zone, the District Court of Guam, and the District Court of the Virgin Islands, or of the judges thereof, granting, continuing, modifying, refusing or dissolving injunctions, or refusing to dissolve or modify injunctions, except where a direct review may be had in the Supreme Court;

(2) Interlocutory orders appointing receivers, or refusing orders to wind up receiverships or to take steps to accomplish the purposes thereof, such as directing sales or other disposals of property;

(3) Interlocutory decrees of such district courts or the judges thereof determining the rights and liabilities of the parties to admiralty cases in which appeals from final decrees are allowed.

(b) When a district judge, in making in a civil action an order not otherwise appealable under this section, shall be of the opinion that such order involves a controlling question of law as to which there is substantial ground for difference of opinion and that an immediate appeal from the order may materially advance the ultimate termination of the litigation, he shall so state in writing in such order. The Court of Appeals which would have jurisdiction of an appeal of such action may thereupon, in its discretion, permit an appeal to be taken from such order, if application is made to it within ten days after the entry of the order: *Provided, however,* That application for an appeal hereunder shall not stay proceedings in the district court unless the district judge or the Court of Appeals or a judge thereof shall so order.

(c) The United States Court of Appeals for the Federal Circuit shall have exclusive jurisdiction—

(1) of an appeal from an interlocutory order or decree described in subsection (a) or (b) of this section in any case over which the court would have jurisdiction of an appeal under section 1295 of this title; and

(2) of an appeal from a judgment in a civil action for patent infringement which would otherwise be appealable to the United States Court of Appeals for the Federal Circuit and is final except for an accounting.

(d)(1) When the chief judge of the Court of International Trade issues an order under the provisions of section 256(b) of this title, or when any judge of the Court of International Trade, in issuing any other interlocutory order, includes in the order a statement that a controlling question of law is involved with respect to which there is a substantial ground for difference of opinion and that an immediate appeal from that order may materially advance the ultimate termination of the litigation, the United States Court of Appeals for the Federal Circuit may, in its discretion, permit an appeal to be taken from such order, if application is made to that Court within ten days after the entry of such order.

(2) When the chief judge of the United States Court of Federal Claims issues an order under section 798(b) of this title, or when any judge of the United States Court of Federal Claims, in issuing an interlocutory order, includes in the order a statement that a controlling question of law is involved with respect to which there is a substantial ground for difference of opinion and that an immediate appeal from that order may materially advance the ultimate termination of the litigation, the United States Court of Appeals for the Federal Circuit may, in its discretion, permit an appeal to be taken from such order, if application is made to that Court within ten days after the entry of such order.

(3) Neither the application for nor the granting of an appeal under this subsection shall stay proceedings in the Court of International Trade or in the Court of Federal Claims, as the case may be, unless a stay is ordered by a judge of the Court of International Trade or of the Court of Federal Claims or by the United States Court of Appeals for the Federal Circuit or a judge of that court.

(4)(A) The United States Court of Appeals for the Federal Circuit shall have exclusive jurisdiction of an appeal from an interlocutory order of a district court of the United States, the District Court of Guam, the District Court of the Virgin Islands, or the District Court for the Northern Mariana Islands, granting or denying, in whole or in part, a motion to transfer an action to the United States Court of Federal Claims under section 1631 of this title.

(B) When a motion to transfer an action to the Court of Federal Claims is filed in a district court, no further proceedings shall be taken in the district court until 60 days after the court has ruled upon the motion. If an appeal is taken from the district court's grant or denial of the motion, proceedings shall be further stayed until the appeal has been decided by the Court of Appeals for the Federal Circuit. The stay of proceedings in the district court shall not bar the granting of preliminary or injunctive relief, where appropriate and where expedition is reasonably necessary. However, during the period in which proceedings are stayed as provided in this subparagraph, no transfer to the Court of Federal Claims pursuant to the motion shall be carried out.

(e) The Supreme Court may prescribe rules, in accordance with section 2072 of this title, to provide for an appeal of an interlocutory decision to the courts of appeals that is not otherwise provided for under subsection (a), (b), (c), or (d).

(As amended Oct. 31, 1951, c. 655, § 49, 65 Stat. 726; July 7, 1958, Pub.L. 85–508, § 12(e), 72 Stat. 348; Sept. 2, 1958, Pub.L. 85–919, 72 Stat. 1770; Apr. 2, 1982, Pub.L. 97–164, Title I, § 125, 96 Stat. 36; Nov. 8, 1984, Pub.L. 98–620, Title IV, § 412, 98 Stat. 3362; Nov. 19, 1988, Pub.L. 100–702, Title V, § 501, 102 Stat. 4652; Oct. 29, 1992, Pub.L. 102–572, Title I, § 101, Title IX, § 906(c), 106 Stat. 4506, 4518.)

§ 1330. Actions Against Foreign States

(a) The district courts shall have original jurisdiction without regard to amount in controversy of any nonjury civil action against a foreign state as defined in section 1603(a) of this title as to any claim for relief in personam with respect to which the foreign state is not entitled to immunity either under sections 1605–1607 of this title or under any applicable international agreement.

(b) Personal jurisdiction over a foreign state shall exist as to every claim for relief over which the district courts have jurisdiction under subsection (a) where service has been made under section 1608 of this title.

(c) For purposes of subsection (b), an appearance by a foreign state does not confer personal jurisdiction with respect to any claim for relief not arising out of any transaction or occurrence enumerated in sections 1605–1607 of this title.

(Added Oct. 21, 1976, Pub.L. 94–583, § 2(a), 90 Stat. 2891.)

§ 1331. Federal Question

The district courts shall have original jurisdiction of all civil actions arising under the Constitution, laws, or treaties of the United States.

(As amended July 25, 1958, Pub.L. 85–554, § 1, 72 Stat. 415; Oct. 21, 1976, Pub.L. 94–574, § 2, 90 Stat. 2721; Dec. 1, 1980, Pub.L. 96–486, § 2(a), 94 Stat. 2369.)

§ 1332. Diversity of Citizenship; Amount in Controversy; Costs

(a) The district courts shall have original jurisdiction of all civil actions where the matter in controversy exceeds the sum or value of $50,000, exclusive of interest and costs, and is between—

    (1) citizens of different States;

    (2) citizens of a State and citizens or subjects of a foreign state;

    (3) citizens of different States and in which citizens or subjects of a foreign state are additional parties; and

    (4) a foreign state, defined in section 1603(a) of this title, as plaintiff and citizens of a State or of different States.

For the purposes of this section, section 1335, and section 1441, an alien admitted to the United States for permanent residence shall be deemed a citizen of the State in which such alien is domiciled.

(b) Except when express provision therefor is otherwise made in a statute of the United States, where the plaintiff who files the case originally in the Federal courts is finally adjudged to be entitled to recover less than the sum or value of $50,000, computed without regard to any setoff or counterclaim to which the defendant may be adjudged to be entitled, and exclusive of interest and costs, the district court may deny costs to the plaintiff and, in addition, may impose costs on the plaintiff.

(c) For the purposes of this section and section 1441 of this title—

(1) a corporation shall be deemed to be a citizen of any State by which it has been incorporated and of the State where it has its principal place of business, except that in any direct action against the insurer of a policy or contract of liability insurance, whether incorporated or unincorporated, to which action the insured is not joined as a party-defendant, such insurer shall be deemed a citizen of the State of which the insured is a citizen, as well as of any State by which the insurer has been incorporated and of the State where it has its principal place of business; and

(2) the legal representative of the estate of a decedent shall be deemed to be a citizen only of the same State as the decedent, and the legal representative of an infant or incompetent shall be deemed to be a citizen only of the same State as the infant or incompetent.

(d) The word "States", as used in this section, includes the Territories, the District of Columbia, and the Commonwealth of Puerto Rico.

(As amended July 26, 1956, c. 740, 70 Stat. 658; July 25, 1958, Pub.L. 85–554, § 2, 72 Stat. 415; Aug. 14, 1964, Pub.L. 88–439, § 1, 78 Stat. 445; Oct. 21, 1976, Pub.L. 94–583, § 3, 90 Stat. 2891, Nov. 19, 1988, Pub.L. 100–702, § 201, 102 Stat. 4642.)

§ 1335. Interpleader

(a) The district courts shall have original jurisdiction of any civil action of interpleader or in the nature of interpleader filed by any person, firm, or corporation, association, or society having in his or its custody or possession money or property of the value of $500 or more, or having issued a note, bond, certificate, policy of insurance, or other instrument of value or amount of $500 or more, or providing for the delivery or payment or the loan of money or property of such amount or value, or being under any obligation written or unwritten to the amount of $500 or more, if

(1) Two or more adverse claimants, of diverse citizenship as defined in section 1332 of this title, are claiming or may claim to be entitled to such money or property, or to any one or more of the benefits arising by virtue of any note, bond, certificate, policy or other instrument, or arising by virtue of any such obligations; and if

(2) the plaintiff has deposited such money or property or has paid the amount of or the loan or other value of such instrument or the amount due under such obligation into the registry of the court, there to abide the judgment of the court, or has given bond payable to the clerk of the court in such amount and with such surety as the court or judge may deem proper, conditioned upon the compliance by the plaintiff with the future order or judgment of the court with respect to the subject matter of the controversy.

(b) Such an action may be entertained although the titles or claims of the conflicting claimants do not have a common origin, or are not identical, but are adverse to and independent of one another.

§ 1337. Commerce and Antitrust Regulations; Amount in Controversy, Costs

(a) The district courts shall have original jurisdiction of any civil action or proceeding arising under any Act of Congress regulating commerce or protecting trade and commerce against restraints and monopolies: *Provided, however,* That the district courts shall have original jurisdiction of an action brought under section 11707 of title 49, only if the matter in controversy for each receipt or bill of lading exceeds $10,000, exclusive of interest and costs.

(b) Except when express provision therefor is otherwise made in a statute of the United States, where a plaintiff who files the case under section 11707 of title 49, originally in the Federal courts is finally adjudged to be entitled to recover less than the sum or value of $10,000, computed without regard to any setoff or counterclaim to which the defendant may be adjudged to be entitled, and exclusive of any interest and costs, the district court may deny costs to the plaintiff and, in addition, may impose costs on the plaintiff.

(c) The district courts shall not have jurisdiction under this section of any matter within the exclusive jurisdiction of the Court of International Trade under chapter 95 of this title.

(As amended Oct. 20, 1978, Pub.L. 95–486, § 9(a), 92 Stat. 1633; Oct. 10, 1980, Pub.L. 96–417, Title V, § 505, 94 Stat. 1743; Jan. 12, 1983, Pub.L. 97–449, § 5(f), 96 Stat. 2442.)

§ 1338. Patents, Plant Variety Protection, Copyrights, Mask Works, Trade-Marks, and Unfair Competition

(a) The district courts shall have original jurisdiction of any civil action arising under any Act of Congress relating to patents, plant variety protection, copyrights and trade-marks. Such jurisdiction shall be exclusive of the courts of the states in patent, plant variety protection and copyright cases.

(b) The district courts shall have original jurisdiction of any civil action asserting a claim of unfair competition when joined with a substantial and related claim under the copyright, patent, plant variety protection or trade-mark laws.

(c) Subsections (a) and (b) apply to exclusive rights in mask works under chapter 9 of title 17 to the same extent as such subsections apply to copyrights.

(As amended Dec. 24, 1970, Pub.L. 91–577, Title III, § 143(b), 84 Stat. 1559; Nov. 19, 1988, Pub.L. 100–702, § 1020, 102 Stat. 4642.)

§ 1343. Civil Rights and Elective Franchise

(a) The district courts shall have original jurisdiction of any civil action authorized by law to be commenced by any person:

(1) To recover damages for injury to his person or property, or because of the deprivation of any right or privilege of a citizen of the United States, by any act done in furtherance of any conspiracy mentioned in section 1985 of Title 42;

(2) To recover damages from any person who fails to prevent or to aid in preventing any wrongs mentioned in section 1985 of Title 42 which he had knowledge were about to occur and power to prevent;

(3) To redress the deprivation, under color of any State law, statute, ordinance, regulation, custom or usage, of any right, privilege or immunity secured by the Constitution of the United States or by any Act of Congress providing for equal rights of citizens or of all persons within the jurisdiction of the United States;

(4) To recover damages or to secure equitable or other relief under any Act of Congress providing for the protection of civil rights, including the right to vote.

(b) For purposes of this section—

(1) the District of Columbia shall be considered to be a State; and

(2) any Act of Congress applicable exclusively to the District of Columbia shall be considered to be a statute of the District of Columbia.

(As amended Sept. 3, 1954, c. 1263, § 42, 68 Stat. 1241; Sept. 9, 1957, Pub.L. 85–315, Part III, § 121, 71 Stat. 637; Dec. 29, 1979, Pub.L. 96–170, § 2, 93 Stat. 1284.)

§ 1359. Parties Collusively Joined or Made

A district court shall not have jurisdiction of a civil action in which any party, by assignment or otherwise, has been improperly or collusively made or joined to invoke the jurisdiction of such court.

§ 1367. Supplemental Jurisdiction

(a) Except as provided in subsections (b) and (c) or as expressly provided otherwise by Federal statute, in any civil action of which the district courts have original jurisdiction, the district courts shall have supplemental jurisdiction over all other claims that are so related to claims in the action within such original jurisdiction that they form part of the same case or controversy under Article III of the United States Constitution. Such supplemental jurisdiction shall include claims that involve the joinder or intervention of additional parties.

(b) In any civil action of which the district courts have original jurisdiction founded solely on section 1332 of this title, the district courts shall not have supplemental jurisdiction under subsection (a) over claims by plaintiffs against persons made parties under Rule 14, 19, 20, or 24 of the Federal Rules of Civil Procedure, or over claims by persons proposed to be joined as plaintiffs under Rule 19 of such rules, or seeking to intervene as plaintiffs under Rule 24 of such rules, when exercising supplemental jurisdiction over such claims would be inconsistent with the jurisdictional requirements of section 1332.

(c) The district courts may decline to exercise supplemental jurisdiction over a claim under subsection (a) if—

(1) the claim raises a novel or complex issue of State law,

(2) the claim substantially predominates over the claim or claims over which the district court has original jurisdiction,

(3) the district court has dismissed all claims over which it has original jurisdiction, or

(4) in exceptional circumstances, there are other compelling reasons for declining jurisdiction.

(d) The period of limitations for any claim asserted under subsection (a), and for any other claim in the same action that is voluntarily dismissed at the same time as or after the dismissal of the claim under subsection (a), shall be tolled while the claim is pending and for a period of 30 days after it is dismissed unless State law provides for a longer tolling period.

(e) As used in this section, the term 'State' includes the District of Columbia, the Commonwealth of Puerto Rico, and any territory or possession of the United States.

(Added Dec. 1, 1990, Pub.L. 101–650, § 310(a), 104 Stat. 5089.)

§ 1391. Venue Generally

(a) A civil action wherein jurisdiction is founded only on diversity of citizenship may, except as otherwise provided by law, be brought only in (1) a judicial district where any defendant resides, if all defendants reside in the same State, (2) a judicial district in which a substantial part of the events or omissions giving rise to the claim occurred, or a substantial part of property that is the subject of the action is situated, or (3) a judicial district in which the defendants are subject to personal jurisdiction at the time the action is commenced, if there is no district in which the action may otherwise be brought.

(b) A civil action wherein jurisdiction is not founded solely on diversity of citizenship may, except as otherwise provided by law, be brought only in (1) a judicial district where any defendant resides, if all defendants reside in the same State, (2) a judicial district in which a substantial part of the events or omissions giving rise to the claim occurred, or a substantial part of property that is the subject of the action is situated, or (3) a judicial district in which any defendant may be found, if there is no district in which the action may otherwise be brought.

(c) For purposes of venue under this chapter, a defendant that is a corporation shall be deemed to reside in any judicial district in which it is subject to personal jurisdiction at the time the action is commenced. In a State which has more than one judicial district and in which a defendant that is a corporation is subject to personal jurisdiction at the time an action is commenced, such corporation shall be deemed to reside in any district in that State within which its contacts would be sufficient to subject it to personal jurisdiction if that district were a separate State, and, if there is no such district, the corporation shall be deemed to reside in the district within which it has the most significant contacts.

(d) An alien may be sued in any district.

(e) A civil action in which a defendant is an officer or employee of the United States or any agency thereof acting in his official capacity or under color of legal authority, or an agency of the United States, or the United States, may, except as otherwise provided by law, be brought in any judicial district in which (1) a defendant in the action resides, (2) a substantial part of the events or omissions giving rise to the claim occurred, or a substantial part of property that is the subject of the action is situated, or (3) the plaintiff resides if no real property is involved in the action. Additional persons may be joined as parties to any such action in accordance with the Federal Rules of Civil Procedure and with such other venue requirements as would be applicable if the United States or one of its officers, employees, or agencies were not a party.

The summons and complaint in such an action shall be served as provided by the Federal Rules of Civil Procedure except that the delivery of the summons and complaint to the officer or agency as required by the rules may be made by certified mail beyond the territorial limits of the district in which the action is brought.

(f) A civil action against a foreign state as defined in section 1603(a) of this title may be brought—

> **(1)** in any judicial district in which a substantial part of the events or omissions giving rise to the claim occurred, or a substantial part of property that is the subject of the action is situated;

> **(2)** in any judicial district in which the vessel or cargo of a foreign state is situated, if the claim is asserted under section 1605(b) of this title;

> **(3)** in any judicial district in which the agency or instrumentality is licensed to do business or is doing business, if the action is brought against an agency or instrumentality of a foreign state as defined in section 1603(b) of this title; or

> **(4)** in the United States District Court for the District of Columbia if the action is brought against a foreign state or political subdivision thereof.

(As amended Oct. 5, 1962, Pub.L. 87–748, § 2, 76 Stat. 744; Dec. 23, 1963, Pub.L. 88–234, 77 Stat. 473; Nov. 2, 1966, Pub.L. 89–714, §§ 1, 2, 80 Stat. 1111; Oct. 21, 1976, Pub.L. 94–574, § 3, 90 Stat. 2721; Oct. 21, 1976, Pub.L. 94–583, § 5, 90 Stat. 2897; Nov. 19, 1988, Pub.L. 100–702, § 1013, 102 Stat. 4642; Dec. 1, 1990, Pub.L. 101–650, § 311, 104 Stat. 5089; Dec. 9, 1991, Pub.L. 102–198, § 3, 105 Stat. 1623; Oct. 29, 1992, Pub.L. 102–572, Title V, § 504, 106 Stat. 4513.)

§ 1392. Defendants or Property in Different Districts in Same State

(a) Any civil action, not of a local nature, against defendants residing in different districts in the same State, may be brought in any of such districts.

(b) Any civil action, of a local nature, involving property located in different districts in the same State, may be brought in any of such districts.

§ 1397. Interpleader

Any civil action of interpleader or in the nature of interpleader under section 1335 of this title may be brought in the judicial district in which one or more of the claimants reside.

§ 1400. Patents and Copyrights

(a) Civil actions, suits, or proceedings arising under any Act of Congress relating to copyrights or exclusive rights in mask works may be instituted in the district in which the defendant or his agent resides or may be found.

(b) Any civil action for patent infringement may be brought in the judicial district where the defendant resides, or where the defendant has committed acts of infringement and has a regular and established place of business.

(As amended Nov. 19, 1988, Pub.L. 100–702, § 1020, 102 Stat. 4642.)

§ 1401. Stockholder's Derivative Action

Any civil action by a stockholder on behalf of his corporation may be prosecuted in any judicial district where the corporation might have sued the same defendants.

§ 1404. Change of Venue

(a) For the convenience of parties and witnesses, in the interest of justice, a district court may transfer any civil action to any other district or division where it might have been brought.

(b) Upon motion, consent or stipulation of all parties, any action, suit or proceeding of a civil nature or any motion or hearing thereof, may be transferred, in the discretion of the court, from the division in which pending to any other division in the same district. Transfer of proceedings in rem brought by or on behalf of the United States may be transferred under this section without the consent of the United States where all other parties request transfer.

(c) A district court may order any civil action to be tried at any place within the division in which it is pending.

(d) As used in this section, "district court" includes the United States District Court for the District of the Canal Zone; and "district" includes the territorial jurisdiction of that court.

(As amended Oct. 18, 1962, Pub.L. 87–845, § 9, 76A Stat. 699.)

§ 1406. Cure or Waiver of Defects

(a) The district court of a district in which is filed a case laying venue in the wrong division or district shall dismiss, or if it be in the interest of justice, transfer such case to any district or division in which it could have been brought.

(b) Nothing in this chapter shall impair the jurisdiction of a district court of any matter involving a party who does not interpose timely and sufficient objection to the venue.

(c) As used in this section, "district court" includes the United States District Court for the District of the Canal Zone; and "district" includes the territorial jurisdiction of that court.

(As amended May 24, 1949, c. 139, § 81, 63 Stat. 101; Sept. 13, 1960, Pub.L. 86–770, § 1, 74 Stat. 912; Oct. 18, 1962, Pub.L. 87–845, § 10, 76A Stat. 699; Apr. 2, 1982, Pub.L. 97–164, Title I, § 132, 96 Stat. 39.)

§ 1407. Multidistrict Litigation

(a) When civil actions involving one or more common questions of fact are pending in different districts, such actions may be transferred to any district for coordinated or consolidated pretrial proceedings. Such transfers shall be made by the judicial panel on multidistrict litigation authorized by this section upon its determination that transfers for such proceedings will be for the convenience of parties and witnesses and will promote the just and efficient conduct of such actions. Each action so transferred shall be remanded by the panel at or before the conclusion of such pretrial proceedings to the district from which it was transferred unless it shall have been previously terminated: *Provided, however,* That the panel may separate any claim, cross-claim, counter-claim, or third-party claim and remand any of such claims before the remainder of the action is remanded.

(b) Such coordinated or consolidated pretrial proceedings shall be conducted by a judge or judges to whom such actions are assigned by the judicial panel on multidistrict litigation. For this purpose, upon request of the panel, a circuit judge or a district judge may be designated and assigned temporarily for service in the transferee district by the Chief Justice of the United States or the chief judge of the circuit, as may be required, in accordance with the provisions of chapter 13 of this title. With the consent of the transferee district court, such actions may be assigned by the panel to a judge or judges of such district. The judge or judges to whom such actions are assigned, the members of the judicial panel on multidistrict litigation, and other circuit and district judges designated when needed by the panel may exercise the powers of a district judge in any district for the purpose of conducting pretrial depositions in such coordinated or consolidated pretrial proceedings.

(c) Proceedings for the transfer of an action under this section may be initiated by—

(i) the judicial panel on multidistrict litigation upon its own initiative, or

(ii) motion filed with the panel by a party in any action in which transfer for coordinated or consolidated pretrial proceedings under this section may be appropriate. A copy of such motion shall be filed in the district court in which the moving party's action is pending.

The panel shall give notice to the parties in all actions in which transfers for coordinated or consolidated pretrial proceedings are contemplated, and such notice shall specify the time and place of any hearing to determine whether such transfer shall be made. Orders of the panel to set a hearing and other orders of the panel issued prior to the order either directing or denying transfer shall be filed in the office of the clerk of the district court in which a transfer hearing is to be or has been held. The panel's order of transfer shall be based upon a record of such hearing at which material evidence may be offered by any party to an action pending in any district that would be affected by the proceedings under this section, and shall be supported by findings of fact and conclusions of law based upon such record. Orders of transfer and such other orders as the panel may make thereafter shall be filed in the office of the clerk of the district court of the transferee district and shall be effective when thus filed. The clerk of the transferee district court shall forthwith transmit a certified copy of the panel's order to transfer to the clerk of the district court from which the action is being transferred. An order denying transfer shall be filed in each district wherein there is a case pending in which the motion for transfer has been made.

(d) The judicial panel on multidistrict litigation shall consist of seven circuit and district judges designated from time to time by the Chief Justice of the United States, no two of whom shall be from the same circuit. The concurrence of four members shall be necessary to any action by the panel.

(e) No proceedings for review of any order of the panel may be permitted except by extraordinary writ pursuant to the provisions of title 28, section 1651, United States Code. Petitions for an extraordinary writ to review an order of the panel to set a transfer hearing and other orders of the panel issued prior to the order either directing or denying transfer shall be filed only in the court of appeals having jurisdiction over the district in which a hearing is to be or has been held. Petitions for an extraordinary writ to review an order to transfer or orders subsequent to transfer shall be filed only in the court of appeals having jurisdiction over the transferee district. There shall be no appeal or review of an order of the panel denying a motion to transfer for consolidated or coordinated proceedings.

(f) The panel may prescribe rules for the conduct of its business not inconsistent with Acts of Congress and the Federal Rules of Civil Procedure.

(g) Nothing in this section shall apply to any action in which the United States is a complainant arising under the antitrust laws. "Antitrust laws" as used herein include those acts referred to in the Act of October 15, 1914, as amended (38 Stat. 730; 15 U.S.C. 12), and also include the Act of June 19, 1936 (49 Stat. 1526; 15 U.S.C. 13, 13a, and 13b) and the Act of September 26, 1914, as added March 21, 1938 (52 Stat. 116, 117; 15 U.S.C. 56); but shall not include section 4A of the Act of October 15, 1914, as added July 7, 1955 (69 Stat. 282; 15 U.S.C. 15a).

(h) Notwithstanding the provisions of section 1404 or subsection (f) of this section, the judicial panel on multidistrict litigation may consolidate and transfer with or without the consent of the parties, for both pretrial purposes and for trial, any action brought under section 4C of the Clayton Act.

(Added Apr. 29, 1968, Pub.L. 90–296, § 1, 82 Stat. 109, and amended Sept. 30, 1976, Pub.L. 94–435, Title III, § 303, 90 Stat. 1396.)

§ 1441.   Actions Removable Generally

(a) Except as otherwise expressly provided by Act of Congress, any civil action brought in a State court of which the district courts of the United States have original jurisdiction, may be removed by the defendant or the defendants, to the district court of the United States for the district and division embracing the place where such action is pending. For purposes of removal under this chapter, the citizenship of defendants sued under fictitious names shall be disregarded.

(b) Any civil action of which the district courts have original jurisdiction founded on a claim or right arising under the Constitution, treaties or laws of the United States shall be removable without regard to the citizenship or residence of the parties. Any other such action shall be removable only if none of the parties in interest properly joined and served as defendants is a citizen of the State in which such action is brought.

(c) Whenever a separate and independent claim or cause of action within the jurisdiction conferred by section 1331 of this title is joined with one or more otherwise non-removable claims or causes of action, the entire case may be removed and the district court may determine all issues therein, or, in its discretion, may remand all matters in which State law predominates.

(d) Any civil action brought in a State court against a foreign state as defined in section 1603(a) of this title may be removed by the foreign state to the district court of the United States for the district and division embracing the place where such action is pending. Upon removal the action shall be tried by the court without jury. Where removal is based upon this subsection, the time limitations of section 1446(b) of this chapter may be enlarged at any time for cause shown.

(e) The court to which such civil action is removed is not precluded from hearing and determining any claim in such civil action because the State court from which such civil action is removed did not have jurisdiction over that claim.

(As amended Oct. 21, 1976, Pub.L. 94–583, § 6, 90 Stat. 2898; June 19, 1986, Pub.L. 99–336, § 3(a), 100 Stat. 637; Nov. 19, 1988, Pub.L. 100–702, § 1016, 102 Stat. 4642; Dec. 1, 1990, Pub.L. 101–650, § 312, 104 Stat. 5089; Dec. 9, 1991, Pub.L. 102–198, § 4, 105 Stat. 1623.)

§ 1443. Civil Rights Cases

Any of the following civil actions or criminal prosecutions, commenced in a State court may be removed by the defendant to the district court of the United States for the district and division embracing the place wherein it is pending:

> **(1)** Against any person who is denied or cannot enforce in the courts of such State a right under any law providing for the equal civil rights of citizens of the United States, or of all persons within the jurisdiction thereof;

> **(2)** For any act under color of authority derived from any law providing for equal rights, or for refusing to do any act on the ground that it would be inconsistent with such law.

§ 1446. Procedure for Removal

(a) A defendant or defendants desiring to remove any civil action or criminal prosecution from a State court shall file in the district court of the United States for the district and division within which such action is pending a notice of removal signed pursuant to Rule 11 of the Federal Rules of Civil Procedure and containing a short and plain statement of the grounds for removal, together with a copy of all process, pleadings, and orders served upon such defendant or defendants in such action.

(b) The notice of removal of a civil action or proceeding shall be filed within thirty days after the receipt by the defendant, through service or otherwise, of a copy of the initial pleading setting forth the claim for relief upon which such action or proceeding is based, or within thirty days after the service of summons upon the defendant if such initial pleading has then been filed in court and is not required to be served on the defendant, whichever period is shorter.

If the case stated by the initial pleading is not removable, a notice of removal may be filed within thirty days after receipt by the defendant, through service or otherwise, of a copy of an amended pleading, motion, order or other paper from which it may first be ascertained that the case is one which is or has become removable, except that a case may not be removed on the basis of jurisdiction conferred by section 1332 of this title more than 1 year after commencement of the action.

(c)(1) A notice of removal of a criminal prosecution shall be filed not later than thirty days after the arraignment in the State court, or at any time before trial, whichever is earlier, except that for good cause shown the United States district court may enter an order granting the petitioner leave to file the notice at a later time.

(2) A notice of removal of a criminal prosecution shall include all grounds for such removal. A failure to state grounds which exist at the time of the filing of the notice shall constitute a waiver of such grounds, and a second notice may be filed only on grounds not existing at the time of the original notice. For good cause shown, the United States district court may grant relief from the limitations of this paragraph.

(3) The filing of a notice of removal of a criminal prosecution shall not prevent the State court in which such prosecution is pending from proceeding further, except that a judgment of conviction shall not be entered unless the prosecution is first remanded.

(4) The United States district court to which such notice is filed shall examine the notice promptly. If it clearly appears on the face of the notice and any exhibits annexed thereto that removal should not be permitted, the court shall make an order for summary remand.

(5) If the United States district court does not order the summary remand of such prosecution, it shall order an evidentiary hearing to be held promptly and after such hearing shall make such disposition of the prosecution as justice shall require. If the United States district court determines that removal shall be granted, it shall so notify the State court in which prosecution is pending, which shall proceed no further.

(d) Promptly after the filing of such petition for removal of a civil action the defendant or defendants shall give written notice thereof to all adverse parties and shall file a copy of the notice with the clerk of such State court, which shall effect the removal and the State court shall proceed no further unless and until the case is remanded.

(e) If the defendant or defendants are in actual custody on process issued by the State court, the district court shall issue its writ of habeas corpus, and the marshal shall thereupon take such defendant or defendants into his custody and deliver a copy of the writ to the clerk of such State court.

(As amended May 24, 1949, c. 139, § 83, 63 Stat. 101; Sept. 29, 1965, Pub.L. 89–215, 79 Stat. 887; July 30, 1977, Pub.L. 95–78, § 3, 91 Stat. 321; Nov. 19, 1988, Pub.L. 100–702, § 1016(b), 102 Stat. 4669; Dec. 9, 1991, Pub.L. 102–198, § 10a, 105 Stat. 1623.)

§ 1447. Procedure After Removal Generally

(a) In any case removed from a State court, the district court may issue all necessary orders and process to bring before it all proper parties whether served by process issued by the State court or otherwise.

(b) It may require the removing party to file with its clerk copies of all records and proceedings in such State court or may cause the same to be brought before it by writ of certiorari issued to such State court.

(c) A motion to remand the case on the basis of any defect in removal procedure must be made within 30 days after the filing of the notice of removal under section 1446(a). If at any time before final judgment it appears that the district court lacks subject matter jurisdiction, the case shall be remanded. An order remanding the case may require payment of just costs and any actual expenses, including attorney fees, incurred as a result of the removal. A certified copy of the order of remand shall be mailed by the clerk to the clerk of the State court. The State court may thereupon proceed with such case.

(d) An order remanding a case to the State court from which it was removed is not reviewable on appeal or otherwise, except that an order remanding a case to the State court from which it was removed pursuant to section 1443 of this title shall be reviewable by appeal or otherwise.

(e) If after removal the plaintiff seeks to join additional defendants whose joinder would destroy subject matter jurisdiction, the court may deny joinder, or permit joinder and remand the action to the State court.

(As amended May 24, 1949, c. 139, § 84, 63 Stat. 102; July 2, 1964, Pub.L. 88–352, Title IX, § 901, 78 Stat. 266; Nov. 19, 1988, Pub.L. 100–702, § 1016, 102 Stat. 4670; Dec. 9, 1991, Pub.L. 102–198, § 10(b), 105 Stat. 1626.)

§ 1448. Process After Removal

In all cases removed from any State court to any district court of the United States in which any one or more of the defendants has not been served with process or in which the service has not been perfected prior to removal, or in which process served proves to be defective, such process or service may be completed or new process issued in the same manner as in cases originally filed in such district court.

This section shall not deprive any defendant upon whom process is served after removal of his right to move to remand the case.

§ 1631. Transfer to Cure Want of Jurisdiction

Whenever a civil action is filed in a court as defined in section 610 of this title or an appeal, including a petition for review of administrative action, is noticed for or filed with such a court and that court finds that there is a want of jurisdiction, the court shall, if it is in the interest of justice, transfer such action or appeal to any other such court in which the action or appeal could have been brought at the time it was filed or noticed, and the action or appeal shall proceed as if it had been filed in or noticed for the court to which it is transferred on the date upon which it was actually filed in or noticed for the court from which it is transferred.

(Added Pub.L. 97–164, Title III, § 301(a), Apr. 2, 1982, 96 Stat. 55.)

§ 1651. Writs

(a) The Supreme Court and all courts established by Act of Congress may issue all writs necessary or appropriate in aid of their respective jurisdictions and agreeable to the usages and principles of law.

(b) An alternative writ or rule nisi may be issued by a justice or judge of a court which has jurisdiction.

(As amended May 24, 1949, c. 139, § 90, 63 Stat. 102.)

§ 1652. State Laws as Rules of Decision

The laws of the several states, except where the Constitution or treaties of the United States or Acts of Congress otherwise require or provide, shall be regarded as rules of decision in civil actions in the courts of the United States, in cases where they apply.

§ 1653. Amendment of Pleadings to Show Jurisdiction

Defective allegations of jurisdiction may be amended, upon terms, in the trial or appellate courts.

§ 1658. Time Limitations on the Commencement of Civil Actions Arising Under Acts of Congress

Except as otherwise provided by law, a civil action arising under an Act of Congress enacted after the date of the enactment of this section may not be commenced later than 4 years after the cause of action accrues.

(Added Dec. 1, 1990, Pub.L. 101–650, § 313, 104 Stat. 5089.)

§ 1738. State and Territorial Statutes and Judicial Proceedings; Full Faith and Credit

The Acts of the legislature of any State, Territory, or Possession of the United States, or copies thereof, shall be authenticated by affixing the seal of such State, Territory or Possession thereto.

The records and judicial proceedings of any court of any such State, Territory or Possession, or copies thereof, shall be proved or admitted in other courts within the United States and its Territories and Possessions by the attestation of the clerk and seal of the court annexed, if a seal exists, together with a certificate of a judge of the court that the said attestation is in proper form.

Such Acts, records and judicial proceedings or copies thereof, so authenticated, shall have the same full faith and credit in every court within the United States and its Territories and Possessions as they have by law or usage in the courts of such State, Territory or Possession from which they are taken.

§ 1738A. Full Faith and Credit Given to Child Custody Determinations

(a) The appropriate authorities of every State shall enforce according to its terms, and shall not modify except as provided in subsection (f) of this section, any child custody determination made consistently with the provisions of this section by a court of another State.

(b) As used in this section, the term—

(1) "child" means a person under the age of eighteen;

(2) "contestant" means a person, including a parent, who claims a right to custody or visitation of a child;

(3) "custody determination" means a judgment, decree, or other order of a court providing for the custody or visitation of a child, and includes permanent and temporary orders, and initial orders and modifications;

(4) "home State" means the State in which, immediately preceding the time involved, the child lived with his parents, a parent, or a person acting as parent, for at least six consecutive months, and in the case of a child less than six months old, the State in which the child lived from birth with any of such persons. Periods of temporary absence of any of such persons are counted as part of the six-month or other period;

(5) "modification" and "modify" refer to a custody determination which modifies, replaces, supersedes, or otherwise is made subsequent to, a prior custody determination concerning the same child, whether made by the same court or not;

(6) "person acting as a parent" means a person, other than a parent, who has physical custody of a child and who has either been awarded custody by a court or claims a right to custody;

(7) "physical custody" means actual possession and control of a child; and

(8) "State" means a State of the United States, the District of Columbia, the Commonwealth of Puerto Rico, or a territory or possession of the United States.

(c) A child custody determination made by a court of a State is consistent with the provisions of this section only if—

(1) such court has jurisdiction under the law of such State; and

(2) one of the following conditions is met:

(A) such State (i) is the home State of the child on the date of the commencement of the proceeding, or (ii) had been the child's home State within six months before the date of the commencement of the proceeding and the child is absent from such State because of his removal or retention by a contestant or for other reasons, and a contestant continues to live in such State;

(B)(i) it appears that no other State would have jurisdiction under subparagraph (A), and (ii) it is in the best interest of the child that a court of such State assume jurisdiction because (I) the child and his parents, or the child and at least one contestant, have a significant connection with such State other than mere physical presence in such State, and (II) there is available in such State substantial evidence concerning the child's present or future care, protection, training, and personal relationships;

(C) the child is physically present in such State and (i) the child has been abandoned, or (ii) it is necessary in an emergency to protect the child because he has been subjected to or threatened with mistreatment or abuse;

(D)(i) it appears that no other State would have jurisdiction under subparagraph (A), (B), (C), or (E), or another State has declined to exercise jurisdiction on the ground that the State whose jurisdiction is in issue is the more appropriate forum to determine the custody of the child, and (ii) it is in the best interest of the child that such court assume jurisdiction; or

(E) the court has continuing jurisdiction pursuant to subsection (d) of this section.

(d) The jurisdiction of a court of a State which has made a child custody determination consistently with the provisions of this section continues as long as the requirement of subsection (c)(1) of this section continues to be met and such State remains the residence of the child or of any contestant.

(e) Before a child custody determination is made, reasonable notice and opportunity to be heard shall be given to the contestants, any parent whose parental rights have not been previously terminated and any person who has physical custody of a child.

(f) A court of a State may modify a determination of the custody of the same child made by a court of another State, if—

(1) it has jurisdiction to make such a child custody determination; and

(2) the court of the other State no longer has jurisdiction, or it has declined to exercise such jurisdiction to modify such determination.

(g) A court of a State shall not exercise jurisdiction in any proceeding for a custody determination commenced during the pendency of a proceeding in a court of another State where such court of that other State is exercising jurisdiction consistently with the provisions of this section to make a custody determination.

(Added Dec. 28, 1980, Pub.L. 96–611, § 8(a), 94 Stat. 3569.)

§ 1746. Unsworn Declarations Under Penalty of Perjury

Wherever, under any law of the United States or under any rule, regulation, order, or requirement made pursuant to law, any matter is required or permitted to be supported, evidenced, established, or proved by the sworn declaration, verification, certificate, statement, oath, or affidavit, in writing of the person making the same (other than a deposition, or an oath of office, or an oath required to be taken before a specified official other than a notary public), such matter may, with like force and effect, be supported, evidenced, established, or proved by the unsworn declaration, certificate, verification, or statement, in writing of such person which is subscribed by him, as true under penalty of perjury, and dated, in substantially the following form:

> (1) If executed without the United States: "I declare (or certify, verify, or state) under penalty of perjury under the laws of the United States of America that the foregoing is true and correct. Executed on (date).
>
> (Signature)".
>
> (2) If executed within the United States, its territories, possessions, or commonwealths: "I declare (or certify, verify, or state) under penalty of perjury that the foregoing is true and correct. Executed on (date).
>
> (Signature)".

(Added Pub.L. 94–550, § 1(a), Oct. 18, 1976, 90 Stat. 2534.)

§ 1861. Declaration of Policy

It is the policy of the United States that all litigants in Federal courts entitled to trial by jury shall have the right to grand and petit juries selected at random from a fair cross section of the community in the district or division wherein the court convenes. It is further the policy of the United States that all citizens shall have the opportunity to be considered for service on grand and petit juries in the district courts of the United States, and shall have an obligation to serve as jurors when summoned for that purpose.

(As amended Sept. 9, 1957, Pub.L. 85–315, Part V, § 152, 71 Stat. 638; Mar. 27, 1968, Pub.L. 90–274, § 101, 82 Stat. 54.)

§ 1862. Discrimination Prohibited

No citizen shall be excluded from service as a grand or petit juror in the district courts of the United States or in the Court of International Trade on account of race, color, religion, sex, national origin, or economic status.

(As amended Mar. 27, 1968, Pub.L. 90–274, § 101, 82 Stat. 54; Oct. 10, 1980, Pub.L. 96–417, Title III, § 302(c), 94 Stat. 1739.)

§ 1863. Plan for Random Jury Selection

(a) Each United States district court shall devise and place into operation a written plan for random selection of grand and petit jurors that shall be designed to achieve the objectives of sections 1861 and 1862 of this title, and that shall otherwise comply with the provisions of this title. The plan shall be placed into operation after approval by a reviewing panel consisting of the members of the judicial council of the circuit and either the chief judge of the district whose plan is being reviewed or such other active district judge of that district as the chief judge of the district may designate. The panel shall examine the plan to ascertain that it complies with the provisions of this title. If the reviewing panel finds that the plan does not comply, the panel shall state the particulars in which the plan fails to comply and direct the district court to present within a reasonable time an alternative plan remedying the defect or defects. Separate plans may be adopted for each division or combination of divisions within a judicial district. The district court may modify a plan at any time and it shall modify the plan when so directed by the reviewing panel. The district court shall promptly notify the panel, the Administrative Office of the United States Courts, and the Attorney General of the United States, of the initial adoption and future modifications of the plan by filing copies therewith. Modifications of the plan made at the instance of the district court shall become effective after approval by the panel. Each district court shall submit a report on the jury selection process within its jurisdiction to the Administrative Office of the United States Courts in such form and at such times as the Judicial Conference of the United States may specify. The Judicial Conference of the United States may, from time to time, adopt rules and regulations governing the provisions and the operation of the plans formulated under this title.

(b) Among other things, such plan shall—

(1) either establish a jury commission, or authorize the clerk of the court, to manage the jury selection process. If the plan establishes a jury commission, the district court shall appoint one citizen to serve with the clerk of the court as the jury commission: *Provided, however,* That the plan for the District of Columbia may establish a jury commission consisting of three citizens. The citizen jury commissioner shall not belong to the same political party as the clerk serving with him. The clerk or the jury commission, as the case may be, shall act under the supervision and control of the chief judge of the district court or such other judge of the district court as the plan may provide. Each jury commissioner shall, during his tenure in office, reside in the judicial district or division for which he is appointed. Each citizen jury commissioner shall receive compensation to be fixed by the district court plan at a rate not to exceed $50 per day for each day necessarily employed in the performance of his duties, plus reimbursement for travel, subsistence, and other necessary expenses incurred by him in the performance of such duties. The Judicial Conference of the United States may establish standards for allowance of travel, subsistence, and other necessary expenses incurred by jury commissioners.

(2) specify whether the names of prospective jurors shall be selected from the voter registration lists or the lists of actual voters of the political subdivisions within the district or division. The plan shall prescribe some other source or sources of names in addition to voter lists where necessary to foster the policy and protect the rights secured by sections 1861 and 1862 of this title. The plan for the District of Columbia may require the names of prospective jurors to be selected from the city directory rather than from voter lists. The plans for the districts of Puerto Rico and the Canal Zone may

prescribe some other source or sources of names of prospective jurors in lieu of voter lists, the use of which shall be consistent with the policies declared and rights secured by sections 1861 and 1862 of this title. The plan for the district of Massachusetts may require the names of prospective jurors to be selected from the resident list provided for in Chapter 234A, Massachusetts General Laws, or comparable authority, rather than from voter lists.

(3) specify detailed procedures to be followed by the jury commission or clerk in selecting names from the sources specified in paragraph (2) of this subsection. These procedures shall be designed to ensure the random selection of a fair cross section of the persons residing in the community in the district or division wherein the court convenes. They shall ensure that names of persons residing in each of the counties, parishes, or similar political subdivisions within the judicial district or division are placed in a master jury wheel; and shall ensure that each county, parish, or similar political subdivision within the district or division is substantially proportionally represented in the master jury wheel for that judicial district, division, or combination of divisions. For the purposes of determining proportional representation in the master jury wheel, either the number of actual voters at the last general election in each county, parish, or similar political subdivision, or the number of registered voters if registration of voters is uniformly required throughout the district or division, may be used.

(4) provide for a master jury wheel (or a device similar in purpose and function) into which the names of those randomly selected shall be placed. The plan shall fix a minimum number of names to be placed initially in the master jury wheel, which shall be at least one-half of 1 per centum of the total number of persons on the lists used as a source of names for the district or division; but if this number of names is believed to be cumbersome and unnecessary, the plan may fix a smaller number of names to be placed in the master wheel, but in no event less than one thousand. The chief judge of the district court, or such other district court judge as the plan may provide, may order additional names to be placed in the master jury wheel from time to time as necessary. The plan shall provide for periodic emptying and refilling of the master jury wheel at specified times, the interval for which shall not exceed four years.

(5)(A) except as provided in subparagraph (B), specify those groups of persons or occupational classes whose members shall, on individual request therefor, be excused from jury service. Such groups or classes shall be excused only if the district court finds, and the plan states, that jury service by such class or group would entail undue hardship or extreme inconvenience to the members thereof, and excuse of members thereof would not be inconsistent with sections 1861 and 1862 of this title.

(B) specify that volunteer safety personnel, upon individual request, shall be excused from jury service. For purposes of this subparagraph, the term 'volunteer safety personnel' means individuals serving a public agency (as defined in section 1203(6) of title I of the Omnibus Crime Control and Safe Streets Act of 1968) in an official capacity, without compensation, as firefighters or members of a rescue squad or ambulance crew.

(6) specify that the following persons are barred from jury service on the ground that they are exempt: (A) members in active service in the Armed Forces of the United States; (B) members of the fire or police departments of any State, the District of Columbia, any territory or possession of the United States, or any subdivision of a State, the District of Columbia, or such territory or possession; (C) public officers in the executive, legislative, or judicial branches of the Government of the United States, or of any State, the District of Columbia, any territory or possession of the United States, or any subdivision of a State, the District of Columbia, or such territory or possession, who are actively engaged in the performance of official duties.

(7) fix the time when the names drawn from the qualified jury wheel shall be disclosed to parties and to the public. If the plan permits these names to be made public, it may nevertheless permit the chief judge of the district court, or such other district court judge as the plan may provide, to keep these names confidential in any case where the interests of justice so require.

(8) specify the procedures to be followed by the clerk or jury commission in assigning persons whose names have been drawn from the qualified jury wheel to grand and petit jury panels.

(c) The initial plan shall be devised by each district court and transmitted to the reviewing panel specified in subsection (a) of this section within one hundred and twenty days of the date of enactment of the Jury Selection and Service Act of 1968. The panel shall approve or direct the modification of each plan so submitted within sixty days thereafter. Each plan or modification made at the direction of the panel shall become effective after approval at such time thereafter as the panel directs, in no event to exceed ninety days from the date of approval. Modifications made at the instance of the district court under subsection (a) of this section shall be effective at such time thereafter as the panel directs, in no event to exceed ninety days from the date of modification.

(d) State, local, and Federal officials having custody, possession, or control of voter registration lists, lists of actual voters, or other appropriate records shall make such lists and records available to the jury commission or clerks for inspection, reproduction, and copying at all reasonable times as the commission or clerk may deem necessary and proper for the performance of duties under this title. The district courts shall have jurisdiction upon application by the Attorney General of the

United States to compel compliance with this subsection by appropriate process.

(As amended Mar. 27, 1968, Pub.L. 90–274, § 101, 82 Stat. 54; Apr. 6, 1972, Pub.L. 92–269, § 2, 86 Stat. 117; Nov. 2, 1978, Pub.L. 95–572, § 2(a), 92 Stat. 2453; Nov. 19, 1988, Pub.L. 100–702, Title VIII, § 802(b), (c), 102 Stat. 4657, 4658; Oct. 29, 1992, Pub.L. 102–572, Title IV, § 401, 106 Stat. 4511.)

§ 1864. Drawing of Names From the Master Jury Wheel; Completion of Juror Qualification Form

(a) From time to time as directed by the district court, the clerk or a district judge shall publicly draw at random from the master jury wheel the names of as many persons as may be required for jury service. The clerk or jury commission may, upon order of the court, prepare an alphabetical list of the names drawn from the master jury wheel. Any list so prepared shall not be disclosed to any person except pursuant to the district court plan or pursuant to section 1867 or 1868 of this title. The clerk or jury commission shall mail to every person whose name is drawn from the master wheel a juror qualification form accompanied by instructions to fill out and return the form, duly signed and sworn, to the clerk or jury commission by mail within ten days. If the person is unable to fill out the form, another shall do it for him, and shall indicate that he has done so and the reason therefor. In any case in which it appears that there is an omission, ambiguity, or error in a form, the clerk or jury commission shall return the form with instructions to the person to make such additions or corrections as may be necessary and to return the form to the clerk or jury commission within ten days. Any person who fails to return a completed juror qualification form as instructed may be summoned by the clerk or jury commission forthwith to appear before the clerk or jury commission to fill out a juror qualification form. A person summoned to appear because of failure to return a juror qualification form as instructed who personally appears and executes a juror qualification form before the clerk or jury commission may, at the discretion of the district court, except where his prior failure to execute and mail such form was willful, be entitled to receive for such appearance the same fees and travel allowances paid to jurors under section 1871 of this title. At the time of his appearance for jury service, any person may be required to fill out another juror qualification form in the presence of the jury commission or the clerk or the court, at which time, in such cases as it appears warranted, the person may be questioned, but only with regard to his responses to questions contained on the form. Any information thus acquired by the clerk or jury commission may be noted on the juror qualification form and transmitted to the chief judge or such district court judge as the plan may provide.

(b) Any person summoned pursuant to subsection (a) of this section who fails to appear as directed shall be ordered by the district court forthwith to appear and show cause for his failure to comply with the summons. Any person who fails to appear pursuant to such order or who fails to show good cause for noncompliance with the summons may be fined not more than $100 or imprisoned not more than three days, or both. Any person who willfully misrepresents a material fact on a juror qualification form for the purpose of avoiding or securing service as a juror may be fined not more than $100 or imprisoned not more than three days, or both.

(As amended Mar. 27, 1968, Pub.L. 90–274, § 101, 82 Stat. 57; Nov. 19, 1988, Pub.L. 100–702, § 803, 102 Stat. 4642.)

§ 1865. Qualifications for Jury Service

(a) The chief judge of the district court, or such other district court judge as the plan may provide, on his initiative or upon recommendation of the clerk or jury commission, shall determine solely on the basis of information provided on the juror qualification form and other competent evidence whether a person is unqualified for, or exempt, or to be excused from jury service. The clerk shall enter such determination in the space provided on the juror qualification form and in any alphabetical list of names drawn from the master jury wheel. If a person did not appear in response to a summons, such fact shall be noted on said list.

(b) In making such determination the chief judge of the district court, or such other district court judge as the plan may provide, shall deem any person qualified to serve on grand and petit juries in the district court unless he—

(1) is not a citizen of the United States eighteen years old who has resided for a period of one year within the judicial district;

(2) is unable to read, write, and understand the English language with a degree of proficiency sufficient to fill out satisfactorily the juror qualification form;

(3) is unable to speak the English language;

(4) is incapable, by reason of mental or physical infirmity, to render satisfactory jury service; or

(5) has a charge pending against him for the commission of, or has been convicted in a State or Federal court of record of, a crime punishable by imprisonment for more than one year and his civil rights have not been restored.

(As amended Mar. 27, 1968, Pub.L. 90–274, § 101, 82 Stat. 58; Apr. 6, 1972, Pub.L. 92–269, § 1, 86 Stat. 117; Nov. 2, 1978, Pub.L. 95–572, § 3(a), 92 Stat. 2453; Nov. 19, 1988, Pub.L. 100–702, § 803, 102 Stat. 4642.)

§ 1866. Selection and Summoning of Jury Panels

(a) The jury commission, or in the absence thereof the clerk, shall maintain a qualified jury wheel and shall place in such wheel names of all persons drawn from the master jury wheel who are determined to be qualified as jurors and not exempt or excused pursuant to the district court plan. From time to time, the jury commission or the clerk shall publicly draw at random from the qualified jury wheel such number of names of persons as may be required for assignment to grand and petit jury panels. The jury commission or the clerk shall prepare a separate list of names of persons assigned to each grand and petit jury panel.

(b) When the court orders a grand or petit jury to be drawn, the clerk or jury commission or their duly designated deputies shall issue summonses for the required number of jurors.

Each person drawn for jury service may be served personally, or by registered, certified, or first-class mail addressed to such person at his usual residence or business address.

If such service is made personally, the summons shall be delivered by the clerk or the jury commission or their duly designated deputies to the marshal who shall make such service.

If such service is made by mail, the summons may be served by the marshal or by the clerk, the jury commission or their duly designated deputies, who shall make affidavit of service and shall attach thereto any receipt from the addressee for a registered or certified summons.

(c) Except as provided in section 1865 of this title or in any jury selection plan provision adopted pursuant to paragraph (5) or (6) of section 1863(b) of this title, no person or class of persons shall be disqualified, excluded, excused, or exempt from service as jurors: *Provided,* That any person summoned for jury service may be (1) excused by the court, or by the clerk under supervision of the court if the court's jury selection plan so authorizes, upon a showing of undue hardship or extreme inconvenience, for such period as the court deems necessary, at the conclusion of which such person either shall be summoned again for jury service under subsections (b) and (c) of this section or, if the court's jury selection plan so provides, the name of such person shall be reinserted into the qualified jury wheel for selection pursuant to subsection (a) of this section, or (2) excluded by the court on the ground that such person may be unable to render impartial jury service or that his service as a juror would be likely to disrupt the proceedings, or (3) excluded upon peremptory challenge as provided by law, or (4) excluded pursuant to the procedure specified by law upon a challenge by any party for good cause shown, or (5) excluded upon determination by the court that his service as a juror would be likely to threaten the secrecy of the proceedings, or otherwise adversely affect the integrity of jury deliberations. No person shall be excluded under clause (5) of this subsection unless the judge, in open court, determines that such is warranted and that exclusion of the person will not be inconsistent with sections 1861 and 1862 of this title. The number of persons excluded under clause (5) of this subsection shall not exceed one per centum of the number of persons who return executed jury qualification forms during the period, specified in the plan, between two consecutive fillings of the master jury wheel. The names of persons excluded under clause (5) of this subsection, together with detailed explanations for the exclusions, shall be forwarded immediately to the judicial council of the circuit, which shall have the power to make any appropriate order, prospective or retroactive, to redress any misapplication of clause (5) of this subsection, but otherwise exclusions effectuated under such clause shall not be subject to challenge under the provisions of this title. Any person excluded from a particular jury under clause (2), (3), or (4) of this subsection shall be eligible to sit on another jury if the basis for his initial exclusion would not be relevant to his ability to serve on such other jury.

(d) Whenever a person is disqualified, excused, exempt, or excluded from jury service, the jury commission or clerk shall note in the space provided on his juror qualification form or on the juror's card drawn from the qualified jury wheel the specific reason therefor.

(e) In any two-year period, no person shall be required to (1) serve or attend court for prospective service as a petit juror for a total of more than thirty days, except when necessary to complete service in a particular case, or (2) serve on more than one grand jury, or (3) serve as both a grand and petit juror.

(f) When there is an unanticipated shortage of available petit jurors drawn from the qualified jury wheel, the court may require the marshal to summon a sufficient number of petit jurors selected at random from the voter registration lists, lists of actual voters, or other lists specified in the plan, in a manner ordered by the court consistent with sections 1861 and 1862 of this title.

(g) Any person summoned for jury service who fails to appear as directed shall be ordered by the district court to appear forthwith and show cause for his failure to comply with the summons. Any person who fails to show good cause for noncompliance with a summons may be fined not more than $100 or imprisoned not more than three days, or both.

(As amended May 24, 1949, c. 139, § 96, 63 Stat. 103; Mar. 27, 1968, Pub.L. 90–274, § 101, 82 Stat. 58; Dec. 11, 1970, Pub.L. 91–543, 84 Stat. 1408; Nov. 2, 1978, Pub.L. 95–572, § 2(b), 92 Stat. 2453; Jan. 12, 1983, Pub.L. 97–463, § 2, 96 Stat. 2531; Nov. 19, 1988, Pub.L. 100–702, § 801, 102 Stat. 4642.)

§ 1870. Challenges

In civil cases, each party shall be entitled to three peremptory challenges. Several defendants or several plaintiffs may be considered as a single party for the purposes of making challenges, or the court may allow additional peremptory challenges and permit them to be exercised separately or jointly.

All challenges for cause or favor, whether to the array or panel or to individual jurors, shall be determined by the court.

(As amended Sept. 16, 1959, Pub.L. 86–282, 73 Stat. 565.)

§ 1915. Proceedings in Forma Pauperis

(a) Any court of the United States may authorize the commencement, prosecution or defense of any suit, action or proceeding, civil or criminal, or appeal therein, without prepayment of fees and costs or security therefor, by a person who makes affidavit that he is unable to pay such costs or give security therefor. Such affidavit shall state the nature of the action, defense or appeal and affiant's belief that he is entitled to redress.

An appeal may not be taken in forma pauperis if the trial court certifies in writing that it is not taken in good faith.

(b) Upon the filing of an affidavit in accordance with subsection (a) of this section, the court may direct payment by the United States of the expenses of (1) printing the record on appeal in any civil or criminal case, if such printing is required by the appellate court; (2) preparing a transcript of proceedings before a United States magistrate in any civil or criminal case, if such transcript is required by the district court, in the case of proceedings conducted under section 636(b) of this title or under section 3401(b) of title 18, United States Code; and (3) printing the record on appeal if such printing is required by the appellate court, in the case of proceedings conducted pursuant to section 636(c) of this title. Such expenses shall be paid when authorized by the Director of the Administrative Office of the United States Courts.

(c) The officers of the court shall issue and serve all process, and perform all duties in such cases. Witnesses shall attend as in other cases, and the same remedies shall be available as are provided for by law in other cases.

(d) The court may request an attorney to represent any such person unable to employ counsel and may dismiss the case if the allegation of poverty is untrue, or if satisfied that the action is frivolous or malicious.

(e) Judgment may be rendered for costs at the conclusion of the suit or action as in other cases, but the United States shall not be liable for any of the costs thus incurred. If the United States has paid the cost of a stenographic transcript or printed record for the prevailing party, the same shall be taxed in favor of the United States.

(As amended May 24, 1949, c. 139, § 98, 63 Stat. 104; Oct. 31, 1951, c. 655, § 51(b, c), 65 Stat. 727; Sept. 21, 1959, Pub.L. 86–320, 73 Stat. 590; Oct. 10, 1979, Pub.L. 96–82, § 6, 93 Stat. 645.)

§ 1920. Taxation of Costs

A judge or clerk of any court of the United States may tax as costs the following:

(1) Fees of the clerk and marshal;

(2) Fees of the court reporter for all or any part of the stenographic transcript necessarily obtained for use in the case;

(3) Fees and disbursements for printing and witnesses;

(4) Fees for exemplification and copies of papers necessarily obtained for use in the case;

(5) Docket fees under section 1923 of this title;

(6) Compensation of court appointed experts, compensation of interpreters, and salaries, fees, expenses, and costs of special interpretation services under section 1828 of this title.

A bill of costs shall be filed in the case and, upon allowance, included in the judgment or decree.

(As amended Oct. 28, 1978, Pub.L. 95–539, § 7, 92 Stat. 2044.)

§ 1927. Counsel's Liability for Excessive Costs

Any attorney or other person admitted to conduct cases in any court of the United States or any Territory thereof who so multiplies the proceedings in any case unreasonably and vexatiously may be required by the court to satisfy personally the excess costs, expenses, and attorneys' fees reasonably incurred because of such conduct.

(As amended Sept. 12, 1980, Pub.L. 96–349, § 3, 94 Stat. 1156.)

§ 1961. Interest

(a) Interest shall be allowed on any money judgment in a civil case recovered in a district court. Execution therefor may be levied by the marshal, in any case where, by the law of the State in which such court is held, execution may be levied for interest on judgments recovered in the courts of the State. Such interest shall be calculated from the date of the entry of the judgment, at a rate equal to the coupon issue yield equivalent (as determined by the Secretary of the Treasury) of the average accepted auction price for the last auction of fifty-two week United States Treasury bills settled immediately prior to the date of the judgment. The Director of the Administrative Office of the United States Courts shall distribute notice of that rate and any changes in it to all Federal judges.

(b) Interest shall be computed daily to the date of payment except as provided in section 2516(b) of this title and section 1304(b) of title 31, and shall be compounded annually.

(c)(1) This section shall not apply in any judgment of any court with respect to any internal revenue tax case. Interest shall be allowed in such cases at the underpayment rate or overpayment rate (whichever is appropriate) established under section 6621 of the Internal Revenue Code of 1954.

(2) Except as otherwise provided in paragraph (1) of this subsection, interest shall be allowed on all final judgments against the United States in the United States Court of Appeals for the Federal circuit, at the rate provided in subsection (a) and as provided in subsection (b).

(3) Interest shall be allowed, computed, and paid on judgments of the United States Court of Federal Claims only as provided in paragraph (1) of this subsection or in any other provision of law.

(4) This section shall not be construed to affect the interest on any judgment of any court not specified in this section.

(As amended Apr. 2, 1982, Pub.L. 97–164, Title III, § 302(a), 96 Stat. 55; Sept. 13, 1982, Pub.L. 97–258, § 2(m)(1), 96 Stat. 1062; Jan. 12, 1983, Pub.L. 97–452, § 2(d)(1), 96 Stat. 2478; Oct. 22, 1986, Pub.L. 99–514, Title XV, § 1511(c)(17), 100 Stat. 2745; Oct. 29, 1992, Pub.L. 102–572, Title IX, § 902(b)(1), 106 Stat. 4516.)

§ 2071. Rule–Making Power Generally

(a) The Supreme Court and all courts established by Act of Congress may from time to time prescribe rules for the conduct of their business. Such rules shall be consistent with Acts of Congress and rules of practice and procedure prescribed under section 2072 of this title.

(b) Any rule prescribed by a court, other than the Supreme Court, under subsection (a) shall be prescribed only after giving appropriate public notice and an opportunity for comment. Such rule shall take effect upon the date specified by the prescribing court and shall have such effect on pending proceedings as the prescribing court may order.

(c)(1) A rule of a district court prescribed under subsection (a) shall remain in effect unless modified or abrogated by the judicial council of the relevant circuit.

(2) Any other rule prescribed by a court other than the Supreme Court under subsection (a) shall remain in effect unless modified or abrogated by the Judicial Conference.

(d) Copies of rules prescribed under subsection (a) by a district court shall be furnished to the judicial council, and copies of all rules prescribed by a court other than the Supreme Court under subsection (a) shall be furnished to the Director of the Administrative Office of the United States Courts and made available to the public.

(e) If the prescribing court determines that there is an immediate need for a rule, such court may proceed under this section without public notice and opportunity for comment, but such court shall promptly thereafter afford such notice and opportunity for comment.

(f) No rule may be prescribed by a district court other than under this section.

(As amended May 24, 1949, c. 139, § 102, 63 Stat. 104; Nov. 19, 1988, Pub.L. 100–702, § 403, 102 Stat. 4642.)

§ 2072. Rules of Procedure and Evidence; Power to Prescribe

(a) The Supreme Court shall have the power to prescribe general rules of practice and procedure and rules of evidence for cases in the United States district courts (including proceedings before magistrates thereof) and courts of appeals.

(b) Such rules shall not abridge, enlarge or modify any substantive right. All laws in conflict with such rules shall be of no further force or effect after such rules have taken effect.

(c) Such rules may define when a ruling of a district court is final for the purposes of appeal under section 1291 of this title.

(Added Nov. 19, 1988, Pub.L. 100–702, § 401(a), 102 Stat. 4648. As amended Dec. 1, 1990, Pub.L. 101–650, § 315, 104 Stat. 5089.)

§ 2073. Rules of Procedure and Evidence; Method of Prescribing

(a)(1) The Judicial Conference shall prescribe and publish the procedures for the consideration of proposed rules under this section.

(2) The Judicial Conference may authorize the appointment of committees to assist the Conference by recommending rules to be prescribed under section 2072 of this title. Each such committee shall consist of members of the bench and the professional bar, and trial and appellate judges.

(b) The Judicial Conference shall authorize the appointment of a standing committee on rules of practice, procedure, and evidence under subsection (a) of this section. Such standing committee shall review each recommendation of any other committees so appointed and recommend to the Judicial Conference rules of practice, procedure, and evidence and such changes in rules proposed by a committee appointed under subsection (a)(2) of this section as may be necessary to maintain consistency and otherwise promote the interest of justice.

(c)(1) Each meeting for the transaction of business under this chapter by any committee appointed under this section shall be open to the public, except when the committee so meeting, in open session and with a majority present, determines that it is in the public interest that all or part of the remainder of the meeting on that day shall be closed to the public, and states the reason for so closing the meeting. Minutes of each meeting for the transaction of business under this chapter shall be maintained by the committee and made available to the public, except that any portion of such minutes, relating to a closed meeting and made available to the public, may contain such deletions as may be necessary to avoid frustrating the purposes of closing the meeting.

(2) Any meeting for the transaction of business under this chapter, by a committee appointed under this section, shall be preceded by sufficient notice to enable all interested persons to attend.

(d) In making a recommendation under this section or under section 2072, the body making that recommendation shall provide a proposed rule, an explanatory note on the rule, and a written report explaining the body's action, including any minority or other separate views.

(e) Failure to comply with this section does not invalidate a rule prescribed under section 2072 of this title.

(Added Nov. 19, 1988, Pub.L. 100–702, § 401(a), 102 Stat. 4648.)

§ 2074. Rules of Procedure and Evidence; Submission to Congress; Effective Date

(a) The Supreme Court shall transmit to the Congress not later than May 1 of the year in which a rule prescribed under section 2072 is to become effective a copy of the proposed rule. Such rule shall take effect no earlier than December 1 of the year in which such rule is so transmitted unless otherwise provided by law. The Supreme Court may fix the extent such rule shall apply to proceedings then pending, except that the Supreme Court shall not require the application of such rule to further proceedings then pending to the extent that, in the opinion of the court in which such proceedings are pending, the application of such rule in such proceedings would not be feasible or would work injustice, in which event the former rule applies.

(b) Any such rule creating, abolishing, or modifying an evidentiary privilege shall have no force or effect unless approved by Act of Congress.

(As amended May 24, 1949, c. 139, § 103, 63 Stat. 104; July 18, 1949, c. 343, § 2, 63 Stat. 446; May 10, 1950, c. 174, § 2, 64 Stat. 158; July 7, 1958, Pub.L. 85–508, § 12(m), 72 Stat. 348; Nov. 6, 1966, Pub.L. 89–773, § 1, 80 Stat. 1323; Nov. 19, 1988, Pub.L. 100–702, § 401, 102 Stat. 4642.)

§ 2106. Determination

The Supreme Court or any other court of appellate jurisdiction may affirm, modify, vacate, set aside or reverse any judgment, decree, or order of a court lawfully brought before it for review, and may remand the cause and direct the entry of such appropriate judgment, decree, or order, or require such further proceedings to be had as may be just under the circumstances.

§ 2111. Harmless Error

On the hearing of any appeal or writ of certiorari in any case, the court shall give judgment after an examination of the record without regard to errors or defects which do not affect the substantial rights of the parties.

(Added May 24, 1949, c. 139, § 110, 63 Stat. 105.)

§ 2201. Creation of Remedy

(a) In a case of actual controversy within its jurisdiction, except with respect to Federal taxes other than actions brought under section 7428 of the Internal Revenue Code of 1986, a proceeding under section 505 or 1146 of title 11, or in any civil action involving an antidumping or countervailing duty proceeding regarding a class or kind of merchandise of a free trade area country (as defined in section 516A(f)(10) of the Tariff Act of 1930), as determined by the administering authority, any court of the United States, upon the filing of an appropriate pleading, may declare the rights and other legal relations of any interested party seeking such declaration, whether or not further relief is or could be sought. Any such declaration shall have the force and effect of a final judgment or decree and shall be reviewable as such.

(b) For limitations on actions brought with respect to drug patents see section 505 or 512 of the Federal Food, Drug, and Cosmetic Act.

(As amended May 24, 1949, c. 139, § 111, 63 Stat. 105; Aug. 28, 1954, c. 1033, 68 Stat. 890; July 7, 1958, Pub.L. 85–508, § 12(p), 72 Stat. 349; Oct. 4, 1976, Pub.L. 94–455, Title XIII, § 1306(b)(8), 90 Stat. 1719; Nov. 6, 1978, Pub.L. 95–598, Title II, § 249, 92 Stat. 2672; Sept. 24, 1984, Pub.L. 98–417, Title I, § 106, 98 Stat. 1597; Sept. 28, 1988, Pub.L. 100–449, Title IV, § 402(c), 102 Stat. 1884; Nov. 16, 1988, Pub.L. 100–670, Title 1, § 107(b), 102 Stat. 3984; Dec. 8, 1993, Pub.L. 103–182, § 414(B), 107 Stat. 2057.)

§ 2202. Further Relief

Further necessary or proper relief based on a declaratory judgment or decree may be granted, after reasonable notice and hearing, against any adverse party whose rights have been determined by such judgment.

§ 2283. Stay of State Court Proceedings

A court of the United States may not grant an injunction to stay proceedings in a State court except as expressly authorized by Act of Congress, or where necessary in aid of its jurisdiction, or to protect or effectuate its judgments.

§ 2361. Process and Procedure

In any civil action of interpleader or in the nature of interpleader under section 1335 of this title, a district court may issue its process for all claimants and enter its order restraining them from instituting or prosecuting any proceeding in any State or United States court affecting the property, instrument or obligation involved in the interpleader action until further order of the court. Such process and order shall be returnable at such time as the court or judge thereof directs, and shall be addressed to and served by the United States marshals for the respective districts where the claimants reside or may be found.

Such district court shall hear and determine the case, and may discharge the plaintiff from further liability, make the injunction permanent, and make all appropriate orders to enforce its judgment.

(As amended May 24, 1949, c. 139, § 117, 63 Stat. 105.)

§ 2402. Jury Trial in Actions Against United States

Any action against the United States under section 1346 shall be tried by the court without a jury, except that any action against the United States under section 1346(a)(1) shall, at the request of either party to such action, be tried by the court with a jury.

(As amended July 30, 1954, c. 648, § 2(a), 68 Stat. 589.)

§ 2403. Intervention by United States or a State; Constitutional Question

(a) In any action, suit or proceeding in a court of the United States to which the United States or any agency, officer or employee thereof is not a party, wherein the constitutionality of any Act of Congress affecting the public interest is drawn in question, the court shall certify such fact to the Attorney General, and shall permit the United States to intervene for presentation of evidence, if evidence is otherwise admissible in the case, and for argument on the question of constitutionality. The United States shall, subject to the applicable provisions of law, have all the rights of a party and be subject to all liabilities of a party as to court costs to the extent necessary for a proper presentation of the facts and law relating to the question of constitutionality.

(b) In any action, suit, or proceeding in a court of the United States to which a State or any agency, officer, or employee thereof is not a party, wherein the constitutionality of any statute of that State affecting the public interest is drawn in question, the court shall certify such fact to the attorney general of the State, and shall permit the State to intervene for presentation of evidence, if evidence is otherwise admissible in the case, and for argument on the question of constitutionality. The State shall, subject to the applicable provisions of law, have all the rights of a party and be subject to all liabilities of a party as to court costs to the extent necessary for a proper presentation of the facts and law relating to the question of constitutionality.

(As amended Aug. 12, 1976, Pub.L. 94–381, § 5, 90 Stat. 1120.)

§ 2412. Costs and Fees

(a)(1) Except as otherwise specifically provided by statute, a judgment for costs, as enumerated in section 1920 of this title, but not including the fees and expenses of attorneys, may be awarded to the prevailing party in any civil action brought by or against the United States or any agency or any official of the United States acting in his or her official capacity in any court having jurisdiction of such action. A judgment for costs when taxed against the United States shall, in an amount established by statute, court rule, or order, be limited to reimbursing in whole or in part the prevailing party for the costs incurred by such party in the litigation.

(2) A judgment for costs, when awarded in favor of the United States in an action brought by the United States, may include an amount equal to the filing fee prescribed under section 1914(a) of this title. The preceding sentence shall not be construed as requiring the United States to pay any filing fee.

(b) Unless expressly prohibited by statute, a court may award reasonable fees and expenses of attorneys, in addition to the costs which may be awarded pursuant to subsection (a), to the prevailing party in any civil action brought by or against the United States or any agency or any official of the United States acting in his or her official capacity in any court having jurisdiction of such action. The United States shall be liable for such fees and expenses to the same extent that any other party would be liable under the common law or under the terms of any statute which specifically provides for such an award.

(c)(1) Any judgment against the United States or any agency and any official of the United States acting in his or her official capacity for costs pursuant to subsection (a) shall be paid as provided in sections 2414 and 2517 of this title and shall be in addition to any relief provided in the judgment.

(2) Any judgment against the United States or any agency and any official of the United States acting in his or her official capacity for fees and expenses of attorneys pursuant to subsection (b) shall be paid as provided in sections 2414 and 2517 of this title, except that if the basis for the award is a finding that the United States acted in bad faith, then the award shall be paid by any agency found to have acted in bad faith and shall be in addition to any relief provided in the judgment.

(d)(1)(A) Except as otherwise specifically provided by statute, a court shall award to a prevailing party other than the United States fees and other expenses, in addition to any costs awarded pursuant to subsection (a), incurred by that party in any civil action (other than cases sounding in tort), including proceedings for judicial review of agency action, brought by or against the United States in any court having jurisdiction of that action, unless the court finds that the position of the United States was substantially justified or that special circumstances make an award unjust.

(B) A party seeking an award of fees and other expenses shall, within thirty days of final judgment in the action, submit to the court an application for fees and other expenses which shows that the party is a prevailing party and is eligible to receive an award under this subsection, and the amount sought, including an itemized statement from any attorney or expert witness representing or appearing in behalf of the party stating the actual time expended and the rate at which fees and other expenses are computed. The party shall also allege that the position of the United States was not substantially justified. Whether or not the position of the United States was substantially justified shall be determined on the basis of the record (including the record with respect to the action or failure to act by the agency upon which the civil action is based) which is made in the civil action for which fees and other expenses are sought.

(C) The court, in its discretion, may reduce the amount to be awarded pursuant to this subsection, or deny an award, to the extent that the prevailing party during the course of the proceedings engaged in conduct which unduly and unreasonably protracted the final resolution of the matter in controversy.

(2) For the purposes of this subsection—

(A) "fees and other expenses" includes the reasonable expenses of expert witnesses, the reasonable cost of any study, analysis, engineering report, test, or project which is found by the court to be necessary for the preparation of the party's case, and reasonable attorney fees (The amount of fees awarded under this subsection shall be based upon prevailing market rates for the kind and quality of the services furnished, except that (i) no expert witness shall be compensated at a rate in excess of the highest rate of compensation for expert witnesses paid by the United States; and (ii) attorney fees shall not be awarded in excess of $75 per hour unless the court determines that an increase in the cost of living or a special factor, such as the limited availability of qualified attorneys for the proceedings involved, justifies a higher fee.);

(B) "party" means (i) an individual whose net worth did not exceed $2,000,000 at the time the civil action was filed, or (ii) any owner of an unincorporated business, or any partnership, corporation, association, unit of local government, or organization, the net worth of which did not exceed $7,000,000 at the time the civil action was filed, and which had not more than 500 employees at the time the civil action was filed; except that an organization described in section 501(c)(3) of the Internal Revenue Code of 1954 (26 U.S.C. 501(c)(3)) exempt from taxation under section 501(a) of such Code, or a cooperative association as defined in section 15(a) of the Agricultural Marketing Act (12 U.S.C. 1141j(a)), may be a party regardless of the net worth of such organization or cooperative association;

(C) "United States" includes any agency and any official of the United States acting in his or her official capacity;

(D) "position of the United States" means, in addition to the position taken by the United States in the civil action, the action or failure to act by the agency upon which the civil action is based; except that fees and expenses may not be awarded to a party for any portion of the litigation in which the party has unreasonably protracted the proceedings;

(E) "civil action brought by or against the United States" includes an appeal by a party, other than the United States, from a decision of a contracting officer rendered pursuant to a disputes clause in a contract with the Government or pursuant to the Contract Disputes Act of 1978;

(F) "court" includes the United States Court of Federal Claims and the United States Court of Veterans Appeals;

(G) "final judgment" means a judgment that is final and not appealable, and includes an order of settlement; and

(H) "prevailing party", in the case of eminent domain proceedings, means a party who obtains a final judgment (other than by settlement), exclusive of interest, the amount of which is at least as close to the highest valuation of the property involved that is attested to at trial on behalf of the property owner as it is to the highest valuation of the property involved that is attested to at trial on behalf of the Government.

(3) In awarding fees and other expenses under this subsection to a prevailing party in any action for judicial review of an adversary adjudication, as defined in subsection (b)(1)(C) of section 504 of title 5, United States Code, or an adversary adjudication subject to the Contract Disputes Act of 1978, the court shall include in that award fees and other expenses to the same extent authorized in subsection

(a) of such section, unless the court finds that during such adversary adjudication the position of the United States was substantially justified, or that special circumstances make an award unjust.

(4) Fees and other expenses awarded under this subsection to a party shall be paid by any agency over which the party prevails from any funds made available to the agency by appropriation or otherwise.

(5) The Attorney General shall report annually to the Congress on the amount of fees and other expenses awarded during the preceding fiscal year pursuant to this subsection. The report shall describe the number, nature, and amount of the awards, the claims involved in the controversy, and any other relevant information which may aid the Congress in evaluating the scope and impact of such awards.

(e) The provisions of this section shall not apply to any costs, fees, and other expenses in connection with any proceeding to which section 7430 of the Internal Revenue Code of 1954 applies (determined without regard to subsections (b) and (f) of such section). Nothing in the preceding sentence shall prevent the awarding under subsection (a) of section 2412 of title 28, United States Code, of costs enumerated in section 1920 of such title (as in effect on October 1, 1981).

(f) If the United States appeals an award of costs or fees and other expenses made against the United States under this section and the award is affirmed in whole or in part, interest shall be paid on the amount of the award as affirmed. Such interest shall be computed at the rate determined under section 1961(a) of this title, and shall run from the date of the award through the day before the date of the mandate of affirmance.

(As amended July 18, 1966, Pub.L. 89–507, § 1, 80 Stat. 308; Oct. 21, 1980, Pub.L. 96–481, Title II, § 204(a), (c), 94 Stat. 2327, 2329; Sept. 3, 1982, Pub.L. 97–248, Title II, § 292(c), 96 Stat. 574; Aug. 5, 1985, Pub.L. 99–80, §§ 2, 6, 99 Stat. 184, 186; Oct. 29, 1992, Pub.L. 102–572, Title III, § 301(a), Title V, §§ 502(b), 506(a), 106 Stat. 4511, 4512, 4513.)

SELECTED PROVISIONS OF THE CONSTITUTION OF CALIFORNIA

Article I, § 16.
Article VI, §§ 1–13.

CONSTITUTION OF CALIFORNIA
ARTICLE I, § 16

[Trial by Jury]

Sec. 16. Trial by jury is an inviolate right and shall be secured to all, but in a civil cause three-fourths of the jury may render a verdict. A jury may be waived in a criminal cause by the consent of both parties expressed in open court by the defendant and the defendant's counsel. In a civil cause a jury may be waived by the consent of the parties expressed as prescribed by statute.

[Number of Jurors in Civil Trials]

In civil causes the jury shall consist of 12 persons or a lesser number agreed on by the parties in open court. In civil causes in municipal or justice court the Legislature may provide that the jury shall consist of eight persons or a lesser number agreed on by the parties in open court.

[Number of Jurors in Criminal Trials]

In criminal actions in which a felony is charged, the jury shall consist of 12 persons. In criminal actions in which a misdemeanor is charged, the jury shall consist of 12 persons or a lesser number agreed on by the parties in open court. *[As amended November 4, 1980.]*

ARTICLE VI
JUDICIAL

SECTION 1. *[Repealed November 8, 1966. See Section 1, below.]*
[Judicial Power Vested in Courts]

Sec. 1. The judicial power of this State is vested in the Supreme Court, courts of appeal, superior courts, municipal courts, and justice courts. All except justice courts are courts of record. *[New section adopted November 8, 1966.]*

Sec. 2. The Supreme Court consists of the Chief Justice of California and 6 associate justices. The Chief Justice may convene the court at any time. Concurrence of 4 judges present at the argument is necessary for a judgment.

An acting Chief Justice shall perform all functions of the Chief Justice when the Chief Justice is absent or unable to act. The Chief Justice or, if the Chief Justice fails to do so, the court shall select an associate justice as acting Chief Justice. [*As amended November 5, 1974.*]

[*Judicial Districts—Courts of Appeal*]

Sec. 3. The Legislature shall divide the State into districts each containing a court of appeal with one or more divisions. Each division consists of a presiding justice and 2 or more associate justices. It has the power of a court of appeal and shall conduct itself as a 3–judge court. Concurrence of 2 judges present at the argument is necessary for a judgment.

An acting presiding justice shall perform all functions of the presiding justice when the presiding justice is absent or unable to act. The presiding justice or, if the presiding justice fails to do so, the Chief Justice shall select an associate justice of that division as acting presiding justice. [*As amended November 5, 1974.*]

[*Superior Courts*]

Sec. 4. In each county there is a superior court of one or more judges. The Legislature shall prescribe the number of judges and provide for the officers and employees of each superior court. If the governing body of each affected county concurs, the Legislature may provide that one or more judges serve more than one superior court.

The county clerk is ex officio clerk of the superior court in the county. [*As amended November 5, 1974.*]

[*Municipal and Justice Courts*]

Sec. 5. (a) Each county shall be divided into municipal court and justice court districts as provided by statute, but a city may not be divided into more than one district. Each municipal and justice court shall have one or more judges.

There shall be a municipal court in each district of more than 40,000 residents and a justice court in each district of 40,000 residents or less. The number of residents shall be ascertained as provided by statute.

The Legislature shall provide for the organization and prescribe the jurisdiction of municipal and justice courts. It shall prescribe for each municipal court and provide for each justice court the number, qualifications, and compensation of judges, officers, and employees.

(b) Notwithstanding the provisions of subdivision (a), any city in San Diego County may be divided into more than one municipal court or justice court district if the Legislature determines that unusual geographic conditions warrant such division. [*As amended June 8, 1976.*]

[*Judicial Council—Membership and Powers*]

Sec. 6.   The Judicial Council consists of the Chief Justice and one other judge of the Supreme Court, 3 judges of courts of appeal, 5 judges of superior courts, 3 judges of municipal courts, and 2 judges of justice courts, each appointed by the Chief Justice for a 2–year term; 4 members of the State Bar appointed by its governing body for 2–year terms; and one member of each house of the Legislature appointed as provided by the house.

Council membership terminates if a member ceases to hold the position that qualified the member for appointment.   A vacancy shall be filled by the appointing power for the remainder of the term.

The council may appoint an Administrative Director of the Courts, who serves at its pleasure and performs functions delegated by the council or the Chief Justice, other than adopting rules of court administration, practice and procedure.

To improve the administration of justice the council shall survey judicial business and make recommendations to the courts, make recommendations annually to the Governor and Legislature, adopt rules for court administration, practice and procedure, not inconsistent with statute, and perform other functions prescribed by statute.

The Chief Justice shall seek to expedite judicial business and to equalize the work of judges.   The Chief Justice may provide for the assignment of any judge to another court but only with the judge's consent if the court is of lower jurisdiction.   A retired judge who consents may be assigned to any court.

Judges shall report to the Judicial Council as the Chief Justice directs concerning the condition of judicial business in their courts. They shall cooperate with the council and hold court as assigned.   [*As amended November 5, 1974.*]

[*Commission on Judicial Appointments—Membership*]

Sec. 7.   The Commission on Judicial Appointments consists of the Chief Justice, the Attorney General, and the presiding justice of the court of appeal of the affected district or, if there are 2 or more presiding justices, the one who has presided longest or, when a nomination or appointment to the Supreme Court is to be considered, the presiding justice who has presided longest on any court of appeal.   [*New section adopted November 8, 1966.*]

[*Commission on Judicial Performance—Membership*]

Sec. 8.   The Commission on Judicial Performance consists of 2 judges of courts of appeal, 2 judges of superior courts, and one judge of a municipal court, each appointed by the Supreme Court; 2 members of the State Bar who have practiced law in this State for 10 years, appointed by its governing body; and 2 citizens who are not judges, retired judges, or members of the State Bar, appointed by the Governor and approved by the Senate, a majority of the membership concurring. All terms are 4 years.

Commission membership terminates if a member ceases to hold the position that qualified the member for appointment. A vacancy shall be filled by the appointing power for the remainder of the term. [*As amended November 2, 1976.*]

[*State Bar*]

Sec. 9. The State Bar of California is a public corporation. Every person admitted and licensed to practice law in this State is and shall be a member of the State Bar except while holding office as a judge of a court of record. [*New section adopted November 8, 1966.*]

[*Jurisdiction—Original*]

Sec. 10. The Supreme Court, courts of appeal, superior courts, and their judges have original jurisdiction in habeas corpus proceedings. Those courts also have original jurisdiction in proceedings for extraordinary relief in the nature of mandamus, certiorari, and prohibition.

Superior courts have original jurisdiction in all causes except those given by statute to other trial courts.

The court may make such comment on the evidence and the testimony and credibility of any witness as in its opinion is necessary for the proper determination of the cause. [*New section adopted November 8, 1966.*]

[*Jurisdiction—Appellate*]

Sec. 11. The Supreme Court has appellate jurisdiction when judgment of death has been pronounced. With that exception courts of appeal have appellate jurisdiction when superior courts have original jurisdiction and in other causes prescribed by statute.

Superior courts have appellate jurisdiction in causes prescribed by statute that arise in municipal and justice courts in their counties.

The Legislature may permit appellate courts to take evidence and make findings of fact when jury trial is waived or not a matter of right. [*New section adopted November 8, 1966.*]

[*Transfer of Causes—Jurisdiction—Review of Decisions*]

Sec. 12. (a) The Supreme Court may, before decision, transfer to itself a cause in a court of appeal. It may, before decision, transfer a cause from itself to a court of appeal or from one court of appeal or division to another. The court to which a cause is transferred has jurisdiction.

(b) The Supreme Court may review the decision of a court of appeal in any cause.

(c) The Judicial Council shall provide, by rules of court, for the time and procedure for transfer and for review, including, among other things, provisions for the time and procedure for transfer with instructions, for review of all or part of a decision, and for remand as improvidently granted.

(d) This section shall not apply to an appeal involving a judgment of death. [*As amended November 6, 1984. Operative May 6, 1985.*]

[Judgment—When Set Aside]

Sec. 13. No judgment shall be set aside, or new trial granted, in any cause, on the ground of misdirection of the jury, or of the improper admission or rejection of evidence, or for any error as to any matter of pleading, or for any error as to any matter of procedure, unless, after an examination of the entire cause, including the evidence, the court shall be of the opinion that the error complained of has resulted in a miscarriage of justice. [*New section adopted November 8, 1966.*]

SELECTED CALIFORNIA CIVIL PROCEDURE STATUTES: CODE OF CIVIL PROCEDURE

Includes laws through the 1993 portion of the 1993–1994 Regular and First Extraordinary Sessions and the November 2, 1993, Election

Table of Contents

TITLE 5. PERSONS SPECIALLY INVESTED WITH MINISTERIAL POWERS RELATING TO COURTS OF JUSTICE

Chapter 1. Attorneys and Counselors at Law

PART 2. OF CIVIL ACTIONS

TITLE 2. OF THE TIME OF COMMENCING CIVIL ACTIONS

Chapter 3. The Time of Commencing Actions Other Than for the Recovery of Real Property

TITLE 3. OF THE PARTIES TO CIVIL ACTIONS

Chapter 5. Permissive Joinder

Chapter 6. Interpleader

Chapter 7. Intervention

PART 1.   OF COURTS OF JUSTICE
TITLE 1.   ORGANIZATION AND JURISDICTION
Chapter 4.   Superior Courts

§ 77. Appellate Department of Superior Court; Composition; Designated Judges; Decisions; Transaction of Business; Jurisdiction and Powers; Procedure

(a) In every county and city and county, there is an appellate department of the superior court consisting of three judges or, when the Chairperson of the Judicial Council finds it necessary, four judges.

(1) In a county with three or fewer judges of the superior court, the appellate department shall consist of those judges, one of whom shall be designated as presiding judge by the Chairperson of the Judicial Council, and an additional judge or judges as designated by the Chairperson of the Judicial Council. Each additional judge shall be a judge of the superior court of another county or a judge retired from the superior court or court of higher jurisdiction in this state.

(2) In a county with four or more judges of the superior court, the appellate department shall consist of judges of that court designated by the Chairperson of the Judicial Council, who shall also designate one of the judges as the presiding judge of the department.

(b) In an appellate department with four judges, no more than three judges shall participate in a hearing or decision. The presiding judge of the department shall designate the three judges who shall participate.

(c) In addition to their other duties, the judges designated as members of the appellate department of the superior court shall serve for the period specified in the order of designation. Whenever a judge is designated to serve in the appellate department of the superior court of a county other than the county in which such judge was elected or appointed as a superior court judge, or if he is retired, in a county other than the county in which he resides, he shall receive from the county to which he is designated his expenses for travel, board, and lodging. If the judge is out of his county overnight or longer, by reason of the designation, such judge shall be paid a per diem allowance in lieu of expenses for board and lodging in the same amounts as are payable for such purposes to justices of the Supreme Court under the rules of the State Board of Control. In addition, a retired judge shall receive from the state and the county to which he is designated, for the time so served, amounts equal to that which he would have received from each if he had been assigned to the superior court of the county.

(d) The concurrence of two judges of the appellate department of the superior court shall be necessary to render the decision in every case in, and to transact any other business except such as may be done at chambers by the presiding judge of, such department. The presiding judge shall convene such department at such times as may be necessary. He shall also supervise its business and transact such thereof as may be done at chambers.

(e) Every appellate department under this section shall have jurisdiction on appeal from the municipal and justice courts within the county or city and county in all cases in which an appeal may be taken to the superior court as is now or may hereafter be provided by law, except such appeals as require a retrial in the superior court. The powers of each appellate department shall be the same as are now or may hereafter be provided by law or rule of the Judicial Council relating to appeals to the superior courts.

(f) The Judicial Council may promulgate rules, not inconsistent with law, governing the practice and procedure and the disposition of the business of such appellate departments, or of each class thereof. (*Added by Stats.1955, c. 527, § 1. Amended by Stats.1961, c. 937, § 1; Stats. 1976, c. 1288, § 1; Stats.1984, c. 704, § 1.*)

Former § 77 was repealed by Stats.1933, c. 743, § 61.

Chapter 5. Municipal Courts and Justice Courts

§ 86. Jurisdiction

(a) Each municipal and justice court has original jurisdiction of civil cases and proceedings as follows:

(1) In all cases at law in which the demand, exclusive of interest, or the value of the property in controversy amounts to twenty-five thousand dollars ($25,000) or less, except cases which involve the legality of any tax, impost, assessment, toll, or municipal fine, except the courts have jurisdiction in actions to enforce payment of delinquent unsecured personal property taxes if the legality of the tax is not contested by the defendant.

(2) In actions for dissolution of partnership where the total assets of the partnership do not exceed twenty-five thousand dollars ($25,000); in actions of interpleader where the amount of money or the value of the

property involved does not exceed twenty-five thousand dollars ($25,-000).

(3) In actions to cancel or rescind a contract when the relief is sought in connection with an action to recover money not exceeding twenty-five thousand dollars ($25,000) or property of a value not exceeding twenty-five thousand dollars ($25,000), paid or delivered under, or in consideration of, the contract; in actions to revise a contract where the relief is sought in an action upon the contract if the court otherwise has jurisdiction of the action.

(4) In all proceedings in forcible entry or forcible or unlawful detainer where the whole amount of damages claimed is twenty-five thousand dollars ($25,000) or less.

(5) In all actions to enforce and foreclose liens on personal property where the amount of the liens is twenty-five thousand dollars ($25,000) or less.

(6) In all actions to enforce and foreclose liens of mechanics, materialmen, artisans, laborers, and of all other persons to whom liens are given under the provisions of Chapter 2 (commencing with Section 3109) of Title 15 of Part 4 of Division 3 of the Civil Code, or to enforce and foreclose an assessment lien on a common interest development as defined in Section 1351 of the Civil Code, where the amount of the liens is twenty-five thousand dollars ($25,000) or less. However, where an action to enforce the lien is pending in a municipal or justice court, and affects property which is also affected by a similar action pending in a superior court, or where the total amount of the liens sought to be foreclosed against the same property by action or actions in a municipal or justice court aggregates an amount in excess of twenty-five thousand dollars ($25,000) the municipal or justice court in which any such action, or actions, is, or are, pending, upon motion of any interested party, shall order the action or actions pending therein transferred to the proper superior court. Upon the making of the order, the same proceedings shall be taken as are provided by Section 399 with respect to the change of place of trial.

(7) In actions for declaratory relief when brought pursuant to either of the following:

(A) By way of cross-complaint as to a right of indemnity with respect to the relief demanded in the complaint or a cross-complaint in an action or proceeding otherwise within the jurisdiction of the municipal or justice court.

(B) To conduct a trial after a nonbinding fee arbitration between an attorney and client, pursuant to Article 13 (commencing with Section 6200) of Chapter 4 of Division 3 of the Business and Professions Code, where the amount in controversy is twenty-five thousand dollars ($25,-000) or less.

(8) To issue temporary restraining orders and preliminary injunctions, to take accounts, and to appoint receivers where necessary to

preserve the property or rights of any party to an action of which the court has jurisdiction; to appoint a receiver and to make any order or perform any act, pursuant to Title 9 (commencing with Section 680.010) of Part 2 (enforcement of judgments); to determine title to personal property seized in an action pending in such court.

(9) In all actions under Article 3 (commencing with Section 708.210) of Chapter 6 of Division 2 of Title 9 of Part 2 for the recovery of an interest in personal property or to enforce the liability of the debtor of a judgment debtor where the interest claimed adversely is of a value not exceeding twenty-five thousand dollars ($25,000) or the debt denied does not exceed twenty-five thousand dollars ($25,000).

(10) In all arbitration-related petitions filed pursuant to either of the following:

(A) Pursuant to Article 2 (commencing with Section 1292) of Chapter 5 of Title 9 of Part 3, except for uninsured motorist arbitration proceedings in accordance with Section 11580.2 of the Insurance Code, if the petition is filed before the arbitration award becomes final and the matter to be resolved by arbitration is within the jurisdiction of the municipal or justice court under paragraphs (1) to (9), inclusive, or the petition if filed after the arbitration award becomes final and the amount of the award and all other rulings, pronouncements, and decisions made in the award are within the jurisdiction of the municipal or justice court under paragraphs (1) to (9), inclusive.

(B) To confirm, correct, or vacate a fee arbitration award between an attorney and client that is binding or has become binding, pursuant to Article 13 (commencing with Section 6200) of Chapter 4 of Division 3 of the Business and Professions Code, where the arbitration award is twenty-five thousand dollars ($25,000) or less.

(b) Each municipal and justice court has jurisdiction of cases in equity as follows:

(1) In all cases to try title to personal property when the amount involved is not more than twenty-five thousand dollars ($25,000).

(2) In all cases when equity is pleaded as a defensive matter in any case otherwise properly pending in a municipal or justice court.

(3) To vacate a judgment or order of such municipal or justice court obtained through extrinsic fraud, mistake, inadvertence, or excusable neglect.

(c) In any action that is otherwise within its jurisdiction, the court may impose liability whether the theory upon which liability is sought to be imposed involves legal or equitable principles.

(d) Changes in the jurisdictional ceilings made by amendments to this section at the 1977–78 Regular Session or the 1985–86 Regular Session of the Legislature shall not constitute a basis for the transfer to another court of any case pending at the time such changes become operative. (*Added by Stats.1976, c. 1288, § 5. Amended by Stats.1978, c. 146, § 1; Stats.1979, c. 958, § 1; Stats.1981, c. 714, § 57; Stats.1982, c. 466, § 14; Stats.1982, c. 497, § 25; Stats.1984, c. 538, § 1; Stats. 1984, c. 1719, § 1.1; Stats.1985, c. 879, § 1; Stats.1985, c. 1383, § 1; Stats.1986, c. 88, § 1; Stats.1986, c. 953, § 1; Stats.1987, c. 104, § 1; Stats.1988, c. 463, § 1; Stats.1993, c. 1261, § 1; Stats.1993, c. 1262, § 4.5.)*

§ 90. Application of Law Applicable to Civil Actions

Except where changed by the provisions of this Article and Part 3.5 (commencing with Section 1823), all provisions of law applicable to civil actions generally apply to actions subject to this article. *(Added by Stats.1982, c. 1581, § 1.)*

§ 91. Application to Municipal and Justice Court Civil Actions if Amount in Controversy Is $25,000 or Less; Exceptions; Withdrawal

(a) Except as otherwise provided in this section, the provisions of this article apply to every municipal and justice court civil action, including cases submitted to arbitration or on the arbitration hearing list, pending in the municipal and justice courts, on or after July 1, 1983, in which the amount in controversy is twenty-five thousand dollars ($25,000) or less. "Amount in controversy" means the amount of the demand, or the recovery sought, or the value of the property, or the amount of the lien, which is in controversy in the action, exclusive of attorney fees, interest, and costs. These provisions also apply to any action transferred to a municipal or justice court by reason of lack of jurisdiction in the court in which it was filed.

(b) The provisions of this article do not apply to any action under Chapter 5A (commencing with Section 116) or any proceeding under Chapter 4 (commencing with Section 1159) of Title 3 of Part 3.

(c) Any action may, upon noticed motion, be withdrawn from the provisions of this article, upon a showing that it is impractical to prosecute or defend the action within the limitations of these provisions.

(d) Special demurrers, motions to strike, and requests for discovery, pending or determined prior to July 1, 1983, shall be subject to the law in effect on June 30, 1983. *(Added by Stats.1982, c. 1581, § 1. Amended by Stats.1983, c. 102, § 1; Stats.1985, c. 1383, § 2.)*

§ 92. Pleadings; Answer; Motions

(a) The pleadings allowed are complaints, answers, cross-complaints, answers to cross-complaints and general demurrers.

(b) The answer need not be verified, even if the complaint or cross-complaint is verified.

(c) Special demurrers are not allowed.

(d) Motions to strike are allowed only on the ground that the damages or relief sought are not supported by the allegations of the complaint.

(e) Except as limited by this section, all other motions are permitted. *(Added by Stats.1982, c. 1581, § 1. Amended by Stats.1983, c. 102, § 2.)*

§ 93. Questionnaires

(a) The plaintiff has the option to serve case questionnaires with the complaint, using forms approved by the Judicial Council. The questionnaires served shall include a completed copy of the plaintiff's completed case questionnaire, and a blank copy of the defendant's questionnaire.

(b) Any defendant upon whom a case questionnaire is served shall serve a completed defendant's case questionnaire upon the requesting plaintiff with the answer.

(c) The case questionnaire shall be designed to elicit fundamental information about each party's case, including names and addresses of all witnesses with knowledge of any relevant facts, a list of all documents relevant to the case, a statement of the nature and amount of damages, and information covering insurance coverages, injuries and treating physicians. The Judicial Council shall design and develop forms for case questionnaires.

(d) Approved forms shall be made available by the clerk of the court.

(e) If a party on whom a case questionnaire has been served under subdivision (a) or (b) fails to serve a timely or a complete response to that questionnaire, the party serving the questionnaire may move for an order compelling a response or a further response and for a monetary sanction under Section 2023. If a party then fails to obey an order compelling a response or a further response, the court may make those orders that are just, including the imposition of an issue sanction, an evidence sanction, or a terminating sanction under Section 2023. In lieu of or in addition to that sanction, the court may impose a monetary sanction under Section 2023. *(Added by Stats.1982, c. 1581, § 1. Amended by Stats.1987, c. 86, § 1.)*

§ 94. Discovery

Discovery is permitted only to the extent provided by this section and Section 95. This discovery shall comply with the notice and format requirements of the particular method of discovery, as provided in Article 3 (commencing with Section 2016) of Chapter 3 of Title 4 of Part 4. As to each adverse party, a party may use the following forms of discovery:

(a) Any combination of 35 of the following:

(1) Interrogatories (with no subparts) under Section 2030.

(2) Demands to produce documents or things under Section 2031.

(3) Requests for admission (with no subparts) under Section 2033.

(b) One oral or written deposition under Sections 2025 to 2028, inclusive.

(c) Any party may serve on any person a deposition subpoena duces tecum requiring the person served to mail copies of documents, books or records to the party's counsel at a specified address, along with an affidavit complying with Section 1561 of the Evidence Code.

The party who issued the deposition subpoena shall mail a copy of the response to any other party who tenders the reasonable cost of copying it.

(d) Physical and mental examinations under Section 2032.

(e) The identity of expert witnesses under Section 2034. *(Added by Stats.1982, c. 1581, § 1. Amended by Stats.1987, c. 86, § 1.3.)*

§ 95. Additional Discovery

(a) The court may, on noticed motion and subject to such terms and conditions as are just, authorize a party to conduct additional discovery, but only upon a showing that the moving party will be unable to prosecute or defend the action effectively without the additional discovery. In making a determination under this section, the court shall take into account whether the moving party has used all applicable discovery in good faith, and whether the party has attempted to secure the additional discovery by stipulation or by means other than formal discovery.

(b) The parties may stipulate to additional discovery. *(Added by Stats.1982, c. 1581, § 1.)*

Chapter 5.5   Small Claims Court

§ 116.210   Small Claims Division

In each justice court and each municipal court there shall be a small claims division. *(Added by Stats.1990, c. 1305, § 3.)*

§ 116.220   Jurisdiction

(a) The small claims court shall have jurisdiction in the following actions:

(1) Except as provided in subdivision (c), for recovery of money, if the amount of the demand does not exceed five thousand dollars ($5,000).

(2) Except as provided in subdivision (c), to enforce payment of delinquent unsecured personal property taxes in an amount not to exceed five thousand dollars ($5,000), if the legality of the tax is not contested by the defendant.

(3) To issue the writ of possession authorized by Sections 1861.5 and 1861.10 of the Civil Code if the amount of the demand does not exceed five thousand dollars ($5,000).

(b) In any action seeking relief authorized by subdivision (a), the court may grant equitable relief in the form of rescission, restitution, reformation, and specific performance, in lieu of, or in addition to, money damages. The court may issue a conditional judgment. The court shall retain jurisdiction until full payment and performance of any judgment or order.

(c) Notwithstanding subdivision (a), the small claims court shall have jurisdiction over a defendant guarantor who is required to respond based upon the default, actions, or omissions of another, only if the demand does not exceed two thousand five hundred dollars ($2,500).

(d) In any case in which the lack of jurisdiction is due solely to an excess in the amount of the demand, the excess may be waived, but any waiver shall not become operative until judgment. (*Added by Stats. 1990, c. 1305, § 3. Amended by Stats.1990, c. 1683, § 3; Stats.1991, c. 133, § 1; Stats.1991, c. 915, § 3; Stats.1992, c. 8, § 1, eff. Feb. 19, 1992; Stats.1992, c. 142, § 2; Stats.1993, c. 1262, § 5; Stats.1993, c. 1264, § 95.*)

Chapter 6. General Provisions Respecting Courts of Justice

§ 128. Powers of Court; Execution of Sentence for Contempt; Stay Pending Appeal; Operative Date

(a) Every court shall have the power to do all of the following:

(1) To preserve and enforce order in its immediate presence.

(2) To enforce order in the proceedings before it, or before a person or persons empowered to conduct a judicial investigation under its authority.

(3) To provide for the orderly conduct of proceedings before it, or its officers.

(4) To compel obedience to its judgments, orders, and process, and to the orders of a judge out of court, in an action or proceeding pending therein.

(5) To control in furtherance of justice, the conduct of its ministerial officers, and of all other persons in any manner connected with a judicial proceeding before it, in every matter pertaining thereto.

(6) To compel the attendance of persons to testify in an action or proceeding pending therein, in the cases and manner provided in this code.

(7) To administer oaths in an action or proceeding pending therein, and in all other cases where it may be necessary in the exercise of its powers and duties.

(8) To amend and control its process and orders so as to make them conform to law and justice.

(b) Notwithstanding Section 1211 or any other provision of law, if an order of contempt is made affecting an attorney, his or her agent, investigator, or any person acting under the attorney's direction, in the preparation and conduct of any action or proceeding, the execution of any sentence shall be stayed pending the filing within three judicial days of a petition for extraordinary relief testing the lawfulness of the court's order, the violation of which is the basis of the contempt except for the conduct as may be proscribed by subdivision (b) of Section 6068 of the Business and Professions Code, relating to an attorney's duty to maintain respect due to the courts and judicial officers.

(c) Notwithstanding Section 1211 or any other provision of law, if an order of contempt is made affecting a public safety employee acting within the scope of employment for reason of the employee's failure to comply with a duly issued subpoena or subpoena duces tecum, the execution of any sentence shall be stayed pending the filing within three judicial days of a petition for extraordinary relief testing the lawfulness of the court's order, a violation of which is the basis for the contempt.

As used in this subdivision, "public safety employee" includes any peace officer, firefighter, paramedic, or any other employee of a public law enforcement agency whose duty is either to maintain official records or to analyze or present evidence for investigative or prosecutorial purposes.

(d) Notwithstanding Section 1211 or any other provision of law, if an order of contempt is made affecting the victim of a sexual assault, where the contempt consists of refusing to testify concerning that sexual assault, the execution of any sentence shall be stayed pending the filing within three judicial days of a petition for extraordinary relief testing the lawfulness of the court's order, a violation of which is the basis for the contempt.

(e) Notwithstanding Section 1211 or any other law, if an order of contempt is made affecting the victim of domestic violence, where the contempt consists of refusing to testify concerning that domestic violence, the execution of any sentence shall be stayed pending the filing within three judicial days of a petition for extraordinary relief testing the lawfulness of the court's order, a violation of which is the basis for the contempt.

As used in this subdivision, the term "domestic violence" means "domestic violence" as defined in Section 6211 of the Family Code.

(f) Notwithstanding Section 1211 or any other provision of law, no order of contempt shall be made affecting a county government or any member of its governing body acting pursuant to its constitutional or statutory authority unless the court finds, based on a review of evidence presented at a hearing conducted for this purpose, that either of the following conditions exist:

(1) That the county has the resources necessary to comply with the order of the court.

(2) That the county has the authority, without recourse to voter approval or without incurring additional indebtedness, to generate the additional resources necessary to comply with the order of the court, that compliance with the order of the court will not expose the county, any member of its governing body, or any other county officer to liability for failure to perform other constitutional or statutory duties, and that compliance with the order of the court will not deprive the county of resources necessary for its reasonable support and maintenance. *(Added by Stats.1987, c. 3, § 2, eff. March 11, 1987, operative March 11, 1989. Amended by Stats.1991, c. 866, § 1; Stats.1992, c. 163, § 13; Stats.1992, c. 697, § 2; Stats.1993, c. 219, § 63.3.)*

§ 128.5 Frivolous Actions or Delaying Tactics; Order for Payment of Expenses

(a) Every trial court may order a party, the party's attorney, or both to pay any reasonable expenses, including attorney's fees, incurred by another party as a result of bad-faith actions or tactics that are frivolous or solely intended to cause unnecessary delay. This section also applies to judicial arbitration proceedings under Chapter 2.5 (commencing with Section 1141.10) of Title 3 of Part 3.

(b) For purposes of this section:

(1) "Actions or tactics" include, but are not limited to, the making or opposing of motions or the filing and service of a complaint or cross-complaint. The mere filing of a complaint without service thereof on an opposing party does not constitute "actions or tactics" for purposes of this section.

(2) "Frivolous" means (A) totally and completely without merit or (B) for the sole purpose of harassing an opposing party.

(c) Expenses pursuant to this section shall not be imposed except on notice contained in a party's moving or responding papers; or the court's own motion, after notice and opportunity to be heard. An order imposing expenses shall be in writing and shall recite in detail the conduct or circumstances justifying the order.

(d) In addition to any award pursuant to this section for conduct described in subdivision (a), the court may assess punitive damages against the plaintiff upon a determination by the court that the plaintiff's action was an action maintained by a person convicted of a felony against the person's victim, or the victim's heirs, relatives, estate, or personal representative, for injuries arising from the acts for which the person was convicted of a felony, and that the plaintiff is guilty of fraud, oppression, or malice in maintaining the action.

(e) The liability imposed by this section is in addition to any other liability imposed by law for acts or omissions within the purview of this section. *(Added by Stats.1981, c. 762, § 1.   Amended by Stats.1984, c. 355, § 1; Stats.1985, c. 296, § 1; Stats.1990, c. 887, § 1.)*

TITLE 2.   JUDICIAL OFFICERS
Chapter 4.   Incidental Powers and Duties of Judicial Officers

§ 177.5 Money Sanctions

A judicial officer shall have the power to impose reasonable money sanctions, not to exceed fifteen hundred dollars ($1,500), notwithstanding any other provision of law, payable to the county in which the judicial officer is located, for any violation of a lawful court order by a person, done without good cause or substantial justification. This power shall not apply to advocacy of counsel before the court. For the purposes of this section, the term "person" includes a witness, a party, a party's attorney, or both.

Sanctions pursuant to this section shall not be imposed except on notice contained in a party's moving or responding papers; or on the court's own motion, after notice and opportunity to be heard. An order imposing sanctions shall be in writing and shall recite in detail the conduct or circumstances justifying the order. *(Added by Stats.1982, c. 1564, § 1.)*

§ 178. Punishment for Contempt

For the effectual exercise of the powers conferred by the last section, a judicial officer may punish for contempt in the cases provided in this Code. *(Enacted 1872.   Amended by Code Am.1880, c. 35, § 1.)*

Chapter 5.   Miscellaneous Provisions Respecting Courts of Justice

§ 187. Jurisdiction; Means to Carry Into Effect; Mode of Proceeding

When jurisdiction is, by the Constitution or this Code, or by any other statute, conferred on a Court or judicial officer, all the means necessary to carry it into effect are also given; and in the exercise of this jurisdiction, if the course of proceeding be not specifically pointed out by this Code or the statute, any suitable process or mode of proceeding may be adopted which may appear most conformable to the spirit of this Code. *(Enacted 1872.   Amended by Code Am.1880, c. 35, § 1.)*

TITLE 3.   PERSONS SPECIALLY INVESTED WITH POWERS OF A JUDICIAL NATURE
Chapter 1.   Trial Jury Selection and Management Act

§ 191. State Policy; Random Selection; Opportunity and Obligation to Serve

The Legislature recognizes that trial by jury is a cherished constitutional right, and that jury service is an obligation of citizenship.

It is the policy of the State of California that all persons selected for jury service shall be selected at random from the population of the area served by the court; that all qualified persons have an equal opportunity, in accordance with this chapter, to be considered for jury service in the state and an obligation to serve as jurors when summoned for that purpose; and that it is the responsibility of jury commissioners to manage all jury systems in an efficient, equitable, and cost-effective manner, in accordance with this chapter. (*Added by Stats.1988, c. 1245, § 2.*)

§ 193. Kinds of Juries

Juries are of three kinds:

(a) Grand juries established pursuant to Title 4 (commencing with Section 888) of Part 2 of the Penal Code.

(b) Trial juries.

(c) Juries of inquest. (*Added by Stats.1988, c. 1245, § 2.*)

§ 194. Definitions

The following definitions govern the construction of this chapter:

(a) "County" means any county or any coterminous city and county.

(b) "Court" means the superior, municipal, and justice courts of this state, and includes, when the context requires, any judge of the court.

(c) "Deferred jurors" are those prospective jurors whose request to reschedule their service to a more convenient time is granted by the jury commissioner.

(d) "Excused jurors" are those prospective jurors who are excused from service by the jury commissioner for valid reasons based on statute, state or local court rules, and policies.

(e) "Juror pool" means the group of prospective qualified jurors appearing for assignment to trial jury panels.

(f) "Jury of inquest" is a body of persons summoned from the citizens before the sheriff, coroner, or other ministerial officers, to inquire of particular facts.

(g) "Master list" means a list of names randomly selected from the source lists.

(h) "Potential juror" means any person whose name appears on a source list.

(i) "Prospective juror" means a juror whose name appears on the master list.

(j) "Qualified juror" means a person who meets the statutory qualifications for jury service.

(k) "Qualified juror list" means a list of qualified jurors.

(*l*) "Random" means that which occurs by mere chance indicating an unplanned sequence of selection where each juror's name has substantially equal probability of being selected.

(m) "Source list" means a list used as a source of potential jurors.

(n) "Summons list" means a list of prospective or qualified jurors who are summoned to appear or to be available for jury service.

(o) "Trial jurors" are those jurors sworn to try and determine by verdict a question of fact.

(p) "Trial jury" means a body of persons selected from the citizens of the area served by the court and sworn to try and determine by verdict a question of fact.

(q) "Trial jury panel" means a group of prospective jurors assigned to a courtroom for the purpose of voir dire. (*Added by Stats.1988, c. 1245, § 2.*)

§ 195. Jury Commissioners; Appointment; Term; Ex Officio Commissioners; Clerk/Administrators; Salaries; Duties

(a) In each county, there shall be one jury commissioner who shall be appointed by, and serve at the pleasure of, a majority of the judges of the superior court. In any county where there is a superior court administrator or executive officer, that person shall serve as ex officio jury commissioner. The person so appointed shall serve as jury commissioner for all trial courts within the county. In any municipal or justice court district in the county, a majority of the judges may appoint the clerk/administrator to select jurors for their court pursuant to this chapter. In any court jurisdiction where any person other than a court administrator or clerk/administrator is serving as jury commissioner on the effective date of this section, that person shall continue to so serve at the pleasure of a majority or the judges of the appointing court.

(b) Except where the superior court administrator or executive officer serves as ex officio jury commissioner, the jury commissioner's salary shall be set by joint action of the board of supervisors and a majority of the superior court judges. Any jury commissioner may, whenever the business of court requires, and with consent of the board of supervisors, appoint deputy jury commissioners. Salaries and benefits of such deputies shall be fixed in the same manner as salaries and benefits of other court employees.

(c) The jury commissioner shall be primarily responsible for managing the jury system under the general supervision of the court in conformance with the purpose and scope of this act. He or she shall have authority to establish policies and procedures necessary to fulfill this responsibility. (*Added by Stats.1988, c. 1245, § 2.*)

§ 197. Source Lists of Jurors; Contents; Data From Department of Motor Vehicles; Confidentiality

(a) All persons selected for jury service shall be selected at random, from a source or sources inclusive of a representative cross section of the population of the area served by the court. Sources may include, in addition to other lists, customer mailing lists, telephone directories, or utility company lists.

(b) The list of registered voters and the Department of Motor Vehicles' list of licensed drivers and identification cardholders resident within the area served by the court, are appropriate source lists for selection of jurors. These two source lists, when substantially purged of duplicate names, shall be considered inclusive of a representative cross section of the population, within the meaning of subdivision (a).

(c) The Department of Motor Vehicles shall furnish the jury commissioner of each county with the current list of the names, addresses, and other identifying information of persons residing in the county who are age 18 years or older and who are holders of a current driver's license or identification card issued pursuant to Article 3 (commencing with Section 12800) of, or Article 5 (commencing with Section 13000) of, Chapter 1 of Division 6 of the Vehicle Code. The conditions under which these lists shall be compiled semiannually shall be determined by the director, consistent with any rules which may be adopted by the Judicial Council. This service shall be provided by the Department of Motor Vehicles pursuant to Section 1812 of the Vehicle Code. The jury commissioner shall not disclose the information furnished by the Department of Motor Vehicles pursuant to this section to any person, organization, or agency. (*Added by Stats.1988, c. 1245, § 5.*)

§ 198. Master and Qualified Juror Lists; Random Selection; Use of Lists

(a) Random selection shall be utilized in creating master and qualified juror lists, commencing with selection from source lists, and continuing through selection of prospective jurors for voir dire.

(b) The jury commissioner shall, at least once in each 12–month period, randomly select names of prospective trial jurors from the source list or lists, to create a master list.

(c) The master jury list shall be used by the jury commissioner, as provided by statute and state and local court rules, for the purpose of (1) mailing juror questionnaires and subsequent creation of a qualified juror list, and (2) summoning prospective jurors to respond or appear for qualification and service. (*Added by Stats.1988, c. 1245, § 5.*)

§ 203. Persons Qualified to Be Trial Jurors; Exceptions

(a) All persons are eligible and qualified to be prospective trial jurors, except the following:

(1) Persons who are not citizens of the United States.

(2) Persons who are less than 18 years of age.

(3) Persons who are not domiciliaries of the State of California, as determined pursuant to Article 2 (commencing with Section 200) of Chapter 1 of Division 1 of the Elections Code.

(4) Persons who are not residents of the jurisdiction wherein they are summoned to serve.

(5) Persons who have been convicted of malfeasance in office or a felony, and whose civil rights have not been restored.

(6) Persons who are not possessed of sufficient knowledge of the English language, provided that no person shall be deemed incompetent solely because of the loss of sight or hearing in any degree or other disability which impedes the person's ability to communicate or which impairs or interferes with the person's mobility.

(7) Persons who are serving as grand or trial jurors in any court of this state.

(8) Persons who are the subject of conservatorship.

(b) No person shall be excluded from eligibility for jury service in the State of California, for any reason other than those reasons provided by this section. (*Added by Stats.1988, c. 1245, § 5.*)

§ 204. Exemptions and Excuses From Jury Service

(a) No eligible person shall be exempt from service as a trial juror by reason of occupation, race, color, religion, sex, national origin, or economic status, or for any other reason. No person shall be excused from service as a trial juror except as specified in subdivision (b).

(b) An eligible person may be excused from jury service only for undue hardship, upon themselves or upon the public, as defined by the Judicial Council. (*Added by Stats.1988, c. 1245, § 5.*)

§ 205. Juror Questionnaires; Contents; Use; Additional Questionnaires

(a) If a jury commissioner requires a person to complete a questionnaire, the questionnaire shall ask only questions related to juror identification, qualification, and ability to serve as a prospective juror.

(b) Except as ordered by the court, the questionnaire referred to in subdivision (a) shall be used solely for qualifying prospective jurors, and for management of the jury system, and not for assisting in the courtroom voir dire process of selecting trial jurors for specific cases.

(c) The court may require a prospective juror to complete such additional questionnaires as may be deemed relevant and necessary for assisting in the voir dire process or to ascertain whether a fair cross section of the population is represented as required by law, if such procedures are established by local court rule.

(d) The trial judge may direct a prospective juror to complete additional questionnaires as proposed by counsel in a particular case to assist the voir dire process. (*Added by Stats.1988, c. 1245, § 5.*)

§ 209. Failure to Respond to Summons; Attachment; Compelling Attendance; Contempt

Any prospective trial juror who has been summoned for service, and who fails to attend upon the court as directed or to respond to the court or jury commissioner and to be excused from attendance, may be attached and compelled to attend; and, following an order to show cause hearing, the court may find the prospective juror in contempt of court, punishable by fine, incarceration, or both, as otherwise provided by law. (*Added by Stats.1988, c. 1245, § 5.*)

§ 220. Number of Jurors

A trial jury shall consist of 12 persons, except that in civil actions and cases of misdemeanor, it may consist of 12 or any number less than 12, upon which the parties may agree. (*Added by Stats.1988, c. 1245, § 5.*)

§ 222.5 Prospective Jurors; Examination

To select a fair and impartial jury in civil jury trials, the trial judge shall examine the prospective jurors. Upon completion of the judge's initial examination, counsel for each party shall have the right to examine, by oral and direct questioning, any of the prospective jurors in order to enable counsel to intelligently exercise both peremptory challenges and challenges for cause. During any examination conducted by counsel for the parties, the trial judge should permit liberal and probing examination calculated to discover bias or prejudice with regard to the circumstances of the particular case. The fact that a topic has been included in the judge's examination should not preclude additional nonrepetitive or nonduplicative questioning in the same area by counsel.

The scope of the examination conducted by counsel shall be within reasonable limits prescribed by the trial judge in the judge's sound discretion. In exercising his or her sound discretion as to the form and subject matter of voir dire questions, the trial judge should consider, among other criteria, any unique or complex elements, legal or factual, in the case and the individual responses or conduct of jurors which may evince attitudes inconsistent with suitability to serve as a fair and impartial juror in the particular case. Specific unreasonable or arbitrary time limits shall not be imposed.

The trial judge should permit counsel to conduct voir dire examination without requiring prior submission of the questions unless a particular counsel engages in improper questioning. For purposes of this section, an "improper question" is any question which, as its dominant purpose, attempts to precondition the prospective jurors to a particular result, indoctrinate the jury, or question the prospective jurors concerning the pleadings or the applicable law. A court should not arbitrarily or unreasonably refuse to submit reasonable written questionnaires, the contents of which are determined by the court in its sound discretion, when requested by counsel.

In civil cases, the court may, upon stipulation by counsel for all the parties appearing in the action, permit counsel to examine the prospective jurors outside a judge's presence. *(Added by Stats.1990, c. 1232 (A.B. 3820), § 1.5.)*

§ 224. Disabled Jurors; Presence of Service Providers; Instructions; Appointment

(a) If a party does not cause the removal by challenge of an individual juror who is deaf, hearing impaired, blind, visually impaired, or speech impaired and who requires auxiliary services to facilitate communication, the party shall (1) stipulate to the presence of a service provider in the jury room during jury deliberations, and (2) prepare and deliver to the court proposed jury instructions to the service provider.

(b) As used in this section, "service provider" includes, but is not limited to, a person who is a sign language interpreter, oral interpreter, deaf-blind interpreter, reader, or speech interpreter. If auxiliary services are required during the course of jury deliberations, the court shall instruct the jury and the service provider that the service provider for the juror with a disability is not to participate in the jury's deliberations in any manner except to facilitate communication between the juror with a disability and other jurors.

(c) The court shall appoint a service provider whose services are needed by a juror with a disability to facilitate communication or participation. A sign language interpreter, oral interpreter, or deaf-blind interpreter appointed pursuant to this section shall be a qualified interpreter, as defined in subdivision (f) of Section 754 of the Evidence Code. Service providers appointed by the court under this subdivision shall be compensated in the same manner as provided in subdivision (i) of Section 754 of the Evidence Code. *(Added by Stats.1988, c. 1245, § 2. Amended by Stats.1992, c. 913, § 9; Stats.1993, c. 1214, § 3.)*

§ 225. Challenges; Definition; Classes and Types

A challenge is an objection made to the trial jurors that may be taken by any party to the action, and is of the following classes and types:

(a) A challenge to the trial jury panel for cause.

(1) A challenge to the panel may only be taken before a trial jury is sworn. The challenge shall be reduced to writing, and shall plainly and distinctly state the facts constituting the ground of challenge.

(2) Reasonable notice of the challenge to the jury panel shall be given to all parties and to the jury commissioner, by service of a copy thereof.

(3) The jury commissioner shall be permitted the services of legal counsel in connection with challenges to the jury panel.

(b) A challenge to a prospective juror by either:

(1) A challenge for cause, for one of the following reasons:

(A) General disqualification—that the juror is disqualified from serving in the action on trial.

(B) Implied bias—as, when the existence of the facts as ascertained, in judgment of law disqualifies the juror.

(C) Actual bias—the existence of a state of mind on the part of the juror in reference to the case, or to any of the parties, which will prevent the juror from acting with entire impartiality, and without prejudice to the substantial rights of any party.

(2) A peremptory challenge to a prospective juror. (*Added by Stats. 1988, c. 1245, § 5.*)

§ 226. Challenges to Individual Jurors; Time; Form; Exclusion on Peremptory Challenge

(a) A challenge to an individual juror may only be made before the jury is sworn.

(b) A challenge to an individual juror may be taken orally or may be made in writing, but no reason need be given for a peremptory challenge, and the court shall exclude any juror challenged peremptorily.

(c) All challenges for cause shall be exercised before any peremptory challenges may be exercised.

(d) All challenges to an individual juror, except a peremptory challenge, shall be taken, first by the defendants, and then by the people or plaintiffs. (*Added by Stats.1988, c. 1245, § 5.*)

§ 227. Challenges for Cause; Time; Order

The challenges of either party for cause need not all be taken at once, but they may be taken separately, in the following order, including in each challenge all the causes of challenge belonging to the same class and type:

(a) To the panel.

(b) To an individual juror, for a general disqualification.

(c) To an individual juror, for an implied bias.

(d) To an individual juror, for an actual bias. (*Added by Stats.1988, c. 1245, § 5.*)

§ 228. Challenges for General Disqualification; Grounds

Challenges for general disqualification may be taken on one or both of the following grounds, and for no other:

(a) A want of any of the qualifications prescribed by this code to render a person competent as a juror.

(b) A loss of hearing, or the existence of any other incapacity which satisfies the court that the challenged person is incapable of performing the duties of a juror in the particular action without prejudice to the substantial rights of the challenging party. (*Added by Stats.1988, c. 1245, § 5.*)

§ 229. Challenges for Implied Bias; Causes

A challenge for implied bias may be taken for one or more of the following causes, and for no other:

(a) Consanguinity or affinity within the fourth degree to any party, to an officer of a corporation which is a party, or to any alleged witness or victim in the case at bar.

(b) Standing in the relation of, or being the parent, spouse, or child of one who stands in the relation of, guardian and ward, conservator and conservatee, master and servant, employer and clerk, landlord and tenant, principal and agent, or debtor and creditor, to either party or to an officer of a corporation which is a party, or being a member of the family of either party; or a partner in business with either party; or surety on any bond or obligation for either party, or being the holder of bonds or shares of capital stock of a corporation which is a party; or having stood within one year previous to the filing of the complaint in the action in the relation of attorney and client with either party or with the attorney for either party. A depositor of a bank or a holder of a savings account in a savings and loan association shall not be deemed a creditor of that bank or savings and loan association for the purpose of this paragraph solely by reason of his or her being a depositor or account holder.

(c) Having served as a trial or grand juror or on a jury of inquest in a civil or criminal action or been a witness on a previous or pending trial between the same parties, or involving the same specific offense or cause of action; or having served as a trial or grand juror or on a jury within one year previously in any criminal or civil action or proceeding in which either party was the plaintiff or defendant or in a criminal action where either party was the defendant.

(d) Interest on the part of the juror in the event of the action, or in the main question involved in the action, except his or her interest as a member or citizen or taxpayer of a county, city and county, incorporated city or town, or other political subdivision of a county, or municipal water district.

(e) Having an unqualified opinion or belief as to the merits of the action founded upon knowledge of its material facts or of some of them.

(f) The existence of a state of mind in the juror evincing enmity against, or bias towards, either party.

(g) That the juror is party to an action pending in the court for which he or she is drawn and which action is set for trial before the panel of which the juror is a member.

(h) If the offense charged is punishable with death, the entertaining of such conscientious opinions as would preclude the juror finding the defendant guilty; in which case the juror may neither be permitted nor compelled to serve. (*Added by Stats.1988, c. 1245, § 5.*)

§ 230. Challenges for Cause; Trial; Witnesses

Challenges for cause shall be tried by the court. The juror challenged and any other person may be examined as a witness in the trial of the challenge, and shall truthfully answer all questions propounded to them. (*Added by Stats.1988, c. 1245, § 5.*)

§ 231. Peremptory Challenges; Number; Joint Defendants; Passing Challenges

(a) In criminal cases, if the offense charged is punishable with death, or with imprisonment in the state prison for life, the defendant is entitled to 20 and the people to 20 peremptory challenges. Except as provided in subdivision (b), in a trial for any other offense, the defendant is entitled to 10 and the state to 10 peremptory challenges. When two or more defendants are jointly tried, their challenges shall be exercised jointly, but each defendant shall also be entitled to five additional challenges which may be exercised separately, and the people shall also be entitled to additional challenges equal to the number of all the additional separate challenges allowed the defendants.

(b) If the offense charged is punishable with a maximum term of imprisonment of 90 days or less, the defendant is entitled to six and the state to six peremptory challenges. When two or more defendants are jointly tried, their challenges shall be exercised jointly, but each defendant shall also be entitled to four additional challenges which may be exercised separately, and the state shall also be entitled to additional challenges equal to the number of all the additional separate challenges allowed the defendants.

(c) In civil cases, each party shall be entitled to six peremptory challenges. If there are more than two parties, the court shall, for the purpose of allotting peremptory challenges, divide the parties into two or more sides according to their respective interests in the issues. Each side shall be entitled to eight peremptory challenges. If there are several parties on a side, the court shall divide the challenges among them as nearly equally as possible. If there are more than two sides, the court shall grant such additional peremptory challenges to a side as the interests of justice may require; provided that the peremptory challenges of one side shall not exceed the aggregate number of peremptory challenges of all other sides. If any party on a side does not use his or her full share of peremptory challenges, the unused challenges may be used by the other party or parties on the same side.

(d) Peremptory challenges shall be taken or passed by the sides alternately, commencing with the plaintiff or people; and each party shall be entitled to have the panel full before exercising any peremptory challenge. When each side passes consecutively, the jury shall then be sworn, unless the court, for good cause, shall otherwise order. The number of peremptory challenges remaining with a side shall not be diminished by any passing of a peremptory challenge.

(e) If all the parties on both sides pass consecutively, the jury shall then be sworn, unless the court, for good cause, shall otherwise order. The number of peremptory challenges remaining with a side shall not be diminished by any passing of a peremptory challenge. (*Added by Stats. 1988, c. 1245, § 5. Amended by Stats.1989, c. 1416, § 9.*)

TITLE 5.   PERSONS SPECIALLY INVESTED WITH MINISTERIAL POWERS RELATING TO COURTS OF JUSTICE

Chapter 1.   Attorneys and Counselors at Law

§ 284.   Change or Substitution; Consent; Order of Court

The attorney in an action or special proceeding may be changed at any time before or after judgment or final determination, as follows:

1.   Upon the consent of both client and attorney, filed with the clerk, or entered upon the minutes;

2.   Upon the order of the court, upon the application of either client or attorney, after notice from one to the other. (*Enacted 1872. Amended by Code Am.1873–74, c. 383, § 26; Code Am.1880, c. 35, § 1; Stats. 1935, c. 560, § 1; Stats.1967, c. 161, § 1.*)

PART 2.   OF CIVIL ACTIONS

TITLE 2.   OF THE TIME OF COMMENCING CIVIL ACTIONS

Chapter 3.   The Time of Commencing Actions Other Than for the Recovery of Real Property

§ 335.   Periods of Limitation

Periods of limitation prescribed. The periods prescribed for the commencement of actions other than for the recovery of real property, are as follows: (*Enacted 1872.*)

§ 340.   One Year

Within one year:

(1) Statutory penalty or forfeiture to individual and state. An action upon a statute for a penalty or forfeiture, when the action is given to an individual, or to an individual and the state, except when the statute imposing it prescribes a different limitation.

(2) Statutory forfeiture or penalty to state. An action upon a statute for a forfeiture or penalty to the people of this state.

(3) Libel, slander, assault, battery, false imprisonment, seduction, injury or death from wrongful act or neglect, forged or raised checks, injury to animals by feeder or veterinarian. An action for libel, slander, assault, battery, false imprisonment, seduction of a person below the age of legal consent, or for injury to or for the death of one caused by the wrongful act or neglect of another, or by a depositor against a bank for the payment of a forged or raised check, or a check that bears a forged or unauthorized endorsement, or against any person who boards or feeds an animal or fowl or who engages in the practice of veterinary medicine as defined in Section 4826 of the Business and Professions Code, for such person's neglect resulting in injury or death to an animal or fowl in the course of boarding or feeding such animal or fowl or in the course of the practice of veterinary medicine on such animal or fowl.

(4) **Damages for seizure.** An action against an officer to recover damages for the seizure of any property for a statutory forfeiture to the state, or for the detention of, or injury to property so seized, or for damages done to any person in making any such seizure.

(5) **Action by good faith improver.** An action by a good faith improver for relief under Chapter 10 (commencing with Section 871.1) of Title 10 of Part 2 of the Code of Civil Procedure. The time begins to run from the date upon which the good faith improver discovers that the good faith improver is not the owner of the land upon which the improvements have been made. (*Enacted 1872. Amended by Code Am.1873–74, c. 383, § 34; Code Am.1875–76, c. 29, § 1; Stats.1905, c. 258, § 2; Stats.1929, c. 518, § 1; Stats.1939, c. 1103, § 1; Stats.1949, c. 863, § 1; Stats.1953, c. 1382, § 1; Stats.1963, c. 1681, § 2; Stats.1968, c. 150, § 1; Stats.1973, c. 20, § 1; Stats.1982, c. 517, § 97.*)

§ 340.5 Action Against Health Care Provider; Three Years From Injury or One Year From Discovery; Exceptions; Minors

In an action for injury or death against a health care provider based upon such person's alleged professional negligence, the time for the commencement of action shall be three years after the date of injury or one year after the plaintiff discovers, or through the use of reasonable diligence should have discovered, the injury, whichever occurs first. In no event shall the time for commencement of legal action exceed three years unless tolled for any of the following: (1) upon proof of fraud, (2) intentional concealment, or (3) the presence of a foreign body, which has no therapeutic or diagnostic purpose or effect, in the person of the injured person. Actions by a minor shall be commenced within three years from the date of the alleged wrongful act except that actions by a minor under the full age of six years shall be commenced within three years or prior to his eighth birthday whichever provides a longer period. Such time limitation shall be tolled for minors for any period during which parent or guardian and defendant's insurer or health care provider have committed fraud or collusion in the failure to bring an action on behalf of the injured minor for professional negligence.

For the purposes of this section:

(1) "Health care provider" means any person licensed or certified pursuant to Division 2 (commencing with Section 500) of the Business and Professions Code, or licensed pursuant to the Osteopathic Initiative Act, or the Chiropractic Initiative Act, or licensed pursuant to Chapter 2.5 (commencing with Section 1440) of Division 2 of the Health and Safety Code; and any clinic, health dispensary, or health facility, licensed pursuant to Division 2 (commencing with Section 1200) of the Health and Safety Code. "Health care provider" includes the legal representatives of a health care provider;

(2) "Professional negligence" means a negligent act or omission to act by a health care provider in the rendering of professional services, which act or omission is the proximate cause of a personal injury or wrongful death, provided that such services are within the scope of services for which the provider is licensed and which are not within any restriction imposed by the licensing agency or licensed hospital. (*Added by Stats.1970, c. 360, § 1. Amended by Stats.1975, 2nd Ex.Sess., c. 1, § 25; Stats.1975, 2nd Ex.Sess., c. 2, § 1.192.*)

TITLE 3.   OF THE PARTIES TO CIVIL ACTIONS
Chapter 5.   Permissive Joinder

§ 382.   Nonconsent to Joinder as Plaintiff; Representative Actions

If the consent of any one who should have been joined as plaintiff cannot be obtained, he may be made a defendant, the reason thereof being stated in the complaint; and when the question is one of a common or general interest, of many persons, or when the parties are numerous, and it is impracticable to bring them all before the court, one or more may sue or defend for the benefit of all. (*Enacted 1872. Amended by Stats.1971, c. 244, § 12.*)

Chapter 6.   Interpleader

§ 386.   Interpleader

(a) Defendant in action on contract or for specific personal property; substitution of third party claimant or cross-complaint; deposit in court or delivery; discharge from liability; action against conflicting claimants. A defendant, against whom an action is pending upon a contract, or for specific personal property, may, at any time before answer, upon affidavit that a person not a party to the action makes against him, and without any collusion with him, a demand upon such contract, or for such property, upon notice to such person and the adverse party, apply to the court for an order to substitute such person in his place, and discharge him from liability to either party, on his depositing in court the amount claimed on the contract, or delivering the property or its value to such person as the court may direct; and the court may, in its discretion, make the order; or such defendant may file a verified cross-complaint in interpleader, admitting that he has no interest in such amount or such property claimed, or in a portion of such amount or such property and alleging that all or such portion of the amount or property is demanded by parties to such action or cross-action and apply to the court upon notice to such parties for an order to deliver such property or portion thereof or its value to such person as the court shall direct. And whenever conflicting claims are or may be made upon a person for or relating to personal property, or the performance of an obligation, or any portion thereof, such person may bring an action against the conflicting claimants to compel them to interplead and litigate their several claims. The order of substitution may be made and the action of interpleader may be maintained, and the applicant or interpleading party be discharged from liability to all or any of the conflicting claimants, although their titles or claims have not a common origin, or are not identical but are adverse to and independent of one another.

(b) Entity or person subject to multiple claims which give rise to multiple liability; action against claimants to compel interpleader and litigation of claims. Any person, firm, corporation, association or other entity against whom double or multiple claims are made, or may be made, by two or more persons which are such that they may give rise to double or multiple liability, may bring an action against the claimants to compel them to interplead and litigate their several claims.

When the person, firm, corporation, association or other entity against whom such claims are made, or may be made, is a defendant in an action brought upon one or more of such claims, it may either file a verified cross-complaint in interpleader, admitting that it has no interest in the money or property claimed, or in only a portion thereof, and alleging that all or such portion is demanded by parties to such action, and apply to the court upon notice to such parties for an order to deliver such money or property or such portion thereof to such person as the court shall direct; or may bring a separate action against the claimants to compel them to interplead and litigate their several claims. The action of interpleader may be maintained although the claims have not a common origin, are not identical but are adverse to and independent of one another, or the claims are unliquidated and no liability on the part of the party bringing the action or filing the cross-complaint has arisen. The applicant or interpleading party may deny liability in whole or in part to any or all of the claimants. The applicant or interpleading party may join as a defendant in such action any other party against whom claims are made by one or more of the claimants or such other party may interplead by cross-complaint; provided, however, that such claims arise out of the same transaction or occurrence.

(c) Deposit of amount payable in court; stoppage of interest and damages for detention of property. Any amount which a plaintiff or cross-complainant admits to be payable may be deposited by him with the clerk of the court at the time of the filing of the complaint or cross-complaint in interpleader without first obtaining an order of the court therefor. Any interest on amounts deposited and any right to damages for detention of property so delivered, or its value, shall cease to accrue after the date of such deposit or delivery.

(d) Answer by defendant; allegation of ownership or interest. A defendant named in a complaint to compel conflicting claimants to interplead and litigate their claims, or a defendant named in a cross-complaint in interpleader, may, in lieu of or in addition to any other pleading, file an answer to the complaint or cross-complaint which shall be served upon all other parties to the action and which shall contain allegations of fact as to his ownership of or other interest in the amount or property and any affirmative defenses and the relief requested. The allegations in such answer shall be deemed denied by all other parties to the action, unless otherwise admitted in the pleadings.

(e) Conflicting claims to property on deposit; issue triable by court; deficiency; trial of claim. Except in cases where by the law a right to a jury trial is now given, conflicting claims to funds or property or the value thereof so deposited or delivered shall be deemed issues triable by the court, and such issues may be first tried. In the event the amount deposited shall be less than the amount claimed to be due by one or more of the conflicting claimants thereto, or in the event the property or the value thereof delivered is less than all of the property or the value thereof claimed by one or more of such conflicting claimants, any issues of fact involved in determining whether there is a deficiency in such deposit or delivery shall be tried by the court or a jury as provided in Title 8 (commencing with Section 577) of Part 2 of this code.

(f) Other proceedings; restraining order. After any such complaint or cross-complaint in interpleader has been filed, the court in which it is filed may enter its order restraining all parties to the action from instituting or further prosecuting any other proceeding in any court in this state affecting the rights and obligations as between the parties to the interpleader until further order of the court. (*Enacted 1872. Amended by Stats.1881, c. 23, § 1; Stats.1951, c. 1142, § 1; Stats.1970, c. 563, § 1; Stats.1975, c. 670, § 1.*)

§ 386.1 Investment of Deposits; Allocation of Interest

Where a deposit has been made pursuant to Section 386, the court shall, upon the application of any party to the action, order such deposit to be invested in an insured interest-bearing account. Interest on such amount shall be allocated to the parties in the same proportion as the original funds are allocated. (*Added by Stats.1972, c. 553, § 1. Amended by Stats.1979, c. 173, § 1.*)

§ 386.5 Stakeholder; Dismissal From Action on Deposit With Clerk

Where the only relief sought against one of the defendants is the payment of a stated amount of money alleged to be wrongfully withheld, such defendant may, upon affidavit that he is a mere stakeholder with no interest in the amount or any portion thereof and that conflicting demands have been made upon him for the amount by parties to the action, upon notice to such parties, apply to the court for an order discharging him from liability and dismissing him from the action on his depositing with the clerk of the court the amount in dispute and the court may, in its discretion, make such order. (*Added by Stats.1953, c. 328, § 1.*)

§ 386.6 Costs and Attorney Fees; Attorney Pro Se

(a) A party to an action who follows the procedure set forth in Section 386 or 386.5 may insert in his motion, petition, complaint, or cross complaint a request for allowance of his costs and reasonable attorney fees incurred in such action. In ordering the discharge of such party, the court may, in its discretion, award such party his costs and reasonable attorney fees from the amount in dispute which has been deposited with the court. At the time of final judgment in the action the court may make such further provision for assumption of such costs and attorney fees by one or more of the adverse claimants as may appear proper.

(b) A party shall not be denied the attorney fees authorized by subdivision (a) for the reason that he is himself an attorney, appeared in pro se, and performed his own legal services. (*Added by Stats.1955, c. 951, § 1. Amended by Stats.1974, c. 273, § 1.*)

Chapter 7. Intervention

§ 387. Intervention; Authorization; Procedure

(a) Upon timely application, any person, who has an interest in the matter in litigation, or in the success of either of the parties, or an interest against both, may intervene in the action or proceeding. An intervention takes place when a third person is permitted to become a party to an action or proceeding between other persons, either by joining the plaintiff in claiming what is sought by the complaint, or by uniting with the defendant in resisting the claims of the plaintiff, or by demanding anything adversely to both the plaintiff and the defendant, and is made by complaint, setting forth the grounds upon which the intervention rests, filed by leave of the court and served upon the parties to the action or proceeding who have not appeared in the same manner as upon the commencement of an original action, and upon the attorneys of the parties who have appeared, or upon the party if he has appeared without an attorney, in the manner provided for service of summons or in the manner provided by Chapter 5 (commencing with Section 1010) Title 14 of Part 2. A party served with a complaint in intervention may within 30 days after service move, demur, or otherwise plead to the complaint in the same manner as to an original complaint.

(b) If any provision of law confers an unconditional right to intervene or if the person seeking intervention claims an interest relating to the property or transaction which is the subject of the action and that person is so situated that the disposition of the action may as a practical matter impair or impede that person's ability to protect that interest, unless that person's interest is adequately represented by existing parties, the court shall, upon timely application, permit that person to intervene. (*Enacted 1872. Amended by Code Am. 1873–74, c. 383, § 44; Stats.1907, c. 371, § 1; Stats.1969, c. 1611, § 5; Stats.1970, c. 484, § 1; Stats.1977, c. 450, § 1.*)

TITLE 4. OF THE PLACE OF TRIAL OF CIVIL ACTIONS
Chapter 1. Generally

§ 392. Real Property Actions; Proper Court

(1) Subject to the power of the court to transfer actions and proceedings as provided in this title, the county in which the real property, which is the subject of the action, or some part thereof, is situated, is the proper county for the trial of the following actions:

(a) For the recovery of real property, or of an estate or interest therein, or for the determination in any form, of such right or interest, and for injuries to real property;

(b) For the foreclosure of all liens and mortgages on real property.

(2) The proper court for the trial of any such action, in the county hereinabove designated as the proper county, shall be determined as follows:

If there is a municipal or justice court, having jurisdiction of the subject matter of the action, established in the city and county or judicial district in which the real property which is the subject of the action, or some part thereof, is situated, such court is the proper court for the trial of such action; otherwise any court in such county having jurisdiction of the subject matter of the action, is a proper court for the trial thereof. (*Amended by Stats.1976, c. 73, p. 110, § 3.*)

§ 393. Actions for Penalty or Forfeiture; Actions Against Public Officers; Proper Court

(1) Subject to the power of the court to transfer actions and proceedings as provided in this title, the county in which the cause, or some part thereof, arose, is the proper county for the trial of the following actions:

(a) For the recovery of a penalty or forfeiture imposed by statute; except, that when it is imposed for an offense committed on a lake, river, or other stream of water, situated in two or more counties, the action may be tried in any county bordering on such lake, river, or stream, and opposite to the place where the offense was committed;

(b) Against a public officer or person especially appointed to execute his duties, for an act done by him in virtue of his office; or against a person who, by his command or in his aid, does anything touching the duties of such officer.

(2) The proper court for the trial of any such action, in the county hereinabove designated as the proper county, shall be determined as follows:

If there is a municipal or justice court, having jurisdiction of the subject matter of the action, established in the city and county or judicial district in which the cause, or some part thereof, arose, such court is the proper court for the trial of such action; otherwise, any court in such county, having jurisdiction of the subject matter of the action, is a proper court for the trial thereof. In the case of offenses committed on a lake, river, or stream, hereinabove mentioned, the court, having jurisdiction of the subject matter of the action, nearest to the place where such offense was committed, in any county mentioned in subdivision 1 of this section, is a proper court for the trial of the action. (*Enacted 1872. Amended by Stats.1933, c. 744, § 4; Stats.1951, c. 869, § 2.*)

§ 394. Actions by or Against a City, County, City and County or Local Agency; Transfer of Cases; Proper Court

(1) An action or proceeding against a county, or city and county, a city, or local agency, may be tried in such county, or city and county, or the county in which such city or local agency is situated, unless such action or proceeding is brought by a county, or city and county, a city, or local agency, in which case it may be tried in any county, or city and county, not a party thereto and in which the city or local agency is not situated. Whenever an action or proceeding is brought by a county, city and county, city, or local agency within a certain county, or city and county, against a resident of another county, city and county, or city, or a corporation doing business in the latter, the action or proceeding must be, on motion of either party, transferred for trial to a county, or city and county, other than the plaintiff, if the plaintiff is a county, or city and county, and other than that in which the plaintiff is situated, if the plaintiff is a city, or a local agency, and other than that in which the defendant resides, or is doing business, or is situated. Whenever an action or proceeding is brought against a county, city and county, city, or local agency, in any county, or city and county, other than the defendant, if the defendant is a county, or city and county, or, if the defendant is a city, or local agency, other than that in which the defendant is situated, the action or proceeding must be, on motion of the said defendant, transferred for trial to a county, or city and county, other than that in which the plaintiff, or any of the plaintiffs, resides, or is doing business, or is situated, and other than the plaintiff county, or city and county, or county in which such plaintiff city or local agency is situated, and other than the defendant county, or city and county, or county in which such defendant city or local agency is situated; provided, however, that any action or proceeding against the city, county, city and county, or local agency for injury occurring within the city, county, or city and county, or within the county in which such local agency is situated, to person or property or person and property caused by the negligence or alleged negligence of such city, county, city and county, local agency, or its

agents or employees, shall be tried in such county, or city and county, or if a city is a defendant, in such city or in the county in which such city is situated, or if a local agency is a defendant, in such county in which such local agency is situated. In any such action or proceeding, the parties thereto may, by stipulation in writing, or made in open court, and entered in the minutes, agree upon any county, or city and county, for the place of trial thereof. When the action or proceeding is one in which a jury is not of right, or in case a jury be waived, then in lieu of transferring the cause the court in the original county may request the chairman of the Judicial Council to assign a disinterested judge from a neutral county to hear said cause and all proceedings in connection therewith. When such action or proceeding is transferred to another county for trial, a witness required to respond to a subpoena for a hearing within the original county shall be compelled to attend hearings in the county to which the cause is transferred. If the demand for transfer be made by one party and the opposing party does not consent thereto the additional costs of the nonconsenting party occasioned by the transfer of the cause, including living and traveling expenses of said nonconsenting party and material witnesses, found by the court to be material, and called by such nonconsenting party, not to exceed five dollars $5 per day each in excess of witness fees and mileage otherwise allowed by law, shall be assessed by the court hearing the cause against the party requesting the transfer. To the extent of such excess, such costs shall be awarded to the nonconsenting party regardless of the outcome of the trial. This section shall apply to actions or proceedings now pending or hereafter brought.

(2) Any court in a county hereinabove designated as a proper county, which has jurisdiction of the subject matter of the action or proceeding, is a proper court for the trial thereof.

(3) For the purposes of this section, "local agency" shall mean any governmental district, board, or agency, or any other local governmental body or corporation, but shall not include the State of California or any of its agencies, departments, commissions, or boards. (*Enacted 1872. Amended by Stats.1881, c. 30, § 1; Stats.1891, c. 61, § 1; Stats.1907, c. 369, § 2; Stats.1915, c. 434, § 1; Stats.1921, c. 382, § 1; Stats.1929, c. 112, § 1; Stats.1931, c. 942, § 1; Stats.1933, c. 744, § 5; Stats.1970, c. 604, § 1; Stats.1971, c. 957, § 1.*)

§ 395. Actions Generally; Proper Court; Waiver by Agreement

(a) Except as otherwise provided by law and subject to the power of the court to transfer actions or proceedings as provided in this title, the county in which the defendants or some of them reside at the commencement of the action is the proper county for the trial of the action. If the action is for injury to person or personal property or for death from wrongful act or negligence, either the county where the injury occurs or the injury causing death occurs or the county in which the defendants, or some of them reside at the commencement of the action, shall be a proper county for the trial of the action. In a proceeding for dissolution of marriage, the county in which the petitioner has been a resident for three months next preceding the commencement of the proceeding is the proper county for the trial of the proceeding. In a proceeding to enforce an obligation of support under Section 3900 of the Family Code, the county in which the child resides is the proper county for the trial of the action. In a proceeding to establish and enforce a foreign judgment or court order for the support of a minor child, the county in which the child resides is the proper county for the trial of the action. Subject to the provisions of subdivision (b), when a defendant has contracted to perform an obligation in a particular county, either the county where such obligation is to be performed or in which the contract in fact was entered into or the county in which the defendant or any such defendant resides at the commencement of the action shall be a proper county for the trial of an action founded on such obligation, and the county in which the obligation is incurred shall be deemed to be the county in which it is to be performed unless there is a special contract in writing to the contrary. If none of the defendants reside in the state or if residing in the state and the county in which they reside is unknown to the plaintiff, the action may be tried in any county which the plaintiff may designate in his or her complaint, and, if the defendant is about to depart from the state, the action may be tried in any county where either of the parties reside or service is made. If any person is improperly joined as a defendant or has been made a defendant solely for the purpose of having the action tried in the county or judicial district where he or she resides, his or her residence shall not be considered in determining the proper place for the trial of the action.

(b) Subject to the power of the court to transfer actions or proceedings as provided in this title, in an action arising from an offer or provision of goods, services, loans or extensions of credit intended primarily for personal, family or household use, other than an obligation described in Section 1812.10 or Section 2984.4 of the Civil Code, or an action arising from a transaction consummated as a proximate result of an unsolicited telephone call made by a seller engaged in the business of consummating transactions of that kind, the county in which the buyer or lessee in fact signed the contract, the county in which the buyer or lessee resided at the time the contract was entered into, or the county in which the buyer or lessee resides at the commencement of the action is the proper county for the trial thereof.

(c) If within the county there is a municipal or justice court having jurisdiction of the subject matter established, in the cases mentioned in subdivision (a), in the judicial district in which the defendant or any defendant resides, in which the injury to person or personal property or the injury causing death occurs, or, in which the obligation was contracted to be performed or, in cases mentioned in subdivision (b), in the judicial district which the buyer or lessee resides, in which the buyer or lessee in fact signed the contract, in which the buyer or lessee resided at the time the contract was entered into, or in which the buyer or lessee resides at the commencement of the action, then such court is the proper court for the trial of such action. Otherwise, any municipal or justice court in such county having jurisdiction of the subject matter is a proper court for the trial thereof.

(d) Any provision of an obligation described in subdivision (b) or (c) waiving those subdivisions is void and unenforceable. *(Enacted 1872. Amended by Stats.1907, c. 369, § 3; Stats.1911, c. 421, §' 1; Stats.1933, c. 744, § 6; Stats.1939, c. 981, § 1; Stats.1951, c. 869, § 3; Stats.1955, c. 832, § 1; Stats.1969, c. 1608, § 11; Stats.1970, c. 75, § 1; Stats.1971, c. 1640, § 1; Stats.1972, c. 1117, § 1; Stats.1972, c. 1118, § 3; Stats.1972, c. 1119, § 3; Stats.1976, c. 610, § 1; Stats.1991, c. 228, § 3; Stats.1992, c. 163, § 17.)*

§ 395.1 Executor, Administrator, Guardian, Conservator or Trustee in Official or Representative Capacity

Except as otherwise provided in Section 17005 of the Probate Code pertaining to trustees, when a defendant is sued in an official or representative capacity as executor, administrator, guardian, conservator, or trustee on a claim for the payment of money or for the recovery of personal property, the county which has jurisdiction of the estate which the defendant represents shall be the proper county for the trial of the action. *(Added by Stats.1943, c. 1043, § 1. Amended by Stats.1979, c. 730, § 20; Stats.1986, c. 820, § 16.)*

§ 395.2 Unincorporated Associations

If an unincorporated association has filed a statement with the Secretary of State pursuant to Section 24003 of the Corporations Code listing its principal office in this state, the proper county for the trial of an action against such unincorporated association is the same as it would be if the unincorporated association were a corporation and, for the purpose of determining such county, the principal place of business of the unincorporated association shall be deemed to be the principal office in this state listed in the statement. *(Added by Stats.1967, c. 1324, § 2.)*

§ 395.5 Actions Against Corporations or Associations; Place of Trial

A corporation or association may be sued in the county where the contract is made or is to be performed, or where the obligation or liability arises, or the breach occurs; or in the county where the principal place of business of such corporation is situated, subject to the power of the court to change the place of trial as in other cases. *(Added by Stats.1972, c. 118, § 1.)*

§ 396. Court Without Jurisdiction; Transfer of Case; Cross–Complaint Beyond Jurisdiction; Time Action Deemed Commenced; Remission of Amount of Demand in Excess of Jurisdiction

If an action or proceeding is commenced in a court which lacks jurisdiction of the subject matter thereof, as determined by the complaint or petition, if there is a court of this state which has such jurisdiction, the action or proceeding shall not be dismissed (except as provided in Section 399, and subdivision 1 of Section 581) but shall, on the application of either party, or on the court's own motion, be transferred to a court having jurisdiction of the subject matter which may be agreed upon by the parties, or, if they do not agree, to a court having such jurisdiction which is designated by law as a proper court for the trial or determination thereof, and it shall thereupon be entered and prosecuted in the court to which it is transferred as if it had been commenced therein, all prior proceedings being saved. In any such case, if summons is served prior to the filing of the action or proceeding in the court to which it is transferred, as to any defendant, so served, who has not appeared in the action or proceeding, the time to answer or otherwise plead shall date from service upon such defendant of written notice of filing of such action or proceeding in the court to which it is transferred.

If an action or proceeding is commenced in or transferred to a court which has jurisdiction of the subject matter thereof as determined by the complaint or petition, and it thereafter appears from the verified pleadings, or at the trial, or hearing, that the determination of the action or proceeding, or of a cross-complaint, will necessarily involve the determination of questions not within the jurisdiction of the court, in which the action or proceeding is pending, the court, whenever such lack of jurisdiction appears, must suspend all further proceedings therein and transfer the action or proceeding and certify the pleadings (or if the pleadings be oral, a transcript of the same), and all papers and proceedings therein to a court having jurisdiction thereof which may be agreed upon by the parties, or, if they do not agree, to a court having such jurisdiction which is designated by law as a proper court for the trial or determination thereof.

An action or proceeding which is transferred under the provisions of this section shall be deemed to have been commenced at the time the complaint or petition was filed in the court from which it was originally transferred.

Nothing herein shall be construed to preclude or affect the right to amend the pleadings as provided in this code.

Nothing herein shall be construed to require the superior court to transfer any action or proceeding because the judgment to be rendered, as determined at the trial or hearing, is one which might have been rendered by a municipal or justice court in the same county or city and county.

In any case where the lack of jurisdiction is due solely to an excess in the amount of the demand, the excess may be remitted and the action may continue in the court where it is pending.

Upon the making of an order for such transfer, proceedings shall be had as provided in Section 399 of this code, the costs and fees thereof, and of filing the case in the court to which transferred, to be paid by the party filing the pleading in which the question outside the jurisdiction of the court appears unless the court ordering the transfer shall otherwise direct. *(Added by Stats.1933, c. 744, § 7. Amended by Stats.1935, c. 722, § 1; Stats.1941, c. 454, § 1; Stats.1951, c. 869, § 4; Stats.1959, c. 1487, § 1; Stats.1971, c. 244, § 16; Stats.1974, c. 1369, § 1.)*

§ 397. Change of Place of Trial; Grounds

The court may, on motion, change the place of trial in the following cases:

(a) When the court designated in the complaint is not the proper court.

(b) When there is reason to believe that an impartial trial cannot be had therein.

(c) When the convenience of witnesses and the ends of justice would be promoted by the change.

(d) When from any cause there is no judge of the court qualified to act.

(e) When a proceeding for dissolution of marriage has been filed in the county in which the petitioner has been a resident for three months next preceding the commencement of the proceeding, and the respondent at the time of the commencement of the proceeding is a resident of another county in this state, to the county of the respondent's residence when the ends of justice would be promoted by the change. If a motion to change the place of trial is made pursuant to this paragraph, the court may, prior to the determination of such motion, consider and determine motions for allowance of temporary spousal support, support of children, temporary restraining orders, attorneys' fees, and costs, and make all necessary and proper orders in connection therewith. *(Enacted 1872. Amended by Stats.1907, c. 369, § 5; Stats.1933, c. 744, § 9; Stats.1955, c. 832, § 2; Stats.1969, c. 1608, § 13; Stats.1992, c. 163, § 19.)*

§ 398. Transfer; Proper Court Having Jurisdiction

If, for any cause, specified in subdivisions 2, 3 and 4 of section 397, the court orders the transfer of an action or proceeding, it must be transferred to a court having jurisdiction of the subject matter of the action which the parties may agree upon, by stipulation in writing, or made in open court and entered in the minutes or docket; or, if they do not so agree, then to the nearest or most accessible court, where the like objection or cause for making the order does not exist.

If an action or proceeding is commenced in a court, other than one designated as a proper court for the trial thereof by the provisions of this title, and the same be ordered transferred for that reason, it must be transferred to any such proper court which the parties may agree upon by stipulation in writing, or made in open court and entered in the minutes or docket; if the parties do not so agree, then to any such proper court in the county in which the action or proceeding was commenced which the defendant may designate, or, if there be no such proper court in such county, to any such proper court, in a proper county, designated by the defendant; if the parties do not so agree, and the defendant does not so designate the court, as herein provided, or where the court orders the transfer of an action on its own motion as provided in this title, to such proper court as the court in which the action or proceeding is pending may determine.

The designation of the court by the defendant, herein provided for, may be made in the notice of motion for change of venue or in open court, entered in the minutes or docket, at the time the order for transfer is made. *(Enacted 1872. Amended by Stats.1881, c. 30, § 2; Stats.1897, c. 124, § 1; Stats.1925, c. 438, § 1; Stats.1927, c. 744, § 2; Stats.1933, c. 744, § 10.)*

§ 400. Petition for Writ of Mandate by Party Aggrieved

When an order is made by the superior court granting or denying a motion to change the place of trial, the party aggrieved by such order may, within 20 days after service of a written notice of the order, petition the court of appeal for the district in which the court granting or denying the motion is situated for a writ of mandate requiring trial of the case in the proper court. The superior court may, for good cause, and prior to the expiration of the initial 20-day period, extend the time for one additional period not to exceed 10 days. The petitioner shall file a copy of such petition in the trial court immediately after the petition is filed in the court of appeal. The court of appeal may stay all proceedings in the case, pending judgment on the petition becoming final. The clerk of the court of appeal shall file with the clerk of the trial court, a copy of any final order or final judgment immediately after such order or judgment becomes final. *(Added by Stats.1961, c. 1059, § 3. Amended by Stats.1963, c. 461, § 1; Stats.1967, c. 17, § 12; Stats.1984, c. 145, § 1; Stats.1989, c. 1416, § 12.)*

TITLE 5.   JURISDICTION AND SERVICE OF PROCESS
Chapter 1.   Jurisdiction and Forum

§ 410.10 Basis

A court of this state may exercise jurisdiction on any basis not inconsistent with the Constitution of this state or of the United States. *(Added by Stats.1969, c. 1610, § 3.)*

§ 410.30 Stay or Dismissal of Action; General Appearance

(a) When a court upon motion of a party or its own motion finds that in the interest of substantial justice an action should be heard in a forum outside this state, the court shall stay or dismiss the action in whole or in part on any conditions that may be just.

(b) The provisions of Section 418.10 do not apply to a motion to stay or dismiss the action by a defendant who has made a general appearance. *(Added by Stats.1969, c. 1610, § 3.   Amended by Stats.1972, c. 601, § 1.)*

§ 410.50   Time of Acquisition; General Appearance as Equivalent to Personal Service of Summons

(a) Except as otherwise provided by statute, the court in which an action is pending has jurisdiction over a party from the time summons is served on him as provided by Chapter 4 (commencing with Section 413.10).   A general appearance by a party is equivalent to personal service of summons on such party.

(b) Jurisdiction of the court over the parties and the subject matter of an action continues throughout subsequent proceedings in the action. *(Added by Stats.1969, c. 1610, § 3.)*

Chapter 3. Summons

§ 412.20   Summons; Formalities; Contents

(a) Except as otherwise required by statute, a summons shall be directed to the defendant, signed by the clerk and issued under the seal of the court in which the action is pending, and it shall contain:

(1) The title of the court in which the action is pending.

(2) The names of the parties to the action.

(3) A direction that the defendant file with the court a written pleading in response to the complaint within 30 days after summons is served on him or her.

(4) A notice that, unless the defendant so responds, his or her default will be entered upon application by the plaintiff, and the plaintiff may apply to the court for the relief demanded in the complaint, which could result in garnishment of wages, taking of money or property, or other relief.

(5) The following statement in boldface type: "You may seek the advice of an attorney in any matter connected with the complaint or this summons.   Such attorney should be consulted promptly so that your pleading may be filed or entered within the time required by this summons."

(6) The following introductory legend at the top of the summons above all other matter, in boldface type, in English and Spanish:

"Notice! You have been sued. The court may decide against you without your being heard unless you respond within 30 days.   Read information below."

(b) Each county may, by ordinance, require that the legend contained in paragraph (6) of subdivision (a) be set forth in every summons issued out of the courts of that county in any additional foreign language, if the legend in the additional foreign language is set forth in the summons in the same manner as required in that paragraph.

(c) A summons in a form approved by the Judicial Council is deemed to comply with this section. *(Added by Stats.1969, c. 1610, § 3. Amended by Stats.1974, c. 363, § 1; Stats.1989, c. 79, § 1; Stats.1989, c. 1105, § 6.)*

§ 412.30   Action Against Corporation or Unincorporated Association; Notice; Contents; Default Judgment

In an action against a corporation or an unincorporated association (including a partnership), the copy of the summons that is served shall contain a notice stating in substance: "To the person served: You are hereby served in the within action (or special proceeding) on behalf of (here state the name of the corporation or the unincorporated association) as a person upon whom a copy of the summons and of the complaint may be delivered to effect service on said party under the provisions of (here state appropriate provisions of Chapter 4 (commencing with Section 413.10) of the Code of Civil Procedure)." If service is also made on such person as an individual, the notice shall also indicate that service is being made on such person as an individual as well as on behalf of the corporation or the unincorporated association.

If such notice does not appear on the copy of the summons served, no default may be taken against such corporation or unincorporated association or against such person individually, as the case may be. *(Added by Stats.1969, c. 1610, § 3.)*

Chapter 4.   Service of Summons

§ 413.10   Law Governing Service

Except as otherwise provided by statute, a summons shall be served on a person:

(a) Within this state, as provided in this chapter.

(b) Outside this state but within the United States, as provided in this chapter or as prescribed by the law of the place where the person is served.

(c) Outside the United States, as provided in this chapter or as directed by the court in which the action is pending, or, if the court before or after service finds that the service is reasonably calculated to give actual notice, as prescribed by the law of the place where the person is served or as directed by the foreign authority in response to a letter rogatory. These rules are subject to the provisions of the Convention on the "Service Abroad of Judicial and Extrajudicial Documents" in Civil or Commercial Matters (Hague Service Convention). *(Added by Stats.1969, c. 1610, § 3. Amended by Stats.1984, c. 191, § 1.)*

§ 413.30   Procedure When No Provision Made for Service; Proof of Service

Where no provision is made in this chapter or other law for the service of summons, the court in which the action is pending may direct that summons be served in a manner which is reasonably calculated to give actual notice to the party to be served and that proof of such service be made as prescribed by the court. *(Added by Stats.1969, c. 1610, § 3.)*

§ 414.10 Authorized Persons

A summons may be served by any person who is at least 18 years of age and not a party to the action. *(Added by Stats.1969, c. 1610, § 3.)*

§ 415.10 Personal Delivery of Copy of Summons and Complaint; Date

A summons may be served by personal delivery of a copy of the summons and of the complaint to the person to be served. Service of a summons in this manner is deemed complete at the time of such delivery.

The date upon which personal delivery is made shall be entered on or affixed to the face of the copy of the summons at the time of its delivery. However, service of a summons without such date shall be valid and effective. *(Added by Stats.1969, c. 1610, § 3. Amended by Stats.1976, c. 789, § 1.)*

§ 415.20 Leaving Copy of Summons and Complaint at Office, Dwelling House, Usual Place of Abode or Usual Place of Business; Mailing Copy

(a) In lieu of personal delivery of a copy of the summons and of the complaint to the person to be served as specified in Section 416.10, 416.20, 416.30, 416.40, or 416.50, a summons may be served by leaving a copy of the summons and of the complaint during usual office hours in his or her office with the person who is apparently in charge thereof, and by thereafter mailing a copy of the summons and of the complaint (by first-class mail, postage prepaid) to the person to be served at the place where a copy of the summons and of the complaint were left. Service of a summons in this manner is deemed complete on the 10th day after such mailing.

(b) If a copy of the summons and of the complaint cannot with reasonable diligence be personally delivered to the person to be served as specified in Section 416.60, 416.70, 416.80, or 416.90, a summons may be served by leaving a copy of the summons and of the complaint at such person's dwelling house, usual place of abode, usual place of business, or usual mailing address other than a United States Postal Service post office box, in the presence of a competent member of the household or a person apparently in charge of his or her office, place of business, or usual mailing address other than a United States Postal Service post office box, at least 18 years of age, who shall be informed of the contents thereof, and by thereafter mailing a copy of the summons and of the complaint (by first-class mail, postage prepaid) to the person to be served at the place where a copy of the summons and of the complaint were left. Service of a summons in this manner is deemed complete on the 10th day after the mailing. *(Added by Stats.1969, c. 1610, § 3. Amended by Stats.1989, c. 1416, § 15.)*

§ 415.30 Service by Mail

(a) A summons may be served by mail as provided in this section. A copy of the summons and of the complaint shall be mailed (by first-class mail or airmail, postage prepaid) to the person to be served, together with two copies of the notice and acknowledgment provided for in subdivision (b) and a return envelope, postage prepaid, addressed to the sender.

(b) The notice specified in subdivision (a) shall be in substantially the following form:

(Title of court and cause, with action number, to be inserted by the sender prior to mailing)

NOTICE

To: (Here state the name of the person to be served.)

This summons is served pursuant to Section 415.30 of the California Code of Civil Procedure. Failure to complete this form and return it to the sender within 20 days may subject you (or the party on whose behalf you are being served) to liability for the payment of any expenses incurred in serving a summons upon you in any other manner permitted by law. If you are served on behalf of a corporation, unincorporated association (including a partnership), or other entity, this form must be signed in the name of such entity by you or by a person authorized to receive service of process on behalf of such entity. In all other cases, this form must be signed by you personally or by a person authorized by you to acknowledge receipt of summons. Section 415.30 provides that this summons is deemed served on the date of execution of an acknowledgment of receipt of summons.

———————————————————

Signature of sender

ACKNOWLEDGMENT OF RECEIPT OF SUMMONS

This acknowledges receipt on (insert date) of a copy of the summons and of the complaint at (insert address).

Date: ———————

(Date this acknowledgment is executed)

———————————————————

Signature of person
acknowledging receipt, with title if
acknowledgment is made on
behalf of another person.

(c) Service of a summons pursuant to this section is deemed complete on the date a written acknowledgment of receipt of summons is executed, if such acknowledgment thereafter is returned to the sender.

(d) If the person to whom a copy of the summons and of the complaint are mailed pursuant to this section fails to complete and return the acknowledgment form set forth in subdivision (b) within 20 days from the date of such mailing, the party to whom the summons was mailed shall be liable for reasonable expenses thereafter incurred in serving or attempting to serve the party by another method permitted by this chapter, and, except for good cause shown, the court in which the action is pending, upon motion, with or without notice, shall award the party such expenses whether or not he is otherwise entitled to recover his costs in the action.

(e) A notice or acknowledgment of receipt in form approved by the Judicial Council is deemed to comply with this section. *(Added by Stats.1969, c. 1610, § 3.)*

§ 415.40   Service on Person Outside State

A summons may be served on a person outside this state in any manner provided by this article or by sending a copy of the summons and of the complaint to the person to be served by first-class mail, postage prepaid, requiring a return receipt. Service of a summons by this form of mail is deemed complete on the 10th day after such mailing. *(Added by Stats.1969, c. 1610, § 3. Amended by Stats.1982, c. 249, § 1.)*

§ 415.50   Service by Publication

(a) A summons may be served by publication if upon affidavit it appears to the satisfaction of the court in which the action is pending that the party to be served cannot with reasonable diligence be served in another manner specified in this article and that:

(1) A cause of action exists against the party upon whom service is to be made or he or she is a necessary or proper party to the action; or

(2) The party to be served has or claims an interest in real or personal property in this state that is subject to the jurisdiction of the court or the relief demanded in the action consists wholly or in part in excluding the party from any interest in the property.

(b) The court shall order the summons to be published in a named newspaper, published in this state, that is most likely to give actual notice to the party to be served and direct that a copy of the summons, the complaint, and the order for publication be forthwith mailed to the party if his or her address is ascertained before expiration of the time prescribed for publication of the summons. Except as otherwise provided by statute, the publication shall be made as provided by Section 6064 of the Government Code unless the court, in its discretion, orders publication for a longer period.

(c) Service of a summons in this manner is deemed complete as provided in Section 6064 of the Government Code.

(d) Notwithstanding an order for publication of the summons, a summons may be served in another manner authorized by this chapter, in which event the service shall supersede any published summons. *(Added by Stats.1969, c. 1610, § 3. Amended by Stats.1972, c. 601, § 2; Stats.1984, c. 352, § 1.)*

§ 416.10 Corporations Generally

A summons may be served on a corporation by delivering a copy of the summons and of the complaint:

(a) To the person designated as agent for service of process as provided by any provision in Section 202, 1502, 2105 or 2107 of the Corporations Code (or Sections 3301 to 3303, inclusive, or Sections 6500 to 6504, inclusive, of the Corporations Code as in effect on December 31, 1976 with respect to corporations to which they remain applicable);

(b) To the president or other head of the corporation, a vice president, a secretary or assistant secretary, a treasurer or assistant treasurer, a general manager, or a person authorized by the corporation to receive service of process;

(c) If the corporation is a bank, to a cashier or assistant cashier or to a person specified in subdivision (a) or (b); or

(d) When authorized by any provision in Section 1701, 1702, 2110 or 2111 of the Corporations Code (or Sections 3301 to 3303, inclusive, or Sections 6500 to 6504, inclusive, of the Corporations Code as in effect on December 31, 1976, with respect to corporations to which they remain applicable), as provided by such provision. *(Added by Stats.1969, c. 1610, § 3. Amended by Stats.1975, c. 682, § 3; Stats.1976, c. 641, § 1.1.)*

§ 416.50 Public Entity

(a) A summons may be served on a public entity by delivering a copy of the summons and of the complaint to the clerk, secretary, president, presiding officer, or other head of its governing body.

(b) As used in this section, "public entity" includes the state and any office, department, division, bureau, board, commission, or agency of the state, the Regents of the University of California, a county, city, district, public authority, public agency, and any other political subdivision or public corporation in this state. *(Added by Stats.1969, c. 1610, § 3.)*

§ 417.10 Service Within State; Manner

Proof that a summons was served on a person within this state shall be made:

(a) If served under Section 415.10, 415.20, or 415.30, by the affidavit of the person making such service showing the time, place, and manner of service and facts showing that such service was made in accordance with this chapter. Such affidavit shall recite or in other manner show the name of the person to whom a copy of the summons and of the complaint were delivered, and, if appropriate, his title or the capacity in which he is served, and that the notice required by Section 412.30 appeared on the copy of the summons served, if in fact it did appear.

If service is made by mail pursuant to Section 415.30, proof of service shall include the acknowledgment of receipt of summons in the form provided by that section or other written acknowledgment of receipt of summons satisfactory to the court.

(b) If served by publication pursuant to Section 415.50, by the affidavit of the publisher or printer, or his foreman or principal clerk, showing the time and place of publication, and an affidavit showing the time and place a copy of the summons and of the complaint were mailed to the party to be served, if in fact mailed.

(c) If served pursuant to another statute of this state, in the manner prescribed by such statute or, if no manner is prescribed, in the manner prescribed by this section for proof of a similar manner of service.

(d) By the written admission of the party.

(e) If served by posting pursuant to Section 415.45, by the affidavit of the person who posted the premises, showing the time and place of posting, and an affidavit showing the time and place copies of the summons and of the complaint were mailed to the party to be served, if in fact mailed.

(f) All proof of personal service shall be made on a form adopted by the Judicial Council. (*Added by Stats.1969, c. 1610, § 3. Amended by Stats.1972, c. 719, § 2; Stats.1980, c. 676, § 65; Stats.1986, c. 953, § 2.*)

§ 417.40 Proof of Service Signed by Registered Process Server; Additional Contents

Any proof of service which is signed by a person registered under Chapter 16 (commencing with Section 22350) of Division 8 of the Business and Professions Code or his employee or independent contractor shall indicate the county in which he is registered and the number assigned to him pursuant to Section 22355 of the Business and Professions Code. (*Added by Stats.1971, c. 1661, § 3.*)

Chapter 5.   Objection to Jurisdiction

§ 418.10 Motion to Quash Service of Summons or to Stay or Dismiss Action; Procedure

(a) A defendant, on or before the last day of his or her time to plead or within any further time that the court may for good cause allow, may serve and file a notice of motion for one or more of the following purposes:

(1) To quash service of summons on the ground of lack of jurisdiction of the court over him or her.

(2) To stay or dismiss the action on the ground of inconvenient forum.

(3) To dismiss the action pursuant to the applicable provisions of Chapter 1.5 (commencing with Section 583.110) of Title 8.

(b) The notice shall designate, as the time for making the motion, a date not more than 30 days after filing of the notice. The notice shall be served in the same manner, and at the same times, prescribed by subdivision (b) of Section 1005. The service and filing of the notice shall extend the defendant's time to plead until 15 days after service upon him or her of a written notice of entry of an order denying his motion, except that for good cause shown the court may extend the defendant's time to plead for an additional period not exceeding 20 days.

(c) If the motion is denied by the trial court, the defendant, within 10 days after service upon him or her of a written notice of entry of an order of the court denying his or her motion, or within any further time not exceeding 20 days that the trial court may for good cause allow, and before pleading, may petition an appropriate reviewing court for a writ of mandate to require the trial court to enter its order quashing the service of summons or staying or dismissing the action. The defendant shall file or enter his or her responsive pleading in the trial court within the time prescribed by subdivision (b) unless, on or before the last day of the defendant's time to plead, he or she serves upon the adverse party and files with the trial court a notice that he or she has petitioned for a writ of mandate. The service and filing of the notice shall extend the defendant's time to plead until 10 days after service upon him or her of a written notice of the final judgment in the mandate proceeding. The time to plead may for good cause shown be extended by the trial court for an additional period not exceeding 20 days.

(d) No default may be entered against the defendant before expiration of his or her time to plead, and no motion under this section, or under Section 473 or 473.5 when joined with a motion under this section, or application to the court or stipulation of the parties for an extension of the time to plead, shall be deemed a general appearance by the defendant. *(Added by Stats.1969, c. 1610, § 3. Amended by Stats. 1989, c. 693, § 1; Stats.1993, c. 456, § 1.)*

TITLE 6.   OF THE PLEADINGS IN CIVIL ACTIONS
Chapter 1.   The Pleadings in General

§ 422.10   Allowable Pleadings

The pleadings allowed in civil actions are complaints, demurrers, answers, and cross-complaints. *(Added by Stats.1971, c. 244, § 18.)*

Chapter 2. Pleadings Demanding Relief

§ 425.10 Statement of Facts; Demand for Judgment

A complaint or cross-complaint shall contain both of the following:

(a) A statement of the facts constituting the cause of action, in ordinary and concise language.

(b) A demand for judgment for the relief to which the pleader claims he is entitled. If the recovery of money or damages be demanded, the amount thereof shall be stated, unless the action is brought in the superior court to recover actual or punitive damages for personal injury or wrongful death, in which case the amount thereof shall not be stated. *(Added by Stats.1971, c. 244, § 23. Amended by Stats.1974, c. 1481, § 1; Stats.1979, c. 778, § 2.)*

§ 425.11 Personal Injury or Wrongful Death Actions; Statement of Nature and Amount of Damages; Service of Statement

(a) When a complaint or cross-complaint is filed in an action in the superior court to recover damages for personal injury or wrongful death, the party against whom the action is brought may at any time request a statement setting forth the nature and amount of damages being sought. The request shall be served upon the plaintiff or cross-complainant, who shall serve a responsive statement as to the damages within 15 days thereafter. In the event that a response is not served, the party, on notice to the plaintiff or cross-complainant, may petition the court in which the action is pending to order the plaintiff or cross-complainant to serve a responsive statement.

(b) If no request is made for the statement referred to in subdivision (a), the plaintiff shall serve the statement on the defendant (1) before a default may be taken; or (2) in the event an answer is filed, at least 60 days prior to date set for the trial.

(c) The statement referred to in subdivision (a) shall be served in the following manner:

(1) If a party has not appeared in the action, the statement shall be served in the same manner as a summons.

(2) If a party has appeared in the action, the statement shall be served upon his or her attorney, or upon the party if he or she has appeared without an attorney, in the manner provided for service of a summons or in the manner provided by Chapter 5 (commencing with Section 1010) of Title 14 of Part 2. *(Added by Stats.1974, c. 1481, p. 3239, § 2. Amended by Stats.1993, c. 456, § 2.)*

§ 425.12 Personal Injury, Property Damage, Wrongful Death, Unlawful Detainer, Breach of Contract or Fraud Actions; Forms

The Judicial Council shall develop and approve official forms for use in trial courts of this state for any complaint, cross-complaint or answer in any action based upon personal injury, property damage, wrongful death, unlawful detainer, breach of contract or fraud.

In developing the forms required by this act, the Judicial Council shall consult with a representative advisory committee which shall include, but not be limited to, representatives of the plaintiff's bar, the defense bar, the public interest bar, court administrators and the public. The forms shall be drafted in nontechnical language and shall be made available through the office of the clerk of the appropriate trial court. *(Added by Stats.1979, c. 843, § 1. Amended by Stats.1982, c. 272, § 1; Stats.1984, c. 354, § 1.)*

§ 425.13 Punitive Damages; Negligence Action Against Health Care Provider

(a) In any action for damages arising out of the professional negligence of a health care provider, no claim for punitive damages shall be included in a complaint or other pleading unless the court enters an order allowing an amended pleading that includes a claim for punitive damages to be filed. The court may allow the filing of an amended pleading claiming punitive damages on a motion by the party seeking the amended pleading and on the basis of the supporting and opposing affidavits presented that the plaintiff has established that there is a substantial probability that the plaintiff will prevail on the claim pursuant to Section 3294 of the Civil Code. The court shall not grant a motion allowing the filing of an amended pleading that includes a claim for punitive damages if the motion for such an order is not filed within two years after the complaint or initial pleading is filed or not less than nine months before the date the matter is first set for trial, whichever is earlier.

(b) For the purposes of this section, "health care provider" means any person licensed or certified pursuant to Division 2 (commencing with Section 500) of the Business and Professions Code, or licensed pursuant to the Osteopathic Initiative Act, or the Chiropractic Initiative Act, or licensed pursuant to Chapter 2.5 (commencing with Section 1440) of Division 2 of the Health and Safety Code; and any clinic, health dispensary, or health facility, licensed pursuant to Division 2 (commencing with Section 1200) of the Health and Safety Code. "Health care provider" includes the legal representatives of a health care provider. *(Added by Stats.1987, c. 1498, § 7. Amended by Stats.1988, c. 1204, § 1; Stats.1988, c. 1205, § 1.)*

§ 426.10 Definitions

As used in this article:

(a) "Complaint" means a complaint or cross-complaint.

(b) "Plaintiff" means a person who files a complaint or cross-complaint.

(c) "Related cause of action" means a cause of action which arises out of the same transaction, occurrence, or series of transactions or occurrences as the cause of action which the plaintiff alleges in his complaint. *(Added by Stats.1971, c. 244, § 23.)*

§ 426.30 Waiver of Related Cause of Action; Exceptions

(a) Except as otherwise provided by statute, if a party against whom a complaint has been filed and served fails to allege in a cross-complaint any related cause of action which (at the time of serving his answer to the complaint) he has against the plaintiff, such party may not thereafter in any other action assert against the plaintiff the related cause of action not pleaded.

(b) This section does not apply if either of the following are established:

(1) The court in which the action is pending does not have jurisdiction to render a personal judgment against the person who failed to plead the related cause of action.

(2) The person who failed to plead the related cause of action did not file an answer to the complaint against him. *(Added by Stats.1971, c. 244, § 23.)*

§ 426.40 Application

This article does not apply if any of the following are established:

(a) The cause of action not pleaded requires for its adjudication the presence of additional parties over whom the court cannot acquire jurisdiction.

(b) Both the court in which the action is pending and any other court to which the action is transferrable pursuant to Section 396 are prohibited by the federal or state constitution or by a statute from entertaining the cause of action not pleaded.

(c) At the time the action was commenced, the cause of action not pleaded was the subject of another pending action. *(Added by Stats. 1971, c. 244, § 23.)*

§ 426.50 Failure to Plead Cause of Action; Notice; Amendment

A party who fails to plead a cause of action subject to the requirements of this article, whether through oversight, inadvertence, mistake, neglect, or other cause, may apply to the court for leave to amend his pleading, or to file a cross-complaint, to assert such cause at any time during the course of the action. The court, after notice to the adverse party, shall grant, upon such terms as may be just to the parties, leave to amend the pleading, or to file the cross-complaint, to assert such cause if the party who failed to plead the cause acted in good faith. This subdivision shall be liberally construed to avoid forfeiture of causes of action. *(Added by Stats.1971, c. 244, § 23.)*

§ 426.60　Application to Civil Actions; Exceptions

(a) This article applies only to civil actions and does not apply to special proceedings.

(b) This article does not apply to actions in the small claims court.

(c) This article does not apply where the only relief sought is a declaration of the rights and duties of the respective parties in an action for declaratory relief under Chapter 8 (commencing with Section 1060) of Title 14 of this part. *(Added by Stats.1971, c. 244, § 23.)*

§ 428.10　Filing of Cross-Complaint; Causes of Action

A party against whom a cause of action has been asserted in a complaint or cross-complaint may file a cross-complaint setting forth either or both of the following:

(a) Any cause of action he has against any of the parties who filed the complaint or cross-complaint against him. Nothing in this subdivision authorizes the filing of a cross-complaint against the plaintiff in an action commenced under Title 7 (commencing with Section 1230.010) of Part 3.

(b) Any cause of action he has against a person alleged to be liable thereon, whether or not such person is already a party to the action, if the cause of action asserted in his cross-complaint (1) arises out of the same transaction, occurrence, or series of transactions or occurrences as the cause brought against him or (2) asserts a claim, right, or interest in the property or controversy which is the subject of the cause brought against him. *(Added by Stats.1971, c. 244, § 23. Amended by Stats. 1975, c. 1240, § 4.)*

§ 428.20　Joinder of Person as Cross-Party

When a person files a cross-complaint as authorized by Section 428.10, he may join any person as a cross-complainant or cross-defendant, whether or not such person is already a party to the action, if, had the cross-complaint been filed as an independent action, the joinder of that party would have been permitted by the statutes governing joinder of parties. *(Added by Stats.1971, c. 244, § 23.)*

§ 428.30　Joinder of Other Causes of Action by Cross-Complainant

Where a person files a cross-complaint as authorized by Section 428.10, he may unite with the cause of action asserted in the cross-complaint any other causes of action he has against any of the cross-defendants, other than the plaintiff in an eminent domain proceeding, whether or not such cross-defendant is already a party to the action. *(Added by Stats.1971, c. 244, § 23.)*

§ 428.50 Filing of Cross-Complaint; Leave of Court

(a) A party shall file a cross-complaint against any of the parties who filed the complaint or cross-complaint against him or her before or at the same time as the answer to the complaint or cross-complaint.

(b) Any other cross-complaint may be filed at any time before the court has set a date for trial.

(c) A party shall obtain leave of court to file any cross-complaint except one filed within the time specified in subdivision (a) or (b). Leave may be granted in the interest of justice at any time during the course of the action. *(Added by Stats.1971, c. 244, § 23. Amended by Stats.1983, c. 176, § 1.)*

§ 428.70 Definitions

(a) As used in this section:

(1) "Third-party plaintiff" means a person against whom a cause of action has been asserted in a complaint or cross-complaint, who claims the right to recover all or part of any amounts for which he may be held liable on such cause of action from a third person, and who files a cross-complaint stating such claim as a cause of action against the third person.

(2) "Third-party defendant" means the person who is alleged in a cross-complaint filed by a third-party plaintiff to be liable to the third-party plaintiff if the third-party plaintiff is held liable on the claim against him.

(b) In addition to the other rights and duties a third-party defendant has under this article, he may, at the time he files his answer to the cross-complaint, file as a separate document a special answer alleging against the person who asserted the cause of action against the third-party plaintiff any defenses which the third-party plaintiff has to such cause of action. The special answer shall be served on the third-party plaintiff and on the person who asserted the cause of action against the third-party plaintiff. *(Added by Stats.1971, c. 244, § 23.)*

§ 428.80 Abolition of Counterclaim

The counterclaim is abolished. Any cause of action that formerly was asserted by a counterclaim shall be asserted by a cross-complaint. Where any statute refers to asserting a cause of action as a counterclaim, such cause shall be asserted as a cross-complaint. The erroneous designation of a pleading as a counterclaim shall not affect its validity, but such pleading shall be deemed to be a cross-complaint. *(Added by Stats.1971, c. 244, § 23.)*

Chapter 3. Objections to Pleadings; Denials and Defenses

§ 430.10 Objection by Defendant; Grounds

The party against whom a complaint or cross-complaint has been filed may object, by demurrer or answer as provided in Section 430.30, to the pleading on any one or more of the following grounds:

(a) The court has no jurisdiction of the subject of the cause of action alleged in the pleading.

(b) The person who filed the pleading does not have the legal capacity to sue.

(c) There is another action pending between the same parties on the same cause of action.

(d) There is a defect or misjoinder of parties.

(e) The pleading does not state facts sufficient to constitute a cause of action.

(f) The pleading is uncertain. As used in this subdivision, "uncertain" includes ambiguous and unintelligible.

(g) In an action founded upon a contract, it cannot be ascertained from the pleading whether the contract is written, is oral, or is implied by conduct.

(h) No certificate was filed as required by Section 411.35.

(i) No certificate was filed as required by Section 411.36. *(Added by Stats.1971, c. 244, § 29. Amended by Stats.1973, c. 828, § 2; Stats.1979, c. 973, § 2; Stats.1979, c. 988, § 2; Stats.1980, c. 163, § 2; Stats.1980, c. 500, § 1; Stats.1990, c. 216, § 8; Stats.1993, c. 456, § 3.)*

§ 430.20   Objections by Plaintiff; Grounds

A party against whom an answer has been filed may object, by demurrer as provided in Section 430.30, to the answer upon any one or more of the following grounds:

(a) The answer does not state facts sufficient to constitute a defense.

(b) The answer is uncertain. As used in this subdivision, "uncertain" includes ambiguous and unintelligible.

(c) Where the answer pleads a contract, it cannot be ascertained from the answer whether the contract is written or oral. *(Added by Stats.1971, c. 244, § 29.)*

§ 430.30   Objections by Demurrer and Answer

(a) When any ground for objection to a complaint, cross-complaint, or answer appears on the face thereof, or from any matter of which the court is required to or may take judicial notice, the objection on that ground may be taken by a demurrer to the pleading.

(b) When any ground for objection to a complaint or cross-complaint does not appear on the face of the pleading, the objection may be taken by answer.

(c) A party objecting to a complaint or cross-complaint may demur and answer at the same time. *(Added by Stats.1971, c. 244, § 29.)*

§ 430.40 Demurrer; Time

(a) A person against whom a complaint or cross-complaint has been filed may, within 30 days after service of the complaint or cross-complaint, demur to the complaint or cross-complaint.

(b) A party who has filed a complaint or cross-complaint may, within 10 days after service of the answer to his pleading, demur to the answer. *(Added by Stats.1971, c. 244, § 29.)*

§ 430.50 Demurrer to All or Part of Pleadings

(a) A demurrer to a complaint or cross-complaint may be taken to the whole complaint or cross-complaint or to any of the causes of action stated therein.

(b) A demurrer to an answer may be taken to the whole answer or to any one or more of the several defenses set up in the answer. *(Added by Stats.1971, c. 244, § 29.)*

§ 430.60 Specification of Grounds

A demurrer shall distinctly specify the grounds upon which any of the objections to the complaint, cross-complaint, or answer are taken. Unless it does so, it may be disregarded. *(Added by Stats.1971, c. 244, § 29.)*

§ 430.70 Demurrer Based on Matter of Which Court May Take Judicial Notice; Specification

When the ground of demurrer is based on a matter of which the court may take judicial notice pursuant to Section 452 or 453 of the Evidence Code, such matter shall be specified in the demurrer, or in the supporting points and authorities for the purpose of invoking such notice, except as the court may otherwise permit. *(Added by Stats.1971, c. 244, § 29.)*

§ 430.80 Failure to Object by Demurrer or Answer; Waiver; Exceptions

(a) If the party against whom a complaint or cross-complaint has been filed fails to object to the pleading, either by demurrer or answer, that party is deemed to have waived the objection unless it is an objection that the court has no jurisdiction of the subject of the cause of action alleged in the pleading or an objection that the pleading does not state facts sufficient to constitute a cause of action.

(b) If the party against whom an answer has been filed fails to demur thereto, that party is deemed to have waived the objection unless it is an objection that the answer does not state facts sufficient to constitute a defense. *(Added by Stats.1971, c. 244, § 29. Amended by Stats.1983, c. 1167, § 2.)*

§ 431.10   Material and Immaterial Allegations, Defined

(a) A material allegation in a pleading is one essential to the claim or defense and which could not be stricken from the pleading without leaving it insufficient as to that claim or defense.

(b) An immaterial allegation in a pleading is any of the following:

(1) An allegation that is not essential to the statement of a claim or defense.

(2) An allegation that is neither pertinent to nor supported by an otherwise sufficient claim or defense.

(3) A demand for judgment requesting relief not supported by the allegations of the complaint or cross-complaint.

(c) An "immaterial allegation" means "irrelevant matter" as that term is used in Section 436. *(Added by Stats.1971, c. 244, § 29. Amended by Stats.1982, c. 704, § 2; Stats.1983, c. 1167, § 3; Stats.1986, c. 540, § 2.)*

§ 431.20   Uncontroverted Allegations Deemed True; New Matter in Answer Deemed Controverted

(a) Every material allegation of the complaint or cross-complaint, not controverted by the answer, shall, for the purposes of the action, be taken as true.

(b) The statement of any new matter in the answer, in avoidance or constituting a defense, shall, on the trial, be deemed controverted by the opposite party. *(Added by Stats.1971, c. 244, § 29.)*

§ 431.30   Answer; Contents; Information and Belief; Denials; Defenses

(a) As used in this section:

(1) "Complaint" includes a cross-complaint.

(2) "Defendant" includes a person filing an answer to a cross-complaint.

(b) The answer to a complaint shall contain:

(1) The general or specific denial of the material allegations of the complaint controverted by the defendant.

(2) A statement of any new matter constituting a defense.

(c) Affirmative relief may not be claimed in the answer.

(d) If the complaint is subject to Article 2 (commencing with Section 90) of Chapter 5 of Title 1 of Part 1 or is not verified, a general denial is sufficient but only puts in issue the material allegations of the complaint. If the complaint is verified, unless the complaint is subject to Article 2 (commencing with Section 90) of Chapter 5 of Title 1 of Part 1, the denial of the allegations shall be made positively or according to the information and belief of the defendant. However, if the cause of action is a claim assigned to a third party for collection and the complaint is verified, the denial of the allegations shall be made positively or according to the information and belief of the defendant, even if the complaint is subject to Article 2 (commencing with Section 90) of Chapter 5 of Title 1 of Part 1.

(e) If the defendant has no information or belief upon the subject sufficient to enable him or her to answer an allegation of the complaint, he or she may so state in his or her answer and place his or her denial on that ground.

(f) The denials of the allegations controverted may be stated by reference to specific paragraphs or parts of the complaint; or by express admission of certain allegations of the complaint with a general denial of all of the allegations not so admitted; or by denial of certain allegations upon information and belief, or for lack of sufficient information or belief, with a general denial of all allegations not so denied or expressly admitted.

(g) The defenses shall be separately stated, and the several defenses shall refer to the causes of action which they are intended to answer, in a manner by which they may be intelligibly distinguished. *(Added by Stats.1971, c. 244, § 29. Amended by Stats.1979, c. 212, § 2; Stats.1985, c. 621, § 1; Stats.1986, c. 281, § 1.)*

Chapter 4.   Motion to Strike

§ 435. Notice of Motion to Strike Whole or Part of Complaint

(a) As used in this section:

(1) The term "complaint" includes a cross-complaint.

(2) The term "pleading" means a demurrer, answer, complaint, or cross-complaint.

(b)(1) Any party, within the time allowed to respond to a pleading may serve and file a notice of motion to strike the whole or any part thereof, but this time limitation shall not apply to motions specified in subdivision (e).

(2) A notice of motion to strike the answer or the complaint, or a portion thereof, shall specify a hearing date set in accordance with Section 1005.

(3) A notice of motion to strike a demurrer, or a portion thereof, shall set the hearing thereon concurrently with the hearing on the demurrer.

(c) If a party serves and files a notice of motion to strike without demurring to the complaint, the time to answer is extended and no default may be entered against that defendant, except as provided in Sections 585 and 586.

(d) The filing of a notice of motion to strike an answer or complaint, or portion thereof, shall not extend the time within which to demur.

(e) A motion to strike, as specified in this section, may be made as part of a motion pursuant to subparagraph (A) of paragraph (1) of subdivision (i) of Section 438. *(Added by Stats.1955, c. 1452, § 3a. Amended by Stats.1971, c. 244, § 33; Stats.1982, c. 704, § 3; Stats.1993, c. 456, § 3.5.)*

§ 436. Discretion of Court to Strike Pleadings or Portions of Pleadings

The court may, upon a motion made pursuant to Section 435, or at any time in its discretion, and upon terms it deems proper:

(a) Strike out any irrelevant, false, or improper matter inserted in any pleading.

(b) Strike out all or any part of any pleading not drawn or filed in conformity with the laws of this state, a court rule, or an order of the court. *(Added by Stats.1982, c. 704, § 3.5. Amended by Stats.1983, c. 1167, § 4.)*

§ 437. Grounds for Motion to Strike; Judicial Notice; Specification

(a) The grounds for a motion to strike shall appear on the face of the challenged pleading or from any matter of which the court is required to take judicial notice.

(b) Where the motion to strike is based on matter of which the court may take judicial notice pursuant to Section 452 or 453 of the Evidence Code, such matter shall be specified in the notice of motion, or in the supporting points and authorities, except as the court may otherwise permit. *(Added by Stats.1982, c. 704, § 4.)*

Chapter 5. Summary Judgments and Motions for Judgment on the Pleadings

§ 437c. Grounds for and Effect of Summary Judgment; Procedure on Motion

(a) Any party may move for summary judgment in any action or proceeding if it is contended that the action has no merit or that there is no defense to the action or proceeding. The motion may be made at any time after 60 days have elapsed since the general appearance in the action or proceeding of each party against whom the motion is directed or at any earlier time after the general appearance that the court, with or without notice and upon good cause shown, may direct. Notice of the motion and supporting papers shall be served on all other parties to the action at least 28 days before the time appointed for hearing. However, if the notice is served by mail, the required 28–day period of notice shall be increased by five days if the place of address is within the State of California, 10 days if the place of address is outside the State of California but within the United States, and 20 days if the place of address is outside the United States. The motion shall be heard no later than 30 days before the date of trial, unless the court for good cause orders otherwise. The filing of the motion shall not extend the time within which a party must otherwise file a responsive pleading.

(b) The motion shall be supported by affidavits, declarations, admissions, answers to interrogatories, depositions and matters of which judicial notice shall or may be taken. The supporting papers shall include a separate statement setting forth plainly and concisely all material facts which the moving party contends are undisputed. Each of the material facts stated shall be followed by a reference to the supporting evidence. The failure to comply with this requirement of a separate statement may in the court's discretion constitute a sufficient ground for denial of the motion.

Any opposition to the motion shall be served and filed not less than 14 days preceding the noticed or continued date of hearing, unless the court for good cause orders otherwise. The opposition, where appropriate, shall consist of affidavits, declarations, admissions, answers to interrogatories, depositions, and matters of which judicial notice shall or may be taken. The opposition papers shall include a separate statement which responds to each of the material facts contended by the moving party to be undisputed, indicating whether the opposing party agrees or disagrees that those facts are undisputed. The statement also shall set forth plainly and concisely any other material facts which the opposing party contends are disputed. Each material fact contended by the opposing party to be disputed shall be followed by a reference to the supporting evidence. Failure to comply with this requirement of a separate statement may constitute a sufficient ground, in the court's discretion, for granting the motion.

Any reply to the opposition shall be served and filed by the moving party not less than five days preceding the noticed or continued date of hearing, unless the court for good cause orders otherwise.

Evidentiary objections not made at the hearing shall be deemed waived.

Sections 1005 and 1013, extending the time within which a right may be exercised or an act may be done, do not apply to this section.

Any incorporation by reference of matter in the court's file shall set forth with specificity the exact matter to which reference is being made and shall not incorporate the entire file.

(c) The motion for summary judgment shall be granted if all the papers submitted show that there is no triable issue as to any material fact and that the moving party is entitled to a judgment as a matter of law. In determining whether the papers show that there is no triable issue as to any material fact the court shall consider all of the evidence set forth in the papers, except that to which objections have been made and sustained by the court, and all inferences reasonably deducible from the evidence, except summary judgment shall not be granted by the court based on inferences reasonably deducible from the evidence, if contradicted by other inferences or evidence, which raise a triable issue as to any material fact.

(d) Supporting and opposing affidavits or declarations shall be made by any person on personal knowledge, shall set forth admissible evidence, and shall show affirmatively that the affiant is competent to testify to the matters stated in the affidavits or declarations. Any objections based on the failure to comply with the requirements of this subdivision shall be made at the hearing or shall be deemed waived.

(e) If a party is otherwise entitled to a summary judgment pursuant to the provisions of this section, summary judgment shall not be denied on grounds of credibility or for want of cross-examination of witnesses furnishing affidavits or declarations in support of the summary judgment, except that summary judgment may be denied in the discretion of the court, where the only proof of a material fact offered in support of the summary judgment is an affidavit or declaration made by an individual who was the sole witness to that fact; or where a material fact is an individual's state of mind, or lack thereof, and that fact is sought to be established solely by the individual's affirmation thereof.

(f)(1) A party may move for summary adjudication as to one or more causes of action within an action, one or more affirmative defenses, one or more claims for damages, or one or more issues of duty, if that party contends that the cause of action has no merit or that there is no affirmative defense thereto, or that there is no merit to an affirmative defense as to any cause of action, or both, or that there is no merit to a claim for damages, as specified in Section 3294 of the Civil Code, or that one or more defendants either owed or did not owe a duty to the plaintiff or plaintiffs. A motion for summary adjudication shall be granted only if it completely disposes of a cause of action, an affirmative defense, a claim for damages, or an issue of duty.

(2) A motion for summary adjudication may be made by itself or as an alternative to a motion for summary judgment and shall proceed in all procedural respects as a motion for summary judgment. However, a party may not move for summary judgment based on issues asserted in a prior motion for summary adjudication and denied by the court, unless that party establishes to the satisfaction of the court, newly discovered facts or circumstances supporting the issues reasserted in the summary judgment motion.

(g) Upon the denial of a motion for summary judgment, on the ground that there is a triable issue as to one or more material facts, the court shall, by written or oral order, specify one or more material facts raised by the motion as to which the court has determined there exists a triable controversy. This determination shall specifically refer to the evidence proffered in support of and in opposition to the motion which indicates that a triable controversy exists. Upon the grant of a motion for summary judgment, on the ground that there is no triable issue of material fact, the court shall, by written or oral order, specify the reasons for its determination. The order shall specifically refer to the evidence proffered in support of, and if applicable in opposition to, the motion which indicates that no triable issue exists. The court shall also state its reasons for any other determination. The court shall record its determination by court reporter or written order.

(h) If it appears from the affidavits submitted in opposition to a motion for summary judgment or summary adjudication or both that facts essential to justify opposition may exist but cannot, for reasons stated, then be presented, the court shall deny the motion, or order a continuance to permit affidavits to be obtained or discovery to be had or may make any other order as may be just.

(i) If the court determines at any time that any of the affidavits are presented in bad faith or solely for purposes of delay, the court shall order the party presenting the affidavits to pay the other party the amount of the reasonable expenses which the filing of the affidavits caused the other party to incur. Sanctions shall not be imposed pursuant to this subdivision except on notice contained in a party's papers, or on the court's own noticed motion, and after an opportunity to be heard.

(j) Except where a separate judgment may properly be awarded in the action, no final judgment shall be entered on a motion for summary judgment prior to the termination of the action, but the final judgment shall, in addition to any matters determined in the action, award judgment as established by the summary proceeding herein provided for.

(k) In actions which arise out of an injury to the person or to property, when a motion for summary judgment was granted on the basis that the defendant was without fault, no other defendant during trial, over plaintiff's objection, may attempt to attribute fault to or comment on the absence or involvement of the defendant who was granted the motion.

(*l*) A summary judgment entered under this section is an appealable judgment as in other cases. Upon entry of any order pursuant to this section except the entry of summary judgment, a party may, within 20 days after service upon him or her of a written notice of entry of the order, petition an appropriate reviewing court for a peremptory writ. If the notice is served by mail, the initial period within which to file the petition shall be increased by five days if the place of address is within the State of California, 10 days if the place of address is outside the State of California but within the United States, and 20 days if the place of address is outside the United States. The superior court may, for good cause, and prior to the expiration of the initial period, extend the time for one additional period not to exceed 10 days.

(m)(1) If a motion for summary adjudication is granted, at the trial of the action, the cause or causes of action within the action, affirmative defense or defenses, claim for damages, or issue or issues of duty as to the motion which has been granted shall be deemed to be established and the action shall proceed as to the cause or causes of action, affirmative defense or defenses, claim for damages, or issue or issues of duty remaining.

(2) In the trial of the action, the fact that a motion for summary adjudication is granted as to one or more causes of action, affirmative defenses, claims for damages, or issues of duty within the action shall not operate to bar any cause of action, affirmative defense, claim for damages, or issue of duty as to which summary adjudication was either not sought or denied.

(3) When an objection is made to a motion for summary adjudication, neither a party, nor a witness, nor the court may comment upon the grant or denial of a motion for summary adjudication, or upon the fact that a party did not seek to summarily adjudicate any issue.

(n) A cause of action has no merit if either of the following exists:

(1) One or more of the elements of the cause of action cannot be separately established, even if that element is separately pleaded.

(2) A defendant establishes an affirmative defense to that cause of action.

(o) For purposes of motions for summary judgment and summary adjudication:

(1) A plaintiff or cross-complainant has met his or her burden of showing that there is no defense to a cause of action if that party has proved each element of the cause of action entitling the party to judgment on that cause of action. Once the plaintiff or cross-complainant has met that burden, the burden shifts to the defendant or cross-defendant to show that a triable issue of one or more material facts exists as to that cause of action or a defense thereto. The defendant or cross-defendant may not rely upon the mere allegations or denials of its pleadings to show that a triable issue of material fact exists but, instead, shall set forth the specific facts showing that a triable issue of material fact exists as to that cause of action or a defense thereto.

(2) A defendant or cross-defendant has met his or her burden of showing that a cause of action has no merit if that party has shown that one or more elements of the cause of action, even if not separately pleaded, cannot be established, or that there is a complete defense to that cause of action. Once the defendant or cross-defendant has met that burden, the burden shifts to the plaintiff or cross-complainant to show that a triable issue of one or more material facts exists as to that cause of action or a defense thereto. The plaintiff or cross-complainant may not rely upon the mere allegations or denials of its pleadings to show that a triable issue of material fact exists but, instead, shall set forth the specific facts showing that a triable issue of material fact exists as to that cause of action or a defense thereto.

(p) Nothing in this section shall be construed to extend the period for trial provided by Section 1170.5.

(q) Subdivisions (a) and (b) shall not apply to actions brought pursuant to Chapter 4 (commencing with Section 1159) of Title 3 of Part 3.

(r) For the purposes of this section, a change in law shall not include a later enacted statute without retroactive application. *(Added by Stats.1973, c. 366, § 2. Amended by Stats.1976, c. 675, § 1; Stats. 1978, c. 949, § 2; Stats.1980, c. 57, § 1; Stats.1982, c. 1510, § 1; Stats.1983, c. 490, § 1; Stats.1984, c. 171, § 1; Stats.1986, c. 540, § 3; Stats.1989, c. 1416, § 16; Stats.1990, c. 1561, § 2; Stats.1992, c. 339, § 1; Stats.1992, c. 1348, § 1; Stats.1993, c. 276.)*

Chapter 6. Verification of Pleadings

§ 446. Subscription; Necessity of Verification; Contents of Affidavit; Persons Who May Verify; Answer by State, Political Subdivision, etc.; Verification Under Penalty of Perjury

Every pleading shall be subscribed by the party or his attorney. When the state, any county thereof, city, school district, district, public agency, or public corporation, or any officer of the state, or of any county thereof, city, school district, district, public agency, or public corporation, in his or her official capacity, is plaintiff, the answer shall be verified, unless an admission of the truth of the complaint might subject the party to a criminal prosecution, or, unless a county thereof, city, school district, district, public agency, or public corporation, or an officer of the state, or of any county, city, school district, district, public agency, or public corporation, in his or her official capacity, is defendant. When the complaint is verified, the answer shall be verified. In all cases of a verification of a pleading, the affidavit of the party shall state that the same is true of his own knowledge, except as to the matters which are therein stated on his or her information or belief, and as to those matters that he or she believes it to be true; and where a pleading is verified, it shall be by the affidavit of a party, unless the parties are absent from the county where the attorney has his or her office, or from some cause unable to verify it, or the facts are within the knowledge of his or her attorney or other person verifying the same. When the pleading is verified by the attorney, or any other person except one of the parties, he or she shall set forth in the affidavit the reasons why it is not made by one of the parties.

When a corporation is a party, the verification may be made by any officer thereof. When the state, any county thereof, city, school district, district, public agency, or public corporation, or an officer of the state, or of any county thereof, city, school district, district, public agency, or public corporation, in his or her official capacity is plaintiff, the complaint need not be verified; and if the state, any county thereof, city, school district, district, public agency, or public corporation, or an officer of such state, county, city, school district, district, public agency, or public corporation, in his or her official capacity is defendant, its or his or her answer need not be verified.

When the verification is made by the attorney for the reason that the parties are absent from the county where he or she has his or her office, or from some other cause are unable to verify it, or when the verification is made on behalf of a corporation or public agency by any officer thereof, the attorney's or officer's affidavit shall state that he or she has read the pleading and that he or she is informed and believes the matters therein to be true and on that ground alleges that the matters stated therein are true. However, in those cases the pleadings shall not otherwise be considered as an affidavit or declaration establishing the facts therein alleged.

A person verifying a pleading need not swear to the truth or his or her belief in the truth of the matters stated therein but may, instead, assert the truth or his or her belief in the truth of those matters "under penalty of perjury." *(Enacted 1872. Amended by Stats.1907, c. 372, § 9; Stats.1933, c. 744, § 29; Stats.1939, c. 712, § 1; Stats.1945, c. 505, § 1; Stats.1951, c. 1737, § 54; Stats.1955, c. 873, § 1; Stats.1963, c. 732, § 1; Stats.1967, c. 1242, § 1; Stats.1977, c. 1257, § 12; Stats.1981, c. 714, § 69.)*

Chapter 8. Variance—Mistakes in Pleadings and Amendments

§ 469. Variance; When Material; Order for Amendment

No variance between the allegation in a pleading and the proof is to be deemed material, unless it has actually misled the adverse party to his prejudice in maintaining his action or defense upon the merits. Whenever it appears that a party has been so misled, the Court may order the pleading to be amended upon such terms as may be just. *(Enacted 1872. Amended by Code Am.1873–74, c. 383, § 58.)*

§ 470. Immaterial Variance; Findings; Amendment

Where the variance is not material, as provided in Section 469 the court may direct the fact to be found according to the evidence, or may order an immediate amendment, without costs. *(Enacted 1872. Amended by Stats.1986, c. 540, § 4.)*

§ 472. Amendment Once of Course

Any pleading may be amended once by the party of course, and without costs, at any time before the answer or demurrer is filed, or after demurrer and before the trial of the issue of law thereon, by filing the same as amended and serving a copy on the adverse party, and the time in which the adverse party must respond thereto shall be computed from the date of notice of the amendment. *(Enacted 1872. Amended by Code Am.1873–74, c. 383, § 59; Stats.1933, c. 744, § 31; Stats.1951, c. 1737, § 56; Stats.1972, c. 73, § 3; Stats.1977, c. 1257, § 13; Stats.1983, c. 142, § 4.)*

§ 472a. Demurrers; Motion to Strike; Motion to Dismiss Relating to Service of Summons

(a) A demurrer is not waived by an answer filed at the same time.

(b) Except as otherwise provided by rule adopted by the Judicial Council, when a demurrer to a complaint or to a cross-complaint is overruled and there is no answer filed, the court shall allow an answer to be filed upon such terms as may be just. If a demurrer to the answer is overruled, the action shall proceed as if no demurrer had been interposed, and the facts alleged in the answer shall be considered as denied to the extent mentioned in Section 431.20.

(c) When a demurrer is sustained, the court may grant leave to amend the pleading upon any terms as may be just and shall fix the time within which the amendment or amended pleading shall be filed. When a demurrer is stricken pursuant to Section 436 and there is no answer filed, the court shall allow an answer to be filed on terms that are just.

(d) When a motion to strike is granted pursuant to Section 436, the court may order that an amendment or amended pleading be filed upon terms it deems proper. When a motion to strike a complaint or cross-complaint, or portion thereof, is denied, the court shall allow the party filing the motion to strike to file an answer.

(e) When a motion to dismiss an action pursuant to Article 2 (commencing with Section 583.210) of Chapter 1.5 of Title 8 is denied, the court shall allow a pleading to be filed. *(Added by Stats.1933, c. 744, § 32. Amended by Stats.1951, c. 1737, § 57; Stats.1971, c. 1475, § 1; Stats.1982, c. 704, § 6; Stats.1983, c. 142, § 5; Stats.1983, c. 1167, § 5; Stats.1984, c. 572, § 2; Stats.1989, c. 1416, § 17; Stats.1993, c. 456, § 6.)*

§ 473. Amendments Permitted by Court; Enlargement of Time to Answer or Demurrer; Continuance, Costs; Relief From Judgment, etc., Taken by Mistake, Inadvertence, Surprise, or Excusable Neglect; Clerical Mistakes in Judgment or Order; Vacating Void Judgment or Order

The court may, in furtherance of justice, and on such terms as may be proper, allow a party to amend any pleading or proceeding by adding or striking out the name of any party, or by correcting a mistake in the name of a party, or a mistake in any other respect; and may, upon like terms, enlarge the time for answer or demurrer. The court may likewise, in its discretion, after notice to the adverse party, allow, upon such terms as may be just, an amendment to any pleading or proceeding in other particulars; and may upon like terms allow an answer to be made after the time limited by this code.

When it appears to the satisfaction of the court that the amendment renders it necessary, the court may postpone the trial, and may, when the postponement will by the amendment be rendered necessary, require, as a condition to the amendment, the payment to the adverse party of such costs as may be just.

The court may, upon such terms as may be just, relieve a party or his or her legal representative from a judgment, order, or other proceeding taken against him or her through his or her mistake, inadvertence, surprise, or excusable neglect. Application for this relief shall be accompanied by a copy of the answer or other pleading proposed to be filed therein, otherwise the application shall not be granted, and shall be made within a reasonable time, in no case exceeding six months, after the judgment, order or proceeding was taken; provided, however, that, in the case of a judgment, order or other proceeding determining the ownership or right to possession of real or personal property, without extending the six-months period, when a notice in writing is personally served within the State of California both upon the party against whom the judgment, order or other proceeding has been taken, and upon his or her attorney of record, if any, notifying that party and his or her attorney of record, if any, that the order, judgment or other proceeding was taken against him or her and that any rights the party has to apply for relief under the provisions of Section 473 of the Code of Civil Procedure shall expire 90 days after service of the notice, then the application shall be made within 90 days after service of the notice upon the defaulting party or his or her attorney of record, if any, whichever service shall be later. No affidavit or declaration of merits shall be required of the moving party. Notwithstanding any other requirements of this section, the court shall, whenever an application for relief is made no more than six months after entry of judgment, is in proper form, and is accompanied by an attorney's sworn affidavit attesting to his or her mistake, inadvertence, surprise or neglect, vacate any (1) resulting default entered by the clerk against his or her client, and which will result in entry of a default judgment, or (2) resulting default judgment entered against his or her client unless the court finds that the default was not in fact caused by the attorney's mistake, inadvertence, surprise, or neglect. The court shall, whenever relief is granted based on an attorney's affidavit of fault, direct the attorney to pay reasonable compensatory legal fees and costs to opposing counsel or parties.

Whenever the court grants relief from a default or default judgment based on any of the provisions of this section, the court may: (1) impose a penalty of no greater than one thousand dollars ($1,000) upon an offending attorney or defaulting party, (2) direct that an offending attorney pay an amount no greater than one thousand dollars ($1,000) to the State Bar Client Security Fund or (3) grant such other relief as is appropriate.

However, where the court grants relief from a default or default judgment pursuant to this section based upon the affidavit of the defaulting party's attorney attesting to the attorney's mistake, inadvertence, surprise, or neglect, the relief shall not be made conditional upon the attorney's payment of compensatory legal fees or costs or monetary penalties imposed by the court or upon compliance with other sanctions ordered by the court.

The court may, upon motion of the injured party, or its own motion, correct clerical mistakes in its judgment or orders as entered, so as to conform to the judgment or order directed, and may, on motion of either party after notice to the other party, set aside any void judgment or order. *(Enacted 1872. Amended by Code Am.1873–74, c. 383, § 60; Code Am.1880, c. 14, § 3; Stats.1917, c. 159, § 1; Stats.1933, c. 744, § 34; Stats.1961, c. 722, § 1; Stats.1981, c. 122, § 2; Stats.1988, c. 1131, § 1; Stats.1991, c. 1003, § 1.)*

§ 473.5 Motion to Set Aside Default and for Leave to Defend Action

(a) When service of a summons has not resulted in actual notice to a party in time to defend the action and a default or default judgment has been entered against him or her in the action, he or she may serve and file a notice of motion to set aside the default or default judgment and for leave to defend the action. The notice of motion shall be served and filed within a reasonable time, but in no event exceeding the earlier of: (i) two years after entry of a default judgment against him or her; or (ii) 180 days after service on him or her of a written notice that the default or default judgment has been entered.

(b) A notice of motion to set aside a default or default judgment and for leave to defend the action shall designate as the time for making the motion a date prescribed by subdivision (b) of Section 1005, and it shall be accompanied by an affidavit showing under oath that the party's lack of actual notice in time to defend the action was not caused by his or her avoidance of service or inexcusable neglect. The party shall serve and file with the notice a copy of the answer, motion, or other pleading proposed to be filed in the action.

(c) Upon a finding by the court that the motion was made within the period permitted by subdivision (a) and that his or her lack of actual notice in time to defend the action was not caused by his avoidance of service or inexcusable neglect, it may set aside the default or default judgment on whatever terms as may be just and allow the party to defend the action. *(Added by Stats.1969, c. 1610, § 23. Amended by Stats.1990, c. 1491, § 5.)*

§ 474. Defendant Designated by Fictitious Name; Amendment; Requirements for Default Judgment; Notice to Person Served

When the plaintiff is ignorant of the name of a defendant, he must state that fact in the complaint, or the affidavit if the action is commenced by affidavit, and such defendant may be designated in any pleading or proceeding by any name, and when his true name is discovered, the pleading or proceeding must be amended accordingly; provided, that no default or default judgment shall be entered against a defendant so designated, unless it appears that the copy of the summons or other process, or, if there be no summons or process, the copy of the first pleading or notice served upon such defendant bore on the face thereof a notice stating in substance: "To the person served: You are hereby served in the within action (or proceedings) as (or on behalf of) the person sued under the fictitious name of (designating it)." The certificate or affidavit of service must state the fictitious name under which such defendant was served and the fact that notice of identity was given by endorsement upon the document served as required by this section. The foregoing requirements for entry of a default or default judgment shall be applicable only as to fictitious names designated pursuant to this section and not in the event the plaintiff has sued the defendant by an erroneous name and shall not be applicable to entry of a default or default judgment based upon service, in the manner otherwise provided by law, of an amended pleading, process or notice designating defendant by his true name. *(Enacted 1872. Amended by Stats.1953, c. 1244, § 1; Stats.1955, c. 886, § 1.)*

TITLE 6.5   ATTACHMENT
Chapter 3.   Actions in Which Attachment Authorized

§ 483.010   Claims Subject to Attachment;   Minimum Amount; Secured Claim;   Claim Against Defendant Who Is Natural Person;   Other Relief;   Duration of Section

Text of section operative until Jan. 1, 1996.

(a) Except as otherwise provided by statute, an attachment may be issued only in an action on a claim or claims for money, each of which is based upon a contract, express or implied, where the total amount of the claim or claims is a fixed or readily ascertainable amount not less than five hundred dollars ($500) exclusive of costs, interest, and attorney's fees.

(b) An attachment may not be issued on a claim which is secured by any interest in real property arising from agreement, statute, or other rule of law (including any mortgage or deed of trust of realty and any statutory, common law, or equitable lien on real property, but excluding any security interest in fixtures subject to Division 9 (commencing with Section 9101) of the Commercial Code). However, an attachment may be issued (1) where the claim was originally so secured but, without any act of the plaintiff or the person to whom the security was given, the security has become valueless or has decreased in value to less than the amount then owing on the claim, in which event the amount to be secured by the attachment shall not exceed the lesser of the amount of the decrease or the difference between the value of the security and the amount then owing on the claim, or (2) where the claim was secured by a nonconsensual possessory lien but the lien has been relinquished by the surrender of the possession of the property.

(c) If the action is against a defendant who is a natural person, an attachment may be issued only on a claim which arises out of the conduct by the defendant of a trade, business, or profession. An attachment may not be issued on a claim against a defendant who is a natural person if the claim is based on the sale or lease of property, a license to use property, the furnishing of services, or the loan of money where the property sold or leased, or licensed for use, the services furnished, or the money loaned was used by the defendant primarily for personal, family, or household purposes.

(d) An attachment may be issued pursuant to this section whether or not other forms of relief are demanded.

(e) This section shall remain in effect only until January 1, 1996, and as of that date is repealed, unless a later enacted statute, which is enacted before January 1, 1996, deletes or extends that date. *(Added by Stats.1974, c. 1516, § 9. Amended by Stats.1976, c. 437, § 6; Stats.1982, c. 1198, § 27; Stats.1990, c. 943, § 1; Stats.1993, c. 589, § 26.)*

For text of section operative Jan. 1, 1996, see § 483.010, post.

§ 483.010   Claims Subject to Attachment; Minimum Amount; Secured Claims; Claims Against Defendant Who Is Natural Person; Other Relief; Operative Date of Section

Text of section operative Jan. 1, 1996.

(a) Except as otherwise provided by statute, an attachment may be issued only in an action on a claim or claims for money, each of which is based upon a contract, express or implied, where the total amount of the claim or claims is a fixed or readily ascertainable amount not less than five hundred dollars ($500) exclusive of costs, interest, and attorney's fees.

(b) An attachment may not be issued on a claim which is secured by any interest in real or personal property arising from agreement, statute, or other rule of law (including any mortgage or deed of trust of realty, any security interest subject to Division 9 (commencing with Section 9101) of the Commercial Code, and any statutory, common law, or equitable lien). However, an attachment may be issued (1) where the claim was originally so secured but, without any act of the plaintiff or the person to whom the security was given, the security has become valueless or has decreased in value to less than the amount then owing on the claim, in which event the amount for which the attachment may issue shall not exceed the lesser of the amount of the decrease or the difference between the value of the security and the amount then owing on the claim, or (2) where the claim was secured by a nonconsensual possessory lien but the lien has been relinquished by the surrender of the possession of the property.

(c) If the action is against a defendant who is a natural person, an attachment may be issued only on a claim which arises out of the conduct by the defendant of a trade, business, or profession. An attachment may not be issued on a claim against a defendant who is a natural person if the claim is based on the sale or lease of property, a license to use property, the furnishing of services, or the loan of money where the property sold or leased, or licensed for use, the services furnished, or the money loaned was used by the defendant primarily for personal, family, or household purposes.

(d) An attachment may be issued pursuant to this section whether or not other forms of relief are demanded.

(e) This section shall become operative on January 1, 1996. *(Added by Stats.1990, c. 943, § 1.5.)*

For text of section operative until Jan. 1, 1996, see § 483.010, ante.

Chapter 5. Ex Parte Hearing Procedure for Obtaining Writ of Attachment

§ 485.010 Affidavit; Showing; Review of Issuance of Writ; Time

(a) Except as otherwise provided by statute, no right to attach order or writ of attachment may be issued pursuant to this chapter unless it appears from facts shown by affidavit that great or irreparable injury would result to the plaintiff if issuance of the order were delayed until the matter could be heard on notice.

(b) The requirement of subdivision (a) is satisfied if any of the following are shown:

(1) Under the circumstances of the case, it may be inferred that there is a danger that the property sought to be attached would be concealed, substantially impaired in value, or otherwise made unavailable to levy if issuance of the order were delayed until the matter could be heard on notice.

(2) Under the circumstances of the case, it may be inferred that the defendant has failed to pay the debt underlying the requested attachment and the defendant is insolvent in the sense that the defendant is generally not paying his or her debts as those debts become due, unless the debts are subject to a bona fide dispute. Plaintiff's affidavit filed in support of the ex parte attachment shall state, in addition to the requirements of Section 485.530, the known undisputed debts of the defendant, that the debts are not subject to bona fide dispute, and the basis for plaintiff's determination that the defendant's debts are undisputed.

(3) A bulk sales notice has been recorded and published pursuant to Division 6 (commencing with Section 6101) of the Commercial Code with respect to a bulk transfer by the defendant.

(4) An escrow has been opened pursuant to the provisions of Section 24074 of the Business and Professions Code with respect to the sale by the defendant of a liquor license.

(5) Any other circumstance showing that great or irreparable injury would result to the plaintiff if issuance of the order were delayed until the matter could be heard on notice.

(c) Upon a writ being issued solely on a showing under paragraph (2) of subdivision (b), if the defendant requests the court to review the issuance of the writ, the court shall conduct a hearing within five court days after the plaintiff is served with notice of the defendant's request.

A writ issued solely on a showing under paragraph (3) of subdivision (b) shall be limited to the property covered by the bulk sales notice or the proceeds of the sale of such property. In addition to any other service required by this title, such writ shall be served by the levying officer on the transferee or auctioneer identified by the bulk sales notice not more than five days after the levy of such writ. A writ issued solely on a showing under paragraph (4) of subdivision (b) shall be limited to the plaintiff's pro rata share of the proceeds of the sale in escrow. *(Added by Stats.1974, c. 1516, § 9. Amended by Stats.1976, c. 437, § 14.5; Stats.1988, c. 727, § 1.)*

§ 485.210 Application; Filing; Showing; Supporting Affidavit

(a) Upon the filing of the complaint or at any time thereafter, the plaintiff may apply pursuant to this article for a right to attach order and a writ of attachment by filing an application for the order and writ with the court in which the action is brought.

(b) The application shall satisfy the requirements of Section 484.020 and, in addition, shall include a statement showing that the requirement of Section 485.010 is satisfied.

(c) The application shall be supported by an affidavit showing all of the following:

(1) The plaintiff on the facts presented would be entitled to a judgment on the claim upon which the attachment is based.

(2) The plaintiff would suffer great or irreparable injury (within the meaning of Section 485.010) if issuance of the order were delayed until the matter could be heard on notice.

(3) The property sought to be attached is not exempt from attachment.

(d) An affidavit in support of the showing required by paragraph (3) of subdivision (c) may be based on the affiant's information and belief. *(Added by Stats.1974, c. 1516, § 9.)*

§ 485.220 Issuance of Order and Writ; Findings; Denial of Order

(a) The court shall examine the application and supporting affidavit and, except as provided in Section 486.030, shall issue a right to attach order, which shall state the amount to be secured by the attachment, and order a writ of attachment to be issued upon the filing of an undertaking as provided by Sections 489.210 and 489.220, if it finds all of the following:

(1) The claim upon which the attachment is based is one upon which an attachment may be issued.

(2) The plaintiff has established the probable validity of the claim upon which the attachment is based.

(3) The attachment is not sought for a purpose other than the recovery upon the claim upon which the attachment is based.

(4) The affidavit accompanying the application shows that the property sought to be attached, or the portion thereof to be specified in the writ, is not exempt from attachment.

(5) The plaintiff will suffer great or irreparable injury (within the meaning of Section 485.010) if issuance of the order is delayed until the matter can be heard on notice.

(b) If the court finds that the application and supporting affidavit do not satisfy the requirements of Section 485.010, it shall so state and deny the order. If denial is solely on the ground that Section 485.010 is not satisfied, the court shall so state and such denial does not preclude the plaintiff from applying for a right to attach order and writ of attachment under Chapter 4 (commencing with Section 484.010) with the same affidavits and supporting papers. *(Added by Stats.1974, c. 1516, § 9. Amended by Stats.1976, c. 437, § 15.)*

§ 485.240 Application to Set Aside Order or Reduce Amount Secured; Notice of Motion; Hearing and Determination

(a) Any defendant whose property has been attached pursuant to a writ issued under this chapter may apply for an order (1) that the right to attach order be set aside, the writ of attachment quashed, and any property levied upon pursuant to the writ be released, or (2) that the amount to be secured by the attachment be reduced as provided in Section 483.015. Such application shall be made by filing with the court and serving on the plaintiff a notice of motion.

(b) The notice of motion shall state the grounds on which the motion is based and shall be accompanied by an affidavit supporting any factual issues raised and points and authorities supporting any legal issues raised. It shall not be grounds to set aside an order that the plaintiff would not have suffered great or irreparable injury (within the meaning of Section 485.010) if issuance of the order had been delayed until the matter could have been heard on notice.

(c) At the hearing on the motion, the court shall determine whether the plaintiff is entitled to the right to attach order or whether the amount to be secured by the attachment should be reduced. If the court finds that the plaintiff is not entitled to the right to attach order, it shall order the right to attach order set aside, the writ of attachment quashed, and any property levied on pursuant to the writ released. If the court finds that the plaintiff is entitled to the right to attach order, thereafter the plaintiff may apply for additional writs pursuant to Article 2 (commencing with Section 484.310) or Article 3 (commencing with Section 484.510) of Chapter 4.

(d) The court's determinations shall be made upon the basis of the pleadings and other papers in the record; but, upon good cause shown, the court may receive and consider at the hearing additional evidence, oral or documentary, and additional points and authorities, or it may continue the hearing for the production of such additional evidence or points and authorities.

(e) The hearing provided for in this section shall take precedence over all other civil matters on the calendar of that day except older matters of the same character. *(Added by Stats.1974, c. 1516, § 9. Amended by Stats.1983, c. 155, § 4.)*

Chapter 7.   Property Subject to Attachment

§ 487.010   Subject Property

The following property of the defendant is subject to attachment:

(a) Where the defendant is a corporation, all corporate property for which a method of levy is provided by Article 2 (commencing with Section 488.300) of Chapter 8.

(b) Where the defendant is a partnership or other unincorporated association, all partnership or association property for which a method of levy is provided by Article 2 (commencing with Section 488.300) of Chapter 8.

(c) Where the defendant is a natural person, all of the following property:

(1) Interests in real property except leasehold estates with unexpired terms of less than one year.

(2) Accounts receivable, chattel paper, and general intangibles arising out of the conduct by the defendant of a trade, business, or profession, except any such individual claim with a principal balance of less than one hundred fifty dollars ($150).

(3) Equipment.

(4) Farm products.

(5) Inventory.

(6) Final money judgments arising out of the conduct by the defendant of a trade, business, or profession.

(7) Money on the premises where a trade, business, or profession is conducted by the defendant and, except for the first one thousand dollars ($1,000), money located elsewhere than on such premises and deposit accounts, but, if the defendant has more than one deposit account or has at least one deposit account and money located elsewhere than on the premises where a trade, business, or profession is conducted by the defendant, the court, upon application of the plaintiff, may order that the writ of attachment be levied so that an aggregate amount of one thousand dollars ($1,000) in the form of such money and in such accounts remains free of levy.

(8) Negotiable documents of title.

(9) Instruments.

(10) Securities.

(11) Minerals or the like (including oil and gas) to be extracted.

(d) In the case of a defendant described in subdivision (c), community property of a type described in subdivision (c) is subject to attachment if the community property would be subject to enforcement of the judgment obtained in the action in which the attachment is sought. Unless the provision or context otherwise requires, if community property that is subject to attachment is sought to be attached:

(1) Any provision of this title that applies to the property of the defendant or to obligations owed to the defendant also applies to the community property interest of the spouse of the defendant and to obligations owed to either spouse that are community property.

(2) Any provision of this title that applies to property in the possession or under the control of the defendant also applies to community property in the possession or under the control of the spouse of the defendant. *(Added by Stats.1974, c. 1516, § 9. Amended by Stats.1976, c. 437, § 24; Stats.1982, c. 1198, § 46.)*

§ 487.020   Exempt Property

Except as provided in paragraph (2) of subdivision (a) of Section 3439.07 of the Civil Code, the following property is exempt from attachment:

(a) All property exempt from enforcement of a money judgment.

(b) Property which is necessary for the support of a defendant who is a natural person or the family of such defendant supported in whole or in part by the defendant.

(c) "Earnings" as defined by Section 706.011.

(d) All property not subject to attachment pursuant to Section 487.010. *(Added by Stats.1974, c. 1516, § 9. Amended by Stats.1976, c. 437, § 25; Stats.1982, c. 1198, § 47; Stats.1986, c. 383, § 7.)*

Chapter 9.   Undertakings

§ 489.210   Undertaking Prerequisite to Attachment or Order

Before issuance of a writ of attachment, a temporary protective order, or an order under subdivision (b) of Section 491.415, the plaintiff shall file an undertaking to pay the defendant any amount the defendant may recover for any wrongful attachment by the plaintiff in the action. *(Added by Stats.1974, c. 1516, § 9. Amended by Stats.1976, c. 437, § 37.5; Stats.1984, c. 538, § 7.)*

§ 489.220   Amount of Undertaking

(a) Except as provided in subdivision (b), the amount of an undertaking filed pursuant to this article shall be two thousand five hundred dollars ($2,500) in an action in the municipal or justice court, and seven thousand five hundred dollars ($7,500) in an action in the superior court.

(b) If, upon objection to the undertaking, the court determines that the probable recovery for wrongful attachment exceeds the amount of the undertaking, it shall order the amount of the undertaking increased to the amount it determines to be the probable recovery for wrongful attachment if it is ultimately determined that the attachment was wrongful. *(Added by Stats.1974, c. 1516, § 9. Amended by Stats.1976, c. 437, § 38; Stats.1977, c. 1257, § 14.)*

Chapter 12.   Nonresident Attachment

§ 492.010   Persons and Entities Subject to Attachment

Notwithstanding subdivision (a) of Section 483.010, an attachment may be issued in any action for the recovery of money brought against any of the following:

(a) A natural person who does not reside in this state.

(b) A foreign corporation not qualified to do business in this state under the provisions of Chapter 21 (commencing with Section 2100) of Division 1 of Title 1 of the Corporations Code.

(c) A foreign partnership which has not filed a designation pursuant to Section 15700 of the Corporations Code. *(Added by Stats.1974, c. 1516, § 9. Amended by Stats.1975, c. 682, § 5; Stats.1982, c. 1198, § 58.)*

TITLE 7.   OTHER PROVISIONAL REMEDIES IN CIVIL ACTIONS
Chapter 1.   General Provisions

§ 501.   Imprisonment for Debt or Tort Prohibited

A person may not be imprisoned in a civil action for debt or tort, whether before or after judgment. Nothing in this section affects any power a court may have to imprison a person who violates a court order. *(Added by Stats.1974, c. 1516, § 11.)*

Chapter 3.   Injunction

§ 525.   Definition; Grant; Enforcement

An injunction is a writ or order requiring a person to refrain from a particular act. It may be granted by the court in which the action is brought, or by a judge thereof; and when granted by a judge, it may be enforced as an order of the court. *(Enacted 1872. Amended by Code Am.1880, c. 15, § 3; Stats.1907, c. 272, § 1.)*

§ 526.   Cases in Which Authorized; Restrictions on Grant

(a) An injunction may be granted in the following cases:

(1) When it appears by the complaint that the plaintiff is entitled to the relief demanded, and the relief, or any part thereof, consists in restraining the commission or continuance of the act complained of, either for a limited period or perpetually.

(2) When it appears by the complaint or affidavits that the commission or continuance of some act during the litigation would produce waste, or great or irreparable injury, to a party to the action.

(3) When it appears, during the litigation, that a party to the action is doing, or threatens, or is about to do, or is procuring or suffering to be done, some act in violation of the rights of another party to the action respecting the subject of the action, and tending to render the judgment ineffectual.

(4) When pecuniary compensation would not afford adequate relief.

(5) Where it would be extremely difficult to ascertain the amount of compensation which would afford adequate relief.

(6) Where the restraint is necessary to prevent a multiplicity of judicial proceedings.

(7) Where the obligation arises from a trust.

(b) An injunction cannot be granted in the following cases:

(1) To stay a judicial proceeding pending at the commencement of the action in which the injunction is demanded, unless such restraint is necessary to prevent a multiplicity of proceedings.

(2) To stay proceedings in a court of the United States.

(3) To stay proceedings in another state upon a judgment of a court of that state.

(4) To prevent the execution of a public statute by officers of the law for the public benefit.

(5) To prevent the breach of a contract the performance of which would not be specifically enforced, other than a contract in writing for the rendition of personal services from one to another where the promised service is of a special, unique, unusual, extraordinary, or intellectual character, which gives it peculiar value, the loss of which cannot be reasonably or adequately compensated in damages in an action at law, and where the compensation for the personal services is as follows:

(A) As to contracts entered into on or before December 31, 1993, the minimum compensation provided in the contract for the personal services shall be at the rate of six thousand dollars ($6,000) per annum.

(B) As to contracts entered into on or after January 1, 1994, the criteria of clause (i) or (ii), as follows, are satisfied:

(i) The compensation is as follows:

(I) The minimum compensation provided in the contract shall be at the rate of nine thousand dollars ($9,000) per annum for the first year of the contract, twelve thousand dollars ($12,000) per annum for the second year of the contract, and fifteen thousand dollars ($15,000) per annum for the third to seventh years, inclusive, of the contract.

(II) In addition, after the third year of the contract, there shall actually have been paid for the services through and including the contract year during which the injunctive relief is sought, over and above the minimum contractual compensation specified in subclause (I), the amount of fifteen thousand dollars ($15,000) per annum during the fourth and fifth years of the contract, and thirty thousand dollars ($30,000) per annum during the sixth and seventh years of the contract. As a condition to petitioning for an injunction, amounts payable under this clause may be paid at any time prior to seeking injunctive relief.

(ii) The aggregate compensation actually received for the services provided under a contract that does not meet the criteria of subparagraph (A), is at least 10 times the applicable aggregate minimum amount specified in subclauses (I) and (II) of clause (i) through and including the contract year during which the injunctive relief is sought. As a condition to petitioning for an injunction, amounts payable under this subparagraph may be paid at any time prior to seeking injunctive relief.

(C) Compensation paid in any contract year in excess of the minimums specified in clauses (i) and (ii) of subparagraph (B) shall apply to reduce the compensation otherwise required to be paid under those provisions in any subsequent contract years. However, an injunction may be granted to prevent the breach of a contract entered into between any nonprofit cooperative corporation or association and a member or stockholder thereof, in respect to any provision regarding the sale or delivery to the corporation or association of the products produced or acquired by the member or stockholder.

(6) To prevent the exercise of a public or private office, in a lawful manner, by the person in possession.

(7) To prevent a legislative act by a municipal corporation. *(Enacted 1872. Amended by Stats.1907, c. 272, § 2; Stats.1919, c. 224, § 1; Stats.1925, c. 408, § 1; Stats.1992, c. 177, § 2; Stats.1993, c. 836, § 2.)*

§ 527. Grants Before Judgment Upon Verified Complaint or Affidavits; Service; Notice; Certification; Order to Show Cause; Readiness for Hearing; Continuance; Counter-Affidavits; Precedence of Hearing and Trial; Reissuance of Ex Parte Domestic Relations Protective Order

(a) An injunction may be granted at any time before judgment upon a verified complaint, or upon affidavits if the complaint in the one case, or the affidavits in the other, show satisfactorily that sufficient grounds exist therefor. A copy of the complaint or of the affidavits, upon which the injunction was granted, must, if not previously served, be served therewith.

A temporary restraining order or a preliminary injunction, or both, may be granted in a class action, in which one or more of the parties sues or defends for the benefit of numerous parties upon the same grounds as in other actions, whether or not the class has been certified.

No preliminary injunction shall be granted without notice to the opposite party; nor shall any temporary restraining order be granted without notice to the opposite party, unless (1) it shall appear from facts shown by affidavit or by the verified complaint that great or irreparable injury would result to the applicant before the matter can be heard on notice and (2) the applicant or the applicant's attorney certifies to the court under oath (A) that within a reasonable time prior to the application he or she informed the opposing party or his or her attorney at what time and where the application would be made; (B) that he or she in good faith attempted to inform the opposing party and his or her attorney but was unable to so inform the opposing party or his or her attorney, specifying the efforts made to contact them; or (C) that for reasons specified he or she should not be required to so inform the opposing party or his or her attorney. In case a temporary restraining order shall be granted without notice, in the contingency above specified, the matter shall be made returnable on an order requiring cause to be shown why the injunction should not be granted, on the earliest day that the business of the court will admit of, but not later than 15 days or, if good cause appears to the court, 20 days from the date of the order. When the matter first comes up for hearing the party who obtained the temporary restraining order must be ready to proceed and must have served upon the opposite party at least two days prior to the hearing, a copy of the complaint and of all affidavits to be used in the application and a copy of the points and authorities in support of the application; if the party is not ready, or if he or she fails to serve a copy of his or her complaint, affidavits and points and authorities, as herein required, the court shall dissolve the temporary restraining order. The defendant, however, shall be entitled, as of course, to one continuance for a reasonable period, if he or she desires it, to enable him or her to meet the application for the preliminary injunction. The defendant may, in response to an order to show cause, present affidavits relating to the granting of the preliminary injunction, and if the affidavits are served on the applicant at least two days prior to the hearing, the applicant shall not be entitled to any continuance on account thereof. On the day upon which the order is made returnable, the hearing shall take precedence of all other matters on the calendar of the day, except older matters of the same character, and matters to which special precedence may be given by law. When the cause is at issue it shall be set for trial at the earliest possible date and shall take precedence of all other cases, except older matters of the same character, and matters to which special precedence may be given by law.

(b) This section does not apply to an order described in Section 240 of the Family Code.

(c) There shall be no filing fee for a petition or response relating to a protective order, restraining order, or a permanent injunction restraining violence or threats of violence in any action brought pursuant to this chapter *(Enacted 1872. Amended by Stats.1895, c. 49, § 1; Stats.1907, c. 272, § 3; Stats.1911, c. 42, § 1; Stats.1963, c. 878, § 2; Stats.1970, c. 488, § 1; Stats.1977, c. 720, § 1; Stats.1978, c. 346, § 1; Stats.1979, c.*

129, § 1; Stats.1979, c. 795, § 7; Stats.1981, c. 182, § 1; Stats.1982, c. 812, § 1; Stats.1992, c. 163, § 23; Stats.1993, c. 583, § 1.)

§ 529. Undertaking; Objection; Insufficiency; Dissolution of Injunction; Exceptions

(a) On granting an injunction, the court or judge must require an undertaking on the part of the applicant to the effect that the applicant will pay to the party enjoined any damages, not exceeding an amount to be specified, the party may sustain by reason of the injunction, if the court finally decides that the applicant was not entitled to the injunction. Within five days after the service of the injunction, the person enjoined may object to the undertaking. If the court determines that the applicant's undertaking is insufficient and a sufficient undertaking is not filed within the time required by statute, the order granting the injunction must be dissolved.

(b) This section does not apply to any of the following persons:

(1) Either spouse against the other in a proceeding for legal separation or dissolution of marriage.

(2) The applicant for an order described in Division 10 (commencing with Section 6200 of the Family Code).

(3) A public entity or officer described in Section 995.220. (Enacted 1872. Amended by Code Am.1873–74, c. 624, § 1; Code Am.1880, c. 64, § 1; Stats.1907, c. 272, § 4; Stats.1931, c. 140, § 1; Stats.1933, c. 744, § 66; Stats.1979, c. 795, § 9; Stats.1982, c. 517, § 123; Stats.1992, c. 163, § 25; Stats.1993, c. 219, § 63.7.)

Chapter 5. Receivers

§ 564. Appointment; Cases in Which Authorized; Definitions

(a) A receiver may be appointed, in the manner provided in this chapter, by the court in which an action or proceeding is pending in any case in which the court is empowered by law to appoint a receiver.

(b) In superior court a receiver may be appointed by the court in which an action or proceeding is pending, or by a judge thereof, in the following cases:

(1) In an action by a vendor to vacate a fraudulent purchase of property, or by a creditor to subject any property or fund to the creditor's claim, or between partners or others jointly owning or interested in any property or fund, on the application of the plaintiff, or of any party whose right to or interest in the property or fund, or the proceeds thereof, is probable, and where it is shown that the property or fund is in danger of being lost, removed, or materially injured.

(2) In an action by a secured lender for the foreclosure of the deed of trust or mortgage and sale of the property upon which there is a lien under a deed of trust or mortgage, where it appears that the property is in danger of being lost, removed, or materially injured, or that the

condition of the deed of trust or mortgage has not been performed, and that the property is probably insufficient to discharge the deed of trust or mortgage debt.

(3) After judgment, to carry the judgment into effect.

(4) After judgment, to dispose of the property according to the judgment, or to preserve it during the pendency of an appeal, or pursuant to Title 9 (commencing with Section 680.010) (enforcement of judgments), or after sale of real property pursuant to a decree of foreclosure, during the redemption period, to collect, expend, and disburse rents as directed by the court or otherwise provided by law.

(5) In the cases when a corporation has been dissolved, or is insolvent, or in imminent danger of insolvency, or has forfeited its corporate rights.

(6) In an action of unlawful detainer.

(7) At the request of the Public Utilities Commission pursuant to Section 855 of the Public Utilities Code.

(8) In all other cases where receivers have heretofore been appointed by the usages of courts of equity.

(c) A receiver may be appointed, in the manner provided in this chapter, including, but not limited to, Section 566, by the superior court in an action brought by a secured lender to enforce the rights provided in Section 2929.5 of the Civil Code, to enable the secured lender to enter and inspect the real property security for the purpose of determining the existence, location, nature, and magnitude of any past or present release or threatened release of any hazardous substance into, onto, beneath, or from the real property security. The secured lender shall not abuse the right of entry and inspection or use it to harass the borrower or tenant of the property. Except in case of an emergency, when the borrower or tenant of the property has abandoned the premises, or if it is impracticable to do so, the secured lender shall give the borrower or tenant of the property reasonable notice of the secured lender's intent to enter and shall enter only during the borrower's or tenant's normal business hours. Twenty-four hours' notice shall be presumed to be reasonable notice in the absence of evidence to the contrary.

(d) Any action by a secured lender to appoint a receiver pursuant to this section shall not constitute an action within the meaning of subdivision (a) of Section 726.

(e) For purposes of this section:

(1) "Borrower" means the trustor under a deed of trust, or a mortgagor under a mortgage, where the deed of trust or mortgage encumbers real property security and secures the performance of the trustor or mortgagor under a loan, extension of credit, guaranty, or other obligation. The term includes any successor-in-interest of the trustor or mortgagor to the real property security before the deed of trust or mortgage has been discharged, reconveyed, or foreclosed upon.

(2) "Hazardous substance" means (A) any "hazardous substance" as defined in subdivision (f) of Section 25281 of the Health and Safety Code as effective on January 1, 1991, or as subsequently amended, (B) any "waste" as defined in subdivision (d) of Section 13050 of the Water Code as effective on January 1, 1991, or as subsequently amended, or (C) petroleum, including crude oil or any fraction thereof, natural gas, natural gas liquids, liquefied natural gas, or synthetic gas usable for fuel, or any mixture thereof.

(3) "Real property security" means any real property and improvements, other than a separate interest and any related interest in the common area of a residential common interest development, as the terms "separate interest," "common area," and "common interest development" are defined in Section 1351 of the Civil Code, or real property consisting of one acre or less which contains 1 to 15 dwelling units.

(4) "Release" means any spilling, leaking, pumping, pouring, emitting, emptying, discharging, injecting, escaping, leaching, dumping, or disposing into the environment, including continuing migration, of hazardous substances into, onto, or through soil, surface water, or groundwater.

(5) "Secured lender" means the beneficiary under a deed of trust against the real property security, or the mortgagee under a mortgage against the real property security, and any successor-in-interest of the beneficiary or mortgagee to the deed of trust or mortgage. *(Enacted 1872. Amended by Stats.1919, c. 166, § 1; Stats.1933, c. 744, § 85a; Stats.1941, c. 444, § 1; Stats.1980, c. 1078, § 1; Stats.1982, c. 497, § 34; Stats.1991, c. 1167, § 2; Stats.1992, c. 167, § 2.)*

TITLE 7A.   PRETRIAL CONFERENCES

§ 575.   Promulgation of Rules by Judicial Council

The Judicial Council may promulgate rules governing pretrial conferences, and the time, manner and nature thereof, in civil cases at issue, or in one or more classes thereof, in the superior, municipal, and justice courts. *(Added by Stats.1955, c. 632, § 1.   Amended by Stats.1977, c. 1257, § 17.)*

§ 575.1   Local Rules; Scope; Purpose; Promulgation

(a) The presiding judge of each superior, municipal, and justice court may prepare with the assistance of appropriate committees of the court, proposed local rules designed to expedite and facilitate the business of the court.   The rules need not be limited to those actions on the civil active list, but may provide for the supervision and judicial management of actions from the date they are filed.   Rules prepared pursuant to this section shall be submitted for consideration to the judges of the court and, upon approval by a majority of the judges, the judges shall have the proposed rules published and submitted to the local bar for consideration and recommendations.

(b) After a majority of the judges have officially adopted the rules, 61 copies or a greater number as specified by Judicial Council rule, shall be filed with the Judicial Council as required by Section 68071 of the Government Code. The Judicial Council shall deposit a copy of each rule and amendment with each county law library or county clerk where it shall be made available for public examination. The local rules shall also be published for general distribution in accordance with rules adopted by the Judicial Council. Each court shall make its local rules available for inspection and copying in every location of the court that generally accepts filing of papers. The court may impose a reasonable charge for copying the rules and may impose a reasonable page limit on copying. The rules shall be accompanied by a notice indicating where a full set of the rules may be purchased.

(c) If a judge of a court adopts a rule which applies solely to cases in that judge's courtroom, or a particular branch or district of a court adopts a rule that applies solely to cases in that particular branch or district of a court, the court shall publish these rules as part of the general publication of rules required by the California Rules of Court. The court shall organize the rules so that rules on a common subject, whether individual, branch, district, or courtwide appear sequentially. Individual judges' rules and branch and district rules are local rules of court for purposes of this section and for purposes of the adoption, publication, comment, and filing requirements set forth in the Judicial Council rules applicable to local court rules. *(Added by Stats.1982, c. 1402, § 1. Amended by Stats.1989, c. 1416, § 19; Stats.1993, c. 925, § 1; Stats.1993, c. 926, § 3.5.)*

§ 575.2 Noncompliance With Local Rules; Effects

(a) Local rules promulgated pursuant to Section 575.1 may provide that if any counsel, a party represented by counsel, or a party if in pro se, fails to comply with any of the requirements thereof, the court on motion of a party or on its own motion may strike out all or any part of any pleading of that party, or, dismiss the action or proceeding or any part thereof, or enter a judgment by default against that party, or impose other penalties of a lesser nature as otherwise provided by law, and may order that party or his or her counsel to pay to the moving party the reasonable expenses in making the motion, including reasonable attorney fees.

(b) It is the intent of the Legislature that if a failure to comply with these rules is the responsibility of counsel and not of the party, any penalty shall be imposed on counsel and shall not adversely affect the party's cause of action or defense thereto. *(Added by Stats.1982, c. 1402, § 2.)*

TITLE 8. OF THE TRIAL AND JUDGMENT
IN CIVIL ACTIONS
Chapter 1. Judgment in General

§ 580. Relief Granted; Scope

The relief granted to the plaintiff, if there is no answer, cannot exceed that which he or she shall have demanded in his or her complaint or in the statement required by Section 425.11; but in any other case, the court may grant the plaintiff any relief consistent with the case made by the complaint and embraced within the issue. *(Enacted 1872. Amended by Stats.1993, c. 456, § 8.)*

§ 581. Dismissal; Definitions

(a) As used in this section:

(1) "Action" means any civil action or special proceeding.

(2) "Complaint" means a complaint and a cross-complaint.

(3) "Court" means the court in which the action is pending.

(4) "Defendant" includes a cross-defendant.

(5) "Plaintiff" includes a cross-complainant.

(6) "Trial." A trial shall be deemed to actually commence at the beginning of the opening statement or argument of any party or his or her counsel, or if there is no opening statement, then at the time of the administering of the oath or affirmation to the first witness, or the introduction of any evidence.

(b) An action may be dismissed in any of the following instances:

(1) With or without prejudice, upon written request of the plaintiff to the clerk, filed with papers in the case, or by oral or written request to the court at any time before the actual commencement of trial, upon payment of the costs, if any.

(2) With or without prejudice, by any party upon the written consent of all other parties.

(3) By the court, without prejudice, when no party appears for trial following 30 days' notice of time and place of trial.

(4) By the court, without prejudice, when dismissal is made pursuant to the applicable provisions of Chapter 1.5 (commencing with Section 583.110).

(5) By the court, without prejudice, when either party fails to appear on the trial and the other party appears and asks for dismissal.

(c) A plaintiff may dismiss his or her complaint, or any cause of action asserted in it, in its entirety, or as to any defendant or defendants, with or without prejudice prior to the actual commencement of trial.

(d) Except as otherwise provided in subdivision (e), the court shall dismiss the complaint, or any cause of action asserted in it, in its entirety or as to any defendant, with prejudice, when upon the trial and before the final submission of the case, the plaintiff abandons it.

(e) After the actual commencement of trial, the court shall dismiss the complaint, or any causes of action asserted in it, in its entirety or as to any defendants, with prejudice, if the plaintiff requests a dismissal, unless all affected parties to the trial consent to dismissal without prejudice or by order of the court dismissing the same without prejudice on a showing of good cause.

(f) The court may dismiss the complaint as to that defendant when:

(1) Except where Section 597 applies, after a demurrer to the complaint is sustained without leave to amend and either party moves for dismissal.

(2) Except where Section 597 applies, after a demurrer to the complaint is sustained with leave to amend, the plaintiff fails to amend it within the time allowed by the court and either party moves for dismissal.

(3) After a motion to strike the whole of a complaint is granted without leave to amend and either party moves for dismissal.

(4) After a motion to strike the whole of a complaint or portion thereof is granted with leave to amend the plaintiff fails to amend it within the time allowed by the court and either party moves for dismissal.

(g) The court may dismiss without prejudice the complaint in whole, or as to that defendant, when dismissal is made under the applicable provisions of Chapter 1.5 (commencing with Section 583.110).

(h) The court may dismiss without prejudice the complaint in whole, or as to that defendant, when dismissal is made pursuant to Section 418.10.

(i) No dismissal of an action may be made or entered, or both, under paragraph (1) of subdivision (b) where affirmative relief has been sought by the cross-complaint of a defendant or if there is a motion pending for an order transferring the action to another court under the provisions of Section 396b.

(j) No dismissal may be made or entered, or both, under paragraph (1) or (2) of subdivision (b) except upon the written consent of the attorney for the party or parties applying therefor, or if consent of the attorney is not obtained, upon order of dismissal by the court after notice to the attorney.

(k) No action may be dismissed which has been determined to be a class action under the provisions of this code unless and until notice that the court deems adequate has been given and the court orders the dismissal.

(l) The court may dismiss, without prejudice, the complaint in whole, or as to that defendant when either party fails to appear at the trial and the other party appears and asks for the dismissal.

(m) The provisions of this section shall not be deemed to be an exclusive enumeration of the court's power to dismiss an action or dismiss a complaint as to a defendant. *(Added by Stats.1986, c. 540, § 8. Amended by Stats.1987, c. 1080, § 3; Stats.1993, c. 456, § 9.)*

§ 581c. Nonsuit; Partial Grant of Motion; Effect

(a) After the plaintiff has completed his or her opening statement, or the presentation of his or her evidence in a trial by jury, the defendant, without waiving his right to offer evidence in the event the motion is not granted, may move for a judgment of nonsuit.

(b) If it appears that the evidence presented, or to be presented, supports the granting of the motion as to some but not all of the issues involved in the action, the court shall grant the motion as to those issues and the action shall proceed as to the issues remaining. Despite the granting of the motion, no final judgment shall be entered prior to the termination of the action, but the final judgment in the action shall, in addition to any matters determined in the trial, award judgment as determined by the motion herein provided for.

(c) If the motion is granted, unless the court in its order for judgment otherwise specifies, the judgment of nonsuit operates as an adjudication upon the merits.

(d) In actions which arise out of an injury to the person or to property, when a motion for judgment of nonsuit was granted on the basis that the defendant was without fault, no other defendant during trial, over plaintiff's objection, may attempt to attribute fault to or comment on the absence or involvement of the defendant who was granted the motion. *(Added by Stats.1947, c. 990, § 2. Amended by Stats.1961, c. 692, § 1; Stats.1980, c. 187, § 1; Stats.1982, c. 1510, § 2.)*

Chapter 1.5   Dismissal for Delay in Prosecution

§ 583.130 Plaintiff to Proceed With Reasonable Diligence; Stipulations and Disposition of Action on Merits Favored

It is the policy of the state that a plaintiff shall proceed with reasonable diligence in the prosecution of an action but that all parties shall cooperate in bringing the action to trial or other disposition. Except as otherwise provided by statute or by rule of court adopted pursuant to statute, the policy favoring the right of parties to make stipulations in their own interests and the policy favoring trial or other disposition of an action on the merits are generally to be preferred over the policy that requires dismissal for failure to proceed with reasonable diligence in the prosecution of an action in construing the provisions of this chapter. *(Added by Stats.1984, c. 1705, § 5.)*

§ 583.210 Time for Service and Return

(a) The summons and complaint shall be served upon a defendant within three years after the action is commenced against the defendant. For the purpose of this subdivision an action is commenced at the time the complaint is filed.

(b) Return of summons or other proof of service shall be made within 60 days after the time the summons and complaint must be served upon a defendant. *(Added by Stats.1984, c. 1705, § 5.)*

§ 583.240 Computation of Time

In computing the time within which service must be made pursuant to this article, there shall be excluded the time during which any of the following conditions existed:

(a) The defendant was not amenable to the process of the court.

(b) The prosecution of the action or proceedings in the action was stayed and the stay affected service.

(c) The validity of service was the subject of litigation by the parties.

(d) Service, for any other reason, was impossible, impracticable, or futile due to causes beyond the plaintiff's control. Failure to discover relevant facts or evidence is not a cause beyond the plaintiff's control for the purpose of this subdivision. *(Added by Stats.1984, c. 1705, § 5.)*

§ 583.250 Failure to Make Timely Service; Mandatory Nature of Article

(a) If service is not made in an action within the time prescribed in this article:

(1) The action shall not be further prosecuted and no further proceedings shall be held in the action.

(2) The action shall be dismissed by the court on its own motion or on motion of any person interested in the action, whether named as a party or not, after notice to the parties.

(b) The requirements of this article are mandatory and are not subject to extension, excuse, or exception except as expressly provided by statute. *(Added by Stats.1984, c. 1705, § 5.)*

§ 583.310 Time to Bring Action to Trial

An action shall be brought to trial within five years after the action is commenced against the defendant. *(Added by Stats.1984, c. 1705, § 5.)*

§ 583.330 Extension of Time

The parties may extend the time within which an action must be brought to trial pursuant to this article by the following means:

(a) By written stipulation. The stipulation need not be filed but, if it is not filed, the stipulation shall be brought to the attention of the court if relevant to a motion for dismissal.

(b) By oral agreement made in open court, if entered in the minutes of the court or a transcript is made. *(Added by Stats.1984, c. 1705, § 5.)*

§ 583.340 Computation of Time

In computing the time within which an action must be brought to trial pursuant to this article, there shall be excluded the time during which any of the following conditions existed:

(a) The jurisdiction of the court to try the action was suspended.

(b) Prosecution or trial of the action was stayed or enjoined.

(c) Bringing the action to trial, for any other reason, was impossible, impracticable, or futile. *(Added by Stats.1984, c. 1705, § 5.)*

§ 583.350   Tolling or Extension of Time Resulting in Less Than Six Months to Bring Action

If the time within which an action must be brought to trial pursuant to this article is tolled or otherwise extended pursuant to statute with the result that at the end of the period of tolling or extension less than six months remains within which the action must be brought to trial, the action shall not be dismissed pursuant to this article if the action is brought to trial within six months after the end of the period of tolling or extension. *(Added by Stats.1984, c. 1705, § 5.)*

§ 583.360   Dismissal on Motion of Court or Defendant; Mandatory Nature of Article

(a) An action shall be dismissed by the court on its own motion or on motion of the defendant, after notice to the parties, if the action is not brought to trial within the time prescribed in this article.

(b) The requirements of this article are mandatory and are not subject to extension, excuse, or exception except as expressly provided by statute. *(Added by Stats.1984, c. 1705, § 5.)*

§ 583.410   Discretion to Dismiss Under Appropriate Circumstances; Procedure

(a) The court may in its discretion dismiss an action for delay in prosecution pursuant to this article on its own motion or on motion of the defendant if to do so appears to the court appropriate under the circumstances of the case.

(b) Dismissal shall be pursuant to the procedure and in accordance with the criteria prescribed by rules adopted by the Judicial Council. *(Added by Stats.1984, c. 1705, § 5.)*

§ 583.420   Grounds for Dismissal; Computation of Time

(a) The court may not dismiss an action pursuant to this article for delay in prosecution except after one of the following conditions has occurred:

(1) Service is not made within two years after the action is commenced against the defendant.

(2) The action is not brought to trial within the following times:

(A) Three years after the action is commenced against the defendant unless otherwise prescribed by rule under subparagraph (B).

(B) Two years after the action is commenced against the defendant if the Judicial Council by rule adopted pursuant to Section 583.410 so prescribed for the court because of the condition of the court calendar or for other reasons affecting the conduct of litigation or the administration of justice.

(3) A new trial is granted and the action is not again brought to trial within the following times:

(A) If a trial is commenced but no judgment is entered because of a mistrial or because a jury is unable to reach a decision, within two years after the order of the court declaring the mistrial or the disagreement of the jury is entered.

(B) If after judgment a new trial is granted and no appeal is taken, within two years after the order granting the new trial is entered.

(C) If on appeal an order granting a new trial is affirmed or a judgment is reversed and the action remanded for a new trial, within two years after the remittitur is filed by the clerk of the trial court.

(b) The times provided in subdivision (a) shall be computed in the manner provided for computation of the comparable times under Articles 2 (commencing with Section 583.210) and 3 (commencing with Section 583.310). *(Added by Stats.1984, c. 1705, § 5.)*

Chapter 2.   Judgment Upon Failure to Answer

§ 585. Judgment on Default

Judgment may be had, if the defendant fails to answer the complaint, as follows:

(a) Contract action; personal service. In an action arising upon contract or judgment for the recovery of money or damages only, if the defendant has, or if more than one defendant, if any of the defendants have, been served, other than by publication, and no answer, demurrer, notice of motion to strike (of the character hereinafter specified), notice of motion to transfer pursuant to Section 396b, notice of motion to dismiss pursuant to Article 2 (commencing with Section 583.210) of Chapter 1.5 of Title 8; notice of motion to quash service of summons or to stay or dismiss the action pursuant to Section 418.10, or notice of the filing of a petition for writ of mandate as provided in Section 418.10 has been filed with the clerk or judge of the court within the time specified in the summons, or such further time as may be allowed, the clerk, or the judge if there is no clerk, upon written application of the plaintiff, and proof of the service of summons, shall enter the default of the defendant or defendants, so served, and immediately thereafter enter judgment for the principal amount demanded in the complaint or the statement required by Section 425.11, or a lesser amount if credit has been acknowledged, together with interest allowed by law or in accordance with the terms of the contract, and the costs against the defendant, or defendants, or against one or more of the defendants. If, by rule of court, a schedule of attorneys' fees to be allowed has been adopted, the clerk may include in the judgment attorneys' fees in accordance with such schedule (1) if the contract provides that attorneys' fees shall be allowed in the event of an action thereon, or (2) if the action is one in which the plaintiff is entitled by statute to recover attorneys' fees in addition to money or damages. The plaintiff shall file a written request at the time of application for entry of the default of the defendant or defendants, to have attorneys' fees fixed by the court, whereupon, after the entry of the default, the court shall hear the application for determination of the attorneys' fees and shall render judgment for such fees and for the other relief demanded in the complaint or the statement required by Section 425.11, or a lesser amount if credit has been acknowledged, and the costs against the defendant, or defendants, or against one or more of the defendants.

(b) **Other actions; personal service; hearing.** In other actions, if the defendant has been served, other than by publication, and no answer, demurrer, notice of motion to strike (of the character hereinafter specified), notice of motion to transfer pursuant to Section 396b, notice of motion to dismiss pursuant to Article 2 (commencing with Section 583.210) of Chapter 1.5 of Title 8, notice of motion to quash service of summons or to stay or dismiss the action pursuant to Section 418.10 or notice of the filing of a petition for writ of mandate as provided in Section 418.10 has been filed with the clerk or judge of the court within the time specified in the summons, or such further time as may be allowed, the clerk, or the judge if there is no clerk, upon written application of the plaintiff, shall enter the default of the defendant. The plaintiff thereafter may apply to the court for the relief demanded in the complaint; the court shall hear the evidence offered by the plaintiff, and shall render judgment in his or her favor for such sum (not exceeding the amount stated in the complaint or in the statement required by Section 425.11), as appears by such evidence to be just. If the taking of an account, or the proof of any fact, is necessary to enable the court to give judgment or to carry the judgment into effect, the court may take the account or hear the proof, or may, in its discretion, order a reference for that purpose. If the action is for the recovery of damages, in whole or in part, the court may order the damages to be assessed by a jury; or if, to determine the amount of damages, the examination of a long account is involved by a reference as above provided.

(c) **Published summons.** In all actions where the service of the summons was by publication, upon the expiration of the time for answering, and upon proof of the publication and that no answer, demurrer, notice of motion to strike (of the character hereinafter specified), notice of motion to transfer pursuant to Section 396b, notice of motion to dismiss pursuant to Article 2 (commencing with Section 583.210) of Chapter 1.5 of Title 8, notice of motion to quash service of summons or to stay or dismiss the action pursuant to Section 418.10, or notice of the filing of a petition for writ of mandate as provided in

Section 418.10 has been filed, the clerk, or the judge if there is no clerk, upon written application of the plaintiff, shall enter the default of the defendant. The plaintiff thereafter may apply to the court for the relief demanded in the complaint; and the court shall hear the evidence offered by the plaintiff, and shall render judgment in his or her favor for such sum (not exceeding the amount stated in the complaint or in the statement required by Section 425.11), as appears by such evidence to be just. If the defendant is not a resident of the state, shall require the plaintiff, or his or her agent, to be examined, on oath, respecting any payments that have been made to the plaintiff, or to anyone for his or her use, on account of any demand mentioned in the complaint or the statement required by Section 425.11, and may render judgment for the amount which he or she is entitled to recover. In all cases affecting the title to or possession of real property, where the service of the summons was by publication and the defendant has failed to answer, no judgment shall be rendered upon proof of mere occupancy, unless such occupancy shall have continued for the time and shall have been of the character necessary to confer title by prescription. In all cases where the plaintiff bases his or her claim upon a paper title, the court shall require evidence establishing plaintiff's equitable right to judgment before rendering judgment. In actions involving only the possession of real property where the complaint is verified and shows by proper allegations that no party to the action claims title to the real property involved, either by prescription, accession, transfer, will, or succession, but only the possession thereof, the court may render judgment upon proof of occupancy by plaintiff and ouster by defendant.

(d) Use of affidavits. In the cases referred to in subdivisions (b) and (c), or upon an application to have attorneys' fees fixed by the court pursuant to subdivision (a), the court in its discretion may permit the use of affidavits, in lieu of personal testimony, as to all or any part of the evidence or proof required or permitted to be offered, received, or heard in such cases. The facts stated in such affidavit or affidavits shall be within the personal knowledge of the affiant and shall be set forth with particularity, and each affidavit shall show affirmatively that the affiant, if sworn as a witness, can testify competently thereto.

(e) Cross-complaints. If a defendant files a cross-complaint against another defendant or the plaintiff, a default may be entered against that party on that cross-complaint if the plaintiff or that cross-defendant has been served with that cross-complaint and he or she has failed to file an answer, demurrer, notice of motion to strike of the character specified in subdivision (f), notice of motion to transfer pursuant to Section 396b, notice of motion to dismiss pursuant to Article 2 (commencing with Section 583.210) of Chapter 1.5 of Title 8, notice of motion to quash service of summons or to stay or dismiss the action pursuant to Section 418.10, or notice of the filing of a petition for a writ of mandate as provided in Section 418.10 within the time specified in the summons, or such other time as may be allowed. However, no judgment may separately be entered on that cross-complaint unless a separate judgment may, in fact, be properly awarded on that cross-complaint and the court finds that a separate judgment on that cross-complaint would not substantially delay the final disposition of the action between the parties.

(f) Notice of motion to strike. A notice of motion to strike within the meaning of this section is a notice of motion to strike the whole or any part of a pleading filed within the time which the moving party is required otherwise to plead to such pleading. The notice of motion to strike shall specify a hearing date set in accordance with Section 1005. The filing of a notice of motion does not extend the time within which to demur. *(Enacted 1872. Amended Stats.1905, c. 47, § 1; Stats.1907, c. 376, § 4; Stats.1915, c. 553, § 1; Stats.1931, c. 285, § 1; Stats.1933, c. 744, § 92; Stats.1951, c. 1737, § 85; Stats.1955, c. 512, § 1; Stats.1955, c. 1452, § 6; Stats.1961, c. 393, § 1; Stats.1967, c. 135, § 1; Stats.1969, c. 345, § 3; Stats.1969, c. 567, § 1.5; Stats.1969, c. 1611, § 6.7; Stats.1973, c. 312, § 1; Stats.1980, c. 367, § 2; Stats.1982, c. 704, § 6.5; Stats.1986, c. 540, § 9; Stats.1993, c. 456, § 10.)*

§ 585.5. Affidavit Accompanying Application to Enter Default; Motion to Set Aside Default and For Leave to Defend; Procedure

(a) Every application to enter default under subdivision (a) of Section 585 shall include, or be accompanied by, an affidavit stating facts showing that the action is or is not subject to Section 1812.10 or 2984.4 of the Civil Code or subdivision (b) of Section 395.

(b) When a default or default judgment has been entered without full compliance with Section 1812.10 or 2984.4 of the Civil Code, or subdivision (b) of Section 395, the defendant may serve and file a notice of motion to set aside the default or default judgment and for leave to defend the action in the proper court. The notice of motion shall be served and filed within 60 days after the defendant first receives notice of levy under a writ of execution, or notice of any other procedure for enforcing, the default judgment.

(c) A notice of motion to set aside a default or default judgment and for leave to defend the action in the proper court shall designate as the time for making the motion a date prescribed by subdivision (b) of Section 1005, and it shall be accompanied by an affidavit showing under oath that the action was not commenced in the proper court according to Section 1812.10 or 2984.4 of the Civil Code or subdivision (b) of Section 395. The party shall serve and file with the notice a copy of the answer, motion, or other pleading proposed to be filed in the action.

(d) Upon a finding by the court that the motion was made within the period permitted by subdivision (b) and that the action was not commenced in the proper court, it shall set aside the default or default judgment on such terms as may be just and shall allow such a party to defend the action in the proper court.

(e) Unless the plaintiff can show that the plaintiff used reasonable diligence to avoid filing the action in the improper court, upon a finding that the action was commenced in the improper court the court shall award the defendant actual damages and costs, including reasonable attorney's fees. *(Amended by Stats.1982, c. 497, § 36; Stats.1983, c. 142, § 6; Stats.1991, c. 1090, § 3.)*

§ 586. Proceedings and Judgment as if Defendant Had Failed to Answer; Cases Where Applicable

(a) In the following cases the same proceedings shall be had, and judgment shall be rendered in the same manner, as if the defendant had failed to answer:

(1) If the complaint has been amended, and the defendant fails to answer it, as amended, or demur thereto, or file a notice of motion to strike, of the character specified in Section 585, within 30 days after service thereof or within the time allowed by the court.

(2) If the demurrer to the complaint is overruled and a motion to strike, of the character specified in Section 585, is denied, or where only one thereof is filed, if the demurrer is overruled or the motion to strike is denied, and the defendant fails to answer the complaint within the time allowed by the court.

(3) If a motion to strike, of the character specified in Section 585, is granted in whole or in part, and the defendant fails to answer the unstricken portion of the complaint within the time allowed by the court, no demurrer having been sustained or being then pending.

(4) If a motion to quash service of summons or to stay or dismiss, the action has been filed or writ of mandate sought and notice thereof given, as provided in Section 418.10, and upon denial of such motion or writ, defendant fails to respond to the complaint, within the time provided in such section or as otherwise provided by law.

(5) If the demurrer to the answer is sustained and the defendant fails to amend the answer within the time allowed by the court.

(6)(A) If a motion to transfer pursuant to Section 396b is denied and the defendant fails to respond to the complaint within the time allowed by the court pursuant to subdivision (e) of Section 396b or within the time provided in subparagraph (C).

(B) If a motion to transfer pursuant to Section 396b is granted and the defendant fails to respond to the complaint within 30 days of the mailing of notice of the filing and case number by the clerk of the court to which the action or proceeding is transferred or within the time provided in subparagraph (C).

(C) If the order granting or denying a motion to transfer pursuant to Section 396a or 396b is the subject of an appeal pursuant to Section 904.2 or 904.3 in which a stay is granted or of a mandate proceeding pursuant to Section 400, the court having jurisdiction over the trial, upon application or on its own motion after such appeal or mandate proceeding becomes final or upon earlier termination of a stay, shall allow the defendant a reasonable time to respond to the complaint. Notice of the order allowing the defendant further time to respond to the complaint shall be promptly served by the party who obtained such order or by the clerk if the order is made on the court's own motion.

(7) If a motion to strike the answer in whole, of the character specified in Section 585, is granted without leave to amend, or if a motion to strike the answer in whole or in part, of the character specified in Section 585, is granted with leave to amend and the defendant fails to amend the answer within the time allowed by the court.

(b) For the purposes of this section, "respond" means to answer, to demur, or to move to strike. *(Formerly § 872, enacted 1872. Amended by Stats.1921, c. 127, § 1. Renumbered § 586, and amended by Stats. 1933, c. 744, § 93; Stats.1955, c. 1452, § 7; Stats.1969, c. 345, § 4; Stats.1969, c. 1611, § 7.5; Stats.1970, c. 587, § 1; Stats.1973, c. 167, § 12; Stats.1982, c. 704, § 7; Stats.1983, c. 1167, § 7; Stats.1991, c. 1090, § 4; Stats.1993, c. 456, § 11.)*

Chapter 3.   Issues—The Mode of Trial and Postponements

§ 592. Issue of Fact; Jury Trial; Waiver; Reference; Issues of Law Disposed of First

In actions for the recovery of specific, real, or personal property, with or without damages, or for money claimed as due upon contract, or as damages for breach of contract, or for injuries, an issue of fact must be tried by a jury, unless a jury trial is waived, or a reference is ordered, as provided in this Code. Where in these cases there are issues both of law and fact, the issue of law must be first disposed of. In other cases, issues of fact must be tried by the Court, subject to its power to order any such issue to be tried by a jury, or to be referred to a referee, as provided in this Code. *(Enacted 1872. Amended by Code Am. 1873–74, c. 383, § 74.)*

§ 598. Precedence of Issues; Motion

The court may, when the convenience of witnesses, the ends of justice, or the economy and efficiency of handling the litigation would be promoted thereby, on motion of a party, after notice and hearing, make an order, no later than the close of pretrial conference in cases in which such pretrial conference is to be held, or, in other cases, no later than 30 days before the trial date, that the trial of any issue or any part thereof shall precede the trial of any other issue or any part thereof in the case, except for special defenses which may be tried first pursuant to Sections 597 and 597.5. The court, on its own motion, may make such an order at any time. Where trial of the issue of liability as to all causes of action precedes the trial of other issues or parts thereof, and the decision of the court, or the verdict of the jury upon such issue so tried is in favor of any party on whom liability is sought to be imposed, judgment in favor of such party shall thereupon be entered and no trial of other issues in the action as against such party shall be had unless such judgment shall be reversed upon appeal or otherwise set aside or vacated.

If the decision of the court, or the verdict of the jury upon the issue of liability so tried shall be against any party on whom liability is sought to be imposed, or if the decision of the court or the verdict of the jury upon any other issue or part thereof so tried does not result in a judgment being entered pursuant to this chapter, then the trial of the other issues or parts thereof shall thereafter be had at such time, and if a jury trial, before the same or other jury, as ordered by the court either upon its own motion or upon the motion of any party, and judgment shall be entered in the same manner and with the same effect as if all the issues in the case had been tried at one time. *(Added by Stats.1963, c. 1205, § 1. Amended by Stats.1977, c. 57, § 1; Stats.1979, c. 216, § 3; Stats.1979, c. 349, § 1.)*

Chapter 4.   Trial by Jury

§ 607.   Order of Proceedings

When the jury has been sworn, the trial must proceed in the following order, unless the court, for special reasons otherwise directs:

1.   The plaintiff may state the issue and his case;

2.   The defendant may then state his defense, if he so wishes, or wait until after plaintiff has produced his evidence;

3.   The plaintiff must then produce the evidence on his part;

4.   The defendant may then open his defense, if he has not done so previously;

5.   The defendant may then produce the evidence on his part;

6.   The parties may then respectively offer rebutting evidence only, unless the court, for good reason, in furtherance of justice, permit them to offer evidence upon their original case;

7.   When the evidence is concluded, unless the case is submitted to the jury on either side or on both sides without argument, the plaintiff must commence and may conclude the argument;

8.   If several defendants having separate defenses, appear by different counsel, the court must determine their relative order in the evidence and argument;

9.   The court may then charge the jury. *(Enacted 1872. Amended by Stats.1933, c. 744, § 100; Stats.1965, c. 841, § 1.)*

§ 607a.   Proposed Jury Instructions

In every case which is being tried before the court with a jury, it shall be the duty of counsel for the respective parties, before the first witness is sworn, to deliver to the judge presiding at the trial and serve upon opposing counsel, all proposed instructions to the jury covering the law as disclosed by the pleadings. Thereafter, and before the commencement of the argument, counsel may deliver to such judge, and serve upon opposing counsel, additional proposed instructions to the jury upon questions of law developed by the evidence and not disclosed by the pleadings. All proposed instructions shall be typewritten, each on a separate sheet of paper. Before the commencement of the argument, the court, on request of counsel, must: (1) decide whether to give, refuse, or modify the proposed instructions; (2) decide which instructions shall be given in addition to those proposed, if any; and (3) advise counsel of all instructions to be given. However, if, during the argument, issues are raised which have not been covered by instructions given or refused, the court may, on request of counsel, give additional instructions on the subject matter thereof. *(Added by Stats.1929, c. 481, § 1. Amended by Stats.1933, c. 744, § 101; Stats.1951, c. 1737, § 89; Stats.1957, c. 1698, § 1.)*

§ 608. Charge to Jury; Written Statement of Points of Law

Charge to the jury. Court must furnish in writing, upon request, the points of law contained therein. In charging the jury the Court may state to them all matters of law which it thinks necessary for their information in giving their verdict; and, if it state the testimony of the case, it must inform the jury that they are the exclusive judges of all questions of fact. The Court must furnish to either party, at the time, upon request, a statement in writing of the points of law contained in the charge, or sign, at the time, a statement of such points prepared and submitted by the counsel of either party. *(Enacted 1872.)*

§ 613. Decision in Court; Deliberation; Communications

When the case is finally submitted to the jury, they may decide in Court or retire for deliberation; if they retire, they must be kept together, in some convenient place, under charge of an officer, until at least three-fourths of them agree upon a verdict or are discharged by the Court. Unless by order of the Court, the officer having them under his charge must not suffer any communication to be made to them, or make any himself, except to ask them if they or three-fourths of them are agreed upon a verdict, and he must not, before their verdict is rendered, communicate to any person the state of their deliberations, or the verdict agreed upon. *(Enacted 1872. Amended by Code Am.1880, c. 21, § 1.)*

§ 618. Verdict; Polling Jury

When the jury, or three-fourths of them, have agreed upon a verdict, they must be conducted into court and the verdict rendered by their foreman. The verdict must be in writing, signed by the foreman, and must be read to the jury by the clerk, or by the court, if there be no clerk, and the inquiry made whether it is their verdict. Either party may require the jury to be polled, which is done by the court or clerk, asking each juror if it is his verdict. If upon such inquiry or polling, more than one-fourth of the jurors disagree thereto, the jury must be sent out again, but if no such disagreement be expressed, the verdict is complete and the jury discharged from the case. *(Enacted 1872. Amended by Code Am.1880, c. 21, § 3; Stats.1933, c. 744, § 102; Stats. 1935, c. 722, § 9; Stats.1978, c. 258, § 1.)*

§ 624. General and Special Verdicts Defined

General and special verdicts defined. The verdict of a jury is either general or special. A general verdict is that by which they pronounce generally upon all or any of the issues, either in favor of the plaintiff or defendant; a special verdict is that by which the jury find the facts only, leaving the judgment to the Court. The special verdict must present the conclusions of fact as established by the evidence, and not the evidence to prove them; and those conclusions of fact must be so presented as that nothing shall remain to the Court but to draw from them conclusions of law. *(Enacted 1872.)*

§ 625. Special Verdict or Findings; Punitive Damages; Filing and Entry Upon Minutes; General Verdict Controlled by Special Findings

In all cases the court may direct the jury to find a special verdict in writing, upon all, or any of the issues, and in all cases may instruct them, if they render a general verdict, to find upon particular questions of fact, to be stated in writing, and may direct a written finding thereon. In all cases in which the issue of punitive damages is presented to the jury the court shall direct the jury to find a special verdict in writing separating punitive damages from compensatory damages. The special verdict or finding must be filed with the clerk and entered upon the minutes. Where a special finding of fact is inconsistent with the general verdict, the former controls the latter, and the court must give judgment accordingly. *(Enacted 1872. Amended by Stats. 1905, c. 62, § 1; Stats. 1909, c. 121, § 1; Stats.1957, c. 1443, § 1; Stats.1983, c. 176, § 2.)*

§ 629. Judgment Notwithstanding Verdict

The court, before the expiration of its power to rule on a motion for a new trial, either of its own motion, after five days' notice, or on motion of a party against whom a verdict has been rendered, shall render judgment in favor of the aggrieved party notwithstanding the verdict whenever a motion for a directed verdict for the aggrieved party should have been granted had a previous motion been made.

A motion for judgment notwithstanding the verdict shall be made within the period specified by Section 659 of this code in respect of the filing and serving of notice of intention to move for a new trial. The making of a motion for judgment notwithstanding the verdict shall not extend the time within which a party may file and serve notice of intention to move for a new trial. The court shall not rule upon the motion for judgment notwithstanding the verdict until the expiration of the time within which a motion for a new trial must be served and filed, and if a motion for a new trial has been filed with the court by the aggrieved party, the court shall rule upon both motions at the same time. The power of the court to rule on a motion for judgment notwithstanding the verdict shall not extend beyond the last date upon which it has the power to rule on a motion for a new trial. If a motion for judgment notwithstanding the verdict is not determined before such date, the effect shall be a denial of such motion without further order of the court.

If the motion for judgment notwithstanding the verdict be denied and if a new trial be denied, the appellate court shall, when it appears that the motion for judgment notwithstanding the verdict should have been granted, order judgment to be so entered on appeal from the judgment or from the order denying the motion for judgment notwithstanding the verdict.

Where a new trial is granted to the party moving for judgment notwithstanding the verdict, and the motion for judgment notwithstanding the verdict is denied, the order denying the motion for judgment notwithstanding the verdict shall nevertheless be reviewable on appeal from said order by the aggrieved party. If the court grants the motion for judgment notwithstanding the verdict or of its own motion directs the entry of judgment notwithstanding the verdict and likewise grants the motion for a new trial, the order granting the new trial shall be effective only if, on appeal, the judgment notwithstanding the verdict is reversed, and the order granting a new trial is not appealed from or, if appealed from, is affirmed. *(Added by Stats.1923, c. 366, § 1. Amended by Stats.1935, c. 722, § 10; Stats.1937, c. 551, § 1; Stats.1951, c. 801, § 1; Stats.1961, c. 604, § 1; Stats.1963, c. 205, § 1.)*

§ 630. Motion for Directed Verdict; Granting of Motion for All or Part of Issues Involved; Effect; Ordering Judgment After Discharge of Jury and Failure to Grant Directed Verdict

(a) Unless the court specified an earlier time for making a motion for directed verdict, after all parties have completed the presentation of all of their evidence in a trial by jury, any party may, without waiving his or her right to trial by jury in the event the motion is not granted, move for an order directing entry of a verdict in its favor.

(b) If it appears that the evidence presented supports the granting of the motion as to some, but not all, of the issues involved in the action, the court shall grant the motion as to those issues and the action shall proceed on any remaining issues. Despite the granting of such a motion, no final judgment shall be entered prior to the termination of the action, but the final judgment, in addition to any matter determined in the trial, shall reflect the verdict ordered by the court as determined by the motion for directed verdict.

(c) If the motion is granted, unless the court in its order directing entry of the verdict specifies otherwise, it shall operate as an adjudication upon the merits.

(d) In actions which arise out of an injury to a person or property, when a motion for directed verdict was granted on the basis that a defendant was without fault, no other defendant during trial, over plaintiff's objection, shall attempt to attribute fault to or comment on the absence or involvement of the defendant who was granted the motion.

(e) The order of the court granting the motion for directed verdict is effective without any assent of the jury.

(f) When the jury for any reason has been discharged without having rendered a verdict, the court on its own motion or upon motion of a party, notice of which was given within 10 days after discharge of the jury, may order judgment to be entered in favor of a party whenever a motion for directed verdict for that party should have been granted had a previous motion been made. Except as otherwise provided in Section 12a, the power of the court to act under the provisions of this section shall expire 30 days after the day upon which the jury was discharged, and if judgment has not been ordered within that time the effect shall be the denial of any motion for judgment without further order of the court. *(Added by Stats.1947, c. 984, § 2. Amended by Stats.1967, c. 625, § 1; Stats.1986, c. 540, § 12.)*

Chapter 5. Trial by Court

§ 631. Waiver of Jury Trial; Manner; Demand for Jury Trial; Exception

(a) Trial by jury may be waived by the several parties to an issue of fact in any of the following ways:

(1) By failing to appear at the trial.

(2) By written consent filed with the clerk or judge.

(3) By oral consent, in open court, entered in the minutes or docket.

(4) By failing to announce that a jury is required, at the time the cause is first set for trial, if it is set upon notice or stipulation, or within five days after notice of setting if it is set without notice or stipulation.

(5) By failing to deposit with the clerk, or judge, advance jury fees 25 days prior to the date set for trial, except in unlawful detainer actions where the fees shall be deposited at least five days prior to the date set for trial, or as provided by subdivision (b). The advanced jury fee shall not exceed the amount necessary to pay the average mileage and fees of 20 trial jurors for one day in the court to which the jurors are summoned.

(6) By failing to deposit with the clerk or judge, promptly after the impanelment of the jury, a sum equal to the mileage or transportation (if any be allowed by law) of the jury accrued up to that time.

(7) By failing to deposit with the clerk or judge, at the beginning of the second and each succeeding day's session a sum equal to one day's fees of the jury, and the mileage or transportation, if any.

(b) In a superior court action if a jury is demanded by either party in the memorandum to set the cause for trial and the party, prior to trial, by announcement or by operation of law waives a trial by jury, then all adverse parties shall have five days following the receipt of notice of the waiver to file and serve a demand for a trial by jury and to deposit any advance jury fees which are then due.

(c) When the party who has demanded trial by jury either waives such trial upon or after the assignment for trial to a specific department of the court, or upon or after the commencement of the trial, or fails to deposit the fees as provided in paragraph (6) of subdivision (a), trial by jury shall be waived by the other party either failing promptly to demand trial by jury before the judge in whose department the waiver, other than for the failure to deposit such fees, was made, or by that party's failing promptly to deposit the fees provided in paragraph (6) of subdivision (a).

(d) The court may, in its discretion upon just terms, allow a trial by jury although there may have been a waiver of a trial by jury. *(Added by Stats.1988, c. 10, § 3. Amended by Stats.1988, c. 278, § 1; Stats.1989, c. 15, § 2, eff. May 10, 1989.)*

§ 631.2. County Payment of Jury Fees; Reimbursement

(a) Notwithstanding any other provision of law, the county may pay jury fees in civil cases from general funds of the county available therefor. Nothing in this section shall be construed to change the requirements for the deposit of jury fees in any civil case by the appropriate party to the litigation at the time and in the manner otherwise provided by law. Nothing in this section shall preclude the right of the county to be reimbursed by the party to the litigation liable therefor for any payment of jury fees pursuant to this section.

(b) The party who has demanded trial by jury shall reimburse the county for the fees and mileage of all jurors appearing for voir dire examination, except those jurors who are excused and subsequently on the same day are called for voir dire examination in another case. *(Added by Stats.1988, c. 10, § 4.)*

§ 631.3. Forfeiture of Jury Fees Deposited; Disposition of Fees

Notwithstanding any other provision of law, when a party to the litigation has deposited jury fees with the judge or clerk and the case is settled or a continuance is granted on motion of the party depositing said jury fees, none of said deposit shall be refunded if the court finds there has been insufficient time to notify the jurors that the trial would not proceed at the time set. If said jury fees so deposited are not refunded for the reasons herein specified, or if jury fees deposited with the judge or clerk have not been refunded within three years after the action was dismissed or a final judgment rendered therein because the depositor thereof cannot be found, said fees shall revert to the county and be deposited in the general fund of the county. All jury fees and mileage fees that may accrue by reason of a juror serving on more than one case in the same day shall revert to the county and be deposited in the general fund of the county. *(Added by Stats.1949, c. 444, § 1. Amended by Stats.1955, c. 511, § 1; Stats.1963, c. 678, § 1.)*

§ 631.8. Motion for Judgment; Partial Grant for Motion; Effect

(a) After a party has completed his presentation of evidence in a trial by the court, the other party, without waiving his right to offer evidence in support of his defense or in rebuttal in the event the motion is not granted, may move for a judgment. The court as trier of the facts shall weigh the evidence and may render a judgment in favor of the moving party, in which case the court shall make a statement of decision as provided in Sections 632 and 634, or may decline to render any judgment until the close of all the evidence. The court may consider all evidence received, provided, however, that the party against whom the motion for judgment has been made shall have had an opportunity to present additional evidence to rebut evidence received during the presentation of evidence deemed by the presenting party to have been adverse to him, and to rehabilitate the testimony of a witness whose credibility has been attacked by the moving party. Such motion may also be made and granted as to any cross-complaint.

(b) If it appears that the evidence presented supports the granting of the motion as to some but not all the issues involved in the action, the court shall grant the motion as to those issues and the action shall proceed as to the issues remaining. Despite the granting of such a motion, no final judgment shall be entered prior to the termination of the action, but the final judgment in such action shall, in addition to any matters determined in the trial, award judgment as determined by the motion herein provided for.

(c) If the motion is granted, unless the court in its order for judgment otherwise specifies, such judgment operates as an adjudication upon the merits. *(Added by Stats.1961, c. 692, § 2. Amended by Stats.1971, c. 244, § 53; Stats.1978, c. 372, § 1; Stats.1980, c. 187, § 2; Stats.1986, c. 540, § 13.)*

§ 632. Statement of Decision

In superior, municipal, and justice courts, upon the trial of a question of fact by the court, written findings of fact and conclusions of law shall not be required. The court shall issue a statement of decision explaining the factual and legal basis for its decision as to each of the principal controverted issues at trial upon the request of any party appearing at the trial. The request must be made within 10 days after the court announces a tentative decision unless the trial is concluded within one calendar day or in less than eight hours over more than one day in which event the request must be made prior to the submission of the matter for decision. The request for a statement of decision shall specify those controverted issues as to which the party is requesting a statement of decision. After a party has requested such a statement, any party may make proposals as to the content of the statement of decision.

The statement of decision shall be in writing, unless the parties appearing at trial agree otherwise; however, when the trial is concluded within one calendar day or in less than 8 hours over more than one day, the statement of decision may be made orally on the record in the presence of the parties. *(Enacted 1872. Amended by Code Am.1873–74, c. 383, § 79; Stats.1933, c. 744, § 105; Stats.1951, c. 1737, § 92; Stats.1959, c. 637, § 1; Stats.1968, c. 716, § 1; Stats.1969, c. 339, § 1; Stats.1975, c. 301, § 2; Stats.1977, c. 1257, § 22; Stats.1981, c. 900, § 1; Stats.1987, c. 207, § 1.)*

Chapter 6. Of References and Trials by Referees

§ 638. Reference by Agreement; Purposes

A reference may be ordered upon the agreement of the parties filed with the clerk, or judge, or entered in the minutes or in the docket, or upon the motion of a party to a written contract or lease which provides that any controversy arising therefrom shall be heard by a reference if the court finds a reference agreement exists between the parties:

1. To try any or all of the issues in an action or proceeding, whether of fact or of law, and to report a statement of decision thereon;

2. To ascertain a fact necessary to enable the court to determine an action or proceeding. *(Enacted 1872. Amended by Stats.1933, c. 744, § 107; Stats.1951, c. 1737, § 93; Stats.1982, c. 440, § 1; Stats.1984, c. 350, § 1.)*

§ 639. Direction of Reference; Application; Court's Own Motion

When the parties do not consent, the court may, upon the application of any party, or of its own motion, direct a reference in the following cases:

(a) When the trial of an issue of fact requires the examination of a long account on either side; in which case the referees may be directed to hear and decide the whole issue, or report upon any specific question of fact involved therein.

(b) When the taking of an account is necessary for the information of the court before judgment, or for carrying a judgment or order into effect.

(c) When a question of fact, other than upon the pleadings, arises upon motion or otherwise, in any stage of the action.

(d) When it is necessary for the information of the court in a special proceeding.

(e) When the court in any pending action determines in its discretion that it is necessary for the court to appoint a referee to hear and determine any and all discovery motions and disputes relevant to discovery in the action and to report findings and make a recommendation thereon. *(Enacted 1872. Amended by Stats.1933, c. 744, § 108; Stats. 1951, c. 1737, § 94; Stats.1977, c. 1257, § 23; Stats.1981, c. 299, § 1.)*

Chapter 7.　Provisions Relating to Trials in General

§ 657.　Relief Available on Motion for New Trial; Causes; Specification of Grounds and Reasons; New Trial for Insufficient Evidence; Manner of Making and Entering Order; Appeal

The verdict may be vacated and any other decision may be modified or vacated, in whole or in part, and a new or further trial granted on all or part of the issues, on the application of the party aggrieved, for any of the following causes, materially affecting the substantial rights of such party:

1.　Irregularity in the proceedings of the court, jury or adverse party, or any order of the court or abuse of discretion by which either party was prevented from having a fair trial.

2.　Misconduct of the jury; and whenever any one or more of the jurors have been induced to assent to any general or special verdict, or to a finding on any question submitted to them by the court, by a resort to the determination of chance, such misconduct may be proved by the affidavit of any one of the jurors.

3.　Accident or surprise, which ordinary prudence could not have guarded against.

4.　Newly discovered evidence, material for the party making the application, which he could not, with reasonable diligence, have discovered and produced at the trial.

5.　Excessive or inadequate damages.

6.　Insufficiency of the evidence to justify the verdict or other decision, or the verdict or other decision is against law.

7.　Error in law, occurring at the trial and excepted to by the party making the application.

When a new trial is granted, on all or part of the issues, the court shall specify the ground or grounds upon which it is granted and the court's reason or reasons for granting the new trial upon each ground stated.

A new trial shall not be granted upon the ground of insufficiency of the evidence to justify the verdict or other decision, nor upon the ground of excessive or inadequate damages, unless after weighing the evidence the court is convinced from the entire record, including reasonable inferences therefrom, that the court or jury clearly should have reached a different verdict or decision.

The order passing upon and determining the motion must be made and entered as provided in Section 660 and if the motion is granted must state the ground or grounds relied upon by the court, and may contain the specification of reasons. If an order granting such motion does not contain such specification of reasons, the court must, within 10 days after filing such order, prepare, sign and file such specification of reasons in writing with the clerk. The court shall not direct the attorney for a party to prepare either or both said order and said specification of reasons.

On appeal from an order granting a new trial the order shall be affirmed if it should have been granted upon any ground stated in the motion, whether or not specified in the order or specification of reasons, except that (a) the order shall not be affirmed upon the ground of the insufficiency of the evidence to justify the verdict or other decision, or upon the ground of excessive or inadequate damages, unless such ground is stated in the order granting the motion and (b) on appeal from an order granting a new trial upon the ground of the insufficiency of the evidence to justify the verdict or other decision, or upon the ground of excessive or inadequate damages, it shall be conclusively presumed that said order as to such ground was made only for the reasons specified in said order or said specification of reasons, and such order shall be reversed as to such ground only if there is no substantial basis in the record for any of such reasons. *(Enacted 1872. Amended by Stats.1919, c. 100, § 1; Stats.1929, c. 479, § 2; Stats.1939, c. 713, § 1; Stats.1965, c. 1749, § 1; Stats.1967, c. 72, § 1.)*

§ 659. Notice of Motion; Filing and Service, Time; Contents; Extension of Time

The party intending to move for a new trial must file with the clerk and serve upon each adverse party a notice of his intention to move for a new trial, designating the grounds upon which the motion will be made and whether the same will be made upon affidavits or the minutes of the court or both, either

1. Before the entry of judgment; or

2. Within 15 days of the date of mailing notice of entry of judgment by the clerk of the court pursuant to Section 664.5, or service upon him by any party of written notice of entry of judgment, or within 180 days after the entry of judgment, whichever is earliest; provided, that upon the filing of the first notice of intention to move for a new trial by a party, each other party shall have 15 days after the service of such notice upon him to file and serve a notice of intention to move for a new trial.

Said notice of intention to move for a new trial shall be deemed to be a motion for a new trial on all the grounds stated in the notice. The time above specified shall not be extended by order or stipulation or by those provisions of Section 1013 of this code which extend the time for exercising a right or doing an act where service is by mail. *(Enacted 1872. Amended by Code Am.1873–74, c. 383, § 85; Stats.1907, c. 380, § 2; Stats.1915, c. 107, § 2; Stats.1923, c. 367, § 1; Stats.1929, c. 479, § 3; Stats.1951, c. 801, § 2; Stats.1959, c. 469, § 1; Stats.1961, c. 604, § 2; Stats.1965, c. 1890, § 1.5; Stats.1967, c. 169, § 1; Stats.1970, c. 621, § 1.)*

§ 660. Hearing; Reference to Pleadings, Orders, Depositions, Documentary Evidence, Transcript, Recollection of Judge; Attendance of Reporter; Precedence; Time for Ruling; Automatic Denial; Determination; Minute Order

On the hearing of such motion, reference may be had in all cases to the pleadings and orders of the court on file, and when the motion is made on the minutes, reference may also be had to any depositions and documentary evidence offered at the trial and to the report of the proceedings on the trial taken by the phonographic reporter, or to any certified transcript of such report or if there be no such report or certified transcript, to such proceedings occurring at the trial as are within the recollection of the judge; when the proceedings at the trial have been phonographically reported, but the reporter's notes have not been transcribed, the reporter must upon request of the court or either party, attend the hearing of the motion and shall read his notes, or such parts thereof as the court, or either party, may require.

The hearing and disposition of the motion for a new trial shall have precedence over all other matters except criminal cases, probate matters and cases actually on trial, and it shall be the duty of the court to determine the same at the earliest possible moment.

Except as otherwise provided in Section 12a of this code, the power of the court to rule on a motion for a new trial shall expire 60 days from and after the mailing of notice of entry of judgment by the clerk of the court pursuant to Section 664.5 or 60 days from and after service on the moving party by any party of written notice of the entry of the judgment, whichever is earlier, or if such notice has not theretofore been given, then 60 days after filing of the first notice of intention to move for a new trial. If such motion is not determined within said period of 60 days, or within said period as thus extended, the effect shall be a denial of the motion without further order of the court. A motion for a new trial is not determined within the meaning of this section until an order ruling on the motion (1) is entered in the permanent minutes of the court or (2) is signed by the judge and filed with the clerk. The entry of a new trial order in the permanent minutes of the court shall constitute a determination of the motion even though such minute order as entered expressly directs that a written order be prepared, signed and filed. The minute entry shall in all cases show the date on which the order actually is entered in the permanent minutes, but failure to comply with this direction shall not impair the validity or effectiveness of the order. *(Enacted 1872. Amended by Code Am.1873–74, c. 383, § 86; Stats.1907, c. 380, § 3; Stats.1915, c. 107, § 3; Stats.1917, c. 156, § 1; Stats.1923, c.*

105, § 1; Stats.1929, c. 479, § 5; Stats.1933, c. 29, § 5; Stats.1959, c. 468, § 1; Stats.1969, c. 87, § 1; Stats.1970, c. 621, § 2.)

§ 662. Cause Tried by Court; Powers of Judge on Motion for New Trial

In ruling on such motion, in a cause tried without a jury, the court may, on such terms as may be just, change or add to the statement of decision, modify the judgment, in whole or in part, vacate the judgment, in whole or in part, and grant a new trial on all or part of the issues, or, in lieu of granting a new trial, may vacate and set aside the statement of decision and judgment and reopen the case for further proceedings and the introduction of additional evidence with the same effect as if the case had been reopened after the submission thereof and before a decision had been filed or judgment rendered. Any judgment thereafter entered shall be subject to the provisions of sections 657 and 659. *(Added by Stats.1929, c. 479, § 7. Amended by Stats.1981, c. 900, § 4.)*

§ 662.5 Inadequate or Excessive Damages as Grounds

In any civil action where after trial by jury an order granting a new trial limited to the issue of damages would be proper, the trial court may in its discretion:

(a) If the ground for granting a new trial is inadequate damages, make its order granting the new trial subject to the condition that the motion for a new trial is denied if the party against whom the verdict has been rendered consents to an addition of so much thereto as the court in its independent judgment determines from the evidence to be fair and reasonable.

(b) If the ground for granting a new trial is excessive damages, make its order granting the new trial subject to the condition that the motion for a new trial is denied if the party in whose favor the verdict has been rendered consents to a reduction of so much thereof as the court in its independent judgment determines from the evidence to be fair and reasonable. *(Added by Stats.1967, c. 72, § 2. Amended by Stats.1969, c. 115, § 1.)*

§ 663. Setting Aside Judgment or Decree; Entry of New Judgment; Grounds

A judgment or decree, when based upon a decision by the court, or the special verdict of a jury, may, upon motion of the party aggrieved, be set aside and vacated by the same court, and another and different judgment entered, for either of the following causes, materially affecting the substantial rights of the party and entitling the party to a different judgment:

1.   Incorrect or erroneous legal basis for the decision, not consistent with or not supported by the facts; and in such case when the judgment is set aside, the statement of decision shall be amended and corrected.

2. A judgment or decree not consistent with or not supported by the special verdict. *(Added by Stats.1897, c. 67, § 1. Amended by Stats.1933, c. 744, § 120; Stats.1981, c. 900, § 5.)*

TITLE 9. ENFORCEMENT OF JUDGMENTS

Chapter 3. Period for Enforcement and Renewal of Judgments

§ 683.010 Entry of Judgment

Except as otherwise provided by statute or in the judgment, a judgment is enforceable under this title upon entry. *(Added by Stats. 1982, c. 1364, § 2.)*

§ 683.020 Period of Enforceability

Except as otherwise provided by statute, upon the expiration of 10 years after the date of entry of a money judgment or a judgment for possession or sale of property:

(a) The judgment may not be enforced.

(b) All enforcement procedures pursuant to the judgment or to a writ or order issued pursuant to the judgment shall cease.

(c) Any lien created by an enforcement procedure pursuant to the judgment is extinguished. *(Added by Stats.1982, c. 1364, § 2.)*

§ 683.120 Application for Renewal; Effect

(a) The judgment creditor may renew a judgment by filing an application for renewal of the judgment with the court in which the judgment was entered.

(b) Except as otherwise provided in this article, the filing of the application renews the judgment in the amount determined under Section 683.150 and extends the period of enforceability of the judgment as renewed for a period of 10 years from the date the application is filed.

(c) In the case of a money judgment payable in installments, for the purposes of enforcement and of any later renewal, the amount of the judgment as renewed shall be treated as a lump-sum money judgment entered on the date the application is filed. *(Added by Stats.1982, c. 1364, § 2.)*

§ 683.180 Judgment Liens; Effect of Renewal

(a) If a judgment lien on an interest in real property has been created pursuant to a money judgment and the judgment is renewed pursuant to this article, the duration of the judgment lien is extended until 10 years from the date of the filing of the application for renewal if, before the expiration of the judgment lien, a certified copy of the application for renewal is recorded with the county recorder of the county where the real property subject to the judgment lien is located.

(b) A judgment lien on an interest in real property that has been transferred subject to the lien is not extended pursuant to subdivision (a) if the transfer was recorded before the application for renewal was filed unless both of the following requirements are satisfied:

(1) A copy of the application for renewal is personally served on the transferee.

(2) Proof of such service is filed with the court clerk within 90 days after the filing of the application for renewal. *(Added by Stats.1982, c. 1364, § 2. Amended by Stats.1983, c. 155, § 9.5.)*

Chapter 5. Interest and Costs

§ 685.040 Costs; Attorney's Fees

The judgment creditor is entitled to the reasonable and necessary costs of enforcing a judgment. Attorney's fees incurred in enforcing a judgment are not included in costs collectible under this title unless otherwise provided by law. Attorney's fees incurred in enforcing a judgment are included as costs collectible under this title if the underlying judgment includes an award of attorney's fees to the judgment creditor pursuant to subparagraph (A) of paragraph (10) of subdivision (a) of Section 1033.5. *(Added by Stats.1982, c. 1364, § 2. Amended by Stats.1992, c. 1348, § 3.)*

§ 685.070 Judgment Creditor's Costs; Memorandum; Motion to Tax Costs

(a) The judgment creditor may claim under this section the following costs of enforcing a judgment:

(1) Statutory fees for preparing and issuing, and recording and indexing, an abstract of judgment or a certified copy of a judgment.

(2) Statutory fees for filing a notice of judgment lien on personal property.

(3) Statutory fees for issuing a writ for the enforcement of the judgment to the extent that the fees are not satisfied pursuant to Section 685.050.

(4) Statutory costs of the levying officer for performing the duties under a writ to the extent that the costs are not satisfied pursuant to Section 685.050 and the statutory fee of the levying officer for performing the duties under the Wage Garnishment Law to the extent that the fee has not been satisfied pursuant to the wage garnishment.

(5) Costs incurred in connection with any proceeding under Chapter 6 (commencing with Section 708.010) of Division 2 that have been approved as to amount, reasonableness, and necessity by the judge or referee conducting the proceeding.

(6) Attorney's fees, if allowed by Section 685.040.

(b) Before the judgment is fully satisfied but not later than two years after the costs have been incurred, the judgment creditor claiming costs under this section shall file a memorandum of costs with the court clerk and serve a copy on the judgment debtor. Service shall be made personally or by mail. The memorandum of costs shall be executed under oath by a person who has knowledge of the facts and shall state that to the person's best knowledge and belief the costs are correct, are reasonable and necessary, and have not been satisfied.

(c) Within 10 days after the memorandum of costs is served on the judgment debtor, the judgment debtor may apply to the court on noticed motion to have the costs taxed by the court. The notice of motion shall be served on the judgment creditor. Service shall be made personally or by mail. The court shall make an order allowing or disallowing the costs to the extent justified under the circumstances of the case.

(d) If no motion to tax costs is made within the time provided in subdivision (c), the costs claimed in the memorandum are allowed.

(e) If a memorandum of costs for the costs specified in subdivision (a) is filed at the same time as an application for a writ of execution, these statutory costs not already allowed by the court in an amount not to exceed one hundred dollars ($100) in the aggregate may be included in the amount specified in the writ of execution, subject to subsequent disallowance as ordered by the court pursuant to a motion to tax if filed by the debtor. The memorandum of costs shall contain the following statement: "The fees sought under this memorandum may be disallowed by a court upon a motion to tax filed by the debtor notwithstanding the fees having been included in the writ of execution." The inclusion of the above costs in the writ of execution or the pendency of the motion to tax on these costs shall not be cause for the clerk of the court to delay issuing the writ of execution or for the levying officer to delay enforcing the writ of execution. *(Added by Stats.1982, c. 1364, § 2. Amended by Stats.1990, c. 790, § 1; Stats.1922, c. 1348, § 4.)*

§ 685.080   Motion to Claim Costs; Notice; Service; Order

(a) The judgment creditor may claim costs authorized by Section 685.040 by noticed motion. The motion shall be made before the judgment is satisfied in full, but not later than two years after the costs have been incurred. The costs claimed under this section may include, but are not limited to, costs that may be claimed under Section 685.070 and costs incurred but not approved by the court or referee in a proceeding under Chapter 6 (commencing with Section 708.010) of Division 2.

(b) The notice of motion shall describe the costs claimed, shall state their amount, and shall be supported by an affidavit of a person who has knowledge of the facts stating that to the person's best knowledge and belief the costs are correct, are reasonable and necessary, and have not been satisfied. The notice of motion shall be served on the judgment debtor. Service shall be made personally or by mail.

(c) The court shall make an order allowing or disallowing the costs to the extent justified under the circumstances of the case. *(Added by Stats.1982, c. 1364, § 2.)*

TITLE 11. CONTRIBUTION AMONG JOINT JUDGMENT DEBTORS

Chapter 1. Releases From and Contribution Among Joint Tortfeasors

§ 877. Release of One or More Joint Tortfeasors or Co-obligors; Effect Upon Liability

Where a release, dismissal with or without prejudice, or a covenant not to sue or not to enforce judgment is given in good faith before verdict or judgment to one or more of a number of tortfeasors claimed to be liable for the same tort, or to one or more other co-obligors mutually subject to contribution rights, it shall have the following effect:

(a) It shall not discharge any other such party from liability unless its terms so provide, but it shall reduce the claims against the others in the amount stipulated by the release, the dismissal or the covenant, or in the amount of the consideration paid for it whichever is the greater.

(b) It shall discharge the party to whom it is given from all liability for any contribution to any other parties.

(c) This section shall not apply to co-obligors who have expressly agreed in writing to an apportionment of liability for losses or claims among themselves.

(d) This section shall not apply to a release, dismissal with or without prejudice, or a covenant not to sue or not to enforce judgment given to a co-obligor on an alleged contract debt where the contract was made prior to January 1, 1988. *(Added by Stats.1957, c. 1700, § 1. Amended by Stats.1987, c. 677, § 2.)*

§ 877.5 Sliding Scale Recovery Agreement; Disclosure to Court and Jury; Service of Notice of Intent to Enter

(a) Where an agreement or covenant is made which provides for a sliding scale recovery agreement between one or more, but not all, alleged defendant tortfeasors and the plaintiff or plaintiffs:

(1) The parties entering into any such agreement or covenant shall promptly inform the court in which the action is pending of the existence of the agreement or covenant and its terms and provisions.

(2) If the action is tried before a jury, and a defendant party to the agreement is called as a witness at trial, the court shall, upon motion of a party, disclose to the jury the existence and content of the agreement or covenant, unless the court finds that such disclosure will create substantial danger of undue prejudice, of confusing the issues, or of misleading the jury.

The jury disclosure herein required shall be no more than necessary to inform the jury of the possibility that the agreement may bias the testimony of the witness.

(b) As used in this section, a "sliding scale recovery agreement" means an agreement or covenant between a plaintiff or plaintiffs and one or more, but not all, alleged tortfeasor defendants, which limits the liability of the agreeing tortfeasor defendants to an amount which is dependent upon the amount of recovery which the plaintiff is able to recover from the nonagreeing defendant or defendants. This includes, but is not limited to, agreements within the scope of Section 877, and agreements in the form of a loan from the agreeing tortfeasor defendant or defendants to the plaintiff or plaintiffs which is repayable in whole or in part from the recovery against the nonagreeing tortfeasor defendant or defendants.

(c) No sliding scale recovery agreement is effective unless, at least 72 hours prior to entering into the agreement, a notice of intent to enter into an agreement has been served on all nonsignatory alleged defendant tortfeasors. However, upon a showing of good cause, the court or a judge thereof may allow a shorter time. The failure to comply with the notice requirements of this subdivision shall not constitute good cause to delay commencement of trial. *(Added by Stats.1977, c. 568, § 1. Amended by Stats.1987, c. 1201, § 3; Stats.1987, c. 1202, § 1; Stats. 1990, c. 17, § 1.)*

§ 877.6   Determination of Good Faith of Settlement With One or More Tortfeasors or Co-obligors; Review by Writ of Mandate; Tolling of Time Limitations

(a)(1) Any party to an action wherein it is alleged that two or more parties are joint tortfeasors or co-obligors on a contract debt shall be entitled to a hearing on the issue of the good faith of a settlement entered into by the plaintiff or other claimant and one or more alleged tortfeasors or co-obligors, upon giving notice thereof in the manner provided in subdivision (b) of Section 1005. Upon a showing of good cause, the court may shorten the time for giving the required notice to permit the determination of the issue to be made before the commencement of the trial of the action, or before the verdict or judgment if settlement is made after the trial has commenced.

(2) In the alternative, a settling party may give notice of settlement to all parties and to the court, together with an application for determination of good faith settlement and a proposed order. The application shall indicate the settling parties, and the basis, terms, and amount of the settlement. The notice, application, and proposed order shall be given by certified mail, return receipt requested. Proof of service shall be filed with the court. Within 25 days of the mailing of the notice, application, and proposed order, a nonsettling party may file a notice of motion to contest the good faith of the settlement. If none of the nonsettling parties files a motion within 25 days of mailing of the notice, application, and proposed order, the court may approve the settlement. The notice by a nonsettling party shall be given in the manner provided in subdivision (b) of Section 1005. However, this paragraph shall not apply to settlements in which a confidentiality agreement has been entered into regarding the case or the terms of the settlement.

(b) The issue of the good faith of a settlement may be determined by the court on the basis of affidavits served with the notice of hearing, and any counteraffidavits filed in response thereto, or the court may, in its discretion, receive other evidence at the hearing.

(c) A determination by the court that the settlement was made in good faith shall bar any other joint tortfeasor or co-obligor from any further claims against the settling tortfeasor or co-obligor for equitable comparative contribution, or partial or comparative indemnity, based on comparative negligence or comparative fault.

(d) The party asserting the lack of good faith shall have the burden of proof on that issue.

(e) When a determination of the good faith or lack of good faith of a settlement is made, any party aggrieved by the determination may petition the proper court to review the determination by writ of mandate. The petition for writ of mandate shall be filed within 20 days after service of written notice of the determination, or within such additional time not exceeding 20 days as the trial court may allow.

(1) The court shall, within 30 days of the receipt of all materials to be filed by the parties, determine whether or not the court will hear the writ and notify the parties of its determination.

(2) If the court grants a hearing on the writ, the hearing shall be given special precedence over all other civil matters on the calendar of the court except those matters to which equal or greater precedence on the calendar is granted by law.

(3) The running of any period of time after which an action would be subject to dismissal pursuant to Section 583 shall be tolled during the period of review of a determination pursuant to this subdivision. *(Added by Stats.1980, c. 562, § 1. Amended by Stats.1984, c. 311, § 1; Stats.1985, c. 621, § 2; Stats.1987, c. 677, § 3; Stats.1988, c. 128, § 1; Stats.1989, c. 693, § 5; Stats.1992, c. 876, § 6.)*

TITLE 13. APPEALS IN CIVIL ACTIONS
Chapter 1. Appeals in General

§ 901. Review of Judgment or Order; Authority of Judicial Council

A judgment or order in a civil action or proceeding may be reviewed as prescribed in this title. The Judicial Council shall prescribe rules for the practice and procedure on appeal not inconsistent with the provisions of this title. *(Added by Stats.1968, c. 385, § 2.)*

§ 904.1 Superior Courts; Appealable Judgments and Orders

(a) An appeal may be taken from a superior court in the following cases:

(1) From a judgment, except (A) an interlocutory judgment, other than as provided in paragraphs (8), (9), and (11), (B) a judgment of

contempt which is made final and conclusive by Section 1222, (C) a judgment on appeal from a municipal court or a justice court or a small claims court, or (D) a judgment granting or denying a petition for issuance of a writ of mandamus or prohibition directed to a municipal court or a justice court or the judge or judges thereof which relates to a matter pending in the municipal or justice court. However, an appellate court may, in its discretion, review a judgment granting or denying a petition for issuance of a writ of mandamus or prohibition, or a judgment or order for the payment of monetary sanctions, upon petition for an extraordinary writ.

(2) From an order made after a judgment made appealable by paragraph (1).

(3) From an order granting a motion to quash service of summons or granting a motion to stay or dismiss the action on the ground of inconvenient forum.

(4) From an order granting a new trial or denying a motion for judgment notwithstanding the verdict.

(5) From an order discharging or refusing to discharge an attachment or granting a right to attach order.

(6) From an order granting or dissolving an injunction, or refusing to grant or dissolve an injunction.

(7) From an order appointing a receiver.

(8) From an interlocutory judgment, order, or decree, hereafter made or entered in an action to redeem real or personal property from a mortgage thereof, or a lien thereon, determining the right to redeem and directing an accounting.

(9) From an interlocutory judgment in an action for partition determining the rights and interests of the respective parties and directing partition to be made.

(10) From an order or decree made appealable by the provisions of the Probate Code or the Family Code.

(11) From an interlocutory judgment directing payment of monetary sanctions by a party or an attorney for a party if the amount exceeds five thousand dollars ($5,000).

(12) From an order directing payment of monetary sanctions by a party or an attorney for a party if the amount exceeds five thousand dollars ($5,000).

(b) Sanction orders or judgments of five thousand dollars ($5,000) or less against a party or an attorney for a party may be reviewed on an appeal by that party after entry of final judgment in the main action, or, at the discretion of the court of appeal, may be reviewed upon petition for an extraordinary writ. *(Added by Stats.1968, c. 385, § 2. Amended by Stats.1969, c. 1611, § 21; Stats.1971, c. 1210, § 8; Stats.1978, c. 395, § 1; Stats.1982, c. 931, § 1; Stats.1982, c. 1198, § 63.2; Stats.1983, c. 1159, § 12; Stats.1984, c. 29, § 2; Stats.1988, c. 1447, § 1; Stats.1989, c. 1416, § 25; Stats.1992, c. 163, § 54; Stats.1993, c. 456, § 12.)*

§ 907. Frivolous Appeal; Appeal for Delay; Damages

When it appears to the reviewing court that the appeal was frivolous or taken solely for delay, it may add to the costs on appeal such damages as may be just. *(Added by Stats.1968, c. 385, § 2.)*

§ 909. Factual Determinations on Appeal; Non-jury Cases; Additional Evidence; Giving or Directing Entry of Judgment or Order; Construction of Section

In all cases where trial by jury is not a matter of right or where trial by jury has been waived, the reviewing court may make factual determinations contrary to or in addition to those made by the trial court. The factual determinations may be based on the evidence adduced before the trial court either with or without the taking of evidence by the reviewing court. The reviewing court may for the purpose of making the factual determinations or for any other purpose in the interests of justice, take additional evidence of or concerning facts occurring at any time prior to the decision of the appeal, and may give or direct the entry of any judgment or order and may make any further or other order as the case may require. This section shall be liberally construed to the end among others that, where feasible, causes may be finally disposed of by a single appeal and without further proceedings in the trial court except where in the interests of justice a new trial is required on some or all of the issues. *(Added by Stats.1968, c. 385, § 2. Amended by Stats.1981, c. 900, § 7.)*

Chapter 2.   Stay of Enforcement and Other Proceedings

§ 916. Stay on Perfection of Appeal; Release From Levy; Proceeding Upon Matters Not Affected by Appeal

(a) Except as provided in Sections 917.1 to 917.9, inclusive, and in Section 116.810, the perfecting of an appeal stays proceedings in the trial court upon the judgment or order appealed from or upon the matters embraced therein or affected thereby, including enforcement of the judgment or order, but the trial court may proceed upon any other matter embraced in the action and not affected by the judgment or order.

(b) When there is a stay of proceedings other than the enforcement of the judgment, the trial court shall have jurisdiction of proceedings related to the enforcement of the judgment as well as any other matter embraced in the action and not affected by the judgment or order appealed from. *(Added by Stats.1968, c. 385, § 2. Amended by Stats. 1975, c. 266, § 5; Stats.1982, c. 497, § 64; Stats.1990, c. 1305, § 8.)*

§ 917.1 Appeal From Money Judgment; Undertaking to Stay Enforcement; Subrogation; Costs Awarded by Trial Court

Unless an undertaking is given, the perfecting of an appeal shall not stay enforcement of the judgment or order in the trial court if the judgment or order is for any of the following:

(1) Money or the payment of money, whether consisting of a special fund or not, and whether payable by the appellant or another party to the action.

(2) Costs awarded pursuant to Section 998 which otherwise would not have been awarded as costs pursuant to Section 1033.5.

(3) Costs awarded pursuant to Section 1141.21 which otherwise would not have been awarded as costs pursuant to Section 1033.5.

(b) The undertaking shall be on condition that if the judgment or order or any part of it is affirmed or the appeal is withdrawn or dismissed, the party ordered to pay shall pay the amount of the judgment or order, or the part of it as to which the judgment or order is affirmed, as entered after the receipt of the remittitur, together with any interest which may have accrued pending the appeal and entry of the remittitur, and costs which may be awarded against the appellant on appeal. This section shall not apply in cases where the money to be paid is in the actual or constructive custody of the court; and such cases shall be governed, instead, by the provisions of Section 917.2. The undertaking shall be for double the amount of the judgment or order unless given by an admitted surety insurer in which event it shall be for one and one-half times the amount of the judgment or order. The liability on the undertaking may be enforced if the party ordered to pay does not make the payment within 30 days after the filing of the remittitur from the reviewing court.

(c) If a surety on the undertaking pays the judgment, either with or without action, after the judgment is affirmed, the surety is substituted to the rights of the creditor and is entitled to control, enforce, and satisfy the judgment, in all respects as if the surety had recovered the judgment.

(d) Costs awarded by the trial court under Chapter 6 (commencing with Section 1021) of Title 14 shall be included in the amount of the judgment or order for the purpose of applying paragraph (1) of subdivision (a) and subdivision (b). However, no undertaking shall be required pursuant to this section solely for costs awarded under chapter 6 (commencing with Section 1021) of Title 14. *(Added by Stats.1968, c. 385, § 2. Amended by Stats.1972, c. 546, § 1; Stats.1981, c. 196, § 1; Stats.1982, c. 517, § 155; Stats.1986, c. 1174, § 1; Stats.1993, c. 456, § 13.)*

TITLE 14.   MISCELLANEOUS PROVISIONS
Chapter 2.   Bonds and Undertakings

§ 996.410   Enforcement of Liability; Beneficiary

(a) The beneficiary may enforce the liability on a bond against both the principal and sureties.

(b) If the beneficiary is a class of persons, any person in the class may enforce the liability on a bond in the person's own name, without assignment of the bond. *(Added by Stats.1982, c. 998, § 1.)*

§ 996.420 Surety Submits to Jurisdiction; Application of Section

(a) A surety on a bond given in an action or proceeding submits itself to the jurisdiction of the court in all matters affecting its liability on the bond.

(b) This section does not apply to a bond of a public officer or fiduciary. *(Added by Stats.1982, c. 998, § 1.)*

§ 996.430 Enforcement of Liability; Civil Action; Venue

(a) The liability on a bond may be enforced by civil action. Both the principal and the sureties shall be joined as parties to the action.

(b) If the bond was given in an action or proceeding, the action shall be commenced in the court in which the action or proceeding was pending. If the bond was given other than in an action or proceeding, the action shall be commenced in any court of competent jurisdiction, and the amount of damage claimed in the action, not the amount of the bond, determines the jurisdiction of the court.

(c) A cause of action on a bond may be transferred and assigned as other causes of action. *(Added by Stats.1982, c. 998, § 1.)*

§ 996.440 Bond in Action or Proceeding; Motion to Enforce; Judgment; Trial; Stay

(a) If a bond is given in an action or proceeding, the liability on the bond may be enforced on motion made in the court without the necessity of an independent action.

(b) The motion shall not be made until after entry of the final judgment in the action or proceeding in which the bond is given and the time for appeal has expired or, if an appeal is taken, until the appeal is finally determined. The motion shall not be made or notice of motion served more than one year after the later of the preceding dates.

(c) Notice of motion shall be served on the principal and sureties at least 30 days before the time set for hearing of the motion. The notice shall state the amount of the claim and shall be supported by affidavits setting forth the facts on which the claim is based. The notice and affidavits shall be served in accordance with any procedure authorized by Chapter 5 (commencing with Section 1010).

(d) Judgment shall be entered against the principal and sureties in accordance with the motion unless the principal or sureties serve and file affidavits in opposition to the motion showing such facts as may be deemed by the judge hearing the motion sufficient to present a triable issue of fact. If such a showing is made, the issues to be tried shall be specified by the court. Trial shall be by the court and shall be set for the earliest date convenient to the court, allowing sufficient time for such discovery proceedings as may be requested.

(e) The principal and sureties shall not obtain a stay of the proceedings pending determination of any conflicting claims among beneficiaries. *(Added by Stats.1982, c. 998, § 1.)*

Chapter 3.   Offers by a Party to Compromise

§ 998. Withholding or Augmenting Costs Following Rejection or Acceptance of Offer to Allow Judgment

(a) The costs allowed under Sections 1031 and 1032 shall be withheld or augmented as provided in this section.

(b) Not less than 10 days prior to commencement of trial, any party may serve an offer in writing upon any other party to the action to allow judgment to be taken in accordance with the terms and conditions stated at that time.

(1) If the offer is accepted, the offer with proof of acceptance shall be filed and the clerk or the judge shall enter judgment accordingly.

(2) If the offer is not accepted prior to trial or within 30 days after it is made, whichever occurs first, it shall be deemed withdrawn, and cannot be given in evidence upon the trial.

(3) For purposes of this subdivision, a trial shall be deemed to be actually commenced at the beginning of the opening statement of the plaintiff or counsel, and if there is no opening statement, then at the time of the administering of the oath or affirmation to the first witness, or the introduction of any evidence.

(c) If an offer made by a defendant is not accepted and the plaintiff fails to obtain a more favorable judgment, the plaintiff shall not recover his or her costs and shall pay the defendant's costs from the time of the offer. In addition, in any action or proceeding other than an eminent domain action, the court, in its discretion, may require the plaintiff to pay the defendant's costs from the date of filing of the complaint and a reasonable sum to cover costs of the services of expert witnesses, who are not regular employees of any party, actually incurred and reasonably necessary in either, or both, the preparation or trial of the case by the defendant.

(d) If an offer made by a plaintiff is not accepted and the defendant fails to obtain a more favorable judgment, the court in its discretion may require the defendant to pay a reasonable sum to cover costs of the services of expert witnesses, who are not regular employees of any party, actually incurred and reasonably necessary in either, or both, the preparation or trial of the case by the plaintiff, in addition to plaintiff's costs.

(e) If an offer made by a defendant is not accepted and the plaintiff fails to obtain a more favorable judgment, the costs under this section shall be deducted from any damages awarded in favor of the plaintiff. If the costs awarded under this section exceed the amount of the damages awarded to the plaintiff the net amount shall be awarded to the defendant and judgment shall be entered accordingly.

(f) Police officers shall be deemed to be expert witnesses for the purposes of this section; plaintiff includes a cross-complainant and defendant includes a cross-defendant. Any judgment entered pursuant to this section shall be deemed to be a compromise settlement.

(g) This chapter does not apply to an offer which is made by a plaintiff in an eminent domain action.

(h) The costs for services of expert witnesses for trial under subdivisions (c) and (d) shall not exceed those specified in Section 68092.5 of the Government Code. *(Added by Stats.1971, c. 1679, § 3. Amended by Stats.1977, c. 458, § 1; Stats.1986, c. 540, § 14; Stats.1987, c. 1080, § 8.)*

Chapter 5.   Notices, and Filing and Service of Papers

§ 1010. Notices; Writing; Contents; Supporting Papers; Service; Defaulting Party

Notices must be in writing, and the notice of a motion, other than for a new trial, must state when, and the grounds upon which it will be made, and the papers, if any, upon which it is to be based. If any such paper has not previously been served upon the party to be notified and was not filed by him, a copy of such paper must accompany the notice. Notices and other papers may be served upon the party or attorney in the manner prescribed in this chapter, when not otherwise provided by this code. No bill of exceptions, notice of appeal, or other notice or paper, other than amendments to the pleadings, or an amended pleading, need be served upon any party whose default has been duly entered or who has not appeared in the action or proceeding. *(Enacted 1872. Amended by Stats.1907, c. 327, § 1; Stats.1935, c. 722, § 28.)*

§ 1011. Personal Service; Service Upon Attorney; Service at Party's Residence

The service may be personal, by delivery to the party or attorney on whom the service is required to be made, or it may be as follows:

(a) If upon an attorney, service may be made at the attorney's office, by leaving the notice or other papers in an envelope or package clearly labeled to identify the attorney being served, with a receptionist or with a person having charge thereof. When there is no person in the office with whom the notice or papers may be left for purposes of this subdivision at the time service is to be effected, service may be made by leaving them between the hours of nine in the morning and five in the afternoon, in a conspicuous place in the office, or, if the attorney's office is not open so as to admit of that service, then service may be made by leaving the notice or papers at the attorney's residence, with some person of not less than 18 years of age, if the attorney's residence is in the same county with his or her office, and, if the attorney's residence is not known or is not in the same county with his or her office, or being in the same county it is not open, or there is not found thereat any person of not less than 18 years of age, then service may be made by putting the notice or papers, enclosed in a sealed envelope, into the post office or a mail box, subpost office, substation, or mail chute or other like facility regularly maintained by the Government of the United States directed to the attorney at his or her office, if known and otherwise to the attorney's residence, if known. If neither the attorney's office nor residence is known, service may be made by delivering the notice or papers to the clerk of the court, or to the judge where there is no clerk, for the attorney.

(b) If upon a party, service shall be made in the manner specifically provided in particular cases, or, if no specific provision is made, service may be made by leaving the notice or other paper at the party's residence, between the hours of eight in the morning and six in the evening, with some person of not less than 18 years of age. If at the time of attempted service between those hours a person 18 years of age or older cannot be found at the party's residence, the notice or papers may be served by mail. If the party's residence is not known, then service may be made by delivering the notice or papers to the clerk of the court or the judge, if there is no clerk, for that party. (*Enacted 1872. Amended by Stats.1907, c. 327, § 2; Stats.1919, c. 194, § 1; Stats.1933, c. 744, § 178; Stats.1949, c. 456, § 2; Stats.1951, c. 1737, § 135; Stats.1989, c. 1105, § 8.*)

§ 1014. Appearance Defined; Right to Notices Before and After Appearance

A defendant appears in an action when he answers, demurs, files a notice of motion to strike, files a notice of motion to transfer pursuant to Section 396b, gives the plaintiff written notice of his appearance, or when an attorney gives notice of appearance for him. After appearance, a defendant or his attorney is entitled to notice of all subsequent proceedings of which notice is required to be given. Where a defendant has not appeared, service of notice or papers need not be made upon him. (*Enacted 1872. Amended by Stats.1955, c. 1452, § 8; Stats.1969, c. 345, § 5; Stats.1973, c. 20, § 11.*)

Chapter 6. Of Costs

§ 1021. Attorney's Fees; Determination by Agreement; Right to Costs

Except as attorney's fees are specifically provided for by statute, the measure and mode of compensation of attorneys and counselors at law is left to the agreement, express or implied, of the parties; but parties to actions or proceedings are entitled to their costs, as hereinafter provided. (*Enacted 1872. Amended by Stats.1933, c. 744, § 180; Stats.1986, c. 377, § 2.*)

§ 1021.5 Attorney Fees; Enforcement of Important Rights Affecting Public Interest

Upon motion, a court may award attorney's fees to a successful party against one or more opposing parties in any action which has resulted in the enforcement of an important right affecting the public interest if: (a) a significant benefit, whether pecuniary or nonpecuniary, has been conferred on the general public or a large class of persons, (b) the necessity and financial burden of private enforcement, or of enforcement by one public entity against another public entity, are such as to make the award appropriate, and (c) such fees should not in the interest of justice be paid out of the recovery, if any. With respect to actions involving public entities, this section applies to allowances against, but not in favor of, public entities, and no claim shall be required to be filed therefor, unless one or more successful parties and one or more opposing parties are public entities, in which case no claim shall be required to be filed therefor under Part 3 (commencing with Section 900) of Division 3.6 of Title 1 of the Government Code.

Attorney's fees awarded to a public entity pursuant to this section shall not be increased or decreased by a multiplier based upon extrinsic circumstances, as discussed in Serrano v. Priest, 20 Cal.3d 25, 49. (*Added by Stats.1977, c. 1197, § 1. Amended by Stats.1993, c. 645, § 2.*)

§ 1021.6 Attorneys' Fees; Implied Indemnity; Prevailing Party; Conditions

Upon motion, a court after reviewing the evidence in the principal case may award attorney's fees to a person who prevails on a claim for implied indemnity if the court finds (a) that the indemnitee through the tort of the indemnitor has been required to act in the protection of the indemnitee's interest by bringing an action against or defending an action by a third person and (b) if that indemnitor was properly notified of the demand to bring the action or provide the defense and did not avail itself of the opportunity to do so, and (c) that the trier of fact determined that the indemnitee was without fault in the principal case which is the basis for the action in indemnity or that the indemnitee had a final judgment entered in his or her favor granting a summary judgment, a nonsuit, or a directed verdict. (*Added by Stats.1979, c. 289, § 1. Amended by Stats.1982, c. 1383, § 1.*)

§ 1021.7 Attorney Fees; Actions Against Peace Officers; Actions for Libel or Slander; Award to Defendant Where Action Not Filed in Good Faith

In any action for damages arising out of the performance of a peace officer's duties, brought against a peace officer, as defined in Chapter 4.5 (commencing with Section 830) of Title 3 of Part 2 of the Penal Code, or against a public entity employing a peace officer or in an action for libel or slander brought pursuant to Section 45 or 46 of the Civil Code, the court may, in its discretion, award reasonable attorney's fees to the defendant or defendants as part of the costs, upon a finding by the court that the action was not filed or maintained in good faith and with reasonable cause. (*Added by Stats.1981, c. 980, § 1.*)

§ 1032. Prevailing Party in Any Action or Proceeding; Stipulation to Alternative Procedures

(a) As used in this section, unless the context clearly requires otherwise:

(1) "Complaint" includes a cross-complaint.

(2) "Defendant" includes a cross-defendant or a person against whom a complaint is filed.

(3) "Plaintiff" includes a cross-complainant or a party who files a complaint in intervention.

(4) "Prevailing party" includes the party with a net monetary recovery, a defendant in whose favor a dismissal is entered, a defendant where neither plaintiff nor defendant obtains any relief, and a defendant as against those plaintiffs who do not recover any relief against that defendant. When any party recovers other than monetary relief and in situations other than as specified, the "prevailing party" shall be as determined by the court, and under those circumstances, the court, in its discretion, may allow costs or not and, if allowed may apportion costs between the parties on the same or adverse sides pursuant to rules adopted under Section 1034.

(b) Except as otherwise expressly provided by statute, a prevailing party is entitled as a matter of right to recover costs in any action or proceeding.

(c) Nothing in this section shall prohibit parties from stipulating to alternative procedures for awarding costs in the litigation pursuant to rules adopted under Section 1034. (*Added by Stats.1986, c. 377, § 6.*)

§ 1033.5 Items Allowable

(a) The following items are allowable as costs under Section 1032:

(1) Filing, motion, and jury fees.

(2) Juror food and lodging while they are kept together during trial and after the jury retires for deliberation.

(3) Taking, videotaping, and transcribing necessary depositions including an original and one copy of those taken by the claimant and one copy of depositions taken by the party against whom costs are allowed, and travel expenses to attend depositions.

(4) Service of process by a public officer, registered process server, or other means, as follows:

(A) When service is by a public officer, the recoverable cost is the fee authorized by law at the time of service.

(B) If service is by a process server registered pursuant to Chapter 16 (commencing with Section 22350) of Division 8 of the Business and Professions Code, the recoverable cost is the amount actually incurred in effecting service, including, but not limited to, a stake out or other means employed in locating the person to be served, unless such charges are successfully challenged by a party to the action.

(C) When service is by publication, the recoverable cost is the sum actually incurred in effecting service.

(D) When service is by a means other than that set forth in subparagraph (A), (B) or (C), the recoverable cost is the lesser of the sum actually incurred, or the amount allowed to a public officer in this state for such service, except that the court may allow the sum actually incurred in effecting service upon application pursuant to paragraph (4) of subdivision (c).

(5) Expenses of attachment including keeper's fees.

(6) Premiums on necessary surety bonds.

(7) Ordinary witness fees pursuant to Section 68093 of the Government Code.

(8) Fees of expert witnesses ordered by the court.

(9) Transcripts of court proceedings ordered by the court.

(10) Attorney fees, when authorized by any of the following:

   (A) Contract.

   (B) Statute.

   (C) Law.

(11) Court reporters fees as established by statute.

(12) Models and blowups of exhibits and photocopies of exhibits may be allowed if they were reasonably helpful to aid the trier of fact.

(13) Any other item that is required to be awarded to the prevailing party pursuant to statute as an incident to prevailing in the action at trial or on appeal.

(b) The following items are not allowable as costs, except when expressly authorized by law:

(1) Fees of experts not ordered by the court.

(2) Investigation expenses in preparing the case for trial.

(3) Postage, telephone, and photocopying charges, except for exhibits.

(4) Costs in investigation of jurors or in preparation for voir dire.

(5) Transcripts of court proceedings not ordered by the court.

(c) Any award of costs shall be subject to the following:

(1) Costs are allowable if incurred, whether or not paid.

(2) Allowable costs shall be reasonably necessary to the conduct of the litigation rather than merely convenient or beneficial to its preparation.

(3) Allowable costs shall be reasonable in amount.

(4) Items not mentioned in this section and items assessed upon application may be allowed or denied in the court's discretion.

(5) When any statute of this state refers to the award of "costs and attorney's fees," attorney's fees are an item and component of the costs to be awarded and are allowable as costs pursuant to subparagraph (B) of paragraph (10) of subdivision (a). Any claim not based upon the court's established schedule of attorney's fees for actions on a contract shall bear the burden of proof. Attorney's fees allowable as costs pursuant to subparagraph (B) of paragraph (10) of subdivision (a) may be fixed as follows: (A) upon a noticed motion, (B) at the time a statement of decision is rendered, (C) upon application supported by affidavit made concurrently with a claim for other costs, or (D) upon entry of default judgment. Attorney's fees allowable as costs pursuant to subparagraph (A) or (C) of paragraph (10) of subdivision (a) shall be fixed either upon a noticed motion or upon entry of a default judgment, unless otherwise provided by stipulation of the parties.

Attorney's fees awarded pursuant to Section 1717 of the Civil Code are allowable costs under Section 1032 as authorized by subparagraph (A) of paragraph (10) of subdivision (a). (*Added by Stats.1986, c. 377, § 13. Amended by Stats.1987, c. 1080, § 8.5; Stats.1989, c. 1416, § 26; Stats.1990, c. 804, § 1; Stats.1993, c. 456, § 15.*)

Chapter 7. General Provisions

§ 1048. Consolidation and Severance of Actions

(a) When actions involving a common question of law or fact are pending before the court, it may order a joint hearing or trial of any or all the matters in issue in the actions; it may order all the actions consolidated and it may make such orders concerning proceedings therein as may tend to avoid unnecessary costs or delay.

(b) The court, in furtherance of convenience or to avoid prejudice, or when separate trials will be conducive to expedition and economy, may order a separate trial of any cause of action, including a cause of action asserted in a cross-complaint, or of any separate issue or of any number of causes of action or issues, preserving the right of trial by jury required by the Constitution or a statute of this state or of the United States. (*Enacted 1872. Amended by Stats.1927, c. 320, § 1; Stats.1971, c. 244, § 58.*)

§ 1049. Pending Action Defined

Actions, when deemed pending. An action is deemed to be pending from the time of its commencement until its final determination upon appeal, or until the time for appeal has passed, unless the judgment is sooner satisfied. (*Enacted 1872.*)

Chapter 8. Declaratory Relief

§ 1060. Right of Action; Actual Controversy; Scope; Effect of Declaration

Any person interested under a deed, will or other written instrument, or under a contract, or who desires a declaration of his rights or duties with respect to another, or in respect to, in, over or upon property, or with respect to the location of the natural channel of a watercourse, may, in cases of actual controversy relating to the legal rights and duties of the respective parties, bring an original action or cross-complaint in the superior court or in the municipal or justice court to the extent allowed pursuant to Article 1 (commencing with Section 86) of Chapter 5 of Title 1 of Part 1 for a declaration of his rights and duties in the premises, including a determination of any question of construction or validity arising under such instrument or contract. He may ask for a declaration of rights or duties, either alone or with other relief; and the court may make a binding declaration of such rights or duties, whether or not further relief is or could be claimed at the time. The declaration may be either affirmative or negative in form and effect, and such declaration shall have the force of a final judgment. Such declaration may be had before there has been any breach of the obligation in respect to which said declaration is sought. (*Added by Stats. 1921, c. 463, § 1. Amended by Stats.1965, c. 959, § 2; Stats.1976, c. 1288, § 18; Stats.1993, c. 1262, § 6.*)

PART 3. OF SPECIAL PROCEEDINGS OF A CIVIL NATURE

TITLE 3.   OF SUMMARY PROCEEDINGS

Chapter 2.5. Judicial Arbitration

§ 1141.10 Legislative Findings and Declarations and Intent

(a) The Legislature finds and declares that litigation involving small civil claims has become so costly and complex as to make more difficult the efficient resolution of such civil claims that courts are unable to efficiently resolve the increased number of cases filed each year, and that the resulting delays and expenses deny parties their right to a timely resolution of minor civil disputes. The Legislature further finds and declares that arbitration has proven to be an efficient and equitable method for resolving small claims, and that courts should encourage or require the use of arbitration for such actions whenever possible.

(b) It is the intent of the Legislature that:

(1) Arbitration hearings held pursuant to this chapter shall provide parties with a simplified and economical procedure for obtaining prompt and equitable resolution of their disputes.

(2) Arbitration hearings shall be as informal and private as possible and shall provide the parties themselves maximum opportunity to participate directly in the resolution of their disputes, and shall be held during nonjudicial hours whenever possible.

(3) Members of the State Bar selected to serve as arbitrators should have experience with cases of the type under dispute and are urged to volunteer their services without compensation whenever possible. (*Added by Stats.1978, c. 743, § 2.*)

§ 1141.11   At–Issue Civil Actions in Superior Courts and Municipal Court Districts; Amount in Controversy; Submission to Arbitration; Use of Case Questionnaires

(a) In each superior court with 10 or more judges, all at-issue civil actions pending on or filed after the operative date of this chapter shall be submitted to arbitration, by the presiding judge or the judge designated, under this chapter if the amount in controversy in the opinion of the court will not exceed fifty thousand dollars ($50,000) for each plaintiff, which decision shall not be appealable.

(b) In each superior court with less than 10 judges, the court may provide by local rule, when it determines that it is in the best interests of justice, that all at-issue civil actions pending on or filed after the operative date of this chapter, shall be submitted to arbitration by the presiding judge or the judge designated under this chapter if the amount in controversy in the opinion of the court will not exceed fifty thousand dollars ($50,000) for each plaintiff, which decision shall not be appealable.

(c) In each municipal court district, the municipal court district may provide by local rule, when it is determined to be in the best interests of justice, that all at-issue civil actions pending on or filed after the operative date of this chapter in such judicial district, shall be submitted to arbitration by the presiding judge or the judge designated under this chapter. This section does not apply to any action in small claims court, or to any action maintained pursuant to Section 1781 of the Civil Code or Section 1161 of this code.

(d) In each municipal court district which has adopted judicial arbitration pursuant to subdivision (c), all civil actions pending on or after July 1, 1990, which involve a claim for money damages against a single defendant as a result of a motor vehicle collision, except those heard in the small claims division, shall be submitted to arbitration within 120 days of the filing of the defendant's answer to the complaint (except as may be extended by the court for good cause) before an arbitrator selected by the court, subject to disqualification for cause as specified in Sections 170.1 and 170.6.

The court may provide by local rule for the voluntary or mandatory use of case questionnaires, established under Section 93, in any proceeding subject to these provisions. Where local rules provide for the use of case questionnaires, the questionnaires shall be exchanged by the parties upon the defendant's answer and completed and returned within 60 days.

For the purposes of this subdivision, the term "single defendant" means (1) an individual defendant, whether a person or an entity, (2) two or more persons covered by the same insurance policy applicable to the motor vehicle collision, or (3) two or more persons residing in the same household when no insurance policy exists that is applicable to the motor vehicle collision. The naming of one or more cross-defendants, not a plaintiff, shall constitute a multiple-defendant case not subject to the provisions of this subdivision.

(e) The provisions of this chapter shall not apply to those actions filed in a superior or municipal court which has been selected pursuant to Section 1823.1 and is participating in a pilot project pursuant to Title 1 (commencing with Section 1823) of Part 3.5; provided, however, that any superior or municipal court may provide by local rule that the provisions of this chapter shall apply to actions pending on or filed after July 1, 1979. Any action filed in such court after the conclusion of the pilot project shall be subject to the provisions of this chapter.

(f) No local rule of a superior court providing for judicial arbitration may dispense with the conference required pursuant to Section 1141.16. *(Added by Stats.1978, c. 743, § 2. Amended by Stats.1979, c. 46, § 1; State.1979, c. 948, § 1; Stats.1979, c. 1146, § 2; Stats.1981, c. 1110, § 1; Stats.1982, c. 31, § 1; Stats.1982, c. 921, § 1; Stats.1982, c. 1522, § 2; Stats.1983, c. 978, § 1; Stats.1985, c. 1383, § 3; Stats.1986, c. 287, § 1; Stats.1987, c. 1201, § 4; Stats.1987, c. 1204, § 1; Stats.1989, c. 894, § 1; Stats.1990, c. 1305, § 9.)*

§ 1141.20 Finality of Award; De Novo Trial; Request; Limitation; Calendar

(a) An arbitration award shall be final unless a request for a de novo trial is filed within 30 days after the date the arbitrator files the award with the court.

(b) Any party may elect to have a de novo trial, by court or jury, both as to law and facts. Such trial shall be calendared, insofar as possible, so that the trial shall be given the same place on the active list as it had prior to arbitration, or shall receive civil priority on the next setting calendar. *(Added by Stats.1978, c. 743, § 2. Amended by Stats.1984, c. 1249, § 2.)*

TITLE 5. OF CONTEMPTS

§ 1209. Acts or Omissions Constituting; Stay of Sentence Pending Appeal

(a) The following acts or omissions in respect to a court of justice, or proceedings therein, are contempts of the authority of the court:

1. Disorderly, contemptuous, or insolent behavior toward the judge while holding the court, tending to interrupt the due course of a trial or other judicial proceeding;

2. A breach of the peace, boisterous conduct, or violent disturbance, tending to interrupt the due course of a trial or other judicial proceeding;

3. Misbehavior in office, or other willful neglect or violation of duty by an attorney, counsel, clerk, sheriff, coroner, or other person, appointed or elected to perform a judicial or ministerial service;

4. Abuse of the process or proceedings of the court, or falsely pretending to act under authority of an order or process of the court;

5. Disobedience of any lawful judgment, order, or process of the court;

6. Rescuing any person or property in the custody of an officer by virtue of an order or process of such court;

7. Unlawfully detaining a witness, or party to an action while going to, remaining at, or returning from the court where the action is on the calendar for trial;

8. Any other unlawful interference with the process or proceedings of a court;

9. Disobedience of a subpoena duly served, or refusing to be sworn or answer as a witness;

10. When summoned as a juror in a court, neglecting to attend or serve as such, or improperly conversing with a party to an action, to be tried at such court, or with any other person, in relation to the merits of such action, or receiving a communication from a party or other person in respect to it, without immediately disclosing the same to the court;

11. Disobedience by an inferior tribunal, magistrate, or officer, of the lawful judgment, order, or process of a superior court, or proceeding in an action or special proceeding contrary to law, after such action or special proceeding is removed from the jurisdiction of such inferior tribunal, magistrate, or officer.

(b) No speech or publication reflecting upon or concerning any court or any officer thereof shall be treated or punished as a contempt of such court unless made in the immediate presence of such court while in session and in such a manner as to actually interfere with its proceedings.

(c) Notwithstanding Section 1211 or any other provision of law, if an order of contempt is made affecting an attorney, his agent, investigator, or any person acting under the attorney's direction, in the preparation and conduct of any action or proceeding, the execution of any sentence shall be stayed pending the filing within three judicial days of a petition for extraordinary relief testing the lawfulness of the court's order, the violation of which is the basis of the contempt, except for such conduct as may be proscribed by subdivision (b) of Section 6068 of the Business and Professions Code, relating to an attorney's duty to maintain respect due to the courts and judicial officers.

(d) Notwithstanding Section 1211 or any other provision of law, if an order of contempt is made affecting a public safety employee acting within the scope of employment for reason of the employee's failure to comply with a duly issued subpoena or subpoena duces tecum, the execution of any sentence shall be stayed pending the filing within three judicial days of a petition for extraordinary relief testing the lawfulness of the court's order, a violation of which is the basis for the contempt.

As used in this subdivision, "public safety employee" includes any peace officer, firefighter, paramedic, or any other employee of a public law enforcement agency whose duty is either to maintain official records or to analyze or present evidence for investigative or prosecutorial purposes. (*Enacted 1872. Amended by Stats.1891, c. 9, § 1; Stats.1907, c. 255, § 1; Stats.1939, c. 979, § 1; Stats.1975, c. 836, § 2; Stats.1982, c. 510, § 2.*)

§ 1209.5   Noncompliance With Order for Care or Support of Child

When a court of competent jurisdiction makes an order compelling a parent to furnish support or necessary food, clothing, shelter, medical attendance, or other remedial care for his or her child, proof that the order was made, filed, and served on the parent or proof that the parent was present in court at the time the order was pronounced and proof that the parent did not comply with the order is prima facie evidence of a contempt of court. (*Added by Stats.1955, c. 1359, § 1. Amended by Stats.1961, c. 1307, § 1; Stats.1992, c. 163, § 57.*)

§ 1211.   Summary Punishment; Order; Affidavit or Statement of Facts

When a contempt is committed in the immediate view and presence of the court, or of the judge at chambers, it may be punished summarily; for which an order must be made, reciting the facts as occurring in such immediate view and presence, adjudging that the person proceeded against is thereby guilty of a contempt, and that he be punished as therein prescribed.

When the contempt is not committed in the immediate view and presence of the court, or of the judge at chambers, an affidavit shall be presented to the court or judge of the facts constituting the contempt, or a statement of the facts by the referees or arbitrators, or other judicial officers. (*Enacted 1872. Amended by Stats.1933, c. 745, § 11; Stats. 1951, c. 1737, § 162.*)

§ 1218.   Determination of Guilt; Punishment; Restriction on Enforcement of Order by Party in Contempt

(a) Upon the answer and evidence taken, the court or judge must determine whether the person proceeded against is guilty of the contempt charged, and if it be adjudged that he or she is guilty of the contempt, a fine may be imposed on him or her not exceeding one thousand dollars ($1,000), or he or she may be imprisoned not exceeding five days, or both.

(b) No party, who is in contempt of a court order or judgment in a dissolution of marriage or legal separation action, shall be permitted to enforce such an order or judgment, by way of execution or otherwise, either in the same action or by way of a separate action, against the other party. This restriction shall not affect nor apply to the enforcement of child or spousal support orders.

(c) In any court action in which a party is found in contempt of court for failure to comply with a court order pursuant to the Family Code, or Sections 11350 to 11476.1, inclusive, of the Welfare and Institutions Code, the court shall order the following:

(1) Upon a first finding of contempt, the court shall order the contemner to perform community service of up to 120 hours, in lieu of imprisonment of up to 120 hours, for each count of contempt.

(2) Upon the second finding of contempt, the court shall order the contemner to perform community service of up to 120 hours, in addition to ordering imprisonment of the contemner up to 120 hours or the payment of a fine of up to one thousand dollars ($1,000), or both such imprisonment and fine, for each count of contempt.

(3) Upon the third or any subsequent finding of contempt, the court shall order both of the following:

(A) The court shall order the contemner to serve a term of imprisonment of up to 240 hours, and to pay a fine of one thousand dollars ($1,000) or perform community service of up to 240 hours, or both such fine and community service, for each count of contempt.

(B) The court shall order the contemner to pay an administrative fee, not to exceed the actual cost of the contemner's administration and supervision, while assigned to a community service program pursuant to this paragraph.

(4) The court shall take parties' employment schedules into consideration when ordering either community service or imprisonment, or both. *(Enacted 1872. Amended by Stats.1933, c. 745, § 17; Stats.1951, c. 1737, § 168; Stats.1968, c. 938, § 2; Stats.1977, c. 1257, § 39; Stats.1983, c. 1092, § 72; Stats.1988, c. 969, § 2; Stats.1993, c. 745, § 1; Stats.1993, c. 746, § 1.)*

§ 1219. Imprisonment to Compel Performance of Acts; Exemption of Sexual Assault and Domestic Violence Victims Who Refuse to Testify

(a) Except as provided in subdivisions (b) and (c), when the contempt consists of the omission to perform an act which is yet in the power of the person to perform, he or she may be imprisoned until he or she has performed it, and in that case the act shall be specified in the warrant of commitment.

(b) Notwithstanding any other law, no court may imprison or otherwise confine or place in custody the victim of a sexual assault for contempt when the contempt consists of refusing to testify concerning that sexual assault.

(c) In a finding of contempt for a victim of domestic violence who refuses to testify, the court shall not incarcerate the victim, but may require the victim to attend up to 72 hours of a domestic violence program for victims or require the victim to perform up to 72 hours of appropriate community service, provided that in a subsequent finding of contempt for refusing to testify arising out of the same case, the court shall have the option of incarceration pursuant to subdivision (a).

(d) As used in this section:

(1) "Sexual assault" means any act made punishable by Section 261, 262, 264.1, 285, 286, 288, 288a, or 289 of the Penal Code.

(2) "Domestic violence" means "domestic violence" as defined in Section 6211 of the Family Code. *(Enacted 1872. Amended by Stats. 1980, c. 676, § 68; Stats.1984, c. 1644, § 2; Stats.1991, c. 866, § 4; Stats.1992, c. 163, § 58; Stats.1993, c. 219, § 69.7.)*

TITLE 9.   ARBITRATION
Chapter 2.   Enforcement of Arbitration Agreements

§ 1281. Validity, Enforceability and Irrevocability of Agreements

A written agreement to submit to arbitration an existing controversy or a controversy thereafter arising is valid, enforceable and irrevocable, save upon such grounds as exist for the revocation of any contract. *(Added by Stats.1961, c. 461, § 2.)*

§ 1281.2 Order to Arbitrate Controversy; Petition; Determination of Court

On petition of a party to an arbitration agreement alleging the existence of a written agreement to arbitrate a controversy and that a party thereto refuses to arbitrate such controversy, the court shall order the petitioner and the respondent to arbitrate the controversy if it determines that an agreement to arbitrate the controversy exists, unless it determines that:

(a) The right to compel arbitration has been waived by the petitioner; or

(b) Grounds exist for the revocation of the agreement.

(c) A party to the arbitration agreement is also a party to a pending court action or special proceeding with a third party, arising out of the same transaction or series of related transactions and there is a possibility of conflicting rulings on a common issue of law or fact. For purposes of this section, a pending court action or special proceeding includes an action or proceeding initiated by the party refusing to arbitrate after the petition to compel arbitration has been filed, but on or before the date of the hearing on the petition. This subdivision shall not be applicable to an agreement to arbitrate disputes as to the professional negligence of a health care provider made pursuant to Section 1295.

If the court determines that a written agreement to arbitrate a controversy exists, an order to arbitrate such controversy may not be refused on the ground that the petitioner's contentions lack substantive merit.

If the court determines that there are other issues between the petitioner and the respondent which are not subject to arbitration and which are the subject of a pending action or special proceeding between the petitioner and the respondent and that a determination of such issues may make the arbitration unnecessary, the court may delay its order to arbitrate until the determination of such other issues or until such earlier time as the court specifies.

If the court determines that a party to the arbitration is also a party to litigation in a pending court action or special proceeding with a third party as set forth under subdivision (c) herein, the court (1) may refuse to enforce the arbitration agreement and may order intervention or joinder of all parties in a single action or special proceeding; (2) may order intervention or joinder as to all or only certain issues; (3) may order arbitration among the parties who have agreed to arbitration and stay the pending court action or special proceeding pending the outcome of the arbitration proceeding; or (4) may stay arbitration pending the outcome of the court action or special proceeding. *(Added by Stats.1961, c. 461, § 2. Amended by Stats.1978, c. 260, § 1.)*

§ 1281.4 Stay of Pending Actions or Proceedings

If a court of competent jurisdiction, whether in this State or not, has ordered arbitration of a controversy which is an issue involved in an action or proceeding pending before a court of this State, the court in which such action or proceeding is pending shall, upon motion of a party to such action or proceeding, stay the action or proceeding until an arbitration is had in accordance with the order to arbitrate or until such earlier time as the court specifies.

If an application has been made to a court of competent jurisdiction, whether in this State or not, for an order to arbitrate a controversy which is an issue involved in an action or proceeding pending before a court of this State and such application is undetermined, the court in which such action or proceeding is pending shall, upon motion of a party to such action or proceeding, stay the action or proceeding until the application for an order to arbitrate is determined and, if arbitration of such controversy is ordered, until an arbitration is had in accordance with the order to arbitrate or until such earlier time as the court specifies.

If the issue which is the controversy subject to arbitration is severable, the stay may be with respect to that issue only. *(Added by Stats.1961, c. 461, § 2.)*

TITLE 9.3. ARBITRATION AND CONCILIATION OF INTERNATIONAL COMMERCIAL DISPUTES
Chapter 1. Application and Interpretation

§ 1297.13 International Status of Agreement; Requirements

An arbitration or conciliation agreement is international if any of the following applies:

(a) The parties to an arbitration or conciliation agreement have, at the time of the conclusion of that agreement, their places of business in different states.

(b) One of the following places is situated outside the state in which the parties have their places of business:

(i) The place of arbitration or conciliation if determined in, or pursuant to, the arbitration or conciliation agreement.

(ii) Any place where a substantial part of the obligations of the commercial relationship is to be performed.

(iii) The place with which the subject matter of the dispute is most closely connected.

(c) The parties have expressly agreed that the subject matter of the arbitration or conciliation agreement relates to commercial interests in more than one state.

(d) The subject matter of the arbitration or conciliation agreement is otherwise related to commercial interests in more than one state. *(Added by Stats.1988, c. 23, § 1.)*

TITLE 11.   SISTER STATE AND FOREIGN MONEY—JUDGMENTS
Chapter 1.   Sister State Money—Judgments

§ 1710.10   Definitions

As used in this chapter:

(a) "Judgment creditor" means the person or persons who can bring an action to enforce a sister state judgment.

(b) "Judgment debtor" means the person or persons against whom an action to enforce a sister state judgment can be brought.

(c) "Sister state judgment" means that part of any judgment, decree, or order of a court of a state of the United States, other than California, which requires the payment of money, but does not include a support order as defined in Section 155 of the Family Code. *(Added by Stats.1974, c. 211, § 3.   Amended by Stats.1992, c. 163, § 64.)*

§ 1710.15   Application for Entry;   Statement;   Contents

(a) A judgment creditor may apply for the entry of a judgment based on a sister state judgment by filing an application pursuant to Section 1710.20.

(b) The application shall be executed under oath and shall include all of the following:

(1) A statement that an action in this state on the sister state judgment is not barred by the applicable statute of limitations.

(2) A statement, based on the applicant's information and belief, that no stay of enforcement of the sister state judgment is currently in effect in the sister state.

(3) A statement of the amount remaining unpaid under the sister state judgment and, if accrued interest on the sister state judgment is to be included in the California judgment, a statement of the amount of interest accrued on the sister state judgment (computed at the rate of interest applicable to the judgment under the law of the sister state), a statement of the rate of interest applicable to the judgment under the law of the sister state, and a citation to the law of the sister state establishing the rate of interest.

(4) A statement that no action based on the sister state judgment is currently pending in any court in this state and that no judgment based on the sister state judgment has previously been entered in any proceeding in this state.

(5) Where the judgment debtor is an individual, a statement setting forth the name and last known residence address of the judgment debtor. Where the judgment debtor is a corporation, a statement of the corporation's name, place of incorporation, and whether the corporation, if foreign, has qualified to do business in this state under the provisions of Chapter 21 (commencing with Section 2100) of Division 1 of Title 1 of the Corporations Code. Where the judgment debtor is a partnership, a statement of the name of the partnership, whether it is a foreign partnership, and, if it is a foreign partnership, whether it has filed a statement pursuant to Section 15800 of the Corporations Code designating an agent for service of process. Except for facts which are matters of public record in this state, the statements required by this paragraph may be made on the basis of the judgment creditor's information and belief.

(6) A statement setting forth the name and address of the judgment creditor.

(c) A properly authenticated copy of the sister state judgment shall be attached to the application. (*Added by Stats.1974, c. 211, § 3. Amended by Stats.1977, c. 232, § 1; Stats.1982, c. 150, § 4; Stats.1984, c. 311, § 2; Stats.1985, c. 106, § 11.*)

§ 1710.25   Entry of Judgment; Accrued Interest

(a) Upon the filing of the application, the clerk shall enter a judgment based upon the application for the total of the following amounts as shown therein:

(1) The amount remaining unpaid under the sister state judgment.

(2) The amount of interest accrued on the sister state judgment (computed at the rate of interest applicable to the judgment under the law of the sister state).

(3) The amount of the fee for filing the application for entry of the sister state judgment.

(b) Entry shall be made in the same manner as entry of an original judgment of the court. From the time of entry, interest shall accrue on the judgment so entered at the rate of interest applicable to a judgment entered in this state. (*Added by Stats.1974, c. 211, § 3. Amended by Stats.1977, c. 232, § 2; Stats.1982, c. 150, § 5; Stats.1984, c. 311, § 4.*)

§ 1710.50 Stay of Enforcement

(a) The court shall grant a stay of enforcement where:

(1) An appeal from the sister state judgment is pending or may be taken in the state which originally rendered the judgment. Under this paragraph, enforcement shall be stayed until the proceedings on appeal have been concluded or the time for appeal has expired.

(2) A stay of enforcement of the sister state judgment has been granted in the sister state. Under this paragraph, enforcement shall be stayed until the sister state stay of enforcement expires or is vacated.

(3) The judgment debtor has made a motion to vacate pursuant to Section 1710.40. Under this paragraph, enforcement shall be stayed until the judgment debtor's motion to vacate is determined.

(4) Any other circumstance exists where the interests of justice require a stay of enforcement.

(b) The court may grant a stay of enforcement under this section on its own motion, on ex parte motion, or on noticed motion.

(c) The court shall grant a stay of enforcement under this section on such terms and conditions as are just including but not limited to the following:

(1) The court may require an undertaking in an amount it determines to be just, but the amount of the undertaking shall not exceed double the amount of the judgment creditor's claim.

(2) If a writ of execution has been issued, the court may order that it remain in effect.

(3) If property of the judgment debtor has been levied upon under a writ of execution, the court may order the levying officer to retain possession of the property capable of physical possession and to maintain the levy on other property. (*Added by Stats.1974, c. 211, § 3.*)

§ 1710.55 Restrictions on Entry of Judgment

No judgment based on a sister state judgment may be entered pursuant to this chapter in any of the following cases:

(a) A stay of enforcement of the sister state judgment is currently in effect in the sister state.

(b) An action based on the sister state judgment is currently pending in any court in this state.

(c) A judgment based on the sister state judgment has previously been entered in any proceeding in this state. (*Added by Stats.1974, c. 211, § 3.*)

PART 4. MISCELLANEOUS PROVISIONS
TITLE 2. OF THE KINDS AND DEGREES OF EVIDENCE
Chapter 3. Writings

§ 1908. Judgment or Final Order; Effect; Conclusiveness; Nonparty

(a) The effect of a judgment or final order in an action or special proceeding before a court or judge of this state, or of the United States, having jurisdiction to pronounce the judgment or order, is as follows:

(1) In case of a judgment or order against a specific thing, or in respect to the probate of a will, or the administration of the estate of a decedent, or in respect to the personal, political, or legal condition or relation of a particular person, the judgment or order is conclusive upon the title to the thing, the will, or administration, or the condition or relation of the person.

(2) In other cases, the judgment or order is, in respect to the matter directly adjudged, conclusive between the parties and their successors in interest by title subsequent to the commencement of the action or special proceeding, litigating for the same thing under the same title and in the same capacity, provided they have notice, actual or constructive, of the pendency of the action or proceeding.

(b) A person who is not a party but who controls an action, individually or in cooperation with others, is bound by the adjudications of litigated matters as if he were a party if he has a proprietary or financial interest in the judgment or in the determination of a question of fact or of a question of law with reference to the same subject matter or transaction; if the other party has notice of his participation, the other party is equally bound.

At any time prior to a final judgment, as defined in Section 577, a determination of whether the judgment, verdict upon which it was entered, or a finding upon which it was entered is to be binding upon a nonparty pursuant to this subdivision or whether such nonparty is entitled to the benefit of this subdivision may, on the noticed motion of any party or any nonparty that may be affected by this subdivision, be made in the court in which the action was tried or in which the action is pending on appeal. If no such motion is made before the judgment becomes final, the determination may be made in a separate action. If appropriate, a judgment may be entered or ordered to be entered pursuant to such determination. (*Enacted 1872. Amended by Code Am. 1873–74, c. 383, § 222; Stats.1975, c. 225, § 1.*)

§ 1908.5 Allegation of Conclusive Judgment or Order in Pleadings; Use as Evidence

When a judgment or order of a court is conclusive, the judgment or order must be alleged in the pleadings if there be an opportunity to do so; if there be no such opportunity, the judgment or order may be used as evidence. (*Added by Stats.1965, c. 299, § 74.*)

§ 1909. Judicial Orders; Disputable Presumption

Effect of other judicial orders, when conclusive. Other judicial orders of a Court or Judge of this State, or of the United States, create a disputable presumption, according to the matter directly determined, between the same parties and their representatives and successors in interest by title subsequent to the commencement of the action or special proceeding, litigating for the same thing under the same title and in the same capacity. *(Enacted 1872.)*

§ 1910. Parties; When Deemed to Be the Same

Where parties are to be deemed the same. The parties are deemed to be the same when those between whom the evidence is offered were on opposite sides in the former case, and a judgment or other determination could in that case have been made between them alone, though other parties were joined with both or either. *(Enacted 1872.)*

§ 1911. Judgment; Items Adjudged

What deemed adjudged in a judgment. That only is deemed to have been adjudged in a former judgment which appears upon its face to have been so adjudged, or which was actually and necessarily included therein or necessary thereto. *(Enacted 1872.)*

TITLE 3.   OF THE PRODUCTION OF EVIDENCE
Chapter 2.   Means of Production

§ 1985. Subpoena Defined; Affidavit for Subpoena Duces Tecum; Issuance of Subpoena in Blank

(a) The process by which the attendance of a witness is required is the subpoena. It is a writ or order directed to a person and requiring the person's attendance at a particular time and place to testify as a witness. It may also require a witness to bring with any books, documents, or other things under the witness's control which the witness is bound by law to produce in evidence. When a county recorder is using the microfilm system for recording, and a witness is subpoenaed to present a record, the witness shall be deemed to have complied with the subpoena if the witness produces a certified copy thereof.

(b) A copy of an affidavit shall be served with a subpoena duces tecum issued before trial, showing good cause for the production of the matters and things described in the subpoena, specifying the exact matters or things desired to be produced, setting forth in full detail the materiality thereof to the issues involved in the case, and stating that the witness has the desired matters or things in his or her possession or under his or her control.

(c) The clerk, or a judge, shall issue a subpoena or subpoena duces tecum signed and sealed but otherwise in blank to a party requesting it, who shall fill it in before service. An attorney at law who is the attorney of record in an action or proceeding, may sign and issue a subpoena to require attendance before the court in which the action or proceeding is pending or at the trial of an issue therein, or upon the taking of a deposition in an action or proceeding pending therein; the subpoena in such a case need not be sealed. An attorney at law who is the attorney of record in an action or proceeding, may sign and issue a subpoena duces tecum to require production of the matters or things described in the subpoena. (*Enacted 1872. Amended by Stats.1933, c. 567, § 1; Stats.1961, c. 496, § 1; Stats.1967, c. 431, § 1; Stats.1968, c. 95, § 1; Stats.1979, c. 458, § 1; Stats.1982, c. 452, § 1; Stats.1986, c. 603, § 3; Stats.1990, c. 511, § 1.*)

§ 1986. Subpoena; Obtainable

A subpoena is obtainable as follows:

(a) To require attendance before a court, or at the trial of an issue therein, or upon the taking of a deposition in an action or proceeding pending therein, it is obtainable from the clerk of the court in which the action or proceeding is pending, or if there is no clerk then from a judge or justice of such court.

(b) To require attendance before a commissioner appointed to take testimony by a court of a foreign country, or of the United States, or of any other state in the United States, or before any officer or officers empowered by the laws of the United States to take testimony, it may be obtained from the clerk of the superior court of the county in which the witness is to be examined.

(c) To require attendance out of court, in cases not provided for in subdivision (a), before a judge, justice, or other officer authorized to administer oaths or take testimony in any matter under the laws of this state, it is obtainable from the judge, justice, or other officer before whom the attendance is required.

If the subpoena is to require attendance before a court, or at the trial of an issue therein, it is obtainable from the clerk, as of course, upon the application of the party desiring it. If it is obtained to require attendance before a commissioner or other officer upon the taking of a deposition, it must be obtained, as of course, from the clerk of the superior court of the county wherein the attendance is required upon the application of the party requiring it. (*Enacted 1872. Amended by Stats.1907, c. 391, § 1; Stats.1929, c. 110, § 1; Stats.1957, c. 1904, § 2; Stats.1979, c. 458, § 2.*)

§ 1989. Residency Requirements for Attendance of Witnesses

A witness, including a witness specified in subdivision (b) of Section 1987, is not obliged to attend as a witness before any court, judge, justice or any other officer, unless the witness is a resident within the state at the time of service. (*Enacted 1872. Amended by Stats.1915, c. 162, § 1; Stats.1935, c. 257, § 1; Stats.1957, c. 1560, § 1; Stats.1980, c. 591, § 1; Stats.1981, c. 184, § 3.*)

§ 1991. Disobedience to Subpoena; Refusal to Be Sworn, to Answer as Witness, or to Subscribe Affidavit or Deposition; Contempt; Report of Disobedience

Disobedience to a subpoena, or a refusal to be sworn, or to answer as a witness, or to subscribe an affidavit or deposition when required, may be punished as a contempt by the court issuing the subpoena.

When the subpoena, in any such case, requires the attendance of the witness before an officer or commissioner out of court, it is the duty of the officer or commissioner to report any disobedience or refusal to be sworn or to answer a question or to subscribe an affidavit or deposition when required, to the court issuing the subpoena. The witness shall not be punished for any refusal to be sworn or to answer a question or to subscribe an affidavit or deposition, unless, after a hearing upon notice, the court orders the witness to be sworn, or to so answer or subscribe and then only for disobedience to the order.

Any judge, justice, or other officer mentioned in subdivision (c) of Section 1986, may report any disobedience or refusal to be sworn or to answer a question or to subscribe an affidavit or deposition when required to the superior court of the county in which attendance was required; and the court thereupon has power, upon notice, to order the witness to perform the omitted act, and any refusal or neglect to comply with the order may be punished as a contempt of court.

In lieu of the reporting of the refusal as hereinabove provided, the party seeking to obtain the deposition or to have the deposition or affidavit signed, at the time of the refusal may request the officer or commissioner to notify the witness that at a time stated, not less than five days nor more than 20 days from the date of the refusal, he or she will report the refusal of the witness to the court and that the party will, at that time, or as soon thereafter as he or she may be heard, apply to the court for an order directing the witness to be sworn, or to answer as a witness, or subscribe the deposition or affidavit, as the case may be, and that the witness is required to attend that session of the court.

The officer or commissioner shall enter in the record of the proceedings an exact transcription of the request made of him or her that he or she notify the witness that the party will apply for an order directing the witness to be sworn or to answer as a witness or subscribe the deposition or affidavit, and of his or her notice to the witness, and the transcription shall be attached to his or her report to the court of the refusal of the witness. The report shall be filed by the officer with the clerk of the court issuing the subpoena, and the witness shall attend that session of the court, and for failure or refusal to do so may be punished for contempt.

At the time so specified by the officer, or at a subsequent time to which the court may have continued the matter, if the officer has theretofore filed a report showing the refusal of the witness, the court shall hear the matter, and without further notice to the witness, may order the witness to be sworn or to answer as a witness or subscribe the deposition or affidavit, as the case may be, and may in the order specify the time and place at which compliance shall be made or to which the taking of the deposition is continued. Thereafter if the witness refuses to comply with the order he or she may be punished for contempt. (*Enacted 1872. Amended by Stats.1907, c. 391, § 2; Stats.1941, c. 406, § 1; Stats.1987, c. 56, § 24.*)

§ 1991.1 Depositions; Disobedience to Subpoena or Refusal to Be Sworn; Punishment

Disobedience to a subpoena requiring attendance of a witness before an officer out of court in a deposition taken pursuant to Article 3, Chapter 3, Title 3, Part 4 (commencing at Section 2016), or refusal to be sworn as a witness at such deposition, may be punished as contempt, as provided in Section 2034, without the necessity of a prior order of court directing compliance by the witness. (*Added by Stats.1959, c. 1590, § 13.*)

§ 1992. Disobedience to Subpoena; Forfeiture; Damages

A witness disobeying a subpoena also forfeits to the party aggrieved the sum of five hundred dollars ($500), and all damages which he may sustain by the failure of the witness to attend, which forfeiture and damages may be recovered in a civil action. (*Enacted 1872. Amended by Stats.1978, c. 479, § 1.*)

Chapter 3.   Manner of Production

§ 2015.5 Certification or Declaration Under Penalty of Perjury

Whenever, under any law of this state or under any rule, regulation, order or requirement made pursuant to the law of this state, any matter is required or permitted to be supported, evidenced, established, or proved by the sworn statement, declaration, verification, certificate, oath, or affidavit, in writing of the person making the same (other than a deposition, or an oath of office, or an oath required to be taken before a specified official other than a notary public), such matter may with like force and effect be supported, evidenced, established or proved by the unsworn statement, declaration, verification, or certificate, in writing of such person which recites that it is certified or declared by him or her to be true under penalty of perjury, is subscribed by him or her, and (1), if executed within this state, states the date and place of execution, or (2), if executed at any place, within or without this state, states the date of execution and that is so certified or declared under the laws of the State of California. The certification or declaration may be in substantially the following form:

(a) If executed within this state:

"I certify (or declare) under penalty of perjury that the foregoing is true and correct":

_____   _____
(Date and Place)   (Signature)

(b) If executed at any place, within or without this state:

"I certify (or declare) under penalty of perjury under the laws of the State of California that the foregoing is true and correct":

_____   _____
(Date)   (Signature)

(Added by Stats.1957, c. 1612, § 1. Amended by Stats.1961, c. 495, § 1; Stats.1963, c. 2080, § 1; Stats.1975, c. 666, § 1; Stats.1980, c. 889, § 1.)

§ 2017. Pending Actions; Scope of Discovery; Sanctions

(a) Unless otherwise limited by order of the court in accordance with this article, any party may obtain discovery regarding any matter, not privileged, that is relevant to the subject matter involved in the pending action or to the determination of any motion made in that action, if the matter either is itself admissible in evidence or appears reasonably calculated to lead to the discovery of admissible evidence. Discovery may relate to the claim or defense of the party seeking discovery or of any other party to the action. Discovery may relate to the claim or defense of the party seeking discovery or of any other party to the action. Discovery may be obtained of the identity and location of persons having knowledge of any discoverable matter, as well as of the existence, description, nature, custody, condition, and location of any document, tangible thing, or land or other property.

(b) A party may obtain discovery of the existence and contents of any agreement under which any insurance carrier may be liable to satisfy in whole or in part a judgment that may be entered in the action or to indemnify or reimburse for payments made to satisfy the judgment. This discovery may include the identity of the carrier and the nature and limits of the coverage. A party may also obtain discovery as to whether that insurance carrier is disputing the agreement's coverage of the claim involved in the action, but not as to the nature and substance of that dispute. Information concerning the insurance agreement is not by reason of disclosure admissible in evidence at trial.

(c) The court shall limit the scope of discovery if it determines that the burden, expense, or intrusiveness of that discovery clearly outweighs the likelihood that the information sought will lead to the discovery of admissible evidence. The court may make this determination pursuant to a motion for protective order by a party or other affected person. This motion shall be accompanied by a declaration stating facts showing a good faith attempt at an informal resolution of each issue presented by the motion.

The court shall impose a monetary sanction under Section 2023 against any party, person, or attorney who unsuccessfully makes or opposes a motion for a protective order, unless it finds that the one subject to the sanction acted with substantial justification or that other circumstances make the imposition of the sanction unjust.

(d) In any civil action, alleging conduct that constitutes sexual harassment, sexual assault, or sexual battery, any party seeking discovery concerning the plaintiff's sexual conduct with individuals other than the alleged perpetrator is required to establish specific facts showing good cause for that discovery, and that the matter sought to be discovered is relevant to the subject matter of the action and reasonably calculated to lead to the discovery of admissible evidence. This showing shall be made by noticed motion and shall not be made or considered by the court at an ex parte hearing. This motion shall be accompanied by a declaration stating facts showing a good faith attempt at an informal resolution of each issue presented by the motion.

The court shall impose a monetary sanction under Section 2023 against any party, person, or attorney who unsuccessfully makes or opposes a motion for discovery, unless it finds that the one subject to the sanction acted with substantial justification or that other circumstances make the imposition of the sanction unjust. (*Added by Stats.1986, c. 1334, § 2. Amended by Stats.1987, c. 86, § 2; Stats.1988, c. 160, § 19; Stats.1988, c. 553, § 1.*)

§ 2018. Attorneys' Work Products

(a) It is the policy of the state to: (1) preserve the rights of attorneys to prepare cases for trial with that degree of privacy necessary to encourage them to prepare their cases thoroughly and to investigate not only the favorable but the unfavorable aspects of those cases; and (2) to prevent attorneys from taking undue advantage of their adversary's industry and efforts.

(b) Subject to subdivision (c), the work product of an attorney is not discoverable unless the court determines that denial of discovery will unfairly prejudice the party seeking discovery in preparing that party's claim or defense or will result in an injustice.

(c) Any writing that reflects an attorney's impressions, conclusions, opinions, or legal research or theories shall not be discoverable under any circumstances.

(d) This section is intended to be a restatement of existing law relating to protection of work product. It is not intended to expand or reduce the extent to which work product is discoverable under existing law in any action.

(e) The State Bar may discover the work product of an attorney against whom disciplinary charges are pending when it is relevant to issues of breach of duty by the lawyer, subject to applicable client approval and to a protective order, where requested and for good cause, to ensure the confidentiality of work product except for its use by the State Bar in disciplinary investigations and its consideration under seal in State Bar Court proceedings. For purposes of this section, whenever a client has initiated a complaint against an attorney, the requisite client approval shall be deemed to have been granted.

(f) In an action between an attorney and his or her client or former client, no work product privilege under this section exists if the work product is relevant to an issue of breach by the attorney of a duty to the attorney's client arising out of the attorney-client relationship.

For purposes of this section, "client" means a client as defined in Section 951 of the Evidence Code. (*Added by Stats.1987, c. 86, § 3.5. Amended by Stats.1988, c. 1159, § 34; Stats.1990, c. 207, § 1.*)

§ 2019. Methods of Discovery; Restriction on Frequency or Extent; Actions Regarding Trade Secrets; Service by Mail

(a) Any party may obtain discovery by one or more of the following methods:

(1) Oral and written depositions.

(2) Interrogatories to a party.

(3) Inspections of documents, things, and places.

(4) Physical and mental examinations.

(5) Requests for admissions.

(6) Simultaneous exchanges of expert trial witness information.

(b) The court shall restrict the frequency or extent of use of these discovery methods if it determines either of the following:

(1) The discovery sought is unreasonably cumulative or duplicative, or is obtainable from some other source that is more convenient, less burdensome, or less expensive.

(2) The selected method of discovery is unduly burdensome or expensive, taking into account the needs of the case, the amount in controversy, and the importance of the issues at stake in the litigation.

The court may make those determinations pursuant to a motion for a protective order by a party or other affected person. This motion shall be accompanied by a declaration stating facts showing a good faith attempt at an informal resolution of each issue presented by the motion.

The court shall impose a monetary sanction under Section 2023 against any party, person, or attorney who unsuccessfully makes or opposes a motion for a protective order, unless it finds that the one subject to the sanction acted with substantial justification or that other circumstances make the imposition of the sanction unjust.

(c) Unless there is a rule of the Judicial Council, or a local court rule or local uniform written policy to the contrary, the methods of discovery may be used in any sequence, and the fact that a party is conducting discovery, whether by deposition or another method, shall not operate to delay the discovery of any other party. However, on motion and for good cause shown, the court may establish the sequence and timing of discovery for the convenience of parties and witnesses and in the interests of justice.

(d) In any action alleging the misappropriation of a trade secret under the Uniform Trade Secrets Act (Title 5 (commencing with Section 3426) of Part 1 of Division 4 of the Civil Code), before commencing discovery relating to the trade secret, the party alleging the misappropriation shall identify the trade secret with reasonable particularity subject to any orders that may be appropriate under Section 3426.5 of the Civil Code.

(e) The provisions of subdivision (a) of Section 1013 relating to extensions of time where service is made by mail shall be applicable to any discovery method or motion in this article. *(Added by Stats.1986, c. 1334, § 2. Amended by Stats.1987, c. 86, § 4; Stats.1988, c. 553, § 2.)*

§ 2020. Nonparty Discovery; Deposition Subpoena

(a) The method for obtaining discovery within the state from one who is not a party to the action is an oral deposition under Section 2025, a written deposition under Section 2028, or a deposition for production of business records and things under subdivisions (d) and (e). Except as provided in paragraph (1) of subdivision (h) of Section 2025, the process by which a nonparty is required to provide discovery is a deposition subpoena. The deposition subpoena may command any of the following:

(1) Only the attendance and the testimony of the deponent, under subdivision (c).

(2) Only the production of business records for copying, under subdivision (d).

(3) Both the attendance and the testimony of the deponent, as well as the production of business records, other documents, and tangible things, under subdivision (e).

Except as modified in this section, the provisions of Chapter 2 (commencing with Section 1985), and of Article 4 (commencing with Section 1560) of Chapter 2 of Division 11 of the Evidence Code, apply to a deposition subpoena.

(b) The clerk of the court in which the action is pending shall issue a deposition subpoena signed and sealed, but otherwise in blank, to a party requesting it, who shall fill it in before service. In lieu of the court-issued deposition subpoena, an attorney of record for any party may sign and issue a deposition subpoena; the deposition subpoena in that case need not be sealed.

(c) A deposition subpoena that commands only the attendance and the testimony of the deponent shall specify the time when and the place where the deponent is commanded to attend for the deposition. It shall set forth a summary of (1) the nature of a deposition, (2) the rights and duties of the deponent, and (3) the penalties for disobedience of a deposition subpoena described in subdivision (h). If the deposition will be recorded by video tape under paragraph (2) of subdivision (*l*) of Section 2025, the deposition subpoena shall state that it will be recorded in that manner. If the deponent is an organization, the deposition subpoena shall describe with reasonable particularity the matters on which examination is requested, and shall advise that organization of its duty to make the designation of employees or agents who will attend described in subdivision (d) of Section 2025.

(d)(1) A deposition subpoena that commands only the production of business records for copying shall designate the business records to be produced either by specifically describing each individual item or by reasonably particularizing each category of item. This deposition subpoena need not be accompanied by an affidavit or declaration showing good cause for the production of the business records designated in it. It shall be directed to the custodian of those records or another person qualified to certify the records. It shall command compliance in accordance with paragraph (4) on a date that is no earlier than 20 days after the issuance, or 15 days after the service, of the deposition subpoena, whichever date is later.

(2) If, under Section 1985.3, the one to whom the deposition subpoena is directed is a witness, and the business records described in the deposition subpoena are personal records pertaining to a consumer, the service of the deposition subpoena shall be accompanied either by a copy of the proof of service of the notice to the consumer described in subdivision (e) of Section 1985.3, or by the consumer's written authorization to release personal records described in paragraph (2) of subdivision (c) of Section 1985.3.

(3) The officer for a deposition seeking discovery only of business records for copying under this subdivision shall be a professional photocopier registered under Chapter 20 (commencing with Section 22450) of Division 8 of the Business and Professions Code, or a person exempted from the registration requirements of that chapter under Section 22451 of the Business and Professions Code. This deposition officer shall not be financially interested in the action, or a relative or employee of any attorney of the parties. Any objection to the qualifications of the deposition officer is waived unless made before the date of production or as soon thereafter as the ground for that objection becomes known or could be discovered by reasonable diligence.

(4) Unless directed to make the records available for inspection or copying by the subpoenaing party's attorney or a representative of that attorney at the witness' business address under subdivision (e) of Section 1560 of the Evidence Code, the custodian of the records or other qualified person shall, in person, by messenger, or by mail, deliver only to the deposition officer specified in the deposition subpoena (1) a true, legible, and durable copy of the records, and (2) an affidavit in compliance with Section 1561 of the Evidence Code. If this delivery is made to the office of the deposi-

tion officer, the records shall be enclosed, sealed, and directed as described in subdivision (c) of Section 1560 of the Evidence Code. If this delivery is made at the office of the business whose records are the subject of the deposition subpoena, the custodian of those records or other qualified person shall (1) permit the deposition officer specified in the deposition subpoena to make a copy of the originals of the designated business records, or (2) deliver to that deposition officer a true, legible, and durable copy of the records on receipt of payment in cash or by check, by or on behalf of the party serving the deposition subpoena, of the reasonable costs of preparing that copy as determined under subdivision (b) of Section 1563 of the Evidence Code. This copy need not be delivered in a sealed envelope. Unless the parties, and if the records are those of a consumer as defined in Section 1985.3, the consumer, stipulate to an earlier date, the custodian of the records shall not deliver to the deposition officer the records that are the subject of the deposition subpoena prior to the date and time specified in the deposition subpoena. The following legend shall appear in boldface type on the deposition subpoena immediately following the date and time specified for production: "Do not release the requested records to the deposition officer prior to the date and time stated above."

(5) Promptly on or after the deposition date and after the receipt or the making of a copy of business records under this subdivision, the deposition officer shall provide that copy to the party at whose instance the deposition subpoena was served, and a copy of those records to any other party to the action who then or subsequently notifies the deposition officer that the party desires to purchase a copy of those records.

(6) The provisions of Section 1562 of the Evidence Code concerning the admissibility of the affidavit of the custodian or other qualified person apply to a deposition subpoena served under this subdivision.

(e) A deposition subpoena that commands both the attendance and the testimony of the deponent, as well as the production of business records, documents, and tangible things, shall (1) comply with the requirements of subdivision (c), (2) designate the business records, documents, and tangible things to be produced either by specifically describing each individual item or by reasonably particularizing each category of item, and (3) specify any testing or sampling that is being sought. This deposition subpoena need not be accompanied by an affidavit or declaration showing good cause for the production of the documents and things designated.

Where, as described in Section 1985.3, the person to whom the deposition subpoena is directed is a witness, and the business records described in the deposition subpoena are personal records pertaining to a consumer, the service of the deposition subpoena shall be accompanied either by a copy of the proof of service of the notice to the consumer described in subdivision (e) of Section 1985.3, or by the consumer's written authorization to release personal records described in paragraph (2) of subdivision (c) of Section 1985.3.

(f) Subject to paragraph (1) of subdivision (d), service of a deposition subpoena shall be effected a sufficient time in advance of the deposition to provide the deponent a reasonable opportunity to locate and produce any designated business records, documents, and tangible things, and, where personal attendance is commanded, a reasonable time to travel to the place of deposition. Any person may serve the subpoena by personal delivery of a copy of it (1) if the deponent is a natural person, to that person, and (2) if the deponent is an organization, to any officer, director, custodian of records, or to any agent or employee authorized by the organization to accept service of a subpoena.

If a deposition subpoena requires the personal attendance of the deponent, under subdivision (c) or (e), the party noticing the deposition shall pay to the deponent in cash or by check the same witness fee and mileage required by Chapter 1 (commencing with Section 68070) of Title 8 of the Government Code for attendance and testimony before the court in which the action is pending. This payment, whether or not demanded by the deponent, shall be made, at the option of the party noticing the deposition, either at the time of service of the deposition subpoena, or at the time the deponent attends for the taking of testimony.

Service of a deposition subpoena that does not require the personal attendance of a custodian of records or other qualified person, under subdivision (d), shall be accompanied, whether or not demanded by the deponent, by a payment in cash or by check of the witness fee required by paragraph (6) of subdivision (b) of Section 1563 of the Evidence Code.

(g) Personal service of any deposition subpoena is effective to require of any deponent who is a resident of California at the time of service (1) personal attendance and testimony, if the subpoena so specifies, (2) any specified production, inspection, testing, and sampling, and (3) the deponent's attendance at a court session to consider any issue arising out of the deponent's refusal to be sworn, or to answer any question, or to produce specified items, or to permit inspection or specified testing and sampling of the items produced.

(h) A deponent who disobeys a deposition subpoena in any manner described in subdivision (g) may be punished for contempt under Section 2023 without the necessity of a prior order of court directing compliance by the witness, and is subject to the forfeiture and the payment of damages set forth in Section 1992. *(Added by Stats.1986, c. 1334, § 2. Amended by Stats.1987, c. 86, § 5; Stats.1992, c. 876, § 9; Stats.1993, c. 926, § 8.)*

§ 2021. Written Stipulations Regarding Depositions and Discovery

Unless the court orders otherwise, the parties may by written stipulation (a) provide that depositions may be taken before any person, at any time or place, on any notice, and in any manner, and when so taken may be used like other depositions, and (b) modify the procedures provided by this article for other methods of discovery. *(Added by Stats.1986, c. 1334, § 2.)*

§ 2023. Abuses of Discovery; Sanctions

(a) Misuses of the discovery process include, but are not limited to, the following:

(1) Persisting, over objection and without substantial justification, in an attempt to obtain information or materials that are outside the scope of permissible discovery.

(2) Using a discovery method in a manner that does not comply with its specified procedures.

(3) Employing a discovery method in a manner or to an extent that causes unwarranted annoyance, embarrassment, or oppression, or undue burden and expense.

(4) Failing to respond or to submit to an authorized method of discovery.

(5) Making, without substantial justification, an unmeritorious objection to discovery.

(6) Making an evasive response to discovery.

(7) Disobeying a court order to provide discovery.

(8) Making or opposing, unsuccessfully and without substantial justification, a motion to compel or to limit discovery.

(9) Failing to confer in person, by telephone, or by letter with an opposing party or attorney in a reasonable and good faith attempt to resolve informally any dispute concerning discovery, if the section governing a particular discovery motion requires the filing of a declaration stating facts showing that such an attempt has been made. Notwithstanding the outcome of the particular discovery motion, the court shall impose a monetary sanction ordering that any party or attorney who fails to confer as required pay the reasonable expenses, including attorney's fees, incurred by anyone as a result of that conduct.

(b) To the extent authorized by the section governing any particular discovery method or any other provision of this article, the court, after notice to any affected party, person, or attorney, and after opportunity for hearing, may impose the following sanctions against anyone engaging in conduct that is a misuse of the discovery process.

(1) The court may impose a monetary sanction ordering that one engaging in the misuse of the discovery process, or any attorney advising that conduct, or both pay the reasonable expenses, including attorney's fees, incurred by anyone as a result of that conduct. The court may also impose this sanction on one unsuccessfully asserting that another has engaged in the misuse of the discovery

process, or on any attorney who advised that assertion, or on both. If a monetary sanction is authorized by any provision of this article, the court shall impose that sanction unless it finds that the one subject to the sanction acted with substantial justification or that other circumstances make the imposition of the sanction unjust.

(2) The court may impose an issue sanction ordering that designated facts shall be taken as established in the action in accordance with the claim of the party adversely affected by the misuse of the discovery process. The court may also impose an issue sanction by an order prohibiting any party engaging in the misuse of the discovery process from supporting or opposing designated claims or defenses.

(3) The court may impose an evidence sanction by an order prohibiting any party engaging in the misuse of the discovery process from introducing designated matters in evidence.

(4) The court may impose a terminating sanction by one of the following orders:

(A) An order striking out the pleadings or parts of the pleadings of any party engaging in the misuse of the discovery process.

(B) An order staying further proceedings by that party until an order for discovery is obeyed.

(C) An order dismissing the action, or any part of the action, of that party.

(D) An order rendering a judgment by default against that party.

(5) The court may impose a contempt sanction by an order treating the misuse of the discovery process as a contempt of court.

(c) A request for a sanction shall, in the notice of motion, identify every person, party, and attorney against whom the sanction is sought, and specify the type of sanction sought. The notice of motion shall be supported by a memorandum of points and authorities, and accompanied by a declaration setting forth facts supporting the amount of any monetary sanction sought. *(Added by Stats.1986, c. 1334, § 2. Amended by Stats.1987, c. 86, § 6.)*

§ 2024. Time for Completion of Discovery

(a) Except as otherwise provided in this section, any party shall be entitled as a matter of right to complete discovery proceedings on or before the 30th day, and to have motions concerning discovery heard on or before the 15th day, before the date initially set for the trial of the action. As used in this section, discovery is considered completed on the day a response is due or on the day a deposition begins. Except as provided in subdivision (e), a continuance or postponement of the trial date does not operate to reopen discovery proceedings.

(b) The time limit on completing discovery in an action to be arbitrated under Chapter 2.5 (commencing with Section 1141.10) of Title 3 of Part 3 is subject to Judicial Council Rule. After an award in a case ordered to judicial arbitration, completion of discovery is limited by Section 1141.24.

(c) This section does not apply to (1) summary proceedings for obtaining possession of real property governed by Chapter 4 (commencing with Section 1159) of Title 3 of Part 3, in which discovery shall be completed on or before the fifth day before the date set for trial except as provided in subdivisions (e) and (f), or (2) eminent domain proceedings governed by Title 7 (commencing with Section 1230.010) of Part 3.

(d) Any party shall be entitled as a matter of right to complete discovery proceedings pertaining to a witness identified under Section 2034 on or before the 15th day, and to have motions concerning that discovery heard on or before the 10th day, before the date initially set for the trial of the action.

(e) On motion of any party, the court may grant leave to complete discovery proceedings, or to have a motion concerning discovery heard, closer to the initial trial date, or to reopen discovery after a new trial date has been set. This motion shall be accompanied by a declaration stating facts showing a reasonable and good faith attempt at an informal resolution of each issue presented by the motion.

In exercising its discretion to grant or deny this motion, the court shall take into consideration any matter relevant to the leave requested, including, but not limited to, the following:

(1) The necessity and the reasons for the discovery.

(2) The diligence or lack of diligence of the party seeking the discovery or the hearing of a discovery motion, and the reasons that the discovery was not completed or that the discovery motion was not heard earlier.

(3) Any likelihood that permitting the discovery or hearing the discovery motion will prevent the case from going to trial on the date set, or otherwise interfere with the trial calendar, or result in prejudice to any other party.

(4) The length of time that has elapsed between any date previously set, and the date presently set, for the trial of the action.

The court shall impose a monetary sanction under Section 2023 against any party, person, or attorney who unsuccessfully makes or opposes a motion to extend or to reopen discovery, unless it finds that the one subject to the sanction acted with substantial justification or that other circumstances make the imposition of the sanction unjust.

(f) Parties to the action may, with the consent of any party affected by it, enter into an agreement to extend the time for the completion of discovery proceedings or for the hearing of motions concerning discovery, or to reopen discovery after a new date for trial of the action has been set. This agreement may be informal, but it shall be confirmed in a writing that specifies the extended date. In no event shall this agreement require a court to grant a continuance or postponement of the trial of the action. *(Added by Stats.1986, c. 1334, § 2. Amended by Stats. 1987, c. 86, § 7; Stats.1991, c. 1090, § 9.5.)*

§ 2025. Oral Depositions; Protective Orders; Sanctions; Audio or Video Tapes; Stenographic Transcripts; Use of Deposition at Trial or Hearing

(a) Parties; person deposed. Any party may obtain discovery within the scope delimited by Section 2017, and subject to the restrictions set forth in Section 2019, by taking in California the oral deposition of any person, including any party to the action. The person deposed may be a natural person, an organization such as a public or private corporation, a partnership, an association, or a governmental agency.

(b) Notice; time. Subject to subdivisions (f) and (t), an oral deposition may be taken as follows:

(1) The defendant may serve a deposition notice without leave of court at any time after that defendant has been served or has appeared in the action, whichever occurs first.

(2) The plaintiff may serve a deposition notice without leave of court on any date that is 20 days after the service of the summons on, or appearance by, any defendant. However, on motion with or without notice, the court, for good cause shown, may grant to a plaintiff leave to serve a deposition notice on an earlier date.

(c) Notice; service. A party desiring to take the oral deposition of any person shall give notice in writing in the manner set forth in subdivision (d). However, where under subdivision (d) of Section 2020 only the production by a nonparty of business records for copying is desired, a copy of the deposition subpoena shall serve as the notice of deposition. The notice of deposition shall be given to every other party who has appeared in the action. The deposition notice, or the accompanying proof of service, shall list all the parties or attorneys for parties on whom it is served.

Where, as defined in subdivision (a) of Section 1985.3, the party giving notice of the deposition is a subpoenaing party, and the deponent is a witness commanded by a deposition subpoena to produce personal records of a consumer, the subpoenaing party shall serve on that consumer (1) a notice of the deposition, (2) the notice of privacy rights specified in subdivision (e) of Section 1985.3, and (3) a copy of the deposition subpoena.

(d) Notice; contents; deponent not natural person; subpoena; service. The deposition notice shall state all of the following:

(1) The address where the deposition will be taken.

(2) The date of the deposition, selected under subdivision (f), and the time it will commence.

(3) The name of each deponent, and the address and telephone number, if known, of any deponent who is not a party to the action. If the name of the deponent is not known, the deposition notice shall set forth instead a general description sufficient to identify the person or particular class to which the person belongs.

(4) The specification with reasonable particularity of any materials or category of materials to be produced by the deponent.

(5) Any intention to record the testimony by audio tape or video tape, in addition to recording the testimony by the stenographic method as required by paragraph (1) of subdivision (*l*).

(6) Any intention to reserve the right to use at trial a video tape deposition of a treating or consulting physician or of any expert witness under paragraph (4) of subdivision (u). In this event, the operator of the video tape camera shall be a person who is authorized to administer an oath, and shall not be financially interested in the action or be a relative or employee of any attorney of any of the parties.

If the deponent named is not a natural person, the deposition notice shall describe with reasonable particularity the matters on which examination is requested. In that event, the deponent shall designate and produce at the deposition those of its officers, directors, managing agents, employees, or agents who are most qualified to testify on its behalf as to those matters to the extent of any information known or reasonably available to the deponent. A deposition subpoena shall advise a nonparty deponent of its duty to make this designation, and shall describe with reasonable particularity the matters on which examination is requested.

If the attendance of the deponent is to be compelled by service of a deposition subpoena under Section 2020, an identical copy of that subpoena shall be served with the deposition notice.

(e) Place. (1) The deposition of a natural person, whether or not a party to the action, shall be taken at a place that is, at the option of the party giving notice of the deposition, either within 75 miles of the deponent's residence, or within the county where the action is pending and within 150 miles of the deponent's residence, unless the court orders otherwise under paragraph (3).

(2) The deposition of an organization that is a party to the action shall be taken at a place that is, at the option of the party giving notice of the deposition, either within 75 miles of the organization's principal executive or business office in California, or within the county where the action is pending and within 150 miles of that office. The deposition of any other organization shall be taken within 75 miles of the organization's principal executive or business office in California, unless the organization consents to a more

distant place. If the organization has not designated a principal executive or business office in California, the deposition shall be taken at a place that is, at the option of the party giving notice of the deposition, either within the county where the action is pending, or within 75 miles of any executive or business office in California of the organization.

(3) A party desiring to take the deposition of a natural person who is a party to the action or an officer, director, managing agent, or employee of a party may make a motion for an order that the deponent attend for deposition at a place that is more distant than that permitted under paragraph (1). This motion shall be accompanied by a declaration stating facts showing a reasonable and good faith attempt at an informal resolution of any issue presented by the motion.

In exercising its discretion to grant or deny this motion, the court shall take into consideration any factor tending to show whether the interests of justice will be served by requiring the deponent's attendance at that more distant place, including, but not limited to, the following:

(A) Whether the moving party selected the forum.

(B) Whether the deponent will be present to testify at the trial of the action.

(C) The convenience of the deponent.

(D) The feasibility of conducting the deposition by written questions under Section 2028, or of using a discovery method other than a deposition.

(E) The number of depositions sought to be taken at a place more distant than that permitted under paragraph (1).

(F) The expense to the parties of requiring the deposition to be taken within the distance permitted under paragraph (1).

(G) The whereabouts of the deponent at the time for which the deposition is scheduled.

The order may be conditioned on the advancement by the moving party of the reasonable expenses and costs to the deponent for travel to the place of deposition.

The court shall impose a monetary sanction under Section 2023 against any party, person, or attorney who unsuccessfully makes or opposes a motion to increase travel limits for party-deponent, unless it finds that the one subject to the sanction acted with substantial justification or that other circumstances make the imposition of the sanction unjust.

(f) Time. An oral deposition shall be scheduled for a date at least 10 days after service of the deposition notice. If, as defined in subdivision (a) of Section 1985.3, the party giving notice of the deposition is a subpoenaing party, and the deponent is a witness commanded by a deposition subpoena to produce personal records of a consumer, the deposition shall be scheduled for a date at least 20 days after issuance of that subpoena. However, in unlawful detainer actions, an oral deposition shall be scheduled for a date at least five days after service of the deposition notice, but not later than five days before trial.

On motion or ex parte application of any party or deponent, for good cause shown, the court may shorten or extend the time for scheduling a deposition, or may stay its taking until the determination of a motion for a protective order under subdivision (i).

(g) Notice; error; waiver; objection; stay. Any party served with a deposition notice that does not comply with subdivisions (b) to (f), inclusive, waives any error or irregularity unless that party promptly serves a written objection specifying that error or irregularity at least three calendar days prior to the date for which the deposition is scheduled, on the party seeking to take the deposition and any other attorney or party on whom the deposition notice was served. If an objection is made three calendar days before the deposition date, the objecting party shall make personal service of that objection pursuant to Section 1011 on the party who gave notice of the deposition. Any deposition taken after the service of a written objection shall not be used against the objecting party under subdivision (u) if the party did not attend the deposition and if the court determines that the objection was a valid one.

In addition to serving this written objection, a party may also move for an order staying the taking of the deposition and quashing the deposition notice. This motion shall be accompanied by a declaration stating facts showing a reasonable and good faith attempt at an informal resolution of any issue presented by the motion. The taking of the deposition is stayed pending the determination of this motion.

The court shall impose a monetary sanction under Section 2023 against any party, person, or attorney who unsuccessfully makes or opposes a motion to quash a deposition notice, unless it finds that the one subject to the sanction acted with substantial justification or that other circumstances make the imposition of the sanction unjust.

(h) Attendance; notice; subpoena. (1) The service of a deposition notice under subdivision (c) is effective to require any deponent who is a party to the action or an officer, director, managing agent, or employee of a party to attend and to testify, as well as to produce any document or tangible thing for inspection and copying.

(2) The attendance and testimony of any other deponent, as well as the production by the deponent of any document or tangible thing for inspection and copying, requires the service on the deponent of a deposition subpoena under Section 2020.

(i) Protective order. Before, during, or after a deposition, any party, any deponent, or any other affected natural person or organization may promptly move for a protective order. The motion shall be accompanied by a declaration stating facts showing a reasonable and good faith attempt at an informal resolution of each issue presented by the motion.

The court, for good cause shown, may make any order that justice requires to protect any party, deponent, or other natural person or organization from unwarranted annoyance, embarrassment, or oppression, or undue burden and expense. This protective order may include, but is not limited to, one or more of the following directions:

(1) That the deposition not be taken at all.

(2) That the deposition be taken at a different time.

(3) That a video tape deposition of a treating or consulting physician or of any expert witness, intended for possible use at trial under paragraph (4) of subdivision (u), be postponed until the moving party has had an adequate opportunity to prepare, by discovery deposition of the deponent, or other means, for cross-examination.

(4) That the deposition be taken at a place other than that specified in the deposition notice, if it is within a distance permitted by subdivision (e).

(5) That the deposition be taken only on certain specified terms and conditions.

(6) That the deponent's testimony be taken by written, instead of oral, examination.

(7) That the method of discovery be interrogatories to a party instead of an oral deposition.

(8) That the testimony be recorded in a manner different from that specified in the deposition notice.

(9) That certain matters not be inquired into.

(10) That the scope of the examination be limited to certain matters.

(11) That all or certain of the writings or tangible things designated in the deposition notice not be produced, inspected, or copied.

(12) That designated persons, other than the parties to the action and their officers and counsel, be excluded from attending the deposition.

(13) That a trade secret or other confidential research, development, or commercial information not be disclosed or be disclosed only to specified persons or only in a specified way.

(14) That the parties simultaneously file specified documents enclosed in sealed envelopes to be opened as directed by the court.

(15) That the deposition be sealed and thereafter opened only on order of the court.

If the motion for a protective order is denied in whole or in part, the court may order that the deponent provide or permit the discovery against which protection was sought on those terms and conditions that are just.

The court shall impose a monetary sanction under Section 2023 against any party, person, or attorney who unsuccessfully makes or opposes a motion for a protective order, unless it finds that the one subject to the sanction acted with substantial justification or that other circumstances make the imposition of the sanction unjust.

(j) Failure to attend or proceed. (1) If the party giving notice of a deposition fails to attend or proceed with it, the court shall impose a monetary sanction under Section 2023 against that party, or the attorney for that party, or both, and in favor of any party attending in person or by attorney, unless it finds that the one subject to the sanction acted with substantial justification or that other circumstances make the imposition of the sanction unjust.

(2) If a deponent does not appear for a deposition because the party giving notice of the deposition failed to serve a required deposition subpoena, the court shall impose a monetary sanction under Section 2023 against that party, or the attorney for that party, or both, in favor of any other party who, in person or by attorney, attended at the time and place specified in the deposition notice in the expectation that the deponent's testimony would be taken, unless the court finds that the one subject to the sanction acted with substantial justification or that other circumstances make the imposition of the sanction unjust.

If a deponent on whom a deposition subpoena has been served fails to attend a deposition or refuses to be sworn as a witness, the court may impose on the deponent the sanctions described in subdivision (h) of Section 2020.

(3) If, after service of a deposition notice, a party to the action or an officer, director, managing agent, or employee of a party, or a person designated by an organization that is a party under subdivision (d), without having served a valid objection under subdivision (g), fails to appear for examination, or to proceed with it, or to produce for inspection any document or tangible thing described in the deposition notice, the party giving the notice may move for an order compelling the deponent's attendance and testimony, and the production for inspection of any document or tangible thing described in the deposition notice. This motion (A) shall set forth specific facts showing good cause justifying the production for inspection of any document or tangible thing described in the deposition notice, and (B) shall be accompanied by a declaration stating facts showing a reasonable and good faith attempt at an informal resolution of each issue presented by it. If this motion is granted, the court shall also impose a monetary sanction under Section 2023 against the deponent or the party with whom the deponent is

affiliated, unless it finds that the one subject to the sanction acted with substantial justification or that other circumstances make the imposition of the sanction unjust. On motion of any other party who, in person or by attorney, attended at the time and place specified in the deposition notice in the expectation that the deponent's testimony would be taken, the court shall also impose a monetary sanction under Section 2023, unless it finds that the one subject to the sanction acted with substantial justification or that other circumstances make the imposition of the sanction unjust.

If that party or party-affiliated deponent then fails to obey an order compelling attendance, testimony, and production, the court may make those orders that are just, including the imposition of an issue sanction, an evidence sanction, or a terminating sanction under Section 2023 against that party deponent or against the party with whom the deponent is affiliated. In lieu of or in addition to this sanction, the court may impose a monetary sanction under Section 2023 against that deponent or against the party with whom that party deponent is affiliated, and in favor of any party who, in person or by attorney, attended in the expectation that the deponent's testimony would be taken pursuant to that order.

(k) Supervising officer. Except as provided in paragraph (3) of subdivision (d) of Section 2020, the deposition shall be conducted under the supervision of an officer who is authorized to administer an oath. This officer shall not be financially interested in the action and shall not be a relative or employee of any attorney of any of the parties. Any objection to the qualifications of the deposition officer is waived unless made before the deposition begins or as soon thereafter as the ground for that objection becomes known or could be discovered by reasonable diligence.

(*l*) Oath; audio or video tape; written questions. (1) The deposition officer shall put the deponent under oath. Unless the parties agree or the court orders otherwise, the testimony, as well as any stated objections, shall be taken stenographically. The party noticing the deposition may also record the testimony by audio tape or video tape if the notice of deposition stated an intention also to record the testimony by either of those methods, or if all the parties agree that the testimony may also be recorded by either of those methods. Any other party, at that party's expense, may make a simultaneous audio tape or video tape record of the deposition, provided that other party promptly, and in no event less than three calendar days before the date for which the deposition is scheduled, serves a written notice of this intention to audio tape or video tape the deposition testimony on the party or attorney who noticed the deposition, on all other parties or attorneys on whom the deposition notice was served under subdivision (c), and on any deponent whose attendance is being compelled by a deposition subpoena under Section 2020. If this notice is given three calendar days before the deposition date, it shall be made by personal service under Section

1011. Examination and cross-examination of the deponent shall proceed as permitted at trial under the provisions of the Evidence Code.

(2) If the deposition is being recorded by means of audio tape or video tape, the following procedure shall be observed:

(A) The area used for recording the deponent's oral testimony shall be suitably large, adequately lighted, and reasonably quiet.

(B) The operator of the recording equipment shall be competent to set up, operate, and monitor the equipment in the manner prescribed in this subdivision. The operator may be an employee of the attorney taking the deposition unless the operator is also the deposition officer. However, if a video tape of deposition testimony is to be used under paragraph (4) of subdivision (u), the operator of the recording equipment shall be a person who is authorized to administer an oath, and shall not be financially interested in the action or be a relative or employee of any attorney of any of the parties, unless all parties attending the deposition agree on the record to waive these qualifications and restrictions.

(C) The operator shall not distort the appearance or the demeanor of participants in the deposition by the use of camera or sound recording techniques.

(D) The deposition shall begin with an oral or written statement on camera or on the audio tape that includes the operator's name and business address, the name and business address of the operator's employer, the date, time, and place of the deposition, the caption of the case, the name of the deponent, a specification of the party on whose behalf the deposition is being taken, and any stipulations by the parties.

(E) Counsel for the parties shall identify themselves on camera or on the audio tape.

(F) The oath shall be administered to the deponent on camera or on the audio tape.

(G) If the length of a deposition requires the use of more than one unit of tape, the end of each unit and the beginning of each succeeding unit shall be announced on camera or on the audio tape.

(H) At the conclusion of a deposition, a statement shall be made on camera or on the audio tape that the deposition is ended and shall set forth any stipulations made by counsel concerning the custody of the audio tape or video tape recording and the exhibits, or concerning other pertinent matters.

(I) A party intending to offer an audio taped or video taped recording of a deposition in evidence under subdivision (u) shall notify the court and all parties in writing of that intent and of the parts of the deposition to be offered within sufficient time for objections to be made and ruled on by the judge to whom the case is assigned for trial or hearing, and for any editing of the tape. Objections to all or part of the deposition shall be made in writing. The court may permit further designations of testimony and objections as justice may require. With respect to those portions of an audio taped or video taped deposition that are not designated by any party or that are ruled to be objectionable, the court may order that the party offering the recording of the deposition at the trial or hearing suppress those portions, or that an edited version of the deposition tape be prepared for use at the trial or hearing. The original audio tape or video tape of the deposition shall be preserved unaltered. If no stenographic record of the deposition testimony has previously been made, the party offering a video tape or an audio tape recording of that testimony under subdivision (u) shall accompany that offer with a stenographic transcript prepared from that recording.

(3) In lieu of participating in the oral examination, parties may transmit written questions in a sealed envelope to the party taking the deposition for delivery to the deposition officer, who shall unseal the envelope and propound them to the deponent after the oral examination has been completed.

(m) Objections; privileged information; attorney work product; unanswered question; unproduced document or thing. (1) The protection of information from discovery on the ground that it is privileged or that it is protected work product under Section 2018 is waived unless a specific objection to its disclosure is timely made during the deposition.

(2) Errors and irregularities of any kind occurring at the oral examination that might be cured if promptly presented are waived unless a specific objection to them is timely made during the deposition. These errors and irregularities include, but are not limited to, those relating to the manner of taking the deposition, to the oath or affirmation administered, to the conduct of a party, attorney, deponent, or deposition officer, or to the form of any question or answer. Unless the objecting party demands that the taking of the deposition be suspended to permit a motion for a protective order under subdivision (n), the deposition shall proceed subject to the objection.

(3) Objections to the competency of the deponent, or to the relevancy, materiality, or admissibility at trial of the testimony or of the materials produced are unnecessary and are not waived by failure to make them before or during the deposition.

(4) If a deponent fails to answer any question or to produce any document or tangible thing under the deponent's control that is

specified in the deposition notice or a deposition subpoena, the party seeking that answer or production may adjourn the deposition or complete the examination on other matters without waiving the right at a later time to move for an order compelling that answer or production under subdivision (o).

(n) Misconduct; suspended testimony; protective order. On demand of any party or the deponent, the deposition officer shall suspend the taking of testimony to enable that party or deponent to move for a protective order on the ground that the examination is being conducted in bad faith or in a manner that unreasonably annoys, embarrasses, or oppresses that deponent or party. This motion shall be accompanied by a declaration stating facts showing a reasonable and good faith attempt at an informal resolution of each issue presented by the motion. The court, for good cause shown, may terminate the examination or may limit the scope and manner of taking the deposition as provided in subdivision (i). If the order terminates the examination, the deposition shall not thereafter be resumed, except on order of the court.

The court shall impose a monetary sanction under Section 2023 against any party, person, or attorney who unsuccessfully makes or opposes a motion for this protective order, unless it finds that the one subject to the sanction acted with substantial justification or that other circumstances make the imposition of the sanction unjust.

(o) Compelling answer or production. If a deponent fails to answer any question or to produce any document or tangible thing under the deponent's control that is specified in the deposition notice or a deposition subpoena, the party seeking discovery may move the court for an order compelling that answer or production. This motion shall be made no later than 60 days after the completion of the record of the deposition, and shall be accompanied by a declaration stating facts showing a reasonable and good faith attempt at an informal resolution of each issue presented by the motion. Notice of this motion shall be given to all parties, and to the deponent either orally at the examination, or by subsequent service in writing. If the notice of the motion is given orally, the deposition officer shall direct the deponent to attend a session of the court at the time specified in the notice. Not less than five days prior to the hearing on this motion, the moving party shall lodge with the court a certified copy of any parts of the stenographic transcript of the deposition that are relevant to the motion. If a deposition is recorded by audio tape or video tape, the moving party is required to lodge a certified copy of a transcript of any parts of the deposition that are relevant to the motion. If the court determines that the answer or production sought is subject to discovery, it shall order that the answer be given or the production be made on the resumption of the deposition.

The court shall impose a monetary sanction under Section 2023 against any party, person, or attorney who unsuccessfully makes or opposes a motion to compel answer or production, unless it finds that the one subject to the sanction acted with substantial justification or that other circumstances make the imposition of the sanction unjust.

If a deponent fails to obey an order entered under this subdivision, the failure may be considered a contempt of court. In addition, if the disobedient deponent is a party to the action or an officer, director, managing agent, or employee of a party, the court may make those orders that are just against the disobedient party, or against the party with whom the disobedient deponent is affiliated, including the imposition of an issue sanction, an evidence sanction, or a terminating sanction under Section 2023. In lieu of or in addition to this sanction, the court may impose a monetary sanction under Section 2023 against that party deponent or against any party with whom the deponent is affiliated.

(p) Transcript; copies; audio or video tape; official record. Unless the parties agree otherwise, the testimony at any deposition recorded by stenographic means shall be transcribed. The party noticing the deposition shall bear the cost of that transcription, unless the court, on motion and for good cause shown, orders that the cost be borne or shared by another party. Any other party, at that party's expense, may obtain a copy of the transcript. At the request of any other party to the action, including a party who did not attend the taking of the deposition testimony, any party who records or causes the recording of that testimony by means of audio tape or video tape shall promptly (1) permit that other party to hear the audio tape or to view the video tape, and (2) furnish a copy of the audio tape or video tape to that other party on receipt of payment of the reasonable cost of making that copy of the tape.

If the testimony at the deposition is recorded both stenographically, and by audio tape or video tape, the stenographic transcript is the official record of that testimony for the purpose of the trial and any subsequent hearing or appeal.

(q) Transcript; change; approval. (1) If the deposition testimony is stenographically recorded, the deposition officer shall send written notice to the deponent and to all parties attending the deposition when the original transcript of the testimony for each session of the deposition is available for reading, correcting, and signing, unless the deponent and the attending parties agree on the record that the reading, correcting, and signing of the transcript of the testimony will be waived or that the reading, correcting, and signing of a transcript of the testimony will take place after the entire deposition has been concluded or at some other specific time. For 30 days following each such notice, unless the attending parties and the deponent agree on the record or otherwise in writing to a longer or shorter time period, the deponent may change the form or the substance of the answer to an [sic] question, and may either approve the transcript of the deposition by signing it, or refuse to approve the transcript by not signing it.

Alternatively, within this same period, the deponent may change the form or the substance of the answer to any question and may approve or refuse to approve the transcript by means of a letter to the deposition officer signed by the deponent which is mailed by certified or registered mail with return receipt requested. A copy of that letter shall be sent by first-class mail to all parties attending the deposition. For good cause shown, the court may shorten the 30-day period for making changes, approving, or refusing to approve the transcript.

The deposition officer shall indicate on the original of the transcript, if the deponent has not already done so at the office of the deposition officer, any action taken by the deponent and indicate on the original of the transcript, the deponent's approval of, or failure or refusal to approve, the transcript. The deposition officer shall also notify in writing the parties attending the deposition of any changes which the deponent timely made in person. If the deponent fails or refuses to approve the transcript within the allotted period, the deposition shall be given the same effect as though it had been approved, subject to any changes timely made by the deponent. However, on a reasonable motion to suppress the deposition, accompanied by a declaration stating facts showing a reasonable and good faith attempt at an informal resolution of each issue presented by the motion, the court may determine that the reasons given for the failure or refusal to approve the transcript require rejection of the deposition in whole or in part.

The court shall impose a monetary sanction under Section 2023 against any party, person, or attorney who unsuccessfully makes or opposes a motion to suppress a deposition, unless it finds that the one subject to the sanction acted with substantial justification or that other circumstances make the imposition of the sanction unjust.

(2) If there is no stenographic transcription of the deposition, the deposition officer shall send written notice to the deponent and to all parties attending the deposition that the recording is available for review, unless the deponent and all these parties agree on the record to waive the hearing or viewing of an audio tape or video tape recording of the testimony. For 30 days following this notice the deponent, either in person or by signed letter to the deposition officer, may change the substance of the answer to any question.

The deposition officer shall set forth in a writing to accompany the recording any changes made by the deponent, as well as either the deponent's signature identifying the deposition as his or her own, or a statement of the deponent's failure to supply such signature, or to contact the officer within the allotted period. When a deponent fails to contact the officer within the allotted period, or expressly refuses by a signature to identify the deposition as his or her own, the deposition shall be given the same effect as though signed. However, on a seasonable motion to suppress the deposition, accompanied by a declaration stating facts showing a reasonable and good faith attempt at an informal resolution of each issue presented by the motion, the court may determine that the reasons given for the refusal to sign require rejection of the deposition in whole or in part.

The court shall impose a monetary sanction under Section 2023 against any party, person, or attorney who unsuccessfully makes or opposes a motion to suppress a deposition, unless it finds that the one subject to the sanction acted with substantial justification or that other circumstances make the imposition of the sanction unjust.

(r) Transcript; certification. The deposition officer shall certify on the transcript of the deposition, or in the writing accompanying an audio taped or video taped deposition as described in paragraph (2) of subdivision (q), that the deponent was duly sworn and that the transcript or recording is a true record of the testimony given and of any changes made by the deponent.

(s) Transcript; custody; destruction. (1) The certified transcript of a deposition shall not be filed with the court. Instead, the deposition officer shall securely seal that transcript in an envelope or package endorsed with the title of the action and marked: "Deposition of (here insert name of deponent)", and shall promptly transmit it to the attorney for the party who noticed the deposition. This attorney shall store it under conditions that will protect it against loss, destruction, or tampering.

The attorney to whom the transcript of a deposition is transmitted shall retain custody of it until six months after final disposition of the action. At that time, the transcript may be destroyed, unless the court, on motion of any party and for good cause shown, orders that the transcript be preserved for a longer period.

(2) An audio tape or video tape record of deposition testimony, including a certified tape made by an operator qualified under subparagraph (B) of paragraph (2) of subdivision (*l*), shall not be filed with the court. Instead, the operator shall retain custody of that record and shall store it under conditions that will protect it against loss, destruction, or tampering, and preserve as far as practicable the quality of the tape and the integrity of the testimony and images it contains.

At the request of any party to the action, including a party who did not attend the taking of the deposition testimony, or at the request of the deponent, that operator shall promptly (A) permit the one making the request to hear or to view the tape on receipt of payment of a reasonable charge for providing the facilities for hearing or viewing the tape, and (B) furnish a copy of the audio tape or the video tape recording to the one making the request on receipt of payment of the reasonable cost of making that copy of the tape.

The attorney or operator who has custody of an audio tape or video tape record of deposition testimony shall retain custody of it until six months after final disposition of the action. At that time, the audio tape or video tape may be destroyed or erased, unless the court, on motion of any party and for good cause shown, orders that the tape be preserved for a longer period.

(t) Subsequent deposition. Once any party has taken the deposition of any natural person, including that of a party to the action, neither the party who gave, nor any other party who has been served with a deposition notice pursuant to subdivision (c) may take a subsequent deposition of that deponent. However, for good cause shown, the court may grant leave to take a subsequent deposition, and the parties, with the consent of any deponent who is not a party, may stipulate that a subsequent deposition be taken. This subdivision does not preclude taking one subsequent deposition of a natural person who has previously been examined as a result of that person's designation to testify on behalf of an organization under subdivision (d).

(u) Use. At the trial or any other hearing in the action, any part or all of a deposition may be used against any party who was present or represented at the taking of the deposition, or who had due notice of the deposition and did not serve a valid objection under subdivision (g), so far as admissible under the rules of evidence applied as though the deponent were then present and testifying as a witness, in accordance with the following provisions:

(1) Any party may use a deposition for the purpose of contradicting or impeaching the testimony of the deponent as a witness, or for any other purpose permitted by the Evidence Code.

(2) An adverse party may use for any purpose, a deposition of a party to the action, or of anyone who at the time of taking the deposition was an officer, director, managing agent, employee, agent, or designee under subdivision (d) of a party. It is not ground for objection to the use of a deposition of a party under this paragraph by an adverse party that the deponent is available to testify, has testified, or will testify at the trial or other hearing.

(3) Any party may use for any purpose the deposition of any person or organization, including that of any party to the action, if the court finds any of the following:

(A) The deponent resides more than 150 miles from the place of the trial or other hearing.

(B) The deponent, without the procurement or wrongdoing of the proponent of the deposition for the purpose of preventing testimony in open court, is (i) exempted or precluded on the ground of privilege from testifying concerning the matter to which the deponent's testimony is relevant, (ii) disqualified from testifying, (iii) dead or unable to attend or testify because of existing physical or mental illness or infirmity, (iv) absent from the trial or other hearing and the court is unable to compel the deponent's attendance by its process, or (v) absent from the trial or other hearing and the proponent of the deposition has exercised reasonable diligence but has been unable to procure the deponent's attendance by the court's process.

(C) Exceptional circumstances exist that make it desirable to allow the use of any deposition in the interests of justice and with due regard to the importance of presenting the testimony of witnesses orally in open court.

(4) Any party may use a video tape deposition of a treating or consulting physician or of any expert witness even though the deponent is available to testify if the deposition notice under subdivision (d) reserved the right to use the deposition at trial, and if that party has complied with subparagraph (I) of paragraph (2) of subdivision (*l*).

(5) Subject to the requirements of this section, a party may offer in evidence all or any part of a deposition, and if the party introduces only part of the deposition, any other party may introduce any other parts that are relevant to the parts introduced.

(6) Substitution of parties does not affect the right to use depositions previously taken.

(7) When an action has been brought in any court of the United States or of any state, and another action involving the same subject matter is subsequently brought between the same parties or their representatives or successors in interest, all depositions lawfully taken and duly filed in the initial action may be used in the subsequent action as if originally taken in that subsequent action. A deposition previously taken may also be used as permitted by the Evidence Code. *(Added by Stats.1986, c. 1334, § 2. Amended by Stats.1987, c. 86, § 8; Stats.1988, c. 553, § 13; Stats.1989, c. 1137, § 1; Stats.1989, c. 1360, § 13; Stats.1989, c. 1416, § 29.5; Stats. 1990, c. 1491, § 11.5; Stats.1991, c. 1090, § 10; Stats.1993, c. 926, § 9.)*

§ 2028. Deposition by Written Questions

(a) **Procedures applicable.** Any party may obtain discovery by taking a deposition by written questions instead of by oral examination. Except as modified in this section, the procedures for taking oral depositions set forth in Sections 2025, 2026, and 2027 apply to written depositions.

(b) **Notice of taking.** The notice of a written deposition shall comply with subdivision (d) of Section 2025, except that (1) the name or descriptive title, as well as the address, of the deposition officer shall be stated, and (2) the date, time, and place for commencement of the deposition may be left to future determination by the deposition officer.

(c) Service of deposition, notice and questions; cross, redirect, and recross questions. The questions to be propounded to the deponent by direct examination shall accompany the notice of a written deposition.

Within 30 days after the deposition notice and questions are served, a party shall serve any cross questions on all other parties entitled to notice of the deposition.

Within 15 days after being served with cross questions, a party shall serve any redirect questions on all other parties entitled to notice of the deposition.

Within 15 days after being served with redirect questions, a party shall serve any recross questions on all other parties entitled to notice of the deposition.

The court may, for good cause shown, extend or shorten the time periods for the interchange of cross, redirect, and recross questions.

(d) Objections; service; motion and declaration of attempted informal resolution; waiver; sanctions. (1) A party who objects to the form of any question shall serve a specific objection to that question on all parties entitled to notice of the deposition within 15 days after service of the question. A party who fails to timely serve an objection to the form of a question waives it. The objecting party shall promptly move the court to sustain the objection. This motion shall be accompanied by a declaration stating facts showing a reasonable and good faith attempt at an informal resolution of each issue presented by the objection and motion. Unless the court has sustained that objection, the deposition officer shall propound to the deponent that question subject to that objection as to its form.

The court shall impose a monetary sanction under Section 2023 against any party, person, or attorney who unsuccessfully makes or opposes a motion to sustain an objection, unless it finds that the one subject to the sanction acted with substantial justification or that other circumstances make the imposition of the sanction unjust.

(2) A party who objects to any question on the ground that it calls for information that is privileged or is protected work product under Section 2018 shall serve a specific objection to that question on all parties entitled to notice of the deposition within 15 days after service of the question. A party who fails to timely serve that objection waives it. The party propounding any question to which an objection is made on those grounds may then move the court for an order overruling that objection. This motion shall be accompanied by a declaration stating facts constituting a reasonable and good faith attempt at an informal resolution of each issue presented by the objection and motion. The deposition officer shall not propound to the deponent any question to which a written objection on those grounds has been served unless the court has overruled that objection.

The court shall impose a monetary sanction under Section 2023 against any party, person, or attorney who unsuccessfully makes or opposes a motion to overrule an objection, unless it finds that the one subject to the sanction acted with substantial justification or that other circumstances make the imposition of the sanction unjust.

(e) Questions on direct examination; copy for prior study by deponent. The party taking a written deposition may forward to the deponent a copy of the questions on direct examination for study prior to the deposition. No party or attorney shall permit the deponent to preview the form or the substance of any cross, redirect, or recross questions.

(f) Orders for protection of parties and deponents. In addition to any appropriate order listed in subdivision (i) of Section 2025, the court may order any of the following:

(1) That the deponent's testimony be taken by oral, instead of written, examination.

(2) That one or more of the parties receiving notice of the written deposition be permitted to attend in person or by attorney and to propound questions to the deponent by oral examination.

(3) That objections under subdivision (d) be sustained or overruled.

(4) That the deposition be taken before an officer other than the one named or described in the deposition notice.

(g) Duty of officer before whom depositions taken. The party taking the deposition shall deliver to the officer designated in the deposition notice a copy of that notice and of all questions served under subdivision (c). The deposition officer shall proceed promptly to propound the questions and to take and record the testimony of the deponent in response to the questions. (*Added by Stats.1986, c. 1334, § 2. Amended by Stats.1987, c. 86, § 11.*)

§ 2030. Deposition of Parties Upon Written Interrogatories

(a) Scope of discovery; restrictions. Any party may obtain discovery within the scope delimited by Section 2017, and subject to the restrictions set forth in Section 2019, by propounding to any other party to the action written interrogatories to be answered under oath.

(b) Time; motion to propound earlier. A defendant may propound interrogatories to a party to the action without leave of court at any time. A plaintiff may propound interrogatories to a party without leave of court at any time that is 10 days after the service of the summons on, or in unlawful detainer actions five days after service of the summons on or appearance by, that party, whichever occurs first. However, on motion with or without notice, the court, for good cause shown, may grant leave to a plaintiff to propound interrogatories at an earlier time.

(c) Number of interrogatories; declaration for additional discovery; form and contents; supplemental interrogatories.
(1) A party may propound to another party (1) 35 specially prepared interrogatories, and (2) any additional number of official form interrogatories, as described in Section 2033.5, that are relevant to the subject matter of the pending action. Except as provided in paragraph (8), no party shall, as a matter of right, propound to any other party more than 35 specially prepared interrogatories. If the initial set of interrogatories does not exhaust this limit, the balance may be propounded in subsequent sets. Unless a declaration as described in paragraph (3) has been made, a party need only respond to the first 35 specially prepared interrogatories served, if that party states an objection to the balance, under paragraph 3 of subdivision (f), on the ground that the limit has been exceeded.

(2) Subject to the right of the responding party to seek a protective order under subdivision (e), any party who attaches a supporting declaration as described in paragraph (3) may propound a greater number of specially prepared interrogatories to another party if this greater number is warranted because of any of the following:

(A) The complexity or the quantity of the existing and potential issues in the particular case.

(B) The financial burden on a party entailed in conducting the discovery by oral deposition.

(C) The expedience of using this method of discovery to provide to the responding party the opportunity to conduct an inquiry, investigation, or search of files or records to supply the information sought.

If the responding party seeks a protective order on the ground that the number of specially prepared interrogatories is unwarranted, the propounding party shall have the burden of justifying the number of these interrogatories.

(3) Any party who is propounding or has propounded more than 35 specially prepared interrogatories to any other party shall attach to each set of those interrogatories a declaration containing substantially the following:

DECLARATION FOR ADDITIONAL DISCOVERY

I, _____, declare:

1. I am (a party to this action or proceeding appearing in propria persona) (presently the attorney for _____, a party to this action or proceeding).

2. I am propounding to _____ the attached set of interrogatories.

3. This set of interrogatories will cause the total number of specially prepared interrogatories propounded to the party to whom they are directed to exceed the number of specially prepared interrogatories permitted by paragraph (1) of subdivision (c) of Section 2030 of the Code of Civil Procedure.

4. I have previously propounded a total of _____ interrogatories to this party, of which _____ interrogatories were not official form interrogatories.

5. This set of interrogatories contains a total of _____ specially prepared interrogatories.

6. I am familiar with the issues and the previous discovery conducted by all of the parties in the case.

7. I have personally examined each of the questions in this set of interrogatories.

8. This number of questions is warranted under paragraph (2) of subdivision (c) of Section 2030 of the Code of Civil Procedure because _____. (Here state each factor described in paragraph (2) of subdivision (c) that is relied on, as well as the reasons why any factor relied on is applicable to the instant lawsuit.)

9. None of the questions in this set of interrogatories is being propounded for any improper purpose, such as to harass the party, or the attorney for the party, to whom it is directed, or to cause unnecessary delay or needless increase in the cost of litigation.

I declare under penalty of perjury under the laws of California that the foregoing is true and correct, and that this declaration was executed on _____.

(Signature)
Attorney for _____

(4) A party propounding interrogatories shall number each set of interrogatories consecutively. In the first paragraph immediately below the title of the case, there shall appear the identity of the propounding party, the set number, and the identity of the responding party. Each interrogatory in a set shall be separately set forth and identified by number or letter.

(5) Each interrogatory shall be full and complete in and of itself. No preface or instruction shall be included with a set of interrogatories unless it has been approved under Section 2033.5. Any term specially defined in a set of interrogatories shall be typed with all letters capitalized wherever that term appears. No specially prepared interrogatory shall contain subparts, or a compound, conjunctive, or disjunctive question.

(6) An interrogatory may relate to whether another party is making a certain contention, or to the facts, witnesses, and writings on which a contention is based. An interrogatory is not objectionable because an answer to it involves an opinion or contention that relates to fact or the application of law to fact, or would be based on information obtained or legal theories developed in anticipation of litigation or in preparation for trial.

(7) An interrogatory may not be made a continuing one so as to impose on the party responding to it a duty to supplement an answer to it that was initially correct and complete with later acquired information.

(8) In addition to the number of interrogatories permitted by paragraphs (1) and (2), a party may propound a supplemental interrogatory to elicit any later acquired information bearing on all answers previously made by any party in response to interrogatories (1) twice prior to the initial setting of a trial date, and (2) subject to the time limits on discovery proceedings and motions provided in Section 2024, once after the initial setting of a trial date. However, on motion, for good cause shown, the court may grant leave to a party to propound an additional number of supplemental interrogatories.

(d) **Manner of service.** The party propounding interrogatories shall serve a copy of them (1) on the party to whom they are directed, and (2) on all other parties who have appeared in the action, unless the court on motion with or without notice has relieved that party from this requirement on its determination that service on all other parties would be unduly expensive or burdensome.

(e) **Orders for protection of parties or others; monetary sanction.** When interrogatories have been propounded, the responding party, and any other party or affected natural person or organization may promptly move for a protective order. This motion shall be accompanied by a declaration stating facts showing a reasonable and good faith attempt at an informal resolution of each issue presented by the motion.

The court, for good cause shown, may make any order that justice requires to protect any party or other natural person or organization from unwarranted annoyance, embarrassment, or oppression, or undue burden and expense. This protective order may include, but is not limited to, one or more of the following directions:

(1) That the set of interrogatories, or particular interrogatories in the set, need not be answered.

(2) That, contrary to the representations made in a declaration submitted under paragraph (3) of subdivision (c), the number of specially prepared interrogatories is unwarranted.

(3) That the time specified in subdivision (h) to respond to the set of interrogatories, or to particular interrogatories in the set, be extended.

(4) That the response be made only on specified terms and conditions.

(5) That the method of discovery be an oral deposition instead of interrogatories to a party.

(6) That a trade secret or other confidential research, development, or commercial information not be disclosed or be disclosed only in a certain way.

(7) That some or all of the answers to interrogatories be sealed and thereafter opened only on order of the court.

If the motion for a protective order is denied in whole or in part, the court may order that the party provide or permit the discovery against which protection was sought on terms and conditions that are just.

The court shall impose a monetary sanction under Section 2023 against any party, person, or attorney who unsuccessfully makes or opposes a motion for a protective order, unless it finds that the one subject to the sanction acted with substantial justification or that other circumstances made the imposition of the sanction unjust.

(f) Response by answer, exercise of option or objection. The party to whom interrogatories have been propounded shall respond in writing under oath separately to each interrogatory by (1) an answer containing the information sought to be discovered, (2) an exercise of the party's option to produce writings, or (3) an objection to the particular interrogatory. In the first paragraph of the response immediately below the title of the case, there shall appear the identity of the responding party, the set number, and the identity of the propounding party. Each answer, exercise of option, or objection in the response shall bear the same identifying number or letter and be in the same sequence as the corresponding interrogatory, but the text of that interrogatory need not be repeated.

(1) Each answer in the response shall be as complete and straightforward as the information reasonably available to the responding party permits. If an interrogatory cannot be answered completely, it shall be answered to the extent possible. If the responding party does not have personal knowledge sufficient to respond fully to an interrogatory, that party shall so state, but shall make a reasonable and good faith effort to obtain the information by inquiry to other natural persons or organizations, except where the information is equally available to the propounding party.

(2) If the answer to an interrogatory would necessitate the preparation or the making of a compilation, abstract, audit, or summary of or from the documents of the party to whom the interrogatory is directed, and if the burden or expense of preparing or making it would be substantially the same for the party propounding the interrogatory as for the responding party, it is a sufficient answer to that interrogatory to refer to this subdivision and to specify the writings from which the answer may be derived or ascertained. This specification shall be in sufficient detail to permit the propounding party to locate and to identify, as readily as the responding party can, the documents from which the answer may be ascertained. The responding party shall then afford to the propounding party a reasonable opportunity to examine, audit, or inspect these documents and to make copies, compilations, abstracts, or summaries of them.

(3) If only a part of an interrogatory is objectionable, the remainder of the interrogatory shall be answered. If an objection is made to an interrogatory or to a part of an interrogatory, the specific ground for the objection shall be set forth clearly in the response. If an objection is based on a claim of privilege, the particular privilege invoked shall be clearly stated. If an objection is based on a claim that the information sought is protected work product under Section 2018, that claim shall be expressly asserted.

(g) Signing response under oath. The party to whom the interrogatories are directed shall sign the response under oath unless the response contains only objections. If that party is a public or private corporation, or a partnership, association, or governmental agency, one of its officers or agents shall sign the response under oath on behalf of that party. If the officer or agent signing the response on behalf of that party is an attorney acting in that capacity for the party, that party waives any lawyer-client privilege and any protection for work product under Section 2018 during any subsequent discovery from that attorney concerning the identity of the sources of the information contained in the response. The attorney for the responding party shall sign any responses that contain an objection.

(h) Service of response. Within 30 days after service of interrogatories, or in unlawful detainer actions within five days after service of interrogatories, the party to whom the interrogatories are propounded shall serve the original of the response to them on the propounding party, unless on motion of the propounding party the court has shortened the time for response, or unless on motion of the responding party the court has extended the time for response. In unlawful detainer actions, the party to whom the interrogatories are propounded shall have five days from the date of service to respond unless on motion of the propounding party the court has shortened the time for response. The party to whom the interrogatories are propounded shall also serve a copy of the response on all other parties who have appeared in the action, unless the court on motion with or without notice has relieved that party from this requirement on its determination that service on all other parties would be unduly expensive or burdensome.

(i) Agreement to extend time for service of response. The party propounding interrogatories and the responding party may agree to extend the time for service of a response to a set of interrogatories, or to particular interrogatories in a set, to a date beyond that provided in subdivision (h). This agreement may be informal, but it shall be confirmed in a writing that specifies the extended date for service of a response. Unless this agreement expressly states otherwise, it is effective to preserve to the responding party the right to respond to any interrogatory to which the agreement applies in any manner specified in subdivision (f).

(j) Retention of interrogatories and response by propounding party. The interrogatories and the response thereto shall not be filed with the court. The propounding party shall retain both the original of the interrogatories, with the original proof of service affixed to them, and the original of the sworn response until six months after final disposition of the action. At that time, both originals may be destroyed, unless the court on motion of any party and for good cause shown orders that the originals be preserved for a longer period.

(k) Failure to serve timely response; motion for order; sanctions. If a party to whom interrogatories have been directed fails to serve a timely response, that party waives any right to exercise the option to produce writings under subdivision (f), as well as any objection to the interrogatories, including one based on privilege or on the protection for work product under Section 2018. However, the court, on motion, may relieve that party from this waiver on its determination that (1) the party has subsequently served a response that is in substantial compliance with subdivision (f), and (2) the party's failure to serve a timely response was the result of mistake, inadvertence, or excusable neglect.

The party propounding the interrogatories may move for an order compelling response to the interrogatories. The court shall impose a monetary sanction under Section 2023 against any party, person, or attorney who unsuccessfully makes or opposes a motion to compel a response to interrogatories, unless it finds that the one subject to the sanction acted with substantial justification or that other circumstances make the imposition of the sanction unjust. If a party then fails to obey an order compelling answers, the court may make those orders that are just, including the imposition of an issue sanction, an evidence sanction, or a terminating sanction under Section 2023. In lieu of or in addition to that sanction, the court may impose a monetary sanction under Section 2023.

(l) Compelling further response; motion; notice; sanctions; orders. If the propounding party, on receipt of a response to interrogatories, deems that (1) an answer to a particular interrogatory is evasive or incomplete, (2) an exercise of the option to produce documents under paragraph (2) of subdivision (f) is unwarranted or the required specification of those documents is inadequate, or (3) an objection to an interrogatory is without merit or too general, that party may move for an order compelling a further response. This motion shall be accompanied by a declaration stating facts showing a reasonable and good faith attempt at an informal resolution of each issue presented by the motion.

Unless notice of this motion is given within 45 days of the service of the response, or any supplemental response, or on or before any specific later date to which the propounding party and the responding party have agreed in writing, the propounding party waives any right to compel a further response to the interrogatories.

The court shall impose a monetary sanction under Section 2023 against any party, person, or attorney who unsuccessfully makes or opposes a motion to compel a further response to interrogatories, unless it finds that the one subject to the sanction acted with substantial justification or that other circumstances make the imposition of the sanction unjust.

If a party then fails to obey an order compelling further response to interrogatories, the court may make those orders that are just, including the imposition of an issue sanction, an evidence sanction, or a terminating sanction under Section 2023. In lieu of or in addition to that sanction, the court may impose a monetary sanction under Section 2023.

(m) Amended answer; use of original answer; sanction. Without leave of court, a party may serve an amended answer to any interrogatory that contains information subsequently discovered, inadvertently omitted, or mistakenly stated in the initial interrogatory. At the trial of the action, the propounding party or any other party may use the initial answer under subdivision (n), and the responding party may then use the amended answer.

The party who propounded an interrogatory to which an amended answer has been served may move for an order that the initial answer to that interrogatory be deemed binding on the responding party for the purpose of the pending action. This motion shall be accompanied by a declaration stating facts showing a reasonable and good faith attempt at an informal resolution of each issue presented by the motion. The court shall grant this motion if it determines that (1) the initial failure of the responding party to answer the interrogatory correctly has substantially prejudiced the party who propounded the interrogatory, (2) the responding party has failed to show substantial justification for the initial answer to that interrogatory, and (3) the prejudice to the propounding party cannot be cured either by a continuance to permit further discovery or by the use of the initial answer under subdivision (n).

The court shall impose a monetary sanction under Section 2023 against any party, person, or attorney who unsuccessfully makes or opposes a motion to deem binding an initial answer to an interrogatory, unless it finds that the one subject to the sanction acted with substantial justification or that other circumstances make the imposition of the sanction unjust.

(n) Use of answer or part of answer at trial or hearing. At the trial or any other hearing in the action, so far as admissible under the rules of evidence, the propounding party or any party other than the responding party may use any answer or part of an answer to an interrogatory only against the responding party. It is not ground for objection to the use of an answer to an interrogatory that the responding party is available to testify, has testified, or will testify at the trial or other hearing. *(Added by Stats.1986, c. 1334, § 2. Amended by Stats. 1987, c. 86, § 12; Stats.1988, c. 553, § 4; Stats.1988, c. 575, § 1; Stats.1991, c. 1090, § 11.)*

§ 2031. Production, Inspection and Entry; Documents, Things and Places

(a) Scope and restrictions; procedure. Any party may obtain discovery within the scope delimited by Section 2017, and subject to the restrictions set forth in Section 2019, by inspecting documents, tangible things, and land or other property that are in the possession, custody, or control of any other party to the action.

(1) A party may demand that any other party produce and permit the party making the demand, or someone acting on that party's behalf, to inspect and to copy a document that is in the possession, custody, or control of the party on whom the demand is made.

(2) A party may demand that any other party produce and permit the party making the demand, or someone acting on that party's behalf, to inspect and to photograph, test, or sample any tangible things that are in the possession, custody, or control of the party on whom the demand is made.

(3) A party may demand that any other party allow the party making the demand, or someone acting on that party's behalf, to enter on any land or other property that is in the possession, custody, or control of the party on whom the demand is made, and to inspect and to measure, survey, photograph, test, or sample the land or other property, or any designated object or operation on it.

(b) Time for demand. A defendant may make a demand for inspection without leave of court at any time. A plaintiff may make a demand for inspection without leave of court at any time that is 10 days after the service of the summons on, or in unlawful detainer actions within five days after service of the summons on or appearance by, the party to whom the demand is directed, whichever occurs first. However, on motion with or without notice, the court, for good cause shown, may grant leave to a plaintiff to make an inspection demand at an earlier time.

(c) Form and contents. A party demanding an inspection shall number each set of demands consecutively. In the first paragraph immediately below the title of the case, there shall appear the identity of the demanding party, the set number, and the identity of the responding party. Each demand in a set shall be separately set forth, identified by number or letter, and shall do all of the following:

(1) Designate the documents, tangible things, or land or other property to be inspected either by specifically describing each individual item or by reasonably particularizing each category of item.

(2) Specify a reasonable time for the inspection that is at least 30 days after service of the demand, or in unlawful detainer actions at least five days after service of the demand, unless the court for good cause shown has granted leave to specify an earlier date.

(3) Specify a reasonable place for making the inspection, copying, and performing any related activity.

(4) Specify any related activity that is being demanded in addition to an inspection and copying, as well as the manner in which

that related activity will be performed, and whether that activity will permanently alter or destroy the item involved.

(d) Service of copy on parties. The party demanding an inspection shall serve a copy of the inspection demand on the party to whom it is directed and on all other parties who have appeared in the action.

(e) Protective orders; sanctions. When an inspection of documents, tangible things or places has been demanded, the party to whom the demand has been directed, and any other party or affected person or organization, may promptly move for a protective order. This motion shall be accompanied by a declaration stating facts showing a reasonable and good faith attempt at an informal resolution of each issue presented by the motion.

The court, for good cause shown, may make any order that justice requires to protect any party or other natural person or organization from unwarranted annoyance, embarrassment, or oppression, or undue burden and expense. This protective order may include, but is not limited to, one or more of the following directions:

(1) That all or some of the items or categories of items in the inspection demand need not be produced or made available at all.

(2) That the time specified in subdivision (h) to respond to the set of inspection demands, or to a particular item or category in the set, be extended.

(3) That the place of production be other than that specified in the inspection demand.

(4) That the inspection be made only on specified terms and conditions.

(5) That a trade secret or other confidential research, development, or commercial information not be disclosed, or be disclosed only to specified persons or only in a specified way.

(6) That the items produced be sealed and thereafter opened only on order of the court.

If the motion for a protective order is denied in whole or in part, the court may order that the party to whom the demand was directed provide or permit the discovery against which protection was sought on terms and conditions that are just.

The court shall impose a monetary sanction under Section 2023 against any party, person, or attorney who unsuccessfully makes or opposes a motion for a protective order, unless it finds that the one subject to the sanction acted with substantial justification or that other circumstances make the imposition of the sanction unjust.

(f) Statements of compliance, representations, or objections. The party to whom an inspection demand has been directed shall respond separately to each item or category of item by a statement that the party will comply with the particular demand for inspection and any related activities, a representation that the party lacks the ability to comply with the demand for inspection of a particular item or category of item, or an objection to the particular demand.

In the first paragraph of the response immediately below the title of the case, there shall appear the identity of the responding party, the set number, and the identity of the demanding party. Each statement of compliance, each representation, and each objection in the response shall bear the same number and be in the same sequence as the corresponding item or category in the demand, but the text of that item or category need not be repeated.

(1) A statement that the party to whom an inspection demand has been directed will comply with the particular demand shall state that the production, inspection, and related activity demanded will be allowed either in whole or in part, and that all documents or things in the demanded category that are in the possession, custody, or control of that party and to which no objection is being made will be included in the production.

Any documents demanded shall either be produced as they are kept in the usual course of business, or be organized and labeled to correspond with the categories in the demand. If necessary, the responding party at the reasonable expense of the demanding party shall, through detection devices, translate any data compilations included in the demand into reasonably usable form.

(2) A representation of inability to comply with the particular demand for inspection shall affirm that a diligent search and a reasonable inquiry has been made in an effort to comply with that demand. This statement shall also specify whether the inability to comply is because the particular item or category has never existed, has been destroyed, has been lost, misplaced, or stolen, or has never been, or is no longer, in the possession, custody, or control of the responding party. The statement shall set forth the name and address of any natural person or organization known or believed by that party to have possession, custody, or control of that item or category of item.

(3) If only part of an item or category of item in an inspection demand is objectionable, the response shall contain a statement of compliance, or a representation of inability to comply with respect to the remainder of that item or category. If the responding party objects to the demand for inspection of an item or category of item, the response shall (A) identify with particularity any document, tangible thing, or land falling within any category of item in the demand to which an objection is being made, and (B) set forth clearly the extent of, and the specific ground for, the objection. If an objection is based on a claim of privilege, the particular privilege invoked shall be stated. If an objection is based on a claim that the information sought is protected work product under Section 2018, that claim shall be expressly asserted.

(g) Signature under oath. The party to whom the demand for inspection is directed shall sign the response under oath unless the response contains only objections. If that party is a public or private corporation or a partnership or association or governmental agency, one of its officers or agents shall sign the response under oath on behalf of that party. If the officer or agent signing the response on behalf of that party is an attorney acting in that capacity for a party, that party waives any lawyer-client privilege and any protection for work product under Section 2018 during any subsequent discovery from that attorney concerning the identity of the sources of the information contained in the response. The attorney for the responding party shall sign any responses that contain an objection.

(h) Service by responding party. Within 20 days after service of an inspection demand, or in unlawful detainer actions within five days of an inspection demand, the party to whom the demand is directed shall serve the original of the response to it on the party making the demand, and a copy of the response on all other parties who have appeared in the action, unless on motion of the party making the demand the court has shortened the time for response, or unless on motion of the party to whom the demand has been directed, the court has extended the time for response. In unlawful detainer actions, the party to whom the demand is directed shall have at least five days from the date of service of the demand to respond unless on motion of the party making the demand the court has shortened the time for the response.

(i) Agreement for extended date for service of response. The party demanding an inspection and the responding party may agree to extend the time for service of a response to a set of inspection demands, or to particular items or categories of items in a set, to a date beyond that provided in subdivision (h). This agreement may be informal, but it shall be confirmed in a writing that specifies the extended date for service of a response. Unless this agreement expressly states otherwise, it is effective to preserve to the responding party the right to respond to any item or category of item in the demand to which the agreement applies in any manner specified in subdivision (f).

(j) Retention and preservation of original demand and response. The inspection demand and the response to it shall not be filed with the court. The party demanding an inspection shall retain both the original of the inspection demand, with the original proof of service affixed to it, and the original of the sworn response until six months after final disposition of the action. At that time, both originals may be destroyed, unless the court, on motion of any party and for good cause shown, orders that the originals be preserved for a longer period.

(k) Failure to serve timely response; waiver; orders and sanctions. If a party to whom an inspection demand has been directed fails to serve a timely response to it, that party waives any objection to the demand, including one based on privilege or on the protection for work product under Section 2018. However, the court, on motion, may relieve that party from this waiver on its determination that (1) the party has subsequently served a response that is in substantial compliance with subdivision (f), and (2) the party's failure to serve a timely response was the result of mistake, inadvertence, or excusable neglect.

The party making the demand may move for an order compelling response to the inspection demand. The court shall impose a monetary sanction under Section 2023 against any party, person, or attorney who unsuccessfully makes or opposes a motion to compel a response to an inspection demand, unless it finds that the one subject to the sanction acted with substantial justification or that other circumstances make the imposition of the sanction unjust. If a party then fails to obey the order compelling a response, the court may make those orders that are just, including the imposition of an issue sanction, an evidence sanction, or a terminating sanction under Section 2023. In lieu of or in addition to that sanction, the court may impose a monetary sanction under Section 2023.

(*l*) Order compelling further response; failure to obey. If the party demanding an inspection, on receipt of a response to an inspection demand, deems that (1) a statement of compliance with the demand is incomplete, (2) a representation of inability to comply is inadequate, incomplete, or evasive, or (3) an objection in the response is without merit or too general, that party may move for an order compelling further response to the demand. This motion (1) shall set forth specific facts showing good cause justifying the discovery sought by the inspection demand, and (2) shall be accompanied by a declaration stating facts showing a reasonable and good faith attempt at an informal resolution of any issue presented by it.

Unless notice of this motion is given within 45 days of the service of the response, or any supplemental response, or on or before any specific later date to which the demanding party and the responding party have agreed in writing, the demanding party waives any right to compel a further response to the inspection demand.

The court shall impose a monetary sanction under Section 2023 against any party, person, or attorney who unsuccessfully makes or opposes a motion to compel further response to an inspection demand, unless it finds that the one subject to the sanction acted with substantial justification or that other circumstances make the imposition of the sanction unjust.

If a party fails to obey an order compelling further response, the court may make those orders that are just, including the imposition of an issue sanction, an evidence sanction, or a terminating sanction under Section 2023. In lieu of or in addition to that sanction, the court may impose a monetary sanction under Section 2023.

(m) Order compelling compliance with response; sanction. If a party filing a response to a demand for inspection under subdivision (f) thereafter fails to permit the inspection in accordance with that party's statement of compliance, the party demanding the inspection may move for an order compelling compliance.

The court shall impose a monetary sanction under Section 2023 against any party, person, or attorney who unsuccessfully makes or opposes a motion to compel compliance with an inspection demand, unless it finds that the one subject to the sanction acted with substantial justification or that other circumstances make the imposition of the sanction unjust.

If a party then fails to obey an order compelling inspection, the court may make those orders that are just, including the imposition of an issue sanction, an evidence sanction, or a terminating sanction under Section 2023. In lieu of or in addition to that sanction, the court may impose a monetary sanction under Section 2023. *(Added by Stats.1986, c. 1334, § 2. Amended by Stats.1987, c. 86, § 13; Stats.1988, c. 575, § 2; Stats.1991, c. 1090, § 12.)*

§ 2032. Physical or Mental Examinations

(a) **Parties.** Any party may obtain discovery, subject to the restrictions set forth in Section 2019, by means of a physical or mental examination of (1) a party to the action, (2) an agent of any party, or (3) a natural person in the custody or under the legal control of a party, in any action in which the mental or physical condition (including the blood group) of that party or other person is in controversy in the action.

(b) **Licensed physicians or clinical psychologists.** A physical examination conducted under this section shall be performed only by a licensed physician or other appropriate licensed health care practitioner. A mental examination conducted under this section shall be performed only by a licensed physician, or by a licensed clinical psychologist who holds a doctoral degree in psychology and has had at least five years of postgraduate experience in the diagnosis of emotional and mental disorders. Nothing in this section affects tests under the Uniform Act on Blood Tests to Determine Paternity (Chapter 2 (commencing with Section 7550) of Part 2 of Division 12 of the Family Code).

(c)(1) **Cross-complainants; cross-defendants.** As used in this subdivision, plaintiff includes a cross-complainant, and defendant includes a cross-defendant.

(2) **Demand for physical examination.** In any case in which a plaintiff is seeking recovery for personal injuries, any defendant may demand one physical examination of the plaintiff, provided the examination does not include any diagnostic test or procedure that is painful, protracted, or intrusive, and is conducted at a location within 75 miles of the residence of the examinee. A defendant may make this demand without leave of court after that defendant has been served or has appeared in the action, whichever occurs first. This demand shall specify the time, place, manner, conditions, scope, and nature of the examination, as well as the

identity and the specialty, if any, of the physician who will perform the examination.

(3) Scheduling. A physical examination demanded under this subdivision shall be scheduled for a date that is at least 30 days after service of the demand for it unless on motion of the party demanding the examination the court has shortened this time.

(4) Service. The defendant shall serve a copy of the demand for this physical examination on the plaintiff and on all other parties who have appeared in the action.

(5) Response by plaintiff. The plaintiff to whom this demand for a physical examination has been directed shall respond to the demand by a written statement that the examinee will comply with the demand as stated, will comply with the demand as specifically modified by the plaintiff, or will refuse, for reasons specified in the response, to submit to the demanded physical examination. Within 20 days after service of the demand the plaintiff to whom the demand is directed shall serve the original of the response to it on the defendant making the demand, and a copy of the response on all other parties who have appeared in the action, unless on motion of the defendant making the demand the court has shortened the time for response, or unless on motion of the plaintiff to whom the demand has been directed, the court has extended the time for response.

(6) Failure to respond; waiver of obligations; order compelling response and compliance. If a plaintiff to whom this demand for a physical examination has been directed fails to serve a timely response to it, that plaintiff waives any objection to the demand. However, the court, on motion, may relieve that plaintiff from this waiver on its determination that (A) the plaintiff has subsequently served a response that is in substantial compliance with paragraph (5), and (B) the plaintiff's failure to serve a timely response was the result of mistake, inadvertence, or excusable neglect.

The defendant may move for an order compelling response and compliance with a demand for a physical examination. The court shall impose a monetary sanction under Section 2023 against any party, person, or attorney who unsuccessfully makes or opposes a motion to compel response and compliance with a demand for a physical examination, unless it finds that the one subject to the sanction acted with substantial justification or that other circumstances make the imposition of the sanction unjust.

If a plaintiff then fails to obey the order compelling response and compliance, the court may make those orders that are just, including the imposition of an issue sanction, an evidence sanction, or a terminating sanction under Section 2023. In lieu of or in addition to that sanction the court may impose a monetary sanction under Section 2023.

(7) Receipt of response; order compelling compliance. If a defendant who has demanded a physical examination under this subdivision, on receipt of the plaintiff's response to that demand, deems that any modification of the demand, or any refusal to submit to the physical examination is unwarranted, that defendant may move for an order compelling compliance with the demand. This motion shall be accompanied by a declaration stating facts showing a reasonable and good faith attempt at an informal resolution of each issue presented by the motion.

The court shall impose a monetary sanction under Section 2023 against any party, person, or attorney who unsuccessfully makes or opposes a motion to compel compliance with a demand for a physical examination, unless it finds that the one subject to the sanction acted with substantial justification or that other circumstances make the imposition of the sanction unjust.

(8) Original copies. The demand for a physical examination and the response to it shall not be filed with the court. The defendant shall retain both the original of the demand, with the original proof of service affixed to it, and the original response until six months after final disposition of the action. At that time, the original may be destroyed, unless the court, on motion of any party and for good cause shown, orders that the originals be preserved for a longer period.

(d) Motion for examination; contents; notice; good cause; order granting examination. If any party desires to obtain discovery by a physical examination other than that described in subdivision (c), or by a mental examination, the party shall obtain leave of court. The motion for the examination shall specify the time, place, manner, conditions, scope, and nature of the examination, as well as the identity and the specialty, if any, of the person or persons who will perform the examination. The motion shall be accompanied by a declaration stating facts showing a reasonable and good faith attempt to arrange for the examination by an agreement under subdivision (e). Notice of the motion shall be served on the person to be examined and on all parties who have appeared in the action.

The court shall grant a motion for a physical or mental examination only for good cause shown. If a party stipulates that (1) no claim is being made for mental and emotional distress over and above that usually associated with the physical injuries claimed, and (2) no expert testimony regarding this usual mental and emotional distress will be presented at trial in support of the claim for damages, a mental examination of a person for whose personal injuries a recovery is being sought shall not be ordered except on a showing of exceptional circumstances. The order granting a physical or mental examination shall specify the person or persons who may perform the examination, and the time, place, manner, diagnostic tests and procedures, conditions, scope, and nature of the examination. If the place of the examination is more than

75 miles from the residence of the person to be examined, the order to submit to it shall be (1) made only on the court's determination that there is good cause for the travel involved, and (2) conditioned on the advancement by the moving party of the reasonable expenses and costs to the examinee for travel to the place of examination.

(e) Written agreement of parties. In lieu of the procedures and restrictions specified in subdivisions (c) and (d), any physical or mental examination may be arranged by, and carried out under, a written agreement of the parties.

(f) Failure to submit to examination; sanctions. If a party required by subdivision (c), (d), or (e) to submit to a physical or mental examination fails to do so, the court, on motion of the party entitled to the examination, may make those orders that are just, including the imposition of an issue sanction, an evidence sanction, or a terminating sanction under Section 2023. In lieu of or in addition to that sanction, the court may, on motion of the party, impose a monetary sanction under Section 2023.

If a party required by subdivision (c), (d), or (e) to produce another for a physical or mental examination fails to do so, the court, on motion of the party entitled to the examination, may make those orders that are just, including the imposition of an issue sanction, an evidence sanction, or a terminating sanction under Section 2023, unless the party failing to comply demonstrates an inability to produce that person for examination. In lieu of or in addition to that sanction, the court may impose a monetary sanction under Section 2023.

(g) Attendance at physical examination; presence of observer; motion for protective order; X-rays; recording of mental examination. (1) The attorney for the examinee or for a party producing the examinee, or that attorney's representative, shall be permitted to attend and observe any physical examination conducted for discovery purposes, and to record stenographically or by audio tape any words spoken to or by the examinee during any phase of the examination. This observer may monitor the examination, but shall not participate in or disrupt it. If an attorney's representative is to serve as the observer, the representative shall be authorized to so act by a writing subscribed by the attorney which identifies the representative.

If in the judgment of the observer the examiner becomes abusive to the examinee or undertakes to engage in unauthorized diagnostic tests and procedures, the observer may suspend it to enable the party being examined or producing the examinee to make a motion for a protective order. If the observer begins to participate in or disrupt the examination, the person conducting the physical examination may suspend the examination to enable the party at whose instance it is being conducted to move for a protective order.

The court shall impose a monetary sanction under Section 2023 against any party, person, or attorney who unsuccessfully makes or opposes a motion for a protective order, unless it finds that the one subject to the sanction acted with substantial justification or that other circumstances make the imposition of the sanction unjust.

If the examinee submits or authorizes access to X-rays of any area of his or her body for inspection by the examining physician, no additional X-rays of that area may be taken by the examining physician except with consent of the examinee or on order of the court for good cause shown.

(2) The examiner and examinee shall have the right to record a mental examination on audio tape. However, nothing in this article shall be construed to alter, amend, or affect existing case law with respect to the presence of the attorney for the examinee or other persons during the examination by agreement or court order.

(h) Copies of specified reports; motion to compel delivery; sanctions. If a party submits to, or produces another for, a physical or mental examination in compliance with a demand under subdivision (c), an order of court under subdivision (d), or an agreement under subdivision (e), that party has the option of making a written demand that the party at whose instance the examination was made deliver to the demanding party (1) a copy of a detailed written report setting out the history, examinations, findings, including the results of all tests made, diagnoses, prognoses, and conclusions of the examiner, and (2) a copy of reports of all earlier examinations of the same condition of the examinee made by that or any other examiner. If this option is exercised, a copy of these reports shall be delivered within 30 days after service of the demand, or within 15 days of trial, whichever is earlier. The protection for work product under Section 2018 is waived, both for the examiner's writings and reports and to the taking of the examiner's testimony.

If the party at whose instance the examination was made fails to make a timely delivery of the reports demanded, the demanding party may move for an order compelling their delivery. This motion shall be accompanied by a declaration stating facts showing a reasonable and good faith attempt at an informal resolution of any issue presented by the motion.

The court shall impose a monetary sanction under Section 2023 against any party, person, or attorney who unsuccessfully makes or opposes a motion to compel delivery of medical reports, unless it finds that the one subject to the sanction acted with substantial justification or that other circumstances make the imposition of the sanction unjust.

If a party then fails to obey an order compelling delivery of demanded medical reports, the court may make those orders that are just, including the imposition of an issue sanction, an evidence sanction, or a terminating sanction under Section 2023. In lieu of or in addition to those sanctions, the court may impose a monetary sanction under Section 2023. The court shall exclude at trial the testimony of any examiner whose report has not been provided by a party.

(i) Waiver of privilege. By demanding and obtaining a report of a physical or mental examination under subdivision (h), or by taking the deposition of the examiner, other than under subdivision (i) of Section 2034, the party who submitted to, or produced another for, a physical or mental examination waives in the pending action, and in any other action involving the same controversy, any privilege, as well as any protection for work product under Section 2018, that the party or other examinee may have regarding reports and writings as well as the testimony of every other physician, psychologist, or licensed health care practitioner who has examined or may thereafter examine the party or other examinee in respect of the same physical or mental condition.

(j) Existing or later reports of previous or subsequent examinations relating to same condition; motion to compel delivery of medical reports. A party receiving a demand for a report under subdivision (h) is entitled at the time of compliance to receive in exchange a copy of any existing written report of any examination of the same condition by any other physician, psychologist, or licensed health care practitioner. In addition, that party is entitled to receive promptly any later report of any previous or subsequent examination of the same condition, by any physician, psychologist, or licensed health care practitioner.

If a party who has demanded and received delivery of medical reports under subdivision (h) fails to deliver existing or later reports of previous or subsequent examinations, a party who has complied with subdivision (h) may move for an order compelling delivery of medical reports. This motion shall be accompanied by a declaration stating facts showing a reasonable and good faith attempt at an informal resolution of each issue presented by the motion.

The court shall impose a monetary sanction under Section 2023 against any party, person, or attorney who unsuccessfully makes or opposes a motion to compel delivery of medical reports, unless it finds that the one subject to the sanction acted with substantial justification or that other circumstances make the imposition of the sanction unjust.

If a party then fails to obey an order compelling delivery of medical reports, the court may make those orders that are just, including the imposition of an issue sanction, an evidence sanction, or a terminating sanction under Section 2023. In lieu of or in addition to the sanction, the court may impose a monetary sanction under Section 2023. The court shall exclude at trial the testimony of any health care practitioner whose report has not been provided by a party ordered to do so by the court.

(k) Disclosure of experts. Nothing in this section shall require the disclosure of the identity of an expert consulted by an attorney in order to make the certification required in an action for professional negligence under Sections 411.30 and 411.35. *(Added by Stats.1986, c. 1336, § 1. Amended by Stats.1987, c. 86, § 14; Stats.1988, c. 553, § 5;*

Stats.1992, c. 163, § 65; Stats.1992, c. 615, § 6; Stats.1993, c. 219, § 71.)

§ 2033. Requests for Admission

(a) Parties. Any party may obtain discovery within the scope delimited by Section 2017, and subject to the restrictions set forth in Section 2019, by a written request that any other party to the action admit the genuineness of specified documents, or the truth of specified matters of fact, opinion relating to fact, or application of law to fact. A request for admission may relate to a matter that is in controversy between the parties.

(b) Time for request. A defendant may make requests for admission by a party without leave of court at any time. A plaintiff may make requests for admission by a party without leave of court at any time that is 10 days after the service of the summons on, or, in unlawful detainer actions, five days after the service of the summons on, or appearance by, that party, whichever occurs first. However, on motion with or without notice, the court, for good cause shown, may grant leave to a plaintiff to make requests for admission at an earlier time.

(c) Number; declaration for additional discovery; form and contents; copies. (1) No party shall request, as a matter of right, that any other party admit more than 35 matters that do not relate to the genuineness of documents. If the initial set of admission requests does not exhaust this limit, the balance may be requested in subsequent sets. Unless a declaration as described in paragraph (3) has been made, a party need only respond to the first 35 admission requests served that do not relate to the genuineness of documents, if that party states an objection to the balance under paragraph (2) of subdivision (f) on the ground that the limit has been exceeded.

The number of requests for admission of the genuineness of documents is not limited except as justice requires to protect the responding party from unwarranted annoyance, embarrassment, oppression, or undue burden and expense.

(2) Subject to the right of the responding party to seek a protective order under subdivision (e), any party who attaches a supporting declaration as described in paragraph (3) may request a greater number of admissions by another party if the greater number is warranted by the complexity or the quantity of the existing and potential issues in the particular case.

If the responding party seeks a protective order on the ground that the number of requests for admission is unwarranted, the propounding party shall have the burden of justifying the number of requests for admission.

(3) Any party who is requesting or who has already requested more than 35 admissions not relating to the genuineness of docu-

ments by any other party shall attach to each set of requests for admissions a declaration containing substantially the following words:

DECLARATION FOR ADDITIONAL DISCOVERY

I, _____, declare:

1. I am (a party to this action or proceeding appearing in propria persona) (presently the attorney for _____, a party to this action or proceeding).

2. I am propounding to _____ the attached set of requests for admission.

3. This set of requests for admission will cause the total number of requests propounded to the party to whom they are directed to exceed the number of requests permitted by paragraph (1) of subdivision (c) of Section 2033 of the Code of Civil Procedure.

4. I have previously propounded a total of _____ requests for admission to this party.

5. This set of requests for admission contains a total of _____ requests.

6. I am familiar with the issues and the previous discovery conducted by all of the parties in this case.

7. I have personally examined each of the requests in this set of requests for admission.

8. This number of requests for admission is warranted under paragraph (2) of subdivision (c) of Section 2033 of the Code of Civil Procedure because _____. (Here state the reasons why the complexity or the quantity of issues in the instant lawsuit warrant this number of requests for admission.)

9. None of the requests in this set of requests is being propounded for any improper purpose, such as to harass the party, or the attorney for the party, to whom it is directed, or to cause unnecessary delay or needless increase in the cost of litigation.

I declare under penalty of perjury under the laws of California that the foregoing is true and correct, and that this declaration was executed on _____.

_____
(Signature)
Attorney for _____

(4) A party requesting admissions shall number each set of requests consecutively. In the first paragraph immediately below the title of the case, there shall appear the identity of the party requesting the admissions, the set number, and the identity of the requesting party, the set number, and the identity of the responding

party. Each request for admission in a set shall be separately set forth and identified by letter or number.

(5) Each request for admission shall be full and complete in and of itself. No preface or instruction shall be included with a set of admission requests unless it has been approved under Section 2033.5. Any term specially defined in a request for admission shall be typed with all letters capitalized whenever the term appears. No request for admission shall contain subparts, or a compound, conjunctive, or disjunctive request unless it has been approved under Section 2033.5.

(6) A party requesting an admission of the genuineness of any documents shall attach copies of those documents to the requests, and shall make the original of those documents available for inspection on demand by the party to whom the requests for admission are directed.

(7) No party shall combine in a single document requests for admission with any other method of discovery.

(d) Service of copies on parties. The party requesting admissions shall serve a copy of them on the party to whom they are directed and on all other parties who have appeared in the action.

(e) Protective orders; sanctions. When requests for admission have been made, the responding party may promptly move for a protective order. This motion shall be accompanied by a declaration stating facts showing a reasonable and good faith attempt at an informal resolution of each issue presented by the motion.

The court, for good cause shown, may make any order that justice requires to protect any party from unwarranted annoyance, embarrassment, oppression, or undue burden and expense. This protective order may include, but is not limited to, one or more of the following directions:

(1) That the set of admission requests, or particular requests in the set, need not be answered at all.

(2) That, contrary to the representations made in a declaration submitted under paragraph (3) of subdivision (c), the number of admission requests is unwarranted.

(3) That the time specified in subdivision (h) to respond to the set of admission requests, or to particular requests in the set, be extended.

(4) That a trade secret or other confidential research, development, or commercial information not be admitted or be admitted only in a certain way.

(5) That some or all of the answers to requests for admission be sealed and thereafter opened only on order of the court.

If the motion for a protective order is denied in whole or in part, the court may order that the responding party provide or permit the discovery against which protection was sought on terms and conditions that are just.

The court shall impose a monetary sanction under Section 2023 against any party, person, or attorney who unsuccessfully makes or opposes a motion for a protective order, unless it finds that the one subject to the sanction acted with substantial justification or that other circumstances make the imposition of the sanction unjust.

(f) Answers or objections. The party to whom requests for admission have been directed shall respond in writing under oath separately to each request. Each response shall answer the substance of the requested admission, or set forth an objection to the particular request. In the first paragraph of the response immediately below the title of the case, there shall appear the identity of the responding party, the set number, and the identity of the requesting party. Each answer or objection in the response shall bear the same identifying number or letter and be in the same sequence as the corresponding request, but the text of the particular request need not be repeated.

(1) Each answer in the response shall be as complete and straightforward as the information reasonably available to the responding party permits. Each answer shall (A) admit so much of the matter involved in the request as is true, either as expressed in the request itself or as reasonably and clearly qualified by the responding party, (B) deny so much of the matter involved in the request as is untrue, and (C) specify so much of the matter involved in the request as to the truth of which the responding party lacks sufficient information or knowledge. If a responding party gives lack of information or knowledge as a reason for a failure to admit all or part of a request for admission, that party shall state in the answer that a reasonable inquiry concerning the matter in the particular request has been made, and that the information known or readily obtainable is insufficient to enable that party to admit the matter.

(2) If only a part of a request for admission is objectionable, the remainder of the request shall be answered. If an objection is made to a request or to a part of a request, the specific ground for the objection shall be set forth clearly in the response. If an objection is based on a claim of privilege, the particular privilege invoked shall be clearly stated. If an objection is based on a claim that the matter as to which an admission is requested is protected work product under Section 2018, that claim shall be expressly asserted.

(g) Signature under oath. The party to whom the requests for admission are directed shall sign the response under oath, unless the response contains only objections. If that party is a public or private corporation, or a partnership or association or governmental agency, one of its officers or agents shall sign the response under oath on behalf of that party. If the officer or agent signing the response on behalf of that party is an attorney acting in that capacity for the party, that party waives any lawyer-client privilege and any protection for work product under Section 2018 during any subsequent discovery from that attorney concerning the identity of the sources of the information contained in the response. The attorney for the responding party shall sign any response that contains an objection.

(h) Service by responding party. Within 30 days after service of requests for admission, or in unlawful detainer actions within five days after service of requests for admission, the party to whom the requests are directed shall serve the original of the response to them on the requesting party, and a copy of the response on all other parties who have appeared, unless on motion of the requesting party the court has shortened the time for response, or unless on motion of the responding party the court has extended the time for response. In unlawful detainer actions, the party to whom the request is directed shall have at least five days from the date of service to respond unless on motion of the requesting party the court has shortened the time for response.

(i) Agreement for extended date for service of response. The party requesting admissions and the responding party may agree to extend the time for service of a response to a set of admission requests, or to particular requests in a set, to a date beyond that provided in subdivision (h). This agreement may be informal, but it shall be confirmed in a writing that specifies the extended date for service of a response. Unless this agreement expressly states otherwise, it is effective to preserve to the responding party the right to respond to any request for admission to which the agreement applies in any manner specified in subdivision (f). Notice of this agreement shall be given by the responding party to all other parties who were served with a copy of the request.

(j) Retention and preservation of original demand and response. The requests for admission and the response to them shall not be filed with the court. The party requesting admissions shall retain both the original of the requests for admission, with the original proof of service affixed to them, and the original of the sworn response until six months after final disposition of the action. At that time, both originals may be destroyed, unless the court, on motion of any party and for good cause shown, orders that the originals be preserved for a longer period.

(k) Failure to serve timely response; waiver; orders and sanctions. If a party to whom requests for admission have been directed fails to serve a timely response, that party thereby waives any objection to the requests, including one based on privilege or on the protection for work product under Section 2018. However, the court, on motion, may relieve that party from this waiver on its determination that (1) the party has subsequently served a response that is in substantial compliance with subdivision (f), and (2) the party's failure to serve a timely response was the result of mistake, inadvertence, or excusable neglect.

The requesting party may move for an order that the genuineness of any documents and the truth of any matters specified in the requests be deemed admitted, as well as for a monetary sanction under Section 2023. The court shall make this order, unless it finds that the party to whom the requests for admission have been directed has served, before the hearing on the motion, a proposed response to the requests for admission that is in substantial compliance with paragraph (1) of subdivision (f). It is mandatory that the court impose a monetary sanction under Section 2023 on the party or attorney, or both, whose failure to serve a timely response to requests for admission necessitated this motion.

(*l*) **Orders compelling further response; failure to obey.** If the party requesting admissions, on receipt of a response to the requests, deems that (1) an answer to a particular request is evasive or incomplete, or (2) an objection to a particular request is without merit or too general, that party may move for an order compelling a further response. The motion shall be accompanied by a declaration stating facts showing a reasonable and good faith attempt at an informal resolution of each issue presented by the motion.

Unless notice of this motion is given within 45 days of the service of the response, or any supplemental response, or any specific later date to which the requesting party and the responding party have agreed in writing, the requesting party waives any right to compel further response to the requests for admission.

The court shall impose a monetary sanction under Section 2023 against any party, person, or attorney who unsuccessfully makes or opposes a motion to compel further response, unless it finds that the one subject to the sanction acted with substantial justification or that other circumstances make the imposition of the sanction unjust.

If a party then fails to obey an order compelling further response to requests for admission, the court may order that the matters involved in the requests be deemed admitted. In lieu of or in addition to this order, the court may impose a monetary sanction under Section 2023.

(m) **Amendment or withdrawal of admission; conditions.** A party may withdraw or amend an admission made in response to a request for admission only on leave of court granted after notice to all parties. The court may permit withdrawal or amendment of an admission only if it determines that the admission was the result of mistake, inadvertence, or excusable neglect, and that the party who obtained the admission will not be substantially prejudiced in maintaining that party's action or defense on the merits. The court may impose conditions on the granting of the motion that are just, including, but not limited to, an order that (1) the party who obtained the admission be permitted to pursue additional discovery related to the matter involved in the withdrawn or amended admission, and (2) the costs of any additional discovery be borne in whole or in part by the party withdrawing or amending the admission.

(n) Effect of admission. Any matter admitted in response to a request for admission is conclusively established against the party making the admission in the pending action, unless the court has permitted withdrawal or amendment of that admission under subdivision (m). However, any admission made by a party under this section is (1) binding only on that party, and (2) made for the purpose of the pending action only. It is not an admission by that party for any other purpose, and it shall not be used in any manner against that party in any other proceeding.

(o) Expenses on refusal to admit. If a party fails to admit the genuineness of any document or the truth of any matter when requested to do so under this section, and if the party requesting that admission thereafter proves the genuineness of that document or the truth of that matter, the party requesting the admission may move the court for an order requiring the party to whom the request was directed to pay the reasonable expenses incurred in making that proof, including reasonable attorney's fees. The court shall make this order unless it finds that (1) an objection to the request was sustained or a response to it was waived under subdivision (*l*), (2) the admission sought was of no substantial importance, (3) the party failing to make the admission had reasonable ground to believe that that party would prevail on the matter, or (4) there was other good reason for the failure to admit. (*Added by Stats.1986, c. 1334, § 2. Amended by Stats.1987, c. 86, § 15; Stats.1988, c. 553, § 6; Stats.1988, c. 575, § 3; Stats.1991, c. 1090, § 13.*)

§ 2033.5. Form Interrogatories and Requests for Admission; Rules

The Judicial Council shall develop and approve official form interrogatories and requests for admission of the genuineness of any relevant documents or of the truth of any relevant matters of fact in any civil action in a state court based on personal injury, property damage, wrongful death, unlawful detainer, breach of contract, family law, or fraud. Use of the approved form interrogatories and requests for admission shall be optional.

In developing the form interrogatories and requests for admission required by this section, the Judicial Council shall consult with a representative advisory committee which shall include, but not be limited to, representatives of the plaintiff's bar, the defense bar, the public interest bar, court administrators, and the public. The form interrogatories and requests for admission shall be drafted in nontechnical language and shall be made available through the office of the clerk of the appropriate trial court.

The Judicial Council also shall promulgate any necessary rules to govern the use of the form interrogatories and requests for admission. (*Added by Stats.1986, c. 1334, § 2. Amended by Stats.1987, c. 86, § 16; Stats.1988, c. 71, § 1.*)

§ 2034. Simultaneous Exchange of Information Concerning Expert Trial Witnesses

(a) Demand for exchange. After the setting of a trial date for the action, any party may obtain discovery by demanding that all parties simultaneously exchange information concerning each other's expert trial witnesses to the following extent:

(1) Any party may demand a mutual and simultaneous exchange by all parties of a list containing the name and address of any natural person, including one who is a party, whose oral or deposition testimony in the form of an expert opinion any party expects to offer in evidence at the trial.

(2) If any expert designated by a party under paragraph (1) is a party or an employee of a party, or has been retained by a party for the purpose of forming and expressing an opinion in anticipation of the litigation or in preparation for the trial of the action, the designation of that witness shall include or be accompanied by an expert witness declaration under paragraph (2) of subdivision (f).

(3) Any party may also include a demand for the mutual and simultaneous production for inspection and copying of all discoverable reports and writings, if any, made by any expert described in paragraph (2) in the course of preparing that expert's opinion.

This section does not apply to exchanges of lists of experts and valuation data in eminent domain proceedings under Chapter 7 (commencing with Section 1258.010) of Title 7 of Part 3.

(b) Schedule. Any party may make a demand for an exchange of information concerning expert trial witnesses without leave of court. A party shall make this demand no later than the 10th day after a trial date has been set, or 70 days before that trial date, whichever is closer to the trial date.

(c) Identification of parties and specification of date. A demand for an exchange of information concerning expert trial witnesses shall be in writing and shall identify, below the title of the case, the party making the demand. The demand shall state that it is being made under this section.

The demand shall specify the date for the exchange of lists of expert trial witnesses, expert witness declarations, and any demanded production of writings. The specified date of exchange shall be 50 days before the initial trial date, or 20 days after service of the demand, whichever is closer to the trial date, unless the court, on motion and a showing of good cause, orders an earlier or later date of exchange.

(d) Service of copies. The party demanding an exchange of information concerning expert trial witnesses shall serve the demand on all parties who have appeared in the action.

(e) Motion for protective order; contents; denial; monetary sanctions. A party who has been served with a demand to exchange information concerning expert trial witnesses may promptly move for a protective order. This motion shall be accompanied by a declaration stating facts showing a reasonable and good faith attempt at an informal resolution of each issue presented by the motion.

The court, for good cause shown, may make any order that justice requires to protect any party from unwarranted annoyance, embarrassment, oppression, or undue burden and expense. The protective order may include, but is not limited to, one or more of the following directions:

(1) That the demand be quashed because it was not timely served.

(2) That the date of exchange be earlier or later than that specified in the demand.

(3) That the exchange be made only on specified terms and conditions.

(4) That the production and exchange of any reports and writings of experts be made at a different place or at a different time than specified in the demand.

(5) That some or all of the parties be divided into sides on the basis of their identity of interest in the issues in the action, and that the designation of any experts as described in paragraph (2) of subdivision (a) be made by any side so created.

(6) That a party or a side reduce the list of employed or retained experts designated by that party or side under paragraph (2) of subdivision (a).

If the motion for a protective order is denied in whole or in part, the court may order that the parties against whom the motion is brought, provide or permit the discovery against which the protection was sought on those terms and conditions that are just.

The court shall impose a monetary sanction under Section 2023 against any party, person, or attorney who unsuccessfully makes or opposes a motion for a protective order, unless it finds that the one subject to the sanction acted with substantial justification or that other circumstances make the imposition of the sanction unjust.

(f) Written exchange of information; contents. All parties who have appeared in the action shall exchange information concerning expert witnesses in writing on or before the date of exchange specified in the demand. The exchange of information may occur at a meeting of the attorneys for the parties involved or by a mailing on or before the date of exchange.

(1) The exchange of expert witness information shall include either of the following:

(A) A list setting forth the name and address of any person whose expert opinion that party expects to offer in evidence at the trial.

(B) A statement that the party does not presently intend to offer the testimony of any expert witness.

(2) If any witness on the list is an expert as described in paragraph (2) of subdivision (a), the exchange shall also include or be accompanied by an expert witness declaration signed only by the attorney for the party designating the expert, or by that party if that party has no attorney. This declaration shall be under penalty of perjury and shall contain:

(A) A brief narrative statement of the qualifications of each expert.

(B) A brief narrative statement of the general substance of the testimony that the expert is expected to give.

(C) A representation that the expert has agreed to testify at the trial.

(D) A representation that the expert will be sufficiently familiar with the pending action to submit to a meaningful oral deposition concerning the specific testimony, including any opinion and its basis, that the expert is expected to give at trial.

(E) A statement of the expert's hourly and daily fee for providing deposition testimony and for consulting with the retaining attorney.

(g) Production and exchange of discoverable reports and writings. If a demand for an exchange of information concerning expert trial witnesses includes a demand for production of reports and writings as described in paragraph (3) of subdivision (a), all parties shall produce and exchange, at the place and on the date specified in the demand, all discoverable reports and writings, if any, made by any designated expert described in paragraph (2) of subdivision (a).

(h) Supplemental lists; declarations; discoverable reports and writings. Within 20 days after the exchange described in subdivision (f), any party who engaged in the exchange may submit a supplemental expert witness list containing the name and address of any experts who will express an opinion on a subject to be covered by an expert designated by an adverse party to the exchange, if the party supplementing an expert witness list has not previously retained an expert to testify on that subject. This supplemental list shall be accompanied by an expert witness declaration under paragraph (2) of subdivision (f) concerning those additional experts, and by all discoverable reports and writings, if any, made by those additional experts. The party shall also make those experts available immediately for a deposition under subdivision (i), which deposition may be taken even though the time limit for discovery under Section 2024 has expired.

(i) Oral and written depositions; procedures. On receipt of an expert witness list from a party, any other party may take the deposition of any person on the list. The procedures for taking oral and written depositions set forth in Sections 2025, 2026, 2027, and 2028 apply to a deposition of a listed trial expert witness except as follows:

(1) The deposition of any expert described in paragraph (2) of subdivision (a) shall be taken at a place that is within 75 miles of the courthouse where the action is pending. However, on motion for a protective order by the party designating an expert witness, and on a showing of exceptional hardship, the court may order that the deposition be taken at a more distant place from the courthouse.

(2) A party desiring to depose any expert witness, other than a party or employee of a party, who is either (A) an expert described in paragraph (2) of subdivision (a) except one who is a party or an employee of a party, (B) a treating physician and surgeon or other treating health care practitioner who is to be asked to express an opinion during the deposition, or (C) an architect, professional engineer, or licensed land surveyor, who was involved with the original project design or survey for which he or she is asked to express an opinion within his or her expertise and relevant to the action or proceeding, shall pay the expert's reasonable and customary hourly or daily fee for any time spent at the deposition from the time noticed in the deposition subpoena or from the time of the arrival of the expert witness should that time be later than the time noticed in the deposition subpoena, until the time the expert witness is dismissed from the deposition, whether or not the expert is actually deposed by any party attending the deposition. If any counsel representing the expert or a nonnoticing party is late to the deposition, the expert's reasonable and customary hourly or daily fee for the time period determined from the time noticed in the deposition subpoena until the counsel's late arrival, shall be paid by that tardy counsel. However, the hourly or daily fee shall not exceed the fee charged the party who retained the expert except where the expert donated his or her services to a charitable or other nonprofit organization. A daily fee shall only be charged for a full day of attendance at a deposition or where the expert was required by the deposing party to be available for a full day and the expert necessarily had to forego all business he or she would have otherwise conducted that day but for the request that he or she be available all day for the scheduled deposition. In a worker's compensation case arising under Division 4 (commencing with Section 3201) or Division 4.5 (commencing with Section 6100) of the Labor Code, a party desiring to depose any expert on another party's expert witness list shall pay this fee.

The party taking the deposition shall either accompany the service of the deposition notice with a tender of the expert's fee based on the anticipated length of the deposition or tender that fee at the commencement of the deposition. The expert's fee shall be delivered to the attorney for the party designating the expert. If the deposition of the expert takes longer than anticipated, the party giving notice of the deposition shall pay the balance of the expert's fee within five days of receipt of an itemized statement from the expert. The party designating the expert is responsible for any fee charged by the expert for preparing for the deposition and for traveling to the place of the deposition, as well as for any travel expenses of the expert.

(3) The service of a proper deposition notice accompanied by the tender of the expert witness fee described in paragraph (2) is effective to require the party employing or retaining the expert to produce the expert for the deposition. If the party noticing the deposition fails to tender the expert's fee under paragraph (2), the expert shall not be deposed at that time unless the parties stipulate otherwise.

(4) If a party desiring to take the deposition of an expert witness under this subdivision deems that the hourly or daily fee of that expert for providing deposition testimony is unreasonable, that party may move for an order setting the compensation of that expert. This motion shall be accompanied by a declaration stating facts showing a reasonable and good faith attempt at an informal resolution of each issue presented by the motion. Notice of this motion shall also be given to the expert. In any such attempt at an informal resolution, either the party or the expert shall provide the other with (A) proof of the ordinary and customary fee actually charged and received by that expert for similar services provided outside the subject litigation, (B) the total number of times the presently demanded fee has ever been charged and received by that expert, and (C) the frequency and regularity with which the presently demanded fee has been charged and received by that expert within the two-year period preceding the hearing on the motion.

In addition to any other facts or evidence, the expert or the party designating the expert shall provide, and the court's determination as to the reasonableness of the fee shall be based upon (A) proof of the ordinary and customary fee actually charged and received by that expert for similar services provided outside the subject litigation, (B) the total number of times the presently demanded fee has ever been charged and received by that expert, and (C) the frequency and regularity with which the presently demanded fee has been charged and received by that expert within the two-year period preceding the hearing on the motion. Provisions (B) and (C) shall apply to actions filed after January 1, 1994. The court may also consider the ordinary and customary fees charged by similar experts for similar services within the relevant community and any other factors the court deems necessary or appropriate to make its determination.

Upon a determination that the fee demanded by that expert is unreasonable, and based upon the evidence and factors considered, the court shall set the fee of the expert providing testimony.

The court shall impose a monetary sanction under Section 2023 against any party, person, or attorney who unsuccessfully makes or opposes a motion to set expert witness fee, unless it finds that the one subject to the sanction acted with substantial justification or that other circumstances make the imposition of the sanction unjust.

(j) Exclusion of expert opinion from evidence. Except as provided in subdivisions (k), (*l*), and (m), on objection of any party who has made a complete and timely compliance with subdivision (f), the trial court shall exclude from evidence the expert opinion of any witness that is offered by any party who has unreasonably failed to do any of the following:

(1) List that witness as an expert under subdivision (f).

(2) Submit an expert witness declaration.

(3) Produce reports and writings of expert witnesses under subdivision (g).

(4) Make that expert available for a deposition under subdivision (i).

(k) Motion to augment list or amend declaration. On motion of any party who has engaged in a timely exchange of expert witness information, the court may grant leave to (1) augment that party's expert witness list and declaration by adding the name and address of any expert witness whom that party has subsequently retained, or (2) amend that party's expert witness declaration with respect to the general substance of the testimony that an expert previously designated is expected to give. This motion shall be made at a sufficient time in advance of the time limit for the completion of discovery under Section 2024 to permit the deposition of any expert to whom the motion relates to be taken within that time limit. However, under exceptional circumstances, the court may permit the motion to be made at a later time. This motion shall be accompanied by a declaration stating facts showing a reasonable and good faith attempt at an informal resolution of each issue presented by the motion. The demand, and all expert witness lists and declarations exchanged in response to it, shall be lodged with the court when their contents become relevant to an issue in any pending matter in the action. The court shall grant leave to augment or amend an expert witness list or declaration only after taking into account the extent to which the opposing party has relied on the list of expert witnesses, and after determining that any party opposing the motion will not be prejudiced in maintaining that party's action or defense on the merits, and that the moving party either (1) would not in the exercise of reasonable diligence have determined to call that expert witness or have decided to offer the different or additional testimony of that expert witness, or (2) failed to determine to call that expert witness, or to offer the different or additional testimony of that expert witness as a result of mistake, inadvertence, surprise, or excusable neglect, provided that the moving party (1) has sought leave to augment or amend promptly after deciding to call the expert witness or to offer the different or additional testimony, and (2) has promptly thereafter served a copy of the proposed expert witness information concerning the expert or the testimony described in subdivision (f) on all other parties who have appeared in the action. Leave shall be conditioned on the moving party making the expert available immediately for a deposition under subdivision (i), and on such other terms as may be just, including, but not limited to, leave to any party opposing the motion to designate additional expert witnesses or to elicit additional opinions from those previously designated, a continuance of the trial for a reasonable period of time, and the awarding to any party opposing the motion.

The court shall impose a monetary sanction under Section 2023 against any party, person, or attorney who unsuccessfully makes or opposes a motion to augment or amend expert witness information, unless it finds that the one subject to the sanction acted with substantial justification or that other circumstances made the imposition of the sanction unjust.

(*l*) **Motion to submit tardy information; condition.** On motion of any party who has failed to submit expert witness information on the date specified in a demand for that exchange, the court may grant leave to submit that information on a later date. This motion shall be made a sufficient time in advance of the time limit for the completion of discovery under Section 2024 to permit the deposition of any expert to whom the motion relates to be taken within that time limit. However, under exceptional circumstances, the court may permit the motion to be made at a later time. This motion shall be accompanied by a declaration stating facts showing a reasonable and good faith attempt at an informal resolution of each issue presented by the motion.

The court shall grant leave to submit tardy expert witness information only after taking into account the extent to which the opposing party has relied on the absence of a list of expert witnesses, and determining that any party opposing the motion will not be prejudiced in maintaining that party's action or defense on the merits, and that the moving party (1) failed to submit that information as the result of mistake, inadvertence, surprise, or excusable neglect, (2) sought that leave promptly after learning of the mistake, inadvertence, surprise, or excusable neglect, and (3) has promptly thereafter served a copy of the proposed expert witness information described in subdivision (f) on all other parties who have appeared in the action. This order shall be conditioned on the moving party making that expert available immediately for a deposition under subdivision (i), and on such other terms as may be just, including, but not limited to, leave to any party opposing the motion to designate additional expert witnesses or to elicit additional opinions from those previously designated, a continuance of the trial for a reasonable period of time, and the awarding of costs and litigation expenses to any party opposing the motion.

The court shall impose a monetary sanction under Section 2023 against any party, person, or attorney who unsuccessfully makes or opposes a motion to submit tardy expert witness information, unless it finds that the one subject to the sanction acted with substantial justification or that other circumstances make the imposition of the sanction unjust.

(m) Calling experts at trial not previously designated by party. A party may call as a witness at trial an expert not previously designated by that party if: (1) that expert has been designated by another party and has thereafter been deposed under subdivision (i), or (2) that expert is called as a witness to impeach the testimony of an expert witness offered by any other party at the trial. This impeachment may include testimony to the falsity or nonexistence of any fact used as the foundation for any opinion by any other party's expert witness, but may not include testimony that contradicts the opinion.

(n) Original copies. The demand for an exchange of information concerning expert trial witnesses, and any expert witness lists and declarations exchanged shall not be filed with the court. The party demanding the exchange shall retain both the original of the demand, with the original proof of service affixed, and the original of all expert witness lists and declarations exchanged in response to the demand until six months after final disposition of the action. At that time, all originals may be destroyed unless the court, on motion of any party and for good cause shown, orders that the originals be preserved for a longer period. (*Added by Stats.1986, c. 1336, § 2. Amended by Stats.1987, c. 86, § 17; Stats.1988, c. 533, § 7; Stats.1990, c. 771, § 1, c. 1392, § 2; Stats.1992, c. 1301, § 1; Stats.1993, c. 3, § 1, c. 678, § 1.*)

§ 2035. Perpetuation of Testimony or Preservation of Evidence Before Action

(a) Discovery scope and restrictions. One who expects to be a party to any action that may be cognizable in any court of the State of California, whether as a plaintiff, or as a defendant, or in any other capacity, may obtain discovery within the scope delimited by Section 2017, and subject to the restrictions set forth in Section 2019, for the purpose of perpetuating that party's own testimony or that of another natural person or organization, or of preserving evidence for use in the event an action is subsequently filed. One shall not employ the procedures of this section for the purpose either of ascertaining the possible existence of a cause of action or a defense to it, or of identifying those who might be made parties to an action not yet filed.

(b) Methods available. The methods available for discovery conducted for the purposes set forth in subdivision (a) are (1) oral and written depositions, (2) inspections of documents, things, and places, and (3) physical and mental examinations.

(c) Filing petition. One who desires to perpetuate testimony or preserve evidence for the purposes set forth in subdivision (a) shall file a verified petition in the superior court of the county of the residence of at least one expected adverse party, or, if no expected adverse party is a resident of the State of California, in the superior court of a county where the action or proceeding may be filed.

(d) Form and contents of petition. The petition shall be titled in the name of the one who desires the perpetuation of testimony or the preservation of evidence. The petition shall set forth all of the following:

(1) The expectation that the petitioner will be a party to an action cognizable in a court of the State of California.

(2) The present inability of the petitioner either to bring that action or to cause it to be brought.

(3) The subject matter of the expected action and the petitioner's involvement.

(4) The particular discovery methods described in subdivision (b) that the petitioner desires to employ.

(5) The facts that the petitioner desires to establish by the proposed discovery.

(6) The reasons for desiring to perpetuate or preserve these facts before an action has been filed.

(7) The name or a description of those whom the petitioner expects to be adverse parties so far as known.

(8) The name and address of those from whom the discovery is to be sought.

(9) The substance of the information expected to be elicited from each of those from whom discovery is being sought.

The petition shall request the court to enter an order authorizing the petitioner to engage in discovery by the described methods for the purpose of perpetuating the described testimony or preserving the described evidence.

(e) Notice and service. The petitioner shall cause service of a notice of the petition to be made on each natural person or organization named in the petition as an expected adverse party. This service shall be made in the same manner provided for the service of a summons. The service of the notice shall be accompanied by a copy of the petition. The notice shall state that the petitioner will apply to the court at a time and place specified in the notice for the order requested in the petition. This service shall be effected at least 20 days prior to the date specified in the notice for the hearing on the petition.

If after the exercise of due diligence, the petitioner is unable to cause service to be made on any expected adverse party named in the petition, the court in which the petition is filed shall make an order for service by publication. If any expected adverse party served by publication does not appear at the hearing, the court shall appoint an attorney to represent that party for all purposes, including the cross-examination of any person whose testimony is taken by deposition. The court shall order that the petitioner pay the reasonable fees and expenses of any attorney so appointed.

(f) Order authorizing discovery. If the court determines that all or part of the discovery requested may prevent a failure or delay of justice, it shall make an order authorizing that discovery. The order shall identify any witness whose deposition may be taken, and any documents, things, or places that may be inspected, and any person whose physical or mental condition may be examined. Any authorized depositions, inspections, and physical or mental examinations shall then be conducted in accordance with the provisions of this article relating to those methods of discovery in actions that have been filed.

(g) Use of depositions. If a deposition to perpetuate testimony has been taken either under the provisions of this section, or under comparable provisions of the laws of another state, or the federal courts, or a foreign nation, that deposition may be used, in any action involving the same subject matter that is brought in a court of the State of California, in accordance with subdivision (u) of Section 2025 against any party, or the successor in interest of any party, named in the petition as an expected adverse party. (*Added by Stats.1986, c. 1334, § 2. Amended by Stats.1987, c. 86, § 18.*)

§ 2036. Perpetuation of Testimony or Preserving Information Pending Appeal

(a) If an appeal has been taken from a judgment entered by any court of the State of California, or if the time for taking an appeal has not expired, a party may obtain discovery within the scope delimited by Section 2017, and subject to the restrictions set forth in Section 2019, for the purpose of perpetuating testimony or preserving information for use in the event of further proceedings in that court.

(b) The methods available for discovery for the purpose set forth in subdivision (a) are (1) oral and written depositions, (2) inspections of documents, things, and places, and (3) physical and mental examinations.

(c) A party who desires to obtain discovery pending appeal shall obtain leave of the court that entered the judgment. This motion shall be made on the same notice to and service of parties as is required for discovery sought in an action pending in that court.

(d) The motion for leave to conduct discovery pending appeal shall set forth (1) the names and addresses of the natural persons or organizations from whom the discovery is being sought, (2) the particular discovery methods described in subdivision (b) for which authorization is being sought, and (3) the reasons for perpetuating testimony or preserving evidence.

(e) If the court determines that all or part of the discovery requested may prevent a failure or delay of justice in the event of further proceedings in the action in that court, it shall make an order authorizing that discovery. The order shall identify any witness whose deposition may be taken, and any documents, things, or places that may be inspected, and any person whose physical or mental condition may be examined. Any authorized depositions, inspections, and physical and mental examinations shall then be conducted in accordance with the provisions of this article relating to these methods of discovery in a pending action.

(f) If a deposition to perpetuate testimony has been taken under the provisions of this section, it may be used in any later proceeding in accordance with subdivision (u) of Section 2025. (*Added by Stats.1986, c. 1334, § 2. Amended by Stats.1987, c. 86, § 19.*)

SELECTED CALIFORNIA FORMS— PLEADING AND DISCOVERY

Complaint (Personal Injury, Property Damage, Wrongful Death).
Cause of Action (General Negligence).
Exemplary Damages Attachment.
Cross–Complaint (Personal Injury, Property Damage, Wrongful Death).
Answer (Personal Injury, Property Damage, Wrongful Death).
Form Interrogatories (Personal Injury).

ATTORNEY OR PARTY WITHOUT ATTORNEY (NAME AND ADDRESS)	TELEPHONE:	FOR COURT USE ONLY
ATTORNEY FOR (NAME)		
Insert name of court, judicial district or branch court, if any, and post office and street address:		
PLAINTIFF:		
DEFENDANT:		

☐ DOES 1 TO _____

COMPLAINT—Personal Injury, Property Damage, Wrongful Death

☐ MOTOR VEHICLE   ☐ OTHER *(specify)*:
    ☐ Property Damage   ☐ Wrongful Death
    ☐ Personal Injury   ☐ Other Damages *(specify)*:

CASE NUMBER

1. This pleading, including attachments and exhibits, consists of the following number of pages: _____

2. a. Each plaintiff named above is a competent adult
    ☐ Except plaintiff *(name)*:
      ☐ a corporation qualified to do business in California
      ☐ an unincorporated entity *(describe)*:
      ☐ a public entity *(describe)*:
      ☐ a minor   ☐ an adult
        ☐ for whom a guardian or conservator of the estate or a guardian ad litem has been appointed
        ☐ other *(specify)*:
      ☐ other *(specify)*:

    ☐ Except plaintiff *(name)*:
      ☐ a corporation qualified to do business in California
      ☐ an unincorporated entity *(describe)*:
      ☐ a public entity *(describe)*:
      ☐ a minor   ☐ an adult
        ☐ for whom a guardian or conservator of the estate or a guardian ad litem has been appointed
        ☐ other *(specify)*:
      ☐ other *(specify)*:

   b. ☐ Plaintiff *(name)*:
      is doing business under the fictitious name of *(specify)*:

      and has complied with the fictitious business name laws.
   c. ☐ Information about additional plaintiffs who are not competent adults is shown in Complaint—Attachment 2c.

(Continued)

SHORT TITLE	CASE NUMBER

COMPLAINT—Personal Injury, Property Damage, Wrongful Death   Page two

3. a Each defendant named above is a natural person
☐ **Except** defendant *(name)*:

   ☐ a business organization, form unknown
   ☐ a corporation
   ☐ an unincorporated entity *(describe)*:

   ☐ a public entity *(describe)*:

   ☐ other *(specify)*:

☐ **Except** defendant *(name)*:

   ☐ a business organization, form unknown
   ☐ a corporation
   ☐ an unincorporated entity *(describe)*:

   ☐ a public entity *(describe)*:

   ☐ other *(specify)*:

☐ **Except** defendant *(name)*:

   ☐ a business organization, form unknown
   ☐ a corporation
   ☐ an unincorporated entity *(describe)*:

   ☐ a public entity *(describe)*:

   ☐ other *(specify)*:

☐ **Except** defendant *(name)*:

   ☐ a business organization, form unknown
   ☐ a corporation
   ☐ an unincorporated entity *(describe)*:

   ☐ a public entity *(describe)*:

   ☐ other *(specify)*:

   b The true names and capacities of defendants sued as Does are unknown to plaintiff.

   c ☐ Information about additional defendants who are not natural persons is contained in Complaint—Attachment 3c.

   d ☐ Defendants who are joined pursuant to Code of Civil Procedure section 382 are *(names)*:

4. ☐ Plaintiff is required to comply with a claims statute, and
   a ☐ plaintiff has complied with applicable claims statutes, or
   b ☐ plaintiff is excused from complying because *(specify)*:

5. This court is the proper court because
   ☐ at least one defendant now resides in its jurisdictional area.
   ☐ the principal place of business of a corporation or unincorporated association is in its jurisdictional area.
   ☐ injury to person or damage to personal property occurred in its jurisdictional area.
   ☐ other *(specify)*:

6. ☐ The following paragraphs of this complaint are alleged on information and belief *(specify paragraph numbers)*:

(Continued)   Page two
          (C4401)

Page Two of Form

SHORT TITLE	CASE NUMBER

COMPLAINT—Personal Injury, Property Damage, Wrongful Death (Continued)   Page three

7. ☐ The damages claimed for wrongful death and the relationships of plaintiff to the deceased are
   ☐ listed in Complaint—Attachment 7 ☐ as follows:

8. Plaintiff has suffered
   ☐ wage loss   ☐ loss of use of property
   ☐ hospital and medical expenses   ☐ general damage
   ☐ property damage   ☐ loss of earning capacity
   ☐ other damage (specify):

9. Relief sought in this complaint is within the jurisdiction of this court.

10. PLAINTIFF PRAYS
    For judgment for costs of suit; for such relief as is fair, just, and equitable; and for
    ☐ compensatory damages
       ☐ (Superior Court) according to proof.

       ☐ (Municipal and Justice Court) in the amount of $ _____
    ☐ other (specify):

11. The following causes of action are attached and the statements above apply to each: (Each complaint must have
    one or more causes of action attached.)
    ☐ Motor Vehicle
    ☐ General Negligence
    ☐ Intentional Tort
    ☐ Products Liability
    ☐ Premises Liability
    ☐ Other (specify):

_____   _____
(Type or print name)   (Signature of plaintiff or attorney)

Page Three of Form

SHORT TITLE:	CASE NUMBER:

_____   **CAUSE OF ACTION—General Negligence**   Page _____
   (number)

ATTACHMENT TO ☐ Complaint   ☐ Cross-Complaint

(Use a separate cause of action form for each cause of action.)

GN-1. Plaintiff *(name)*:

    alleges that defendant *(name)*:

      ☐ Does _____ to _____

was the legal (proximate) cause of damages to plaintiff. By the following acts or omissions to act, defendant
negligently caused the damage to plaintiff
on *(date)*:
at *(place)*:

(description of reasons for liability):

Form Approved by the
Judicial Council of California
Effective January 1, 1982
Rule 982 1(3)
       CAUSE OF ACTION—General Negligence   CCP 425.12
                                                       [C4404]

SHORT TITLE:	CASE NUMBER:

Exemplary Damages Attachment   Page _____

ATTACHMENT TO ☐ Complaint ☐ Cross-Complaint

EX-1. As additional damages against defendant *(name)*:

Plaintiff alleges defendant was guilty of
☐ malice
☐ fraud
☐ oppression
as defined in Civil Code section 3294, and plaintiff should recover, in addition to actual damages, damages
to make an example of and to punish defendant.

EX-2. The facts supporting plaintiff's claim are as follows:

EX-3. The amount of exemplary damages sought is
    a. ☐ not shown, pursuant to Code of Civil Procedure section 425.10.
    b. ☐ $

Form Approved by the
Judicial Council of California
Effective January 1, 1982
Rule 982.1(13)   **Exemplary Damages Attachment**   CCP 425.12
[C4408]

ATTORNEY OR PARTY WITHOUT ATTORNEY (NAME AND ADDRESS):   TELEPHONE: FOR COURT USE ONLY

ATTORNEY FOR (NAME):

Insert name of court, judicial district or branch court, if any, and post office and street address:

SHORT TITLE:

CROSS-COMPLAINANT:

CROSS-DEFENDANT:

☐ DOES 1 TO _____

CASE NUMBER:

CROSS-COMPLAINT—Personal Injury, Property Damage, Wrongful Death
☐ Apportionment of Fault   ☐ Declaratory Relief
☐ Indemnification   ☐ Other *(specify)*:

1. This pleading, including exhibits and attachments, consists of the following number of pages: ___ . ___

CROSS-COMPLAINANT *(name)*:

SAYS AGAINST CROSS-DEFENDANT *(name)*:

2. ☐ The following causes of action are attached and the statements below apply to each: *(In the attachments plaintiff means cross-complainant and defendant means cross-defendant.)*
   ☐ Motor Vehicle   ☐ Products Liability
   ☐ General Negligence   ☐ Premises Liability
   ☐ Intentional Tort
   ☐ Other *(specify)*:

3. a. Each cross-complainant named above is a competent adult
   ☐ **Except** cross-complainant *(name)*:

     ☐ a corporation qualified to do business in California
     ☐ an unincorporated entity *(describe)*:
     ☐ a public entity *(describe)*:
     ☐ a minor ☐ an adult
       ☐ for whom a guardian or conservator of the estate or a guardian ad litem has been appointed
       ☐ other *(specify)*:
     ☐ other *(specify)*:

b. ☐ Information about additional cross-complainants who are not competent adults is contained in Cross-Complaint—Attachment 3b.   (Continued)

Form Approved by the
Judicial Council of California
Effective January 1, 1982
Rule 982.1(14)

CROSS-COMPLAINT—Personal Injury, Property Damage,
Wrongful Death

CCP 425.12
[C4409]

Page One of Form

SHORT TITLE:	CASE NUMBER

CROSS-COMPLAINT—Personal Injury, Property Damage, Wrongful Death

Page two

4. a. Each cross-defendant named above is a natural person
　　□ Except cross-defendant (name):　　　　　　□ Except cross-defendant (name):

　　　　□ a business organization, form unknown　　□ a business organization, form unknown
　　　　□ a corporation　　　　　　　　　　　　　□ a corporation
　　　　□ an unincorporated entity (describe):　　　□ an unincorporated entity (describe):

　　　　□ a public entity (describe):　　　　　　　□ a public entity (describe):

　　　　□ other (specify):　　　　　　　　　　　□ other (specify):

　b. The true names and capacities of cross-defendants sued as Does are unknown to cross-complainant.

　c. □ Information about additional cross-defendants who are not natural persons is contained in Cross-Complaint—Attachment 4c.

5. □ Cross-complainant is required to comply with a claims statute, and
　　a. □ has complied with applicable claims statutes, or
　　b. □ is excused from complying because (specify):

6. □ _____ Cause of Action—Indemnification
　　　　(number)

　a. I am informed and believe that cross-defendants were the agents, employees, co-venturers, partners, or in some manner agents or principals, or both, for each other and were acting within the course and scope of their agency or employment.

　b. The principal action alleges among other things conduct entitling plaintiff to compensatory damages against me. I contend that I am not liable for events and occurrences described in plaintiff's complaint.

　c. If I am found in some manner responsible to plaintiff or to anyone else as a result of the incidents and occurrences described in plaintiff's complaint, my liability would be based solely upon a derivative form of liability not resulting from my conduct, but only from an obligation imposed upon me by law; therefore, I would be entitled to complete indemnity from each cross-defendant.

7. □ _____ Cause of Action—Apportionment of Fault
　　　　(number)

　I am informed and believe that each cross-defendant was responsible, in whole or in part, for the injuries, if any, suffered by plaintiff. If I am judged liable to plaintiff, each cross-defendant should be required:

　a. to pay a share of plaintiff's judgment which is in proportion to the comparative negligence of that cross-defendant in causing plaintiff's damages and

　b. to reimburse me for any payments I make to plaintiff in excess of my proportional share of all cross-defendants' negligence.

(Continued)

Page two
[C44 10]

Page Two of Form

SHORT TITLE:

CASE NUMBER

CROSS-COMPLAINT— Personal Injury, Property Damage, Wrongful Death (Continued) Page three

8. ☐ _____ **Cause of Action—Declaratory Relief**
   (number)

   An actual controversy exists between the parties concerning their respective rights and duties because cross-complainant contends and cross-defendant disputes ☐ as specified in Cross-Complaint—Attachment 8
   ☐ as follows:

9. ☐ _____ **Cause of Action—*(Specify):***
   (number)

10. **CROSS-COMPLAINANT PRAYS**
    For judgment for costs of suit; for such relief as is fair, just, and equitable; and for
    ☐ compensatory damages
       ☐ **(Superior Court)** according to proof.
       ☐ **(Municipal and Justice Court)** in the amount of $ _____

    ☐ total and complete indemnity for any judgments rendered against me.

    ☐ judgment in a proportionate share from each cross-defendant.

    ☐ a judicial determination that cross-defendants were the legal cause of any injuries and damages sustained by plaintiff and that cross-defendants indemnify me, either completely or partially, for any sums of money which may be recovered against me by plaintiff.

    ☐ other *(specify):*

. . . .
(Type or print name)

_____
(Signature of cross-complainant or attorney)

Page Three of Form

ATTORNEY OR PARTY WITHOUT ATTORNEY (NAME AND ADDRESS)	TELEPHONE	FOR COURT USE ONLY

ATTORNEY FOR (NAME)

Insert name of court, judicial district or branch court, if any, and post office and street address:

PLAINTIFF:

DEFENDANT:

ANSWER—Personal Injury, Property Damage, Wrongful Death ☐ COMPLAINT OF (name): ☐ CROSS-COMPLAINT OF (name):	CASE NUMBER

1. This pleading, including attachments and exhibits, consists of the following number of pages:

DEFENDANT OR CROSS-DEFENDANT (name):

2. ☐ Generally denies each allegation of the unverified complaint or cross-complaint.

3. a. ☐ DENIES each allegation of the following numbered paragraphs:

    b. ☐ ADMITS each allegation of the following numbered paragraphs:

    c. ☐ DENIES, ON INFORMATION AND BELIEF, each allegation of the following numbered paragraphs:

    d. ☐ DENIES, BECAUSE OF LACK OF SUFFICIENT INFORMATION OR BELIEF TO ANSWER, each allegation of the following numbered paragraphs:

    e. ☐ ADMITS the following allegations and generally denies all other allegations:

(Continued)

SHORT TITLE:	CASE NUMBER:

ANSWER—Personal Injury, Property Damage, Wrongful Death   Page two

f. ☐ DENIES the following allegations and admits all other allegations:

g. ☐ Other *(specify):*

AFFIRMATIVELY ALLEGES AS A DEFENSE

4. ☐ The comparative fault of plaintiff or cross-complainant *(name):*
   as follows:

5. ☐ The expiration of the Statute of Limitations as follows:

6. ☐ Other *(specify):*

7. DEFENDANT OR CROSS-DEFENDANT PRAYS
   For costs of suit and that plaintiff or cross-complainant take nothing.
   ☐ Other *(specify):*

. . . .   _____
(Type or print name)   (Signature of party or attorney)

Page Two of Form

Page two
(C4413)

ATTORNEY OR PARTY WITHOUT ATTORNEY *(Name and Address)*:	TELEPHONE NO.:

ATTORNEY FOR *(Name)*

NAME OF COURT AND JUDICIAL DISTRICT AND BRANCH COURT, IF ANY:

SHORT TITLE OF CASE:

FORM INTERROGATORIES	CASE NUMBER:
Asking Party:	
Answering Party:	
Set No.:	

Sec. 1. Instructions to All Parties

(a) These are general instructions. *For time limitations, requirements for service on other parties, and other details, see Code of Civil Procedure section 2030 and the cases construing it.*

(b) These interrogatories do not change existing law relating to interrogatories nor do they affect an answering party's right to assert any privilege or objection.

Sec. 2. Instructions to the Asking Party

(a) These interrogatories are designed for optional use in the superior courts only. A separate set of interrogatories, Form Interrogatories—Economic Litigation, which have no subparts, are designed for optional use in municipal and justice courts. However, they also may be used in superior courts. See Code of Civil Procedure section 94.

(b) Check the box next to each interrogatory that you want the answering party to answer. Use care in choosing those interrogatories that are applicable to the case.

(c) The interrogatories in section 16.0, Defendant's Contentions—Personal Injury, should not be used until the defendant has had a reasonable opportunity to conduct an investigation or discovery of plaintiff's injuries and damages.

(d) Additional interrogatories may be attached.

Sec. 3. Instructions to the Answering Party

(a) In superior court actions, an answer or other appropriate response must be given to each interrogatory checked by the asking party.

(b) As a general rule, within 30 days after you are served with these interrogatories, you must serve your responses on the asking party and serve copies of your responses on all other parties to the action who have appeared. See Code of Civil Procedure section 2030 for details.

(c) Each answer must be as complete and straightforward as the information reasonably available to you permits. If an interrogatory cannot be answered completely, answer it to the extent possible.

(d) If you do not have enough personal knowledge to fully answer an interrogatory, say so, but make a reasonable and good faith effort to get the information by asking other persons or organizations, unless the information is equally available to the asking party.

(e) Whenever an interrogatory may be answered by referring to a document, the document may be attached as an exhibit to the response and referred to in the response. If the document has more than one page, refer to the page and section where the answer to the interrogatory can be found.

(f) Whenever an address and telephone number for the same person are requested in more than one interrogatory, you are required to furnish them in answering only the first interrogatory asking for that information.

(g) Your answers to these interrogatories must be verified, dated, and signed. You may wish to use the following form *at the end of your answers:*

"I declare under penalty of perjury under the laws of the State of California that the foregoing answers are true and correct.

_____   _____   ''
      (DATE)   (SIGNATURE)

Sec. 4. Definitions

Words in **BOLDFACE CAPITALS** in these interrogatories are defined as follows:

(a) **INCIDENT** includes the circumstances and events surrounding the alleged accident, injury, or other occurrence or breach of contract giving rise to this action or proceeding.

(b) **YOU OR ANYONE ACTING ON YOUR BEHALF** includes you, your agents, your employees, your insurance companies, their agents, their employees, your attorneys, your accountants, your investigators, and anyone else acting on your behalf.

(Continued)   Page 1 of 8

Form Approved by the
Judicial Council of California
FI-120 [Rev. July 1, 1987]

FORM INTERROGATORIES

CCP 2030, 2033.5
[E2642]

(c) **PERSON** includes a natural person, firm, association, organization, partnership, business, trust, corporation, or public entity.

(d) **DOCUMENT** means a writing, as defined in Evidence Code section 250, and includes the original or a copy of handwriting, typewriting, printing, photostating, photographing, and every other means of recording upon any tangible thing and form of communicating or representation, including letters, words, pictures, sounds, or symbols, or combinations of them.

(e) **HEALTH CARE PROVIDER** includes any **PERSON** referred to in Code of Civil Procedure section 667.7(e)(3).

(f) **ADDRESS** means the street address, including the city, state, and zip code.

Sec. 5. Interrogatories

The following interrogatories have been approved by the Judicial Council under section 2033.5 of the Code of Civil Procedure:

CONTENTS

1.0 Identity of Persons Answering These Interrogatories

☐ 1.1 State the name, **ADDRESS**, telephone number, and relationship to you of each **PERSON** who prepared or assisted in the preparation of the responses to these interrogatories. (Do not identify anyone who simply typed or reproduced the responses.)

2.0 General Background Information — Individual

☐ 2.1 State:
(a) your name;
(b) every name you have used in the past;
(c) the dates you used each name.

☐ 2.2 State the date and place of your birth.

☐ 2.3 At the time of the **INCIDENT**, did you have a driver's license? If so, state:
(a) the state or other issuing entity;
(b) the license number and type;
(c) the date of issuance;
(d) all restrictions.

☐ 2.4 At the time of the **INCIDENT**, did you have any other permit or license for the operation of a motor vehicle? If so, state:
(a) the state or other issuing entity;
(b) the license number and type;
(c) the date of issuance;
(d) all restrictions.

☐ 2.5 State:
(a) your present residence **ADDRESS**;
(b) your residence **ADDRESSES** for the last five years;
(c) the dates you lived at each **ADDRESS**.

☐ 2.6 State:
(a) the name, **ADDRESS**, and telephone number of your present employer or place of self-employment;
(b) the name, **ADDRESS**, dates of employment, job title, and nature of work for each employer or self-employment you have had from five years before the **INCIDENT** until today.

☐ 2.7 State:
(a) the name and **ADDRESS** of each school or other academic or vocational institution you have attended beginning with high school;
(b) the dates you attended;
(c) the highest grade level you have completed;
(d) the degrees received.

☐ 2.8 Have you ever been convicted of a felony? If so, for each conviction state:
(a) the city and state where you were convicted;
(b) the date of conviction;
(c) the offense;
(d) the court and case number.

☐ 2.9 Can you speak English with ease? If not, what language and dialect do you normally use?

☐ 2.10 Can you read and write English with ease? If not, what language and dialect do you normally use?

☐ 2.11 At the time of the **INCIDENT** were you acting as an agent or employee for any **PERSON**? If so, state:
(a) the name, **ADDRESS**, and telephone number of that **PERSON**;
(b) a description of your duties.

☐ 2.12 At the time of the **INCIDENT** did you or any other person have any physical, emotional, or mental disability or condition that may have contributed to the occurrence of the **INCIDENT**? If so, for each person state:
(a) the name, **ADDRESS**, and telephone number;

(b) the nature of the disability or condition;

(c) the manner in which the disability or condition contributed to the occurrence of the INCIDENT.

☐ 2.13 Within 24 hours before the INCIDENT did you or any person involved in the INCIDENT use or take any of the following substances: alcoholic beverage, marijuana, or other drug or medication of any kind (prescription or not)? If so, for each person state:

(a) the name, ADDRESS, and telephone number;

(b) the nature or description of each substance;

(c) the quantity of each substance used or taken;

(d) the date and time of day when each substance was used or taken;

(e) the ADDRESS where each substance was used or taken;

(f) the name, ADDRESS, and telephone number of each person who was present when each substance was used or taken;

(g) the name, ADDRESS, and telephone number of any HEALTH CARE PROVIDER that prescribed or furnished the substance and the condition for which it was prescribed or furnished.

3.0 General Background Information — Business Entity

☐ 3.1 Are you a corporation? If so, state:

(a) the name stated in the current articles of incorporation;

(b) all other names used by the corporation during the past ten years and the dates each was used;

(c) the date and place of incorporation;

(d) the ADDRESS of the principal place of business;

(e) whether you are qualified to do business in California.

☐ 3.2 Are you a partnership? If so, state:

(a) the current partnership name;

(b) all other names used by the partnership during the past ten years and the dates each was used;

(c) whether you are a limited partnership and, if so, under the laws of what jurisdiction;

(d) the name and ADDRESS of each general partner;

(e) the ADDRESS of the principal place of business.

☐ 3.3 Are you a joint venture? If so, state:

(a) the current joint venture name;

(b) all other names used by the joint venture during the past ten years and the dates each was used;

(c) the name and ADDRESS of each joint venturer;

(d) the ADDRESS of the principal place of business.

☐ 3.4 Are you an unincorporated association? If so, state:

(a) the current unincorporated association name;

(b) all other names used by the unincorporated association during the past ten years and the dates each was used;

(c) the ADDRESS of the principal place of business.

☐ 3.5 Have you done business under a fictitious name during the past ten years? If so, for each fictitious name state:

(a) the name;

(b) the dates each was used;

(c) the state and county of each fictitious name filing;

(d) the ADDRESS of the principal place of business.

☐ 3.6 Within the past five years has any public entity registered or licensed your businesses? If so, for each license or registration:

(a) identify the license or registration;

(b) state the name of the public entity;

(c) state the dates of issuance and expiration.

4.0 Insurance

☐ 4.1 At the time of the INCIDENT, was there in effect any policy of insurance through which you were or might be insured in any manner (for example, primary, pro-rata, or excess liability coverage or medical expense coverage) for the damages, claims, or actions that have arisen out of the INCIDENT? If so, for each policy state:

(a) the kind of coverage;

(b) the name and ADDRESS of the insurance company;

(c) the name, ADDRESS, and telephone number of each named insured;

(d) the policy number;

(e) the limits of coverage for each type of coverage contained in the policy;

(f) whether any reservation of rights or controversy or coverage dispute exists between you and the insurance company;

(g) the name, ADDRESS, and telephone number of the custodian of the policy.

☐ 4.2 Are you self-insured under any statute for the damages, claims, or actions that have arisen out of the INCIDENT? If so, specify the statute.

5.0 *(Reserved)*

6.0 Physical, Mental, or Emotional Injuries

☐ 6.1 Do you attribute any physical, mental, or emotional injuries to the INCIDENT? If your answer is "no," do not answer interrogatories 6.2 through 6.7.

☐ 6.2 Identify each injury you attribute to the INCIDENT and the area of your body affected.

☐ 6.3 Do you still have any complaints that you attribute to the INCIDENT? If so, for each complaint state:

(a) a description;

(b) whether the complaint is subsiding, remaining the same, or becoming worse;

(c) the frequency and duration.

☐ 6.4 Did you receive any consultation or examination (except from expert witnesses covered by Code of Civil Procedure, § 2034) or treatment from a HEALTH CARE PROVIDER for any injury you attribute to the INCIDENT? If so, for each HEALTH CARE PROVIDER state:

(a) the name, ADDRESS, and telephone number;

(b) the type of consultation, examination, or treatment provided;

(c) the dates you received consultation, examination, or treatment;
(d) the charges to date.

☐ 6.5 Have you taken any medication, prescribed or not, as a result of injuries that you attribute to the INCIDENT? If so, for each medication state:
(a) the name;
(b) the PERSON who prescribed or furnished it;
(c) the date prescribed or furnished;
(d) the dates you began and stopped taking it;
(e) the cost to date.

☐ 6.6 Are there any other medical services not previously listed (for example, ambulance, nursing, prosthetics)? If so, for each service state:
(a) the nature;
(b) the date;
(c) the cost;
(d) the name, ADDRESS, and telephone number of each provider.

☐ 6.7 Has any HEALTH CARE PROVIDER advised that you may require future or additional treatment for any injuries that you attribute to the INCIDENT? If so, for each injury state:
(a) the name and ADDRESS of each HEALTH CARE PROVIDER;
(b) the complaints for which the treatment was advised;
(c) the nature, duration, and estimated cost of the treatment.

7.0 Property Damage

☐ 7.1 Do you attribute any loss of or damage to a vehicle or other property to the INCIDENT? If so, for each item of property:
(a) describe the property;
(b) describe the nature and location of the damage to the property;
(c) state the amount of damage you are claiming for each item of property and how the amount was calculated;
(d) if the property was sold, state the name, ADDRESS, and telephone number of the seller, the date of sale, and the sale price.

☐ 7.2 Has a written estimate or evaluation been made for any item of property referred to in your answer to the preceding interrogatory? If so, for each estimate or evaluation state:
(a) the name, ADDRESS, and telephone number of the PERSON who prepared it and the date prepared;
(b) the name, ADDRESS, and telephone number of each PERSON who has a copy;
(c) the amount of damage stated.

☐ 7.3 Has any item of property referred to in your answer to interrogatory 7.1 been repaired? If so, for each item state:
(a) the date repaired;
(b) a description of the repair;
(c) the repair cost;

(d) the name, ADDRESS, and telephone number of the PERSON who repaired it;
(e) the name, ADDRESS, and telephone number of the PERSON who paid for the repair.

8.0 Loss of Income or Earning Capacity

☐ 8.1 Do you attribute any loss of income or earning capacity to the INCIDENT? If your answer is ''no,'' do not answer interrogatories 8.2 through 8.8.

☐ 8.2 State:
(a) the nature of your work;
(b) your job title at the time of the INCIDENT;
(c) the date your employment began.

☐ 8.3 State the last date before the INCIDENT that you worked for compensation.

☐ 8.4 State your monthly income at the time of the INCIDENT and how the amount was calculated.

☐ 8.5 State the date you returned to work at each place of employment following the INCIDENT.

☐ 8.6 State the dates you did not work and for which you lost income.

☐ 8.7 State the total income you have lost to date as a result of the INCIDENT and how the amount was calculated.

☐ 8.8 Will you lose income in the future as a result of the INCIDENT? If so, state:
(a) the facts upon which you base this contention;
(b) an estimate of the amount;
(c) an estimate of how long you will be unable to work;
(d) how the claim for future income is calculated.

9.0 Other Damages

☐ 9.1 Are there any other damages that you attribute to the INCIDENT? If so, for each item of damage state:
(a) the nature;
(b) the date it occurred;
(c) the amount;
(d) the name, ADDRESS, and telephone number of each PERSON to whom an obligation was incurred.

☐ 9.2 Do any DOCUMENTS support the existence or amount of any item of damages claimed in interrogatory 9.1? If so, state the name, ADDRESS, and telephone number of the PERSON who has each DOCUMENT.

10.0 Medical History

☐ 10.1 At any time before the INCIDENT did you have complaints or injuries that involved the same part of your body claimed to have been injured in the INCIDENT? If so, for each state:
(a) a description;
(b) the dates it began and ended;
(c) the name, ADDRESS, and telephone number of each HEALTH CARE PROVIDER whom you consulted or who examined or treated you.

☐ 10.2 List all physical, mental, and emotional disabilities you had immediately before the **INCIDENT**. (You may omit mental or emotional disabilities unless you attribute any mental or emotional injury to the **INCIDENT**.)

☐ 10.3 At any time after the **INCIDENT**, did you sustain injuries of the kind for which you are now claiming damages. If so, for each incident state:
(a) the date and the place it occurred;
(b) the name, **ADDRESS**, and telephone number of any other **PERSON** involved;
(c) the nature of any injuries you sustained;
(d) the name, **ADDRESS**, and telephone number of each **HEALTH CARE PROVIDER** that you consulted or who examined or treated you;
(e) the nature of the treatment and its duration.

11.0 Other Claims and Previous Claims

☐ 11.1 Except for this action, in the last ten years have you filed an action or made a written claim or demand for compensation for your personal injuries? If so, for each action, claim, or demand state:
(a) the date, time, and place and location of the **INCIDENT** (closest street **ADDRESS** or intersection);
(b) the name, **ADDRESS**, and telephone number of each **PERSON** against whom the claim was made or action filed;
(c) the court, names of the parties, and case number of any action filed;
(d) the name, **ADDRESS**, and telephone number of any attorney representing you;
(e) whether the claim or action has been resolved or is pending.

☐ 11.2 In the last ten years have you made a written claim or demand for worker's compensation benefits? If so, for each claim or demand state:
(a) the date, time, and place of the **INCIDENT** giving rise to the claim;
(b) the name, **ADDRESS**, and telephone number of your employer at the time of the injury;
(c) the name, **ADDRESS**, and telephone number of the worker's compensation insurer and the claim number;
(d) the period of time during which you received worker's compensation benefits;
(e) a description of the injury;
(f) the name, **ADDRESS**, and telephone number of any **HEALTH CARE PROVIDER** that provided services;
(g) the case number at the Worker's Compensation Appeals Board.

12.0 Investigation — General

☐ 12.1 State the name, **ADDRESS**, and telephone number of each individual:
(a) who witnessed the **INCIDENT** or the events occurring immediately before or after the **INCIDENT**;
(b) who made any statement at the scene of the **INCIDENT**;
(c) who heard any statements made about the **INCIDENT** by any individual at the scene;

(d) who **YOU OR ANYONE ACTING ON YOUR BEHALF** claim has knowledge of the **INCIDENT** (except for expert witnesses covered by Code of Civil Procedure, § 2034).

☐ 12.2 Have **YOU OR ANYONE ACTING ON YOUR BEHALF** interviewed any individual concerning the **INCIDENT**? If so, for each individual state:
(a) the name, **ADDRESS**, and telephone number of the individual interviewed;
(b) the date of the interview;
(c) the name, **ADDRESS**, and telephone number of the **PERSON** who conducted the interview.

☐ 12.3 Have **YOU OR ANYONE ACTING ON YOUR BEHALF** obtained a written or recorded statement from any individual concerning the **INCIDENT**? If so, for each statement state:
(a) the name, **ADDRESS**, and telephone number of the individual from whom the statement was obtained;
(b) the name, **ADDRESS**, and telephone number of the individual who obtained the statement;
(c) the date the statement was obtained;
(d) the name, **ADDRESS**, and telephone number of each **PERSON** who has the original statement or a copy.

☐ 12.4 Do **YOU OR ANYONE ACTING ON YOUR BEHALF** know of any photographs, films, or videotapes depicting any place, object, or individual concerning the **INCIDENT** or plaintiff's injuries? If so, state:
(a) the number of photographs or feet of film or videotape;
(b) the places, objects, or persons photographed, filmed, or videotaped;
(c) the date the photographs, films, or videotapes were taken;
(d) the name, **ADDRESS**, and telephone number of the individual taking the photographs, films, or videotapes;
(e) the name, **ADDRESS**, and telephone number of each **PERSON** who has the original or a copy.

☐ 12.5 Do **YOU OR ANYONE ACTING ON YOUR BEHALF** know of any diagram, reproduction, or model of any place or thing (except for items developed by expert witnesses covered by Code of Civil Procedure, § 2034) concerning the **INCIDENT**? If so, for each item state:
(a) the type (i.e., diagram, reproduction, or model);
(b) the subject matter;
(c) the name, **ADDRESS**, and telephone number of each **PERSON** who has it.

☐ 12.6 Was a report made by any **PERSON** concerning the **INCIDENT**? If so, state:
(a) the name, title, identification number, and employer of the **PERSON** who made the report;
(b) the date and type of report made;
(c) the name, **ADDRESS**, and telephone number of the **PERSON** for whom the report was made.

☐ 12.7 Have **YOU OR ANYONE ACTING ON YOUR BEHALF** inspected the scene of the **INCIDENT**? If so, for each inspection state:

(a) the name, **ADDRESS**, and telephone number of the individual making the inspection (except for expert witnesses covered by Code of Civil Procedure, § 2034);

(b) the date of the inspection.

13.0 Investigation — Surveillance

13.1 Have YOU OR ANYONE ACTING ON YOUR BEHALF conducted surveillance of any individual involved in the **INCIDENT** or any party to this action? If so, for each surveillance state:

(a) the name, **ADDRESS**, and telephone number of the individual or party;

(b) the time, date, and place of the surveillance;

(c) the name, **ADDRESS**, and telephone number of the individual who conducted the surveillance.

13.2 Has a written report been prepared on the surveillance? If so, for each written report state:

(a) the title;

(b) the date;

(c) the name, **ADDRESS**, and telephone number of the individual who prepared the report;

(d) the name, **ADDRESS**, and telephone number of each **PERSON** who has the original or a copy.

14.0 Statutory or Regulatory Violations

14.1 Do YOU OR ANYONE ACTING ON YOUR BEHALF contend that any **PERSON** involved in the **INCIDENT** violated any statute, ordinance, or regulation and that the violation was a legal (proximate) cause of the **INCIDENT**? If so, identify each **PERSON** and the statute, ordinance, or regulation.

14.2 Was any **PERSON** cited or charged with a violation of any statute, ordinance, or regulation as a result of this **INCIDENT**? If so, for each **PERSON** state:

(a) the name, **ADDRESS**, and telephone number of the **PERSON**;

(b) the statute, ordinance, or regulation allegedly violated;

(c) whether the **PERSON** entered a plea in response to the citation or charge and, if so, the plea entered;

(d) the name and **ADDRESS** of the court or administrative agency, names of the parties, and case number.

15.0 Special or Affirmative Defenses

15.1 Identify each denial of a material allegation and each special or affirmative defense in your pleadings and for each:

(a) state all facts upon which you base the denial or special or affirmative defense;

(b) state the names, **ADDRESSES**, and telephone numbers of all **PERSONS** who have knowledge of those facts;

(c) identify all **DOCUMENTS** and other tangible things which support your denial or special or affirmative defense, and state the name, **ADDRESS**, and telephone number of the **PERSON** who has each **DOCUMENT**.

16.0 Defendant's Contentions — Personal Injury

[See Instruction 2(c)]

16.1 Do you contend that any **PERSON**, other than you or plaintiff, contributed to the occurrence of the **INCIDENT** or the injuries or damages claimed by plaintiff? If so, for each **PERSON**:

(a) state the name, **ADDRESS**, and telephone number of the **PERSON**;

(b) state all facts upon which you base your contention;

(c) state the names, **ADDRESSES**, and telephone numbers of all **PERSONS** who have knowledge of the facts;

(d) identify all **DOCUMENTS** and other tangible things that support your contention and state the name, **ADDRESS**, and telephone number of the **PERSON** who has each **DOCUMENT** or thing.

16.2 Do you contend that plaintiff was not injured in the **INCIDENT**? If so:

(a) state all facts upon which you base your contention;

(b) state the names, **ADDRESSES**, and telephone numbers of all **PERSONS** who have knowledge of the facts;

(c) identify all **DOCUMENTS** and other tangible things that support your contention and state the name, **ADDRESS**, and telephone number of the **PERSON** who has each **DOCUMENT** or thing.

16.3 Do you contend that the injuries or the extent of the injuries claimed by plaintiff as disclosed in discovery proceedings thus far in this case were not caused by the **INCIDENT**? If so, for each injury:

(a) identify it;

(b) state all facts upon which you base your contention;

(c) state the names, **ADDRESSES**, and telephone numbers of all **PERSONS** who have knowledge of the facts;

(d) identify all **DOCUMENTS** and other tangible things that support your contention and state the name, **ADDRESS**, and telephone number of the **PERSON** who has each **DOCUMENT** or thing.

16.4 Do you contend that any of the services furnished by any **HEALTH CARE PROVIDER** claimed by plaintiff in discovery proceedings thus far in this case were not due to the **INCIDENT**? If so:

(a) identify each service;

(b) state all facts upon which you base your contention;

(c) state the names, **ADDRESSES**, and telephone numbers of all **PERSONS** who have knowledge of the facts;

(d) identify all **DOCUMENTS** and other tangible things that support your contention and state the name, **ADDRESS**, and telephone number of the **PERSON** who has each **DOCUMENT** or thing.

16.5 Do you contend that any of the costs of services furnished by any **HEALTH CARE PROVIDER** claimed as damages by plaintiff in discovery proceedings thus far in this case were unreasonable? If so:

(a) identify each cost;

(b) state all facts upon which you base your contention;

(c) state the names, **ADDRESSES**, and telephone numbers of all **PERSONS** who have knowledge of the facts;

(d) identify all **DOCUMENTS** and other tangible things that support your contention and state the name, **ADDRESS**, and telephone number of the **PERSON** who has each **DOCUMENT** or thing.

☐ **16.6** Do you contend that any part of the loss of earnings or income claimed by plaintiff in discovery proceedings thus far in this case was unreasonable or was not caused by the **INCIDENT**? If so:

(a) identify each part of the loss;

(b) state all facts upon which you base your contention;

(c) state the names, **ADDRESSES**, and telephone numbers of all **PERSONS** who have knowledge of the facts;

(d) identify all **DOCUMENTS** and other tangible things that support your contention and state the name, **ADDRESS**, and telephone number of the **PERSON** who has each **DOCUMENT** or thing.

☐ **16.7** Do you contend that any of the property damage claimed by plaintiff in discovery proceedings thus far in this case was not caused by the **INCIDENT**? If so:

(a) identify each item of property damage;

(b) state all facts upon which you base your contention;

(c) state the names, **ADDRESSES**, and telephone numbers of all **PERSONS** who have knowledge of the facts;

(d) identify all **DOCUMENTS** and other tangible things that support your contention and state the name, **ADDRESS**, and telephone number of the **PERSON** who has each **DOCUMENT** or thing.

☐ **16.8** Do you contend that any of the costs of repairing the property damage claimed by plaintiff in discovery proceedings thus far in this case were unreasonable? If so:

(a) identify each cost item;

(b) state all facts upon which you base your contention;

(c) state the names, **ADDRESSES**, and telephone numbers of all **PERSONS** who have knowledge of the facts;

(d) identify all **DOCUMENTS** and other tangible things that support your contention and state the name, **ADDRESS**, and telephone number of the **PERSON** who has each **DOCUMENT** or thing.

☐ **16.9** Do **YOU OR ANYONE ACTING ON YOUR BEHALF** have any **DOCUMENT** (for example, insurance bureau index reports) concerning claims for personal injuries made before or after the **INCIDENT** by a plaintiff in this case? If so, for each plaintiff state:

(a) the source of each **DOCUMENT**;

(b) the date each claim arose;

(c) the nature of each claim;

(d) the name, **ADDRESS**, and telephone number of the **PERSON** who has each **DOCUMENT**.

☐ **16.10** Do **YOU OR ANYONE ACTING ON YOUR BEHALF** have any **DOCUMENT** concerning the past or present physical, mental, or emotional condition of any plaintiff in this case from a **HEALTH CARE PROVIDER** not previously identified (except for expert witnesses covered by Code of Civil Procedure, § 2034)? If so, for each plaintiff state:

(a) the name, **ADDRESS**, and telephone number of each **HEALTH CARE PROVIDER**;

(b) a description of each **DOCUMENT**;

(c) the name, **ADDRESS**, and telephone number of the **PERSON** who has each **DOCUMENT**.

17.0 Responses to Request for Admissions

☐ **17.1** Is your response to each request for admission served with these interrogatories an unqualified admission? If not, for each response that is not an unqualified admission:

(a) state the number of the request;

(b) state all facts upon which you base your response;

(c) state the names, **ADDRESSES**, and telephone numbers of all **PERSONS** who have knowledge of those facts;

(d) identify all **DOCUMENTS** and other tangible things that support your response and state the name, **ADDRESS**, and telephone number of the **PERSON** who has each **DOCUMENT** or thing.

20.0 How the Incident Occurred — Motor Vehicle

☐ **20.1** State the date, time, and place of the **INCIDENT** (closest street **ADDRESS** or intersection).

☐ **20.2** For each vehicle involved in the **INCIDENT**, state:

(a) the year, make, model, and license number;

(b) the name, **ADDRESS**, and telephone number of the driver;

(c) the name, **ADDRESS**, and telephone number of each occupant other than the driver;

(d) the name, **ADDRESS**, and telephone number of each registered owner;

(e) the name, **ADDRESS**, and telephone number of each lessee;

(f) the name, **ADDRESS**, and telephone number of each owner other than the registered owner or lien holder;

(g) the name of each owner who gave permission or consent to the driver to operate the vehicle.

☐ **20.3** State the **ADDRESS** and location where your trip began, and the **ADDRESS** and location of your destination.

☐ **20.4** Describe the route that you followed from the beginning of your trip to the location of the **INCIDENT**, and state the location of each stop, other than routine traffic stops, during the trip leading up to the **INCIDENT**.

☐ **20.5** State the name of the street or roadway, the lane of travel, and the direction of travel of each vehicle involved in the **INCIDENT** for the 500 feet of travel before the **INCIDENT**.

20.6 Did the **INCIDENT** occur at an intersection? If so, describe all traffic control devices, signals, or signs at the intersection.

20.7 Was there a traffic signal facing you at the time of the **INCIDENT**? If so, state:
(a) your location when you first saw it;
(b) the color;
(c) the number of seconds it had been that color;
(d) whether the color changed between the time you first saw it and the **INCIDENT**.

20.8 State how the **INCIDENT** occurred, giving the speed, direction, and location of each vehicle involved:
(a) just before the **INCIDENT**;
(b) at the time of the **INCIDENT**;
(c) just after the **INCIDENT**.

20.9 Do you have information that a malfunction or defect in a vehicle caused the **INCIDENT**? If so:
(a) identify the vehicle;
(b) identify each malfunction or defect;
(c) state the name, **ADDRESS**, and telephone number of each **PERSON** who is a witness to or has information about each malfunction or defect;
(d) state the name, **ADDRESS**, and telephone number of each **PERSON** who has custody of each defective part.

20.10 Do you have information that any malfunction or defect in a vehicle contributed to the injuries sustained in the **INCIDENT**? If so:
(a) identify the vehicle;
(b) identify each malfunction or defect;
(c) state the name, **ADDRESS**, and telephone number of each **PERSON** who is a witness to or has information about each malfunction or defect;
(d) state the name, **ADDRESS**, and telephone number of each **PERSON** who has custody of each defective part.

20.11 State the name, **ADDRESS**, and telephone number of each owner and each **PERSON** who has had possession since the **INCIDENT** of each vehicle involved in the **INCIDENT**.

50.0 Contract

50.1 For each agreement alleged in the pleadings:
(a) identify all **DOCUMENTS** that are part of the agreement and for each state the name, **ADDRESS**, and telephone number of each **PERSON** who has the **DOCUMENT**;
(b) state each part of the agreement not in writing, the name, **ADDRESS**, and telephone number of each **PERSON** agreeing to that provision, and the date that part of the agreement was made;
(c) identify all **DOCUMENTS** that evidence each part of the agreement not in writing and for each state the name, **ADDRESS**, and telephone number of each **PERSON** who has the **DOCUMENT**;
(d) identify all **DOCUMENTS** that are part of each modification to the agreement, and for each state the name, **ADDRESS**, and telephone number of each **PERSON** who has the **DOCUMENT**;
(e) state each modification not in writing, the date, and the name, **ADDRESS**, and telephone number of each **PERSON** agreeing to the modification, and the date the modification was made;
(f) identify all **DOCUMENTS** that evidence each modification of the agreement not in writing and for each state the name, **ADDRESS**, and telephone number of each **PERSON** who has the **DOCUMENT**.

50.2 Was there a breach of any agreement alleged in the pleadings? If so, for each breach describe and give the date of every act or omission that you claim is the breach of the agreement.

50.3 Was performance of any agreement alleged in the pleadings excused? If so, identify each agreement excused and state why performance was excused.

50.4 Was any agreement alleged in the pleadings terminated by mutual agreement, release, accord and satisfaction, or novation? If so, identify each agreement terminated and state why it was terminated including dates.

50.5 Is any agreement alleged in the pleadings unenforceable? If so, identify each unenforceable agreement and state why it is unenforceable.

50.6 Is any agreement alleged in the pleadings ambiguous? If so, identify each ambiguous agreement and state why it is ambiguous.

CALIFORNIA RULES OF COURT

Including Amendments Effective January 1, 1994

Table of Rules

Rule
1613. Rules of Evidence at Hearing.
1616. Trial After Arbitration.

TITLE ONE. APPELLATE RULES
DIVISION I. RULES RELATING TO THE SUPREME COURT AND COURTS OF APPEAL
Chapter I. Rules on Appeal
Part I. Filing Appeal

Rule 2. Time of Filing Notice of Appeal

(a) **[Normal time]** Except as otherwise provided by Code of Civil Procedure section 870 or other statute or rule 3, a notice of appeal from a judgment shall be filed on or before the earliest of the following dates: (1) 60 days after the date of mailing by the clerk of the court of a document entitled "notice of entry" of judgment; (2) 60 days after the date of service of a document entitled "notice of entry" of judgment by any party upon the party filing the notice of appeal, or by the party filing the notice of appeal; or (3) 180 days after the date of entry of the judgment. For the purposes of this subdivision, a file-stamped copy of the judgment may be used in place of the document entitled "notice of entry".

(b) **[What constitutes entry]** For the purposes of this rule: (1) The date of entry of a judgment shall be the date of its entry in the judgment book or, in a county following the procedure specified in Code of Civil Procedure Section 668.5 in lieu of maintaining a judgment book, the date of filing the judgment with the clerk pursuant to that section. (2) The date of entry of an appealable order which is entered in the minutes shall be the date of its entry in the permanent minutes, unless such minute order as entered expressly directs that a written order be prepared, signed and filed, in which case the date of entry shall be the date of filing of the signed order. (3) The date of entry of an appealable order which is not entered in the minutes shall be the date of filing of the order signed by the court. (4) The date of entry of a decree of distribution in a probate proceeding shall be the date of its entry at length in the judgment book or other permanent record of the court.

(c) **[Premature notice]** A notice of appeal filed prior to entry of the judgment, but after its rendition, shall be valid and shall be deemed to have been filed immediately after entry. A notice of appeal filed prior to rendition of the judgment, but after the judge has announced his intended ruling, may, in the discretion of the reviewing court for good cause, be treated as filed immediately after entry of the judgment.

(d) **[Appealable order]** As used in subdivisions (a) and (c) of this rule, "judgment" means "appealable order" if the appeal is from an appealable order.

As amended, eff. Jan. 1, 1951; Sept. 17, 1965; Dec. 1, 1967; Jan. 1, 1976; Jan. 1, 1982; Sept. 22, 1982; Jan. 1, 1986; Jan. 1, 1990; July 1, 1992.

Rule 3. Extension of Time and Cross–Appeal

(a) [New trial proceeding] When a valid notice of intention to move for a new trial is served and filed by any party, and the motion is denied, the time for filing the notice of appeal from the judgment is extended for all parties until 30 days after either entry of the order denying the motion or denial thereof by operation of law, but in no event may such notice of appeal be filed later than 180 days after the date of entry of the judgment whether or not the motion for new trial has been determined.

(b) [Motion to vacate] When a valid notice of intention to move to vacate a judgment or to vacate a judgment and enter another and different judgment is served and filed by any party on any ground within the time in which, under rule 2, a notice of appeal may be filed, or such shorter time as may be prescribed by statute, the time for filing the notice of appeal from the judgment is extended for all parties until the earliest of 30 days after entry of the order denying the motion to vacate; or 90 days after filing the first notice of intention to move to vacate the judgment; or 180 days after entry of the judgment.

(c) [Cross appeal] When a timely notice of appeal is filed under subdivision (a) of rule 2 or under subdivision (a) or (b) of rule 3, any other party may file a notice of appeal within 20 days after mailing of notification by the superior court clerk of such first appeal or within the time otherwise prescribed by the applicable subdivision, whichever period last expires. If a timely notice of appeal is filed from an order granting a motion for a new trial or granting, within 150 days after entry of judgment, a motion to vacate the judgment or to vacate judgment and enter another and different judgment, any party other than the appellant, within 20 days after mailing of notification by the superior court clerk of such appeal, may file a notice of appeal from the judgment or from an order denying a motion for judgment notwithstanding the verdict, and on that appeal may present any question which he might have presented on an appeal from the judgment as originally entered or from the order denying a motion for judgment notwithstanding the verdict.

(d) [Motion for judgment notwithstanding verdict] When the same party has served and filed valid notices of intention to move for a new trial and to move for entry of a judgment notwithstanding the verdict, and both motions are denied or not decided by the superior court within 60 days after the filing of the notice of intention to move for a new trial, the time for filing the notice of appeal from the judgment or from the denial of the motion to enter a judgment notwithstanding the verdict is extended for all parties until the earlier of 30 days after entry of the order denying the motion for a new trial or its denial by operation of law, or 180 days after entry of the judgment.

When a party has served and filed a notice of intention to move for judgment notwithstanding the verdict, but either does not move for a new trial or is granted a new trial, the time for filing a notice of appeal from the order denying a judgment notwithstanding the verdict, if appealable, is governed by rule 2 unless extended pursuant to subdivision (c) of this rule.

As amended, eff. Jan. 1, 1951; Jan. 1, 1959; Jan. 2, 1962; Sept. 17, 1965; Jan. 1, 1971; Jan. 1, 1976; Jan. 1, 1983.

PART IV. HEARING AND DETERMINATION OF APPEAL

Rule 19. Voluntary Abandonment and Dismissal

(a) [**Before record filed**] At any time before the filing of the record in the reviewing court, the appellant may file in the office of the clerk of the superior court a written abandonment of the appeal; or the parties may file in that office a stipulation for abandonment. The filing of either document shall operate to dismiss the appeal and to restore the jurisdiction of the superior court. Upon such a dismissal, the appellant shall be entitled to the return of that portion of any deposit in excess of the actual cost of preparation of the record on appeal up to that time. The clerk of the superior court shall promptly send a copy or other notice of the abandonment to the clerk of the reviewing court.

(b) [**After record filed**] If the record has been filed in the reviewing court, an abandonment or a stipulation of the parties to dismiss the appeal shall be filed in that court, which may order the dismissal and immediate issuance of the remittitur.

(c) [**Notification by clerk**] The clerk of the court in which the abandonment or dismissal is filed shall immediately notify the adverse party of the filing of the abandonment or the order of dismissal.

(d) [**Approval of compromise**] Whenever the guardian of a minor or of an insane or incompetent person seeks approval of a proposed compromise of a case pending on appeal, the reviewing court may, by order, refer the matter to the trial court with instructions to hear the same and determine whether the proposed compromise is for the best interests of the ward, and to report its findings. On receipt of the report, the reviewing court shall make its order approving or disapproving the compromise.

As amended, eff. Jan. 1, 1951; Jan. 1, 1986; Jan. 1, 1994.

Rule 26. Costs on Appeal

(a) [**Right to costs**] Except as provided in this rule, the prevailing party shall be entitled to costs on appeal as an incident to the judgment on appeal. In the case of a general and unqualified affirmance of the judgment, or the dismissal of an appeal, the respondent shall be deemed the prevailing party; in the case of a reversal, in whole or in part, or of a modification of the judgment, the appellant shall be deemed the prevailing party. In any case in which the interests of justice require it, the reviewing court may make any award or apportionment of costs it deems proper. In probate cases, in the absence of an express direction for costs by the reviewing court, costs on appeal shall be awarded to the prevailing party, but the superior court shall decide against whom the award shall be made. The foregoing provisions do not apply in criminal cases. Where the appeal is frivolous or taken solely for the purpose of delay or where any party has required in the typewritten or printed record on appeal the inclusion of any matter not reasonably material to the determination of the appeal, or has been guilty of any other unreasonable infraction of the rules governing appeals, the reviewing court may impose upon offending attorneys or parties such penalties, including the withholding or imposing of costs, as the circumstances of the case and the discouragement of like conduct in the future may require.

If there is more than one notice of appeal or if the judgment of the trial court is reversed in whole or in part, or modified, the opinion shall specify the award or denial of costs.

(b) [Entry of judgment for costs] In any case in which the reviewing court directs the manner in which costs shall be awarded or denied, the clerk shall enter on the record and insert in the remittitur a judgment in accordance with such directions. In the absence of such directions by the reviewing court the clerk shall enter on the record and insert in the remittitur a judgment for costs as follows: (1) in the case of a general and unqualified affirmance of the judgment, for the respondent; (2) in the case of a dismissal of the appeal, for the respondent. If the clerk fails to enter judgment for costs as provided in this subdivision, the reviewing court, on motion made not later than 30 days after issuance of the remittitur or on its own motion, may recall the remittitur for correction.

(c) [Items recoverable as costs] The party to whom costs are awarded may recover only the following, when actually incurred: (1) the cost of preparation of an original and one copy of any type of record on appeal authorized by these rules if the party is the appellant, or one copy of such record if the party is the respondent, subject to reduction by order of the reviewing court pursuant to subdivision (a) of this rule; provided, however, that the expense of any method of preparation in excess of the cost of preparing the record in typewriting shall not be recoverable as costs, unless the parties so stipulate, and provided, further, that the expense of copying exhibits and affidavits under rule 5(b), or of copying parts of a prior record that could be incorporated by reference under rule 11(b), shall not be recoverable as costs unless the copying is ordered by the reviewing court; (2) the reasonable cost of printing or reproduction of briefs by other process of duplication; (3) the cost of production of additional evidence; (4) filing and notary fees and the expense of service, transmission, and filing of the record, briefs, and other papers; (5) the premium on any surety bond procured by the party recovering costs, unless the court to which the remittitur is transmitted determines that the bond was unnecessary; and (6) other expense reasonably necessary to procure the surety bond, such as the expense of acquiring a letter of credit required as collateral for the bond.

(d) [Procedure for claiming costs] A party who claims costs awarded by a reviewing court shall, within 40 days after the clerk of the reviewing court mails that party notice of the issuance of the remittitur, serve and file in the trial court a memorandum of costs verified as prescribed by rule 870(a)(1).

A party may move to have costs taxed in the same manner and within a like time after service of a copy of the memorandum of costs, as prescribed by rule 870(b). After the costs have been taxed, or after the time for taxing the costs has expired, the award of costs may be enforced in the same manner as a money judgment.

As amended, eff. Jan. 1, 1951; Jan. 1, 1959; July 1, 1968; July 1, 1986; Jan. 1, 1987; July 1, 1989; Jan. 1, 1994.

PART VI. GENERAL PROVISIONS

Rule 40. Definitions

In these rules, unless the context or subject matter otherwise requires:

(a) The past, present and future tenses shall each include the other; the masculine, feminine and neuter gender shall each include the other; and the singular and plural number shall each include the other.

(b) The words "superior court" mean the court from which an appeal is taken pursuant to these rules; the words "reviewing court" apply to the court in which an appeal or original proceeding is pending, and mean the Supreme Court or the Court of Appeal to which an appeal is taken, or to which an appeal or an original proceeding is transferred, or in which an original proceeding is commenced.

(c) The party appealing is known as the "appellant," and the adverse party as the "respondent."

(d) The word "shall" is mandatory and the word "may" is permissive.

(e) The terms "party," "appellant," "respondent," "petitioner" or other designation of a party include such party's attorney of record. Whenever under these rules a notice is required to be given to or served on a party such notice or service shall be made on his attorney of record, if he has one.

(f) The words "serve and file" mean that a document filed in a court is to be accompanied by proof of prior service, in a manner permitted by law, of one copy of the document on counsel for each adverse party who is represented by separate counsel, except that proof of service of briefs on each party represented by separate counsel shall be made.

(g) "Judgment" includes any judgment, order or decree from which an appeal lies.

(h) The words "Chief Justice" include the acting Chief Justice, and the words "Presiding Justice" include the acting Presiding Justice.

(i) The terms "written," "writing," "typewriting" and "typewritten" include other methods of duplication equivalent in legibility to typewriting. When applied to briefs, "typewriting" includes originals produced by letter-quality word processing equipment, by photocomposition equipment, and by other means producing characters of equal clarity and similar typeface, but excludes originals obviously produced by a dot-matrix process.

(j) Rule and subdivision headings do not in any manner affect the scope, meaning or intent of the provisions of these rules.

(k) The word "briefs" includes petitions for rehearing, petitions for review, and answers thereto. It does not include petitions for extraordinary relief in original proceedings.

(*l*) The terms "other duplication process" and "other process of duplication" mean any reproduction of typewriting (except typewriter ribbon and carbon copies) which produces a clear black-on-white image equally legible to a ribbon copy of typewriting with a well-inked ribbon.

(m) "Register" and "register of actions" means the permanent record of cases maintained by electronic, magnetic, microphotographic, or similar means.

(n) "Date of filing" of a brief (as defined in subdivision (k)) is the date of delivery to the clerk's office during normal business hours. The brief is timely, however, if the time for its filing had not expired on the date of its mailing by certified or express mail as shown on the postal receipt or postmark, or the date of its delivery to a common carrier promising overnight delivery as shown on the carrier's receipt.

(o) The word "recycled" as applied to paper means "recycled paper product" as defined by section 42202 of the Public Resources Code. Whenever the use of recycled paper is required by these rules, the attorney, party, or other person filing or serving a document certifies, by the act of filing or service, that the document was produced on paper purchased as recycled paper as defined by that section.

As amended, eff. Jan. 1, 1951; Jan. 1, 1959; Jan. 1, 1961; Nov. 11, 1966; Jan. 1, 1983; July 1, 1989; July 1, 1991; Jan. 1, 1994.

Rule 45. Extension and Shortening of Time

(a) [**Computation of time**] The time for doing any act required or permitted under these rules shall be computed and extended in the manner provided by the Code of Civil Procedure.

(b) [**Extension by superior court prohibited**] Judges of the superior court shall not extend the time for doing any act involved in the preparation of the record on appeal. Those times may be extended as provided in subdivision (c).

(c) [**Extension of time**] The time for filing a notice of appeal, filing a petition for Supreme Court review of a Court of Appeal decision or the granting or denial of a rehearing in the Court of Appeal shall not be extended. The time for the granting or denial of Supreme Court review of a decision of a Court of Appeal shall only be extended as provided in subdivision (a) of rule 28. The time for the granting or denial of a rehearing in the Supreme Court shall only be extended as provided in subdivision (a) of rule 24. The time for ordering a case transferred from the superior court to the Court of Appeal as provided in rule 62 shall not be extended, and the time for a superior court to certify the transfer of a case to the Court of Appeal shall not be extended except as provided in subdivision (d) of rule 63. The Chief Justice or Presiding Justice, for good cause shown, may extend the time for doing any other act required or permitted under these rules. The Chief Justice or Presiding Justice may relieve a party from a default for failure to file a timely petition for review or rehearing if the time within which the court could order review or rehearing on its own motion has not expired. An application for extension of time shall be made as provided in rule 43.

(d) [Shortening time] The Chief Justice or Presiding Justice, for good cause shown, may shorten the time for serving or filing a notice of motion or other paper incident to an appeal or an original proceeding in the reviewing court. An application to shorten time shall be made as provided in rule 43.

(e) [Relief from default] The reviewing court for good cause may relieve a party from a default occasioned by any failure to comply with these rules, except the failure to give timely notice of appeal. This rule is applicable to any order granting relief from default made after January 1, 1962.

(f) [Notification to client] Counsel in civil cases shall mail or otherwise deliver to the party represented a copy of each stipulation or application for additional time for a step in the preparation of the record or for filing briefs, and affix evidence of doing so to the application or stipulation. In class actions, delivering a copy to one represented party is adequate. The evidence of mailing or other delivery need not state the address of the party to whom copies were sent.

As amended, eff. Jan. 1, 1951; Jan. 1, 1957; Jan. 1, 1961; Jan. 2, 1962; July 1, 1963; Nov. 11, 1966; Jan. 1, 1974; Jan. 1, 1976; Jan. 1, 1979; May 6, 1985; July 1, 1989; July 1, 1990.

TITLE TWO. PRETRIAL AND TRIAL RULES
DIVISION I. RULES FOR THE SUPERIOR COURTS
Part 2. Caseflow Management

Rule 209. Memorandum That Civil Case Is at Issue

(a) [At-issue memorandum] A civil case shall be placed on the civil active list or be set for trial when the court deems the case to be at issue or, if the court so requires, (i) when the parties have filed a joint at-issue memorandum, or (ii) when a party has served and filed an at-issue memorandum. The at-issue memorandum shall include the following:

(1) the title and number of the case;

(2) the nature of the case;

(3) a statement that all essential parties have been served with process or have appeared and that the case is at issue as to those parties;

(4) whether the case is entitled to legal preference, and, if so, a citation to the section of the code or statute granting the preference;

(5) whether a jury trial is demanded;

(6) the time estimated for trial; and

(7) the names, addresses, and telephone numbers of the attorneys for the parties or of parties appearing without counsel.

For purposes of this rule and rule 210, a case may be considered at issue notwithstanding any cross-complaint that is not at issue.

This rule shall not affect the authority of the court to order a severance of a cross-complaint pursuant to Code of Civil Procedure section 1048.

(b) [Judicial arbitration] In courts having judicial arbitration under Code of Civil Procedure section 1141.11, the at-issue memorandum shall state

(1) whether the case is suitable for placement on the arbitration hearing list, and a statement of reasons if a party claims that it is not;

(2) whether the plaintiff elects or the parties stipulate that the case be placed on the arbitration hearing list; and

(3) the type of injury and special damages in a personal injury case, and the amount of damages and relief sought in any other case.

(c) [Countermemorandum] A party not in agreement with the information or estimates given in an at-issue memorandum shall within 10 days after the service thereof serve and file a memorandum on the party's behalf.

Adopted, eff. Jan. 1, 1985. As amended, eff. Jan. 1, 1991.

Rule 222. Mandatory Settlement Conferences

(a) [Settlement conference within three weeks before trial] In courts having three or more judges, a settlement conference shall be held in all long cause matters within three weeks before the date set for trial.

(b) [Other or additional conferences] On the joint request of all parties or by order of court, other or additional conferences may be held at any time.

(c) [Persons attending] Trial counsel, parties, and persons with authority to settle the case shall personally attend the conference, unless excused by the court for good cause.

(d) [Settlement conference statement] No later than five days before the date set for the settlement conference, each party claiming damages shall file and serve on each party a statement containing a settlement demand and an itemization of special and general damages, and comply with any additional requirement imposed by local rule.

Adopted, eff. Jan. 1, 1985.

Part 4.   Sanctions

Rule 227.   Sanctions in Respect to Rules, Local Rules, and Court Orders

The failure of any person to comply with these rules, local rules, or order of the court, unless good cause is shown, or failure to participate in good faith in any conference those rules or an order of the court require, is an unlawful interference with the proceedings of the court. The court may order the person at fault to pay the opposing party's reasonable expenses and counsel fees and to reimburse or make payment to the county, may order an appropriate change in the calendar status of the action, and for failure to comply with local rules may impose sanctions authorized under section 575.2 of the Code of Civil Procedure and under section 68608(b) of the Government Code, in addition to any other sanction permitted by law.

Adopted, eff. Jan. 1, 1985. As amended, eff. Jan. 1, 1994.

Rule 228.   Examination of Prospective Jurors in Civil Cases

This rule applies to all civil jury trials. To select a fair and impartial jury, the trial judge shall examine the prospective jurors orally, or by written questionnaire, or by both methods. The Juror Questionnaire for Civil Cases (Judicial Council form MC–001) may be used. Upon completion of the initial examination the trial judge shall permit counsel for each party who so requests to submit additional questions which the judge shall put to the jurors. Upon request of counsel, the trial judge shall permit counsel to supplement the judge's examination by oral and direct questioning of any of the prospective jurors. The scope of the additional questions or supplemental examination shall be within reasonable limits prescribed by the trial judge in the judge's sound discretion.

The court may, upon stipulation by counsel for all parties appearing in the action, permit counsel to examine the prospective jurors outside a judge's presence.

As amended, eff. Jan. 1, 1972; Jan. 1, 1974; Jan. 1, 1975; Jan. 1, 1988; Jan. 1, 1990; June 6, 1990; July 1, 1993.

DIVISION II.   CIVIL LAW AND MOTION RULES

Chapter 4.   Particular Motions

Part 2.   Discovery and Discovery Motions

Rule 331.   Format of Supplemental and Further Discovery

(a) **[Supplemental interrogatories and responses, etc.]** In each set of (1) supplemental interrogatories, (2) supplemental responses to interrogatories, (3) amended answers to interrogatories, and (4) further responses to interrogatories, inspection demands, and admission requests, the following shall appear in the first paragraph immediately below the title of the case: the identity of the propounding, demanding, or requesting party, the identity of the responding party, the set number being propounded or responded to, and the nature of the paper.

(b) [Sequence of responses] Each supplemental or further response and each amended answer shall be identified by the same number or letter and be in the same sequence as the corresponding interrogatory, inspection demand, or admission request, but the text shall not be repeated.

As amended, eff. Jan. 1, 1986; July 1, 1987.

Part 7.   Miscellaneous Motions

Rule 372.   Motion for Discretionary Dismissal After Two Years for Delay in Prosecution

(a) [Discretionary dismissal two years after filing] The court on its own motion or on motion of the defendant may dismiss an action under article 4 (§ 583.410 et seq.) of chapter 1.5 of title 8 of part 2 of the Code of Civil Procedure for delay in prosecution if the action has not been brought to trial or conditionally settled within two years after the action was commenced against the defendant.   If the court intends to dismiss an action on its own motion, the clerk shall set a hearing on the dismissal and mail notice to all parties at least 20 days before the hearing date.

"Conditionally settled" means (i) a settlement agreement conditions dismissal on the satisfactory completion of specified terms that are not to be fully performed within two years after the filing of the case, and (ii) notice of the settlement is filed with the court as provided in rule 225.

(b) [Purpose of rule] This rule is adopted under sections 583.-410(b) and 583.420(a)(2)(B) of the Code of Civil Procedure to reduce unnecessary delay in the resolution of litigation and to improve the administration of justice.

Adopted, eff. Jan. 1, 1990.

Rule 516.   Examination of Prospective Jurors in Civil Cases

This rule applies to all civil jury trials.   To select a fair and impartial jury, the trial judge shall examine the prospective jurors and upon completion of the initial examination the trial judge shall permit counsel for each party who so requests to submit additional questions which the judge shall put to the jurors.   Upon request of counsel, the trial judge shall permit counsel to supplement the judge's examination by oral and direct questioning of any of the prospective jurors.   The scope of the additional questions or supplemental examination shall be within reasonable limits prescribed by the trial judge in the judge's sound discretion.

The court may, upon stipulation by counsel for all parties appearing in the action, permit counsel to examine the prospective jurors outside a judge's presence.

As amended, eff. Jan. 1, 1972; Jan. 1, 1974; Jan. 1, 1975; June 6, 1990.

TITLE FOUR.   SPECIAL RULES FOR TRIAL COURTS
DIVISION III.   JUDICIAL ARBITRATION RULES
FOR CIVIL CASES

Rule 1600.   Actions Subject to Arbitration

Except as provided in rule 1600.5 the following actions shall be arbitrated:

(a) Upon stipulation, any action in any court, regardless of the amount in controversy.

(b) Upon filing of an election by a plaintiff, any action in any court in which the plaintiff agrees that the arbitration award shall not exceed $50,000.

(c) In each superior court with 10 or more judges, all civil actions where the amount in controversy does not exceed $50,000 as to any plaintiff.

(d) In each superior court with fewer than 10 judges that so provides by local rule, all actions where the amount in controversy does not exceed $50,000 as to any plaintiff.

(e) All actions in a municipal court that so provides by local rule.

Adopted, eff. July 1, 1979. As amended, eff. Jan. 1, 1982; Jan. 1, 1986; Jan. 1, 1988.

Rule 1600.5   Actions Exempt From Arbitration

The following actions are exempt from arbitration:

(a) Actions that include a prayer for equitable relief that is not frivolous or insubstantial;

(b) Class actions;

(c) Small claims actions or trials de novo on appeal from the small claims court;

(d) Unlawful detainer proceedings;

(e) Family Law Act proceedings;

(f) Any action otherwise subject to arbitration that is found by the court to be not amenable to arbitration on the ground that arbitration would not reduce the probable time and expense necessary to resolve the litigation;

(g) Any category of actions otherwise subject to arbitration but excluded by local rule as not amenable to arbitration on the ground that under the circumstances relating to the particular court arbitration of such cases would not reduce the probable time and expense necessary to resolve the litigation;

(h) Actions involving multiple causes of action or a cross-complaint if the court determines that the amount in controversy as to any given cause of action or cross-complaint exceeds $50,000.

Adopted, eff. July 1, 1979. As amended, eff. Jan. 1, 1982; Jan. 1, 1986; Jan. 1, 1988; July 1, 1988.

Rule 1612. Discovery

The parties to the arbitration shall have the right to take depositions and to obtain discovery, and to that end may exercise all of the same rights, remedies, and procedures, and shall be subject to all of the same duties, liabilities, and obligations as provided in Part 4, Title 3, Chapter 3 of the Code of Civil Procedure, except that all discovery shall be completed not later than 15 days prior to the date set for the arbitration hearing unless the court, upon a showing of good cause, makes an order granting an extension of time within which discovery must be completed.

As amended, eff. July 1, 1979.

Rule 1613. Rules of Evidence at Hearing

(a) All evidence shall be taken in the presence of the arbitrator and all parties, except where any of the parties has waived the right to be present or is absent after due notice of the hearing.

(b) The rules of evidence governing civil actions apply to the conduct of the arbitration hearing, except:

(1) Any party may offer written reports of any expert witness, medical records and bills (including physiotherapy, nursing, and prescription bills), documentary evidence of loss of income, property damage repair bills or estimates, police reports concerning an accident which gave rise to the case, other bills and invoices, purchase orders, checks, written contracts, and similar documents prepared and maintained in the ordinary course of business. The arbitrator shall receive them in evidence if copies have been delivered to all opposing parties at least 20 days prior to the hearing. Any other party may subpoena the author or custodian of the document as a witness and examine the witness as if under cross-examination. Any repair estimate offered as an exhibit, and the copies delivered to opposing parties, shall be accompanied (i) by a statement indicating whether or not the property was repaired, and, if it was, whether the estimated repairs were made in full or in part, and (ii) by a copy of the receipted bill showing the items of repair made and the amount paid. The arbitrator shall not consider any opinion as to ultimate fault expressed in a police report.

(2) The written statements of any other witness may be offered and shall be received in evidence if:

(i) they are made by affidavit or by declaration under penalty of perjury,

(ii) copies have been delivered to all opposing parties at least 20 days prior to the hearing, and

(iii) no opposing party has, at least 10 days before the hearing, delivered to the proponent of the evidence a written demand that the witness be produced in person to testify at the hearing.

The arbitrator shall disregard any portion of a statement received pursuant to this rule that would be inadmissible if the witness were testifying in person, but the inclusion of inadmissible matter does not render the entire statement inadmissible.

(3) The deposition of any witness may be offered by any party and shall be received in evidence, subject to objections available under Code of Civil Procedure section 2025(g), notwithstanding that the deponent is not "unavailable as a witness" within the meaning of section 240 of the Evidence Code and no exceptional circumstances exist, if

(i) the deposition was taken in the manner provided for by law or by stipulation of the parties and within the time provided for in these rules, and

(ii) not less than 20 days prior to the hearing the proponent of the deposition delivered to all opposing parties notice of intention to offer the deposition in evidence.

The opposing party, upon receiving the notice, may subpoena the deponent and, at the discretion of the arbitrator, either the deposition may be excluded from evidence or the deposition may be admitted and the deponent may be further cross-examined by the subpoenaing party. These limitations are not applicable to a deposition admissible under the terms of section 2025(u) of the Code of Civil Procedure.

(c) Subpoenas shall issue for the attendance of witnesses at arbitration hearings as provided in the Code of Civil Procedure, in Section 1985 and elsewhere of Part 4, Title 3, Chapters 2 and 3. It shall be the duty of the party requesting the subpoena to modify the form of subpoena so as to show that the appearance is before an arbitrator, and to give the time and place set for the arbitration hearing. At the discretion of the arbitrator, nonappearance of a properly subpoenaed witness may be a ground for an adjournment or continuance of the hearing. If any witness properly served with a subpoena fails to appear at the arbitration hearing or, having appeared, refuses to be sworn or to answer, proceedings to compel compliance with the subpoena on penalty of contempt may be had before the superior court as provided in Code of Civil Procedure Section 1991 for other instances of refusal to appear and answer before an officer or commissioner out of court.

(d) For purposes of this rule, "delivery" of a document or notice may be accomplished manually or by mail in the manner provided by Code of Civil Procedure section 1013. If service is by mail, the times prescribed in this rule for delivery of documents, notices, and demands are increased by five days.

As amended, eff. July 1, 1979; Jan. 1, 1984; Jan. 1, 1988; July 1, 1990.

standards specified in section 1141.21 of the Code of Civil Procedure.

As amended, eff. July 1, 1979; Jan. 1, 1985; July 1, 1990.

LONG ARM STATUTES OF ILLINOIS AND NEW YORK

Illinois Code of Civil Procedure

735 ILCS § 5/2–209. Act submitting to jurisdiction—Process

(a) Any person, whether or not a citizen or resident of this State, who in person or through an agent does any of the acts hereinafter enumerated, thereby submits such person, and, if an individual, his or her personal representative, to the jurisdiction of the courts of this State as to any cause of action arising from the doing of any of such acts:

(1) The transaction of any business within this State;

(2) The commission of a tortious act within this State;

(3) The ownership, use, or possession of any real estate situated in this State;

(4) Contracting to insure any person, property or risk located within this State at the time of contracting;

(5) With respect to actions of dissolution of marriage, declaration of invalidity of marriage and legal separation, the maintenance in this State of a matrimonial domicile at the time this cause of action arose or the commission in this State of any act giving rise to the cause of action;

(6) With respect to actions brought under the Illinois Parentage Act of 1984, as now or hereafter amended, the performance of an act of sexual intercourse within this State during the possible period of conception;

(7) The making or performance of any contract or promise substantially connected with this State;

(8) The performance of sexual intercourse within this State which is claimed to have resulted in the conception of a child who resides in this State;

(9) The failure to support a child, spouse or former spouse who has continued to reside in this State since the person either formerly resided with them in this State or directed them to reside in this State;

(10) The acquisition of ownership, possession or control of any asset or thing of value present within this State when ownership, possession or control was acquired;

(11) The breach of any fiduciary duty within this State;

(12) The performance of duties as a director or officer of a corporation organized under the laws of this State or having its principal place of business within this State;

(13) The ownership of an interest in any trust administered within this State; or

(14) The exercise of powers granted under the authority of this State as a fiduciary.

(b) A court may exercise jurisdiction in any action arising within or without this State against any person who:

(1) Is a natural person present within this State when served;

(2) Is a natural person domiciled or resident within this State when the cause of action arose, the action was commenced, or process was served;

(3) Is a corporation organized under the laws of this State; or

(4) Is a natural person or corporation doing business within this State.

(c) A court may also exercise jurisdiction on any other basis now or hereafter permitted by the Illinois Constitution and the Constitution of the United States.

(d) Service of process upon any person who is subject to the jurisdiction of the courts of this State, as provided in this Section, may be made by personally serving the summons upon the defendant outside this State, as provided in this Act, with the same force and effect as though summons had been personally served within this State.

(e) Service of process upon any person who resides or whose business address is outside the United States and who is subject to the jurisdiction of the courts of this State, as provided in this Section, in any action based upon product liability may be made by serving a copy of the summons with a copy of the complaint attached upon the Secretary of State. The summons shall be accompanied by a $5 fee payable to the Secretary of State. The plaintiff shall forthwith mail a copy of the summons, upon which the date of service upon the Secretary is clearly shown, together with a copy of the complaint to the defendant at his or her last known place of residence or business address. Plaintiff shall file with the circuit clerk an affidavit of the plaintiff or his or her attorney stating the last known place of residence or the last known business address of the defendant and a certificate of mailing a copy of the summons and complaint to the defendant at such address as required by this subsection (e). The certificate of mailing shall be prima facie evidence that the plaintiff or his or her attorney mailed a copy of the summons and complaint to the defendant as required. Service of the summons shall be deemed to have been made upon the defendant on the date it is served upon the Secretary and shall have the same force and effect as though summons had been personally served upon the defendant within this State.

(f) Only causes of action arising from acts enumerated herein may be asserted against a defendant in an action in which jurisdiction over him or her is based upon subsection (a).

(g) Nothing herein contained limits or affects the right to serve any process in any other manner now or hereafter provided by law.

P.A. 82–280, § 2–209, eff. July 1, 1982. Amended by P.A. 82–783, Art. III, § 43, eff. July 13, 1982; P.A. 85–907, Art. II, § 1, eff. Nov. 23, 1987; P.A. 85–1156, Art. I, § 7, eff. Jan. 1, 1989; P.A. 86–840, § 1, eff. Sept. 1, 1989.

New York Civil Practice Law and Rules

§ 301.   Jurisdiction over persons, property or status

A court may exercise such jurisdiction over persons, property, or status as might have been exercised heretofore.

(L.1962, c. 308.)

§ 302.   Personal jurisdiction by acts of non-domiciliaries

(a) Acts which are the basis of jurisdiction.   As to a cause of action arising from any of the acts enumerated in this section, a court may exercise personal jurisdiction over any nondomiciliary, or his executor or administrator, who in person or through an agent:

1.   transacts any business within the state or contracts anywhere to supply goods or services in the state; or

2.   commits a tortious act within the state, except as to a cause of action for defamation of character arising from the act; or

3.   commits a tortious act without the state causing injury to person or property within the state, except as to a cause of action for defamation of character arising from the act, if he

(i) regularly does or solicits business, or engages in any other persistent course of conduct, or derives substantial revenue from goods used or consumed or services rendered, in the state, or

(ii) expects or should reasonably expect the act to have consequences in the state and derives substantial revenue from interstate or international commerce; or

4.   owns, uses or possesses any real property situated within the state.

(b) Personal jurisdiction over non-resident defendant in matrimonial actions or family court proceedings.   A court in any matrimonial action or family court proceeding involving a demand for support, alimony, maintenance, distributive awards or special relief in matrimonial actions may exercise personal jurisdiction over the respondent or defendant notwithstanding the fact that he or she no longer is a resident or domiciliary of this state, or over his or her executor or administrator, if the party seeking support is a resident of or domiciled in this state at the time such demand is made, provided that this state was the matrimonial domicile of the parties before their separation, or the defendant abandoned the plaintiff in this state, or the claim for support, alimony, maintenance, distributive awards or special relief in matrimonial actions accrued under the laws of this state or under an agreement executed in this state. The family court may in any proceeding under article ten of the family court act exercise personal jurisdiction over a non-resident respondent as provided in such article.

(c) **Effect of appearance.** Where personal jurisdiction is based solely upon this section, an appearance does not confer such jurisdiction with respect to causes of action not arising from an act enumerated in this section.

(As amended L.1974, c. 859, § 1; L.1979, c. 252, §§ 1, 2; L.1980, c. 281, § 22; L.1982, c. 505, § 1; L.1991, c. 69, § 7.)

SELECTED CALIFORNIA CASES

FORUM NON CONVENIENS

ARCHIBALD v. CINERAMA HOTELS

Supreme Court of California, In Bank, 1976.
15 Cal.3d 853, 544 P.2d 947, 126 Cal.Rptr. 811.

TOBRINER, JUSTICE.

Plaintiff Archibald appeals from a trial court order dismissing her class action against all defendants on grounds of Forum non conveniens * * *. We explain that because plaintiff is a California resident, the trial court erred in granting defendants' motion to dismiss on grounds of Forum non conveniens; even if Hawaii would provide a more convenient forum, as defendants contend, the authority of the trial court is limited to staying the California action pending proceedings in Hawaii. * * *

Plaintiff Archibald, a California resident, filed the present action on behalf of herself and other California residents who visit the State of Hawaii. Defendants include companies which own or operate over 40 hotels and motels in Hawaii, as well as American Express Company, an agency which procured hotel reservations for plaintiff and other members of her class. She alleges that hotels in Hawaii have established by agreement a discriminatory rate structure which imposes on mainland visitors a higher room rental than the rate, called the Kamaaina rate, charged to residents of Hawaii.

Plaintiff visited Hawaii in 1971 and 1972 and was charged room rentals higher than the Kamaaina rate; she alleges that other California residents have fallen victim to the same practice. Asserting that the alleged price discrimination is illegal under both California and Hawaii law, plaintiff seeks recovery of compensatory and punitive damages on behalf of the class she represents.

All the defendants joined in a motion to dismiss the action on the ground of Forum non conveniens. * * * The trial court granted [the] motion, and plaintiff appealed.

1. *The superior court erred in dismissing the suit on the ground of forum non conveniens.*

The doctrine of Forum non conveniens, established in California by judicial decision (Goodwine v. Superior Court (1965) 63 Cal.2d 481, 47 Cal.Rptr. 201, 407 P.2d 1; Price v. Atchison, T. & S.F. Ry. Co. (1954) 42 Cal.2d 577, 268 P.2d 457), is codified in Code of Civil Procedure section 410.30. This section provides that "When a court upon motion of a party or its own motion finds that in the interest of substantial justice an action should be heard in a forum outside this state, the court shall stay or dismiss the action in whole or in part on any conditions that may be just."

As we noted in Ferreira v. Ferreira (1973) 9 Cal.3d 824, 838, 109 Cal.Rptr. 80, 89, 512 P.2d 304, 313, "Both the terms of section 410.30 and the prior decisional law ... distinguish between the dismissal of an action on grounds of forum non conveniens, and the stay of an action on that ground." This distinction, we explained, "does not merely lie in terminology. The staying court retains jurisdiction over the parties and the cause; ... it can compel the foreign (party) to cooperate in bringing about a fair and speedy hearing in the foreign forum; it can resume proceedings if the foreign action is unreasonably delayed or fails to reach a resolution on the merits.... In short, the staying court can protect ... the interests of the California resident pending the final decision of the foreign court." A court which has dismissed a suit on grounds of Forum non conveniens, on the other hand, has lost jurisdiction over the action and in relinquishing that jurisdiction deprived itself of the power to protect the interests of the California resident.

Because a court which has dismissed a suit cannot thereafter protect the interests of the litigants, we have consistently held that except in extraordinary cases a trial court has no discretion to dismiss an action brought by a California resident on grounds of forum non conveniens. In *Goodwine v. Superior Court,* we said that "A determination that a plaintiff is domiciled here would ordinarily preclude granting the defendant's motion for dismissal on the ground of forum non conveniens." * * * *Ferreira v. Ferreira,* stated that "in the ordinary case, the doctrine of forum non conveniens does not permit the dismissal of an action itself, as distinguished from a stay of that action, brought by a California resident."

Noting that our decisions have indicated that in an extraordinary case the court could dismiss an action by a California resident on grounds of Forum non conveniens, defendants assert that the present action is such an extraordinary case; they support this assertion by pointing to considerations which suggest that Hawaii might be a more convenient place of trial.[3] In so asserting, defendants necessarily assume that the extraordinary case * * * is simply a case in which the foreign forum is very much more convenient.

Defendants' assumption overlooks the reasoning underlying our refusal to permit the dismissal of actions brought by California residents. This limitation of the Forum non conveniens doctrine does not rest on any conclusion derived from a balancing of conveniences; it reflects an overriding state policy of assuring California residents an adequate forum for the redress of grievances. In light of that policy, the exceptional case which justifies the dismissal of a suit under the doctrine of Forum non conveniens is one in which California cannot provide an adequate forum or has no interest in doing so. Examples would include cases in which no party is a California resident or in which the nominal California resident sues on behalf of foreign beneficiaries or creditors.

The present case does not fall within the exception to the rule barring dismissal. Plaintiff here sues on behalf of herself and other California residents, not as the representative of foreign beneficiaries or creditors; she asserts that she and other California residents have been victimized by unlawful and oppressive price discrimination. California unquestionably has an interest in assuring plaintiff a forum adequate to resolve this controversy and can, if necessary, provide that forum itself.[7]

Defendants respond that to refuse to permit the trial court to dismiss a suit by a true California resident even when the foreign forum is much the more convenient turns the doctrine of Forum non conveniens on its head, and transforms it into an inflexible rule compelling trial in an inconvenient forum. Their argument overlooks the power of the trial court, applying the doctrine of Forum non conveniens, to stay a suit by a California resident even when it lacks the power to dismiss that suit. In considering whether to stay an action, in contrast to dismissing

---

3. Defendants claim that Hawaii will be more convenient to the majority of witnesses and a less expensive place of trial; that plaintiff can obtain unquestioned jurisdiction over all defendants in Hawaii; and that an Hawaiian class action need not be limited to California plaintiffs. They further contend that plaintiff's causes of action based upon common law or on the Hawaii innkeepers' law will be governed by Hawaii decisions, and that, since the outcome of the case will affect the pricing policies of many Hawaiian hotels, Hawaii has a great-

er interest than California in the controversy.

Although plaintiff questions the weight to be given the considerations cited by defendants, her primary objection to a Hawaii proceeding arises from her uncertainty whether Hawaii class action procedures are adequate to provide a practical remedy for her class claim.

7. California can assert personal jurisdiction over most if not all of the defendants, and defendants do not contend that any absent defendants are indispensable.

it, the plaintiff's residence is but one of many factors which the court may consider. The court can also take into account the amenability of the defendants to personal jurisdiction, the convenience of witnesses, the expense of trial, the choice of law, and indeed any consideration which legitimately bears upon the relative suitability or convenience of the alternative forums. (See Gulf Oil Co. v. Gilbert (1947) 330 U.S. 501, 508–509, 67 S.Ct. 839, 91 L.Ed. 1055; * * *.) In short, the trial court retains a flexible power to consider and weigh all factors relevant to determining which forum is the more convenient, and to stay actions by true California residents when it finds that the foreign forum is preferable. The only procedure it cannot follow is that which the trial court attempts in the present case—a dismissal of a suit by a true California resident on grounds of Forum non conveniens.

We conclude, therefore, that the trial court erred in granting defendants' motion to dismiss the present action. Anticipating this conclusion, the parties urge that we instruct the trial court whether it should grant or deny a motion to stay the instant action. To the extent that the parties' request requires us to consider and weigh the numerous factors which we have suggested above that should resolve whether trial in Hawaii is more or is less convenient than trial in California, we decline the task. * * * Since defendants have not presented a motion for a stay to the trial judge, that judge has not yet had the opportunity to exercise his discretion.

We do, however, address one argument presented by plaintiff since its determination would preclude the exercise of any discretion by the trial court in the matter. Plaintiff argues that defendants have failed to show the existence of a suitable alternative forum (see *Gulf Oil Co. v. Gilbert*), and consequently that the trial court lacks the discretion to stay proceedings in California.

Plaintiff's argument rests on a comparison of class action procedures in California and Hawaii. As plaintiff points out, California decisions permit a class plaintiff to aggregate individual claims to bring his action within the monetary jurisdiction of the superior court. (Collins v. San Francisco (1952) 112 Cal.App.2d 719, 724, 247 P.2d 362; see Daar v. Yellow Cab Co. (1967) 67 Cal.2d 695, 63 Cal.Rptr. 724, 433 P.2d 732; * * *.) Moreover, the representative plaintiff in a California class action is not required to notify individually every readily ascertainable member of his class without regard to the feasibility of such notice; he need only provide meaningful notice in a form that "should have a reasonable chance of reaching a substantial percentage of the class members." Thus California class action procedures pose no unreasonable barriers to the trial of plaintiff's class suit on its merits.

Plaintiff questions, however, whether her class suit will receive a hospitable reception under Hawaiian procedure. Class actions in Hawaii are governed by rule 23 of the Hawaii Rules of Civil Procedure, which is modeled upon rule 23 of the federal rules. Supreme Court decisions interpreting federal rule 23 have held that individual claims cannot be aggregated to overcome a monetary minimum required for subject matter jurisdiction and that the representative plaintiff bears the burden of notifying individually every readily identifiable member of the class. Since no Hawaii appellate decisions adjudicate the issue, plaintiff fears that if the Hawaii courts follow these federal decisions she will be unable either to comply with the $500 minimum claim required for a suit in the Hawaii courts of general jurisdiction, or to afford the expense of notifying individually the thousands of members of her class.

Any attempt on our part to predict how Hawaiian courts will resolve unsettled issues of class action procedure would be purely speculative. But, contrary to plaintiff's contention, the existence of unsettled questions of Hawaiian procedure does not compel the trial court to conclude as a matter of law that Hawaii is not a suitable alternative forum. Uncertainties such as this concerning the suitability of the foreign forum have prompted our holding that a court cannot dismiss a suit by a true California plaintiff, but can stay that suit: the staying court can resume proceedings if the foreign forum proves unsuitable. California's appetite for litigation must not be so gluttonous as to compel it to engage in the trial of causes that are found by the court of first resort to be more conveniently resolved elsewhere, since if redress in the foreign jurisdiction proves abortive, California courts retain the option to resume proceedings.

Since a request for a stay is a matter which must first be addressed to the discretion of the trial court, we do not decide how that discretion should be exercised if such a request is urged. To resolve the issue presented on this appeal it is sufficient to hold that the court has no discretion to dismiss the instant action on grounds of Forum non conveniens, and that its order of dismissal must therefore be reversed.

* * *

Note

In 1986, the California Legislature temporarily modified CCP § 410.30, the inconvenient forum statute, by adding: "The domicile or residence in this state of any party to the action shall not preclude the court from staying or dismissing the action." While this amendment was effective, the California courts interpreted it as legislative rejection of cases like *Archibald*. E.g., Credit Lyonnais Bank Nederland, N.V. v. Manatt, Phelps, Rothenberg & Tunney, 202 Cal.App.3d 1424, 249 Cal.Rptr. 559 (1988). The amendment expired of its own terms on January 1, 1992, and the Legislature did not renew it. As a result, California courts have determined that the statute is to be interpreted as it was prior to 1986. Beckman v. Thompson, 4 Cal.App.4th 481, 6 Cal.Rptr.2d 60 (1992).

PLEADING

COMMITTEE ON CHILDREN'S TELEVISION, INC. v. GENERAL FOODS CORPORATION

Supreme Court of California, In Bank, 1983.
35 Cal.3d 197, 673 P.2d 660, 197 Cal.Rptr. 783.

BROUSSARD, JUSTICE.

Plaintiffs appeal from a judgment of dismissal following a trial court order sustaining demurrers without leave to amend to their fourth amended complaint. The complaint essentially charges defendants— General Foods Corporation, Safeway Stores, and two advertising agencies—with fraudulent, misleading and deceptive advertising in the marketing of sugared breakfast cereals. The trial court found its allegations insufficient because they fail to state with specificity the advertisements containing the alleged misrepresentations. We review the allegations of the complaint and conclude that the trial court erred in sustaining demurrers without leave to amend to plaintiffs' causes of action charging fraud and violation of laws against unfair competition and deceptive advertising.

I. SUMMARY OF THE PLEADINGS AND PROCEDURE

Plaintiffs filed their original complaint on June 30, 1977, as a class action on behalf of "California residents who have been misled or deceived, or are threatened with the likelihood of being deceived or misled," by defendants in connection with the marketing of sugared cereals.[1] The named plaintiffs included five organizations (The Committee on Children's Television, Inc; the California Society of Dentistry for Children; the American G.I. Forum of California; the Mexican–American Political Association; the League of United Latin American Citizens), individual adults, and individual children.

The principal defendant is General Foods Corporation, the manufacturer of five "sugared cereals"—Alpha Bits, Honeycomb, Fruity Pebbles, Sugar Crisp, and Cocoa Pebbles—which contain from 38 to 50 percent sugar by weight. The other corporate defendants are two advertising agencies—Benton and Bowles, Inc., and Ogilvy & Mather International, Inc.—which handled advertising of these cereals, and Safeway Stores, which sold the products to plaintiffs. Finally, the complaint includes as defendants numerous officers and employees of the corporate defendants.

When the court sustained a demurrer to the third amended complaint, it ruled that no cause of action could be stated on behalf of the organizational plaintiffs. The individual plaintiffs remaining then filed

---

1. Defendants' demurrers did not attack the description of the class or the suitability of the case as a class action. Questions concerning the certification of the class remain to be resolved in further proceedings.

their fourth amended complaint; the validity of this complaint is the principal issue on appeal.

The fourth amended complaint presents seven causes of action: two based upon consumer protection statutes, four sounding in fraud, and one for breach of warranty. The first cause of action is based on Business and Professions Code sections 17200–17208, the unfair competition law. Paragraph 34 alleges that defendants "engaged in a sophisticated advertising and marketing program which is designed to capitalize on the unique susceptibilities of children and preschoolers in order to induce them to consume products which, although promoted and labelled as 'cereals,' are in fact more accurately described as sugar products, or candies." The complaint thereafter refers to sugared cereals as "candy breakfasts."

Paragraph 35 lists some 19 representations allegedly made in television commercials aimed at children. Most of these representations are not explicit but, according to plaintiffs, implicit in the advertising.
* * *[3]

3. Paragraph 35 of the complaint reads as follows:

35. The advertising scheme routinely and repeatedly employs and utilizes, in commercials aimed at children, each of the following representations which are conveyed both visually and verbally:

(a) Children and young children who regularly eat candy breakfasts are bigger, stronger, more energetic, happier, more invulnerable, and braver than they would have been if they did not eat candy breakfasts.

(b) Eating candy breakfasts is a "fun" thing for children to do, and is invariably equated with entertainment and adventure.

(c) The sweet taste of a product ensures or correlates with nutritional merit.

(d) Eating candy breakfasts will make children happy.

(e) Bright colors in foods ensure or correlate with nutritional merit.

(f) Candy breakfasts are grain products.

(g) Candy breakfasts are more healthful and nutritious for a child than most other kinds and types of cereals.

(h) Adding small amounts of vitamins and minerals to a product automatically makes it "nutritious".

(i) Candy breakfasts inherently possess and/or impart to those ingesting them magical powers, such as the capacity to cause apes and fantastic creatures to appear or disappear.

(j) Candy breakfasts contain adequate amounts of the essential elements of a growing child's diet, including protein.

(k) The "premiums" (small toys packaged in with the candy breakfast as an inducement to the child) are very valuable and are offered free as a prize in each box of candy breakfast.

(l) Candy breakfasts are the most important part of a "well-balanced breakfast" and are at least as nutritious as milk, toast and juice.

(m) Candy breakfasts calm a child's fears and dispel a child's anxiety. . . .

(n) Candy breakfasts have visual characteristics which they do not in fact possess, such as vivid colors and the capacity to glitter or to enlarge from their actual size to a larger size.

In addition to the foregoing representations specified in Paragraph 35(a) through (n), in each of the commercials for each of the products specified below the advertising scheme repeatedly, uniformly and consistently utilizes and relies upon the following representations with respect to particular products:

(o) Cocoa Pebbles are good for a child to eat whenever he or she is hungry, and it is a sound nutritional practice to eat chocolatey tasting foods, such as Cocoa Pebbles, for breakfast.

(p) Honeycomb (i) contains honey and (ii) consists of pieces which are each at least two (2) inches in diameter and (iii) will make a child big and strong.

(q) Alpha–Bits (i) will enable a child to conquer his or her enemies, (ii) can be

Plaintiffs allege that commercials containing these representations are broadcast daily. Although the commercials changed every 60 days, "they retain consistent themes and each convey . . . the representations as set forth." Defendants, but not plaintiffs, know the exact times, dates, and places of broadcasts. Plaintiffs further allege that the same representations appear in other media, and on the cereal packages themselves.

Paragraph 42 asserts that defendants concealed material facts, such as the sugar content of their products, that "[t]here is no honey in Honeycomb, no fruit in Fruity Pebbles," that sugared cereals contribute to tooth decay and can have more serious medical consequences, and that they cost more per serving than breakfast foods of greater nutritional value. Such concealment, plaintiffs allege, when joined with the affirmative misrepresentations listed in paragraph 35, render the advertisements misleading and deceptive.

The complaint asserts at length the special susceptibility of children to defendants' "advertising scheme," and explains how defendants take advantage of this vulnerability. It further asserts that, as defendants know, the desires and beliefs of children influence and often determine the decision of adults to buy certain breakfast foods. Finally, claiming that defendants will continue deceptive practices unless enjoined, the first cause of action seeks injunctive relief, plus restitution of monies paid for "candy breakfasts."

* * *

The third through sixth causes of action set out various aspects of the tort of fraud. The third cause of action charges deliberate fraud in violation of Civil Code section 1710, subdivision 1. Incorporating the allegations of the first cause of action, it adds allegations of plaintiffs' reasonable reliance upon defendants' representations, especially in light of defendants' claim to superior knowledge about the nutritional value of foods. The fourth cause of action adds allegations of negligent misrepresentation (Civ.Code, § 1710, subd. 2); the fifth cause of action adds fraudulent concealment (Civ.Code, § 1710, subd. 3). The sixth cause of action is based on common law fraud. Each of these causes of action asserts proximate causation, and claims compensatory damages of $10 million; those counts asserting intentional misrepresentation include a prayer for punitive damages.

The prayer for relief is extensive, and includes some novel requests. In addition to seeking damages, restitution, and injunctive relief, plain-

used by a child easily to spell words in his or her spoon, (iii) are an effective cure for the child's anxieties, and (iv) have magical powers and can impart magical powers to a child. . . .

(r) Fruity Pebbles (i) contain fruit and (ii) emit auras, rainbows or mesmerizing colors.

(s) Super Sugar Crisp (i) should be eaten as a snack food without danger to dental health, (ii) should be eaten as a nutritious snack whenever a child is hungry, (iii) makes a child smart and (iv) is coated with golden sugar and such sugar is very valuable.

tiffs seek warning labels in stores and on packages, creation of funds for research on the health effects of sugar consumption by young children, public interest representatives on defendants' boards of directors, and public access to defendants' research on the health effects of their products.

Defendants demurred to the fourth amended complaint for failure to state a cause of action and for uncertainty. The trial court sustained the demurrers without leave to amend. The trial judge explained the basis for his ruling: "[I]n order to state a cause of action for fraud or for breach of warranty, there must be alleged with specificity the basis for the cause and that is, if there are advertisements which contain fraudulent matters, those advertisements must be set out. [¶] In paragraph 35, which is the heart of the allegations concerning the conveying of the representations, we have just a series of very general allegations to which there is no reference of an advertisement actually made.... [¶] Paragraph 38 which makes the allegations concerning media dissemination sets out no television stations, no other media, except for the fact that these ads were run on television stations every day in Southern California for a four-year period. [¶] This gives the defendant practically no kind of information concerning that which the defendant must answer, and it doesn't give the court a sufficient factual basis for its administration of the case."

Appealing from the judgment of dismissal, plaintiffs contend that their fourth amended complaint states, or can be amended to state, a valid cause of action. * * *

II. CAUSES OF ACTION BASED ON CONSUMER PROTECTION STATUTES

* * * [P]laintiffs rely on three statutes—the unfair competition law, the false advertising law, and the Sherman Food, Drug and Cosmetic Law—all of which in similar language prohibit false, unfair, misleading, or deceptive advertising. * * *

To state a cause of action under these statutes for injunctive relief, it is necessary only to show that "members of the public are likely to be deceived." (Chern v. Bank of America (1976) 15 Cal.3d 866, 876, 127 Cal.Rptr. 110, 544 P.2d 1310.) Allegations of actual deception, reasonable reliance, and damage are unnecessary. The court may also order restitution without individualized proof of deception, reliance, and injury if it "determines that such a remedy is necessary 'to prevent the use or employment' of the unfair practice...." (Fletcher v. Security Pacific National Bank [(1979)] 23 Cal.3d 442, 453, 153 Cal.Rptr. 28, 591 P.2d 51.)

Insofar as plaintiffs seek injunctive relief and restitution under the cited consumer protection statutes, defendants' principal basis for demurrer is the charge that the complaint fails to describe the alleged deceptive practices with sufficient particularity. Defendants assert that plaintiffs should not merely describe the substance of the misrepresentations, but should state the specific deceptive language employed, identify the persons making the misrepresentations and those to whom they were made, and indicate the date, time and place of the deception.

The complaint in a civil action serves a variety of purposes, of which two are relevant here: it serves to frame and limit the issues and to apprise the defendant of the basis upon which the plaintiff is seeking recovery. In fulfilling this function, the complaint should set forth the ultimate facts constituting the cause of action, not the evidence by which plaintiff proposes to prove those facts.[11]

* * *

The fourth amended complaint in the present case describes the alleged deceptive scheme in considerable detail. Paragraph 35 alleges some 19 misrepresentations—some general, others relatively specific. Paragraph 42 lists material facts which are not disclosed. Finally, plaintiffs allege that each misrepresentation appears (and every listed material fact is concealed) in every advertisement for the specified product during the period in question.[13] There is thus no doubt as to what advertisements are at issue, nor as to what deceptive practices are called into question.[14] We believe these allegations are sufficient to notify the defendants of the claim made against them, and to frame the issues for litigation.

Defendants' objection, as we see it, is not really one of lack of specificity or notice. Basically defendants believe that the allegations of paragraph 35 are not a fair paraphrase of the actual language of the advertisements, and that if plaintiffs could be compelled to state the exact language, it would be clear, for example, that defendants are not really representing that Cocoa Puffs will make children braver or that Alpha Bits impart magical powers.

It is not the ordinary function of a demurrer to test the truth of the plaintiff's allegations or the accuracy with which he describes the defendant's conduct. A demurrer tests only the legal sufficiency of the pleading. It "admits the truth of all material factual allegations in the complaint . . .; the question of plaintiff's ability to prove these allegations, or the possible difficulty in making such proof does not concern the reviewing court." (Alcorn v. Anbro Engineering, Inc. (1970) 2 Cal.3d 493, 496, 86 Cal.Rptr. 88, 468 P.2d 216.) We must therefore assume that defendants did in substance make each of the representations listed in paragraph 35 (and omit to state material facts as described in paragraph 42) in each advertisement within the period described by

---

11. The requirement that fraud be pleaded with specificity, discussed in part III of this opinion, does not apply to causes of action under the consumer protection statutes.

13. We are skeptical of plaintiffs' claim that every advertisement includes every misrepresentation. But to require plaintiffs in their complaint to review every advertisement to determine, for example,

whether the April 1977 advertisements for Fruity Pebbles implied that they would dispel a child's anxiety, would greatly increase the complexity of the pleading without adding any significant increase in clarity.

14. Plaintiffs' complaint may be uncertain, however, as to what media, other than television and cereal boxes, were employed to advertise the sugared cereals.

the complaint. Defendants' contention that the words and images used do not constitute such misrepresentations, and did not conceal material facts, frames an issue for trial, not demurrer.

The unsuitability of a demurrer to test the accuracy of a complaint is particularly marked in the present case. Plaintiffs do not, for the most part, claim that defendants made explicit oral or written representations. Instead, they claim that defendants used language, and presented images, in a form such that a particularly susceptible and naive audience—one composed largely of preschool children—would believe defendants were making those representations. Even if plaintiffs pled the exact language and sequence of visual images making up a television advertisement, it would be difficult for judges unaided by expert testimony to determine how a three-year-old would interpret that advertisement.

Important policy considerations also argue against requiring plaintiffs to set out the specific language of each advertisement. Plaintiffs allege that defendants carried out a large scale program of deceptive advertising in which the specific advertisements change constantly, but all follow a pattern of making, in one form or another, certain misleading and deceptive representations. If such is the case, to require plaintiffs to plead the specifics of each advertisement would render a suit challenging the overall program impractical. The complaint would have to include thousands of pages setting out specifics which are largely within defendants' knowledge. The cost and difficulty of compiling, organizing, and setting down the information would seriously deter the filing of any such complaint. The effect of such a pleading requirement, moreover, would not be limited to discouraging private suits; it would also seriously hamper suits by public officials seeking to enjoin schemes of unfair competition and deceptive advertising.

We conclude that the allegations of plaintiffs' fourth amended complaint are sufficient to overcome a general demurrer and to state causes of action for injunctive relief and restitution under both the unfair competition law and the false advertising law. * * *

III. CAUSES OF ACTION BASED ON FRAUD

Plaintiffs base their third, fourth, fifth and sixth causes of action on the tort of fraud. * * * Defendants, citing the rule that fraud must be pleaded specifically, claim plaintiffs' allegations of misrepresentation, reasonable reliance, and damages are insufficient to comply with that rule.

"Fraud actions . . . are subject to strict requirements of particularity in pleading. The idea seems to be that allegations of fraud involve a serious attack on character, and fairness to the defendant demands that he should receive the fullest possible details of the charge in order to prepare his defense. Accordingly the rule is everywhere followed that fraud must be specifically pleaded. The effect of this rule is twofold: (a) General pleading of the legal conclusion of 'fraud' is insufficient; the facts constituting the fraud must be alleged. (b) Every element of the cause of action for fraud must be alleged in the proper manner (i.e., factually and specifically), and the policy of liberal construction of the pleadings ... will not ordinarily be invoked to sustain a pleading defective in any material respect." (3 Witkin, Cal.Procedure (2d ed. 1971) Pleading, § 574.) [17]

The specificity requirement serves two purposes. The first is notice to the defendant, to "furnish the defendant with certain definite charges which can be intelligently met." (Lavine v. Jessup, *supra,* 161 Cal. App.2d 59, 69, 326 P.2d 238;) The pleading of fraud, however, is also the last remaining habitat of the common law notion that a complaint should be sufficiently specific that the court can weed out nonmeritorious actions on the basis of the pleadings. Thus the pleading should be sufficient " 'to enable the court to determine whether, on the facts pleaded, there is any foundation, prima facie at least, for the charge of fraud.' " (Scafidi v. Western Loan and Building Co., [(1946)] 72 Cal. App.2d 550, 553, 165 P.2d 260;)

We observe, however, certain exceptions which mitigate the rigor of the rule requiring specific pleading of fraud. Less specificity is required when "it appears from the nature of the allegations that the defendant must necessarily possess full information concerning the facts of the controversy," (Bradley v. Hartford Acc. & Indem. Co. (1973) 30 Cal. App.3d 818, 825, 106 Cal.Rptr. 718); "[e]ven under the strict rules of common law pleading, one of the canons was that less particularity is required when the facts lie more in the knowledge of the opposite party...." (Turner v. Milstein (1951) 103 Cal.App.2d 651, 658, 230 P.2d 25.)

Additionally, in a case such as the present one, considerations of practicality enter in. A complaint should be kept to reasonable length, and plaintiffs' fourth amended complaint, 64 pages long, strains at that limit. Yet plaintiffs allege thousands of misrepresentations in various media over a span of four years—representations which, while similar in substance, differ in time, place, and detail of language and presentation. A complaint which set out each advertisement verbatim, and specified the time, place, and medium, might seem to represent perfect compliance with the specificity requirement, but as a practical matter, it would provide less effective notice and be less useful in framing the issues than would a shorter, more generalized version.

---

17. Witkin adds, however, that: "In reading the cases one gains the impression that entirely too much emphasis has been laid upon the requirement of specific pleading. The characterization of some actions as 'disfavored' has little to recommend it ... and actions based on fraud are so numerous and commonplace that the implications of immoral conduct are seldom considered more serious than those involved in other intentional torts. Hence, while it seems sound to require specific pleading of the facts of fraud rather than general conclusions, the courts should not look askance at the complaint, and seek to absolve the defendant from liability on highly technical requirements of form in pleading. Pleading facts in ordinary and concise language is as permissible in fraud cases as in any others, and liberal construction of the pleading is as much a duty of the court in these as in other cases." (3 Witkin, op. cit. *supra,* Pleading, § 575, quoted in Lacy v. Laurentide Finance Corp. (1972) 28 Cal.App.3d 251, 258, fn. 2, 104 Cal.Rptr. 547.)

Defendants object to the allegations of misrepresentation on the ground that the complaint fails to state the time and place of each misrepresentation, to identify the speaker and listener, and to set out the representation verbatim or in close paraphrase. The place and time of the advertisements, however, is fully known to defendant General Foods, but became available to plaintiffs only through discovery. That defendant equally knows the distribution of cereal box advertisements. A lengthy list of the dates and times of cereal ads on California television stations would add nothing of value to the complaint; the same is true for a list of California grocers marketing General Foods cereals. The language of the complaint—all ads for sugared cereals within a given four-year period—is sufficient to define the subject of the complaint and provide notice to defendants.

General Foods also knows the content of each questioned advertisement. Plaintiffs initially lacked such detailed knowledge, and although they have now obtained copies of the television storyboards through discovery, quotation or attachment of such copies to the complaint would consume thousands of pages. Attachment of the storyboards, moreover, would not redress defendants' grievance, which is, as we understand it, not that they lacked knowledge of the content of the commercials but that they do not understand what it is in the images and words that gives rise to the alleged misrepresentations.

For plaintiffs to provide an explanation for every advertisement would be obviously impractical. We believe, however, that the trial court could reasonably require plaintiffs to set out or attach a representative selection of advertisements, to state the misrepresentations made by those advertisements, and to indicate the language or images upon which any implied misrepresentations are based. This is a method of pleading which has been endorsed in other cases involving numerous misrepresentations. It represents a reasonable accommodation between defendants' right to a pleading sufficiently specific "that the court can ascertain for itself if the representations ... were in fact material, and of an actionable nature" (8 Grossman & Van Alstyne, [Cal.Practice (1981)], § 984 (fns. omitted)), and the importance of avoiding pleading requirements so burdensome as to preclude relief in cases involving multiple misrepresentations.[19]

* * *

We turn finally to the question of damages. In an action for fraud, damage is an essential element of the cause of action; the successful plaintiff recovers damages as a matter of right.

* * * The allegations of the complaint are clearly sufficient to state a cause of action for restitution of the money spent to purchase the

---

19. We did not suggest the necessity of plaintiffs pleading a representative selection of advertisements when we discussed their causes of action under the consumer protection laws. The requirement of specificity in pleading does not apply to those causes of action; the use of pleadings as a method by which the court can inquire into the merits of the case is confined to fraud actions.

sugared cereals. The complaint also seeks additional damages, claiming that plaintiffs and members of their class encountered medical or dental injury from consuming sugared cereals and incurred expenses to treat those injuries. It does not, however, assert that any of the named children sustained any specific injury or that any of the named parents spent money to treat such injury. As a result, the allegations appear sufficient to assert injury to a subclass of parents and children (the class being all parents who purchased and children who consumed, even if no injury was incurred), but does not clearly place any of the individually named plaintiffs within their subclass. In view of the requirement for specific pleading in fraud actions, we believe the trial court could view the complaint as uncertain in its failure to make clear whether the individual child plaintiffs have incurred any specific health injury from the consumption of the sugared cereals, and whether their parents have spent any specific sums to treat those injuries.

In summary, the * * * allegations on behalf of the individual plaintiffs—both parents and children—are insufficiently certain and specific, but those deficiencies can be cured by amendment. We recognize that plaintiffs have already had opportunities to amend, but without the guidance of this opinion, their failure to make the specific amendments we now require is excusable. * * * The judgment must be reversed to permit plaintiffs to correct any uncertainty or lack of required specificity in their fraud causes of action. * * *

V. CONCLUSION

Although the parties argue primarily the sufficiency and specificity of the pleadings, the underlying controversy is of much greater dimension. Defendants engaged in a nationwide, long-term advertising campaign designed to persuade children to influence their parents to buy sugared cereals. Adapted to its audience, the campaign sought to persuade less by direct representation than by imagery and example. While maintaining a constant theme, the particular advertisements changed frequently. Plaintiffs now contend that these advertisements were deceptive and misleading, and while we do not know the actual truth of those charges, we must assume them true for the purpose of this appeal. Yet, if we apply strict requirements of specificity in pleading as defendants argue, the result would be to eliminate the private lawsuit as a practical remedy to redress such past deception or prevent further deception. By directing their advertisements to children, and changing them frequently, defendants would have obtained practical immunity from statutory and common law remedies designed to protect consumers from misleading advertising.

It can be argued that administrative investigation and rule making would be a better method of regulating advertising of this scope and character. The California Legislature, however, has not established the necessary administrative structure. It has enacted consumer protection statutes and codified common law remedies which in principle apply to all deceptive advertising, regardless of complexity and scale, and, we believe, regardless of whether the advertisement seeks to influence the consumer directly or through his children. Established rules of pleading should not be applied so inflexibly that they bar use of such remedies.

We therefore conclude that plaintiffs' complaint states a cause of action for injunctive relief and restitution under the unfair competition law (Bus. & Prof.Code, § 17200 et seq.) and the false advertising law (Bus. & Prof.Code, § 17500 et seq.) Plaintiffs should be permitted to amend their complaint on behalf of the parent and child plaintiffs under the causes of action for fraud. * * *

MOSK, RICHARDSON, KAUS, REYNOSO and GRODIN, JJ., concur.

BIRD, CHIEF JUDGE, concurring and dissenting.

[omitted]

DISCOVERY

VINSON v. SUPERIOR COURT

Supreme Court of California, In Bank, 1987.
43 Cal.3d 833, 740 P.2d 404, 239 Cal.Rptr. 292.

MOSK, JUSTICE.

* * *

Plaintiff is a 59–year–old widow who in 1979 applied for a job in Oakland with a federally funded program, administered at the time by defendant Peralta Community College District, under the direction of codefendant Grant. Plaintiff alleges that Grant, during an interview with her in a private cubicle, commented on how attractive she appeared for a woman of her age. He assertedly made some salacious observations regarding her anatomy and expressed his desires with regard thereto. He allegedly concluded the interview by intimating that acquiring the position was subject to a condition precedent: her acquiescence to his sexual yearnings. Plaintiff claims she declined his advances as unconscionable and left greatly distraught.

Unknown to Grant, plaintiff was later hired by defendant college district as a certification technician. She asserts that once he discovered she was working for the program, he had her transferred to the payroll unit, a position for which he apparently knew she had no training. Soon thereafter he terminated her employment.

Plaintiff filed suit on several causes of action, among them sexual harassment, wrongful discharge, and intentional infliction of emotional distress. Defendants' actions are said to have caused her to suffer continuing emotional distress, loss of sleep, anxiety, mental anguish, humiliation, reduced self-esteem, and other consequences.

Defendants moved for an order compelling her to undergo a medical and a psychological examination. The examinations were meant to test the true extent of her injuries and to measure her ability to function in the workplace. Plaintiff opposed the motion as a violation of her right to privacy. In the alternative, if the court were to permit the examination she requested a protective order shielding her from any probing into her sexual history or practices, and asked that her attorney be allowed to attend in order to assure compliance with the order. The court granted the motion without imposing any of these limitations. Plaintiff petitioned the Court of Appeal for a writ of prohibition and/or mandate to direct the trial court to forbid the examination or to issue appropriate protective orders. The Court of Appeal denied the petition.

I. The Appropriateness of a Mental Examination

Plaintiff first contends the psychiatric examination should not be permitted because it infringes on her right to privacy. Before we can entertain this constitutional question, we must determine the statutory scope of the discovery laws.[2]

Code of Civil Procedure section 2032, subdivision (a), permits the mental examination of a party in any action in which the mental condition of that party is in controversy. Plaintiff disputes that her mental condition is in controversy. She points to Cody v. Marriott Corp. (D.Mass.1984) 103 F.R.D. 421, 422, a case interpreting rule 35(a) of the Federal Rules of Civil Procedure. Like the California rule that was patterned on it, rule 35 requires that physical or mental condition be "in controversy" before an examination is appropriate. Cody was an employment discrimination case in which the plaintiffs alleged mental and emotional distress. The court held that the claim of emotional distress did not ipso facto place the plaintiff's mental state in controversy.

The reasoning of Cody rested in large part on Schlagenhauf v. Holder (1964) 379 U.S. 104, 85 S.Ct. 234, 13 L.Ed.2d 152, in which the United States Supreme Court examined the "in controversy" requirement. In Schlagenhauf the plaintiffs were passengers injured when their bus collided with the rear of a truck. The defendant truck company, in answer to a cross-claim by the codefendant bus company, charged that the bus driver had been unfit to drive and moved to have him undergo a mental and physical examination. The Supreme Court recognized that at times the pleadings may be sufficient to put mental or physical condition in controversy, as when a plaintiff in a negligence action alleges mental or physical injury. But it determined that the driver had not asserted his mental condition in support of or in a defense of a claim, nor did the general charge of negligence put his mental state in controversy. Schlagenhauf thus stands for the proposition that one

---

2. Part 4, title 3, chapter 3, article 3, of the Code of Civil Procedure (§§ 2016–2036.-5), the applicable legislation on depositions and discovery at the time this action began, has been repealed. The repeal was operative July 1, 1987, on which date a new article 3 (entitled the Civil Discovery Act of 1986) came into effect. The act provides, however, that the use of a discovery method initiated before July 1, 1987, will be governed by the law regulating that method at the time it was initiated. We must therefore apply the superseded discovery procedures to this case. But as we shall show by appropriate references to the new act, many of its relevant provisions are substantially similar.

party's unsubstantiated allegation cannot put the mental state of another in controversy.

It is another matter entirely, however, when a party places his *own* mental state in controversy by alleging mental and emotional distress. Unlike the bus driver in *Schlagenhauf,* who had a controversy thrust upon him, a party who chooses to allege that he has mental and emotional difficulties can hardly deny his mental state is in controversy. To the extent the decision in *Cody, supra,* 103 F.R.D. 421, is inconsistent with this conclusion, we decline to follow it.

In the case at bar, plaintiff haled defendants into court and accused them of causing her various mental and emotional ailments. Defendants deny her charges. As a result, the existence and extent of her mental injuries is indubitably in dispute. In addition, by asserting a causal link between her mental distress and defendants' conduct, plaintiff implicitly claims it was not caused by a preexisting mental condition, thereby raising the question of alternative sources for the distress. We thus conclude that her mental state is in controversy.

We emphasize that our conclusion is based solely on the allegations of emotional and mental damages in this case. A simple sexual harassment claim asking compensation for having to endure an oppressive work environment or for wages lost following an unjust dismissal would not normally create a controversy regarding the plaintiff's mental state. To hold otherwise would mean that every person who brings such a suit implicitly asserts he or she is mentally unstable, obviously an untenable proposition.

Determining that the mental or physical condition of a party is in controversy is but the first step in our analysis. In contrast to more pedestrian discovery procedures, a mental or physical examination requires the discovering party to obtain a court order. The court may grant the motion only for good cause shown.

* * * The requirement of a court order following a showing of good cause is doubtless designed to protect an examinee's privacy interest by preventing an examination from becoming an annoying fishing expedition. While a plaintiff may place his mental state in controversy by a general allegation of severe emotional distress, the opposing party may not require him to undergo psychiatric testing solely on the basis of speculation that something of interest may surface.

Plaintiff in the case at bar asserts that she continues to suffer diminished self-esteem, reduced motivation, sleeplessness, loss of appetite, fear, lessened ability to help others, loss of social contacts, anxiety, mental anguish, loss of reputation, and severe emotional distress. In their motion defendants pointed to these allegations. Because the truth of these claims is relevant to plaintiff's cause of action and justifying facts have been shown with specificity, good cause as to these assertions has been demonstrated. Subject to limitations necessitated by plaintiff's right to privacy, defendants must be allowed to investigate the continued existence and severity of plaintiff's alleged damages.

II. PRIVACY LIMITATIONS ON THE SCOPE OF A MENTAL EXAMINATION

If we find, as we do, that an examination may be ordered, plaintiff urges us to circumscribe its scope to exclude any probing into her sexual history, habits, or practices. Such probing, she asserts, would intrude impermissibly into her protected sphere of privacy. Furthermore, it would tend to contravene the state's strong interest in eradicating sexual harassment by means of private suits for damages. An examination into a plaintiff's past and present sexual practices would inhibit the bringing of meritorious sexual harassment actions by compelling the plaintiff—whose privacy has already been invaded by the harassment—to suffer another intrusion into her private life.

* * *

Defendants acknowledge plaintiff's right to privacy *in abstracto* but maintain she has waived it for purposes of the present suit. In addition, they urge us to take heed of their right to a fair trial, which they claim depends on a "meaningful" examination of plaintiff. Defendants contend they would not have requested a mental examination if plaintiff had simply brought a sexual harassment suit; but because she claims emotional and mental damage, they should be entitled to present expert testimony on the extent of the injury. Preparing such testimony, they suggest, requires not simply a mental examination, but one without substantial restrictions on its scope.

We cannot agree that the mere initiation of a sexual harassment suit, even with the rather extreme mental and emotional damage plaintiff claims to have suffered, functions to waive all her privacy interests, exposing her persona to the unfettered mental probing of defendants' expert. Plaintiff is not compelled, as a condition to entering the courtroom, to discard entirely her mantle of privacy. At the same time, plaintiff cannot be allowed to make her very serious allegations without affording defendants an opportunity to put their truth to the test.

* * *

Plaintiff's present mental and emotional condition is directly relevant to her claim and essential to a fair resolution of her suit; she has waived her right to privacy in this respect by alleging continuing mental ailments. But she has not, merely by initiating this suit for sexual harassment and emotional distress, implicitly waived her right to privacy in respect to her sexual history and practices. Defendants fail to explain why probing into this area is directly relevant to her claim and essential to its fair resolution. * * *

But even though plaintiff retains certain unwaived privacy rights, these rights are not necessarily absolute. On occasion her privacy interests may have to give way to her opponent's right to a fair trial. Thus courts must balance the right of civil litigants to discover relevant facts against the privacy interests of persons subject to discovery.

Before proceeding, we note the Legislature recently enacted a measure designed to protect the privacy of plaintiffs in cases such as these. Section 2036.1 (operative until July 1, 1987; presently, substantially the same provision is contained in § 2017, subdivision (d)), provides that in a civil suit alleging conduct that constitutes sexual harassment, sexual assault, or sexual battery, any party seeking discovery concerning the plaintiff's sexual conduct with individuals other than the alleged perpetrator must establish specific facts showing good cause for that discovery, and that the inquiry is relevant to the subject matter and reasonably calculated to lead to the discovery of admissible evidence. We must determine whether the general balancing of interests embodied in this new legislation has obviated the need for us to engage in an individualized balancing of privacy with discovery in the case at bar.

In enacting the measure, the Legislature took pains to declare that "The discovery of sexual aspects of complainant's [sic] lives, as well as those of their past and current friends and acquaintances, has the clear potential to discourage complaints and to annoy and harass litigants. . . . without protection against it, individuals whose intimate lives are unjustifiably and offensively intruded upon might face the 'Catch–22' of invoking their remedy only at the risk of enduring further intrusions into the details of their personal lives in discovery. . . . [¶] . . . Absent extraordinary circumstances, inquiry into those areas should not be permitted, either in discovery or at trial." (Stats.1985, ch. 1328, § 1.) [8]

Nowhere do defendants establish specific facts justifying inquiry into plaintiff's zone of sexual privacy or show how such discovery would be relevant. Rather they make only the most sweeping assertions regarding the need for wide latitude in the examination. Because good cause has not been shown, discovery into this area of plaintiff's life must be denied.

Section 2036.1 thus amply protects plaintiff's privacy interests. We anticipate that in the majority of sexual harassment suits, a separate weighing of privacy against discovery will not be necessary. It should normally suffice for the court, in ruling on whether good cause exists for probing into the intimate life of a victim of sexual harassment, sexual battery, or sexual assault, to evaluate the showing of good cause in light of the legislative purpose in enacting this section and the plaintiff's constitutional right to privacy.

---

8. Plaintiff suggests that section 2036.1 does not adequately protect her privacy interests because section 2032 already requires "good cause" for a mental examination, and nothing is added by again requiring good cause for inquiry into a plaintiff's sexual history and practices. But the above-quoted legislative declaration accompanying section 2036.1, i.e., that inquiry into sexuality should not be permitted absent "extraordinary circumstances," suggests that a stronger showing of good cause must be made to justify inquiry into this topic than is needed for a general examination. Furthermore, section 2032 merely requires good cause for the examination as a whole; in emotional distress cases that will often be present. By contrast, a defendant in a sexual harassment case desiring to ask sex-related questions must show specific facts justifying that particular inquiry.

III. Presence of Counsel

In the event a limited psychiatric examination is proper, plaintiff urges us to authorize the attendance of her attorney. She fears that the examiner will stray beyond the permitted area of inquiry. Counsel would monitor the interview and shield her from inappropriate interrogation. And depicting the examination as an "alien and frankly hostile environment," she asserts that she needs her lawyer to provide her with aid and comfort.

Defendants, joined by amici California Psychiatric Association and Northern California Psychiatric Association, counter that a meaningful mental examination cannot be conducted with an attorney interposing objections. And if plaintiff's counsel is present, defense counsel would also seek to attend. Defendants maintain these adversaries would likely convert the examination into a chaotic deposition.

We contemplated whether counsel must be allowed to attend the psychiatric examination of a client in Edwards v. Superior Court (1976) 16 Cal.3d 905, 130 Cal.Rptr. 14, 549 P.2d 846. The plaintiff in *Edwards* alleged that because of the defendant school district's failure to properly instruct and supervise users of school equipment, she sustained physical and emotional injuries. The trial court granted a motion compelling her to undergo a psychiatric examination alone. Holding that the plaintiff could not insist on the presence of her counsel, a majority of this court denied her petition for a peremptory writ.

The plaintiff in *Edwards* raised many of the points urged upon us here. She asserted that her attorney should be present to protect her from improper inquiries. We were skeptical that a lawyer, unschooled in the ways of the mental health profession, would be able to discern the psychiatric relevance of the questions. And the examiner should have the freedom to probe deeply into the plaintiff's psyche without interference by a third party. The plaintiff further suggested counsel should be present to lend her comfort and support in an inimical setting. We responded that an examinee could view almost any examination of this sort, even by her own expert, as somewhat hostile. Whatever comfort her attorney's handholding might afford was substantially outweighed by the distraction and potential disruption caused by the presence of a third person. Finally, we concluded counsel's presence was not necessary to ensure accurate reporting. Verbatim transcription might inhibit the examinee, preventing an effective examination. Furthermore, other procedural devices—pretrial discovery of the examiner's notes or cross-examination, for example—were available for the plaintiff's protection.

* * *

Despite the dissent in *Edwards,* 16 Cal.3d 905, 914, 130 Cal.Rptr. 14, 549 P.2d 846 (dis. opn. by Sullivan, J. and Mosk, J.), we conclude that a reconsideration of that decision—which is barely 10 years old—is not justified.[9] We emphasize, however, that *Edwards* should be viewed

---

9. Section 2032, subdivision (g) (operative July 1, 1987), now specifically provides for the attendance of an attorney at a *physical* examination. Subdivision (g)(2) states,

as standing for the proposition that the presence of an attorney is not *required* during a mental examination. In light of their broad discretion in discovery matters, trial courts retain the power to permit the presence of counsel or to take other prophylactic measures when needed.

Plaintiff makes no showing that the court abused its discretion in excluding her counsel from the examination. Her fears are wholly unfounded at this point; not a shred of evidence has been produced to show that defendants' expert will not respect her legitimate rights to privacy or might disobey any court-imposed restrictions. Plaintiff's apprehension appears to derive less from the reality of the proposed analysis than from the popular image of mental examinations.

Plaintiff's interests can be adequately protected without having her attorney present. In the first place, section 2032 requires the court granting a physical or mental examination to specify its conditions and scope. We must assume, absent evidence to the contrary, that the examiner will proceed in an ethical manner, adhering to these constraints. And if plaintiff truly fears that the examiner will probe into impermissible areas, she may record the examination on audio tape. This is an unobtrusive measure that will permit evidence of abuse to be presented to the court in any motion for sanctions.[10]

Plaintiff refers us to the history of psychiatric examinations for victims of sexual assault. Such examinations were widely viewed as inhibiting prosecutions for rape by implicitly placing the victim on trial, leading to a legislative prohibition of examinations to assess credibility. The victim of sexual harassment is analogous to the prosecutrix in a rape case, plaintiff asserts, and she points to legislative findings that discovery of sexual aspects of complainants' lives "has the clear potential to discourage complaints." (Stats.1985, ch. 1328, § 1.) If we conclude on the basis of general considerations that a mental examination is appropriate and that it should occur without the presence of counsel, plaintiff urges us to adopt a special rule exempting those who bring harassment charges from either or both of these requirements.

We believe that in these circumstances such a special rule is unwarranted. In the first place, we should be guided by the maxim that *entia non sunt multiplicanda praeter necessitatem:* we should carve out exceptions from general rules only when the facts require it. The state admittedly has a strong interest in eradicating the evil of sexual harassment, and the threat of a mental examination could conceivably dampen a plaintiff's resolve to bring suit. But we have seen that those who allege harassment have substantial protection under existing procedural

however, that nothing in the discovery statutes shall be construed to alter, amend, or affect existing case law with respect to the presence of counsel or other persons during a mental examination by agreement or court order. * * * [I]n the course of that revision the Legislature considered and rejected a provision that would have annulled our decision in *Edwards* by permitting counsel to attend a mental examination.

10. We note that the new discovery act explicitly provides both examiners and examinees the opportunity to perpetuate the interview on audio tape. (§ 2032, subd. (g)(2) (operative July 1, 1987).)

rules. In general it is unlikely that a simple sexual harassment suit will justify a mental examination. Such examinations may ordinarily be considered only in cases in which the alleged mental or emotional distress is said to be ongoing. When an examination is permitted, investigation by a psychiatrist into the private life of a plaintiff is severely constrained, and sanctions are available to guarantee those restrictions are respected.

Finally, the mental examination in this case largely grows out of plaintiff's emotional distress claim. We do not believe the state has a greater interest in preventing emotional distress in sexual harassment victims than it has in preventing such distress in the victims of any other tort.

The judgment of the Court of Appeal is reversed with directions to issue a peremptory writ of mandate compelling respondent court to limit the scope of the mental examination in accordance with the views expressed herein.

BP ALASKA EXPLORATION, INC. v. SUPERIOR COURT
California Court of Appeal, Fifth District, 1988.
199 Cal.App.3d 1240, 245 Cal.Rptr. 682.

FRANSON, PRESIDING JUSTICE.

INTRODUCTION
Two basic issues are involved in this appeal: (1) whether the crime-fraud exception to the lawyer-client privilege provided in Evidence Code section 956 applies to writings protected by the attorney work product rule and (2) the proper standard for determining whether the party seeking discovery of an otherwise privileged attorney-client communication has made the prima facie showing of crime or fraud required to negate the privilege.

THE CASE
Petitioner, BP Alaska Exploration, Inc. (BPAE), seeks a writ of prohibition directing the respondent Kern County Superior Court to vacate its order requiring production of several documents and compelling BPAE's president to answer deposition questions. BPAE claims the communications are protected by the attorney-client privilege (Evid. Code, § 954) and the attorney work product rule (formerly Code Civ. Proc., § 2016, subd. (b), now § 2018). Real parties in interest, Nahama & Weagant Energy Company 1984 Exploratory Drilling Limited Partnership and Nahama & Weagant Company (collectively referred to as NWEC), argues the privileges were vitiated by Evidence Code section 956 because BPAE sought counsel's services to commit a fraud. * * *

THE FACTS
NWEC claims it had unique, confidential geological ideas based on many years of research and analysis to develop underground oil and gas

reserves in an area known in the industry as the Bakersfield Arch in Kern County. On March 4, 1985, NWEC proposed to BPAE that they join in a large-scale exploration venture in the Arch area controlled by Tenneco Oil Company. To persuade BPAE to participate, NWEC disclosed confidential information about five prospects on Tenneco land and other prospects on adjoining property. [Subsequently, BPAE and Tenneco entered into an exploration agreement which excluded NWEC. NWEC claimed it had a right to participate in the "Tenneco play". BPAE representatives met with NWEC employees to discuss the matter. In addition, the claims were investigated by BPAE's general counsel with the help of outside counsel before BPAE rejected them in a letter dated December 23, 1985.] * * *

NWEC filed suit in August 1986. The second amended complaint alleges multiple causes of action—that BPAE breached an implied-in-fact agreement that BPAE would not use NWEC's confidential information without granting NWEC an interest in the Tenneco play, that BPAE acted in bad faith and without probable cause in denying the existence of the contractual obligation to NWEC; that BPAE breached a confidential relationship with NWEC, misappropriated trade secrets, engaged in unfair competition and received unjust enrichment all as a result of its conduct in not including NWEC in the Tenneco project.

NWEC sought discovery from BPAE about its investigation of NWEC's claim. BPAE refused to divulge four communications related to the investigation on the ground they were protected by the attorney-client privilege and the work product rule. The communications are as follows:

(1) The written report prepared by Bright and Brown, outside counsel, retained by BPAE to assist in evaluating NWEC's claims.

(2) The written report of Dorey, BPAE's general counsel, allegedly prepared for BPAE during the investigation.

(3) The memo of Brownhill, BPAE's vice president in charge of exploration, prepared at the direction of general counsel Dorey, and describing the November 27, 1985, meeting with Nahama and Dryden [from NWEC].

(4) The testimony of Gibson–Smith, BPAE's president, in response to deposition questions concerning the investigation. BPAE maintains that the information sought by the questions is protected by the attorney-client privilege because it was channeled through Attorney Dorey or in Dorey's presence.

NWEC moved respondent court for an order compelling BPAE to produce the documents and testimony. NWEC contended the communications had lost their privileged status because they were obtained in furtherance of a fraud, citing Evidence Code section 956. NWEC's theory of fraud is that the alleged misrepresentations in the December

23, 1985, letter from BPAE to NWEC were made for the purpose of dissuading NWEC from pursuing its claim against BPAE.

Respondent court granted the motion finding NWEC had made a prima facie showing of fraud so the attorney-client privilege and the work product rule did not apply.

DISCUSSION
THE "OLD" DISCOVERY ACT GOVERNS THIS MOTION

The new discovery act, which became operative July 1, 1987, provides that any particular use of a discovery method initiated before July 1, 1987, is governed by preexisting provisions. (Stats.1987, ch. 86, § 20.) NWEC's motion to compel involved discovery methods initiated before the operative date of the new discovery act. Thus, the "old" act controls the parties' claims in this case.

* * *

I. The Evidence Code Section 956 Crime-fraud Exception Does Not Apply to Documents Protected by the Work Product Rule

Evidence Code section 956 codifies the common law rule that the privilege protecting confidential attorney-client communications is lost if the client seeks legal assistance to plan or perpetrate a crime or fraud. The crime-fraud exception expressly applies to communications ordinarily shielded by the attorney-client privilege.

The work product rule encompasses a companion but separate document protection.

The work product of an attorney shall not be discoverable unless the court determines that denial of discovery will unfairly prejudice the party seeking discovery in preparing his claim or defense or will result in an injustice, and *any writing that reflects an attorney's impressions, conclusions, opinions, or legal research or theories shall not be discoverable under any circumstances.* (Code Civ.Proc., § 2016, subd. (b), emphasis added.)

The work product rule in California creates for the attorney a qualified privilege against discovery of general work product and an absolute privilege against disclosure of writings containing the attorney's impressions, conclusions, opinions or legal theories.

The purpose of the rule appears in Code of Civil Procedure section 2016, subdivision (h), "It is the policy of this state (i) to preserve the rights of attorneys to prepare cases for trial with that degree of privacy necessary to encourage them to prepare their cases thoroughly and to investigate not only the favorable but the unfavorable aspects of such cases and (ii) to prevent an attorney from taking undue advantage of his adversary's industry or efforts." At the hearing below, the parties assumed the Evidence Code section 956 crime-fraud exception applied to the work product doctrine as well as to the attorney-client privilege protecting documents, and the court so found.

The parties relied on federal case law which holds that even an attorney's "opinion" work product can be penetrated under exceptional circumstances. However, federal law is not controlling in California because the federal rule (Fed.Rules Civ.Proc., rule 26(b)(3)) differs substantially from the California rule. Rule 26(b)(3) states "... the court shall protect against disclosure of the mental impressions, conclusions, opinions, or legal theories of an attorney ... concerning the litigation." The federal provision leaves room for argument that the immunity conferred on "hard-core" work product is not absolute, and federal cases so hold. *See* Upjohn Co. v. United States (1981) 449 U.S. 383, 400, 401–402, 101 S.Ct. 677, 688, 688–89, 66 L.Ed.2d 584: "While we are not prepared at this juncture to say that such material is always protected by the work-product rule, we think a far stronger showing of necessity and unavailability ... would be necessary to compel disclosure"; and In re Sealed Case (D.C.Cir.1982) 676 F.2d 793, 809–810: Under rule 26 of Federal Rules of Civil Procedure, a party can obtain "opinion" work product upon a showing of "extraordinary justification."

On the other hand, California courts have held that an attorney's opinion work product is absolutely insulated from discovery by virtue of the "shall not be discoverable under any circumstances" language of Code of Civil Procedure section 2016, subdivision (b). However, it appears that no California court has addressed the issue whether the crime-fraud exception applies to opinion work product documents.

Evidence Code section 956 refers only to attorney-client privileged matter. There is no similar statute for work product protected documents. * * *

By analogy, the absence of a statutory crime-fraud exception to the work product rule implies that the exception does not apply to work product documents. In addition, the language of section 2016, subdivision (b) is absolute. If the statute is clear, the Legislature is presumed to have meant what it said and the plain meaning of the language governs.

Accordingly, respondent court erred in ordering disclosure of documents which reflect the absolute work product of BPAE's attorneys based on the crime-fraud exception of Evidence Code section 956.

II. The Work Product Rule Applies to the Requested Documents

* * *

A question arises at this point as to whether an attorney's opinion letter or memorandum to a client loses its absolute work product status once the letter or memorandum is delivered in confidence to the client. This is not a question of waiver of the work product rule by the attorney's act of delivering the document to the client (under the cases, such a communication in confidence does not constitute a waiver) but rather is a question of whether the document loses its character as work product once it is delivered to the client.

The question is relevant in the present case because if the writings containing the attorney's legal opinions and impressions about BPAE's defense to NWEC's claim are outside the statutory definition of work product, then the issue of whether the crime-fraud exception applies to work product becomes moot.

We conclude that the attorney's absolute work product protection continues as to the contents of a writing delivered to a client in confidence. [The court noted that attorneys have broader work product protection under California law than they do under Hickman v. Taylor (1947) 329 U.S. 495, 67 S.Ct. 385, 91 L.Ed. 451, and F.R.C.P. 26(b)(3).]
* * *

The Legislature presumably intended to protect the attorney's privacy in the opinion writing after its delivery to the client because this would free the attorney from the fear of a subsequent disclosure of the writing to third parties where the client for some reason did not assert the attorney-client privilege to prevent disclosure. In a sense, this legislative purpose furthers the stated policy of preserving the right of attorneys to prepare their cases for trial "with that degree of privacy necessary to . . . investigate not only the favorable but the unfavorable aspects of such cases. . . ." (Code Civ.Proc., § 2016, subd. (h).) It also encourages the attorney to deliver his or her opinions in writing to the client for the client's further consideration rather than merely communicating orally the contents of the writing to the client. This practice strengthens the attorney-client relationship.

* * *

We conclude from * * * [California and federal] cases that the attorney's absolute work product protection continues as to the contents of a writing delivered to a client in confidence. The protection precludes third parties not representing the client from discovery of the writing. The fact that the client does not object to disclosure of the contents of the writing does not lessen the attorney's need for privacy. The recognition of an attorney's right to assert a work product protection in the contents of a writing after it is delivered to the client strengthens the attorney-client relationship by enabling the attorney to evaluate his client's case and to communicate his opinions to the client without fear that his opinions and theories will thereafter be exposed to the opposing party or to the public in general for criticism or ridicule.

* * *

Thus, the only exception to the absolute work product protection of an attorney's confidential opinion letter to a client is where there has been a waiver of the protection by *the attorney's* voluntary disclosure or consent to disclosure of the writing to a person other than the client who has no interest in maintaining the confidentiality of the contents of the writing. A claim of work product may also be waived by failure to make the claim, by tendering certain issues and by conduct between discovery and trial that is inconsistent with such claim. The present case does not fit within the parameters of the waiver exception because the alleged memorandum of general counsel Dorey and the opinion letter of outside counsel Bright and Brown were delivered only to their client, BPAE. Hence, the writings are entitled to protection as the attorney's work product.

However, this court cannot evaluate BPAE's work product assertions because the documents and testimony are not in the record. We will remand the matter to the trial court with directions to determine which documents contain work product. The determination of the work product protection should be made on an item-by-item basis. The remand will require the trial court to conduct an in camera inspection of the documents. It also will require BPAE to prove the preliminary facts essential to the applicability of the work product rule to each of the documents.

* * *

Let a writ of prohibition issue restraining respondent court from enforcing its discovery order as to documents protected by the attorney work product rule and requiring further responses by Mr. Gibson–Smith to deposition questions pertaining to the work product.

The matter is remanded to respondent court for an in camera hearing to determine the work product portion of each of the documents which shall not be discoverable. Real party in interest NWEC will then be free to bring a motion to compel further answers by Gibson–Smith to specified deposition questions concerning any part of the documents not protected by the work product rule.

In all other respects, the discovery order is affirmed.

MARTIN, J., concurs.

BEST, ASSOCIATE JUSTICE, concurring and dissenting.

* * *

It seems clear that the purpose of the absolute portion of the attorney's work product rule is to protect from discovery the industry and efforts of the attorney as reflected in his or her work papers in which he or she has reduced to writing his or her "impressions, conclusions, opinions, or legal research or theories" in the preparation of the client's case. I have been unable to find any indication that it was ever intended to apply to the written product furnished to the client, which, upon delivery to the client, belongs to the client. Nor does logic or necessity require the extension of the attorney's work product rule to such material. If the written product is a contract, lease or other document not intended to be confidential, no protection from discovery is needed or desired. If the finished product consists of a letter or legal memorandum intended to be confidential, the writing is a confidential communication within the attorney-client privilege and falls under the protective cloak of that privilege. The holding of the majority in this case would bestow upon writings of the latter type a dual character—

both attorney's work product and a confidential communication within the attorney-client privilege. Assuming the majority's holding that the crime-fraud exception does not apply to the attorney's work product to be correct, and I believe it is, the exception would never be applicable when the confidential communication from attorney to client was in writing but it would be applicable if the communication was simply oral; and the exception would still apply to both written and oral confidential communications from the client to the attorney. If the confidential communication from the attorney to the client was in writing, and under the present holding work product absolutely privileged from discovery, would the remaining Evidence Code exceptions likewise be inapplicable (Evid.Code, § 957—parties claiming through a deceased client; § 958—breach of duty arising out of lawyer-client relationship; § 959—lawyer as attesting witness; § 960—intention of deceased client concerning writing affecting property; § 961—validity of writing affecting property interest; and § 962—joint clients)?

If such writings were possessed of a dual character (both attorney's work product falling within the absolute portion of the rule and a confidential communication within the attorney-client privilege), logic would dictate that these exceptions would be inapplicable to the attorney's work product and preclude discovery of the contents even though discovery would be possible if the writings were only confidential communications within the attorney-client privilege.

I submit that such a result would not only be contrary to the Legislature's intent but border upon the absurd.

Accordingly, I would hold that none of the communications sought to be discovered constituted attorney's work product within the meaning of former Code of Civil Procedure section 2016, subdivision (b). * * *

SANCTIONS

LESSER v. HUNTINGTON HARBOR CORPORATION

California Court of Appeal, Second District, 1985.
173 Cal.App.3d 922, 219 Cal.Rptr. 562.

KLEIN, PRESIDING JUSTICE.

Plaintiff and appellant Louis Lesser (Lesser) appeals from an order awarding defendants and respondents Huntington Harbor Corporation and The Christiana Companies (collectively respondents) attorney's fees and costs of $59,148.10 incurred in defense of a fraud action.

Because Lesser was not afforded adequate notice and opportunity to be heard, the judgment is reversed and remanded for a new hearing.

PROCEDURAL AND FACTUAL BACKGROUND

The trial court awarded attorney's fees and costs under the authority of Code of Civil Procedure section 128.5 (section 128.5) to respondents after they prevailed in a suit brought by Lesser.

Lesser initiated the lawsuit in the summer of 1977, alleging a breach of fiduciary duty, fraud, and interference with prospective economic advantage. A second amended complaint was filed in March 1978.

In June 1978, Lesser filed a lis pendens against the subject matter of the action, the Huntington Harbor Beach Club. In August 1978, the lis pendens was expunged with Huntington Harbor required to post a bond of $100,000.

Lesser sought relief by writs of mandate on certain issues before the appellate court and the California Supreme Court. Interrogatories were taken by both parties, as well as four sets of depositions.

After the five-year statute was waived, the case proceeded to trial on May 16, 1983. The respondents submitted a trial brief which asked for an award under section 128.5.

Lesser presented his case in one and one-half days and at the conclusion, the respondents moved for a nonsuit. After hearing argument, the trial court granted the motion, finding the evidence was unbelievable and did not substantiate Lesser's claims.

The trial court concluded by stating the case was a proper one for an award of attorney's fees and costs and thereby sanctions under section 128.5 and it would hold a hearing the next morning to determine the amounts thereof.

Shortly after the outset of the hearing, Lesser's counsel moved for a continuance so as to afford Lesser an opportunity to employ new counsel, which was denied.

After hearing testimony by respondents' counsel concerning the expenses of defending the suit during the six years, and from Lesser about the propriety of the award, the trial court awarded Huntington Harbor $59,148.10 in attorney's fees and costs incurred in the action.

CONTENTIONS

Lesser contends the trial court erred in making an award pursuant to section 128.5 because: (1) he did not receive adequate notice; (2) he was denied an adequate opportunity to be heard; (3) his lawsuit was not frivolous or in bad faith; and (4) the order was insufficient in detail as to the conduct or circumstances justifying the award.

* * *

DISCUSSION

1. SECTION 128.5 EXPENSES ARE APPROPRIATE WHEN THE TRIAL COURT FINDS THE ENTIRE LAWSUIT TO BE FRIVOLOUS

Section 128.5 was passed in direct response to the Supreme Court ruling in Bauguess v. Paine (1978) 22 Cal.3d 626, 150 Cal.Rptr. 461, 586 P.2d 942. In *Bauguess,* after plaintiff's attorney's conduct caused a mistrial, the attorney was ordered by the trial court to pay $700 to defendant's counsel. The Supreme Court reversed, holding the award of such attorney's fees was not within the equitable or supervisory power of the trial court, and *was not authorized by any statute*. The *Bauguess* decision was based in large part on the possibility of "serious due process problems" if monetary sanctions were imposed "without appropriate safeguards and guidelines." (*Id.*, at pp. 638–639, 150 Cal.Rptr. 461, 586 P.2d 942.)

To remedy this lack of statutory authority, the California Legislature passed section 128.5 in 1981. The Legislature stated: " '[i]t is the intent of this legislation to broaden the powers of the trial courts to manage their calendars and provide for the expeditious processing of civil actions by authorizing monetary sanctions now not presently authorized by the interpretation of the law in *Bauguess* * * *.' " (Ellis v. Roshei Corp. (1983) 143 Cal.App.3d 642, 648, 192 Cal.Rptr. 57 citing Stats. 1981, ch. 762, § 2.)

An order to pay reasonable expenses, including attorney's fees and costs, pursuant to section 128.5 is in effect an award of sanctions.

Section 128.5 does not specifically mention frivolous *lawsuits*, but the Supreme Court has recognized that section 128.5 sanctions might serve to take the place of a malicious prosecution suit. In City of Long Beach v. Bozek (1982) 31 Cal.3d 527, 530, 183 Cal.Rptr. 86, 645 P.2d 137, [certiorari granted, vacated and remanded 459 U.S. 1095, 103 S.Ct. 712 [74 L.Ed.2d 943], reaffirmed and reissued (1983) 33 Cal.2d 727, 190 Cal.Rptr. 918, 661 P.2d 1072], * * * [the California Supreme Court] explicitly recognized that section 128.5's purpose was to discourage "frivolous litigation" and in some instances it "is a clearly preferable remedy to an independent action for malicious prosecution with its costs in terms of additional attorney's fees and imposition upon judicial resources." (*Id.*, at p. 538, 183 Cal.Rptr. 86, 645 P.2d 137.)

* * *

Nothing in section 128.5's language limits the section's application only to tactics or motions. In fact, the section specifically states frivolous actions are not limited to making or opposing motions without good faith. A reasonable interpretation is that the section also applies to *entire actions* not based on good faith which are frivolous or cause unnecessary delay in the resolution of a dispute.[3]

3. * * * In connection therewith, the Legislative Counsel's Digest reported, "[e]xisting law authorizes a trial court to require a party or a party's attorney, or both to pay any reasonable expenses incurred by another party as a result of tactics or actions not based on good faith which are frivolous or cause unnecessary delay, as specified. Existing law also provides separate actions for abuse of judicial process and malicious prosecution. [¶] This bill would revise the above provisions for award of expenses by making these provisions applicable to bad-faith tactics or actions which are intended to cause unnecessary delay or are employed solely to harass an opposing party or are totally and completely without merit, rather than tactics or actions that cause unnecessary delay. The bill would define "actions and tactics" to include, but not be limited to, the making or opposing of motions and the filing and service of a complaint or cross-complaint. "Actions and tactics" would not include the mere filing of a complaint without service upon an opposing party."

2. NOTICE REQUIRED BEFORE IMPOSING EXPENSES IS DEPENDENT UPON THE CIRCUMSTANCES

Lesser contends neither respondents nor the trial court gave adequate notice before the imposition of expenses.

* * *

The Legislature recognized the notice and opportunity to be heard concerns expressed in *Bauguess,* when it specifically provided for such in subdivision (b) of section 128.5. * * * However, the section is not specific as to the measure of notice necessary.

* * *

Here, the notice respondents gave Lesser was in the trial brief served on the day of the trial, and the demand for expenses was buried on page 17 of the trial brief, without any special heading or notice language.

Also, there is a question as to the adequacy of notice in the alternative provided by the trial court, since the trial court purported to award attorney's fees and costs on its own motion as well. The trial court gave Lesser notice sometime mid-day on the second day of trial, and ordered the hearing to take place at 9:00 a.m. the following morning.

* * *

After an analysis of the cases that either affirm or reverse the award of section 128.5 sanctions, it appears adequacy of notice should be determined on a case-by-case basis to satisfy basic due process requirements. The act or circumstances giving rise to the imposition of expenses must be considered together with the potential dollar amount. The existing cases mostly involve frivolous or bad faith motions or failures to appear.

In re Marriage of Flaherty, [(1982) 31 Cal.3d 637, 183 Cal.Rptr. 508, 646 P.2d 179], is precedent for allowing an additional measure of notice when the entire lawsuit is questioned as frivolous. *Flaherty* recognized due process as a flexible concept that must be tailored to the requirements of each particular situation. Relying in part on section 128.5, the Supreme Court held the appellate courts must allow for notice and hearing before imposing sanctions.

In the instant case, the trial court found the entire lawsuit to be without good faith and frivolous and therefore imposed respondents' attorney's fees and costs of defending the suit as sanctions. Because the question of good faith in the bringing and maintaining of the *$7 million* lawsuit, which had been ongoing for six years, was the subject of the hearing, and because the expenses in defense were substantial, more than one or two days notice is deemed necessary. Lesser was unable to get declarations prepared on less than a day's notice to show his lawsuit was brought in good faith. Therefore, the trial court abused its discretion in the matter of notice.

3. Lesser Did Not Have Adequate Opportunity to Be Heard

* * *

a. The Trial Court May Have Predetermined an Important Issue

At the end of the trial when reciting its finding, the trial court stated this was a proper case for the imposition of expenses under section 128.5 and "[t]he court will hold a hearing at 9:00 a.m. tomorrow morning on the issue of the amount of attorney fees to be awarded and costs against * * * [Lesser] in this case."

When questioned by Lesser's counsel at the beginning of the next day's proceedings concerning the purpose of the hearing, the trial court responded "I think this case is not only frivolous but close to a malicious prosecution of a civil matter. That's why I imposed 128.5, and we are here on the amount I will award." It further stated "[t]he only reason for this hearing, so far as I am concerned, is to determine the amount of attorney fees."

These statements indicate the trial court may have determined the issue prior to receiving evidence at the hearing and was only concerned with the *amount* of expenses to be awarded.

Obviously a trial court would be considering imposing sanctions when it notices such a hearing, but it must nonetheless maintain objectivity while conducting the hearing. Lesser should have been provided an opportunity to be heard, even though the trial court did not believe Lesser's testimony or that of his witnesses during trial. Lesser *may* have been able to present evidence in addition to his own testimony in support of his alleged good faith in bringing his lawsuit.

b. Lesser Did Not Have an Opportunity to Fully Present His Case at the Hearing

Lesser also maintains he was unable to defend against an award. As discussed, the one-day time constraint severely limited his ability to marshal any evidence.

Respondents take the position that Lesser waived any objection to the sanction by failing to raise objections at the hearing. However, Lesser's counsel made several objections. When counsel asked for a continuance, the trial court denied the motion as a delaying tactic. Lesser's counsel objected that he had inadequate notice. When the trial court remarked that Lesser's counsel was "hopelessly entwined" with the case because he was a relative of Lesser's, counsel took exception to that remark, but was ordered to "sit down."

The peremptory manner in which the hearing took place negates a finding that Lesser waived any objection to the award.

4. Section 128.5 Expenses Should Not Be Imposed on a Meritless Action if Not Initiated for an Improper Motive

Lesser contends the trial court erred by comparing a meritless action with a frivolous one and thereby improperly imposed sanctions.

As discussed, Lesser's hearing was not adequate because of the short notice and lack of opportunity to be heard; therefore we cannot determine on this record whether Lesser's initiating and pursuing the action warranted imposition of section 128.5 sanctions.

Section 128.5 allows for expenses for "tactics or actions not based on good faith which are frivolous or which cause unnecessary delay." * * * [Atchison, Topeka & Santa Fe Ry. Co. v. Stockton Port Dist. (1983) 140 Cal.App.3d 111, 189 Cal.Rptr. 208] held the "fact that an action is determined to be 'without merit' does not, a fortiori, place it in the category of frivolous." A further determination is necessary to ascertain whether an action was brought with an improper motive.

Relying on *Flaherty,* the *Atchison* court further recognized "[t]he Legislature did not intend, [in passing section 128.5] however, to chill the valid assertion of a litigant's rights against ... any ... defendant. For this reason, it is clear sanctions should not be imposed except in the clearest of cases." (*Atchison* * * * at p. 117.)

Because due process requirements as to notice and opportunity to be heard were not met here, we do not reach either the *propriety* of the trial court's imposition of sanctions in this fact situation or the sufficiency of the order.

DISPOSITION

The judgment is reversed and remanded to the trial court to hold a hearing consistent with this opinion.

Each party to bear respective costs on appeal.

JOINDER

SIMPSON REDWOOD COMPANY· v. STATE

California Court of Appeal, First District, 1987.
196 Cal.App.3d 1192, 242 Cal.Rptr. 447.

NEWSOM, ASSOCIATE JUSTICE.

Respondent Simpson Lumber Company (hereafter Simpson) initiated this action by filing a complaint to quiet title and for declaratory relief against the State of California (hereafter the State), seeking title to specified parcels of real property located in Humboldt County in Township 12 North, Range 1 East, Humboldt Meridian. Promptly thereafter, appellant Save–The–Redwoods League (hereafter appellant or the League) filed a motion for leave to intervene (Code Civ.Proc., § 387, subd. (a)) in the action, asserting an interest in the old growth redwood forest sought by Simpson in its complaint. * * *

[The court provided a history of the primary dispute, which concerned title to valuable forest land in and near Prarie Creek Redwoods State Park. In 1932, appellant had donated some of the land to the state as an addition to the state park system. The following year, the park was established with the property donated by appellant and with some acquired through purchase. Simpson claimed title to some parcels of the park property under one land survey; the state claimed title under another survey.]

* * *

Appellant contends that the trial court erred in denying its motion to intervene in Simpson's quiet title action under section 387, subdivision (a) of the Code of Civil Procedure * * *. The purpose of allowing intervention is to promote fairness by involving all parties potentially affected by a judgment. The right to intervene granted by section 387, subdivision (a) is not absolute, however; intervention is properly permitted only if the requirements of the statute have been satisfied. The trial court is vested with discretion to determine whether the standards for intervention have been met.

Simpson argues that appellant's interest in the underlying action is indirect and remote, and so does not justify intervention. It is well-settled that the intervener's interest in the matter in litigation must be direct, not consequential, and that it must be an interest which is proper to be determined in the action in which intervention is sought. The "interest" referred to in section 387, subdivision (a), "must be of such direct or immediate character, that the intervener will either gain or lose by the direct legal operation and effect of the judgment." (Knight v. Alefosio [(1984)] 158 Cal.App.3d at p. 721, 205 Cal.Rptr. 42 * * *.)

But the nature of the necessary direct interest in the litigation is undescribed by the statute. Nor is the decisional law helpful. As has been said: "[T]he point at which one's interest in the success of one of the parties to the action becomes direct, and not consequential, is not easily fixed. It has been the subject of much judicial discussion." (Fireman's Fund Ins. Co. v. Gerlach (1976) 56 Cal.App.3d 299, 302, 128 Cal.Rptr. 396.) Whether the intervenor's interest is sufficiently direct must be decided on the facts of each case. But it is established that the intervener need neither claim a pecuniary interest nor a specific legal or equitable interest in the subject matter of the litigation. And section 387 should be liberally construed in favor of intervention.

We find in the record ample evidence of appellant's direct, substantial interest in the case. Appellant has asserted that its members frequently use the Park for recreational purposes. We learn too from the record that the League was instrumental in the establishment of the Park; in fact, all of the parcels in dispute once belonged to the League, and were donated to the State for the sole and express purpose of inclusion in the Park. Memorial groves, named after members of the League, lie within the disputed area and would certainly not be maintained in their present pristine condition under Simpson's ownership. The League has also claimed, without contradiction, that its reputation and integrity as a conservation organization will suffer if property which it acquired through donation and targeted for preservation is transferred to private ownership for exploitation.

That appellant's members are frequent users of the Park, will not, standing alone, justify intervention. Intervention cannot be predicated *solely* on the League's contribution to the creation of the Park, and while appellant donated the land which comprised a part of the park, it no longer claims a legal or equitable interest in the property in dispute. Moreover, appellant's support for the State's claim to the property is an insufficient basis for intervention. Still, appellant's interests in the underlying litigation extend far beyond a general and historical preference for preservation of the current borders of the Park. The League was formed and continues to exist for the purpose of conserving lands such as those in dispute here in their natural state, and has so represented itself to members and donors. If property acquired by donation in an effort to create and preserve a park is privately exploited, the impact upon appellant's reputation might well translate into loss of future support and contributions.

That appellant will not suffer direct *pecuniary* harm, and has failed to establish with absolute certainty the detriment an adverse judgment might cause, does not defeat its right to intervene. It is not necessary that an intervener's interest "be such that he will *inevitably* be affected by the judgment. It is enough that there be a substantial *probability* that his interests will be so affected." Here, we think appellant has demonstrated a cognizable interest in perpetuating its role and furthering its avowed policies.

Yet another factor which favors a finding of appellant's direct interest in the subject litigation is its present right to control development of the property, which would of course be altered by a judgment in favor of respondent. As one of the exhibits demonstrate, in donating land to the State the League placed a recital in the deed specifying that such property be used for "state park purposes." " 'It is well settled that where a grant deed is for a specified, limited and definite purpose, the subject of the grant cannot be used for another and different purpose.' [Citations.]" (Big Sur Properties v. Mott (1976) 62 Cal. App.3d 99, 103, 132 Cal.Rptr. 835.) Hence, only as long as the State owns the property in dispute, can appellant rely upon the restrictive language to prevent an inconsistent use of the donated parcels. For this and the related reasons earlier described, we conclude that appellant has demonstrated the requisite specific and direct interest in the outcome of the litigation justifying intervention, and that the trial court's contrary finding was error.

We turn next to the issue of potential delay and confusion which arguably might flow from intervention. Even if otherwise proper, "intervention will not be allowed when it would retard the principal suit, or require a reopening of the case for further evidence, or delay the trial of the action, or change the position of the original parties. [Citation.]" Respondent argues that such is the case here, in that appellant will raise issues of implied dedication which have not heretofore been presented by the State as part of its claim to the disputed property, thereby impermissibly enlarging the scope of the litigation.

While appellant undeniably intends to introduce new causes of action, our analysis of the nature of such new matters convinces us it will not delay the litigation, change the position of the parties, or even require introduction of additional evidence. Thus, appellant will claim that respondent, in law or in fact, dedicated the land in dispute to the public. Resolution of that issue will center upon essentially the same facts as those involved in the State's claims of adverse possession and agreed boundaries. We perceive no danger that the dedication issue will prolong, confuse or disrupt the present lawsuit.

Nor do we find that intervention would subvert the salutary purposes of section 387, subdivision (b), to obviate delays and prevent a multiplicity of suits arising out of the same facts, while protecting the interests of those affected by the judgment. On the contrary, were intervention to be denied in the present case, appellant would be forced to bring a separate action against Simpson.

A final telling factor in our decision is the conviction that appellant's own substantial interests probably cannot be adequately served by the State's sole participation in the suit, since it here seeks merely to protect its fee interest in the property, which may turn out to be simply pecuniary in nature. The State might, for example, choose to settle the case for a monetary consideration in exchange for relinquishment of its claims of title to the land. But appellant's interest in the litigation—to preserve the property in its natural condition—is singular and indeed unique, and powerfully militates in favor of intervention.

* * *

REYES v. SAN DIEGO COUNTY BOARD OF SUPERVISORS

California Court of Appeal, Fourth District, 1987.
196 Cal.App.3d 1263, 242 Cal.Rptr. 339.

WORK, ASSOCIATE JUSTICE.

Blas Reyes and the Welfare Rights Organization of San Diego, Inc. (Plaintiffs) brought this class action for declaratory and injunctive relief against the San Diego County Board of Supervisors and Department of Social Services (County) to stop the practice of depriving general relief recipients of benefits for failing to comply with work project rules without distinguishing between willful and nonwillful violators and to recover past benefits lost from such illegal terminations. They appeal that portion of the trial court's order denying its motion for class certification as to retroactive relief. They contend the class for retroactive benefits is ascertainable and meets all proper community of interest requirements necessary for certification, asserting the trial court improperly relied on the County's potential administrative burdens at the remedy stage of determining class identity and individual claimant entitlements. For the reasons which follow, we conclude the trial court abused its discretion in denying Plaintiffs' motion for class certification as to retroactive relief. Accordingly, we reverse its order in part.

FACTUAL AND PROCEDURAL BACKGROUND

Welfare and Institutions Code [1] section 17000, requires every county to provide general relief to all incompetent, poor, indigent and incapacitated individuals who are not supported by relatives, friends or state or private relief. Financed entirely out of County general funds, this program was designed to be the residual financial "safety net" for indigents who cannot obtain relief from any private sources and cannot qualify for aid under any specialized state or private program.

Pursuant to this mandate, the County established a general relief program divided into two essential parts, providing assistance to those employable and eligible for benefits under section 17000 and those who are incapacitated and unemployable by reason of age, disease, or accident. Those recipients who are employable must participate in work projects as a condition of obtaining relief. Employable recipients work up to 72 hours per month on a county work project at the federal minimum wage to repay any grant. During their off-hours, these employable recipients must seek employment and accept any job paying the minimum wage. They are required to submit job applications to different employers each month and provide proof of such job contact to the County. * * * Failure to comply with any welfare program requirement without good cause results in a recipient being "sanctioned" by a period of ineligibility or denial of relief for three months on the first noncompliance and six months for a second within a twelve-month period. Failure to timely return a job-search verification results in the loss of aid for one month.

* * * Plaintiffs' lawsuit essentially contends the sanctioning process of the County's program fails to distinguish between the competent healthy recipients who *willfully* fail to comply with the underlying requirements of the program and those whose failure is the result of mere negligence, inadvertence, or mental or physical disability. The class action complaint seeks injunctive and declaratory relief, claiming the County's practice of terminating general relief benefits without distinguishing between willful and nonwillful violations of its work project rules violate substantive due process. The action further asks the court to require the County to provide advance notice of terminations for alleged work project violations so recipients can request continued benefits pending an administrative hearing consistent with the constitutional guarantee of procedural due process. Petitioners also seek a peremptory writ of mandate ordering the County to provide timely and adequate notice of actions to sanction individuals, to provide full discovery of evidence for and during hearings, to cease enforcement of its sanctioning process, to implement regulations requiring County to

1. All statutory references are to the   wise specified.
Welfare and Institutions Code unless other-

sanction only healthy, competent individuals who willfully fail to comply with the program requirements, and to identify and set aside all actions sanctioning class members since April 10, 1983, restoring prospective benefit to currently sanctioned individuals, providing notice of eligibility to apply for retroactive benefits to class members, and providing hearings for such individuals to determine eligibility for benefits.

Plaintiffs' motion for class certification was granted insofar as it sought to certify a class of all individuals who will be sanctioned by the County and deprived general relief benefits on or after the date of entry of final judgment. However, with regard to retroactive relief to *all individuals who have been sanctioned by the County's relief program since April 10, 1983, to the date of entry of the final judgment,* certification was denied. The trial court rationalized its denial of retroactive benefits to a class estimated to be comprised of 15,000 individuals, because determination of class identity and entitlement to relief at the remedy stage rendered the class unascertainable and unmanageable.
* * *

Governing Law
* * *

In California, Code of Civil Procedure section 382 authorizes class action suits "when the question is one of a common or general interest, of many persons, or when the parties are numerous, and it is impracticable to bring them all before the court...." This provision has been construed to require the showing of an ascertainable class and a well-defined community of interest in questions of law and fact among the members of that class. However, in light of the general character of Code of Civil Procedure section 382 which fails to define a procedural framework for class certification, the courts have sought guidance from both Civil Code section 1781 regarding consumer class actions and the Federal Rules of Civil Procedure, rule 23, in the absence of state precedent.

Whether a class is ascertainable is determined by examining (1) the class definition, (2) the size of the class, and (3) the means available for identifying class members. (Vasquez v. Superior Court [(1971)] 4 Cal.3d at pp. 821–822, 94 Cal.Rptr. 796, 484 P.2d 964; Miller v. Woods [(1983)] 148 Cal.App.3d at p. 873, 196 Cal.Rptr. 69.) As to the community of interest requirement, it consists of three factors: "(1) predominate common questions of law or fact; (2) class representatives with claims or defenses typical of the class; and (3) class representatives who can adequately represent the class. * * * " (Richmond v. Dart Industries, Inc. [(1981)] 29 Cal.3d at p. 470, 174 Cal.Rptr. 515, 629 P.2d 23; Miller v. Woods, *supra,* 148 Cal.App.3d at p. 874, 196 Cal.Rptr. 69.)

The decision whether to certify a class rests within the sound discretion of the trial court and will not be disturbed on appeal if supported by substantial evidence, unless either improper criteria were employed or erroneous legal assumptions were made. Trial courts have been admonished to carefully weigh the respective benefits and burdens and to allow maintenance of the class action only where substantial benefits accrue both to the litigants as well as the courts. The party seeking class certification bears the burden of not only showing that substantial benefits, both to the litigants and to the court, will result from class certification but also proving the adequacy of its representation. At the certification stage, just as the trial court is not to examine the merits of the case, our inquiry on review is strictly limited to whether plaintiffs have carried their burden of establishing the prerequisites of a class action. * * *

PLAINTIFFS' CONTENTIONS AND THE COUNTY'S RESPONSE

Plaintiffs contend they have met their burden of establishing not only an ascertainable class, but also a well-defined community of interests among their class members. They assert the trial court erroneously relied on the County's *potential* administrative burdens at the post-judgment remedy stage of determining class identity and individual claimant entitlement to relief, when it denied class certification for retroactive benefits. They argue the determination of class certification in government benefits cases involves the primary concern of the *court's* role in trying the case, not the *administrative agency's* duties in providing legally required relief to those who prove they are members of the class. Consequently, because the issues of class member identity and relief entitlement are not determined by the court, they are irrelevant to the class certification decision. Moreover, they contend the County's remedial concerns here were based upon unsupported assumptions that determinations regarding past benefits would be unduly administratively burdensome.

The County responds certification was properly denied because the validity of its actions as to any specific recipient must be individually factually determined and thus it is possible the challenged sanctioning process may have been invalidly applied to only a few members of the broadly defined class. * * *

The County also argues manageability is a proper factor for the court to consider in determining class certification, citing the total administrative cost here of processing approximately 7,600 claims (approximately one-half of the 15,200 sanctions imposed during the time involved) would be approximately $257,000 and exhaust six and one-half years of staff time. It claims retroactive relief here would be without substantial benefit to the class members in comparison to the administrative burden imposed. Citing section 17403, the County explains that because general relief must be repaid by a recipient when one has the means to do so, retroactive payments to rehabilitated individuals would result in simply debts due to the County.[8] Moreover, it contends current general relief recipients would suffer from the enormous expenditure of

---

8. The validity of this contention is doubtful. * * * [T]he fatal flaw to this comment is the County has not proffered any statistical evidence as to how many former recipients meet the qualifications of section 17403, are no longer in need of, or interested in obtaining further assistance.

administrative resources in attempting to afford retroactive relief because it would be better for the general public to keep the funds in the public treasury for public use than to consume them in attempting to award retroactive relief where the administrative burden is severe and the potential benefit is small.

AN ASCERTAINABLE CLASS

Mindful in determining whether a class is ascertainable we examine the class definition, the size of the class and the means of identifying class members (Vasquez v. Superior Court, *supra,* 4 Cal.3d at pp. 821–822, 94 Cal.Rptr. 796, 484 P.2d 964; Miller v. Woods, *supra,* 148 Cal.App.3d at p. 873, 196 Cal.Rptr. 69), we conclude Plaintiffs' proffered class of "all individuals sanctioned from the County's general relief program since April 10, 1983," is sufficiently defined to meet the "ascertainable" standard.

The County concedes the proposed class as defined is not "unduly complex". It clearly includes all individuals potentially affected by the challenged administrative sanctioning process. (Compare Employment Development Dept. v. Superior Court [(1981)] 30 Cal.3d at p. 260, 178 Cal.Rptr. 612, 636 P.2d 575, where the class was defined as "all other women 'subjected' to the provisions of [Unemployment Insurance Code] section 1264"; Miller v. Woods, *supra,* 148 Cal.App.3d at p. 873, 196 Cal.Rptr. 69, where the class was defined as " 'all applicants, recipients and providers of IHSS in California who have been or will be disqualified from receiving or providing protective supervision based solely on MPP § 30–463.233c.' ") Moreover, the County does not challenge the size of the class, conceding it exceeds 15,000 individuals. Rather, the County asserts the class is not easily ascertainable because it would take approximately eight months of staff time at a cost of $14,000 to manually cross-compare the statistical records of the approximately 60,000 general relief cases closed since April 10, 1983, to identify those individuals whose cases which were closed as a result of a sanction.

Preliminarily, it is firmly established a plaintiff is not required at this stage of the proceedings to establish the existence and identity of class members. In fact, prejudgment notice is not required in welfare class actions where declaratory and injunctive relief are the primary objectives. "California decisions follow the analysis of the federal courts; prejudgment notice 'serves no apparent purposes' in welfare class actions where there are no factual disputes and the class is adequately represented by counsel." (Miller v. Woods, *supra,* 148 Cal. App.3d at p. 875, 196 Cal.Rptr. 69; *see also* Gonzales v. Jones (1981) 116 Cal.App.3d 978, 985–987, 171 Cal.Rptr. 567.) However, within the context of manageability, the issue is whether there exists sufficient means for identifying class members at the remedial stage. (*See* Daar v. Yellow Cab Co. [(1967)] 67 Cal.2d at p. 706, 63 Cal.Rptr. 724, 433 P.2d 732.) Here, the means are available in that the County does have the records from which to identify those past general relief recipients who were sanctioned out of the welfare program.

However, the County essentially argues the class is unmanageable because of the cited administrative cost in identification at the remedial stage. * * * [W]here the administrative cost in identification and processing of past general relief recipients' claims is so substantial to render the likely appreciable benefits to the class de minimis in comparison, the class action should not be certified. * * * However, a court should not decline to certify a class simply because it is afraid that insurmountable problems may later appear at the remedy stage. "But where the court finds, on the basis of substantial evidence ... that there are serious problems now appearing, it should not certify the class merely on the assurance of counsel that some solution will be found." (Windham v. American Brands, Inc. (4th Cir.1977) 565 F.2d 59, 70.) Consequently, unless the unmanageability of the class action is essentially without dispute or clearly established, it should not foreclose class certification.

Here, the County has not shown the administrative cost of retroactive relief outweighs appreciable benefits to the class. Preliminarily, we are unpersuaded the County's selected method of identification and notice is the most practicable and cost-efficient; for, in comparison, how effective and costly would simple notice to all general relief recipients during that period of time be? Moreover, the size of the class in regards to the starting date for payment of retroactive benefits to class members is not established and binding until the trial court grants final relief. Indeed, in order for the County to show the administrative costs are disproportionate to the potential benefits to the class if the latter should prevail, the County must determine the potential class benefits and compare them to the administrative cost. Disproportionality can only be established by comparing administrative cost figures with the total potential retroactive benefits to the class; for, all such class actions inevitably accrue administrative costs. Consequently, if we take as unchallenged the County's claim of $257,000 in administrative costs, then that figure is not so overwhelming in light of the Plaintiffs' estimate the class has been illegally denied $3.4 million in retroactive benefits. Granted, both parties challenge each other's figures; however, it is precisely these disputes which illustrate the County has failed to establish disproportionality and the propriety of leaving these issues to the discretion of the trial court at the remedial stage. There, the County may raise a specific objection to any remedial mechanism the court, in the exercise of its discretion, fashions to cope with the identification and notice problems arising from the government records and the individual determinations of liability and damages. * * *

THE CLASS SHARES A WELL-DEFINED COMMUNITY OF INTEREST IN QUESTIONS OF LAW AND FACT

In determining whether the class satisfies the community of interest requirement, we look to whether common questions of law or fact dominate, the claims of the class representative are typical of the class and the class representative can adequately represent the class in its entirety. We conclude the class for retroactive benefits meets all proper criteria, as the trial court will decide the legality of the County's sanctioning process and the County's existing administrative agency will decide the remaining issues of individual recipient qualification, entitlement and amount of damages. It is undisputed Plaintiffs' claims are representative with qualified and experienced counsel able to conduct the proposed litigation. Accordingly, the sole issue presented here is whether there are predominate questions of law or fact common to the class as a whole.

This second statutory requirement of a "community of interest" revolves on "whether the common questions are sufficiently pervasive to permit adjudication in a class action rather than in a multiplicity of suits." (Vasquez v. Superior Court, *supra,* 4 Cal.3d at p. 810, 94 Cal.Rptr. 796, 484 P.2d 964; Miller v. Woods, *supra,* 148 Cal.App.3d at pp. 873–874, 196 Cal.Rptr. 69.) This common question requirement is patently satisfied here by the class claim the County has violated state law by failing to distinguish between *willful* violations of work rules by competent healthy adults who may be sanctioned and *nonwillful* violations caused by negligence, inadvertence or mental or physical disability which may not serve as a basis for sanctioning. In other words, the common goal of the entire class is to invalidate this sanctioning process and require the implementation of regulations requiring the County to sanction only healthy, competent individuals who willfully fail to comply with program requirements.

The County challenges this assessment, contending class-wide liability cannot be established by the declaratory/injunctive relief phase of this case, because each class member's right to recover depends on facts peculiar to his/her case. The County explains that in order for a class member to recover, that individual must establish at the remedy phase not only damages, but liability—that he/she was a victim of unlawful conduct, to wit sanctioned for nonwillful conduct. Finally, the County stresses that as to each class member, the separate factual issues of eligibility, nature and willfulness of the violation, and the existence of any defenses must be determined.

Granted, there lacks a sufficient community of interest within a class where each member would be required to individually litigate numerous and substantial questions to determine his/her right to recover following the class judgment determining issues common before the class. However, the necessity for class members to individually establish eligibility and damages does not mean individual fact questions predominate. * * * [I]t is firmly established that "a class action is not inappropriate simply because each member of the class may at some point be required to make an individual showing as to his or her eligibility for recovery or as to the amount of his or her damages. [Citations.] ... [A] court can devise remedial procedures which channel the individual determinations that need to be made through existing administrative forums. [Citations.]" (Employment Development Dept. v. Superior Court, *supra,* 30 Cal.3d at p. 266, 178 Cal.Rptr. 612, 636 P.2d 575.)

Moreover, this community of interest requirement is especially satisfied here, because the trial court would have to redetermine the legality of the County's sanctioning process in each case individually pursued. For, "[t]he courts will not apply ... [the principle of res judicata] to foreclose the relitigation of an issue of law covering a public agency's ongoing obligation to administer a statute enacted for the public benefit and affecting members of the public not before the court. [Citations.]" (California Optometric Assn. v. Lackner (1976) 60 Cal. App.3d 500, 505, 131 Cal.Rptr. 744.)

Finally, we find unpersuasive the County's assertion that the "common issue" cannot be decided without examining the facts of each individual case. * * * Rather, whether the County applied an unlawful sanctioning process can be proved by reviewing the County's regulations, the testimony of the County's welfare employees as to the standard practices followed in making sanctioning decisions, as well as a *sampling* of representative cases probative of the County's practice of sanctioning for nonwillful noncompliance with work program requirements.

THE GENERAL APPROPRIATENESS OF CLASS CERTIFICATION

As already noted, it is especially appropriate to proceed with a class action to provide effective relief when, as here, a large number of welfare recipients have been allegedly, improperly denied governmental benefits on the basis of an invalid administrative practice. The true appropriateness of proceeding with a class action here rests solely not in the ascertainability of a class of past welfare recipients under section 17000 et seq., but rather the underlying reality that those indigent and disabled who qualify for general relief are utterly desperate and impoverished, dependent as a last resort upon the County grant for the rudimentary necessities of life. * * * If the gravamen of this litigation is legally correct and many past general relief recipients were illegally denied benefits, such victims as a practical matter without class certification will individually neither seek nor obtain redress because they are too poor, their claims too small and the legal issues too arcane to obtain private counsel. The remaining public policy considerations supporting class actions, such as judicial economy, finality of judgment binding all parties to the decree, and enforceability of class judgments through contempt or supplemental decree, all support the appropriateness of a class action here. Indeed, we must not forget "[t]he class action is a product of the court of equity. 'It rests on considerations of necessity and convenience, adopted to prevent a failure of justice.'" (Lowry v. Obledo [(1980)] 111 Cal.App.3d at p. 26, 169 Cal.Rptr. 732, quoting City of San Jose v. Superior Court [(1974)] 12 Cal.3d at p. 458, 115 Cal.Rptr. 797, 525 P.2d 701.) The trial court certification of the class for purposes of prospective relief does not promote justice in that it deprives a potentially substantial class the barest of necessities, a means by which to enforce a vindicated right, and notice one has been invalidly denied general welfare benefits. Accordingly, let us not speculate on the size of the resulting eligible class or how many valid claims will be made, but rather let this matter proceed as a class action as to both prospective and retroactive relief. The nature of the complaint and those who comprise the class compel us to leave to the discretion of the trial court at the remedial phase the fashioning of a cost-effective and practical administrative procedure designed to identify and notify the class members and to resolve individual issues of eligibility and damages, because the County has failed to establish the cost in administering retroactive relief would be disproportionate to the benefits received by class members individually and the class as a whole warranting the denial of class certification as to retroactive relief.

* * *

BENKE, ASSOCIATE JUSTICE.

I concur.

* * * [T]he difficulty and danger in examining the number of issues at the class certification stage lies in determining at what point the number of substantial issues passes from the permissible number into the impermissible and whether the multiple issues problem will present itself at the liability or remedial stage of the proceedings. While it is certainly possible, and the court is duty bound to detect an unascertainable class at the certification stage, incorrect focusing at that time on the number of substantial issues potentially involved or when they will arise may in doubtful cases serve to prematurely foreclose a legitimate class action which might more properly be limited or eliminated by decertification in later proceedings on the merits.

* * *

One potential danger is that multiple issues which may arise and which can properly be absorbed into administrative proceedings and forums at the remedial stage, will be mistaken for an impermissible number of issues for purposes of the litigation on the merits. I believe this is what occurred below.

Whether the multiple issues will arise at the liability or remedial stages depends in large part upon the theory of liability to be advanced by the proposed class. * * * In this case, the plaintiff's theory of liability is that the county illegally sanctioned individuals without first drawing a distinction between those acting willfully and those acting nonwillfully. The proposed class—everyone "sanctioned"—is objectively discernible and co-extensive with the theory of liability.

Although the county's ultimate liability to each class member may well depend upon individual factual circumstances, the county's existing administrative forums do provide a suitable means of protecting individual interests without sacrificing the efficacy of a class proceeding. * * *

RES JUDICATA

TAKAHASHI v. BOARD OF EDUCATION OF LIVINGSTON, UNION SCHOOL DISTRICT

California Court of Appeal, Fifth District, 1988.
202 Cal.App.3d 1464, 249 Cal.Rptr. 578, *cert. denied*,
1989, 490 U.S. 1011, 109 S.Ct. 1654, 104 L.Ed.2d 168.

HAMLIN, ASSOCIATE JUDGE.

Plaintiff Mitsue Takahashi appeals from a judgment dismissing her causes of action against defendants Livingston Union School District, Board of Education of Livingston Union School District, Harold Thompson, Dale Eastlee and Hamilton Brannan after the trial court granted defendants' motions for summary judgment in consolidated proceedings Nos. 70836 and 71869.

The basic issue on appeal is whether or not the judgments in the litigation previously initiated by plaintiff in both California and federal courts against one or more of the defendants in these consolidated actions operate as a bar to the present actions under res judicata principles. Decision on the issue presented requires us to determine the relationship between the procedures under the California Fair Employment Practices Act (Gov.Code, § 12900 et seq.) and the schoolteacher dismissal procedures. We will conclude that the judgments in the previous litigation are res judicata on the issues in the consolidated actions and will affirm the judgment.

PROCEDURAL BACKGROUND

Our statement of the procedural background is based upon the record before this court in case No. F000235 as well as the record in the present action, F008684. The record in case number F00235 provided the basis for this court's decision in California Teachers Assn. v. Governing Board (1983) 144 Cal.App.3d 27, 192 Cal.Rptr. 358. This court takes judicial notice of its own record in that case.

Plaintiff was employed by the Livingston Union School District (district) in 1960 and continued in employment there until the fall of 1980, rendering her at the time of the hearing a permanent or tenured teacher.

[In 1978 and 1979, plaintiff received three negative evaluations of her job performance in the classroom and was warned that dismissal proceedings might be initiated.] * * *

On May 12, 1980, plaintiff was issued a document entitled "notice of intent to dismiss," along with a statement of charges indicating that cause existed to dismiss her on the basis of incompetency and that the district intended to do so. Attached to the notice of charges was a copy of the [last] * * * evaluation.

* * *

At the termination hearing plaintiff challenged the Commission [on Professional Competence's] jurisdiction based on the district's failure to comply with the Stull Act (Ed.Code, § 44660 et seq.). That challenge was denied. In addition to the jurisdictional challenge, plaintiff raised at the administrative hearing the following issues in her defense: (1) that her students had good test scores; (2) that certain disruptive students who should not have been in the same room had been put in her classroom; (3) that other classes were also noisy; (4) that the criteria for judging incompetency were inadequate and not uniform so that no objective, verifiable determination of plaintiff's competency or incompetency could be established; and (5) that she believed she was doing as good a job as the other teachers.

There was no mention nor suggestion in the transcript of the administrative hearing of any defense based on violation of plaintiff's civil or constitutional rights.

After the administrative hearing was completed, the Commission rendered its decision * * * and ordered that plaintiff be dismissed from her position effective forthwith.

On December 4, 1980, plaintiff filed in the Superior Court of Merced County a petition for writ of mandate (first action) alleging that (1) the Commission committed a prejudicial abuse of discretion in that the findings of the Commission were not supported by the evidence and the findings did not support the decision of incompetency; (2) the Commission proceeded without or in excess of its jurisdiction because incompetency may only be proved by reference to uniform, objective standards, which the district did not have; and (3) the district lacked jurisdiction to proceed because it failed to include with the 90–day notice an Education Code section 44660 evaluation (Ed.Code, § 44938), and since the focus of a charge of teacher incompetence is whether or not the students learned the required material, the charge was rebutted by evidence that plaintiff's students accomplished their academic goals. (Code Civ.Proc., § 1094.5, subd. (b).) That petition named both the California Teachers' Association (CTA) and Mitsue Takahashi as plaintiffs.

On May 1, 1981, the petition in the first action was argued and denied. The reporter's transcript of that hearing shows that plaintiff elected to argue only the lack of jurisdiction of the Commission to dismiss plaintiff because of the failure of the district to comply with the provisions of the Stull Act. The action was dismissed and judgment entered on June 9, 1981.

* * * This court affirmed the trial court's denial of the petition in the first action. That opinion was certified for publication and appears as California Teachers Assn. v. Governing Board, supra, 144 Cal.App.3d 27, 192 Cal.Rptr. 358. A petition for rehearing in this court and a petition for hearing in the California Supreme Court were denied. Plaintiff also petitioned the United States Supreme Court; certiorari was denied by the United States Supreme Court (1984) 465 U.S. 1008, 104 S.Ct. 1003, 79 L.Ed.2d 235.

On November 10, 1983, plaintiff filed an action in the United States District Court for the Eastern District of California for damages and injunctive relief based on 42 United States Code sections 1981 and 1983 (hereafter federal court case). The district court held that the decision in the first action precluded plaintiff's federal court case. The United States Court of Appeals for the Ninth Circuit affirmed that holding in Takahashi v. Bd. of Trustees of Livingston (9th Cir.1986) 783 F.2d 848, and certiorari was denied by the United States Supreme Court (1986) 476 U.S. 1182, 106 S.Ct. 2916, 91 L.Ed.2d 545.

On November 15, 1982, plaintiff filed a complaint in the Superior Court of Merced County for damages, case number 70836. That complaint (hereafter the common law case) alleged causes of action for breach of employment contract and conspiracy to defraud. It specifically alleged that plaintiff's employment contract was breached by the district's "terminating the plaintiff without just cause" and cited seven specific instances of such breach. The second cause of action alleged that various district employees conspired to "set the plaintiff up" to "attempt to show justification in terminating the plaintiff." The complaint in the common law case was amended on September 22, 1983, to add causes of action for intentional and negligent infliction of emotional distress.

On March 31, 1983, a separate complaint, case number 71869, was filed seeking "monetary, injunctive and declaratory relief." That complaint (hereafter the civil rights case) alleged causes of action for (1) wrongful discharge from employment for exercise of plaintiff's First Amendment rights of freedom of speech and association; (2) unconstitutional discharge from employment for exercise of right of liberty and property in employment in violation of the right to due process (the complaint specifically alleged that: (a) plaintiff was terminated from her employment because she held a job outside of her teaching job, and (b) her right to due process was violated since no allegations or charges relating to her outside employment were made); (3) termination of employment in violation of equal protection of the laws, specifically that she was terminated for holding outside employment and that other people holding outside employment were not similarly terminated; (4) discrimination in employment on account of race and ancestry, alleging that plaintiff was terminated from her employment because defendants were "motivated by pejorative stereotypes and biases as to Japanese persons"; (5) discrimination in employment on account of sex, alleging that defendants terminated plaintiff because they used "sex differential criteria in evaluation and criticism of Takahashi"; (6) discrimination in employment on account of age, alleging "in terminating Takahashi's employment based upon alleged 'incompetence' purportedly consisting of an inability to control student behavior, defendants employed age-differential criteria."

* * *

After the common law and civil rights cases were consolidated pursuant to stipulation, defendants moved for summary judgment. The motion was heard, and about three weeks later an untitled document was filed in the consolidated action reading in its entirety as follows: "Defendants have moved for summary judgment in these consolidated actions. [¶] This court concludes that previous State and Federal court litigation bars these actions on the basis of res judicata. [¶] There are no material facts in dispute and defendants are entitled to a judgment as a matter of law. [¶] The issues here present were litigated or could have been litigated in prior administrative and mandamus proceeding. [¶] The motion is granted in both these actions." Based on this grant of the motion for summary judgment, the trial court entered a judgment dismissing the consolidated actions.

DISCUSSION

Did the trial court err in concluding that the judgment in the first action and/or the federal court case operates as a bar to these consolidated actions?

To determine if either judgment operates as a bar, we will examine the doctrines of res judicata and collateral estoppel and the relationship of those principles to the administrative hearing and the petition in the first action. We then apply the elements of res judicata to these consolidated actions to determine whether the same primary right is being asserted here as in the former cases and if it is being asserted against the same parties or those in privity with such parties. Finally, we will consider the effect of issues that were not litigated and the impact of claims that plaintiff asserts could not have been raised at the time of the administrative hearing or the first action.

* * *

Plaintiff seems to be saying in part that the underlying action cannot be res judicata since the original action was an administrative rather than a judicial proceeding. People v. Sims [(1982) 32 Cal.3d 468, 186 Cal.Rptr. 77, 651 P.2d 321] stands for the proposition that the final judgment of an administrative hearing may have collateral estoppel effect in a subsequent court proceeding (in that case a criminal proceeding). However, plaintiff is mistaken in believing that it is the administrative proceeding that serves as the bar in this case. The first action (in the superior court) is the state court proceeding upon which the trial court based its finding of res judicata as to the consolidated actions. As discussed, that first action was brought by plaintiff in December 1980. The trial court independently reviewed the record of the administrative hearing, held a hearing at which plaintiff had the opportunity to present any argument to the court, and determined independently that cause existed to dismiss plaintiff on the basis of incompetency. That judgment has long since become final.

A. The Primary Right Involved Here Is the Same as in the First Action

Plaintiff has argued that she is not precluded from bringing the present actions since she did not assert the violation of the same rights as defenses to termination for cause in the first action. She points out that her actions involve a different primary right and the Commission did not have the authority to award her punitive damages, thus precluding an appropriate remedy in that forum.

To determine the scope of causes of action, California courts employ the "primary rights" theory. Under this theory, the underlying right sought to be enforced determines the cause of action. In determining the primary right, "the significant factor is the harm suffered." (Agarwal v. Johnson (1979) 25 Cal.3d 932, 954, 160 Cal.Rptr. 141, 603 P.2d 58.)

The United States Court of Appeals for the Ninth Circuit in Takahashi v. Bd. of Trustees of Livingston, *supra,* 783 F.2d 848 concluded that plaintiff's federal court case was barred by the res judicata effect of the prior state court judgment denying plaintiff's petition in the first action. Plaintiff's complaint in the federal court case alleged that the district violated her rights under the Fourteenth Amendment to the United States Constitution and 42 United States Code sections 1981 and 1983 by (1) terminating her employment on account of her sex and ethnic origin, (2) terminating her employment on the basis of the impermissibly vague requirement that she maintain a suitable learning environment in her classroom, and (3) employing methods of evaluating her job performance that were different from those employed to evaluate the performance of others similarly situated.

That court characterized plaintiff's first action as an action based on the invasion of her contractual right to employment by the district. It then determined that the identical primary right, the contractual right to employment, was at stake both in the first action and in the federal court case. Quoting from *Agarwal v. Johnson, supra,* the court noted that in determining the primary right at stake, " 'the significant factor is the harm suffered.' " (Takahashi v. Bd. of Trustees of Livingston, supra, 783 F.2d at p. 851.) The court went on to say, "Absent termination of her employment contract, Takahashi suffered no harm. Takahashi's allegations of mental distress caused as a result of her dismissal do not present a separate injury. Rather, any such distress would be a consequence of the District's violation a [sic] Takahashi's primary contractual right. Consequential damages cannot support a separate cause of action." (*Ibid.,* fn. omitted.)

Plaintiff has again cited *Agarwal* as support for her position that separate primary rights are involved. *Agarwal* does appear to support plaintiff's position, but it is distinguishable. In that case, the plaintiff was terminated from private employment without notice. * * * The plaintiff's former employer made unfavorable statements about him to prospective employers. Agarwal then sued his employer for defamation and emotional distress. Before the state court case came to trial, a federal court action on the individual and class claims of discrimination under title VII of the Civil Rights Act of 1964 (42 U.S.C. § 2000e et seq.) was concluded.

The California Supreme Court concluded in *Agarwal* that the federal court's determination of the claims under title VII of the Civil Rights Act of 1964 was not res judicata as to the issues raised in the state court proceeding because the harm for which Agarwal recovered damages in the state court action was different. It pointed out:

"Our review of the district court's findings of fact discloses that its attention was primarily directed to McKee's [the defendant's] employment practices and the corresponding impact on racial minorities, and to statistical analyses of the McKee employee population. Although Agarwal's state court claims for defamation and intentional infliction of emotional distress arose in conjunction with the alleged violation of title VII, the fact remains that in the present action he was awarded damages for harm distinct from employment discrimination."

All of plaintiff's alleged causes of action in this consolidated action arise in conjunction with or as a result of the alleged wrongful termination of her employment. Indeed, plaintiff specifically alleges that each act complained of caused the dismissal (wrongful discharge, conspiracy, unconstitutional discharge, discharge in violation of state civil rights) or was a consequence of the termination (emotional distress, damages), part and parcel of the violation of the single primary right, the single harm suffered. Plaintiff's allegations of consequential injuries are not based upon infringement of a separate primary right.

Plaintiff has further argued that even if the same primary right is involved, the Commission could not have awarded punitive damages and she should therefore be able to bring a separate suit for punitive damages.

We agree that the Commission did not have jurisdiction to award damages, either consequential or punitive. * * *

However, we disagree that the Commission's lack of authority to award damages somehow excuses plaintiff's failure to present her defenses to the district's charges of incompetency at the termination hearing. There can hardly be justification for such a position. Government Code sections 11505 and 11506 give the plaintiff the right to interpose any defense, and the Commission is required to make findings of fact and determination of issues. Right of discovery is the same in proceedings before the Commission as in civil lawsuits and continuances may be had.

If violation of constitutional and civil rights had been alleged and proved in proceedings before the Commission to determine whether the district had cause to terminate plaintiff for incompetency, such violation would have made the termination wrongful. Plaintiff would then have been in a position to bring a lawsuit against defendants based on violation of her constitutional rights alleging the damages she suffered thereby, supported by the findings of the Commission. She would also have retained her position and mitigated any possible damages.

B. *The District's Employees May Assert the First Action as a Bar to Plaintiff's Causes of Action in This Consolidated Action Even Though They Were Not Parties to the First Action*

Plaintiff has additionally contended that even if the doctrine of res judicata or collateral estoppel bars her causes of action against the district in these proceedings, her causes of action against the individually named defendants who were not defendants in the first action are not similarly barred. However, since Bernhard v. Bank of America (1942) 19 Cal.2d 807, 122 P.2d 892, mutuality has not been a prerequisite to asserting the defense of res judicata in California. One not a party to a prior suit may successfully assert collateral estoppel as a defense if: (1) the issue decided in the prior action is identical to the one presented in the action in which the defense is asserted; (2) a final judgment has been entered in the prior action on the merits; and (3) the party against whom the defense is asserted was a party to the prior adjudication. Here, all three of the individually named defendants were employees of the district and were acting within the course and scope of their employment in terminating plaintiff from her teaching position. They are sued solely because of their involvement in the termination process. The party against whom the bar is being asserted is identical to the one in the prior lawsuit. Since all of the prerequisites to asserting the defense of res judicata or collateral estoppel as stated in *Bernhard v. Bank of America, supra,* are satisfied, the district's employees are entitled to assert the decision in the first action as a bar to these consolidated actions.

* * *

D. *The Final Judgment in the First Action Is Res Judicata as to All Issues That Were or Could Have Been Litigated in That Action*

It is axiomatic that a final judgment serves as a bar not only to the issues litigated but to those that could have been litigated at the same time. In Sutphin v. Speik (1940) 15 Cal.2d 195, 202, 99 P.2d 652, the California Supreme Court stated the California rule regarding the scope of res judicata as follows:

If the matter was within the scope of the action, related to the subject matter and relevant to the issues, so that it *could* have been raised, the judgment is conclusive on it despite the fact that it was not in fact expressly pleaded or otherwise urged. [Emphasis in original.] The reason for this is manifest. A party cannot by negligence or design withhold issues and litigate them in consecutive actions. Hence the rule is that the prior judgment is *res judicata* on matters which were raised or could have been raised, on matters litigated or litigatable. [Citations.] ... "This principle also operates to demand of a defendant that all of its defenses to the cause of action urged by the plaintiff be asserted under the penalty of forever losing the right to thereafter so urge them."

* * * Simply put, plaintiff cannot prevail against defendants on the basis that their conduct toward her that caused her termination was wrongful in the face of a final state court determination in the first action that the district had the right to terminate her for incompetency. That plaintiff elected not to litigate at the hearing before the Commission her claims that she was discriminated against in violation of her constitutional and civil rights does not detract from the finding by the Commission, and independently by the superior court, that the district had cause to dismiss her.

* * *

F. The Federal Decision Is Res Judicata

As we have seen, the United States Court of Appeals, Ninth Circuit, in *Takahashi v. Bd. of Trustees of Livingston, supra,* 783 F.2d 848 concluded that plaintiff's federal court action was barred by the res judicata effect of the prior state court judgment in the first action.

Plaintiff has cited the case of Merry v. Coast Community College Dist., (1979) 97 Cal.App.3d 214, 158 Cal.Rptr. 603 as support for her assertion that the court's acceptance of the res judicata defense in the federal court case does not compel the striking of her causes of action in this consolidated action on the basis of res judicata. In the cited case, the plaintiff alleged that the defendant college had deprived him of his property interest in a television film series without due process by coercing him through threats and intimidation to sign a contract waiving his interest in the series. He filed an action in federal court under the Civil Rights Act and the First and Fourteenth Amendments to the United States Constitution. A summary judgment was granted, the court finding no genuine issues of material fact and concluding that the complaint did not state a federal cause of action. The plaintiff then filed in state court seeking rescission of the contract for fraud, undue influence and mistake of law. The state court sustained defendant's demurrer without leave to amend on the force of the res judicata effect of the federal court judgment.

The plaintiff contended that res judicata did not operate as a bar to his action since the federal court failed to pass on state claims and that different primary rights were involved. The defendant countered that the state claim could have been raised and considered under pendent jurisdiction and the rule against splitting causes of action should preclude plaintiff's suit in the state court. The court first noted that "It clearly appears that the federal court would have declined to exercise its pendent jurisdiction to adjudicate plaintiff's state claims had they been raised." (*Merry v. Coast Community College Dist., supra,* 97 Cal.App.3d at p. 221, 158 Cal.Rptr. 603.) The court then concluded that the summary judgment in the federal action was not a bar to the state action.

There is a very significant difference here that plaintiff ignores: the summary judgment in her federal court action was based precisely on the preclusive effect of the prior state judgment in the first action on the same cause of action. It would be absurd to say that the federal court should have granted summary judgment and dismissed the state claims for adjudication in state court when the dismissal of the federal claims was based on the preclusive effect of the existing state court final judgment in the first action. However we do not need to decide whether the federal court judgment is res judicata since we have concluded that the state court's denial of plaintiff's petition for writ of mandate in the first action does bar these consolidated actions.

* * *

BRAKE v. BEECH AIRCRAFT CORPORATION
California Court of Appeal, First District, 1986.
184 Cal.App.3d 930, 229 Cal.Rptr. 336.

SMITH, ASSOCIATE JUSTICE.

The 1976 crash of a twin-engine aircraft, a Beechcraft Baron 58, took the lives of William P. Brake and Donald E. McCarter. Their widows, as administrators of the estates, brought independent actions for wrongful death against the plane's manufacturer, Beech Aircraft Corporation, and the actions were consolidated for jury trial. Plaintiff widows (plaintiffs) appeal from a judgment entered on a special verdict in favor of defendant manufacturer (Beech) and from a subsequent order denying their motion to tax costs.

BACKGROUND

The aircraft crashed in rugged high-desert terrain north of a ridge of the San Gabriel Mountains, near the town of Pearblossom in Los Angeles County, about one hour after a 9:05 a.m. takeoff from Hawthorne Municipal Airport. * * *

Plaintiffs attempted to prove negligent or defective design. * * *

Beech's theory was pilot negligence or error. * * *

The jury returned a special verdict in favor of Beech, finding no negligence and no defect. Judgment on the verdict was entered * * *. [T]he court * * * allowed, as reasonable and necessary, $45,470.70 of the costs claimed [by Beech]. * * *

* * *

IX

Of the $45,470 awarded to Beech as costs, plaintiffs challenge all but about $4,000, representing jury and filing fees.

The court made its award pursuant to Code of Civil Procedure section 998, subdivision (c), which provides: "If an offer made [pursuant to this section] by a defendant is not accepted and the plaintiff fails to obtain a more favorable judgment, the plaintiff shall not recover his costs and shall pay the defendant's costs from the time of the offer. In addition, ... the court, in its discretion, may require the plaintiff to pay the defendant's costs from the date of filing of the complaint and a reasonable sum to cover costs of the services of expert witnesses, who are not regular employees of any party, actually incurred and reasonably necessary in either, or both, the preparation or trial of the case by the defendant." Plaintiffs rejected Beech's section 998 settlement offer of $75,000.01 made at the start of trial.[18]

The court determined that each allowed item was reasonable and necessarily incurred in defense of the action. Those conclusions and the determination of what items were allowable under the statute were discretionary decisions that cannot be upset without a showing of abuse of discretion.

The largest sum challenged is a total of $22,720.60 for aircraft rental and insurance needed to flight test and videotape the Baron 58. Plaintiffs challenge the necessity for those expenses. However, as Beech notes, the test flights and videotaping were essential at trial; plaintiffs incurred the same type of expenses for their own experts to test the plane. Finally, while plaintiffs query in the abstract why an aircraft manufacturer _ke Beech had to rent "one of its own" aircraft, they do not direct our attention to any showing in the trial court that the expense was not necessary. It was plaintiffs' burden, in the face of Beech's verified costs memorandum, which established prima facie evidence that the expenses were necessarily incurred, to overcome that showing. They did not. We cannot assume that Beech had a Baron 58 available to it for less than the cost it claimed.

Similarly, plaintiffs did not make any showing of how the sums claimed for videotape equipment rental (before and at trial) were unnecessary or excessive, as they now maintain, or how the two fees paid to expert White were cumulative.

Next, plaintiffs are legally mistaken to assert that costs of deposing experts are "unnecessary" where their testimony is ultimately not disputed at trial. The need for a deposition must be viewed from the pretrial vantage point of a litigant who does not yet know whether or not to oppose the expert's opinions. Plaintiffs do not explain why Beech should have been required to await surprise at trial—their apparent position on appeal. It was their burden to show that the depositions were unnecessary. Moreover, plaintiffs are factually mistaken in asserting that their experts were uncontradicted at trial.

---

18.   * * * Also frivolous is their alternative claim that some of the cost items are unsupportable, even under section 998, because Beech failed to show that those costs were incurred *after* the offer. The statute, quoted above, provides for discretionary awards of costs incurred anytime after the action was *filed*.

Plaintiff Brake asserts that she should not have been required to pay witness fees for two experts designated only by plaintiff McCarter. However, the court had discretion under Code of Civil Procedure section 998 to apportion those costs between plaintiffs (cf. Rappenecker v. Sea–Land Service, Inc. (1979) 93 Cal.App.3d 256, 265, 155 Cal.Rptr. 516 [plaintiff in one of six consolidated actions entitled to recover full costs so long as defendant not charged more than once]) and apparently chose to do that here. Similarly, we believe that the court had discretion to charge plaintiffs with the witness fee, costs of service of process, and deposition costs of an expert (Northrop employee Harry O'Connor) designated by plaintiff-in-intervention Industrial Indemnity Company (IIC), even though IIC settled shortly before trial.

Finally, plaintiffs do not even attempt to explain by what calculations they conclude that witness fees and mileage expenses were excessive * * *.

X

As a final matter, we address an issue of collateral estoppel lately urged upon us by plaintiffs. In the week before oral argument on this appeal, plaintiffs filed an application for leave to file a supplemental brief in which they contend that Beech should be barred by the judgment in Elsworth v. Beech Aircraft Corp. [(1984)] 37 Cal.3d 540, 208 Cal.Rptr. 874, 691 P.2d 630 (hereafter *Elsworth*), from maintaining that the Baron 58 is not defectively designed.

We hereby grant their application and will consider the merits of their supplemental briefing, but we do so convinced that denial of the application would be well within our discretion in light of the timing and other circumstances of the application. This case has been fully briefed on appeal since January 1985. The *Elsworth* decision became final in our Supreme Court that same month (Cal.Rules of Court, rule 24(a)) and was extensively cited in plaintiffs' response brief, on issues other than collateral estoppel. The United States Supreme Court subsequently denied certiorari on May 13, 1985, leaving the case final for all purposes; yet plaintiffs waited 11 months, until the eve of oral argument in April 1986, to raise the collateral estoppel issue. At oral argument, counsel for plaintiffs' only explanation for the delay was that they had not realized the collateral estoppel significance of *Elsworth* earlier. That is hard to accept, however, especially since Mr. Cathcart, trial and appellate counsel for plaintiff Brake herein, was also counsel for the successful plaintiffs-respondents in *Elsworth*.

* * *

We nevertheless consider the claim and find it to be meritless. *Elsworth,* a wrongful death action arising out of the stall-spin crash of a Travel Air model twin-engine plane, was tried to a jury on a theory, among others, that the plane's wing (airfoil) was defectively designed in that it caused the plane to easily enter nonrecoverable flat spins under single-engine flying conditions—one of the same theories presented in the instant case with respect to the Baron 58 model. Plaintiffs argue that because the Supreme Court in *Elsworth* upheld a jury verdict finding Beech liable, and since the airfoil design is identical on the Travel Air and Baron 58 models, we should find Beech collaterally estopped to deny the claimed airfoil defect in the Baron 58 and remand the case for the limited purpose of trying the issues of causation and damages.

It is not so simple. In order to prevail in their collateral estoppel claim, plaintiffs must establish, among other things, that the issue in *Elsworth* was both *necessarily decided* and *identical* to the issue in this case. Without passing on the perhaps more difficult question of whether the two models of aircraft in these two cases perform the same by virtue of having the same airfoil and therefore posed "identical" issues (despite other design differences), we conclude that plaintiffs cannot establish that the *Elsworth* jury necessarily found the Travel Air airfoil to be defectively designed.

Elsworth was submitted to the jury on several alternative theories of recovery, and the jury returned a general verdict from which we cannot tell which theory or theories were found applicable. This is critical because one of the theories was "negligence for Beech's failure to adequately warn pilots of the Travel Air's 'undue spinning tendencies' during single engine stalls." (*Elsworth, supra* at p. 546, fn. 4, 208 Cal.Rptr. 874, 691 P.2d 630.) If the jury relied on that theory alone—a possibility we cannot rule out—then the airfoil was not necessarily found to be defectively designed. * * * Because we cannot tell from the general verdict in *Elsworth* that the airfoil was necessarily determined to be defectively designed, the doctrine of collateral estoppel cannot apply.

* * *

ATTORNEYS' FEES AND COSTS

BRANDT v. SUPERIOR COURT

Supreme Court of California, 1985.
37 Cal.3d 813, 693 P.2d 796, 210 Cal.Rptr. 211.

KAUS, JUSTICE.

When an insurer tortiously withholds benefits, are attorney's fees, reasonably incurred to compel payment of the policy benefits, recoverable as an element of the damages resulting from such tortious conduct? We hold that they are and accordingly issue a writ of mandate directing the trial court to reinstate the portion of the complaint seeking attorney's fees as damages.

According to the complaint real party in interest Standard Insurance Company (Standard) issued a group disability income insurance policy to Vicom Associates, petitioner's employer, under which petitioner was insured. Petitioner sustained a loss covered by the policy when he became totally disabled. He made a timely demand on Standard for benefits, which it unreasonably refused to pay. Petitioner therefore filed an action against Standard for (1) breach of contract, (2) breach of the covenant of good faith and fair dealing, and (3) for violation of the statutory prohibitions against unfair claims practices.

In his causes of action for breach of the duty of good faith and fair dealing and for the statutory violations, petitioner listed attorney's fees incurred in connection with the contract cause of action as part of the resulting damage. Standard successfully moved to strike the portions of the complaint seeking attorney's fees. Petitioner then filed the present mandate proceeding.

* * *

"It is well settled that if an insurer, in discharging its contractual responsibilities, 'fails to deal *fairly and in good faith* with its insured by refusing, without proper cause, to compensate its insured for a loss covered by the policy, such conduct may give rise to a cause of action in tort for breach of an implied covenant of good faith and fair dealing.' When such a breach occurs, the insurer is 'liable for any damages which are the proximate result of that breach.' " (Austero v. Washington National Insurance Co. [(1982)] 132 Cal.App.3d at pp. 419–420, 182 Cal.Rptr. 919 [dis. opn. of Morris, P.J.].)

When an insurer's tortious conduct reasonably compels the insured to retain an attorney to obtain the benefits due under a policy, it follows that the insurer should be liable in a tort action for that expense. The attorney's fees are an economic loss—damages—proximately caused by the tort. These fees must be distinguished from recovery of attorney's fees *qua* attorney's fees, such as those attributable to the bringing of the bad faith action itself. What we consider here is attorney's fees that are recoverable as damages resulting from a tort in the same way that medical fees would be part of the damages in a personal injury action.

"When a pedestrian is struck by a car, he goes to a physician for treatment of his injuries, and the motorist, if liable in tort, must pay the pedestrian's medical fees. Similarly, in the present case, an insurance company's refusal to pay benefits has required the insured to seek the services of an attorney to obtain those benefits, and the insurer, because its conduct was tortious, should pay the insured's legal fees." (*Austero, supra* at 421.)

Code of Civil Procedure section 1021 does not preclude an award of attorney's fees under these circumstances. "Section 1021 leaves to the agreement of the parties 'the measure and mode of compensation of attorneys.' However, here, as in the third party tort situation, 'we are not dealing with "the measure and mode of compensation of attorneys" but with damages wrongfully caused by defendant's improper actions.' " (*Austero, supra* at 420.) In such cases there is no recovery of attorney's fees *qua* attorney's fees. This is also true in actions for false arrest and malicious prosecution, where damages may include attorney's fees incurred to obtain release from confinement or dismissal of the unjustified charges or to defend the prior suit.

The fact that—here as well as in *Austero*—the fees claimed as damages are incurred in the very lawsuit in which their recovery is sought, does not in itself violate section 1021's general requirement that parties bear their own costs of legal representation, though it may make the identification of allowable fees more sophisticated. If the insured were to recover benefits under the policy in a separate action before suing on the tort, the distinction between fees incurred in the policy action, recoverable as damages, and those incurred in the tort action, nonrecoverable, would be unmistakable. As pointed out in Prentice v. North Amer. Title Guar. Corp. [(1963)] 59 Cal.2d at page 621, 30 Cal.Rptr. 821, 381 P.2d 645, "[i]n the usual case, the attorney's fees will have been incurred in connection with a prior action; but there is no reason why recovery of such fees should be denied simply because the two causes ... are tried in the same court at the same time. There was no disadvantage to defendant in the fact that the causes, although separate, were concurrently tried."

The dual nature of the present action distinguishes this case from Lowell v. Maryland Casualty Co. (1966) 65 Cal.2d 298, 54 Cal.Rptr. 116, 419 P.2d 180, Patterson v. Insurance Co. of North America (1970) 6 Cal.App.3d 310, 85 Cal.Rptr. 665, and Carroll v. Hanover Insurance Co. (1968) 266 Cal.App.2d 47, 71 Cal.Rptr. 868. "*Lowell, Patterson,* and *Carroll* were not bad faith cases. The plaintiffs' entire actions there were comparable only to the first part of the present action, i.e., for benefits due under insurance policies. In none of those cases was any allegation of bad faith made, which is the gravamen of the second part of the present action. Thus [the] plaintiffs in *Lowell, Patterson,* and *Carroll* sought attorney's fees in an action for prosecution of that very action, or ... attorney's fees *qua* attorney's fees. Plaintiff[s] here, however, seek[s] recovery of attorney's fees as damages, like any other damages, proximately caused by defendant's breach of its duty to deal in good faith." (*Austero* [dis. opn. by Morris, P.J.].)

The *Austero* majority's reliance on *Lowell, Patterson,* and *Carroll* blurred the distinction between bad faith conduct and nontortious but erroneous withholding of benefits. "[A]n erroneous interpretation of an insurance contract by an insurer does not necessarily make the insurer liable in tort for violating the covenant of good faith and fair dealing; to be liable in tort, the insurer's conduct must also have been *unreasonable.* When no bad faith has been alleged and proved, *Lowell, Patterson,* and *Carroll* preclude the award of attorney's fees incurred in obtaining benefits that the insurer erroneously, but in good faith, withheld from the insured. However, when the insurer's conduct is unreasonable, a plaintiff is allowed to recover for all detriment proximately resulting from the insurer's bad faith, which detriment *Mustachio* has correctly held includes those attorney's fees that were incurred to obtain the policy benefits and that would not have been incurred but for the insurer's tortious conduct." (Austero, *supra* at 422.) The fees recoverable, however, may not exceed the amount attributable to the attorney's efforts to obtain the rejected payment due on the insurance contract. Fees attributable to obtaining any portion of the plaintiff's award which exceeds the amount due under the policy are not recoverable.

* * *

BIRD, C.J., and BROUSSARD, REYNOSO and GRODIN, JJ., concur.

MOSK, JUSTICE, concurring.

[omitted]

LUCAS, JUSTICE, dissenting.

I respectfully dissent. In my view, the trial court properly denied petitioner's request for attorney fees.

The American rule has long been that each party to litigation should bear his own attorney fees. The California Legislature first adopted this rule in 1851. * * *

Although this court may have an inherent equitable power to award attorney fees in certain cases, we have "moved cautiously in expanding the nonstatutory bases on which awards of attorney's fees may be predicated." We have acknowledged limited exceptions only "when overriding considerations of justice seemed to compel such a result." "Three of these exceptions, discussed at length in Serrano v. Priest (1977) 20 Cal.3d 25, 34–47 [141 Cal.Rptr. 315, 569 P.2d 1303], base recovery of attorney fees to the prevailing party on the fact that the litigation has conferred benefits on others. Thus, if the litigation has succeeded in creating or preserving a common fund for the benefit of a number of persons, the plaintiff may be awarded attorney fees out of that fund. Likewise, if a judgment confers a substantial benefit on a defendant, such as in a corporate derivative action, the defendant may be required to pay the attorney fees incurred by the plaintiff. Finally, under the 'private attorney general' concept attorney fees may be awarded to those who by litigation secure benefits for a broad class of persons by effectuating a strong public policy." (Gray v. Don Miller & Associates, Inc. (1984) 35 Cal.3d 498, 505, 198 Cal.Rptr. 551, 674 P.2d 253.) Petitioner does not contend that his request for attorney fees comes within any of these exceptions.

A fourth exception is the "third-party tort" situation. "A person who through the tort of another has been required to act in the protection of his interests by bringing or defending an action *against a third person* is entitled to recover compensation for the reasonably necessary loss of time, attorney's fees, and other expenditures thereby suffered or incurred." (Italics added, Prentice v. North Amer. Title Guar. Corp. (1963) 59 Cal.2d 618, 620, 30 Cal.Rptr. 821, 381 P.2d 645.) Likewise, petitioner does not claim his request for attorney fees comes within this exception.

Petitioner suggests, however, that section 1021 would not preclude recovery of attorney fees *as damages* incurred "independently" of the litigation in which the right to damages is established. According to petitioner, the "third-party tort" exception is only one example of the broader "collateral litigation" exception. Other examples include recovery of attorney fees occasioned by false imprisonment or by malicious prosecution. Thus, petitioner asserts that in general a party should be allowed to recover attorney fees for legal services independently incurred, and that any limitations on this rule are the exceptions.

But in fact section 1021 applies with equal force to collateral litigation. In each of the examples mentioned above, it was not the fact of collateral litigation per se that led to the award. Attorney fees are given in false imprisonment or malicious prosecution suits not because collateral litigation is involved, but as sanctions against the abuse of process those two torts represent. Likewise, in the third party tort exception, it is the presence of the third party, not the existence of collateral litigation, that is the important factor. It is one thing for a tortfeasor to force the victim to sue him; in such a case the victim must bear his own attorney fees. But it is quite another thing for the tortfeasor to inject the victim into litigation with another person. * * *

Furthermore, even if there were some general exception for collateral litigation, the present type of case would not appear to qualify. It is contended that we can find collateral litigation in the fact that the insured has two causes of action against the insurance company: one for breach of contract and one for violation of the duty of good faith and fair dealing. The contract suit is regarded as if it were a prior suit and the tort suit as if it were a later suit; since the insurer's tort is what caused it to deny benefits, the suit to recover benefits was occasioned by the tort and therefore in the tort suit the insured should be allowed to recover the attorney fees he expended in the contract suit.

But this analysis appears to mistake the nature of the bad faith tort. When an insurance company withholds payments in bad faith its actions amount to both a breach of contract and a tort, but two separate breaches of duty are not involved. The single duty breached—the covenant of good faith and fair dealing—"springs from the contractual relationship between the parties." The plaintiff may bring suit on both contract and tort theories, but ultimately he must elect which remedy to pursue. There simply is no collateral suit from which attorney fees may be recovered.

The analysis of the Court of Appeal in Mustachio v. Ohio Farmers Ins. Co. (1975) 44 Cal.App.3d 358, 118 Cal.Rptr. 581, is similarly flawed. Focusing on the fact that the insurer's breach of the duty of good faith constitutes a tort, the court concluded that plaintiff insured was entitled to attorney fees because his employment of an attorney was proximately caused by the insurer's tort. Admittedly, plaintiff's employment of an attorney was a foreseeable consequence of defendant insurer's breach, but this logic would apply to any tort suit to which a collateral cause of action is attached, effectively allowing the exception to swallow the American rule on attorney fees.

The *Mustachio* opinion failed to follow the logic of the proposed collateral litigation exception to its end. Rather, the court argued that there is something special about an insurance contract that requires its bad faith breach by an insurer to be treated differently from any other tort suit. The relationship between an insured and his insurer may involve a fiduciary relationship, but we have recently held that tortious breach of such a relationship is not a sufficient basis for creating an exception to section 1021. (Gray v. Don Miller & Associates, Inc., *supra.*)

The mere fact that an insurance contract is bought to secure peace of mind is not a sufficient reason to create an exception to section 1021. In *Crisci,* we discussed the peace of mind of the insured as a basis for granting the type of damages most appropriate to compensate an insured for the disturbance of his tranquility: damages for emotional distress. (See Crisci v. Security Ins. Co., 66 Cal.2d at pp. 432–434, 58 Cal.Rptr. 13, 426 P.2d 173.) Such damages alone should be enough to compensate for an insured's loss of peace of mind.

Even if emotional distress damages are insufficient, an insured may seek numerous additional items of damage in an action for bad faith breach of contract that he could not obtain for simple breach of contract. He may recover for awards against him in excess of the policy limits if the insurer has refused in bad faith to settle within the policy limits. He may recover all economic loss proximately caused. If he can prove oppression, fraud or malice, he may recover punitive damages. Given the numerous types of damages that the plaintiff may recover for a tortious breach of his insurance contract, any or all of which can and often do exceed the policy limits, I can see no persuasive need to create an exception to the general rule that each party must bear his own attorney fees.

The *Mustachio* opinion implies that tortious breach of an insurance contract is such a serious abuse that attorney fees must be awarded as well: "If the insurer, instead of bargaining with the insured in good faith, tortiously violates its covenant of good faith and fair dealing and thereby makes it reasonable for the insured to seek the protection of counsel, plain justice demands that the insurer be financially responsible for an expense which but for its tortious conduct would not have been incurred."

But it must be remembered that an insured need not establish the level of misconduct shown by the insurance company in *Mustachio* in order to recover on a bad faith tort. He must prove only that the insurance company acted negligently, i.e., that a "prudent insurer" would have paid the claim. Mere breach of the duty of good faith is "not meant to connote the absence or presence of positive misconduct of a malicious or immoral nature...." Such negligence on the part of the insurer is enough to warrant an award of damages for emotional distress, economic loss, and the like because of the special nature of the insurance contract, but it is not such an abuse of process as to justify an award of attorney fees. The argument is more convincing when the insurer has acted with malice, but in that case punitive damages may be awarded; when punitive damages are not justified, I can see little reason for an award of attorney fees.

For the reasons stated, I would deny the peremptory writ.

BRAKE v. BEECH AIRCRAFT CORPORATION
California Court of Appeal, First District, 1986.
184 Cal.App.3d 930, 229 Cal.Rptr. 336.

[This case is reproduced *supra* at page 545.]

RIGHT TO TRIAL BY JURY

CROUCHMAN v. SUPERIOR COURT
Supreme Court of California, In Bank, 1988.
45 Cal.3d 1167, 755 P.2d 1075, 248 Cal.Rptr. 626.

LUCAS, CHIEF JUSTICE:

We granted review to decide whether a defendant in a small claims action at law for money damages has a right to a jury trial in the de novo proceeding in superior court when he appeals from the small claims court judgment.[1] We conclude the Court of Appeal correctly held that the appealing defendant has no right to trial by jury.

I. FACTS

Real party in interest,[2] defendant's former landlord, sued in small claims court for money due on the rental contract between it and defendant, and for damages for injury to the property rented to defendant. Possession of the property was not in issue; defendant had previously vacated the premises. After trial, the small claims court awarded real party $1,500 plus costs. Defendant appealed to the respondent superior court, to have the action "tried anew." (Code.Civ.Proc., § 117.10; all further statutory references are to this code unless otherwise indicated.) He demanded a jury trial, which the superior court denied. Defendant then unsuccessfully petitioned the Court of Appeal for a writ of mandate to compel the superior court to grant him a jury trial. * * *

II. ANALYSIS

A. Small Claims Procedure

Each justice and municipal court in the state includes a small claims division (§ 116, subd. (a)), which has jurisdiction over claims for the

---

1. Petitioner (hereafter defendant) does not assert he had a right to a jury in the original small claims court hearing. It has been assumed that to the extent a right to trial by jury exists, it is satisfied by a two-tiered procedure which affords a jury trial in the de novo proceeding in superior court." Maldonado v. Superior Court (1984) 162 Cal.App.3d 1259, 1266, fn. 9, 209 Cal.Rptr. 199; * * *

2. Real party in interest, El Dorado Investors, did not participate in the proceedings in the Court of Appeal or before this court.

recovery of money when the amount of the demand does not exceed $1,500. (§ 116.2, subd. (a).) The Legislature created small claims courts to provide an accessible judicial forum for the resolution of disputes involving small amounts of money in "an expeditious, inexpensive, and fair manner." (§ 116.1.)

The statutory scheme governing small claims court provides for simplified, informal procedures. (§§ 116–117.41.) "The chief characteristics of [small claims court] proceedings are that there are no attorneys, no pleadings and no legal rules of evidence; there are no juries, and no formal findings are made on the issues presented. At the hearings the presentation of evidence may be sharply curtailed, and the proceedings are often terminated in a short space of time. The awards—although made in accordance with substantive law—are often based on the application of common sense; and the spirit of compromise and conciliation attends the proceedings." (Sanderson v. Niemann (1941) 17 Cal.2d 563, 573, 110 P.2d 1025.) Attorneys are prohibited from representing litigants in small claims court.[3] (§ 117.4.) The small claims court judge may permit the parties to offer evidence by witnesses outside of the hearing, and may "consult witnesses informally and otherwise investigate the controversy." (§ 117, subd. (a).) The judge is authorized to "give judgment and make such orders" as he "deems to be just and equitable for disposition of the controversy." (*Ibid.*)

The plaintiff in a small claims action has no right to appeal. (§ 117.8, subd. (a).) The defendant may appeal to the superior court (§ 117.8, subd. (b)), for a trial de novo. (§ 117.10.) This right is limited in that "if the defendant seeks any affirmative relief by way of a claim in the small claims court, he shall not have the right to appeal from the judgment on the claim." (§ 117.8, subd. (b).) The superior court judgment is not appealable. (§ 117.12.)

Section 117.10 directs the Judicial Council to "prescribe by rule the practice and procedure" to be followed in appeals to the superior court in small claims cases. The Judicial Council has accordingly promulgated California Rules of Court, rules 151–158, governing small claims appeals. Under these rules, the trial de novo "shall be conducted informally as provided in Code of Civil Procedure section 117 except that attorneys may participate. No tentative decision or statement of decision shall be required." (Cal.Rules of Court, rule 155.)

B. Right to Jury in Trial De Novo

1. Small Claims Statute Does Not Provide for Jury Trial.

The Legislature's emphasis on informal and expeditious proceedings makes it clear that it did not contemplate a jury trial in small claims court itself. Indeed, defendant does not dispute this point. (See ante, * * * fn. 1.) As to the procedure on appeal, no provision of the

---

3. This deprivation of assistance of counsel has been held not to deny the litigants due process: the plaintiff has waived such assistance by his choice of forum, and the defendant's right is protected because he may retain a lawyer for the appeal.

applicable statute or court rules makes any reference to a jury in the superior court trial de novo.

* * * [I]t is apparent that the scheme created by statute and rules requires the superior court trial de novo to be conducted pursuant to the same summary procedures as govern the small claims court itself (except that attorneys may participate.) It follows that there is no right to a jury trial at any point in a small claims proceeding under the small claims statute and rules.

2. There Is No Statutory or Constitutional Right to Jury Trial on Appeal From Small Claims Court.

Defendant argues that regardless of the legislative intent underlying the small claims statute, the state Constitution (art. I, § 16) and section 592 (generally guaranteeing a trial by jury in legal actions), afford him the right to a jury trial in his appeal. The Court of Appeal concluded defendant has no right to a jury in the trial de novo under either section 592 or the state Constitution. Upon careful consideration of the issue, we conclude that the Court of Appeal was correct. Accordingly, we adopt the following portion of Justice Agliano's opinion for the Court of Appeal in this case, with modifications as indicated:[6]

Article I, section 16, of the California Constitution provides in pertinent part that "[t]rial by jury is an inviolate right and shall be secured to all...." This constitutional right to jury trial "is the right as it existed at common law in 1850, when the Constitution was first adopted, 'and what that right is, is a purely historical question, a fact which is to be ascertained like any other social, political or legal fact.' [Citations.]" (C & K Engineering Contractors v. Amber Steel Co. (1978) 23 Cal.3d 1, 8–9, 151 Cal.Rptr. 323, 587 P.2d 1136; * * *.) "The common law at the time the Constitution was adopted includes not only the lex non scripta but also the written statutes enacted by Parliament." (*Id.*, at p. 287, 231 P.2d 832.) "As a general proposition, '[T]he jury trial is a matter of right in a civil action at law, but not in equity.' [Citations.]" (C & K Engineering Contractors v. Amber Steel Co., supra, 23 Cal.3d 1, 8, 151 Cal.Rptr. 323, 587 P.2d 1136.) But if a proceeding otherwise identifiable in some sense as a "civil action at law" did not entail a right to jury trial under the common law of 1850, then the modern California counterpart of that proceeding will not entail a *constitutional* right to trial by jury. And of course there will be no *constitutional* right to jury trial in special proceedings unknown to the common law of 1850.

The statute on which [defendant] relies is Code of Civil Procedure section 592, which provides in pertinent part that "[i]n actions for the recovery of specific, real, or personal property, with or without damages, or for money claimed as due upon contract, or as damages for breach of contract, or for injuries, an issue of fact must be tried by a jury, unless a

---

6. Brackets together, in this manner [ ], are used to indicate deletions from the Court of Appeal's opinion; brackets enclos-ing material (other than the editor's parallel citations), unless otherwise indicated, denote insertions or additions.

jury trial is waived, or a reference is ordered, as provided in this code.... In other cases, issues of fact must be tried by the Court" with provisos not relevant here. The 1873–74 amendment by which section 592 was put into its present form "was evidently framed with a view of adopting the principle ... that the constitutional guaranty of the right to jury trial ... applies only to common law actions and that it does not confer such right with respect to any action as to which it did not previously exist." (Vallejo etc. R.R. Co. v. Reed Orchard Co. (1915) 169 Cal. 545, 556, 147 P. 238.) [Thus, section 592, like the constitutional provision, is historically based, and does not expand the jury trial right beyond its common law scope.] * * *

[Defendant]'s argument is straightforward. He contends that [real party's] action is for money claimed due upon the rental contract and for injuries to property, and thus that it comes within the plain language of section 592, and that in any event these claims were historically the subjects of actions at law to which the constitutional guaranty would directly apply.

[ ]

[The right to jury trial in the de novo appeal in a small claims action does not turn on the *legal* nature of the claim. Instead, our analysis under both section 592 and the constitutional guarantee in this case must turn on a more basic historical analysis. Our state Constitution essentially *preserves* the right to a jury in those actions in which there was a right to a jury trial at common law at the time the Constitution was first adopted. Thus, the scope of the constitutional right to jury trial depends on the provisions for jury trial at common law. The historical analysis of the common law right to jury often relies on the traditional distinction between courts at law, in which a jury sat, and courts of equity, in which there was no jury. When analyzing whether there is a constitutional entitlement to a jury in a small claims case, however, we must look beyond the legal/equitable dichotomy, because that distinction was irrelevant, at common law, to the provision of a jury for a small monetary claim.]

[Historical inquiry reveals that there were various special juryless small claims tribunals in England and the American colonies, territories, and states, many of them well established before the adoption of our state Constitution. (See Pound, Organization of Courts (1940) pp. 150–156, 245–246.) Significantly, in the years preceding 1850, a litigant in a special small claims proceeding was not necessarily entitled to a jury even if the claim at issue was legal and could alternatively have been brought in a common law court and heard by a jury. (See Barrett, The Constitutional Right to Jury Trial: A Historical Exception for Small Monetary Claims (1987) 39 Hastings L.J. 125, 154.) Under the English system, "when remedies were available simultaneously in both tribunals [i.e., the common law court and a special small claims tribunal], the prevailing practice not only permitted summary relief in the juryless small claims tribunals but strongly encouraged it: in some jurisdictions there were laws expressly penalizing the litigant who persisted in seeking the common law procedure for a small monetary claim. The very purpose of small claims courts was to provide the kind of relief the common law courts provided—money judgments—through a procedure simplified to accommodate the small amount-in-controversy." (*Ibid.*, fn. omitted.)]

[Thus,] [t]he small claims court concept is by no means new: A concern that access to courts of general jurisdiction was beyond the means of poor plaintiffs with small claims can be tracked back in English legal history at least to the fifteenth century. (Cf. 1 Holdsworth, A History of English Law (7th ed. 1956) pp. 186–187.) "The establishment of small claims courts was intended to provide speedy, inexpensive, and informal disposition of small actions through simple proceedings conducted with an eye toward compromise and conciliation. The court was to be designed particularly to help the 'poor' litigant. An informal court procedure was thought to reduce expense and delay 'in cases involving small amounts and often no real issue of law.' Further, it was believed that by securing justice to ordinary citizens in small cases, the integrity of our judicial system would be meaningfully demonstrated. [¶] The small claims movement led to the statutory creation of a small debt court in London in 1606. In 1846, the new county courts were created in England to provide speedy and informal disposition of small causes." ([Comment], The California Small Claims Court, 52 Cal.L.Rev. 876, 876–877 [fns. omitted].) In the new county courts as they existed in 1850 by virtue of the Act of 1846, there was no right to trial by jury if the amount at issue was five pounds or less, and there appears to have been no right of appeal at all. (Cf. * * * Pound, *supra,* at p. 269 [Noting that "[a]t one time or another legislation has forbidden any appeal where the sum or property in controversy did not exceed some small fixed amount or value," and suggesting that the preferable solution with regard to review of small claims court judgments is "to provide an appeal as simple, speedy, and inexpensive as the original proceeding...."].)

[As summarized by Professor Barrett, "[D]uring the seventeenth, eighteenth, and nineteenth centuries an understanding existed both in England and in many of the American colonies and territories that special provisions could and should be made to resolve small monetary claims without the right to a jury at any stage of the proceedings. These provisions were needed to provide practical, useful remedies for persons with very small claims. Under the historical test for the extent of the state constitutional right to jury, this early practice of resolving small claims without a jury would justify comparable juryless procedures today." (Barrett, *supra,* at p. 151.)]

* * *

The principle established by the English common law as it existed in 1850 was that small claims, as legislatively defined within limits reasonably related to the value of money and the cost of litigation in the contemporary economy, were to be resolved expeditiously, without a jury and without recourse to appeal.

We do not attempt to determine whether five British pounds of 1850 are the equivalent of $1,500 in today's economy. [ ] In any event, the amount in controversy is not the issue here. [Defendant]'s contention is the same whether the small claims jurisdictional sum is $1 or $1,500. [We note, however, that the Legislature's power to raise the small claims court jurisdictional amount is limited by constitutional parameters, and any attempt to raise the small claims limit to a level which could no longer be considered a very small monetary amount, would probably necessitate a re-evaluation of whether a jury trial is constitutionally required for the de novo appeal. We find the current small claims ceiling to be a reasonable legislative enactment to allow claimants with small monetary demands to resolve their cases expeditiously, while preserving the defendant's right to jury trial, as historically defined. The $1,500 limit falls comfortably within the constitutional guidelines.]

[Finally, defendant] argues that it is not clear that the Act of 1846 should be considered in defining the common law right to trial by jury as it existed in 1850, and that "[i]f there are any decisions of [our court] which hold that English statutes enacted just prior to adoption of our Constitution in 1849 were incorporated into the jury trial guarantee, those decisions should not be followed. Recent acts of a legislature on the other side of the world were surely known to neither the framers of our Constitution nor the people who voted for ratification." His arguments are not so persuasive as to warrant a departure from our [ ] unqualified and long-accepted rule that the common law of 1850 includes "the written statutes enacted by Parliament." (People v. One 1941 Chevrolet Coupe [(1951)] 37 Cal.2d 283, 287, 231 P.2d 832 [, citing Moore v. Purse Seine Net (1941) 18 Cal.2d 835, 838, 118 P.2d 1 ("It is well established in California that the common law of England includes not only the *lex non scripta* but also the written statutes enacted by Parliament.")].)

[We emphasize also that the small claims exception to the right to jury trial did not originate with the 1846 statute. The parliamentary act of 1846, rather than establishing a new concept, simply "continue[d] the tradition of denying a jury in suits for very small amounts." (Barrett, *supra*, 39 Hastings L.J. at p. 142.) Thus, "throughout the period relevant to our present inquiry, England had a system of small claims courts to resolve small monetary disputes without recourse to a jury at any point in the proceedings." (*Id.*, at p. 144.) * * *]

Finding neither a right to jury trial in comparable proceedings under English common law in 1850, nor express statutory provision for jury trial on appeal from a California small claims judgment, we conclude that [defendant] has neither a constitutional nor a statutory right to jury trial in this proceeding.

* * *

WILLIAMS v. SUPERIOR COURT

Supreme Court of California, 1989.
49 Cal.3d 736, 781 P.2d 557, 263 Cal.Rptr. 503.

PANELLI, JUSTICE.

The issue in this case is whether jury selection procedures in Los Angeles County violate a criminal defendant's right to an impartial jury, that is, a jury representative of a cross-section of the community. Specifically, we must decide whether, for purposes of cross-section analysis, "community" is defined as the county, the superior court ("judicial") district, or an area extending 20 miles from the courthouse. As explained hereafter, we conclude that the appropriate definition of community for cross-section analysis is the judicial district.[1]

Edward Williams (defendant) is charged with the first degree murder of Bruce Horton. Defendant is Black; Horton was White. The crime occurred in the West Superior Court District of Los Angeles County (West District); trial was scheduled for that district's superior court, located in Santa Monica.[2]

Defendant moved to quash the venire on the ground that Black persons on jury panels in the West District were unconstitutionally underrepresentative of the Black population of Los Angeles County. Defendant sought transfer of the case to either the Central District in downtown Los Angeles or the South Central District in Compton, where a greater number of Blacks could reasonably be expected to appear in the venire.

At the hearing on the motions, defendant called Raymond Arce, Director of Juror Services for Los Angeles County, who testified that since 1981 the county has used its list of registered voters and the Department of Motor Vehicles list of licensed drivers to compile a master list of eligible jurors for both the superior and municipal courts. Arce testified that Black persons presumptively eligible to serve as jurors comprise 11.4 percent of the total county population; in the West District, 5.6 percent of the total population is Blacks presumptively eligible to serve as jurors.[3] A survey of jurors in the Santa Monica courthouse for the three-month period preceding defendant's trial indicated that 4.5 percent appearing for jury duty was Black.

Arce also described the Bullseye System, a computer program used by the county for assigning jurors: Although an eligible juror may be assigned to virtually any superior or municipal court in the county, the

---

1. We note at the outset that this case presents no issue concerning the requirement of a jury of the vicinage. In a companion case filed on this day (Hernandez v. Municipal Court (1989) 49 Cal.3d 713, 263 Cal.Rptr. 513, 781 P.2d 547) we hold that boundaries of the county define the vicinage.

2. Pursuant to the provisions of Government Code sections 69640–69650, Los Angeles County has been divided into 11 superior court or judicial districts.

3. Arce estimated that Blacks comprise over 11.4 percent of the Central District jurors and approximately 25 percent of the South Central District jurors.

program assigns the prospective juror to the court nearest the juror's residence. If that court does not require jurors, the juror is assigned to the next nearest courthouse in need of jurors. If that court is located over 20 miles from his residence, the juror is informed that, under Code of Civil Procedure section 203, he has a right to be excused.[4]

Defendant did not argue that the percentage of Blacks on his jury panels was unfair in relation to the percentage of Blacks within the West District or within a 20–mile radius of its courthouse. He argued only that Blacks were underrepresented on the panels in relation to the percentage of Blacks within the entire county.

The trial court denied defendant's motions. The court found the county's jury selection procedure to be "fair and reasonable" and further stated:

> "It appears ... that Los Angeles County is making a reasonable and good faith effort to meet the constitutional requirements here.

> "In any event, there is no showing of any significant underrepresentation of a cognizable group based on the figures presented here."

Defendant then filed a petition for writ of prohibition and/or mandate in the Court of Appeal. The Court of Appeal denied the petition and agreed with the trial court's finding that defendant had not made the required prima facie showing of systematic underrepresentation. Significantly, however, the Court of Appeal held that a criminal defendant in Los Angeles County, in order to establish systematic underrepresentation of a distinctive group, must show that representation of the group is not fair and reasonable in relation to the percentage of such persons residing within a 20–mile radius of that particular courthouse.

REPRESENTATIVE JURY—CROSS-SECTION OF COMMUNITY

In California, the right to trial by a jury drawn from a representative cross-section of the community is guaranteed equally and independently by the Sixth Amendment to the federal Constitution (Taylor v. Louisiana (1975) 419 U.S. 522, 530, 95 S.Ct. 692, 697, 42 L.Ed.2d 690) and by article I, section 16 of the California Constitution. (People v. Wheeler (1978) 22 Cal.3d 258, 272, 148 Cal.Rptr. 890, 583 P.2d 748.)

* * *

It is well settled that no litigant has the right to a jury that mirrors the demographic composition of the population, or necessarily includes members of his own group, or indeed is composed of any particular individuals. What the representative cross-section requirement does mean, however, is that a litigant "is constitutionally entitled to a petit jury that is as near an approximation of the ideal cross-section of the community as the process of random draw permits."[5]

4. After we granted review in this case, the Legislature repealed former section 203. (Stats.1988, ch. 1245, § 1.)

5. The fair cross-section principles set forth in *Wheeler* were codified by the Legislature in 1980. As amended in 1988, section 197, subdivision (a), requires in part

Defendant argues that his right to a jury panel drawn from a representative cross-section of the community is abridged by the jury selection procedures in Los Angeles County. Defendant cites the testimony of Raymond Arce. Blacks comprise 11.4 percent of the countywide, juror-eligible population. Defendant did not argue that the jurors called in his case were not representative of the juror-eligible Black population of the West District, which Arce testified averaged 5.6 percent in the three months preceding defendant's trial. In fact, Blacks comprised 8.6 percent of the jurors appearing for defendant's case.

Under Duren v. Missouri, [439 U.S. 357, 99 S.Ct. 664, 58 L.Ed.2d 579 (1979),] in order to establish a prima facie violation of the fair cross-section requirement, "the defendant must show (1) that the group alleged to be excluded is a 'distinctive' group in the community; (2) that the representation of this group in venires from which juries are selected is not fair and reasonable in relation to the number of such persons in the community; and (3) that this underrepresentation is due to systematic exclusion of the group in the jury-selection process."

We are not concerned with the first prong of the *Duren* test for the People concede that Blacks are a cognizable, distinctive group for purposes of fair cross-section analysis.

To meet the second prong of the *Duren* test, defendant must show that Blacks were underrepresented in jury venires in relation to the number of such persons in the community. Before this court can evaluate the statistical showing of underrepresentation made by defendant, however, we must first determine what community the jury venire must fairly represent. It is here that we confront the central issue of this case.

Defendant argues that community is defined as the entire county. The People argue that community means the judicial district. As noted, the Court of Appeal rejected both definitions, preferring instead a provocative compromise that defines community as that area within a 20–mile radius of the courthouse.[6] Inasmuch as the basis for the decision of the Court of Appeal has been eliminated, no purpose is served by an extended discussion of the propriety of using the 20–mile–radius community in determining the population for cross-section analysis.[7]

---

that jurors be selected "at random, from a source or sources inclusive of a representative cross section of the population of the area served by the court." Section 204 (former section 197.1) prohibits exclusion from jury service "by reason of occupation, race, color, religion, sex, national origin, or economic status, or for any other reason."

6. The Court of Appeal found support for its definition of community in the provisions of the Code of Civil Procedure relating to jurors (§ 190 et seq.), especially section 203 which provided that persons listed for service as trial jurors "shall be fairly repre-

sentative of the population of the area served by the court, and shall be selected upon a random basis. ... In counties of more than one court location, the rules shall reasonably minimize the distance traveled by jurors. In addition, in the County of Los Angeles no juror shall be required to serve at a distance greater than 20 miles from his or her residence." Section 203 has been repealed in the Trial Jury Selection and Management Act, Stats.1988, ch. 1245.

7. Suffice it to say that the appellate court found evidence of legislative intent to

We turn, instead, to the arguments of the People and defendant who, respectively, propose the judicial district and county. We conclude that the judicial district best serves the constitutional and statutory considerations at issue in the determination of the appropriate community for cross-section analysis as well as the practical problems posed by a far-flung megapolis—Los Angeles County.

County as Community.[8]

Defendant contends that the relevant community is the county. In O'Hare v. Superior Court (1987) 43 Cal.3d 86, 233 Cal.Rptr. 332, 729 P.2d 766, we addressed the issue whether the Sixth Amendment entitled a defendant to a venire drawn from, and representative of, the entire county. We squarely held that it does not.

O'Hare was to be tried on a felony charge in the North County Branch of the San Diego Superior Court, which drew its jurors from an area limited by the boundaries of the North County Municipal Court Judicial District. O'Hare complained that the limited venire contained a significantly lower percentage of jury-eligible Blacks than did the county as a whole.

We held that "the constitutional cross-section requirement is a procedural and not a substantive requirement" and found no constitutional limitation on the government's power to define the "community" against which the demographics of the venire is measured. * * * [W]e concluded in *O'Hare* that the Sixth Amendment imposes no limitation on the legislative definition of community for the cross-section requirement: "What the Sixth Amendment does guarantee to every defendant, regardless of his personal characteristics, is a jury drawn from a venire from which no member of the local community was arbitrarily or unnecessarily excluded."

Albeit in another context, in *People v. Harris,* Justice Mosk noted the balkanized nature of Los Angeles County and the "significant deceptiveness" of the use of countywide statistical data. "Our code uses the term 'area served by the court' (CCP § 197), not the county in which the court is situated. It takes only a cursory knowledge of the demography of Southern California to realize that Long Beach courts serve an area completely distinct in population characteristics from the totality of

make particular provisions for the jury draw in Los Angeles County in the provision that "... no juror shall be required to serve at a distance greater than 20 miles from his or her residence." Given the plain language of the statute, however, we may infer that the 20–mile–radius provision was simply intended to facilitate jury convenience by giving jurors an elective exemption if they resided outside the 20–mile radius.

8. The definition of community (no matter what it is) establishes a standard of comparison, not a method of selection. Jurors, selected from a countywide draw, will serve at various courthouse locations and with varying frequencies depending on where they reside in the county, no matter what method is used to determine the representativeness of the resulting jury venires. Cross-section analysis does not address where the jurors are sent to serve, but rather examines the relevant community for determination of its composition.

Los Angeles County.... Figures for the entire County of Los Angeles are not only irrelevant but in this instance significantly deceptive."

Judicial District as Community.

Having concluded that there is no constitutional limitation on the Legislature to create a relevant community for cross-section purposes, we must determine whether in creating superior court (or "judicial") districts in Los Angeles County, the Legislature intended to define community in that county as the judicial district where the case is tried.

* * *

While the Legislature did not explicitly designate the superior court districts as communities for the purpose of assessing the representativeness of jury panels, the considerations that prompted creation of the districts in the first place—the practical realities of the county's unique demographics, its geographical expanse, and the need for judicial efficiency—convince us that the Legislature intended that the districts serve as the community for determination of jury impartiality. In a sense, the districts were to be microcosms of an entity—the Los Angeles Superior Court—that had become unmanageable and inefficient as a single unit.

* * *

Having defined the community which the jury venires must fairly represent, we return to the second prong of the *Duren* test which the defendant must satisfy to establish a prima facie violation of the fair cross-section requirement. The defendant must show that the representation of the excluded group in venires from which juries are selected is not "fair and reasonable in relation to the number of such persons in the community."

Defendant challenged the jury venires as underrepresentative of the Black population of Los Angeles County. At no time did he argue that the percentage of Blacks on the jury panels in the West District was unfair in relation to the percentage of Blacks in the jury eligible population of the West District. Accordingly, defendant has failed to show that the representation of Blacks in venires from which juries are selected is not fair and reasonable in relation to the number of such persons in the community.

Finally, absent a finding of underrepresentation, we do not reach the third prong of *Duren,* i.e., whether the "underrepresentation is due to systematic exclusion of the group in the jury selection process."

CONCLUSION

The judgment of the Court of Appeal is affirmed. The Court of Appeal is directed to remand the cause to the West Superior Court District for trial.

KAUFMAN, JUSTICE, concurring.

I concur fully in the decision and opinion of the majority authored by Justice Panelli. I write separately to respond to the concurring and dissenting opinion penned by Justice Broussard (hereafter the dissent). Justice Broussard, apparently frustrated at his inability to persuade a majority to his view, implies that a majority of the members of this court are insensitive to problems of racial and ethnic discrimination and in a series of decisions have embarked upon an agenda of diminishing the constitutional rights of minority residents of this state. His frustration may be understandable, but his attack on the motives and integrity of the other members of the court is unjustified, improvident and wholly unworthy of him.

Today's decisions in this case and Hernandez v. Municipal Court (1989) 49 Cal.3d 713, 263 Cal.Rptr. 513, 781 P.2d 547 and the other decisions criticized by the dissent are not and were not based on racial considerations at all, much less racial discrimination. They represent reasoned and reasonable resolutions of procedural problems, adopting rules that will afford trial courts the discretion they require to operate the trial court system and conduct criminal trials in a fair yet expeditious manner. Several of the decisions, basically unrelated, reject arguments based on an unwarranted distrust of the trial judges and public prosecutors of our state that this court should adopt ever more impossibly complex standards of review for appellate courts and procedural rules that would continue to ensnare our criminal courts, trial and appellate, in protracted, resource-consuming proceedings having little to do with guilt or innocence or ultimate justice in the particular case. We should have learned from the experience of the past that justice is not achieved by rules and procedures which sound perfect in theory but are unworkable in practice.

In the specific case of jury selection procedures, this means that while the defendant must be afforded a reasonable opportunity to demonstrate invidious or systematic exclusion of members of a cognizable group, a showing of some underrepresentation at a given time is not enough. Neither the venire nor the jury need mirror the racial, ethnic, or religious composition of the community. Once the jury has been fairly selected the law assumes that its members, whether Black, White, Hispanic, Catholic, Jew, rich or poor, are equally capable of representing the entire community. The right to trial by a jury of one's peers does not mean and has never meant that a Black defendant is entitled to be tried by Blacks or a White defendant by Whites. Nor does the right to trial within the vicinage mean that a defendant who commits a crime in Watts has the right to be tried in Watts or that a crime committed in Beverly Hills must be tried in Beverly Hills.

No member of this court, and no thoughtful person in this country today, can be ignorant of the powerful and corrosive force of racism. Nor is there any disagreement on the goal we all seek: a society in which no advantage or disadvantage results from an individual's race, religion, sex, or ethnic background. There is, however, an emotionally-charged debate raging in this country regarding the best means to reach this common goal. According to some, we should eliminate all forms of racial criteria and use only race-neutral procedures. According to others, past wrongs can be redressed and subtle forms of discrimination rooted out only by the use of racial preferences and a heightened race consciousness, hopefully, benign.

It is my personal view that heightened race consciousness and utilization of criteria preferring one race over another, no matter how well intentioned, will in the long run be counterproductive to the common goal and will tend to perpetuate racial bias and hostility. But as justices it is not our function in judicial decisions to take sides in this acrimonious debate, although from time to time we are presented with cases which impinge on some aspect of it. References to the supposed purposes, beliefs, convictions or intentions of other justices, however, are no more than ad hominem attacks and should play no part in the opinions of any member of the judiciary. Refraining from such tactics has been a cherished tradition of this court; it pains me deeply that Justice Broussard now appears to cast this tradition aside.

This is not a matter merely of etiquette or decorum. Forceful and reasoned dissents are, of course, valuable tools in the shaping of the law. But attacks on the purposes and assumed intent of one's colleagues destroy the collegiality essential to the proper functioning of an appellate court and undermine the public respect and confidence so essential to the rule of law. It would be well remembered that each of us, and indeed every judge of this state, took an oath to uphold the Constitutions of the United States and the State of California and that each of us is as equally devoted to fulfilling that oath as any other.

BROUSSARD, JUSTICE, concurring and dissenting.

* * *

II.

This is the latest of a series of recent decisions in which this court has discussed the right to a representative jury, and thus a suitable time to review those decisions as a whole.

The first to be filed was People v. Johnson (1989) 47 Cal.3d 1194, 255 Cal.Rptr. 569, 767 P.2d 1047, which concerned the prosecution's use of peremptory challenges to remove minority members from the jury. Prosecutors will generally attempt to justify such challenges by pointing to individual characteristics of the challenged jurors. Our prior decisions recognized that the most effective way to test the truth of those statements is to see if the prosecutor also challenged nonminority jurors with similar individual characteristics. (People v. Trevino (1985) 39 Cal.3d 667, 217 Cal.Rptr. 652, 704 P.2d 719.) *Johnson,* however, overruled *Trevino,* depriving the appellate courts of the most effective way to review a trial judge's decision upholding the challenges.

Johnson went on to state in dictum that the poor do not constitute a cognizable class, which in context means that the prosecution may systematically exclude poor persons from a jury. That conclusion seems to be contrary to the United States Supreme Court decision in Thiel v. Southern Pacific Co. (1946) 328 U.S. 217, 66 S.Ct. 984, 90 L.Ed. 1181, which held that the state could not systematically exclude economic groups from jury service. Then, in an astonishing footnote, *Johnson* suggests that although Blacks and Hispanics cannot be excluded from juries, Asians and Jews can. If a prosecutor wants a 17th century jury of Christian freeholders, the Constitution, if interpreted as suggested in *Johnson,* is no barrier.

The next case, People v. Morales (1989) 48 Cal.3d 527, 257 Cal.Rptr. 64, 770 P.2d 244, concerned exclusion of minorities from the jury venire. The majority held that a statistical sample of 3,600 jurors was too small to prove systematic exclusion, even though statistical experts testified without dispute that the sample was sufficient to prove the point with a risk of error of only 1 in 1,000. *Morales* further stated that a defendant could not show a constitutional violation by proving that a facially neutral practice had the effect of excluding a cognizable class. What this means is that the state cannot expressly exclude Blacks, but it can exclude all persons of characteristic "x" (low income, for example), even if "x" so closely correlates with race that the practice results in disproportionate exclusion of Blacks.

People v. Bell (1989) 49 Cal.3d 502, 262 Cal.Rptr. 1, 778 P.2d 129 holds a showing of substantial and continuous underrepresentation of Blacks from a county's juries is insufficient even to put the county to the burden of explaining the underrepresentation. Instead, a defendant must now point to a constitutionally impermissible aspect of the county's jury selection procedure and show that this is the cause of the racial disproportionality. Such a specific showing is beyond the resources of most, if not all, defendants. Moreover, the holding itself assumes that the county, confronted with a showing that something in its method of selecting jurors is having the effect of excluding a cognizable group, has no duty to investigate and correct the system; it may continue to exclude minorities until someone is able to prove the exact cause of the problem.

Bell goes on to speak favorably of the "absolute disparity" test for determining when a defendant has made a prima facie showing of exclusion, and unfavorably of all other tests. (49 Cal.3d at p. 527, fn. 14, 262 Cal.Rptr. at p. 14, fn. 14, 778 P.2d at p. 142, fn. 14.) The absolute-disparity test measures the disparity as a percentage of total population. (I.e., if Blacks constitute 8 percent of county population, and all are excluded, this is "only" an 8 percent, not a 100 percent, exclusion.) It is the most restrictive of the competing tests, and in practical effect will make it impossible for a defendant to present a prima facie showing on behalf of a minority group which comprises less than 10 percent or so of the community.

Finally, Hernandez v. Municipal Court, supra, 49 Cal.3d page 713, 263 Cal.Rptr. 513, 781 P.2d 547, together with the present case, deny a defendant the right to a jury chosen from or representative of the community where the crime was committed; he receives instead a jury representative of such community as the prosecutor or courts select.

This court has an obligation to consider the practical consequences of its decisions. Yet none of these decisions show any awareness of their impact on the right of a defendant to obtain a jury which is in fact representative of the community and the vicinage of the crime. None show any recognition that racial bias, conscious or unconscious, is or ever was a matter of concern in this state. None show any sensitivity for the minority defendant facing trial before a predominately White jury. To the contrary, the decisions simply seem to assume that judges, jurors, jury commissioners and prosecutors lack any feelings of racial bias. They erect procedural barriers to make it difficult or impossible to prove subtle forms of bias. And they dismantle, step by step, the legal doctrines which have been created over the years to make the right to a representative jury an effective and enforceable right. I have dissented to each of these decisions, and now register my dissent to the ongoing process of undermining the right of the defendant and the community to a truly representative jury.

MOSK, J., I agree in principle with the views of JUSTICE BROUSSARD.

†